Life-Span Developmental Psychology

RESEARCH AND THEORY

CONTRIBUTORS

PAUL B. BALTES

JACK BOTWINICK

D. B. BROMLEY

DON C. CHARLES

PETER E. COMALLI, JR.

JOHN H. FLAVELL

L. R. GOULET

KARL J. GROFFMANN

JOHN L. HORN

DONALD H. KAUSLER

LEWIS P. LIPSITT

HARRY MUNSINGER

JOHN R. NESSELROADE

WILLIS F. OVERTON

DAVID S. PALERMO

HAYNE W. REESE

GUNTHER REINERT

KLAUS F. RIEGEL

K. WARNER SCHAIE

JOACHIM F. WOHLWILL

LIFE-SPAN DEVELOPMENTAL PSYCHOLOGY

RESEARCH AND THEORY

Edited by

L. R. GOULET and PAUL B. BALTES

Department of Psychology
West Virginia University
Morgantown, West Virginia

 1970

ACADEMIC PRESS   New York and London

ACADEMIC PRESS, INC.
111 Fifth Avenue, New York, New York 10003

United Kingdom Edition published by
ACADEMIC PRESS, INC. (LONDON) LTD.
Berkeley Square House, London W1X 6BA

LIBRARY OF CONGRESS CATALOG CARD NUMBER: 78-117093

PRINTED IN THE UNITED STATES OF AMERICA

73 01429

Contents

List of Contributors   xi

Preface   xiii

CONCEPTUAL STATUS AND HISTORY

1. **Status and Issues of a Life-Span Developmental Psychology**

    Paul B. Baltes and L. R. Goulet

I.	Introduction	4
II.	Developmental Disciplines: The Study of Change	4
III.	General Developmental Psychology	6
IV.	Human Life-Span Developmental Psychology	12
V.	Conclusions and Perspectives	19

2. **Historical Antecedents of Life-Span Developmental Psychology**

    Don C. Charles

I.	Introduction	24
II.	American Beginnings	26
III.	Clinical Work with Children	29
IV.	Educational Psychology	35
V.	Behaviorism	37
VI.	Developmental Psychology in the 1920s and 1930s	38

VII.   Child-Study Institutes   39
VIII.   Other Early Influences   41
IX.   Maturity and Old Age   43
X.   Child Psychology through the Middle of the Century   45
XI.   Post World War II   47
XII.   Who Studies the Life-Span?   48
XIII.   Longitudinal Studies of the Life-Span   48
XIV.   Conclusion   51

3.   **Life-Span Developmental Psychology in Europe: Past and Present**

Karl J. Groffmann

I.   Introduction   54
II.   Prescientific Origins of Life-Span Developmental Psychology   55
III.   Scientific Origins of Life-Span Developmental Psychology   59
IV.   Concluding Remarks   67

THEORY CONSTRUCTION

4.   **An Approach to Theory Construction in the Psychology of Development and Aging**

D. B. Bromley

I.   Introduction   72
II.   Evidence and Inference: A Case History and Commentary   73
III.   The Deductive Function of Theories   81
IV.   Theories and the Analysis of Arguments   87
V.   A Simple Exercise in Theory Construction: The Internal Logic of a
          Theory of the Effects of Age on Creative Thinking   93
VI.   A Difficult Exercise in Theory Construction: The Internal Logic of
          the Theory of Disengagement   96
VII.   The Role of Models and Analogies in Theory Construction   108
VIII.   Commentary on Birren's Counterpart Theory of Aging   111
IX.   Conclusions   114

5.   **Models of Development and Theories of Development**

Hayne W. Reese and Willis F. Overton

I.   Introduction   116
II.   Models and Theories   117
III.   The Concept of Development   126
IV.   The Mechanistic and Organismic Models of Development   130
V.   Summary and Conclusions   144

GENERAL METHODOLOGY

6. **Methodology and Research Strategy in the Study of Developmental Change**

   Joachim F. Wohlwill

I.	Introduction: The Age Variable in Developmental Research	150
II.	The Formulation and Assessment of the Dependent Variable in Developmental Studies	151
III.	The Longitudinal Method: Its Value and Limitations and Some Compromise Solutions	167
IV.	The Descriptive Analysis of Developmental Functions	176
V.	The Study of Functional Relations among Developmental Variables	180
VI.	The Study of Individual Differences within the Developmental-Functional Framework	186
VII.	Conclusion	190

7. **Application of Multivariate Strategies to Problems of Measuring and Structuring Long-Term Change**

   John R. Nesselroade

I.	Introduction	194
II.	Implications of Multivariate Techniques for Studying Patterns of Change	194
III.	Implications of Factor Analysis for Structuring Qualitative and Quantitative Change: Factor Loading Patterns and Factor Scores	196
IV.	Correlational Techniques which Bear directly on the Problems of Structuring Change	201
V.	Overview of More Generalized Correlational Techniques	204
VI.	Areas of Convergence between Multivariate Techniques and Developmental Concepts	205
VII.	Conclusion	207

PERCEPTION AND COGNITION

8. **Life-Span Changes in Visual Perception**

   Peter E. Comalli, Jr.

I.	Introduction	211
II.	Visual Illusion	212
III.	Spatial Orientation	215
IV.	Part-Whole Differentiation	221
V.	Perceptual Closure	224
VI.	Speed of Recognition	225
VII.	Conclusion	226

9. **Light Detection and Pattern Recognition: Some Comments on the Growth of Visual Sensation and Perception**

Harry Munsinger

I.	Introduction	228
II.	Some History of Sensation and Perception	228
III.	The Mechanisms of Detection and Recognition	229
IV.	Detection and Recognition in Neonates	235
V.	Simultaneous Detection and Recognition	237
VI.	Detection, Recognition, and Method	238
VII.	Perception and Judgment	239
VIII.	Detection Theory	240
IX.	Muddy and Cloudy Developmental Data	244

10. **Cognitive Changes in Adulthood**

John H. Flavell

I.	Differences between Child and Adult Cognitive Changes	248
II.	The Role of Experience in Adult Cognitive Change	250

LEARNING AND RETENTION

11. **Learning in Children and in Older Adults**

Jack Botwinick

I.	Conditioning	258
II.	Discrimination Learning	269
III.	Paired-Associate and Serial Learning	277
IV.	Incidental Learning	279

12. **The Experiential Origins of Human Behavior**

Lewis P. Lipsitt

I.	Introduction	285
II.	Unconditioned and Conditioned Behavior	287
III.	A Brief Review of Selected Facts about Infant Behavior Plasticity	293
IV.	Comments on the Concept of "State"	301
V.	Summary	302

13.   Retention-Forgetting as a Nomological Network for Developmental
      Research

      Donald H. Kausler

      I.   Introduction   306
      II.   Verbal Learning: Models, Processes, and Paradigms   307
      III. A Nomological Network for Retention-Development Relationships   314
      IV.   Interference Theory and Retention-Development Relationships   331
      V.   Retention-Development Relationships for Recognition Learning   350
      VI.   Concluding Comments   353

LANGUAGE

14.   The Language Acquisition Process: A Reinterpretation of Selected
      Research Findings

      Klaus F. Riegel

      I.   Introduction   358
      II.   Intralingual Relations   367
      III. Psycholinguistic Operations   390

15.   Research on Language Acquisition: Do We Know Where We Are Going?

      David S. Palermo

      I.   Historical Introduction   401
      II.   Psycholinguistics   406

INTELLECTUAL ABILITIES

16.   Organization of Data on Life-Span Development of Human Abilities

      John L. Horn

      I.   Introduction   424
      II.   Unity and Differentiation among Abilities   425
      III. Processes Basic to Intellectual Functioning   428
      IV.   Development of Abilities in Childhood   431
      V.   Development of Abilities in Adulthood and Old Age   445
      VI.   General Summary   464

17.   **Comparative Factor Analytic Studies of Intelligence throughout
      The Human Life-Span**

      Gunther Reinert

      I.   Introduction   468
      II.   Relevant Hypotheses and Results   468
      III.   Methodological Aspects and Problems   475
      IV.   Discussion and Conclusions   479

18.   **A Reinterpretation of Age Related Changes in Cognitive Structure
      and Functioning**

      K. Warner Schaie

      I.   Introduction   486
      II.   Age Changes versus Age Differences versus Cultural Change   486
      III.   The Impact of Generational Differences   492
      IV.   Empirical Evidence Bearing upon Generation Differences in
             Intelligence   498
      V.   Conclusions   506

References   509

Author Index   563
Subject Index   577

List of Contributors

Numbers in parentheses indicate the pages on which the authors' contributions begin.

PAUL B. BALTES (3), West Virginia University, Morgantown, West Virginia

JACK BOTWINICK (257), Washington University, St. Louis, Missouri

D. B. BROMLEY (71), The University of Liverpool, Liverpool, England

DON C. CHARLES (23), Iowa State University, Ames, Iowa

PETER E. COMALLI, JR. (211), Temple University, Philadelphia, Pennsylvania

JOHN H. FLAVELL (247), University of Minnesota, Minneapolis, Minnesota

L. R. GOULET (3), University of Illinois, Urbana, Illinois

KARL J. GROFFMANN (53), University of Mannheim, Mannheim, West Germany

JOHN L. HORN (423), University of Denver, Denver, Colorado

DONALD H. KAUSLER (305), St. Louis University, St. Louis, Missouri

LEWIS P. LIPSITT (285), Brown University, Providence, Rhode Island

HARRY MUNSINGER (227), University of California, San Diego, California

JOHN R. NESSELROADE (193), West Virginia University, Morgantown, West Virginia

WILLIS F. OVERTON (115), State University of New York, Buffalo, New York

DAVID S. PALERMO (401), Pennsylvania State University, University Park, Pennsylvania

HAYNE W. REESE (115), University of Kansas, Lawrence, Kansas*

GUNTHER REINERT (467), University of Mannheim, Mannheim, West Germany

KLAUS F. RIEGEL (357), The University of Michigan, Ann Arbor, Michigan

K. WARNER SCHAIE (485), West Virginia University, Morgantown, West Virginia

JOACHIM F. WOHLWILL (149), Clark University, Worcester, Massachusetts†

---

* Now at West Virginia University, Morgantown, West Virginia.

† Now at Pennsylvania State University, University Park, Pennsylvania.

Preface

The contemporary period marks an exciting phase in the history of developmental psychology. For the first time the discipline is firmly entrenched as a graduate option in most of the major programs in this country and abroad and the discipline is generating Ph.D.s at a rapidly increasing rate. The upsurge of interest in developmental problems is also marked by the increasing number of "converts" to the field, each of whom brings his own "shotgun" and/or arsenal of research methods and theoretical models and a concern with studying the correlates and determinants of time-ordered changes in behavior.

Developmental psychology is changing but the appropriate description of this change is not of evolution, but quiet revolution. Time-honored conceptions of developmental psychology are being rejected by some and reevaluated by almost all others. A field whose history has been marked by borrowing methods, concepts, and theories from other specializations within psychology (and other disciplines for that matter) is formulating both a separate identity and those methods, concepts and theories that are unique to its problems.

The recent frontal attack on developmental problems has had both desirable and undesirable consequences. For the first time massive amounts of data are being collected which bear on the explication of basic developmental processes. And, developmentalists are responding in increasing numbers to the call for solutions to societal problems. However, the contemporary period has seen little progress beyond the attempts of A. Quetelet and Charlotte Bühler in Europe and Sidney Pressey and Raymond Kuhlen in the United States at a life-span conceptualization of developmental psychology. There has been no clear and unified effort to countermand the *recent* trend to subdivide developmental psychology into separate disciplines encompassing individually the chronological age determined periods of infancy, childhood, adolescence, adulthood, and old age.

It is difficult to specify what has precipitated these divisions. There are, of course, a number of substantive and methodological reasons, some of which include the complexity of the task, "basic" differences between infants and the aged, methodological problems implicit in the comparison of behavior in humans who vary widely in their response repertoire, the problem of subject availability, and the difficulties associated with long-term longitudinal research. There are also the separate demands made by society to provide answers to the unique problems of individuals at varying points in the life cycle (e.g., problems associated with maternal care, the need for educational innovation in elementary and secondary schools, problems associated with retirement, the training or retraining of workers in the face of a changing technology, etc.). However, none of these reasons provide a logical basis for the chronological divisions of the life span. Rather, they highlight the necessity for innovative, and perhaps completely new, ways of studying time-related behavior change in its continuity and potential discontinuity throughout the entire life span.

The present volume is the result of a conference whose primary purpose was to provide a forum for the discussion of the issues and problems associated with a life-span conceptualization of developmental psychology. The contributors to the conference represent a heterogeneous group of psychologists reflecting diverse theoretical orientations and differential concern with various sections of the life span. They were given the charge of preparing a paper within their own specialty which integrated, wherever possible, the available data and/or theoretical conceptions heretofore associated with smaller sections of the life span. The goals of the conference were quite ambitious—the concurrent exploration of new (and a few old) models of development, and a synthesis of data relevant to basic psychological processes throughout the human life span. The papers together represent the multiple approaches to the study of development, and for most areas, a first attempt to deal simultaneously with developmental processes encompassing the period from birth to natural death.

Acknowledgments

The editors received valuable assistance in all phases of planning for the conference. Robert F. Munn, Provost for Research and Graduate Affairs, and K. Warner Schaie, Chairman of the Department of Psychology at West Virginia University, arranged for University sponsorship and provided encouragement and support from the point of initial planning through the final phase of manuscript preparation. At one time or another, a number of graduate students including Ronald Bone, John Burke, Nicholas Cavoti, Chiu Cheung, Juanita Field, Barbara Grimm, Wayne Frohring, Eric Labouvie, Gisela Labouvie, Steve Lubin, Barbara Marquette, Anne Nardi, Diane Papalia, Henry Schneider, and Harvey Sterns, assisted or assumed responsibility for a host of chores associated with the conference. It is a pleasure to acknowledge them here. The editors also gratefully acknowledge the excellent secretarial assistance of Mrs. Jackie Frum and Miss Nancy Fast. Special thanks are due to our wives, Carol Goulet, who assisted in editing and proofreading, and Margret Baltes, who had primary responsibility for the translation of two chapters and the preparation of the reference section.

CONCEPTUAL STATUS
AND
HISTORY

Status and Issues of a Life-Span Developmental Psychology

PAUL B. BALTES

WEST VIRGINIA UNIVERSITY
MORGANTOWN, WEST VIRGINIA

L. R. GOULET

UNIVERSITY OF ILLINOIS
URBANA, ILLINOIS

ABSTRACT

Human life-span developmental psychology is concerned with the description and explication of ontogenetic (age-related) behavioral change from birth to death. With this referent, life-span developmental psychology is related to other developmental disciplines which differ in terms of the entity studied, the attributes measured and the antecedent-consequent relationships used to explicate the time continuum. In addition, major objectives and assumptions of a life-span approach to the study of ontogenetic change are elaborated and implications for methodology and theory are derived. Throughout, particular emphasis is accorded to the discussion of experimental strategies in the study of developmental phenomena.

I. INTRODUCTION

The recent decade has witnessed an explosion of research concerned with the study of developmental change. This explosion, indexed for example by the disproportionate growth of citations in *Psychological Abstracts*, has been paralleled by a series of changes in emphases and perspectives. One aspect of this change concerns the increasing interest in age-related behavior associated with all segments of the age span. With some exceptions, however, few attempts have been made to develop a comprehensive life-span developmental psychology (e.g., M. Bloom, 1964; Bühler & Massarik, 1968; Hurlock, 1968; Pressey & Kuhlen, 1957) incorporating ontogenetic change from conception to death. On the contrary, for the vast majority of developmentally-oriented researchers, the subject matter of ontogenetic change is divided into a set of nominally related, but functionally separate disciplines dealing either with smaller sections of the age span (e.g., infancy, childhood, adolescence, adulthood, old age) or with the psychological processes underlying human behavior (e.g., learning, perception, memory, etc.). In fact, the individual researcher typically specializes in and identifies with one cell of the age-segment—process matrix (e.g., learning in neonates, aging and memory, etc.).

Most of the chapters of the present volume coordinate various process-oriented research efforts heretofore related only to specific age groups. This brief introductory chapter will attempt to take a more abstract look at the status of a life-span developmental psychology. First, the concept of a life-span developmental psychology will be further delineated and placed into the more general frame of reference of comparative developmental research; second, an attempt will be made to identify commonalities in research previously identified with restricted points of the age continuum; third, some general methodological problems and some of the major research issues related to the study of long-term developmental change will be summarized. Finally, some implications of a life-span developmental psychology for other behavioral sciences will be highlighted. Through all this runs the thread of conceiving of the human organism as an ordered system showing stability but also continuous change throughout his terrestrial existence.

II. DEVELOPMENTAL DISCIPLINES: The Study of Change

It is easily forgotten by psychologists that there are many scientific disciplines (e.g., history, geology, anthropology) which address themselves primarily to the study of change. As a matter of fact, one might doubt whether there are any scientific areas that deal only with stable, unchanging phenomena. In this regard, all the disciplines which deal with developmental phenomena orient themselves (at least at the outset) on a time continuum, and thus fulfill the basic developmental paradigm that $C = f(T)$, where C stands for observed change in a given attribute, T indexes time, and f denotes a functional relationship between C and T.

Borrowing terms from both measurement theory (e.g., Torgerson, 1958) and general system theory (e.g., J. E. Anderson, 1957; J. G. Miller, 1955; Nagel, 1957; von Bertalanffy, 1968; also see Reese & Overton, Chapter 5), it is proposed that the research approaches of the various developmental disciplines differ primarily with regard to three aspects:

1. the *entity* (system) of observation,
2. the kind of *attributes* (measurement variables) of the entity that are observed, and
3. the nature of *explication* of the *time continuum* (type of independent or process variables).

There are, of course, other distinctive criteria, but these three appear to be the most significant for the present purpose. With the risk of oversimplification, the entity or system refers to the identification of *who* is changing, while the attributes refer to the specification of *what* is changing with respect to the entity. Finally, the nature of explication of the time continuum reflects the *when* and *why* of any observed change.

Specifically, the concept of an entity is used here to indicate a functional unit, possessing distinctive reality (for example, an aggregation of elements as combined by nature into an integrated whole moving forward in time and space), which can be subjected to scientific inquiry through observation of its attributes. When living organisms are involved, one tends to speak of entities as systems. Furthermore, in regard to the nature of attributes, it is useful to distinguish between the constituent or basic variables that define the system and those attributes that are used in describing any changes occurring in the system.

The explication of the time continuum is of primary importance since time itself is rarely conceptualized as a causative factor. Rather, time serves as a preliminary index for the complex network of interacting influences operating in time (e.g., Birren, 1959b; Wohlwill, 1970; Zigler, 1963; see also Bromley, Chapter 4; Wohlwill, Chapter 6). Thus, the first task of a developmental discipline consists of specifying functional relationships between time and attributes in the entity under investigation. Such description, however, must be supplemented by specification of the why of change, that is, of antecedent-process-consequent relationships, in order to arrive at a network of causal inferences. When comparing various developmental disciplines, it appears useful to further distinguish between two aspects related to the explication of the time continuum. The first concerns the nature of independent variables involved (e.g., genetic, environmental), while the second refers to the nature of the processes or mechanisms that are used in linking antecedent conditions to consequent change in attributes.

Thus, a developmental biologist might be interested in organisms of a certain species as an entity or system, and observe as attributes characteristics related to the morphology or the central nervous system of these organisms. When proceeding to explicate the time continuum, the biologist might focus on a network of physiological mechanisms (largely indicating hereditary mechanisms such as maturation) to account for ontogenetic changes. An anthropologist, on the other hand, may take a particular African tribe as an entity and investigate religious attitudes as attributes. The emphasis of the anthropologist in explicating the time continuum might center about such process concepts as acculturation or innovation.

The life-span of the entity under study specifies to a large degree the number of subdivisions of the time continuum. Compare, for example, the life-span of cultures, often measured in centuries, with that of biological units such as cells, measured in hours or days. This is not to say that chronological subdivisions of the life-span of an entity are both artificial and unnecessary. While such is the case in many instances, the nature of the entity, the theoretical framework, and the attributes with which the researcher is working sometimes dictate the number and placement of these subdivisions.

It is conceded that this discussion of differences and commonalities among various developmental disciplines is oversimplified. It is not easy to reach consensus as to what constitutes the entity and what constitutes the attributes. The above discussion, like any metatheoretical exercise, may also be seen as somewhat arbitrary because it, of necessity, imposes a structure on the subject matter of developmental disciplines. Nevertheless, it is argued that it is a major task of theorizing in any developmental discipline to structure its basic data relational system (R. B. Cattell, 1966a) in terms of entities, attributes, and the major variables and mechanisms used in explication of the time continuum.

Such an endeavor will permit further clarification of our own conceptualization of developmental psychology. It also has ramifications for other developmental disciplines, the discussion of which, however, is not a major concern of this chapter. Moreover, the delineation of a number of other major developmental disciplines might open new theoretical and methodological perspectives related to the study of developmental change.

III. GENERAL DEVELOPMENTAL PSYCHOLOGY

It is generally agreed that the entity or system on which psychology focuses is the living organism, with particular emphasis on the human organism. At first glance, the living organism is easily identifiable, that is, it constitutes a functional unit which moves together in space and time (or time-space) from birth to death and it is easily distinguishable from its environment.

Difficulties arise, however, when various scientists (or sciences) are forced to qualify this entity in terms of what they consider to be its basic elements, attributes, and their relationships. In this context, it can be briefly mentioned that none of the sciences involved in studying living organisms deals with the *total* organism. Instead, each selectively investigates and organizes (construes) those attributes of the entity that are considered relevant for the theoretical system (biology, sociology, psychology) in question. Thus, through the process of scientific investigation by researchers with different orientations, organisms are seen as a selected set of abstractions consisting of a network of interrelated constructs.

In this context it must suffice to state that a developmental enterprise might be called "purely" psychological in nature if both the nature of attributes and the nature of explicating the time continuum are within the scope of psychology, that is, if independent variables, process mechanisms, and the dependent variables under consideration are generally accepted as being a part of psychology. If one of these aspects involved in describing change in an organism reflects the conceptualizations of another discipline, we may speak of an interdisciplinary developmental approach.

A. Structure of Entities

A life-span developmental psychology of human organisms, as it is discussed in the present volume, does not embrace all of developmental psychology. Rather it is part of a general developmental psychology in the sense of Yerkes (1913) and H. Werner (1948) who both emphasized that developmental psychology considers *all* living organisms as they move forward in time. Such a position necessarily requires a classification of organisms into subentities (subsystems).

The process of classifying living organisms into a structured set of subentities (similar to Linneaus' classification scheme in biology) on the basis of psychological criteria has barely begun in psychology. To illustrate the implications of such a classification into subentities, we may consider three subentities of organisms which appear to show differences regarding their age development. These are *species* (e.g., Bitterman, 1965; Schneirla, 1957), *generation* (e.g., Bakwin, 1964; also see Schaie, Chapter 18), and *culture* (e.g., Holtzman, 1965; Piaget, 1966; H. Werner, 1948). The resulting categorization of organisms in terms of species membership, cultural membership, and generational membership is summarized in Table 1.

First, such a preliminary classification of organisms exemplifies the restricted scope of conventional textbooks on developmental psychology which typically deal with one species (e.g., human beings), one generation (e.g., cohort 1950), and one set of cultures (e.g., North America). Moreover, this preliminary classification permits the specification of a set of distinct developmental psychologies, all of which are concerned with life-span behavioral change. Thus, one may group together organisms from any of the subentities (species, generation, culture), while neglecting the other two. Accordingly, one would arrive at a *species-specific*, a *generation-specific*, and a *culture-specific* developmental psychology. All these age-developmental psychologies are, of course, worthy of being considered independently. However, it must be noted that up to the present there has been a heavy concentration of research in only a few cells of Table 1.

TABLE 1

General Developmental Psychology and Its
Formal Relationship to Specific Developmental Psychologies [a]

Species (S)	Culture (C)	Life-span		
		Generation$_1$	Generation$_2$	Generation$_m$
S$_1$	C$_1$ C$_2$ C$_k$	R$_{1,2,\ldots,r}$	R$_{1,2,\ldots,r}$	R$_{1,2,\ldots,r}$
S$_2$	C$_1$ C$_2$ C$_k$	R$_{1,2,\ldots,r}$	R$_{1,2,\ldots,r}$	R$_{1,2,\ldots,r}$
S$_n$	C$_1$ C$_2$ C$_k$	R$_{1,2,\ldots,r}$	R$_{1,2,\ldots,r}$	R$_{1,2,\ldots,r}$

[a] Represents a five-dimensional framework. The framework specifies a distinct set of developmental psychologies which are all life-span developmental in nature. For further explanation, see text.

A second set of life-span developmental psychologies identifiable in Table 1 may be classified as comparative in nature. On the one hand, it is possible to compare the age development within each subentity and arrive at a *comparative-species* developmental psychology, a *comparative-generation* developmental psychology, and a *comparative-culture* developmental psychology. On the other hand, it may be possible to make comparisons among subentities, an approach rarely considered.

It should be noted again that the proposed structure of entities should not be seen as final, but only as an attempt to introduce some kind of systematization into the bulk of life-span developmental questions, and to illustrate the task that lies ahead of us. As is true for all models, revisions will be necessary when additional information suggests an alternative classification. Of particular interest would seem to be the development of classifications based on behavioral aspects, since the existing attempts rely largely upon criteria formulated outside the realm of psychology (e.g., biology and sociology).

B. Structure of Attributes

Neglecting additional issues involved in setting apart psychological attributes from those attributes which are under the domain of related disciplines, psychologists seem to agree that psychological attributes refer to responses (R) of the organism. This restriction transforms the original developmental paradigm into $C_R = f(T)$, where C_R indicates that the subject matter (or major dependent variable) of developmental psychology is the study of change in behavior of the organism as a function of time (e.g., Baltes, 1968b; Kessen, 1960). The potential number of such responses or attributes ($R_{1, 2 \ldots, r}$), however, is very large. More precisely, since attributes are to be conceived of as being construed (invented) rather than detected, the universe of psychological attributes is yet undefined. Since the task of delineating the basic structure of psychological attributes is itself still in its early infancy, any attempt to propose a set of categories is only preliminary and necessarily reflects the idiosyncracies of a selected group or even a single psychologist. Categories that are, for example, discussed in the present volume are perception, learning, memory, cognition, language, and intellectual abilities.

The incorporation of the component "categories of attributes" expands the basic data relational system of developmental psychology and leads to the formulation of two additional sets of developmental psychologies as represented in Table 1. A first set might be called *behavior-specific* and represents all those approaches that consider life-span changes within particular categories of attributes, such as developmental perception, developmental learning, developmental intelligence, or developmental cognition. A second approach is again comparative in nature and might be denoted as *comparative-behavior* developmental psychology. Such an approach would concentrate on comparing developmental changes between a distinct set of categories such as perception and intelligence (e.g., Piaget, 1947a).

A major task in categorizing the universe of attributes into a set of behavioral categories will consist in examining the extent to which the structure of attributes can be assumed to be developmentally invariant, both with regard to ontogenesis and phylogenesis. In other words, the question is whether observed life-span changes in a fixed set of attributes consist of differences in level only (quantitative change) or whether the structure of attributes itself is undergoing developmental transformations (number of attributes, relationship among attributes) in the sense of structural change (see Baltes & Nesselroade, 1970; also see Nesselroade, Chapter 7), as inherent, for example, in Piaget's theory of cognitive development. Unfortunately, the question of invariance of the structure of attributes (across entities and age levels) has barely been touched, except for a series of studies in the area of intelligence (see Horn, Chapter 16; Reinert, Chapter 17) and personality development (e.g., Emmerich, 1968; Schaie & Marquette, 1970). Some research, however, is now also being directed, for example, to the issue of the invariance of linguistic abilities in children of different cultures (e.g., McNeil, 1968; Slobin, 1966b; also see Palermo, Chapter 15). In this context it appears particularly fruitful to heed some recent work in cross-cultural psychology (e.g., Berrien, 1968; Boesch & Eckenberger, 1969) presenting thoughtful discussions and suggestions related to the examination of cross-cultural equivalence of measurement instruments which have significant bearing on developmental research methodology.

C. Explication of Time Continuum

1. The Study of Age-Related Change

The descriptive aspect of explicating the time continuum refers to the assessment of age-functional relationships according to Kessen's (1960) paradigm that $C_R = f(A)$, where A indicates the chronological age of the organism under study. Implicit in this paradigm is a delimitation of which time-related change should be labeled as developmental in nature.

Fundamentally, the concept of development can be traced to both biological and philosophical sources (e.g., J. E. Anderson, 1957; D. B. Harris, 1957b; also see Charles, Chapter 2; Groffmann, Chapter 3) and its meaning is ambiguous when used as a theoretical concept (see Reese and Overton, Chapter 5). When used as a theoretical concept, the term development typically implies some essential ideas about the nature of change, such as a change toward a higher level of complexity or an end state of organization. In this instance the concept of aging is sometimes contrasted with development (e.g., Birren, 1959b), with the former including those changes that occur after maturity and the latter including those changes associated with the growth period.

It is argued here that this distinction between developmental change and aging change generates more heat than light. The only major criterion that seems necessary to define developmental change is whether there exists a systematic age-functional relationship (Kessen, 1960; Spiker, 1966) from birth to death, whatever the shape of this relationship (linear, nonlinear, increasing, decreasing, U-shaped, inverted U-shaped, etc.) may be. In case developmental change needs further specification, this may be accomplished by restricting it to those attributes that show long-term changes, that is, changes through a major part of the life-span. This restriction would exclude a number of short-term behavioral changes that, although they are tied to the time variable, do not exhibit the kind of change that is long-term (measured with regard to the life-span) in nature. Examples for such short-term changes would be the menstrual cycle, fluctuations in attention, motivational cycles (hunger, thirst), or the sleep-wakefulness cycle. Such short-term changes, of course, are of special significance in a developmental framework if it is necessary to consider age as a parameter in describing individual differences.

2. The Age Variable and Explanatory Mechanisms

The next aspect related to the explication of the time continuum refers to the meaning of the age variable. Birren (1959b) and Wohlwill (Chapter 6) provide excellent discussions of some of the problems involved in the investigation of such age-functional relationships and point to the need of taking a new look at the status of the age variable.

A first step toward refining and explicating age-functional relationships consists of structuring the universe of antecedent conditions associated with age into major categories. Longstreth (1968), for example, proposes a division into three categories: heredity, past environment, and present environment. This would expand the developmental paradigm to

$$C_R = f(H, E_{pa}, E_{pr})$$

where H denotes heredity, E_{pa} past environmental events, and E_{pr} the present environmental conditions. Undoubtedly, such a paradigm needs further refinement. One crucial problem is, of course, that the basic dimensions of heredity and environment are largely unknown and that, except for some elements of E_{pr}, the core variables making up heredity and environment are biotic in nature and not under full control of the experimenter. As a consequence, most of the research with humans must invoke indirect methods for the assessment of nature-nurture relations. Examples here are studies concerned with the effects of natural cross-fostering (reared together versus reared apart) and variation in the family constellation (identical twins, nonidentical twins, siblings, unrelated children) as implicit, for example, in Cattell's Multiple Abstract Variance Analysis (R. B. Cattel, 1960; Vandenberg, 1966a,b). It should be noted, however, that in a strict sense the bulk of nature-nurture research is *not* developmental, since the age variable (or age-related change) is rarely incorporated into these designs. On the other hand, it is reasonable to expect nature-nurture ratios to vary as a function of age and, moreover, as a function of the species, generation, and culture which is considered.

The final aspect of explicating the time continuum concerns the specification of the mechanisms or processes involved in linking antecedent to consequent conditions. Basically, such processes cannot be directly observed, but are to be inferred and distinguished on the basis of process-specific antecedents and consequents. Although this task appears to be the most intriguing, at least for experimentally-oriented psychologists, it is also troublesome. The major processes that have been postulated thus far are *learning* and *maturation* which, in addition are assumed to interact (e.g., Spiker, 1966). This distinction, however, leads to a number of intricate problems. One is that both learning and maturation are not unitary processes but are to be conceived as indicating a series of distinct mechanisms, such as specific and nonspecific transfer in the case of learning. Moreover, the issue arises whether these processes are invariant across age levels, or whether the mechanisms that link antecedents and consequents vary from one age level to the next (see Comalli, Chapter 8; Munsinger, Chapter 9; Botwinick, Chapter 11; Riegel, Chapter 14). By and large, it seems fair to conclude that the research oriented to the study of changes in process mechanisms in an age-developmental framework is most scarce. However, if living organisms are conceived of as representing *open* systems (not finally determined as are machines) which are engaged in continuous interchange with the environment, it seems justifiable to hypothesize that the operating mechanisms may be subject to change as well. Here, issues inherent in the discussion of organismic versus mechanistic models (see Reese & Overton, Chapter 5) are of crucial significance.

IV. HUMAN LIFE-SPAN DEVELOPMENTAL PSYCHOLOGY

A provisional definition of the topic of the present volume might then read: "Human life-span developmental psychology is concerned with the description and explication of ontogenetic (age-related) behavioral change from birth to death."

The definition suggests that developmental change might occur throughout the entire age span, whereas the focus of conventional developmental psychology has emphasized the first two decades of the life-span. Furthermore, the definition stresses the need for explication; that is, the identification of antecedent-consequent relationships, and not only description. Thus, developmental psychology, in general, has emphasized the description of age functions only in terms of the nature and rate of growth, and only in the last decade or so (e.g., Birren, 1969; Bronfenbrenner, 1963; McCandless & Spiker, 1956; Zigler, 1963) has the mainstream of developmental psychology been turned to the explication of ontogenetic change in the framework of causative networks. Undoubtedly, the increasing interest of experimentally trained researchers in developmental questions is a major reason for this historical trend. This trend, however, might also be taken as signaling the rise of mature theorizing in the field of developmental psychology.

A. Major Assumptions and Objectives

Basically, the major objectives and assumptions of a life-span approach to human development are no different from those in any age-specific developmental psychology (except for extending the age range) in that the primary objective is the investigation of *intraindividual variability.*

In general, the study of intraindividual variability (Fiske & Rice, 1955) rests on two major assumptions: (a) that intraindividual variability is systematic and not random and (b) that intraindividual variability is not negligible when contrasted with the magnitude of interindividual differences. Specific to a life-span approach are the further assumptions that: (c) the human organism exhibits continuous intraindividual change, and (d) that a significant portion of intraindividual variability is age-related, that is, ontogenetic in nature. Both the latter assumptions are supported by a sizeable but largely uncoordinated amount of research, which shows marked changes within all age periods (e.g., Birren, 1964; Botwinick, 1967; Bromley, 1966; Kagan & Moss, 1962; Pressey & Kuhlen, 1957). However, extremely little research encompasses the entire life-span and incorporates methodology appropriate to the study of ontogenetic change.

A second objective of life-span developmental psychology is the *integrative conceptualization of the totality of ontogenetic behavioral changes.* As previously mentioned, the bulk of research efforts in developmental psychology has been conducted thus far by researchers whose primary orientation was toward specific age periods such as infancy, etc., without any comprehensive attempts to integrate the findings within the framework of the life-span. As a consequence, and with few exceptions, these age-specific research efforts have remained fairly insular and uncoordinated, even though they appear to be intrinsically related through their common goal, the study of age-related behavioral change.

There is a third objective of any developmental psychology. At face value it appears to be rather dull and nondevelopmental in nature. This objective refers to the examination of the *generalizability of behavioral data and lawful relationships* across people, one aspect of what D. T. Campbell and Stanley (1963) have called "external validity." The behavioral data that are available and the laws or phenomena that are known have been largely obtained and developed within the framework of young adult subject populations, and little systematic information is available regarding their generality. To what extent, however, do infants, children, adolescents, adult, and old-aged people exhibit the same kind of perceptual, learning, and cognitive phenomena or share the same processes? One has only to mention the nomothetic versus idiographic controversy to appreciate the question whether behavioral data and processes are subject invariant. From another perspective, the question of generalizability illustrates the intrinsic relationships between developmental psychology, comparative psychology, and the psychology of individual differences.

B. Issues in Theory Construction

As Reese and Overton (Chapter 5) convincingly argue, there is a whole gamut of orientations or models (e.g., organismic versus mechanistic) from which to choose in construing developmental networks. Any comprehensive developmental theory, however, needs to incorporate the basic criteria of general developmental psychology. Furthermore, operational clarity, parsimony, and predictive power will delineate the life-span of such theories.

Let us now turn to some issues which appear of particular significance for theorizing in life-span developmental psychology. At the outset, it seems fair to state that there is no integrated body of theory in sight that offers a set of statements including laws and concepts (see Bromley, Chapter 4) encompassing the entire age span; this is particularly true if such a theory is expected to incorporate a multitude of behavioral attributes and the criteria specified above. As a matter of fact, one might even question whether there are any theoretical attempts which would permit the beginning of an internal logical analysis as demonstrated by Bromley (Chapter 4) with the disengagement theory of Cumming and Henry (1961) which, incidentally, covers only the later part of life.

What is at hand are age-specific theories, such as Piaget's theory of cognitive development, which become miniature or even dry (see Flavell, Chapter 10) when explored for life-span developmental implications. In fact, one might question whether age-specific developmental theories can be easily expanded to incorporate the life-span, or whether any life-span approach might not require a novel conceptualization of intraindividual behavioral change. In other words, can we expect a life-span developmental psychology to consist simply of some kind of additive combination of age-specific attempts, or is it so that it requires alternative ways of organizing and construing reality? Here, the old, but far from dead, issue of reductionism versus constructionism comes into the picture and deserves serious consideration. Does one become a life-span developmental psychologist by simply asking the same questions for different age ranges, by combining studies conducted with children, adolescents, adults, and old people? Undoubtedly, such a strategy represents a first step, but it seems reasonable to expect that in the not too distant future, a life-span approach might have to lead to kinds of inquiries which cannot directly be deduced from age-specific developmental theories.

In this context, two related aspects seem particularly relevant; one concerns the status of the age variable in developmental theorizing, the other the question of homology both with regard to the structure of attributes and the set of

processes that are postulated to account for antecedent-consequent
ships. As alluded to earlier, age (as an organismic, subject-related variable, might
represent one of many parameters (Kessen, 1962) to be considered in otherwise
unaltered antecedent-consequent relationships (e.g., Hull, 1943; Noble, Baker, &
Jones, 1964). Alternatively, the systematic explication of the age concept may
reveal the necessity to construct different, perhaps disparate theoretical
networks (incorporating structural changes in attributes and processes) for
different developmental levels in order to arrive at a parsimonious set of
statements about long-term ontogenetic change. Here, the notions of homology
(e.g., Nissen, 1951), indicating the degree of invariance of concepts, processes,
and laws, and of quantitative versus qualitative change (e.g., Beilin, 1969; also
see Nesselroade, Chapter 7) are of crucial significance and deserve to be revisited,
especially by methodologically-minded researchers.

C. Issues in Research Methodology

The present volume includes a number of chapters which directly or indirectly
bear on aspects of research methodology which are specific to the investigation
of developmental change (Wohlwill, Chapter 6; Nesselroade, Chapter 7; Kausler,
Chapter 13; Schaie, Chapter 18). Thus, the issues highlighted (e.g., construct
validation, measurement of change, analysis of developmental functions, analysis
of sequential change, sequential strategies, measurement of the multiple
determinants of behavior, structuring of change, etc.) clearly demonstrate that
developmental psychology is in need of a particular methodology suited for the
examination of structural and quantitative change.

A first aspect of the conventional research approach that needs reconsidera-
tion is the *status of the age variable*, as most persuasively demonstrated by
Wohlwill (Chapter 6; Wohlwill, 1970). A new perspective regarding the age
variable is indeed important. First, chronological age, though a powerful index,
appears to be a rather dull variable (e.g., McCandless & Spiker, 1956) for
developmental theorizing. On the one hand, it is a nonpsychological variable and,
as discussed earlier, its psychological meaning must always be deduced from
further research aimed at its systematic explication in terms of age-associated
conditions and processes.

Chronological age also shares the experimental shortcomings of all biotic
(organismic) variables in that it is not under full control of the experimenter.
Furthermore, few age-related developmental theories assign importance or
theoretical status to a specific age (e.g., five years old) in the life span. Rather,
the developmentalist is concerned with the sequence of change. The fact that
the sequence of change occurs at predetermined times after birth is of no
necessary relevance, nor does it alter the importance or nature of developmental
research. Therefore, any attempts to develop alternative age concepts such as

biological age, sociological age, or psychological age (e.g., Birren, 1959b) are welcomed.

Alternatively, it is theoretically possible to introduce "age simulations" through the incorporation of specific experimental procedures. As an example, Parrish, Lundy, and Leibowitz (1968) have explored the fruitfulness of manipulating age by means of hypnotic age-regression. Goulet (1968a, b) has suggested the use of massed practice as a method to equate for the effects of differential prior experience (learning) that characterizes samples varying in age. It is apparent that hypnosis as a potential method is limited to retrospective studies (for example, the study of behavior characterizing an earlier level of development) and that the use of this technique in developmental research is, as yet, unvalidated. Massed training, on the other hand, as a technique to compensate for the differential effects of prior experience in developmental research, is limited to prospective studies. Furthermore, the method would not influence biological maturation *per se*.

Such approaches have the potential both to alter the nature of age-developmental research and to provide new insights into the psychological meaning of age changes. One implication for research strategy that follows from such a reevaluation of the age variable is, for example, that any descriptive age differences or age changes that are observed are not to be taken as fixed and final. Thus, inquiries should be directed toward those parameters which, when manipulated, affect ontogenetic change. What is, for example, necessary to speed up or even reverse age changes in short-term memory from 20 to 80 years of age; or, what manipulations are necessary to equate 20- and 80-year-olds with regard to memory performance given that descriptive, age-developmental research suggests pronounced age differences.

A second aspect of research methodology concerns the *measurement of intraindividual change*, an issue recently cast in the distinction between age changes and age differences (e.g., Bromley, 1966; Schaie, 1967), and the conclusion that both the cross-sectional and longitudinal methods are preexperimental designs as defined by D. T. Campbell and Stanley (1963). Both Wohlwill (Chapter 6) and Schaie (Chapter 18) deal extensively with this issue.

In this chapter it has been argued strongly that the basic objective of any ontogenetic developmental psychology is the study of intraindividual change. The bulk of developmental research, however, still involves designs most appropriate to the study of interindividual differences, for example, the conventional cross-sectional method. A cross-sectional study, however, must be considered as a weak strategy as long as more information is desired than the comparison of mean differences between age samples. Moreover, conventional cross-sectional studies (particularly, when covering the life-span) are bound to confound age differences with a number of uncontrolled factors, e.g., individual differences in life-span (selective survival), differences between generations, or age-specific selective sampling effects which preclude the comparability of the age groups involved. Thus, only in rare instances can it be assumed that cross-sectional age differences are a result of the aging process, that is, do reflect age changes. What is necessary in research of this nature is the incorporation of a series of control groups to check the assumption that age differencs obtained using cross-sectional designs reflect *average* and unbiased intraindividual age changes.

The direct measurement of intraindividual variability (and of course, of interindividual differences in such ontogenetic intraindividual variability) clearly requires the use of repeated measurement designs. Both Wohlwill and Nesselroade, in their respective chapters, have discussed some of the more potent strategies. Again, it is important to stress the fact that a single longitudinal study is also rather unsatisfactory unless a series of control groups for such effects as selective sampling, selective drop-out, or testing are incorporated. One further point is that the use of a repeated measurement design alone is not sufficient. It is also necessary to utilize the information inherent in repeated measures when analyzing the data. In this context, much more attention should be given to design strategies which explicitly vary age and time of measurement as is true, for example, for Cattell's (see Wohlwill, Chapter 6; Nesselroade, Chapter 7), *O, P, S,* and *T* techniques. Moreover, significant information might be obtained by combining the various correlational techniques in order to examine not only intraindividual variability in the framework of a single individual (*O, P*) but also interindividual differences in intraindividual variability.

The problems associated with the study of long-term intraindividual change also force attention to issues related to *methods and instruments for data collection.* For example, is it possible to "compress" the time interval of observation that is needed to obtain information on ontogenetic change. It is typically argued that any long-term longitudinal approach suffers from the fact that the subjects will likely outlive the experimenter. Such an argument, however, is only far-reaching when it is assumed that the process of observation and the behavior itself need to occur concurrently or at least very close in time. Although concurrent observation might be superior for most questions, particularly when experimental manipulations are involved, a life-span approach must explore the fruitfulness of alternative strategies of observation. Thus, it might be feasible in certain circumstances to compress the time interval by use of retrospective and prospective reports by the subject himself (e.g., Ahammer, 1970). As a matter of fact, C. Bühler (1935), one of the pioneers of life-span developmental psychology, based her theorizing largely on retrospective reports in the form of autobiographies. Much more effort, however, will have to center on examining the reliabilities and validities of retrospective (e.g., Robbins, 1961; Rosenthal, 1963) and prospective observations. One intriguing approach relevant to retrospective measurement is the strategy of hypnotic age-regression (Barber,

1962), mentioned earlier. Furthermore, it appears useful to investigate the fruitfulness of using informants (parents, friends, teachers) other than the subject whose ontogenetic change is under study. In this context it might be particularly useful to look to scientists in other developmental fields (e.g., history, anthropology, or even geology) for appropriate models.

A second issue related to problems of data collection is that of developing measurement instruments that are age invariant in terms of their validities and reliabilities. Ideally, tasks or instruments that are age equivalent would provide measures of the same attributes and processes in subjects from all segments of the life-span. With certain observational media and tasks (e.g., questionnaires) such requirements are impossible to meet, since the demands of the task exceed the capabilities of at least some of the subjects. On the other hand, the application of the same task (e.g., eyelid conditioning) does not necessarily guarantee that the measures reflect the same processes when age is varied (see Comalli, Chapter 8; Botwinick, Chapter 11; Kausler, Chapter 13). Here, the different strategies of appraising the validity of a test (content, concurrent, predictive, construct validity) are of significance and more attention needs to be directed toward a systematic examination of age differences in such test characteristics. One issue is of particular interest in this context. It relates to the question whether age differences in validities (and reliabilities for that matter) are seen as being associated with changes inherent in the measurement instruments or in the persons. For example, do age differences in performance on a questionnaire indicate that the questionnaire measures different attributes in different age groups or do the age differences in performance reflect only changes in the subject's position (more or less) on a particular attribute? In line with the distinction between a physical and a functional stimulus, both assumptions might be reasonable as long as designs for the separation of age-associated change in validity of measurement instruments and change in persons are available.

In case it is not possible to develop a single task or a measurement instrument that shows equivalent validities throughout the total life-span, the feasibility of cross-linking measurement instruments will have to be explored. Such cross-linking might involve the systematic variation of attributes and associated instruments following Campbell and Fiske's convergent versus discriminant validation approach by the multitrait-multimethod matrix (D. T. Campbell & Fiske, 1959). Moreover, to obtain continuous coverage of the life-span it will be necessary to use particular age levels for cross-linking. For example, task A is given at age levels I and II, task B at age levels II and III, task C at age levels III and IV, in order to examine corresponding validities for those tasks that overlap at specific age levels (e.g., A and B are compared on age level II). Here, techniques of comparative and interbattery factor analysis (Baltes & Nessel-roade, 1970; Kristof, 1967; also see Nesselroade, Chapter 7) and strategies to disentangle method variance from attribute variance (e.g., D. N. Jackson, 1969) will be of value. To realize the lack of emphasis with respect to validation studies in developmental psychology, one has only to mention the fact that the question of validity is largely ignored by process-oriented (learning, perception, cognition, etc.) developmental researchers.

V. CONCLUSIONS AND PERSPECTIVES

Considering the life-span as the domain in which to study developmental change immediately makes apparent the restricted nature of our usual conceptualization of developmental psychology. This appears to be the primary reason why editors of developmental journals (e.g., A. E. Siegel, 1967) continue to lament the restricted age groups which are currently receiving the preponderance of attention. The restriction in scope becomes even more evident when human developmental psychology is examined in the framework of general developmental psychology, which is itself concerned with species, generation, and cultural changes of a long-term nature.

Although the issues and problems of research in life-span developmental psychology in principle are not different from those of any age-range-specific developmental psychology, there are some features of methodology, theory construction, and content, which, when viewed in the perspective of the life-span, become more conspicuous. First, the comparative nature of life-span psychology points to the need for a systematic analysis of the universe of attributes and processes that define the matrix for describing ontogenetic change. Particular emphasis needs to be given to questions of both structural and quantitative changes when comparing, for example, infants with adults and the elderly. Moreover, intensive efforts regarding the examination of age differences in the validity and reliability of measurement instruments must be made. Furthermore, attention must be directed to the development of measurement networks that permit cross-linking of observations that would otherwise be restricted to particular age ranges. Last but not least, it appears highly desirable to investigate the usefulness of measurement devices that permit compressing the time interval of observation by means of techniques associated with retrospective but also prospective measurement.

Second, the investigation of long-term, intraindividual change underlines the now well-documented demand for more sophisticated research designs in the analysis of antecedent-consequent relationships, particularly when cause-effect sequences are sought. In this regard, the restriction inherent in the conventional age-descriptive studies (cross-sectional and longitudinal) can hardly be underestimated, and attempts at manipulating and controlling age changes are highly desirable to enhance mature theorizing in developmental psychology. In this context, a life-span model also forces attention to systematic changes in the composition of the population under investigation, both in regard to age changes in a single cohort (e.g., selective survival) and to changes over generations. Thus, with respect to the latter, admitting the role of experiential determinants of developmental change is to admit the sizeable impact on behavior of advances in the communication media, the continuously increasing levels of education, standard of living, etc. Furthermore, advances in the medical sciences have resulted both in better health and increased life expectancy (e.g., Platt & Parkes, 1967; Pressey & Kuhlen, 1957), factors which potentially can change the characteristics of the population under study. Such a perspective also highlights the generation- and culture-specific nature of available theories relating to developmental change, not to mention the available texts in the area.

A life-span conceptualization also elicits a number of intriguing hypotheses and issues not necessarily apparent within the context of an age-specific conceptualization. Contrast, to give two examples, the statements by Lipsitt (Chapter 12) that infancy constitutes the period most conducive to learning with Flavell's (Chapter 10) that environmental influences on behavior are most important during the span from adulthood to death and maturational factors are of primary importance before this point. Or, compare the generally accepted notion of continuity and stability in change with Neugarten's (1969) contention that one might be impressed more by the discontinuities than the continuities in behavior when taking a look at current life-span research. While such discrepancies are partially a function of the scarcity of data, they do provide illustrations of assumptions about the nature of life-span changes and underline a problem raised in a previous section: whether we can expect life-span developmental psychology to consist in a simple additive combination of the phenomena and laws appropriate to the set of age-range-specific developmental psychologies, or whether life-span developmental psychology requires an alternative, fresh conceptualization (in terms of concepts and laws) in integrating long-term ontogenetic change. If the latter is true, the present volume clearly represents an exploratory venture since the bulk of hypotheses and data discussed still has its primary roots in age-specific research.

Finally, it might be interesting to highlight some implications of a life-span developmental psychology for related disciplines and vice versa. In this context it should not be overlooked that the tendency to take a life-span look at ontogenetic change is not idiosyncratic to psychology. On the contrary, other fields interested in the living organism, such as biology, medicine, psychiatry, sociology, and education, share this interest as well. Thus, information on adult and old-age changes in learning or perception will be important for educational psychologists who increasingly focus a major part of their endeavor to the formulation of curricula for adult education. Conversely, the introduction of adult education will significantly alter the type of age functions to be expected in, for exampie, life-span research on cognitive functioning in future generations. Similarly, the study of age changes in the physiology of sense organs will undoubtedly contribute to the understanding of age changes in psychological aspects of perception and vice versa. Such examples reflect the notion that a multidisciplinary approach is necessary for the development of a parsimonious network of developmental phenomena and laws.

CHAPTER 2

Historical Antecedents of Life-Span Developmental Psychology[1]

DON C. CHARLES
IOWA STATE UNIVERSITY
AMES, IOWA

ABSTRACT

Contemporary developmental psychology studies children or aged persons and rarely considers the whole of life. Child psychology originated in baby biographies, genetic psychology, child-clinical, and educational psychology. These origins have maintained the focus on childhood and on the person. Educational measurement and behaviorism started the trend toward scientific rigor in research. Although some studies of maturity and old age were conducted early, most postadolescent research originated after World War II and emphasizes the medical, physiological, and social problems of old age. The entire life-span has become an area for concern primarily by those researchers involved in longitudinal studies: As their subjects have matured and aged, the researchers' interests have kept pace.

[1] Although developmental psychology has by no means been entirely an American enterprise nor limited solely to the study of human subjects, limitations of time and space make it necessary to confine this paper almost exclusively to the study of human beings in the United States. A succeeding paper will consider European developments.

I. INTRODUCTION

A scientific discipline, like a person or institution, reflects in its present state the experiences and influences of its past. Examination of its history may provide some insight into its strengths and weaknesses, some explanations for its day-to-day performance, and perhaps some forecast of its future. The present conference, the first to my knowledge called to examine the whole life, suggests that an appropriate time has arrived to examine the antecedents of psychology's concern with the life-span. Perhaps thereby both present state and future development may be somewhat illumined.

Before we look at history, we should determine just what is the present state of the interest area, or indeed, whether there exists an interest area, that we can call life-span developmental psychology. The papers in the present volume indicate that (a) there is a body of relevant literature and (b) there are numbers of scientists concerned with the problems of the area. In these days when almost every activity is highly structured and organized, we would expect common membership by these scientists in a society or association devoted to the discipline. At this point the identity of life-span psychologists becomes less clear.

Since there is no division of the American Psychological Association for life-span psychologists, one would expect common membership in those two divisions encompassing all the ages of man: Division 7, labeled Developmental Psychology (formerly the division on Childhood and Adolescence) and Division 20, Maturity and Old Age. In fact, one might logically expect an eventual merging of these two divisions. Wolfle (1949) recommended that merger, but it has not occurred. A few years later, Adkins (1954) factor analyzed multiple membership in APA divisions and at least one other organization. She found practically no overlap between Division 7 and Division 20 memberships. One factor, described as concerning "Scholarly pursuit of theoretical knowledge without concern for practical applications" included the Psychometric Society and divisions on Esthetics, Evaluation, and Measurement, General Psychology, and Maturity and Old Age (Division 20). Another factor consisted primarily of Division 7, Developmental Psychology, and Division 15, Educational Psychology. A reworking of Adkin's data (Ransom, 1956) revealed differences in both origins and interests of members of the two divisions of our concern.

An examination of the membership list of Divisions 7 and 20 in a complete APA Directory (American Psychological Association, 1966) reveals that there were 810 Members and Fellows in Division 7 and a total of 288 in Division 20. Only 45 psychologists held overlapping membership in the two divisions; that is, a little more than 5% of Division 7 affiliates were also in Division 20, and 15% of Division 20 affiliates were in Division 7. Identification with divisions concerned with all the life-span is held by a very small minority of psychologists.

There are few texts that cover more than the periods of infancy, childhood, and adolescence separately or combined. A few texts have appeared in which the "life-span" aspect has consisted of a chapter or two on maturity and old age tacked onto the end of a child and adolescent text. Some genuine life-span texts have appeared over a thirty-year period. What was probably the first such book was developed between 1934 and 1939 by Sidney Pressey at Ohio State aided by two of his students. This was *Life: A Psychological Survey* (Pressey, Janney & Kuhlen, 1939). Pressey reported, "Using this volume as text, I began offering a course on psychological development through the life span; this became a required five hour course for all departmental majors. . ." (Pressey, 1969 personal communication). The book was later revised (Pressey & Kuhlen, 1957). Pressey (1967) commented, ". . .the book was a radical departure from those then current. Most seemed to assume that development stopped at eighteen; one venturesome author gave fifteen pages to all the years from puberty till death, but forty-five pages to development from conception till birth. . . [pp. 326-327]." Noteworthy texts besides Pressey's exhibiting a genuine concern for changes through life include those by J. E. Anderson (1949), Zubek and Solberg (1954) and Hurlock (1968).

An anonymous reviewer for a major publisher commented in 1968 on a partially completed manuscript of a life-span psychology text, ". . . it is fine to argue that developmental psychology course instructors ought to expose students to the problems of old age, but how many people are interested in teaching that kind of course? . . .very few professors teach a 'full-life' developmental course. In fact many developmental courses even omit adolescence as a topic area."

It would appear from these and other observations of the current scene that life-span psychology as a clearly defined interest area is still in an early and formative stage of development. It seems desirable then to examine the history of the various life-segment interest areas to find the origins of our concerns. Developmental psychology has in its past nineteenth century descriptions of infant development, the genetic psychology enthusiasm of Hall and his followers, the child psychology movement of the twenties and thirties, educational psychology's continuing need for evidence on the characteristics of pupils, the employment of children as research subjects by general-experimental psychologists, and most recently, medical, social, and psychological interest in the problems of aging. Perhaps most significant has been the involvement maintained by some developmental researchers with subjects they first examined as long as four decades ago; as the subjects have matured and aged, so have the researchers' interests. Continuities and discontinuities in development of individuals has sometimes provided intriguing conflict with existing cross-sectional data and longitudinal studies would seem to have been a major factor in drawing researchers' interests along from one age and stage to the next.

II. AMERICAN BEGINNINGS

Concern with human development appeared in two major manifestations in the late nineteenth and early twentieth centuries. One of these was the description of day-by-day changes in structure and functioning of children known as "baby biographies," although some went well beyond babyhood in their age coverage. The other was the "genetic psychology" movement of G. S. Hall and his students.

A. Baby Biographies and Other Child Descriptions

In Europe in the nineteenth century, a number of biographical studies of young children appeared, but until the time of Darwin and Preyer, these were generally sentimental accounts, rather than careful descriptions of growth and development. While Preyer (1882) is sometimes cited as author of the first, or one of the first, baby biographies, at least twelve such records preceded his in publication (Dennis, 1949). The earliest baby biography in English apparently was Willard's "Observations on an Infant in its First Year by a Mother" (Willard, 1835). The relatively complete coverage of individual child development in European and American biographies was supplemented by studies with a narrower focus in the United States, e.g., the two early longitudinal studies of language development by Holden (1877) and Humphries (1880).

Another very early, but unpublished, baby biography was that kept by the New England eccentric, utopian, and transcendentalist Bronson Alcott on his daughter who was born in 1831. The account was published later in summary form (Talbot, 1882). Among Alcott's many ventures was the establishment of a school based on his original educational ideas. In the course of his educational operation, an assistant recorded and later published nearly verbatim conversations he carried on with children (Alcott & Peabody, 1835, 1836-1837). His questions and stimulation elicited responses which revealed the child's reasoning processes in a manner not unlike that followed by Piaget a century later.

An extraordinarily complete description of a female child from birth to age three was made by Shinn. The study included early measurements and continuing reports on growth, health, sense development, movements and motor development, speech, and what would today be called cognitive and perceptual development. It was originally published in two volumes including nearly 700 journal pages (Shinn, 1893–1899, 1907) and in another version as a book (Shinn, 1900). Shinn utilized functionalist concepts and showed special sensitivity to the mother-child interaction. In the journal version there is a thoughtful discussion of methods in child study, and some restrained criticism of then-current theory, especially that of Baldwin. She comments:

The moral of all this is that people should be very cautious indeed in drawing parallels between the child and the race, and especially in basing educational theories on them. But if one is cautious enough and patient enough, there are many hints about our race history to be found in the nursery [Shinn, 1900, p. 8] ;

An early (perhaps the first) statement of support for longitudinal study of the individual also comes from her book:

If I should find out that a thousand babies learned to stand at an average age of forty-six weeks and two days, I should not know as much that is important about standing, as a stage in human progress, as I should after watching a single baby carefully through the whole process of achieving balance on his little soles [Shinn, 1900, p. 11].

Another scholarly study of a quality similar to Shinn's was one by K. C. Moore (1896).

In 1883, G. S. Hall published a major study called "The contents of children's minds" (Hall, 1883). This was a better and more thorough repetition of an earlier study by the same title in Germany (Bartholomäi, 1870). The study was an attempt to determine children's familiarity with a large number of relatively ordinary objects and concepts at the time of entry into first grade. The study was noteworthy in its methods: Children were interrogated on 134 topics by trained and supervised kindergarten teachers. This study was well received and was reprinted frequently for the next twenty-five years.

Developmental psychology has always drawn on other disciplines, especially physiology and medicine. The Harvard physiologist Henry P. Bowditch was one of the originators of the child study movement in the United States. Bowditch presented diagrams of children's growth to the Boston Medical Society in 1872 and conducted a normative study in 1875. His data were published as "The Growth of Children" in 1877 and 1879 (Bowditch, 1877, 1879-1880). The study revealed, among other new insights into growth, that large children began their period of accelerated growth earlier than small (Cannon, 1924).

B. The Genetic Psychology Movement

Baby biographies and other descriptions of growth did not lead directly to a science of human development. However interesting or useful, they did not fit into any overall theory, nor fall into a pattern for analysis. The work of Darwin and his supporters along with the notion of pangenesis provided the stimulus for a theory that aroused great enthusiasm in the late nineteenth and early twentieth centuries and, although erroneous, led eventually to the discipline of developmental psychology. Pangenesis was the theory that every cell, tissue, and organ secreted minute particles called gemmules, which were concentrated in the semen and were the basis of fecundation. G. S. Hall and students borrowed evolutionary ideas from Darwin, Haeckel, Spencer, and Lamarck, combined ideas from botany, biology, geology, paleontology, and embryology and fashioned "genetic psychology" from these components.

Hall's theory was summed up in the catch-phrase, "ontogeny recapitulates phylogeny." That is, each human organism, from conception to birth, was supposed to recapitulate the evolutionary rise of the human race from lower organism to human infant. Then, in childhood, the social evolution of man was repeated; only at adolescence could one begin to modify or mold the person. As G. S. Hall (1904) phrased it, one had to allow "the fundamental traits of savagery their fling till twelve [p. x] ." During adolescence and early maturity however, society had a heavy burden because, according to Hall's interpretation of Lamarckian theory, genetic changes could be effected during this period. A natural scientist of the time expressed the idea:

All modifications and variations in progressive series tend to appear first in the adolescent or adult stages of growth, and then to be inherited in successive descendents at earlier and earlier stages according to the law of acceleration, until they either become embryonic, or are crowded out of the organizations, and replaced in the development of characteristics of later origin [Hyatt, 1890, p. ix] .

While revolutionary evolutionists did not attend much to Rousseau, the idea that nature should have its way until adolescence was espoused by Hall and by John Fiske and other students who "found Rousseau a wellspring of profound insight when they recognized, as he had, that focus on development might well be diverged into childhood and adolescent stages [Grinder, 1967, p. 26] ." Therefore childhood was to be free until about twelve, when society could begin to improve the genetic stock by modifying and controlling it.

Hall began teaching at Johns Hopkins, but did most of his work at Clark, where he was also president. As a psychologist he attracted a long list of students who themselves grew into eminence: Dewey, Cattell, Sanford, Burnham, and Jastrow were at Hopkins when he was and both Terman and Gesell became his students at Clark. He established laboratories and was the founder of several journals which were important for a new science's identity as well as for its communication. In the developmental area there was the *Pedagogical Seminary*, established in 1891, renamed *The Journal of Genetic Psychology* in 1927. Sigmund Freud and psychoanalysis were first given a hearing in the United States in 1909 through Hall's efforts.

Genetic psychology helped to differentiate adolescence as a life-period of psychological concern, and one of Hall's major efforts was his massive and encyclopedic two-volume *Adolescence* (G. S. Hall, 1904). This work was a mixture of description and genetic psychology theory, with little scientific foundation, but it was immensely popular. Hall's interests and writing appealed to educators, as did his use of the Galton questionnaire technique. Thus, educational psychology also received much of its early stimulation from the genetic psychology movement.

J. M. Baldwin was another aggressive speaker for genetic psychology. He was a theoretician and writer whose book *Mental Development in the Child and the Race (J. M. Baldwin, 1895)* was one of the major source books for the movement. The experimentalists criticized him vigorously for his elaboration of genetic theories in absence of a sound empirical basis, but in defense he reported later, "Questionnaires, experimental studies, theoretical interpretations, have all taken on a more serious and scientific look since the day of the publication of Darwin's and Preyer's careful observations [J. M. Baldwin, 1913, pp. 124-125]."

Genetic psychology faded as natural scientists discredited pangenesis and acquired characteristics, making it necessary to discard the theory of recapitulation. Then Mendel's 1865 paper on dominant and recessive traits was rediscovered and genetics began its scientific advance, discarding Lamarckian influence. While the theory itself had to be abandoned, the efforts exerted in its behalf helped to develop a science of child study—a functional psychology which has continued in that tradition. Grinder (1967) evaluates the movement:

Genetic psychology makes sparse linkage with contemporary issues; its enduring importance, however, does not inhere in its specific endowments to psychological theory. The genetic psychology movement dispatched the transition of the study of man's psychical development from biology to psychology and the social sciences, and its historical significance is revealed in the pattern by which assumptions drawn from the earlier natural sciences were focused upon man [p. viii].

III. CLINICAL WORK WITH CHILDREN

A. Introduction

Psychological concern for children with problems began to develop during the same period that the baby biographers and genetic psychologists were producing their work. Lightner Witmer, who had studied under Cattell and Wundt, founded a clinic for children at the University of Pennsylvania in 1896. His original concern and emphasis was on learning defects, however displayed; his early cases included a chronic poor speller, a boy with a speech impediment, and disruptive children suffering from what was termed "moral defects." In all cases the child was examined by a physician and then given a "mental examination" including anthropometric measures, eye tests, reaction time study, and the like. Witmer's treatment was pedagogical and similar to that which Itard and Seguin had developed in their work with mentally retarded children in Europe and the United States (Fernberger, 1931; Phillips, 1931; Witmer, 1907). Despite some evangelism at the 1896 APA meeting, clinical application of psychology was not then attractive to most psychologists. One psychologist, William Krohn, did found a laboratory for study of the mentally ill in Illinois in 1897, but he later moved on to medical and psychiatric study (Wallin, 1961).

Clinical work with children received a significant impetus from the establishment of the Juvenile Psychopathic Institute in Chicago in 1909. The Institute was headed by William Healy, whose training was medical and psychiatric, and it had a staff of one, psychologist Grace Fernald (Healy & Bronner, 1948). The Healy clinic attracted wide attention, and led to the establishment of similar units over the country. Healy and Augusta Bronner left Chicago for Boston and the Judge Baker Foundation in 1917.

Another figure who was active in work with abnormal and retarded children was J. E. W. Wallin, who fought for professional recognition of clinical psychologists and wrote one of the early mental health texts (Wallin, 1914).

Between the establishment of Healy's clinic in 1909 and the beginning of World War I, at least nineteen child guidance clinics were established, including those at the University of Iowa, Yale, the University of Pittsburgh, Tulane, Rutgers, Cornell, and in the cities of Albany, Trenton, Philadelphia, Los Angeles, Oakland, and also in connection with children's hospitals (T. L. Smith, 1914; Wallin, 1911).

It is noteworthy that clinical concern for children at this early twentieth century period emphasized school and general social adjustment rather than psychosis. A number of European works of the late nineteenth century discussed the existence of psychoses in children (e.g., Maudsley, 1880), although there was popular objection to the concept. Kanner, a major figure in child psychiatry, reported that concern with severe emotional disturbance in children—primarily schizophrenia—was not consistent nor widespread among clinicians until the 1930's (Kanner, 1962).

Concern with the moderately retarded child was also neglected. Since the eighteenth century, obviously abnormal and severely retarded children had been institutionalized, studied, and some attempts at palliative treatment had been attempted. Not until the development of mental tests, however, was there awareness of the large number of children who looked and even acted "normal," but who could not learn well in school. While occasional concern for these retardates was exercised in the new clinics, extensive study and therapeutic effort were generally left to specialists at institutions like the Vineland Training School in New Jersey.

In his 1911 article Wallin praised the work being done in the child-guidance clinics, but lamented the lack of attention given to scientific research: "[It is] . . . to our shame that they have lagged considerably behind the institutions for the abnormal and defective in respect to the establishment of *laboratories for discovery and research* [Wallin, 1911, p. 196] ."

One effect of the clinical movement was concentration of attention on the individual child. Where the genetic psychologists were looking for laws and universals, and trying to develop a new science, the clinicians were looking at persons and trying to solve problems. Witmer (1907) summarized the point of view.

The clinical psychologist is interested primarily in the individual child. . . . the clinical psychologist examines a child with a single definite object in view—the next step in the child's mental and physical development . . . the purpose of the clinical psychologist, as a contributor to science, is to discover the relation between cause and effect in applying the various pedagogical remedies to a child who is suffering from general or special retardation [pp. 6-7].

This stance elicited criticism from science-oriented psychologists; the defense rejoinder was mostly a referral to the youth of the applied movement (Sylvester, 1913-1914).

But developmental psychology has maintained its strong concern for the welfare of the whole person: The searching for the causes of present behavior has encouraged a truly developmental point of view, and the discovery of the complexity of behavioral cause has helped avoid too-simple explanations. The negative aspect of this clinical influence has been in methodology: the complexity and effect of change over time have rendered research difficult, and the "helping attitude" has not always furthered the establishment of a sound theoretical and empirical basis for a science of human development.

An allied effect of the continuing strength of clinical interest by child psychologists has been a preference for psychoanalytic theory, perhaps because of early closeness to medical and psychiatric practice. Whatever its virtues in diagnosis and therapy, psychoanalysis did not lead psychologists into the mainstream of behavioral research. By the same token, there has been, during much of the history of the developmental psychology movement, a clinical emphasis on abnormality and on problems rather than on the course and progress of normal development.

A third effect of the clinical orientation was involvement of developmentalists in the mental measurement movement that developed with the new century.

B. Mental Measurement

Origin of the mental testing movement is usually attributed to Binet and the date cited about 1904 or 1905. Like many historical generalizations this one is true, but does not tell the whole story. Related perhaps to European laboratory activity in measuring sensory function, considerable testing was going on there and in the United States before Binet's work was developed.

In about 1890, F. Boas at Clark University had made anthropological measurements on 1500 school children, and then tested them on vision, hearing, and memory. The latter capacity was inferred from performance on what later became a standard subtest in intelligence batteries—a digit-span test. This approach to memory-span evaluation was devised by J. Jacobs (1887). Boas was perhaps first to attempt to relate his subjects' performance on the various tests to independent judgments of the children's teachers. The technique was described by Bolton (1891). Similarly, testing was going on in Europe; Münsterberg (1891), for example, gave a series of tests to school children on reading, controlled association, judgment, memory and the like.

The major early stimulus for mental testing in the United States came from J. McKeen Cattell. After working with Wundt, and more importantly, Galton, Cattell returned to the University of Pennsylvania as a professor of psychology. He was convinced that psychology should advance on the basis of measurement and experimentation. He introduced the term "mental test" in 1890. His own testing included measures of dynamometer pressure, rate of movement, sensation areas, least noticeable differences in weight, reaction time for sound, time for naming colors, bisection of a 50-cm line, judgment of 10-seconds time, and numbers of letters remembered on one hearing. In a comment appended to the Cattell report, Galton argued that, in addition to the type of tests used, independent estimates should be added of such things as personality characteristics—"mobile, eager, energetic"—physical impression of subject, notes on activity such as "good at games requiring good eye and hand," and similar judgments.

The results of Cattell's tests, which took 40 minutes to administer, were given individually to one hundred freshmen at Columbia and were published in 1896. Cattell's investigations of individual differences were used, along with others, in Spearman's early correlational work as a supplement to his own (Spearman's) data. In general, Cattell defined the place of quantitative work in American psychology. Later, at Columbia, he taught E. L. Thorndike who continued quantitative and experimental study of abilities (J. McK. Cattell, 1890; Cattell & Farrand, 1896; Spearman, 1904).

Another early attempt to relate test performance to ability estimates by teachers was conducted by J. A. Gilbert (1894). In 1893, he gave several mental tests to 1200 New Haven school children. The measures included height, weight, lung capacity, and tests of sensation, tapping, reaction time, memory for tone duration, and suggestibility. Gilbert observed steady improvement to pubescence, followed by more gradual improvement. Binet may have been influenced by this research for he reported discussing the pattern of development and the criterion of teacher judgments with Henri (Binet & Henri, 1896).

Another early tester was J. Jastrow, who reported results of testing on a number of University of Wisconsin students (Jastrow, 1891-1892). Obviously, the "psychology of the college sophomore" has a venerable history in American psychology! In 1893, Jastrow set up a battery of fifteen tests—five touch and cutaneous sensibility, five touch and vision, five vision—to be taken by any interested person passing by at the Columbian Exposition in Chicago. Unfortunately he did not publish his findings (Phillippe, 1894). Kirkpatrick was still another who tested children and made comparisons of scores to an academic criterion—in his case, to school work (Kirkpatrick, 1900).

Mental testing work was part of the *Zeitgeist* of the turn of the century. Binet, who had been interested in testing in the 1890s, was appointed to a commission to study failures in the Paris schools in 1904. He and Simon produced the first version of the famous test, and by 1908 produced a revision scaled according to item difficulty and age which gave rise to the "mental age" concept (Binet & Simon, 1905a,b, 1908).

American psychologists reacted quickly to Binet's efforts. Goddard translated and adapted the items for American use (Goddard, 1910). Healy and Fernald (1910) published their set of tests the same year.

It is noteworthy that, at this point, neither research nor school application was motivating most of the testers using versions of the Binet. Goddard was working with mentally deficient children at the Vineland school, and Healy and Fernald were working with delinquent and disturbed children in Chicago. Tests were not yet well standardized and were used as clinical tools for diagnosis and as aids in problem solving. A psychologist who worked with Healy (Worcester, 1969, personal communication) recalls:

...I worked with Healy one summer at the Psychopathic Institute of the Juvenile Court of Chicago. That was, I believe, the summer of 1916. . . . We used Goddard's translation of the Binet-Simon, the Healy Pictorial and one or two other tests, always supplemented by what Healy called some common-sense questions. These latter were often quite revealing.

In order to achieve a measure of subnormality, Binet had subtracted the mental age from the chronological age. In 1912, Stern developed the concept of intelligence as a relative state (i.e., MA/CA), and thus suggested the IQ (W. Stern, 1914).

Ability testing was limited to a few clinics and university laboratories until 1916, when Terman published his revision of Binet's test. Terman provided norms based on 1000 subjects ranging in age from 3 to 18. He set age 16 as normal adult achievement, and age 18 as "superior adult" level. Binet items were moved up or down and new items were added. There was a battery at each age, with each item credited with two to six months each. Stern's idea of the IQ was utilized for the first time (Terman, 1916).

One of the major virtues of the test, from a developmental point of view, was the attempt to select a representative sample of subjects for standardizing the instrument. Thus, it became possible not only to make fair comparisons between children of similar and different ages, like and opposite sex, different social classes and the like, but as testing became more common, repeated testing of the same children over time became possible, and individual mental growth could be studied.

World War I brought the next major development in mental testing. A committee of five psychologists, under Robert Yerkes' direction, was appointed to construct a group intelligence test for military use. Derived largely from a device developed earlier by Otis, a paper-and-pencil test was developed and administered to millions of men; the instrument was called the Army Alpha (Yerkes, 1921). The Alpha opened the gates. After the war, tests of greatly varying quality were developed and were widely administered. While too much was expected of the tests, they did hasten developmental psychology's concern with measurement, and provided vast quantities of data to evaluate.

One of the questions generated by the testing movement was, "At what age does a person reach mental maturity?" Doll (1919), for example, studied 500 subjects ranging in age from 9.9 to 15.5 years and concluded that "on the average, or for 50 percent of presumably unselected cases, intelligence growth is practically complete at 13 years [p. 323]." Yerkes' group also reported that maturity was reached at age 13, stimulating both dismay and controversy because of the surprisingly early peak. The issue continued to excite interest for decades. Thorndike (1923) set the peak at 18 or later. Until subjects tested as children grew into middle and older age, data on intellectual growth could be gathered only by testing population samples of different ages, or by retesting individual subjects after a short period of time. One of the most extensive cross-sectional studies of intelligence and age was begun by H. E. Jones in 1925; he was joined the following year by H. Conrad.

The pair tested 1191 subjects with the Army Alpha in rural New England communities, a population somewhat lower in social class and educational achievement than Terman's standardization group had been. About one-half of the subjects were adults. Peak performance for the group was reached at about age 20, with decline seen thereafter (H. E. Jones & Conrad, 1933). Walter Miles, using the Otis test, found similar results in subjects aged from 10 to 80 (W. R. Miles, 1931).

The Jones and Miles studies exemplified much that became characteristic of post-World-War I developmental psychology: the description, by testing, of large numbers of subjects. Concern with age beyond adolescence at best was, however, not characteristic of the period.

It appears from the early history of mental testing that interest in psychological measurement, in general, was in part precipitated and expanded by the growth of mental testing, which, after Terman's test and the Army Alpha became available, quickly outgrew the clinics and excited the interest of school people. Tests, and measurement in general, became a significant aspect of educational psychology, which in turn contributed greatly to the general concern for the nature of children's development.

IV. EDUCATIONAL PSYCHOLOGY

Educational psychology begins, as does so much of American psychology in general, with William James. In the first place, practically every student of psychology and related disciplines read his *Principles* (James, 1890). In 1892, he was asked to discuss psychology in relation to school with the teachers of Cambridge. The lectures were successful and were frequently presented in the next few years. (James needed the money gained from the lectures, but some lack of enthusiasm for the activity might be inferred from his comment about his listeners after returning from a lecture series, "I have never seen more women and less beauty, heard more voices and less sweetness, perceived more earnestness and less triumph than I ever supposed possible [James, 1896]"). In 1899, the lectures were published as *Talks to Teachers on Psychology and to Students on Some of Life's Ideals* (James, 1899).

The psychology James promoted was, of course, functional. The child was seen as an active, behaving organism. The purpose of education was to be consistent with his instincts, and it should be designed to fit him for life in his society. The child's interests were to be awakened and broadened, his will strengthened, and of course, much emphasis was to be exerted in developing appropriate habits. Education should be ultimately practical. While James' instinct orientation fell by the wayside, his influence did make serious inroads into the old faculty psychology, and helped to bring the attention of later psychologists to the child in the classroom (B. T. Baldwin, 1911).

G. S. Hall was a student of James, but could not be described as a follower. As noted earlier, Hall's genetic psychology had considerable appeal to educators but his approach was much different from James'. In an early statement on education, G. S. Hall (1901-1902), emphasized the difference between a "scholiocentric" and a "pedocentric" orientation; instead of fitting the child to the school, the school should fit the child.

The guardians of the young should strive first of all to keep out of nature's way and to prevent harm. . .they should feel profoundly that childhood. . .is not corrupt. . .there is nothing else so worthy of love, reverence, and service as the body and soul of the growing child [pp. 24-25].

G. S. Hall's books, *Adolescence* (1904) and *Educational Problems* (1911) helped to accomplish what his 1901 paper recommended: to shift the focus of attention to the child's characteristics, development, and needs. Once educators were convinced of the primacy of the child's nature in determining school curriculum and methods, there was a demand for research evidence on the child. Developmental psychology, as an important segment of educational psychology, flourished in response to these needs. Genetic psychology was not of lasting scientific importance, but the attitude it generated in turn helped produce a scientific discipline of developmental psychology.

E. L. Thorndike brought scientific research to bear on the problems of both the school and nature of the child. As a student at Western Reserve, he read James' *Principles* and soon went to Harvard to study with him. While a student under James, he worked with instinctive and intelligent behavior in chickens. (His research was done largely in the James' basement, because of lack of appropriate facilities in the university.) He moved to Columbia and completed his work with Cattell; there he was stimulated by both Cattell and by Franz Boas to develop quantitative treatment of psychological data. His quantitative work became a lifelong interest and was one of his major contributions. His dissertation, published as *Animal Intelligence* (Thorndike, 1898), was a scientific landmark. Out of his problem-box experiments came a theory and a new "law" concerning the wedding of a specific stimulus and a specific response through neural conditioning, stamped in by reward. "Connectionism" was the label he used for the idea and the "law of effect" became a major force in educational and developmental psychology. Through the "law of effect," behavior was seen as dependent upon the organism's success or failure, reward or punishment, or satisfaction or annoyance. By putting responsibility for behavior on learning, which in turn was conditioned by experience, Thorndike freed psychology from its dependence on "mind" and instincts to explain behavior.

Thorndike taught at Western Reserve briefly, but was brought back to Columbia by Cattell and J. E. Russell. They encouraged him to develop his theory using human rather than animal subjects. He soon organized his ideas and data into a book on educational psychology (Thorndike, 1903). This first edition was concerned primarily with the origin and nature of individual uniqueness in children. He expanded both his work and his writing, and in a decade, published his massive three-volume *Educational Psychology* (1913). In this work he brushed aside past theories of man's nature—those of the Old Testament, Rousseau, Locke, *et al.*—with his assertion that man starts with certain original tendencies that can be shaped and modified by learning. He went on to study transfer of training with Woodworth, to detailed study of individual differences by way of intelligence research and test construction, and to production and encouragement of quantitative methods in research. He published hundreds of papers on topics related to childhood and education in his long career (Murchison, 1929b; Thorndike, 1901, 1936).

Thorndike's work had direct and long-term influence on developmental psychology. His point of view that children are in large part the product of their learning experiences turned attention of researchers in child behavior toward identifying the experiences that were antecedent to, or causes of, given knowledge, skill, and traits. His laboratory work both in content and example provided the stimulus for experimental child psychology. After Thorndike there was a gradual increase in the amount and proportion of experimental laboratory work in child psychology, and an increasing focus on learning as a major aspect of that research.

The influential John Dewey was one of those who asked that the child's nature be the source of inspiration for curriculum (Dewey, 1902).

A movement somewhat related to Thorndike's connectionist theory and laboratory work, though not derived from it, was behaviorism. While behaviorism's originator, J. B. Watson, found his major inspiration elsewhere, he referred frequently to Thorndike's work in his major (J. B. Watson, 1919) statement of his position.

V. BEHAVIORISM

Watson was a laboratory psychologist working with animals at Chicago before World War I. Rejecting the entire concept of mind and consciousness, he developed a materialistic point of view which he presented in his first paper on the theory, "Psychology as a Behaviorist Views it" (J. B. Watson, 1913). The paper was presented at Columbia, at Cattell's invitation, but the point of view was first expressed in a Chicago seminar in 1908. A more detailed presentation of the theory was made later in a book with a title similar to that of the paper (J. B. Watson, 1919). Most of Watson's work of interest to developmental psychology was done at Johns Hopkins in Baltimore. It was there, at the Phipps Clinic in 1916, that he was given a small sum to study behavior of newborn human infants; his interests lay in both innate behavior and conditioning.

Watson demonstrated the origin of a specific emotion—in this case, fear—in a laboratory experiment in which an infant was conditioned to fear a furry animal through association with a sudden, loud noise (J. B. Watson & Raynor, 1920). The study had a great impact on psychology: Watson had demonstrated that behavior ranging from simple motor responses to complex emotional and personality traits could literally be "taught."

He also promoted the idea that the child's language development is the product of conditioning. His hypothesis was that sounds made by the child that caused—or were associated with—satisfaction of his needs by other persons, would tend to be repeated more than nonproductive sounds. Thus babbling, through conditioning, evolved into true speech. He was less successful in promoting the idea that thinking was merely the action of the language mechanism, and thus would be available for study and, presumably, conditioning (J. B. Watson, 1920). After he left academic psychology in 1920, he wrote extensively on child rearing in both book and popular magazine form. (J. B. Watson, 1936).

The conditioned-response method quickly became popular among psychologists, and since infants and young children are ideal subjects, almost every conceivable aspect of early behavior was subject to laboratory study.

Thus, Watson's behaviorism and Thorndike's connectionism together ushered in an era of scientific developmental psychology. Control and modification of behavior through learning experiences was emphasized; the laboratory experiment was seen as appropriate (or ideal) in the study of children; and quantification and measurement (from Thorndike, Thurstone, and others) was emphasized. In general there was among both researchers and the public a feeling that scientific explanations were forthcoming—or available—for most aspects of behavior.

While both systems were transitional, and we are today perhaps less confident than in the 1920s and 1930s, great impetus was given to scientific study of human development. The volume of research increased sharply. Public confidence in the scientific quality of the work was reflected in the establishment of a number of child-study institutes, both tax supported and private. These institutes contributed heavily to both the quantity and quality of child research in the country; they disseminated information on child-rearing and teaching practices, and were places of origin of most of the longitudinal studies that proved to be influential in the development of a life-span psychology. Before they are described, an overview of developmental psychology in the 1920s and 1930s would seem appropriate.

VI. DEVELOPMENTAL PSYCHOLOGY IN THE 1920s AND 1930s

It should not be inferred from the above statements that developmental psychology became exclusively or even primarily laboratory- and experiment-oriented in the two decades after World War I. That orientation was a trend, not an accomplished fact. Diversity has always been characteristic of American psychology in general, and the developmental psychology of the period was representative of this diversity. Surveying journals of the period, handbooks, or collections of topical chapters gives an impression of several trends.

First, it was apparent that no single unifying theory, theme, or idea was being tested or examined. Individual researchers (or institutions) would follow an interest without regard to fitting it to any overall research plan. Ideas and topics were tried out and discarded or pursued, without much attempt at study in depth. As a result, the number of different topics studied was great. For example, in a volume of *Pedagogical Seminary and Journal of Genetic Psychology* taken from a library shelf at random (Volume 35, 1928), there were 38 articles. Slightly more than half could be placed in three very broad categories: tests and clinical reports, intelligence and other ability studies (especially mental deficiency), and learning, both human and animal. The remaining articles could not be lumped even in very broad categories, ranging in topic from children's attitudes to dogs versus cats, to the relation of Bible study and character. Of the 38 studies, 12 were laboratory reports on either animals or children, 21 were to some degree at least concerned with quantitative treatment of data (generally descriptive), and the other five were discussions of various topics.

Another approach to summarizing work during this period is to look at handbooks or reviews of literature. One such volume was *The Foundations of Experimental Psychology* (Murchison, 1929a). Of 23 articles, three were devoted to developmental psychology. These covered infancy in one report, and intelligence in two—general ability and special abilities. The infancy piece described both methods of study and provided some data on development. The other two reviews were test-oriented. More relevant was the *Handbook of Child Psychology* (Murchison, 1931).[2] In this compilation of 22 reviews, there was one methods chapter, one chapter each devoted to general descriptions of language development, learning and social behavior, and theory statements by Lewin, Piaget, and Anna Freud. The rest of the articles were on specific topics like twins, birth order, morals, children's drawings, dreams, and the like.

While the breadth, descriptive nature, and frequent shallowness of work during this period did not add up to a coherent science of developmental psychology, the broad base of data gathering was, in total, probably desirable and necessary before more highly structured research could be done. There is at least a starting place in the literature for evidence on most aspects of human development.

It should be observed, at least in passing, that by no means all the research during this period (or any other, for that matter) using infants or children as subjects was truly "developmental," that is, concerned with change, growth, and development. Children are useful and convenient subjects for all kinds of research, but it is the nature of the research, not the age of the subjects, that determines whether the data are useful in understanding human development.

VII. CHILD-STUDY INSTITUTES

Some of the institutes where program research could be carried on—as opposed to piecemeal, individual efforts—evolved out of child guidance clinics, others were developed in public and private universities as administrative units separate from academic departments, and still others were privately funded. Most had not only a research orientation, but a charge or expectation of providing child-rearing

[2] Reading the literature of this period, one is struck by the high proportion of women psychologists active in research and writing. For example, in the 1931 Murchison *Handbook*, half—11 of 22—authors of reviews of literature are women. In a comparable recent work, *Review of Child Development Research* (Hoffman & Hoffman, 1964-1966), out of 30 authors of 23 review articles, only four women are sole authors, and another four are joint authors—slightly more than 25% of the total number. Similar proportions of female authorship seem to appear in the journals of the twenties and thirties, although no journal count has been made.

advice and help for parents. Up to this time, only medically-oriented books were generally available for child-rearing advice. Best known perhaps was *Care and Feeding of Children*, by L. M. Holt, first published in 1894 and continued in a series of editions into the 1920s (L. M. Holt, 1894). In later years, the revisions were made by the son of the original author. These books had a simple and direct answer to most questions parents might have, but of course had scanty or no evidence on which to base the advice on behavior.

One of the first of the institutes was the Yale Psycho-Clinic, begun in 1911 under Gesell. It became a major research center with early focus on infancy, but gradually raised the age of interest to include all of childhood and adolescence. Gesell's early work was noteworthy especially for innovations in observational techniques, especially the one-way vision screen and the photographic observation dome. Infant behavior patterns were charted through painstaking analysis of stills from movie film (Gesell, 1931). Several books were produced in which the clinic's research was summarized.

The Iowa Child Welfare Research Station (sponsored by the Womens Christian Temperence Union) was established in 1917 under Bird T. Baldwin from Yale, where he had studied under Dearborn. He was soon joined by Beth Wellman. Research focused early on physical and mental development in young, school-age and institutionalized children. George Stoddard was director later, followed by R. Sears from Yale. The Iowa group was at the center of the nature-nurture controversy of the 1930s.

The Merrill-Palmer Institute at Detroit was another early center, and was one of the first to have a nursery school. (Iowa also had a preschool unit.) Edna White was the first leader at Merrill-Palmer.

In 1925, child development centers were established at Teacher's College, Columbia, followed by Minnesota, California, Toronto, and somewhat later by Michigan and Denver, Colorado. In the Early 1930s, other units were established at the Harvard School of Public Health, the Washington Child Research Center, the Fels Institute at Antioch, and one at the Columbia Medical School. All carried out extensive research programs, but it is noteworthy that nursery schools were operated and parent and extension classes were established at the institutes. The concentration on the whole person, and the individual focus of clinical work in general, as well as the helping orientation, were not abandoned in favor of an exclusive research orientation.

John Anderson came to Minnesota from Yale where he had studied the effect of diet on rats. He started a program with R. Scammon and E. Boyd on the morphology of growth. One study at Minnesota cited frequently in the literature was that of Shirley (1933a), whose study of the first two years of life for 25 babies resulted in predictions and forecasts that held up remarkably well in spite of the methodological problems with the study.

At Western Reserve, T. Wingate Todd, an anatomist, began the x-ray study of the bones of growing children. The work was continued by Greulich (later at Stanford) and by Pyle. At Michigan, Willard Olson, an educational psychologist, concerned himself with the organismic concept of development in school children, and the relation of physical growth to school learning. Washburne instituted longitudinal studies of children for the Denver Research Council (L. K. Frank, 1962).

An Institute of Child Welfare was established at Berkeley in 1927, under a grant from the Laura Spelman Rockefeller fund. The main activity there has been associated with three longitudinal studies which were begun in the 1920s and have continued in operation. In 1958, the name was changed to Institute of Human Development, to reflect the maturing of the original subjects. H. Stolz, a pediatrician, was the original director, and the psychologist H. E. Jones led the organization from 1935 to 1960. The work there has been interdisciplinary and the staff has included medical, physiological, and social scientists as well as psychologists (Institute of Human Development, 1968).

The Fels Research Institute was established at Yellow Springs, Ohio in 1929. The layman who sponsored the institute, S. Fels, was impressed by the variety of individual differences in human beings. He founded the institute to study these differences and specified that the research was to begin before subjects' birth and was to include biochemistry, psychology, physical anthropology, and medicine. The institute has continued its involvement with many subjects into maturity. The staff in 1963 included 65 people ranging from senior research investigators to research assistants in four departments: growth and genetics psychophysiology-neurophysiology, biochemistry, psychology and psychiatry. The long-time director has been L. W. Sontag, M. D. (L. W. Sontag, 1963).

The impact of the institutes was great because of their obvious advantages: a staff selected to work together, the possibility of doing program research, generally good access to subjects (even if somewhat limited in range of social class and ability), and through involvement in both planned and fortuitous longitudinal research. The influence of these latter studies will be examined shortly.

VIII. OTHER EARLY INFLUENCES

Some variety in methods and content of American developmental study entered from sources outside psychology. Especially prominent were pediatrics, anthropology, and psychoanalysis.

A. Pediatrics

The historical influence of pediatrics was reflected primarily in the area of neurological developments. However, this interest grew into concern for broad developmental sequences. Several directors of child research institutes were medically trained, including Gesell, Sontag, and Stolz, for example. In later years there was collaboration and training with psychiatrists, an educational experience that was relevant to dealing with emotional disturbance, psychosomatic ailments, etc. Psychological-medical collaboration was common in the clinic as well as in the research institutes (Senn, 1948).

B. Psychoanalysis

Although Freud himself did little work with children, the movement he originated affected the perception of childhood held by both professionals and laymen. The idea of distinct developmental stages was adopted enthusiastically by many: Classifying and categorizing seems to be a pleasurable human activity. Psychoanalysis gave a particular (and somewhat standardized) focus to the search for earlier antecedents or causes of present behavior. Play techniques (as substitute for free association) came from Freud but were modified and elaborated by M. Klein (1932) and Anna Freud (1946).

Psychoanalysis itself was not a science nor was it research oriented. Some psychologists did generate hypotheses for research from the theory, but for the most part, it was not empirical, data- or number-oriented.

C. Anthropology

Facts on primitive cultures were gathered early, but without much organization or focus. Developmental psychologists were of course especially interested in primitive children, and in family and child rearing characteristics of primitive cultures. Reports like Mead's *Coming of Age in Samoa* (1928) and *Growing Up in New Guinea* (1930) had a great impact on developmental psychology since they indicated that some "laws" of behavior were obviously not universal, e.g., the *"sturm und drang"* theory of adolescence, and that some "givens" of the child-parent relationship had to be reexamined. From the late 1920s onward, child psychology texts and handbooks typically had a chapter on primitive children.

To this point, no mention has been made of concern for development beyond adolescence. The reason is that little interest existed in the mature and older ages. Only scattered research was done prior to World War II. The reasons for this neglect are at least partially apparent from the foregoing discussion. The origins of developmental psychology made emphasis or exclusive concern with children almost inevitable, just as conditions around the World War II period produced interest in older persons—"older" here meaning quite old, generally.

IX. MATURITY AND OLD AGE

Interest in the aging process is probably as old as man, and recorded discussions of the problems go back at least as far as ancient Greece and Rome. Concern for the characteristics and changes common to early or middle maturity are hard to identify in pre-twentieth-century times. In a way, one might say that all psychology concerned with man, not specifying youth or old age, is a psychology of maturity. However, the early literature is sparse. Psychologists have, not surprisingly, concentrated on the periods of most rapid or dramatic developmental change.

The history of scientific study of aging usually is said to begin with Quetelet, the French scientist, and the date cited is that of his best-known work, *Sur L'Homme et le Développement de ses Facultés* (Quetelet, 1835). Quetelet was, in modern terminology, a mathematician, sociologist, and psychologist. He presented all sorts of population and probability data, much of it adequate for comparison with contemporary figures. He studied the relation of age to creativity a century before Lehman, helped develop mathematics, and influenced Galton.

Francis Galton, the gentleman scientist-hobbyist, gathered quantitative data on several aspects of aging. One of his best-known ventures was his *Inquiries into Human Faculty and its Development* (Galton, 1883), which explored individual differences in relation to development and age. He furnished an early report on the loss of high-frequency sound perception in old age. His most important work probably was the data gathered in 1884 at his anthropometric laboratory in the International Health Exhibition in London (Galton, 1885).

Quetelet and Galton together provided documentation for some of the changes that occur with age, and also made apparent the degree to which individuals differ in the aging process. Birren (1961a, p. 73) comments, Galton and Quetelet "made it legitimate, desirable, and possible to study man's psychological development and aging."

The first publication on aging of psychological importance emerging in the United States was G. S. Hall's *Senescence, the Last Half of Life* (G. S. Hall, 1922). Hall wrote this book in his own antiquity. He was 78 at the time of publication, and he died within two years of its appearance. In part the book was personal and retrospective, but it contained much of interest, including a history of aging, a certain amount of philosophizing, a discussion of medical and physiological aspects of aging (including a considerable discussion of the problems of constipation), statistics on mortality, and even a chapter containing excerpts from literature: "sayings," bits of poetry, and the like. Of particular interest was a chapter reporting results of a questionnaire administered to aged persons on their self-perceptions, problems, and attitudes. The subjects were generally from the upper-middle class, since Hall explained that his attempts to get data from inmates of old people's homes resulted in trivial and complaining remarks.

Work in aging of good scientific quality began emerging soon after Hall's book was published. One early sophisticated study of aging evaluated visual and auditory reaction time through multiple regression techniques (Koga & Morant, 1923). E. L. Thorndike was active in research on mature persons in the 1920s. He published *Adult Learning* (E. L. Thorndike, 1928) which was a summary of studies concerned with the influence of age on ability, and achievement of mature persons in adult education. This was followed by *Adult Interests* (E. L. Thorndike, 1935), a report on studies, conducted in 1931-1934, on changes in intensity of interests with age, and concerned with the possibility of modifying and improving personal characteristics at various ages. At about the same time, a doctoral study at Columbia under Woodworth's direction was carried out on mental efficiency in senescence, in which comparison was made of the functioning of age samples in the 20s and 60s (J. G. Gilbert, 1935). Other reports on mental functions in adults and older persons in this period include studies by Babcock (1930), Beeson (1920), J. O. Foster (1920), Ruch (1934), Sorenson (1930), and others.

The first major research unit devoted to psychological aspects of aging was established at Stanford in 1928. W. R. Miles reported becoming concerned when he learned that workers over 40 were having difficulty obtaining jobs in California. Under Terman (then department head) a committee including Calvin Stone, E. K. Strong, Terman, and Miles, chairman, was established to study the problem. Research funds were secured to study "later maturity" and eight PhD dissertations were completed in the 1930s (Birren, 1961b, p. 131). In addition to the dissertations, noteworthy staff research was going on, including Miles' "Measures of Certain Human Abilities through the Life Span" (W. R. Miles, 1931), his "Age and Human Ability" (W. R. Miles, 1933), and Strong's *Change of Interests with Age* (E. K. Strong, 1931).

Late in this period, a major contribution to the biological and medical aspects of aging appeared with the publication of Cowdry's *Problems of Aging* (Cowdry, 1939). From about this time onward, there has been a continuing close relationship between medical-biological and psychological study of aging.

After the hiatus of World War II, research on psychological aspects of maturity and old age grew rapidly. In 1946, the Nuffield Institute for Research into the Problems of Aging was established at Cambridge University. During its six-year history, research, in line with its charter, concentrated primarily on measurement of skills and application to industry. Two books by Welford, *Skill and Age* (1951), and a 1958 revision summarized much of this work (Welford, 1951, 1958).

In 1946, a productive research unit was organized by the National Institute of Health in the United States. One noteworthy accomplishment was the published report of the 1955 Bethesda Conference on Psychological Aspects of Aging, which provided both research summaries and stimulation for future work. (J. E. Anderson, 1956). Another publication of great importance to the field was the *Handbook of Aging and the Individual* (Birren, 1959a), which provided the kind of literature review and statement of position in the field that the Murchison handbook had presented for child psychology thirty years earlier. The aging handbook was supported by NIH funds, and was developed by a group under the chairmanship of R. Kleemeier of the Gerontological Society.

In 1945, Division 20, on Maturity and Old Age, was formed, the first in APA to be approved under the new bylaws. Sidney Pressey was largely responsible for stimulating this approval (Pressey, 1948).

The University of Chicago became one of the centers for research on maturity and aging. In 1943, a committee on social adjustment in old age was formed under Havighurst's leadership. The group—indeed the whole Committee on Human Development—has been highly productive. The social adjustment group published a report entitled *Personal Adjustment in Old Age* (Cavan, Burgess, Havighurst, & Goldhammer, 1949). Havighurst and Albrecht (1953) reported on the Prairie City study. In 1951, funds were secured for the Kansas City Study of Adult Life, a combined cross-sectional and longitudinal study of aging. Among the many reports from this continuing study were Cumming and Henry's (1961) book, Havighurst's (1957) monograph on the social competence of middle-aged people, and Williams and Wirth's (1965) *Lives Through the Years*.

Another active research center has been the Duke University medical center under the leadership of E. W. Busse. Their first grant for aging research (a study on the central nervous system) was made in 1950. While there has been a continuing medical and psychiatric orientation, much of the work has represented other disciplines from the behavioral and social sciences. The Duke group has seemed especially adept at securing varied samples of subjects representing the general population. However, it was the Department of Psychology at Ohio State that, until the time of Pressey's retirement, turned out more PhD's in the aging area than any other school in the United States.

Summarizing activities in the field in 1961, Birren reported, "More research seems to have been published in the decade of 1950-1959 than had been published in the entire preceding 115 years the subject may be said to have existed (Birren, 1961b, p. 131).

X. CHILD PSYCHOLOGY THROUGH THE MIDDLE OF THE CENTURY

From the time of Murchison's (1931) handbook to the post-World-War-II period, both quantity and quality of research in childhood increased. The quantity and variety of research is so great that it is difficult to summarize in any coherent fashion. One approach is to look at the studies most frequently cited in texts on developmental psychology. Using this technique, a number of topical interests become apparent.

One pervading interest is a concern for the relative effects of genetic inheritance in relation to those of experience or learning. Studies of physical and intellectual similarity in persons of varying degrees of familial relationship were numerous and continuous; twin studies were especially popular, and these ranged from the early research by Gesell to more extensive data-collecting studies. The effects of deprivation have been described, and these have ranged from early reports of mountain children to later urban and institutional studies. The effects on IQ of inheritance versus experience was a major concern of such work.

Learning was a prime topic after Thorndike and Watson; here studies ranged from those concerned with laboratory investigations of the effects of reinforcement schedules, to more complex approaches.

Watson's behaviorism was succeeded by the more complex formulations of his logical successor, Clark Hull (1943). The Yale Institute of Human Relations, where Hull worked, produced several researchers who attempted to build personality theory on a scientific laboratory-testable basis. The work of N. E. Miller and Dollard (1941) on social learning, the frustration-aggression hypothesis (Dollard, Miller, Doob, Mowrer, & Sears, 1939), and the Whiting and Child (1953) child socialization approach attracted a number of researchers.

The research on the primitive-child of earlier days was largely superseded by studies of social class and subculture. Sociological studies like A. Davis and Dollard's (1940) *Children of Bondage* are typical of this research approach.

Effects of family-life patterns on child behavior was another area of concern. Maternal influence (and maternal deprivation) was of continuing interest, especially to those of psychoanalytic persuasion. Descriptive-analytical studies of the relation of child-rearing practices to child personality and social behavior were also popular (A. L. Baldwin, Kalhorn, & Breese, 1945). Interest in physical development declined rather steadily during the period. Concern with psychosocial adjustment of children was of continuing high interest, but approaches and methods remained largely clinical in orientation through the years.

A second approach to evaluating a period is to look at differences in collections or literature reviews published some years apart. Bronfenbrenner has done this, comparing the 1931 Murchison *Handbook* to the 1954 Carmichael *Manual of Child Psychology*. He noted first a shift away from "sheer description of molecular phenomena" toward concern with more abstract processes and constructs, for example dropping "child drawings" or "dreams" in favor of chapters (still largely descriptive) on comprehensive topics like "emotional development." Another modification was exemplified by change in descriptive statistics used: Frequency tables were still most apparent, but correlations were used more often in the attempt to determine cause, or at least relationship.

A third change was related to theory; while theories lost popularity as systems, their constructs and hypotheses were applied in research on specific problems. This is best exemplified in the work of Piaget, Lewin, and Freud (Bronfenbrenner, 1963).

XI. POST WORLD WAR II

Perhaps the major impression to be gained from the research of the late 1950s and 1960s is the rapid movement in the direction of greater scientific rigor. Descriptive study, while not abandoned, has lost popularity in favor of hypothesis-testing research and many studies far more complex in design and quantitative analysis are available than was true only a few years earlier. The expansion of computer availability has, of course, contributed greatly to evaluation of the typically numerous variables in developmental studies. *A Handbook of Research Methods in Child Psychology* (Mussen, 1960) presents far more sophisticated discussion of methods than was found in any earlier publication in the developmental area, yet this volume does not take into account the range of possibilities available today.

The change in focus is somewhat circular, or spiral: that is, where post-war effort seemed to be aimed toward a larger grasp of concepts and away from fragmented, discrete topics, today's literature reveals infrequent discussion of broad topic areas like "infancy" or "early development," and focuses attention more narrowly on topics like "effects of infant care," "separation from parents during early childhood," and "effects of early group experience." The foregoing are chapter headings from a two-volume *Review of Child Development Research* (Hoffman & Hoffman, 1964-1966).

Topical content in psychological research with children in the last two decades has emphasized especially cognitive development, the somewhat related area of language development, and varied approaches to understanding the socialization process.

The Piaget-Geneva-school work in cognitive development has become immensely popular. Interpretative books have appeared and local theoretical variants have been evolving. All the developmental journals have been inundated with manuscripts reporting Genevan research.

Language development has been a standard topic in child psychology since its beginning, but in the past few years research has gone beyond the description of the child's acquisition of vocabulary and verbal accuracy and has focused on the nature of the language itself and its structure and meaning as it is revealed by the child's acquisition of communitive skills, and especially of syntax and grammar.

Brown and Bellugi, Chomsky, Ervin-Tripp, and Slobin have all been influential in this field.

Research in the socialization process has taken many forms; two widely-practiced approaches are related to modeling behavior in studies and research into moral development.

Adolescence occupies a somewhat anomalous position in developmental psychology. Almost every psychology department (especially those serving teacher-trainees) has a course called "Psychology of Adolescence," and there are numerous texts by that title. Yet, although there is some original work, an attempt to review research literature in the area yields little. The research leans heavily toward social development. Much of the content of courses and texts is extrapolation or repetition of child psychology data. Since 1966, there has been a quarterly journal, *Adolescence*, to provide an outlet for work in this developmental period.

XII. WHO STUDIES THE LIFE-SPAN?

The evolution of scientific study of human development has been described in at least a cursory fashion in the preceding sections of this paper. But what has been revealed, with little exception, is the evolution of concern with children by one group, and of concern with old people by another group. Where are the psychologists who are concerned with the whole of life?

Perhaps the only psychologists who have exhibited interest—and consequently carried out research—on change through the life-span are those who have been involved in longitudinal studies. Despite the perplexing methodological problems of longitudinal studies, they have provided us with our only glimpses of what it means to grow up, mature, and grow old. It is unlikely that many (if any) of the longitudinal researchers *planned* to become life-span psychologists, but as their subjects matured and aged, the researchers' interests were pulled along into the new developmental period. A quick look at some of the major studies may be suggestive at this point.

XIII. LONGITUDINAL STUDIES OF THE LIFE-SPAN

Certain assumptions of continuity of behavior over time are made by psychologists, implicitly or explicitly, whenever generalizations or predictions are made. Only when the same persons are evaluated over time are these assumptions tested. Major questions engaging longitudinal researchers have included response stability in areas such as intelligence, personal characteristics, and the relation between parental attitude and practice, and developing behavior.

Some longitudinal research has been planned as such from the beginning, other studies have been fortuitous "follow-up" reevaluations of subjects originally studied with no expectation of continuing involvement. Probably few studies were originally designed with expectation of continued evaluation into the old age of the subjects. Yet, this has occurred. While an established research institute or foundation is most likely to be able to carry on longitudinal study, some important studies have been done by individual scientists, or by a series of individuals over time.

A. Major Institutional Research

1. Stanford Studies of Gifted Children.

In 1921, Lewis Terman set out to study approximately 1500 children with high IQs. Intelligence and achievement tests and a personality inventory were administered to the children. The study, originally titled "Genetic Studies of Genius" has continued to the present and thus to the late middle-age of the subjects. Directors have included Terman from 1921 to 1956, R. Sears from 1956 to 1962, and F. J. McDonald from 1962 to the present. Five volumes of reports have been published, and 1600 offspring of the original subjects have been studied (Kagan, 1964).

2. University of California

The three longitudinal studies at the Institute of Human Development are going into the fifth decade of longitudinal research. The Oakland Growth Study began in 1932 under H. Stolz and H. Jones. Physiological growth, abilities and functions, social behavior, patterns of emotional expressiveness, interests, attitudes, and other personal characteristics have all been examined, but physical functioning and adolescent social behavior were emphasized in early stages of the study. Work has continued under John Clausen.

The Berkeley Growth Study has maintained records on physical, motor, and mental development on subjects first observed in neonatal life and at monthly intervals during infancy. Subjects were born in 1928-1929. Emphasis has been on physical and intellectual development. Work continued under the originator of the study, Nancy Bayley, until 1968 and she has been replaced as director by D. Eichorn. Much of the early data have been reevaluated in recent years, using more sophisticated techniques than were available at the time of original study, and attempts have been made to examine sex differences in development and to look at long-term patterns of consistency, especially of intelligence.

The Guidance Study under J. W. MacFarland began in 1929. This has been a complex, multidisciplinary study of biological-environmental-behavioral data on individuals who have been not only subjects for research, but who have in many cases been involved in a clinical relationship with the original researcher. Study of the adult lives of these subjects continues at a time when they are involved in rearing their own children. Interest in personality and parent-child relations have been strong points of this research. The study is now under the direction of Marjorie Honzik.

One of the unique aspects of the California studies is the continued involvement, to the present or recent past, of most of the original investigators and of others who have worked with the subjects many years. J. Clausen replaced H. Jones as director of the Institute, and was in turn replaced by M. B. Smith, who served until 1968. A long bibliography of reports on the various studies exists.

The Institute's program of Intergenerational Studies of Development and Aging was funded in full in June 1968 through NICHD, so work will continue (H. E. Jones, 1958a; Institute of Human Development, 1968).

3. Fels Research Institute

Since 1929, the institute has continued under direction of L. Sontag. From 1929 to 1944, six to eight newborn infants were enrolled in the study each year; from 1944 on, about 10 each year were added. There are now more than 300 subjects ranging in age from birth to the mid-thirties in age. Mental and personality tests, observations of children and of mother-child interactions, and interviews with mothers and children are all on file. At least one study of a mature group of subjects has been carried out. A noteworthy book-length report was *Birth to Maturity* (Kagan & Moss, 1962). New subjects will continue to be enrolled, and further adult evaluations will be made (Kagan, 1964; L. W. Sontag, 1963).

Other institutions have carried out longitudinal studies including those of the Menninger Foundation, Harvard, New York University School of Medicine, Colorado School of Medicine. However, none has been concerned with development beyond adolescence. A number of follow-up studies involving reevaluations of adult subjects originally chosen without plans for further study have produced valuable data on consistency and change.

B. Significant Follow-Up Studies

For more than two decades after he came to the United States, Franz Kallmann was primarily concerned with similarities in twins, but he continued studying some pairs over several years and thus provided longitudinal evidence on changes in old age. There has generally been little data on these pairs from their early

An adult follow-up, after 28 years, of subjects who had attended the University of Minnesota Nursery School was instituted by John Anderson. Test and observational records made in the school have been compared to adult data in an attempt to evaluate prediction of adult variables from child data (J. E. Anderson, 1960).

Before World War II, E. L. Kelly had begun a dating and engagement study of University of Michigan students. The war interrupted, and later when the subjects were in their late thirties he queried many of them to learn of consistency and change in attitudes and values through the years of early maturity (E. L. Kelly, 1955).

One widely cited study has been the follow-up made by Owens in 1950 of a group of men first tested with the Army Alpha in 1919. Their improved scores excited considerable interest; in general their high performance was maintained into their sixties, as determined by a second follow-up (Owens, 1953, 1966).

Also in the area of intelligence is the series of studies on a group of more than 200 school children originally judged mentally deficient. Their social and intellectual characteristics have been examined at several periods since childhood. Like Owens' college students, they have shown consistent and surprising improvement (Baller, 1936; Charles 1953; Baller, Charles, & Miller, 1967).

Another study of retardates is that of H. Skeels, whose early report of improvement after environmental manipulation excited interest in the 1930s. Skeels located and studied his subjects again in their mature years, and was able to compare them with his original control group (Skeels, 1966).

Longitudinal research is not very fashionable these days. Methodological problems abound, making data interpretation hazardous. Topics that were of major interest at the beginning of studies have in many cases lost their charm for contemporary researchers. There has been, for example, a plethora of intelligence test reports on individuals over time. Yet, practically no data have been collected on changes in cognitive functioning. Most longitudinal studies have emphasized description when we want analysis. With all the deficiencies and inadequacies, studies of the on-going lives of persons have provided insight into some aspects of development, have provided both confirmation of expectation and some surprises, and have generated questions of major importance to developmental psychologists. Methodological innovations like those discussed later in this volume may emphasize the virtues and reduce the deficiencies of future longitudinal research. Regardless of future advances, interest in the whole span of life to a large extent come from studies that gradually encompassed more and more of the life-span of the subjects—and of the researchers.

XIV. CONCLUSION

Like all disciplines or institutions, contemporary developmental psychology reflects its origins. It has been strongly person oriented over the years and a clinical or "helping" emphasis has pervaded in much of its activity. Baby biographies were the earliest manifestation of the child study movement. Genetic psychology focused interest on childhood and adolescence, and generated concern among school people for evidence on the nature of development. The establishment and growth of child guidance clinics furthered concern for the unique individual and his adjustment, but did not do much to encourage scientific study. Educational psychology grew out of the mental measurement movement, clinical concern with children, and the educator's need for understanding of their charges in the new "child-centered" school.

A second characteristic of developmental psychology has been its growing concern for scientific respectability. When Thorndike and Watson turned from animal to child study in their laboratories, they quickly gained a host of followers. The combination of improved measurement techniques and controlled research energized the field and research institutes became numerous in the 1920s. Both volume and quality of research increased steadily but without much pattern or focus.

Like child psychologists, gerontologists have been motivated by adjustment problems of their subject group—industrial, retirement, and housing concerns for example, as well as the delineation of physiological change with age. Medicine and social science have been deeply involved in the growth of concern over old persons in our society.

However, child psychology and gerontology have achieved much scientific rigor in the past decade and have lost some of their concern for the person's life.

Child psychology and gerontology: May and December. How do they get together? Longitudinal studies seem to be, historically, the one source of concern for psychological characteristics and change from birth to old age. Though often lacking in methodological adequacy, they have focused our interests on the person as he grows, matures, and ages.

At this point in time, we may be ready to develop research attacks on the intriguing problems that are revealed as the person moves through his life.

CHAPTER 3

Life-Span Developmental Psychology in Europe: Past and Present

KARL J. GROFFMANN

UNIVERSITY OF MANNHEIM
MANNHEIM, WEST GERMANY

ABSTRACT

The historical development of life-span developmental psychology in Europe is traced through the last three centuries with particular consideration of the German language area. It is shown that the concern with human development as a continuous process from birth to death can be observed in the literary, philosophical, and scientific works of the eighteenth century. In the first half of the nineteenth century, the foundations of a psychology of the human life-span in the modern sense were laid by Quetelet, even before the introduction of a modern child psychology in the Preyer and Hall tradition at the end of the same century. In Germany, the problem of the psychological development of adults attracted considerable attention before the First World War in connection with differential psychology. After 1920, large-scale research into the changes of behavior in adults and old people were conducted. In particular, Charlotte Bühler contributed toward a comprehensive psychology of the whole course of life. Finally, current German research in life-span psychology and psychogerontology is discussed emphasizing methodological issues.

I. INTRODUCTION

The scientific study of the psychology of the total human life-span is a characteristic of the twentieth century. A review of the history of psychology over the last one hundred years reveals in general three different sources from which developmental psychology has emerged:

1. The strong stimulation which came from the progress of biology in the nineteenth century, including the discussion about the theory of evolution.
2. The methodological consolidation of psychology as a science and its simultaneous institutionalization at the universities.
3. Humanitarian practical needs; e.g., the improvement of education, therapy, and social work.

Keeping these facts in mind, it is not surprising that systematic research related to human ontogenesis did not get under way until the end of the nineteenth century. Starting with the study of infant development, it rapidly grew to include school children and adolescents and finally, relatively late, turned its attention to adults and the elderly. Once the work on developmental psychology had begun, it had a systematic effect, arising as a logical consequence of the research to focus upon changes in adults and older people. This extension can be seen, for instance, in the longitudinal studies of children, which started in the 1920s, especially in the United States, and which necessarily had to cover a period greater than childhood and adolescence. However, at least with regard to the motivations of research, we must not forget the therapeutic aims of psychoanalysis, or the problems of medical, psychological, and social care which followed as a consequence of the strongly increased life expectancies in the industrial countries.

The scientific study of the human life-span is, like developmental psychology in general, a very new chapter of scientific history. When we attempt to trace it back from the present state to its origins, we find ourselves very soon in the prescientific phase of artistic and literary description and in the general history of philosophy, where the phenomenon of development appears again and again as a central theme. Historical papers on developmental psychology, like those of C. Bühler and Hetzer (1929) and Dennis (1949), restrict themselves, like many others, to childhood and adolescence. Höhn (1959) describes the history of child and adolescent psychology comprehensively, and gives some pointers on the psychology of the human life-span. An exception is the article of Hofstätter (1938), which strongly emphasizes the psychology of the total life-span. Hofstätter stresses especially the merits of Quetelet (1838) and from there attempts to synthesize the work which was accumulated in this field until 1938.

II. PRESCIENTIFIC ORIGINS OF LIFE-SPAN DEVELOPMENTAL PSYCHOLOGY

While the scientific treatment of problems of the human life-span was not evident before Quetelet's work, attention was directed much earlier to specific characteristics of the various sections of the life-span. Birth, death, growth, and decline are, in fact, too conspicuous to have been overlooked by any culture. The fact of succession of generations, together with its fundamental significance for the social organization of a society, has given rise to age-specific roles and behavior expectations which have been recognized as socially important and which have been applied in practice, e.g., by the ancient cultures.

A. Examples of Differential Evaluations of Various Sections of the Life-Span

Mering and Weniger (1959) discuss the evaluation of old age in the Greek and Roman cultures. Interestingly, these authors, comparing these older viewpoints to those of some modern authors, concluded that the opinions of the Greeks and Romans are still found in modern literature. It follows from this observation that new theories and an extensive gathering of new data are presently needed.

With regard to the political role of the various age sections, examples can be found in ancient Greece. The Spartan society, for instance, not only adhered to principles of education stressing the military abilities of the adolescents of both sexes, but also restricted admission at the public meetings (parliament) to members who were more than 30 years old. Also, the Board of Seniors consisted of citizens who were older than 60 years. These provisions probably reflect the rejection of juvenile thoughtlessness and a simultaneous appreciation of maturity and life experiences with regard to political decisions.

Plato (427-347B.C.), whose model of a society was influenced by the Spartan model, developed very specific ideas not only about an adequate education of children and adolescents, but also about different stages of the adults' life as differentially qualified for public service in the polis. The differentiated period of education should, according to Plato, last to the age of 30, and for a small elite of exceptionally able, even to the age of 35. These highly gifted individuals were, after the age of 50, to be dedicated to scientific research and should also take over the government of the state—this despite Plato's hopeless failure as a practical politician (Stanka, 1951).

Hofstätter (1938) has also discussed the significance of the pre-socratic hebdomas system. The Romans differentiated five sections of the life-span: *pueritia, adolescentia, juventus, virilitas,* and *senectus*; this division was based not only on biological, but also on psychological and social criteria. Cicero's (106-43 B.C.) paper *De Senectute*, for example, may be mentioned in this context. Other examples of prescientific views on old age can be found in Munnichs' (1966) work.

B. The German Entwicklungs and Bildungs Novel

Among the prescientific attempts to describe the human life-span is included a genre of literature typical of Germany; it was developed mainly in the eighteenth century and reflects the philosophical and scientific discussion of the concept of development.

The series of German *Entwicklungs* novels begins with the medieval epic poem "Parzival" of Wolfram von Eschenbach (Gerhard, 1926; Stahl, 1934). This epic describes, in a still unpsychological way, the development and experiences of a naïve boy, passing through various stages until he reaches maturity. The series continues with von Grimmelshausen's adventure novel *Simplicius Simplicissimus*, which appeared in the seventeenth century and which describes an individual course of development with first attempts at psychological analysis.

In the eighteenth century, a series of *Entwicklungs* novels appeared, developing more and more into the *Bildungs* novel of the German classic period and culminating in Goethe's (1749-1832) *Wilhelm Meisters theatralische Sendung* (1777-1784) and *Wilhelm Meisters Lehrjahre* (1795-1796). This tradition was continued to the present century, for example, by Thomas Mann (1875-1955).

The literary origins of the classic German *Bildungs* novel were the *Entwicklungs* novel on the one hand, and autobiographical works on the other, starting with those of St. Augustine and continuing over the mystic period to the sensualistic and pietistic confessions of the seventeenth and eighteenth centuries and to Rousseau (1712-1778). Misch notes that the *Confessions of St. Augustine* (354-430) is the first book to emphasize the homogeneity of human existence (see Pascal, 1965, p. 33). The philosophic origins were the preformistic and epigenetic theories of development in the eighteenth century and the ideal of humanity of Winckelmann (1717-1768), Herder (1744-1803), and Kant (1724-1804).

The *Bildungs* novel describes the development of the "human" man. It is not only concerned with development and sophisticated styles of education. The spontaneity of the individual is also emphasized. The environmental patterns are random and the individual selects among them and tries to come to terms with them in a creative analysis. (see Stahl, 1934). Man possesses those creative forces which are able to determine what he shall be. Religious, practical, and aesthetic humanity are but opening stages "Only the final stage brings the ideal: an ethical, active influence in the human-social community, responsibility and work in the interests of all [Martini, 1968, p. 258 (citation translated)] ."

C. Formulation and Refinement of the Concept of Development

It took a long time to come up with theoretical formulations of a specific, scientifically defined concept of development from the naïve knowledge of antiquity about the psychological characteristics of different age groups. More than two-thousand years were necessary to reach the stage at which modern psychological research was possible. This evolution is marked by an initial process toward higher abstraction and a following return to more concreteness.

The Greeks did not have a clearly defined concept of development. Nevertheless, from the time of the pre-Socratics, their ideas focused upon the phenomenon of "kinesis," the problem of growth and decline (Ballauff, 1954). Their work did not aim so much at explanations of single processes—the motive for doing research was the desire for understanding rather than for practical application of knowledge—and was, therefore, directed merely toward a general explanation of nature. Thus resulted "the basic problem of the Greek philosophy: How to conceive of a unitarian and permanent being underlying all manifold changes of the phenomena. . . [Windelband & Heimsoeth, 1957, p. 119 (citation translated)]." It was Aristotle (384-322 B.C.), the 'Vater der Logik' who solved this problem by introducing the concept of development.

Contrary to his forerunners, Aristotle postulated no distinction between the being and the phenomena. The general is realized in the particular. Both are combined as form and material. Through the process of the *entelecheia*, the being is reflected in the phenomena.

The artist shapes material and, prior to the creative act, form and material are separated. With regard to the organismic beings, the form is already laid down in the material from the beginning and is systematically unfolded. In this case, form and material are merely separated through abstraction. The form is, at the same time, antecedent and consequence of the process of development. From this point of view, development is teleologically determined. This teleological process proceeds from the lower to the higher, whereby Aristotle introduced an evaluative standard in the process of development.

Rickert (1929) reviewed the logical criteria which constitute the concept of development. According to his criteria, the Aristotelian concept is "metaphysical" because the value to be realized is at the same time cause and purpose. This metaphysical-teleogical point of view is not acceptable for psychology. However, a conditional teleological concept of development, as proposed by Rickert perhaps cannot be avoided.

During the next 1500 years, the Aristotelian concept of development remained dominant within European philosophy. This lack of progress was partly caused by Aristotle himself. Because of his outstanding authority, following generations adopted his approach of laying emphasis on the development of the general rather than the particular. The lack of progress, however, was due mainly to the attitude of the philosophy of the Middle Ages which was completely different from that of the present day.

It was not until the Renaissance that traditional authority was abolished through an increase in observations and detailed research. With regard to scientific and philosophical problems, new theories emerged. Descartes (1596-1650) and Bacon (1561-1626) attempted to find new theoretical foundations and rationalism and empiricism formed the fundamental positions of cognizance. Influenced by the development of modern physics, movement was explained within a mechanistic framework, but Leibniz (1646-1716), at the end of the seventeenth century, attempted again to reconcile mechanics and teleology in a metaphysical system of development.

At the beginning of the eighteenth century, after a period of theorizing, philosophy turned toward anthropological questions. The problem of development reappeared. Leibniz was the founder of the doctrine of preformation, which was also adopted by Bonnet (1720-1793) and Haller (1708-1777). According to this theory, the sperm and the ovum already contain all the possibilities of development, which are only manifested in a process of evolution. Therefore, no new and progressive forms of development were possible if they were not already potentially present. The germ already includes all organs. This doctrine was accepted in order to explain not only the development of the individual, but also the development of the species (see Ballauff, 1954).

At the same time, the controversial viewpoints of the animalculists [represented by Leeuwenhoek (1632-1723)] and the ovulists [e.g., Schwammerdam (1637-1723)] were propogated. The former believed that the spermatozoa were the main bearers of the organism and were supplied with nourishment from the ovum. The latter were convinced of the importance of the ovum; they believed that the spermatazoa had only the function of stimulating the beginning of the development in the ovum.

The preformation doctrine during the eighteenth century, often referred to as the theory of evolution, was opposed by the theory of epigenesis, which was especially represented by the embryologist C. F. Wolff (1733-1794). According to this theory, organisms are generated through a continued new formation of unorganized material, through a differentiation of parts, but not through the evolution of an already complete whole. For the first time, the epigenetic theory could claim to be scientific, although it was not defensible in its original form.

This progress was the consequence of an approximation toward reality, was based on observations and (to a certain extent) experiments, but not on philosophical ideas. Corresponding to this new attitude—during the eighteenth century—the biologists began to describe and classify the variability of the organic nature [e.g., Linné (1707-1778) and his opponent Buffon (1707-1788), though the latter was not convinced of the importance of a classificatory system]. It was not until this time that the contributions of Aristotle were exceeded (Anker & Dahl, 1938). Comparative morphology and comparative anatomy began and were developed. Plausible astrophysical theories were also formulated, e.g., the Kant-Laplace theory of the origin of the solar system.

Finally, at the end of the eighteenth century, Tetens (1736-1807) attempted to organize the theoretical conceptions of his time. Discussing the human life-span, Tetens (1777) talks about rise and decline in the progress of human development, about physical and psychical development, about differences in the process of development, and about the loss of energy in old age. He was one of the first to attempt to deal comprehensively and consistently with the phenomenon of human development in a more scientific publication.

The concept of development was the subject of both philosophy and science. The eighteenth century laid the theoretical and scientific foundation for the modern conception of development of the nineteenth century. These new ideas aimed at an explanation of the growth of mankind and were manifested scientifically in the theory of evolution and philosophically in the theory of history as formulated by German philosophy of the early nineteenth century. The problem of development was a main topic in the nineteenth century. One may mention here the philosophy of Hegel (1770-1831), the historic-materialistic theory of Marx (1818-1883), the positivism of Comte (1798-1857), and the biological theories of Lamarck (1744-1829) and Darwin (1809-1882). Darwin's theory, stressing the notions of variability and selection, was particularly successful. The vehement discussions provoked by Darwinism during the nineteenth century certainly influenced the beginnings of modern ontogenetic research within psychology.

This biological concept of development is no longer a metaphysical one. Development is conceived phylogenetically as a function of genetic and environmental determination, and ontogenetically as a function of maturation (heredity plus age) and environment; growth and decline are interpreted as a coherent series of changes. Still, however, this concept had a teleological connotation, a belief in evolution as progress. The old notion of an evolution toward a higher end state was revived in a new form.

III. SCIENTIFIC ORIGINS OF LIFE-SPAN DEVELOPMENTAL PSYCHOLOGY

The preceding presentation has shown that the phenomenon of development has been discussed and reflected about for millennia. It has been shown, too, that there have been only a few attempts—and these in literary and auto-biographic works—to trace the course of human life from a psychological viewpoint in the larger sense. These approaches often are casuistric, and combine "poetry and reality." Other knowledge did not go beyond everyday experience. Systematic approaches often consisted in the application of astrological analogies, or the seriation of mystical numbers to arrive at a division of the life-span.

A. The Contributions of Quetelet (1796-1874) to the Psychology of the Human Life-Span

During the first half of the nineteenth century—as far as I can see—the first approach toward the modern scientific analysis of the human life span was made. Responsible for this approach was neither a philosopher nor an artist, but the astronomer and mathematician, Quetelet. He was also regarded as one of the outstanding pioneers in social statistics.

Quetelet was convinced of the usefulness of statistics with regard to scientific, social, and political problems, and demanded the systematic collection of empirical data. We know that Galton was stimulated by the work of Quetelet. Both have in common the same enthusiasm for measurement and quantitative research.

Quetelet's fundamental idea was to regard age as an independent variable and to assign to it dependent variables through observation, measurement, and counting. Obviously, he conceived of development within the framework of the model of quantitative changes. He used a cross-sectional method according to the concept of the average individual observed at different ages. Quetelet already intended to predict functional relationships between age and dependent variables. Hofstätter (1938) enumerated the following nine points which seem in Quetelet's work to be important with regard to the psychology of the life-span:

1. The concept of the average individual.
2. The mortality rate with its minimum in the second decade of life.
3. The age of about 25 as the age of strong emotions and a period of greater tendency to delinquency.
4. The growth of muscular strength at about the same period of life.
5. Mental activities of man (indicated by socially successful achievements, e.g., dramas) and mental illness tend to develop at the age of about 25.
6. Quetelet (1838, p. 424 ff.) concludes the discussion of the developmental curve of intellectual abilities with the following preview: "Our intellectual abilities have their origin, grow and decline, each of them reaching its maximum at a certain age. It would be important to know which of them matures first and which one last. . . ." Furthermore, he is aware of the complex structure of the "intellectual abilities" and recognizes the fact that only after a great number of empirical studies would a precise analysis be possible.
7. Maximal frequencies of mental illness and the least chances of their recovery and also the climax of production of dramas occur simultaneously within the period between 30 years and 50 years of age.
8. The existence of age specific criminal acts and a maximum of delinquency at about the age of 25.

9. The number of suicides relative to the population of an age group increases continually from the age of 20 to that of 70. The various forms of suicide are clearly age specific.

Quetelet related dependent variables such as constitution, body strength, intelligence, emotions, interests, etc. to age, and anticipated the methods of most of the cross-sectional studies concerned with relationships between psychical and physical functions on the one hand and age on the other. He also recognized that variance is affected not only by age, but also by other sampling characteristics such as sex, geographical, national, and social influence. Interestingly, there is mentioned in a footnote (Quetelet, 1838, p. 333 ff.) a critique of Quetelet's cross-sectional investigations and longitudinal studies are recommended.

B. Psychoanalytic Contributions to Life-Span Research

Today, developmental psychology and psychology in general adhere more or less to the conceptions and research techniques which were launched by Quetelet. His research style could be implemented more intensively only after the methods of measuring psychological functions were sufficiently refined and after the progress in the social sciences made it clear that behavioral changes were also largely determined by the confrontation of the individual with his sociocultural evironment. This issue was well known to philosophers and writers of the eighteenth century who were especially interested in problems of education. But only with psychoanalysis was it brought into the focus of modern developmental research (C. Thompson, 1952; Wyss, 1966).

According to C. S. Hall and Lindzey (1957), Freud (1856-1939) was the first to see the problems of personality and development as closely interrelated. His theory was partly mechanistic and partly Darwinistic, that is, he incorporated both the tradition of the Age of Enlightenment and the ideas of biology in the nineteenth century in a productive synthesis. His theory of personality development was basically a theory of the development of the libido, which he attempted to explain in terms of both a phylogenetic and an ontogenetic process.

Freud's conception of the stages of libido development and the participating psychological mechanisms are known and need not be repeated. It is known, too, that this conception was based upon therapeutic casework, and developed by interpretations of single cases, even though it was guided by systematic viewpoints. This speculative approach accounts for the many well-founded critical reservations toward psychoanalysis from the standpoint of scientific theory construction and methodology. Nevertheless, clinical experience introduced Freud to the conflicts of adult patients and encouraged him to try to establish a causal relationship in development from infancy to adulthood at a time when the developmental research of educational psychology was occupied exclusively with the child.

Because of Freud's search for causal relationships, we have heard more from him about the developmental possibilities of early childhood and less about the successive ages. Later, Freud (1920) made the attempt to complement the dynamic function of the libido with the theory of the death drive. However, as far as I can see, this concept was not related to his ontogenetic theory in any concrete manner. Potentially, the sentence: "Das Ziel allen Lebens ist der Tod. . . [p. 40)" implies the extension of the developmental theory of psychoanalysis to the whole life-span.

The emphasis on early childhood remains characteristic for psychoanalysis but not necessarily for neo-psychoanalysis, e.g., Erikson (1957) expanded the conception to the whole life-span. Erikson's ideas, however, were already influenced by certain trends of scientific thinking of the last decades.

A. Adler (1870-1937) and C. G. Jung (1875-1961) differ from Freud in some respects. Adler supplements Freud by the emphasis of such concepts as minority feelings, power striving, and compensation; he also indicates a finalistic orientation in the concept of "Lebensleitlinie" and tried to cope with the mechanistic definition of development by introducing the concept of the "creative self." The concept of the creative self emphasized the spontaneous character of human development and led to a humanistic psychology. Spontaneity of development, which was in the foreground in the eighteenth century, is often overlooked in modern developmental psychology.

With Jung, the finalistic orientation and the individual spontaneity come to the fore. Jung saw development as a complex differentiation process which continues into old age. According to Jung, the goal of development is self-realization, which occurs in this process of "individuation." Jung also distinguished between two life sections, with the age of 40 as a turning point. In the first life cycle, the *ego* is formed; in the second life-cycle, the inner world is formed, and the developmental process is completed.

The psychoanalysts were usually outsiders. As physicians they were confronted mainly with the psychological disorders of adult persons. Freud devised an analysis of the etiology of disorders in a basically psychogenetic framework. It is doubtful whether he was influenced by early developmental psychology. However, in the French view of psychopathology in the nineteenth century, the developmental idea had been recognized in connection with the problem of mental deficiency (Groffmann, 1964).

C. Contributions of Developmental Psychology to Life-Span Research

The start of developmental psychology as a scientific field is usually related to publications by Preyer (1882) and G. S. Hall (1883). Dennis (1949), however, shows that both Preyer and Hall had forerunners. The oldest child diary was written by Tiedemann (1787), taking the publication date as criterion. The child diary by Heroard (1868), a physician and teacher at the French court, was started in 1601 but was published much later. Furthermore, Dennis indicated that Galton (1822-1911) should, indeed, be ranked together with Preyer and Hall. Several publications of Galton (1875, 1879, 1880a, 1880b) deal with performances and psychological abilities in different ages to adulthood and senility.

The influence of Galton, like that of Quetelet, on German developmental psychology appears to be relatively small. First, child psychology was of main interest. W. Stern (1871-1938) even in 1908, gives a description of the concept of development in which he sees ontogenetic development as encompassing only childhood and adolescence. However, two years later he stated that "genetic psychography" should not restrict itself to childhood and adolescence, since adulthood is not a state of stagnation (W. Stern, 1910).

This psychographic research stimulated by Stern is of interest to developmental psychology in several respects. First, the terms "cross-sectional" and "longitudinal" analysis were not first introduced into psychological literature in the 1920s (Baltes, 1967), but were used before that time by Stern and his students (Margis, 1911; W. Stern, 1910). Furthermore, it is interesting to note that W. Stern (1921, p. 18; 1910), with his concepts of "variation," "correlational," "psychographic," and "comparative" research designs, has anticipated, at least in principle, R. B. Cattell's (1952) covariation chart developed in the context of factor analysis. A further point should be mentioned in connection with "living" and "historical" objects. This analysis of historical objects necessarily implies the use of historical data and the observation of changes over time. In fact, such longitudinally conducted analyses of individuals were started at about this time (Margis, 1911).

After 1920, there was a growing body of research in Germany on psychological aspects of aging (e.g., Giese, 1928; Gruhle, 1938; Heydt, 1925; Marbe, 1926; Moede, 1926; Schorn, 1930; Skutsch, 1925; E. Stern, 1928, 1931; von Bracken, 1939; E. Weiss, 1927). This was the time at which the classical studies of Thorndike (1928), E. K. Strong (1931), W. R. Miles (1933), and H. E. Jones and Conrad (1933) were performed in the United States, and at which the large-scale longitudinal studies, summarized by Kagan (1964), were begun.

Except for Gottschaldt's large twin study beginning in 1936, which will be discussed later, comparable longitudinal studies were not conducted in Germany before World War II. In the early 1930s, however, Charlotte Bühler's work on *"Der Menschliche Lebenslauf als psychologisches Problem"* (C. Bühler, 1933, 1959) appeared, after K. Bühler's (1929) earlier publication of a textbook on developmental psychology. Charlotte Bühler was the head of the Vienna Research Center in Child Psychology; her main interest was the psychology of childhood and adolescence (C. Bühler, 1922, 1928) and a large number of developmental studies had been performed at this institute prior to the publication of the *Lebenslauf* (Höhn, 1959). This book can, therefore, been seen as an extension of her earlier work on childhood and adolescence. The *Lebenslauf* was made public in the United States by C. Bühler (1935) and E. Frenkel (1936).

It is impossible to give a summary of this book in this context. It is based on the analyses of 250 individual life-spans, 50 of which were gathered in an institution for aged people; the remaining 200 were taken from biographies and autobiographies. Numerous members of the Vienna Institute provided partial monographs to complete this research on the life-span (see C. Bühler, 1933; Frenkel, 1936). The papers of Frenkel (1931, 1936) offer examples of the method of data quantification used.

Contrary to the studies centered on limited sections of the life-span which were typical of this period, Charlotte Bühler's study rests on her interpretation of the *whole* course of life. She distinguishes between two developmental curves: The first is biological and describes the physical growth and decline in five periods, while the second comprises various aspects of biographical data.

Biographical changes seem to be a function of biological changes, but only relatively, since both curves do not necessarily proceed synchronously. This relationship is exemplified by a sequential analysis of performance. Both biological and biographical curves of development seem to proceed in phases, which can be defined as "chronotypic changes" (Hofstätter, 1938) with stages of transition, that is, as age-specific dominance of activities, interests, and experiences. A major aim of the book is to arrive at regularities ruling the life-span. The notion of "short lives," for instance, is interesting in this context: Whereas a normal structure is found for the usual period of long life, short lives are characterized either by complete, though shortened, life curves, or else by incomplete and interrupted ones. Remarkable, too, is the more general conclusion that childhood and adolescence not only constitute a recapitulation of phylogenesis, but also are an outline and anticipation of the whole course of life.

A critique of this research has already been presented by E. Stern (1933). He called attention to peculiarities of the data, sampling errors, problems of quantification, etc. Contrary to the rather philosophical ways of interpretation sometimes found in developmental psychology at that period (e.g., Spranger, 1925), Bühler's methodology offered a compromise between this and the tendency merely to gather and juxtapose facts: She tried to combine quantitative data and qualitative interpretation by transcending the empirical facts and raising the question of the purpose of life. These studies started in Vienna were interrupted when both the Bühlers were forced by political circumstances to emigrate. Since then, Charlotte Bühler's book has been reworked and reinterpreted, especially with regard to the "purpose structure" of human life, and newly published after the Second World War (C. Bühler, 1959).

Hofstätter (1938), too, was a member of the Vienna Circle. However, he seemed to prefer a different way of research. This preference can be inferred from his return to Quetelet, from his emphasis on quantitative analysis, and from his independence in attacking the problem of a life-span developmental psychology.

In 1936, Gottschaldt (1939, 1942, 1960, 1968) started a large-scale twin study on pairs of mono- and dizygotic twins mainly aged 10 to 18 years. These subjects had been assembled at a children's holiday home for a two month period, during which they were subjected to extensive observation and diagnostic testing. Gradually a longitudinal study developed out of this approach, and in 1950-1951, 70 pairs of twins out of the original sample (ages 25-30) were retested. The Ss had undergone largely diverse experiences due to the war. The Ss still available after 1966 (mean age 45) have been retested, using intelligence tests, problem solving tasks, EEG measures, projective tests, and 18-20-hours interview with consequent scaling on 320 attributes. According to Gottschaldt, the personality development of twins will be covered from puberty to the period of involution when his study is concluded. More recently, Gottschaldt (1968) concluded that, although there is a high concordance in the beginning, even monozygotic twins differ more and more in socially dependent functions as age increases.

D. The Time after the Second World War

In World War II, psychological research, especially in the developmental area, was interrupted in Germany. Research in this area started again very slowly and then only after the economic reconstruction (Höhn, 1959).

R. Meili (1953, 1955, 1957; G. Meili & Meili, 1969; R. Meili, Lohr, & Pulver, 1964; Pulver & Lang, 1961) began a longitudinal research project in 1950 in Switzerland. This project involved the investigation of relationship between distortions of the "perceptual Response" (PR) on 3-4 month-old children and their later behavior. PR was measured by ratings based on filmed scenes. Behavior was measured by several tests and ratings in play situations on children aged 3, 6, 8, and 15. In 1959, a new series of data collection ($n = 34$) was started; the new data collection was supposed to examine the prediction of PR distortions of the first group ($n = 26$) with broader test materials (G. Meili & Meili, 1969). The data were analyzed by correlational and factor analytical procedures. Single variables did not show consistent relations to PR; composed variables, however, yielded significant results. The assumption is made that early behavior is related to later personality traits. This attempt is interesting, but methodologically difficult.

Meili attempts to predict behavior from a very early sensory-motor reaction. Different from this approach is another longitudinal project on children started by Coerper, Hagen, and Thomae (1955) in 1951. This project is more in line with the classical-descriptive developmental psychology in terms of the methodology used. The research is a joint medical and psychological longitudinal endeavor only the psychological part of which was sponsored by Thomae (W. Hagen, Thomae, & Ronge, 1962; Thomae, 1965). This project originally included nearly 2800 subjects born in 1945-46 and 1938, in six different areas of West Germany. In the last retesting, the subjects were 15-16 years old. Only about half of the original participants were available (Thomae, 1965).

The psychological analysis is based upon sociological data, intelligence tests, drawings, sentence completion test, psychomotor test, interviews, and behavior ratings on eight different 9-point scales (see Coerper et al., 1955; W. Hagen, 1964; W. Hagen et al., 1962). Although Thomae accepts the importance of statistical analyses, the difficulties of which he is well aware (i.e., problems of quantification of some data), he also emphasizes the value of longitudinal single case studies and research in real-life situations. In a recent book (Thomae, 1968a), he suggests that psychology runs the risk, as a consequence of the strict methodological requirements, of missing the reality of life.

Many monographs have come from this longitudinal project (shown in the references). The advantages of this project lie in the great number of subjects used and in the possibility of describing the process of physical development and general adjustment on a broad basis. Questions of continuity and discontinuity and questions of the influence of many sociocultural variables were treated in detail.

As far as I know, there are today only two such programs: The twin research program started in 1936 and directed by Gottschaldt, and the program "German Post-War Children" by Coerper, Hagen, and Thomae. Independent of these investigations on children and adolescents, Thomae and his staff launched research on problems of aging (see e.g., Lehr, 1966; Lehr & Dreher, 1968; Lehr & Thomae, 1958, 1965, 1968; Scharmann, 1955; Thomae, 1959, 1968b, 1968c, 1968d, 1968e; Thomae & Lehr, 1968). The Bonn research group works together with the German Society of Gerontology which fosters interdisciplinary cooperation on "aging" problems. In 1969, a special research center of the German Research Society was established at the Department of Psychology of the University of Bonn. This center is concerned with the coordination of the "already and partly still proceeding longitudinal investigations on subjects from the 1st to the 8th decade of life" (Thomae, 1968d).

Besides the Bonn research on developmental psychology of the adult and old, there are a number of publications, such as the monographs by Moers (1953) and E. Stern (1955). Both books are representative, even though for different reasons, of the more classical tradition of German developmental psychology. As examples of individual research, some German titles of K. F. and R. M. Riegel (K. F. Riegel, 1958, 1959a; K. F. Riegel, Riegel, & Skiba, 1962; R. M. Riegel, 1960; R. M. Riegel & Riegel, 1959) should be noted.

A review of present initiatives in Germany in the area of psychological research on aging is given in the report on the congress of the German Society for Gerontology (Schubert, 1968). Further references to articles past and present can be found in a reader, edited by Thomae and Lehr (1968).

IV. CONCLUDING REMARKS

There is almost no specialized historical research on psychological problems of the life-span. Historians of psychology were typically not very interested in developmental psychology; historians of developmental psychology concentrated mainly on the origins of child psychology. As a result, one gains the impression that the historical roots of developmental psychology encompassed only child psychology. This impression is not quite correct.

At the end of the eighteenth century, the first child biography (Tiedemann, 1787) and the first attempt to discuss life-span problems (Tetens, 1777) appeared within a short time of each other. The methodological approach was that of longitudinal description.

The cross-sectional method was used one-half century later by Quetelet (1838), who can be called the founder of life-span psychology in the modern sense. According to him, development followed a model of quantitative changes and he used quantitative methods to show the age dependancy of many variables.

Galton's contribution to life-span psychology began in 1875. Up to that time, developmental psychology did not consist only of child psychology. Taking Quetelet into account, it can be seen that life-span developmental psychology was methodologically more advanced than child psychology. The latter increased in importance with the works of Preyer (1882) and G. S. Hall (1883).

In Germany life-span developmental psychology developed mainly from preliminary studies of W. Stern (1921), who dealt with, among other things, the methodological problems of "genetic psychography." Of special importance are C. Bühler (1933) and her research group in Vienna. Here, probably for the first time, an attempt was made at a comprehensive, descriptive, longitudinal analysis of behavior.

The present situation in Germany can be summarized as follows: A center for research on aging, also including life-span psychology, has been established and is supported by the *"Deutsche Forschungsge-meinschaft"* at the University of Bonn. This center, directed by H. Thomae, works in close connection with the *"Deutsche Gesellschaft für Gerontologie,"* which coordinates research on old age.

In Germany, the general approach to research is more often "empirical" than "experimental." Quantitative data are collected, but the qualitative data are not neglected. As Munnichs (1966) found, research in Germany in this field is frequently closer to real life than, for example, American research. On the other hand, methodological difficulties often arise for this very reason.

ACKNOWLEDGMENT

The author gratefully acknowledges the assistance of Ingeborg Wender. Latter sections of this chapter are restricted to historical trends in Germany.

THEORY
CONSTRUCTION

CHAPTER 4

An Approach to Theory Construction in the Psychology of Development and Aging

D. B. BROMLEY

DEPARTMENT OF PSYCHOLOGY
THE UNIVERSITY OF LIVERPOOL, ENGLAND

ABSTRACT

Theory construction in life-span psychology takes place within a context of scientific method and philosophy of science appropriate to the social and behavioral sciences. Some of the complexities of theorizing are illustrated in a case history dealing with the psychopathology and developmental psychology of cognitive processes. The rules of formal logic, which are external or field independent, show what is required of an analytical argument, but provide little guidance in the construction of substantial arguments—arguments dealing with empirical facts and scientific conjectures—where the logical rules are internal or field dependent. Toulmin has proposed a method for the analysis of substantial arguments, and the method is illustrated by applying it to (a) a theory of the effects of age on creative thinking and (b) the theory of disengagement. The technique is to work out the implicit or latent content of the initial, explicit or manifest, argument. The resulting network of interconnected statements constitutes an explanation and reveals the functions of theoretical and other terms in relation to each other and in relation to empirical data; it also provides opportunities for creative conjecture, critical evaluation, and logical deduction. The role of models and analogies in theory construction is illustrated by reference to computer processes. Birren's counterpart theory is discussed. It is concluded that the problems of theory construction in life-span psychology are no different in principle from those in other scientific disciplines.

I. INTRODUCTION

The topic of theory construction in life-span psychology can be dealt with in a number of ways. I have chosen to adopt a novel approach by keeping as close as possible to the actual machinery of argument and by using examples with which I am familiar drawn largely from the psychology of aging. I have tried to give a "worm's eye" view of theory construction—describing what seems to go on in the process of theorizing, but excluding problem solving and creative thinking. This is not to say that philosophy of science issues are neglected, but rather that they provide a context for a consideration of the practical problems of theory construction. Among the publications relating to philosophy of science that I happen to have found particularly useful are the following: Beveridge (1950), Conant (1947), Hempel (1965, 1966), Mandler and Kessen (1959), Popper (1959, 1962), Toulmin (1953, 1958), and M. B. Turner (1967). An alternative approach to the topic would have been to make a comparative study of existing theories. Unfortunately, existing theories do not lend themselves easily to comparative analysis, and in any case it would be impossible to achieve this in anything less than a full volume—along the lines of, say, D. B. Harris (1957a), A. L. Baldwin (1967), Maier (1965), or Langer (1969). In a related chapter, Reese and Overton adopt yet another approach.

Life-span psychology is an empirical, multidisciplinary science. Thus, by definition, it constitutes an endeavor to investigate, describe, understand, predict, control, and explain those events and processes which we commonly refer to as "development and aging." As in other sciences, statements in life-span psychology must be firmly based upon observation and reason and must be subject, directly or indirectly, to corroboration by competent persons working independently of one another. The sorts of evidence used in rational arguments about the processes of development and aging are various. They include clinical observations, experimental observations and measurements, survey data, psychometric results, and, in fact, any relevant materials supplied by a credible source. Thus, in order to encompass the wide range of facts, the diversity of observational techniques, and the various sorts of explanation that are found in the psychology of development and aging, scientific method will be broadly defined as, "A system of rational and empirical procedures designed to test claims against evidence and thereby progressively reduce error."

Adopting such a definition means that one need not restrict one's attention narrowly to theories which demand quantifiable data or close laboratory control of observation. One can treat the topic of "theory construction" as a kind of empirical problem by examining representative examples and discovering what is required of a good theory. Thus, although the term "theory" tends to conjure up notions of systems of ideas associated with the natural sciences—especially systems of ideas falling into mathematico-deductive patterns of argument—the broad definition of scientific method just proposed enables one to take account not only of theories modeled on those of the natural and biological sciences, but also of theories which may be less formal and less analytic than one would wish but are nevertheless heuristically valuable—or, at worst, all that one has—theories not unlike those found in law, history, and social science generally.

Since the topic of theory construction cannot be easily separated from the topic of philosophy of science, in the next section a detailed illustration will be given of the philosophical context within which the construction of theories about development and aging occurs.

II. EVIDENCE AND INFERENCE:
A CASE HISTORY AND COMMENTARY

I shall briefly describe, in the form of a case history, a small set of related studies with which I am familiar. Although the studies are of little importance in themselves, they are, I believe, fairly typical and illustrate to some extent the manner of scientific inquiry and the associated theorizing.

A. Pilot Study

In the early 1950s, I was interested in the psychological aspects of thought disorder (Bromley, 1953). I had conducted a pilot inquiry into the relationships between aging and intellectual changes using simple measures of choice reaction time, intelligence, short-term memory, vocabulary, and concept formation. The Ss were drawn from two psychiatric observation wards in a general hospital and I tested every S between the ages of 40 and 80 years who was capable of cooperating and understanding the test instructions. The reason for choosing this particular kind of group was that I expected intellectual changes associated with normal aging to show up more clearly, in aggravated form as it were, in abnormal (deteriorated) Ss.

Notice that the theory behind the investigator's choice of problem and method helps to determine even the early stages of a scientific inquiry. Such a "proto-theory" is loosely formulated and consists of a small number of basic assumptions, some of which may be implicit, i.e., not recognized as such by the investigator. Thus, I had assumed that the effects of normal aging would be emphasized rather than masked by the concomitant psychiatric condition; and I had assumed that intellectual deterioration was a homogeneous process, i.e., that it would follow a similar basic pattern regardless of etiology. The background of ideas giving rise to this latter assumption was derived from a number of sources: H. Werner (1948, also see 1957), Goldstein and Scheerer (1941), Hanfmann and Kasanin (1942), and others. The common theme concerns the relatively primitive forms of thought supposedly characteristic of patients suffering from certain kinds of mental disease or brain injury, and characteristic of elderly people, young children, and people in primitive communities; it seems to assume: (a) that intellectual functions become organized into hierarchical-developmental patterns, (b) that the basic processes are normally superseded or assimilated by more advanced or inclusive intellectual functions, and (c) that *any* process of deterioration would bring about a reversion to earlier and more primitive forms of thought.

As presently conceived, Piaget's theory (see Flavell, 1963) says nothing about the developmental aspects of intelligence in maturity and old age, save a study by Dennis and Mallinger (1949) and a study by S. Sanders, Laurendeau, and Bergeron (1966); it says nothing about abnormalities and variations in the developmental process. In retrospect, it seems that I was correct in supposing that structural features such as concreteness, syncretism, and rigidity were a proper focus for an investigation into the psychology of thought disorder in late life. The theory, however, left much to be desired, since it did not specify in sufficient detail what kinds of changes should occur and it did not provide an adequate basis for predicting what might be observed—except insofar as it predicted some kind of reversion to inferior or developmentally earlier patterns of cognition that would be revealed as errors and abnormalities in performance. Notice the implicit theorizing here too, for even if systematic patterns of error and abnormality were observed (as was, in fact, the case), they would indicate a reversion to earlier developmental structures only if it could be shown that such late-life patterns (of errors and abnormalities) were characteristic of, or analogous to, similar patterns during development. My initial theory, therefore, was far from explicit, since it did not distinguish between (a) observations indicating a reversion to earlier stages of intellectual development, and (b) observations indicating some kind of deterioration or simplification of cognitive processes arising from one or another cause, such as "aging," mental disease, or brain damage.

In the investigation under review, the Progressive Matrices Test (Raven, 1938, 1951) was the principal instrument. It consists of a series of diagrams with logical relationships holding across elements in the rows and elements in the columns, and with the element in the last row and column missing. Ss are required to complete the pattern by selecting the correct element from the group of six or eight numbered elements placed below each matrix. It was supposed that their responses might reveal systematic errors and abnormalities in performance. The test was individually administered to each member of the sample. Ss were encouraged to explain their reasons for choosing one answer rather than another. The expectation behind this procedure was that Ss with normal intellectual functions would give rational and logical explanations for their choice of solution to each problem, whereas Ss with abnormal intellectual functions, or Ss whose cognitive structures had reverted to earlier or simpler forms would give irrational, primitive, abnormal explanations, and make systematic errors. It did not occur to me at the time that, except for obvious aphasia, the Ss' verbal capacities might themselves be impaired independently of their cognitive capacities. I assumed that abnormal explanations would reflect abnormal thought processes.

Since the investigation had been conceived merely as a pilot inquiry, only 35 Ss were tested. The frequency distribution of correct responses, as judged by the selection of correct alternatives from the choice of answers given, seemed to indicate not a smooth decrease from the easiest problem to the most difficult, but rather a steady decrease accompanied by abrupt falls at intervals throughout the series of 60 items. These abrupt falls were construed as marking shifts from one cognitive level to another, e.g., a shift from singular to multiple operations, or a shift from simple matching to reasoning by analogy. No doubt other constructions could be placed upon this finding, e.g., inadequate or insufficient items; this aspect of the case history illustrates another feature of theory construction, namely, that more than one construction (interpretation) can be put upon the same set of observations (data). The problem then becomes one of discovering which of several explanations (theories) is the correct one. This particular aspect of theory construction is now very familiar in philosophy of science. It has been dealt with in considerable detail by Popper (1959), and it helps us to understand the weakness of inductive arguments. Popper's principle of falsification requires that hypotheses derived from a theory should be tested to see if they can be shown to be wrong. If they are shown to be wrong, then the theory from which they were derived must be reexamined and possibly rejected, or at least supported by auxiliary assumptions. If they are not shown to be wrong, then the theory is not proved right but becomes more confidently accepted by the investigator.

In addition to suggesting abrupt shifts in levels of cognitive functioning, the observational evidence relating to the Progressive Matrices Test showed that the *wrong* answers to the items were not distributed in the way one would have expected if the wrong alternatives were all equally wrong from a "logical" point of view. Instead, Ss tended to select similar responses even when the responses were wrong. Furthermore, even the layout of the multiple choice answers seemed to influence the S's responses, since, regardless of the correctness of the alternatives, alternatives in certain physical positions were selected more frequently: Ss tended to choose alternatives from the top line rather than the bottom, and from the right-hand side rather than the left, but also preferred the first and last alternatives.

The pilot inquiry provided the investigator with evidence relevant to his inquiries. At that stage it was not necessary for his theory to be well articulated or for his methods of inquiry and analysis to be very rigorous, since he was not intending that his results would be definitive. One might even argue that loosely formulated theories and methods are more appropriate in the early stages of an inquiry, since the investigator is not too committed and can more easily allow the data to shape his ideas and methods (see Barker, 1965). But this is not to say that the investigator is not theorizing (implicitly) or that he is not being misled by his methods.

So far, I have explained that the performance of the Ss on the Progressive Matrices Test was, in some respects, not normal, i.e., not what you would expect from adult Ss capable of average intellectual operations. There were step-wise decreases in the frequency distribution of scores, the distribution of wrong answers was not random, i.e., there were positional preferences, and the "explanations" offered by the Ss were frequently illogical and abnormal. Except for the last mentioned item, these particular findings had not been explicitly predicted by the vague "theory" of intellectual deterioration which gave rise to the investigation, but they were compatible with it. So here, again, we find another aspect of scientific theorizing illustrated by the case history; that is to say, the actual observations which we are led to make frequently provide us with evidence that we had not anticipated, even though, when the evidence is made available, we see that we *might have* expected it. What is missing in occurrences of this sort usually is either a lack of sustained deductive theorizing on the part of the investigator or a lack of "bridging principles" which would enable him to work out more thoroughly the empirical implications of his theory.

In the pilot inquiry, however, the theory had predicted that the cognitive processes of the Ss, as judged by their reasons for choosing particular answers, would reveal abnormalities. Notice that, even here, the theory did not enable the investigator to predict exactly what sorts of abnormal "reasons" would be given, although, of course, any subsequent investigation could specify them. Such a subsequent investigation, however, would then merely corroborate, though in a rather precise way, the empirical findings of the earlier investigation, and this could be achieved without any progress in theorizing. What would have been achieved would be a kind of consistency in the evidence which would reveal an opportunity for creative theorizing by calling for an answer to the question, "Why should Ss make such responses?" Consistent findings also stimulate the investigator to make comparative studies—to test whether other sorts of Ss make the same responses, or whether the same sorts of Ss make the same responses in different conditions. The investigator hopes to extend by these means the range and variety of evidence relevant to his expectations and, eventually, to develop the internal logic of his theory, so that he can deduce what should occur under specified conditions.

The problem of cataloging the sorts of reasons given by the patients for choosing one answer rather than another illustrates other aspects of scientific theorizing: terminology, taxonomy, and operational definitions. It is clear that simply listing the observations is not enough—the facts of observation do not speak for themselves, they have to be spoken for; and they are spoken for by a theory which imposes upon them a pattern of meaning, a logical structure. Without going into too much detail, it can be said that the reasons given by the patients could be classified into two main categories: normal and primitive. The normal responses were those that appeared to make use of the logical relationships embedded in each item; the primitive responses were those that failed to do so. As in other systems of classification, the distinction is somewhat arbitrary and imperfect. The Ss were able, to a limited extent, to pay attention to those aspects of the Matrices problems that the normal adult considers relevant, and to work out the answers in a rational logical way. But Ss were also inclined to give responses based on personal associations, concrete imagery, global (undifferentiated) impressions, oversimplifications, and stereotyped (repetitive) reactions. It was in these respects that their cognitive level was described as "primitive," i.e., undeveloped, undifferentiated.

Position preferences similar to those observed among Ss in the pilot inquiry had been observed in normal school children (F. M. Miller & Raven, 1939), thus providing at least a little support for the theory of reversion to developmentally earlier cognitive structures. The theory stated that in Ss with more primitive cognitive structures, their "boundedness to outer-world stimuli," i.e., field dependence, takes the form of an inability to analyze a complex situation into its component parts or to restructure it, and their "egocentricity" restricts their behavior by strongly predisposing them to personal and habitual forms of response. In normal Ss, attention is influenced, but not fixed, by the stimulus properties of the problem, and is similarly influenced, but not fixed, by subjective factors such as expectation and habit.

Further analysis of the data revealed that, apart from correct answers, which, as judged by the explanations given, were mainly determined by eductive (logically rational) processes, Ss were likely to choose in order of preference from among the alternatives: first, a part of the matrix; second, a figure embodying all or several features of the total matrix; third, a figure similar to the correct one; fourth, a figure simular to some part of the matrix, but a distortion of it; and fifth, very infrequently, an unrelated figure. These "content preference" effects were somewhat obscured by positional influences. Here again, one sees that there can be no description relevant to a scientific theory without some attempt to classify and organize the data. In fact, the classification adopted attempted to improve on one developed by F. M. Miller and Raven (1939). It could be argued that if sufficient evidence of a representative sort had been collected, then the facts would have fallen into place, almost, as it were, of their own accord. But this is not so. The facts (of observation) have to be given a place in a theory. It is the theory which supplies the meaning; and whether the facts fall into place easily or not depends not only upon the adequacy of the theory and the sorts and amounts of evidence, but also upon the scientific skill of the investigator as he moves between theory construction on the one hand and data collection on the other.

Perhaps at the most basic level of observation one can only describe what is perceived (given the context and the assumptions), and hope that gradually some pattern will become apparent (see Barker, 1965). In the pilot inquiry, such descriptive observation was carried out systematically, and several classes of primitive response were distinguished and exemplified: global responses, concrete responses, mechanization (rigidity), inability to explain, motoric (pointing, tracing) responses, loss of decision criteria, confusion and fluidity of thought, avoidance of reality. Such responses appeared to coexist with other, more logically rational, responses. A valid theory would call for a proper taxonomy, i.e., an exhaustive and exclusive set of categories for classifying all responses.

Thus, although the pilot inquiry did not reach a very sophisticated level of theory construction and data collection, it did represent a legitimate form of theorizing and procedure, i.e., the sort you need when you want to look into a problem without restricting your terms of reference too closely. What you hope to gain from such loose theorizing and simple procedures is not a definite answer to your question, but rather an opportunity to reformulate your questions and your terms of reference so that they become more explicit and more narrowly focused, and an opportunity to revise your methods of data collection so that the evidence you collect on the next occasion is more pertinent and more easily handled. For example, one could test whether intellectual deterioration in conditions of old age, mental disease or brain injury showed systematic trends as regards the appearance of primitive forms of thought, and whether the three sorts of condition brought about comparable forms of intellectual deterioration. If so, one would then test whether the observed changes were retrograde, i.e., systematically related to developmental changes.

The Matrices Test results showed that normal and primitive cognitive responses could be elicited from the same S, which suggested that primitive forms of thought might function in two ways: (a) as "compensatory" modes of functioning (cf. Welford, 1958) when higher intellectual operations are no longer possible because of deterioration, and (b) as "intrusive" modes of functioning disrupting already weakened processes of intellectual control. Here we have an example of creative theorizing—a simple investigation yields rather more relevant evidence than was anticipated, but the evidence can be assimilated to the theory by developing its internal principles.

B. Further Research

The scientific issues raised in the study of primitive forms of response to the Matrices Test were taken up by Maher (1960) and Wetherick (1964). Maher confined his analysis to sets A and B of the Progressive Matrices Test, but compared young mentally retarded Ss with college students with regard to positional preferences for wrong answers. He pointed out that positions occupied by correct alternatives in easy problems early in the series are occupied by incorrect alternatives in difficult later problems; hence, it is these positions which appear to have a high probability of appearing as position errors when results are combined for a series of problems. Maher demonstrated that the results obtained by F. M. Miller and Raven (1939) and Bromley (1953) in respect of position preferences could have been a statistical artifact, and argued that position preferences must be tested for item by item. When this was done, he was able to show that there was no conclusive evidence of position preferences, and it seemed reasonable to suppose that the explanation for systematic errors, whether among normal children, adults, or patients, must lie elsewhere, i.e., in some other kind of preference. Maher referred to the differential attractiveness of the "content" of frequently chosen erroneous alternatives, and so, although disproving the position preference hypothesis, left the content preference hypothesis intact.

Maher's findings illustrate two aspects of theory construction. The first is that with loosely organized theories it is often possible to disprove one part of the system without altering other parts. The second is that it is only too easy to find ex post facto theoretical "rationalizations" for empirical findings. For example, the assumed position preferences had been "explained" in part by notions such as egocentricity, boundedness to outer-world stimuli, and boundary effects. Consider also Cronbach's (1955) demonstration that the results of many studies of accuracy in the perception of others were better explained as statistical artifacts than in terms of mechanisms affecting interpersonal perception. So there is a double danger in theory construction—the empirical data upon which the theory is initially based may be in error, and even when they are not, more than one construction can be imposed on them.

Wetherick (1964) examined wrong answers (content preferences) in the Matrices Test item by item given by a large sample of adults of different ages. He found that Ss of higher intelligence did not invariably choose the same wrong responses as Ss of lower intelligence, and at first sight this appeared as an age trend, since intelligence declines with age. But further analysis showed that adult Ss made the same kinds of errors in the Progressive Matrices Test, i.e., had the same content preferences. Wetherick considered the sources of error to be, for example, the inability of a S to educe a relation or correlate of the required complexity, inadequate short-term memory, or carrying out the wrong logical operation. He showed, however, that the pattern of errors (content preferences) of his normal to above average elderly Ss was similar to the pattern of errors characteristic of Bromley's small sample of older psychiatric patients. This meant either (a) that the forms of thought exhibited by the patients were not really primitive or abnormal, or (b) that the normal elderly Ss were exhibiting primitive or abnormal forms of thought (Wetherick speculated about the reasons for his Ss' errors but obtained no verbal reports from them), or (c) that the intellectual processes of the psychiatric patients were normal but their verbal processes were impaired—patients might have been unable to "render an intelligible account" of themselves, even though their logical operations were normal. Evidence collected in the main inquiry (Bromley, 1963) shows that elderly "normal" Ss do in fact give some pathological responses to some mental tests. And subsequent studies (e.g., Reitan, 1955, Davies, 1968), have shown that from the age of about 40, normal Ss perform "abnormally" on tests designed to assess brain damage.

Wetherick's contribution to our case history illustrates some aspects of scientific method and theorizing to which I have already referred. In particular, it shows that what one observes depends to a large extent on what one is looking for. Wetherick was looking for evidence relevant to his ideas concerning inductive (unavoidable) and deductive (avoidable) errors in problem solving. He claimed to have found similarities between responses to items in the Progressive Matrices Test and to items in his own Letter Group Test, though he was using the Matrices Test mainly as a measure of nonverbal intelligence and only incidentally as a way of examining intellectual processes by analyzing errors in performance. On reflection, however, Wethericks's results, like those of Maher, do clarify the situation, for now we know that although there are consistent patterns of error in response to the Matrices Test which point to some underlying structural (or mediational) factors in cognition (which, if we could conceptualize them adequately, would constitute a partial theory of cognition), such patterns do not arise because of positional preferences and seem to be related to development and aging only indirectly, through the association of intelligence with chronological age. As regards the pathology of thought, it may be that the intellectual impairment associated with mental disease, brain injury, and normal aging is connected in some way with developmental processes—for example, through the erosion of later developed, more inclusive mental processes.

C. Outcome

Unfortunately, as must be true of many other case-histories in scientific method, there has been no definite outcome, only a shift of interests and methods (see Bromley, 1963, 1967, 1968b). Topics in science are taken up and then dropped if they do not yield results quickly, since it is difficult (though sometimes rewarding) to persist with inquiries which do not show interesting and meaningful results in the early stages. Scientific investigators are constantly casting around for conceptual clarification which will lead to more effective prediction and control of events. This is another way of saying that scientific investigators, whether they realize it or not, are constantly engaged in theory construction.

Like most scientific inquiries, the one I have described in some detail, which was conceived in the early 1950s, naturally was influenced by the prevailing concepts and methods relevant to the study of aging, brain damage, and intellectual deficit. Since that time, although relatively little progress has been achieved in theory or in the actual techniques of assessment, there have been considerable advances in methodology and statistical analysis. But in addition, interest has shifted more toward functions other than thought disorder, toward short-term memory (STM) (e.g, Craik, 1968a; Inglis, Sykes, & Ankus, 1968b), conceptual processes and problem solving (e.g., Wetherick, 1965, Arenberg, 1968), and verbal behavior (e.g., Canestrari, 1968b; K. F. Riegel, 1968a).

III. THE DEDUCTIVE FUNCTION OF THEORIES

We need not concern ourselves with the technical details of analytical logic because, as we shall see, theories in life-span psychology do not consist of rigorously defined, closely-knit conceptual systems for which analytic logic is particularly appropriate. Nevertheless, logical fallacies are proscribed even in weakly formulated theories and it is therefore necessary to consider some aspects of deduction. The formal (external) rules of deductive inference are of peripheral interest, however, since we shall be concerned mainly with what might be called the "internal logic" or "field dependent logic" of scientific arguments.

First, it is usually necessary to generalize one's findings. For example, from observing the particular responses of particular patients, one generalizes to a class of responses of a class of patients: "Elderly psychiatric patients make primitive responses to the Matrices test." Though this is only one of a set of generalizations which might account for the initial data. In order to corroborate the observational data, one would have to replicate the original investigation. Such corroboration is based on the assumption that nature is consistent or uniform; and if it turned out that equivalent samples of elderly psychiatric patients did not make equivalent primitive responses to the Matrices test, then no such generalization would be legitimate. The kind of generalization that is made by the E to assimilate, or make sense of, the observational evidence depends a great deal upon the E's personal qualities and experience—but we need not concern ourselves with the creative aspects of induction. Even without replicating the investigation, it is often possible to point to other relevant evidence which supports or fails to support the generalization; thus, many hasty generalizations can be quickly disposed of. For example, if the elderly female psychiatric patients in the sample had not made primitive responses, then it would be obvious that the relationship had been overstated. Thus, in a very direct way, either by adducing additional evidence or by examining the first evidence more closely, it is possible to dispose of or to modify the original generalization.

But the generalization, whether original or modified, is more than a summary statement of a relationship detected by the E and exemplified in his observational evidence. It is, in addition, a rule, which the E can use to draw conclusions in a deductive argument. Not that Es are prone to see themselves playing such a pedantic role; they are more likely to see themselves as making claims or stating the implications of their findings, usually without going to the trouble of setting out the full logic of their argument. That is to say, much of the argument supporting their scientific claims is implicit (premises are supressed), and it might come as a surprise to some investigators, for example, those who use clinical and case methods, to find that they have been practicing the hypothetico-deductive method. In fact, of course, there is no other method of arriving at the rational consequences of one's initial beliefs—hence the definition of scientific method proposed at the beginning of this article. Constructing a theory is, to my way of thinking, simply making explicit the whole array of statements (of which empirical generalizations are only a part) which enable one to deduce rational implications, i.e., make scientific claims, regarding some relatively limited empirical issues. The empirical issues have a bearing on, i.e., are relevant to, the theory (premises) insofar as they are implied by the theory, since relevant empirical evidence is, by definition, either for or against the theory.

One simple sort of hypothetico-deductive argument is described by Hempel (1966, p. 7) as follows, where H stands for a hypothesis, and I for an implication of that hypothesis:

> If H is true, then so is I.
> *But (as the evidence shows) I is not true.*
> H is not true

The same simple form of argument can be displayed in another way (Toulmin, 1958); where D stands for data or evidence, C stands for claim or conclusion, and W stands for inference warrant (this premise is suppressed in the above argument):

> If D, then C, since W.
> *But (as the evidence shows) not C.*
> So not D (or not W).

Thus, to take a concrete example:

> If the statement that Ss making wrong responses to the Matrices test are affected by
> position preferences is true, then so is the statement that position preferences occur even
> when tested for item by item (or when the positions of the multiple choice responses are
> experimentally varied). But (as the evidence shows) the implied statement (conclusion) is
> not true, therefore the hypothesis (or at least one premise) is not true (regardless of the
> truth of any reason adduced to explain the supposed connection between the belief and the
> expectation—H and I, or D and C above).

It is important to remember that such arguments are valid only if one affirms the
antecedent (to conclude that I is true) or denies the consequent (to conclude
that H is false). As Hempel points out (1966, p. 8), no amount of confirmation
of the consequent (I) can lead to an analytically valid affirmation of the
hypothesis (H). What repeated confirmation of the implications can do,
however, is to increase the E's confidence in his hypothesis—provided, of course,
that such repeated confirmations constitute a sufficiently varied sample of tests.

The connecting link between the belief and the expectation (H and I) has
been referred to above as an inference warrant (W). An inference warrant is the
reason given by the E for expecting his hypothesis, if true, to have one set of
implications, or, if false, another set. The inference warrant can be construed as
a kind of justification for linking the theoretical statement to the relevant
empirical evidence; or it can be thought of as a statement which explains how
the cause-effect relationship operates, i.e., how the theory works in practice.

Events are "explained" when it is explicitly stated that, given certain
circumstances, certain effects will occur—provided the explanation shows (even
if only vaguely) what conditions are necessary and sufficient to produce the
effects. For example, "If a test of conceptual thought is administered to elderly
normal Ss, they will make responses similar to those made by young patients
suffering from certain kinds of mental disease or brain injury, since normal old
age is accompanied by similar cortical deterioration."

As Hempel (1966, p. 20) points out, we are dealing with conditional
statements or material implications, and such statements can frequently lead to
experimental tests in which the conditions (C) are set up and the effects (E)
observed, so that evidence relevant to law-like statements (L) can be collected.
When the expected relationships have been formulated, and especially when the
variables can be quantified, experimental tests of the hypothesis can be achieved
by systematically varying the conditions and measuring the effects to see
whether, or to what extent, the expected relationships hold.

The total array of interrelated statements comprising the theory is intended
to describe the conditions governing the appearance or nonappearance of the
effect. Such statements refer not only to the ingenious mechanisms and
relationships proposed by the E but also to the more mundane requirements
regarding instrumentation, procedure, credibility of informants, assumptions,

and the like. For example, in experimental studies of creativity, the behavior of Ss can be influenced by the way the instructions are phrased (and, or course, this is true of many other kinds of experimental studies with human Ss); so any theory which attempts to explain, say, age differences or the effects of training in relation to creativity must somehow be able to incorporate statements about the effects, if any, produced by variations in test instructions.

Any one of the statements incorporated in a theory or any one of its testable implications may be shown to be deficient or false; this does not necessarily lead to the abandonment of the whole conceptual system, but it does call for some kind of adjustment, e.g., a qualifying phrase restricting the implications that can be deduced, or a statement making explicit a suppressed premise. Thus, adapting Hempel's example (1966, p. 23):

> If H_1, H_2, H_3, . . . , H_k are all true, then so is I.
> *But (as the evidence shows) I is not true.*
> Therefore, at least one H is not true.

What the E has to do in such circumstances is to adjust his theory until the offending evidence can be incorporated or rendered irrelevant. Thus, theories which do not live up to the expectations we have of them can often be rehabilitated after a course of corrective treatment, which is why, as Hempel (1966, p. 28) points out, crucial experiments to decide between two or more theories are impossible. At best the E may prefer one theory over another because, all things considered, it has distinct advantages. He may even, if he chooses, shift his preference from one theory to another, depending upon circumstances. There may be many ways of conceptualizing the same events, and it is only when these different conceptualizations give rise to contradictory implications that the stage is set for an important test, the outcome of which should lead the E to prefer one theory rather than another.

One cannot legitimately introduce a modification for the sole purpose of protecting the conceptual system from the offending evidence. Rather, any modification must lead to a better explanation, i.e., one must ask what has been gained in the way of prediction, control, and understanding. As is well known, one of the objections to psychoanalysis is that so many protective features have been introduced into the conceptual system to fend off adverse criticism that it is difficult, if not impossible, to state what evidence would, if adduced, refute any part of the theory. If a theory does not allow for the possibility of refutation, then it cannot be regarded as scientific, i.e., as a rational and empirical method of settling issues by appeal to reason and observation. The poverty of theory construction in psychology generally and in life-span psychology in particular means that some of the philosophy of science issues concerning theoretical simplicity, or mutual support between theories developed independently of one another, or credibility, scarcely arise.

Since there are no rules governing the *kind* of explanation that can be offered to account for natural events (save the criteria for judging the soundness of arguments), one need not feel obliged to construct theories modeled on those developed in the physical sciences. Nor need one, at this stage in the history of scientific psychology, worry unduly if one's theory does not lend itself readily to quantification and mathematical treatment. It is more important to gain insight than to worry about the respectability of one's conceptual system. Any kind of conceptualization is permitted, provided it shows how an effect arises under prescribed conditions, and provided the implications of the conceptualization can be confirmed or falsified by empirical observations. But, as already stated, more than one conceptualization may adequately account for the relevant observations, and the problem is to decide on the relative merits of these competing theories by working out their implications and attempting to falsify them.

For Hempel (1965, pp. 335-376; 1966, pp. 49-58), explanations which consist in deducing a conclusion or implication from an array of law-like statements describing empirical uniformities and statements about particular facts or conditions are classed as deductive-nomological (D-N) explanations. Often, the deductive argument is not given in full, i.e., some of the premises remain implicit or suppressed; this may be because they would be too tedious to work out, e.g., a child's fear might be "explained" by reference to a previous traumatic experience—the associated theory of learning being taken for granted. To ask for an explanation is usually to ask for some information which one lacks; when that information is forthcoming, one is able to complete the pattern of meaning. But, in a sense, there is never a *complete* explanation for the events, and to ask for one is to ask for the impossible, since the ramifications of the implicit argument are infinite—a skeptic will be prepared to push his objections to an argument so far as to question the very bases of one's experience and logic. Nevertheless, there are practical limits to the reasons one can give for not accepting a theory; and to accept such limits is to be prepared in principle to adopt the cause-effect account which the theory expounds.

One important aspect of theory construction in the empirical sciences concerns the persistent liability to falsification. Thus, even if generalizations are expressed in a modified universal form, there is always the risk that they have been overstated. Similarly, although theoretical statements are treated as if they were true, they may, in fact, be false. The cumulative effect of these risks and errors, allied with unfortunate gaps in the theory and the evidence, is to make any scientific framework of ideas merely an approximation to the true state of affairs (as judged by subsequent findings), and to attach to any deduction an associated degree of likelihood or credibility.

Life-span psychology abounds with evidence of apparent relationships and uniformities, and this wealth of empirical material has stimulated many kinds of theorizing, e.g., the role of early experience and behavior as a determinant of adult functions; the interaction of heredity and environment in neurosis; the origins and consequences of disengagement. The data pertaining to each of these areas can be used as evidence for or against some theoretical construction that purports to explain the data, i.e., the E tries to show that the data fall into one pattern of meaning rather than another. In order to do this, he makes use of theoretical terms (laws, principles, mechanisms, entities) to organize the data, e.g., the Yerkes-Dodson law describing the relation between performance and degree of anxiety, the principles of developmental differentiation and integration, mechanisms such as the reticular activating system or repression, and entities such as reference group or short-term memory. These theoretical terms, in addition to seeming to account for the evidence which stimulated their invention, may also account for other data and give rise to expectations about possible data.

Hempel (1966, pp. 72-75), makes a distinction between internal principles and bridge principles in theory construction. Internal principles are those "basic entities and processes invoked by the theory and the laws to which they are assumed to conform." In Piaget's developmental theory, for example, assimilation and accommodation are internal principles. Bridge principles show "how the processes envisaged by the theory are related to empirical phenomena. . . ." In Eysenck's theory of personality, (Eysenck, 1966) for example, the notion of "involuntary rest pause" is a bridge principle connecting the theoretical term "inhibition" with experimentally observable changes in rate of performance. Bridge principles relate different sorts of statement, e.g., they connect novel theoretical concepts with already established theoretical notions or with empirical findings and techniques.

A theory should have the effect of organizing a wide range of facts and principles, and of condensing and clarifying them, e.g., by providing a suitable taxonomy, by subsuming particular instances under a few general rules, by employing statements limiting or qualifying the applicability of the theory. Eventually, adequately validated scientific theories become linked, by suitable bridge principles, with common sense. In the process, both scientific theory and common sense are transformed; the former is called upon to account for the evidence of our senses, the latter is called upon to assimilate verified scientific findings and to abandon beliefs which are demonstrably false.

In order to get a grip on and further develop some relatively new conceptualization, it may be necessary to invent new terms. But these terms have to be anchored, initially at least, in already established scientific knowledge. Analogy and metaphor are sometimes employed for this purpose, and so are "operational definitions." It does not follow that a concept will have theoretical value simply because it can be anchored to an operational definition, but the converse holds: A concept will have no value if it cannot be anchored.

Normally, the interrelationships between concepts and evidence in the overall fabric of scientific knowledge will provide a number of anchorage points for a given concept, so that it is not tied to one specific operational definition. Of particular importance in life-span developmental psychology are those bridge principles which link concepts in two or more disciplines, e.g., psycho-physiological and psychosocial generalizations, for life-span studies must, in the long run at least, be multidisciplinary and bring about coalescing of diverse concepts and findings by means of more embracing theories.

When a theory has been adequately formulated, it should be largely independent of the original empirical data that stimulated its invention. The theory should specify the kinds of observations that need to be made in order to confirm or refute the implications of its internal logic. It should include some rules for classifying and ordering empirical data, i.e., there should be at least some rudimentary taxonomy and metric, so that variables can be reliably distinguished, related, and measured, giving rise eventually to a systematic causal or functional analysis, preferably with quantitative relationships and independently verifiable laws and mechanisms. The meaning of a theoretical term is derived from the system of which it forms a part; this conceptual system (calculus or grammar) dictates the rules for well-formed sentences containing the term. Such theoretical terms are linked with relevant empirical data (evidence) by means of deductive (or quasi-deductive) theorems and bridge principles.

IV. THEORIES AND THE ANALYSIS OF ARGUMENTS

One approach to the study of scientific reasoning has been described by Toulmin (1958), who says that the syllogism and analytical logic generally have been mistakenly regarded as setting standards of proof for *all* rational inquiry. Standards which are effective and appropriate for mathematical arguments, however, are not necessarily effective and appropriate for arguments in psychology or jurisprudence; similarly, the canons of proof in physics are inappropriate in history or sociology. In a sense each discipline has its own logic, and scientific method operates differently in each even while sharing a common aim.

It is of particular relevance that several interesting phenomena in life-span psychology arise as natural events, some of which can be studied only retrospectively by what are basically historical and quasi-judicial methods of investigation, e.g., reactions to bereavement, maladjustment in middle age and later life, and delinquency. Historical and judicial investigations, in their own way, set standards of proof as demanding as any found in the natural and the biological sciences; so we should not allow presuppositions about methodology or theory construction to restrict our scientific endeavors.

The kind of scientific method proposed permits any kind of observation, any method of inquiry, and any kind of concept, provided that the observations are made by credible observers and can be corroborated; and provided that the observations are relevant to a rational argument, the terms of which can be made explicit as facts, propositions, definitions, and rules. The consequence of adopting such a broad definition is not to open the door to all kinds of pseudoscientific theory and practice but rather to avoid dismissing material as unscientific simply because it does not bear the familiar hallmarks of natural science: experimental demonstration, quantifiable variables, and analytical reasoning.

Scientific method and scientific knowledge are not detached from common sense; they are rather the vanguard of common sense. Scientific theorizing similarly has its roots in common sense, and where we are concerned with matters which have progressed little beyond common knowledge, it is not surprising that theories are little more than explicit statements and extensions of common sense. But how are such quasitheories to be developed and evaluated? Obviously, theories pertaining to language development, delinquency, and disengagement do not set out to be axiomatic-deductive systems, especially in their initial stages. Even theories which are revolutionary by common-sense standards, e.g., psychoanalysis and some aspects of learning theory, are usually expressed in the language of everyday life, save for a few novel concepts which require some definition and translation. Where one is dealing with theories of this sort, there are advantages to be gained by regarding the theory as an "argument" rather than as a "formal deductive system" with its own specialized notation because, as implied at the beginning of this section, the reasons for rejecting an argument as unsound vary widely from one discipline to another. This is not to say that some disciplines permit invalid conclusions or fail to eradicate fallacies, but rather that, after the obvious formal checks on logic have been carried out, some disciplines have a more developed "internal logic" which depends in part on the substance and procedures of its arguments. So, the internal logic of physics and chemistry is more developed than that of psychology and sociology; the internal logic of learning theory is more developed than that of motivational theory. The internal logic of life-span psychology is scarcely explicit at all—our present purpose is to develop its internal logic, much of which is probably already implicit in the way we think about developmental processes. For example, one of the main objections to the theory that age changes late in life are "regressive" is that it contravenes that part of the internal logic of life-span psychology which specifies that development is unidirectional and can only move forward in time. This merely restates one of the requirements for causal explanations in science; but the effect of the objection is to require a conceptual analysis of the term "regression" before it can be used effectively in connection with psychological disorders in late life or the psychodymanics of development.

Toulmin has formulated a general scheme for the analysis of arguments relating to substantial issues, i.e., arguments in which observational data and theoretical notions combine to form a more of less coherent system. The scheme has particular relevance to sciences which lack well-developed theoretical structures and established general laws. It appears well suited to the analysis of arguments in clinical psychology, legal arguments, and arguments about historical events. I am currently using it (Bromley, 1968; Livesley & Bromley, 1967) in connection with an approach to personality study through person perception. Toulmin's scheme can be described briefly and simply; it sets out the general structure of a substantial argument and describes the function of each of its components. I have taken a few liberties with Toulmin's work, but my outline is basically the same as that described in Toulmin (1958).

Let us recall what we are doing: We are trying to work out how theories are constructed (and reconstructed) in life-span psychology; and, because this discipline lacks theories of a formal comprehensive sort, we are obliged to work with quasitheories couched largely in the language of everyday life and differing little from any ordinary serious and sustained sensible commonsense argument.

We can think of an argument as a set of interlocking ideas, analogous to a jigsaw puzzle or a meccano set. It is possible to distinguish six sorts of components which fit together in a way symbolized by the following mnemonic diagram.

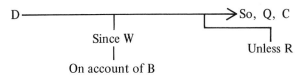

Label	Name of assertion	Role or description
D	Data	Offers data (relevant evidence), i.e., foundations for the claim.
C	Claim	States a claim or conclusion.
Q	Qualification	Qualifies a claim or conclusion by the use of modal terms, i.e., modifies a claim by stating the degree of belief or the kind of confidence one may have in it.
W	Warrant	Refers to a license to infer C from D, i.e., the step from D to C is justified by appealing to any legitimate rules of inference such as: accepted standards, theoretical relationships, analogies, definitions.
R	Rebuttal	Rebuts a claim or conclusion under the conditions specified or introduces reservations about the circumstances under which the argument holds, i.e., introduces auxiliary hypotheses or assumptions.
B	Backing	Provides backing or support for the inference warrant (W), i.e., justifies the stated connection between D and C by appealing to facts or principles of one sort or another.

Colloquially:

D	answers the question	"What have you to go on?"
C	answers the question	"What are you saying?"
Q	answers the question	"How sure are you?"
W	answers the question	"How do you make that out?"
R	answers the question	"What are you assuming?"
B	answers the question	"What proof have you?"

Thus, a simple argument in standard form contains six sorts of components each fulfilling a distinct role, for example:

D   Jones has a tested mental age of eight and is about eight years old.
C   So, Jones is of average intelligence.
Q   Presumably.
W   Since young persons whose MA and CA are equal or nearly equal have average intelligence.
R   Unless the intelligence test was wrongly administered or wrongly scored; unless there has been a mistake made about Jones's age; unless Jones was not feeling well or cooperative; or unless there are other reasons for supposing that the data are false.
B   On account of the accepted theory and practice of intelligence testing which defines intelligence in terms of IQ.

In a long complex argument, however, such as one finds in jurisprudence, or in a clinical case history or in a report of a psychological experiment, there are several sets of components which should interlock by means of a simple linking device whereby a statement fulfills one function in one set and a different function in another set. For instance, in the above example, if some of the ramifications of the argument are traced, W and B enter into a new set of statements, forming a subsidiary argument, again in standard form, but now W becomes C, and B becomes D, as follows:

D   The accepted theory and practice of intelligence testing defines intelligence in terms of IQ.
C   So, young persons whose MA and CA are equal or nearly equal have average intelligence.
Q   Necessarily, i.e., by definition.
W   Since $IQ = (MA/CA) \times 100$ with $\bar{X}_{IQ} = 100$ and $S_{IQ} = 15$.
R   Unless the CA falls outside the range of values allowed for in standard tests; and excluding those persons who, because of special circumstances such as disabilities or deprivation, cannot be satisfactorily tested by the usual methods.

B   On account of the assessment procedures pioneered by Binet and developed by others, which have been published, together with norms of performance for children of different ages, and are widely used in clinical and educational practice.

Thus one unit of argument in standard form can be linked with another unit of argument also in standard form. Since any component in the initial argument can be called in question, any component may have to fulfill another function, e.g., C, in a subsidiary argument. Furthermore, it is often possible to justify a conclusion by more than one line of argument, so that the conclusion is, as it were, overdetermined. In a sound argument, when a number of subsidiary arguments have been developed, the sets of components become cross-linked and form a firm conceptual framework giving powerful support to the original claim. Thus, arguments of this sort are analogous to webs, cables, or jigsaw puzzles and not quite so analogous to chains, mazes or chess.

It should be understood that the component R need not introduce *all* the reservations necessary to protect the claim against rebuttal, but only those which demarcate the range of convenience of the underlying theory and offer some protection against unwarranted generalization. In practice, i.e., when arguments are being expounded, component functions are often omitted. Sometimes, B, Q, and R are "taken for granted" or omitted in the interests of economy of effort or ease of communication. At other times, they are omitted through carelessness or because the backing is weak or nonexistent, or because implicit (unspoken) assumptions are made. In practice, furthermore, the initial explicit argument is like the tip of the iceberg; or, to put it another way: The initial explicit (manifest) argument depends upon a much larger implicit (latent) argument, the validity of which can be examined only when its ramifications are made explicit.

A component in an argument may require several sentences for its expression, and it can be thought of as belonging to a logical network together with other components in the same set of arguments. Some components, and some units of argument in standard form, will be more obvious and scientifically acceptable than others and so provide anchorage points supporting less obvious conclusions. The scheme provides an open conceptual system in which data, definitions, rules, and concepts of all kinds can find a place. The problem is to trace out all the important subsidiary arguments that form the latent (implicit) content of the initial manifest (explicit) argument. This is not an easy task; it can rarely be done except by an expert in the appropriate discipline; and, as we have seen, the same statements may function differently in different contexts.

The problem of constructing or reconstructing theories in life-span psychology is solved by this kind of conceptual analysis which requires statements and their relationships to be made clear and, if necessary, justified by reference to subsidiary statements and relationships. A theory is an explanation for something, and to ask for an explanation is to ask for some evidence or connection of which one is ignorant. When the information is forthcoming, one is able to impose a pattern of meaning on what was previously incomprehensible—the pieces of the jigsaw puzzle fall into place. In one sense, however, there can be no *complete* explanation for a phenomenon, and to ask for one is to ask for the impossible since the ramifications of the implicit argument are infinite and the very foundations of empirical science and rational inquiry are not immune from scepticism.

It is possible, in some circumstances, to eliminate the components Q and R and to disregard certain features of W and B, so as to reduce the number of components to three and produce a syllogism. In other words, by eliminating a great deal of what is important and relevant in a substantial argument, one can transform it into a simplified analytical one. The following example shows the components D, W, and C arranged as a valid analytic argument:

> John is born of long-lived parents
> Long-lived parents have children with a long life expectation
> So John has a long life expectation.

But the next argument, which uses B instead of W, and introduces an R clause, is not a syllogism; yet it is a reasonable (substantial) argument—the argument in fact from which the first is derived:

> John is born of long-lived parents.
> Social statistics indicate* that long-lived parents tend* to have children
>   who survive to a late age, provided they are not late-born.
> So, unless John was late-born, he can be expected* to live to a late age.

(The asterisks denote the use of probabilistic and psychological terms.) Thus arguments about substantial issues can be shaped to an analytical form, but little is achieved thereby except perhaps making explicit the general statements and the chain of implication—and this may or may not be important to the overall soundness of the argument, relative, that is, to other aspects of the argument.

To show that an argument contains no formal errors, no material fallacies, and no semantic confusions is merely clearing the ground before critically examining the strengths and weaknesses of its substance. The substance of such an argument includes the following: statements of what has been observed, empirical generalizations, theoretical conjectures, predictive statements, procedural rules, definitions and assumptions, reservations, qualifications, and so on.

V. A SIMPLE EXERCISE IN THEORY CONSTRUCTION:
THE INTERNAL LOGIC OF A THEORY OF
THE EFFECTS OF AGE ON CREATIVE THINKING

The first detailed application of the method to an argument in life-span psychology concerns an investigation of the relationship between the frequency of occurrence and the serial order of appearance of responses to several tests of creativity (Bromley, 1957, 1967, 1969). The aims of the investigation were to demonstrate and explain the effects of age on creative intellectual output. The general life-span trends were described in detail by Lehman (1953) in *Age and Achievement.* Lehman suggested a variety of explanations for his findings, but failed to emphasize the likely effects of a reduction with age in problem solving ability and speed of intellectual processes. He also failed to account adequately for the differential effects of age on the quantity and quality of intellectual output.

The results of Bromley's investigation showed that, even when no time limits were imposed, older Ss had a lower total output on the tests of creativity than did younger Ss. If the degree of originality of a response is measured in terms of its frequency of occurrence, then it can be shown that older Ss produce responses that are, on average, less original than those produced by younger Ss, i.e., older Ss produce fewer low frequency, rational responses. The explanation is simple: There is a general correlation between the frequency of occurrence of a response and its serial order of appearance—late appearing responses are relatively infrequent. Since older Ss produce fewer responses than do younger Ss, these responses are *necessarily* restricted to a narrower range of serial position numbers, namely, to those which are associated with relatively common and more frequently occurring responses appearing early in the series.

In order to achieve a creative solution to a problem, it is usually necessary to work through a number of preliminary formulations, making successive transformations or shifts, until some sort of conceptual or practical limit is reached, as in searching for a solution to a scientific problem, or in formulating a military or business strategy. As age advances, the number of such shifts and transformations is reduced because of adverse changes in the speed and power of intellectual processes. The serial order of appearance of successive attempts to find a better solution to a problem is associated with qualities such as difficulty, ingenuity, cleverness, originality, and rarity—all of which help to define the general term "quality." Since older Ss make fewer responses (fewer shifts and transformations), they do not achieve the higher levels of quality associated with responses appearing toward the end of a long series of preliminary formulations, i.e., older Ss become less capable of finding progressively more ingenious solutions to problems. In addition, older Ss become intellectually slower, so that if time limits are imposed, as they are in real-life intellectual endeavor, then they must necessarily make fewer responses, further lowering the level of excellence they can reach.

The formal validity of the above argument can be demonstrated in a series of linked conditional statements, but the "internal logic" of the argument is revealed more adequately by Toulmin's method of analysis. Thus:

D1   Older Ss make fewer responses in tests of creativity than do younger Ss.

C2 = D2   In tests of creativity, responses which tend to have higher serial position numbers i.e., appear later in the series, tend also to be more original.

D3   In tests of creativity, responses which tend to appear later in the series also tend to be more infrequent.

Q1   . . . necessarily.

C1   . . . older Ss tend to produce fewer original responses than do younger Ss.

W1   . . . older Ss produce fewer responses with higher serial position numbers, i.e., produce fewer responses later in the series.

W2   . . . the degree of originality of a response can be defined and measured in terms of its frequency of occurrence.

B1   . . . the normal scoring system ensures that Ss with higher scores have responses with higher serial position numbers.

B2   . . . the apparent or assumed relationship between the frequency of occurrence of a response and its independently assessed quality (ingenuity).

R1   . . . the effect is not because of differences in chronological age directly, but rather because of differences in total output, since older and younger Ss with the same total output in tests of creativity do not differ as regards the quality of that output.

R2   . . . only those responses which are compatible with the test instructions, and meet certain requirements of rationality, are to be counted.

The structure of this argument, i.e., its internal logic, is shown below. Naturally, its ramifications could be worked out more fully.

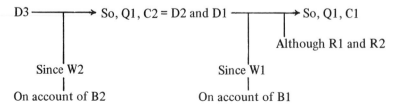

In the above example, the statements are closely tied to observational evidence. No theoretical terms are introduced, unless the notion of originality itself or the notion of rationality, is regarded as a theoretical term. Nevertheless, it still seems reasonable to regard the above explanation as a theory, or at least a quasitheory, since it explains a relationship and enables one to predict an effect. It is conceivable, moreover, that another investigator might come along with a different interpretation of the evidence; and the construction he might place upon the stated facts, and other related facts, would constitute a competing theory.

The argument as it stands, however satisfactory it may be from the standpoint of formal logic and substantial logic, is not satisfactory from the standpoint of behavioral science, since although it demonstrates a logically necessary linkage in the relationships between operationally defined variables and relevant empirical data, it introduces no explanation as to (a) why there should be a close association between (i) the frequency of occurrence of a response, (ii) its creative quality, and (iii) its position in the serial order of appearance of the set of responses; and (b) why there should be a normal decrease with age in the quantity of output in tests of creativity. (Note that the argument set out in detail above shows that if there is a decrease in quantity of output then there must *necessarily* be a decrease in quality.) In other words, it is not sufficient that D1 and D3 be supported by empirical data, i.e., inductively; they must also be supported by a theoretical argument which explains why the effects should be as they are and not otherwise. These problems are easier to pose than to solve, but, for example, effect (b) might be a consequence of diminished cortical tissue or arousal, or increased reactive inhibition, in older Ss, though it would be difficult to demonstrate the causal connections between effect (b) and these age changes. Effect (a) might be a consequence of some psychobiological response mechanism giving adaptive flexibility, whereby efficiency is achieved by the early, rapid, and orderly production of a small number of salient responses which differ substantially in probability of occurrence among themselves but have higher probabilities than the nonsalient (reserve) responses which can be called out later in situations where the salient (high priority) responses have either failed or have been used up. An ample reserve of potential responses (with a low probability of occurrence) makes it possible for behavior to vary widely, and this is generally regarded as leading to more effective adjustment. There is some evidence (Bromley, 1969) to suggest that the response probabilities are distributed over the set of serial positions in the way suggested, i.e., frequently occurring (high probability) responses have their total probability of occurrence spread rather thickly over a few early serial positions, whereas infrequently occurring (low probability) responses have their total probability of occurrence spread rather thinly over many late serial positions. The biological and psychological advantage of this seems to be that it combines efficiency (speed and confidence) with variability (flexibility and creativity). It is conceivable that such a mechanism of "adaptive flexibility" could be related to mechanisms of learning, but it would have to explain how novel (creative) responses could emerge out of past learning. The point at issue, however, is that if psychobiological mechanisms such as "reactive inhibition" or "adaptive flexibility" could be adequately conceptualized, we should be able to *deduce* from our conceptualization the conclusions for which we already have empirical support; we should also be able to deduce further conclusions and subject them to empirical test. Unfortunately, the theoretical notions just introduced are not sufficiently developed to permit such deductions. And, as Hempel has pointed out, there is nothing in the empirical data or even in the existing theoretical notions which will show the direction that appropriate conceptual innovation might take.

VI. A DIFFICULT EXERCISE IN THEORY CONSTRUCTION: THE INTERNAL LOGIC OF THE THEORY OF DISENGAGEMENT

A. Procedure

In this section readers are assumed to be familiar with the theory of disengagement as formulated by Cumming and Henry (1961), Cumming (1964), and Henry (1966), and discussed by A. M. Rose (1964), Maddox (1964), and Havighurst, Neugarten, and Tobin (1963).

If we use Toulmin's method of analysis, the argument (theory), briefly, is as follows:

D   Society and most individuals engage in various activities which have age-related consequences in late life.

Q, C   So, apparently, society and most individuals are preparing in advance for the consequences of the largely inevitable and universal biological and psychological changes which occur in late life.

W   Since, in this way, society tries to provide for the systematic replacement of individuals in their social roles, and individuals try to maintain good living standards and personal adjustment.

B   On account of the self-maintaining mechanisms operating in large, complex human communities.

The theory of disengagement is interesting because of its "life-span" ecological context and because of the analogy, by contrast, with the theory of adolescent development. The intention is to display, by example, the infrastructure of this important theory and thereby further demonstrate the nature of the proposed method.

Damianopoulos (1961) presents what is termed, "A formal statement of disengagement theory." The formal statement contains nine postulates and ten corollaries and one might suppose that the system would constitute a logically coherent analytical argument. As soon as one begins to examine the logical character of this "formal statement," however, it becomes clear that, first, the theory does not lend itself to this kind of analysis, and that, second, even when the necessary revisions are made in order to establish formally valid logical implications, the result is trivial in comparison with the substance, i.e., the internal logic, of the theory.

I have attempted to restate the elements of disengagement theory as a "substantial argument" following the procedure proposed by Toulmin and briefly described in a previous section. I have restricted the argument to those issues raised in the formal statement by Damianopoulos, keeping as close as possible to the original phraseology. The analysis requires six separate networks containing, respectively, 13, 3, 6, 6, 4, and 10 basic arguments in standard form. The analysis can be displayed either as a series of coded and tabulated statements, or preferably as a diagram with connections between labels referring to the coded statements. The analysis reveals that some conclusions are each arrived at from several starting points; that some starting points each generate several conclusions; that empirical data and definitions are required as "anchorage points" for the network of arguments; that some statements each occur several times and fulfil various roles depending upon their positions in the network. The networks, when completed to the first level of justification, i.e., when the first subsidiary arguments are worked out, require 42 distinct but interconnected basic arguments containing 327 statements (some of which occur more than once). These 327 statements comprise 68 Ds (data statements), 42 Qs (confidence statements), 46 Cs (conclusions), 56 Ws (inference warrants), 62 Bs (backing statements), and 53 Rs (reservations or conditions of rebuttal). Since some of these statements occur several times, the number of *different* statements in much less. For example, for simplicity and convenience only three *different* Qs (modal qualifiers) are employed: necessarily (Q1), probably (Q2), and presumably (Q3). The reason why there are not 46 Qs (to match 46 Cs) is that some conclusions occur in pairs. In the formal account by Daminanopoulos there are 98 statements (excluding contextual material), which gives a rough indication of the initial explicit argument as compared with the extent of even the simplest version of the implicit argument. In the formal account, however, most of the statements occur only once, so the proper comparison is with the number of *different* statements in the analysis of the implicit argument. Thus, there are 56 different D statements, 17 different C statements (additional to those listed in the D class), 48 different and additional W statements, 12 different and additional B statements, 31 different and additional R statements, and 3 Q statements, making 167 different statements altogether.

TABLE 1

Classification of Statements in the Disengagement Argument

Code	Data elements (D), i.e., It is observed that . . .
1	. . . in late life, there is a mutual, permanent, and inevitable severing and altering of the ties between a person and others in his society, known as "disengagement."
1m	. . . 1, e.g., following retirement for men (See also D33m).
1f	. . . 1, e.g., following widowhood for women (See also D33f).
2	. . . the expectation of death, usually in late life, is universal, but age at death is somewhat unpredictable.
3	. . . in late life, decrement of ability is probable.
4	. . . people differ in physiology.
5	. . . people differ in temperament.
6	. . . people differ in personality.
7	. . . people differ in life situation.
8	. . . in late life, the number and variety of central interactions between a person and others in his society are permanently reduced.
9	. . . in late life, people often suffer a dramatic reduction in social life space.
10	. . . in late life, there is an increased freedom from the control of the norms governing everyday behavior.
11	. . . interactions create and reaffirm norms.
12	. . . norms help to sustain interactions and ties.
13	. . . there are psychobiological and environmental differences among people.
16	. . . the disengaged individual has a wider choice of relational rewards than the person who is still engaged.
17	. . . the disengaged individual's social relationships shift from vertical solidarities to horizontal solidarities.
19m	. . . the central role of men is to work for economic gain, to relate themselves functionally to members of appropriate occupational groups, and to derive status identity from their work.
19f	. . .the central role of women is to work for husband and family, to relate themselves emotionally to kin and friends, and to derive status identity from their husband.
20m	. . . the central role of men is instrumental–they normally acquire and maintain their social status identity through their occupation.
20f	. . . the central role of women is socioemotional–their social status identity is normally derived from and maintained by that of their husband.
23	. . . some individuals have high prestige and considerable power.
30m	. . . in late life, problem (i) is that men normally lose membership in a peer group.
30f	. . . in late life, problem (i) is that women normally lose a highly cathected spouse.
31m	. . . in late life, problem (ii) is that men normally lack the instrumental skills through which to relate themselves to others in society.
31f	. . . in late life, problem (ii) is that women normally lose the status derived from their husband's occupation.
32m	. . . in late life, problem (iii) is that men normally lose social status identity.
32f	. . . in late life, problem (iii) is that women normally shift from obligatory to voluntary relationships.

TABLE 1–*Continued*

Code	Data elements (D), i.e., It is observed that . . .
33m	. . . in late life, men normally retire from work (See also D1m).
33f	. . . in late life, women are normally widowed (See also D1f).
35m	. . . for men, none of the conditions (D30m, D31m, D32m) remains problematical for the very old.
35f	. . . for women, none of the conditions (D30f, D31f, D32f) remains problematical for the very old.
41	. . . ego changes eventually lead to preoccupation with inner states.
42	. . . ego changes eventually lead to the narcissism of the very old.
46	. . . there are ego changes (in knowledge and skill) of an adverse kind in the later phases of the human life cycle.
47	. . . success in an industrial society is based on knowledge and skill.
48	. . . age grading ensures that the young are sufficiently well trained to assume authority and the old are retired before they lose their skill.
49	. . . D47 and D48 are concurrent.
53	. . . disengagement may be initiated by both the individual and society simultaneously.
54	. . . at times, both the individual and society are ready for disengagement.
55 (or not 55)	. . . echelons of individuals may (not) be ready for disengagement and may (not) instigate it by attempting to retire.
56 (or not 56)	. . . society may (not) be ready for the disengagement of echelons of individuals and (may not) initiate(s) it by permitting or enforcing their retirement.
63	. . . there are ecological differences between human societies.
64	. . . societies differ in size.
65	. . . societies differ in technology.
66	. . . societies differ in culture.
67	. . . societies differ in age composition.
68	. . . disengagement of the elderly is earlier and more widespread in some societies than in others.
69	. . . concepts which can be applied to virtually all members of a relevant class are said to be "free," i.e., not restricted in application.
70	. . . in late life, the individual becomes sharply aware of the shortness of life.
71	. . . in late life, the individual becomes sharply aware of the scarcity of time remaining to him.
72	. . . in late life, the individual becomes aware that his social life space is decreasing dramatically.
73	. . . in late life, the individual's ego energy is lessened.
74	. . . there are requirements of the rational-legal occupational system that society must fulfil.
75	. . . the nuclear family helps to maintain age grading.
76	. . . there is a differential death rate between men and women.

Code	Confidence elements or modal qualifiers (Q)
1	Necessarily
2	Probably
3	Presumably

TABLE 1—*Continued*

Code	Claim or conclusion elements (C), i.e., So, (Q) . . .[a]
1a (or not 1a)	. . . disengagement (does not) result(s).
1b	. . . disengagement occurs earlier for some people than for others.
1c	. . . disengagement is a circular, i.e., self-perpetuating, process.
1d	. . . the process of disengagement differs between men and women.
18	. . . in late life, there is often a disjunction (crisis) between the expectations of the individual and those of others in society.
21	. . . there is a shift in the quality of the relationships in the remaining roles.
22	. . . the shift to the nonobligatory, egalitarian, horizontal relationship is, for some individuals, a serious disjunction, i.e., crisis.
24	. . . the number of bonds broken differs from person to person.
25	. . . the number of bonds remaining differs from person to person.
26	. . . qualitative changes in relationships with the people to whom the aging individual is still bonded vary from person to person.
34m	. . . in late life, men face at least three problems of adjustment to retirement.
34f	. . . in late life, women face at least three problems of adjustment to widowhood.
36m	. . . for men, solutions to these problems (as for women) need only be temporary.
36f	. . . for women, solutions to these problems (as for men) need only be temporary..
57	. . . in late life, often, morale is lowered.
61	. . . the form of disengagement is culture bound.
62	. . . the concept of disengagement is culture free as regards function.

[a]Note: Since $Ci = Di$, e.g., C1 = D1, C13 = D13, the only C elements listed here are those not listed as D elements.

Code	Inference warrant elements (W), i.e., Since . . .
1	= . . . D1
11	= . . . D11.
12	= . . . D12.
20m	= . . . D20m.
20f	= . . . D20f.
d101a	. . . this defines and exemplifies "mutual severing of ties."
d101b	. . . this defines and exemplifies "ecological differences."
d101c	. . . this defines and exemplifies "psychobiological and environmental differences."
d101d	. . . this defines and exemplifies the "form" of disengagement.
d101e	. . . this defines and exemplifies "problems of adjustment to retirement" (and they are enumerated in the usual way).
d101f	. . . this defines and exemplifies "problems of adjustment to widowhood" (and they are enumerated in the usual way).
d101g	. . . this defines and exemplifies "personal readiness for disengagement."
d101h	. . . this defines and exemplifies "social readiness for disengagement."
d101i	. . . this defines and exemplifies "quality of relationship."
d101j	. . . this defines and exemplifies "instrumental."

TABLE 1–*Continued*

Code	Inference warrant elements (W), i.e., Since . . .
d101k	. . . this defines and exemplifies "socioemotional."
102	. . . society tries to maintain itself independently of the life-span of particular members.
103	. . . individuals must make some readjustment to their changed abilities and circumstances.
104	. . . the consequences of such differences between individuals may occur at different ages.
105	. . . individuals differ with regard to baseline measures of social interaction.
106	. . . the causal consequences are complex and interdependent.
107	. . . individuals differ with regard to the kind (as well as the number) of social relationships they have.
109	. . . disengagement often occurs abruptly with insufficient preparation or subsequent effort on the part of society to look after the interests of the older individual.
116	. . . the individual's central roles normally restrict his choice of relational rewards.
117	. . . the individual's central roles normally require vertical rather than horizontal solidarities.
120	. . . the social roles of men and women are different, i.e., require different sorts of activities and satisfactions.
123	. . . they associate the image of their own success, i.e., their standards, with the taking of responsibility (central roles) and the management of hierarchical relationships. And the old standards conflict with the new standards.
127m	. . . men depend upon work for peer relations.
127f	. . . for women, the marital relationship is normally of focal importance and tends to be exclusive.
128m	. . . men have no purely sociable skills.
129m	. . . men must mediate social relationships through instrumental activity.
129f	. . . previously, the social relationships of women were tied to the status position derived from the husband.
130m	. . . the solution to problem (i) is provided by certain recreational groups and by kinsmen.
130f	. . . there is no solution to problem (i) short of remarriage.
131m	. . . solutions to problem (ii) are provided by temporary or parttime reengagement with the occupational world and by recreation that has instrumental aspects.
131f	. . . the solution to problem (ii) is automatic as women are given enough consideration in this society to compensate for loss of status.
132m	. . . the solution to problem (iii) is provided by a strategy of "passive mastery" which yields satisfaction in what has been rather than a pride in what is.
132f	. . . the solution to problem (iii) is easy as the higher death rate among men leaves an available peer group of widows, and membership in such a group allows a kind of nonobligatory, horizontal, peer relationship compatible with the process of disengagement.
136	. . . voluntary relationships are available and satisfying.
137	. . . obligatory relationships are defined as those arising from central roles.

TABLE 1–*Continued*

Code	Inference warrant elements (W), i.e., Since . . .
143	. . . the terminal phases of life restrict the person to self-maintaining activities which take priority over the problems of adjustment associated with disengagement.
146	. . . the individual becomes aware of and tries to adapt to these changes.
147	. . . society's "organizational imperatives" require its members to become aware of and to adapt to adverse changes (in knowledge and skill) among its older members.
152	. . . W146 and W147 are concurrent and often work toward compatible ends.
153	. . . efforts are directed toward reducing conflicts of interest between the person and his society, and these interests will at times coincide in a common wish for the individual's retirement.
154	. . . the common wish for retirement (W153) gives rise to practical and successful efforts to achieve this aim.
155	. . . D56 and not D55.
156	. . . efforts are directed toward reducing conflicts of interest between the person and his society and these interests will at times coincide in a common wish for the individual's continued employment.
157	. . . the common wish for continued employment (W156) gives rise to practical and successful efforts to achieve this aim.
158	. . . social interests generally override individual interests (to the detriment of the individual).
161	. . . ecological factors affect the employment of individuals in the society.
163	. . . ecological factors affect relationships between people.
169	. . . the terms used to define and exemplify the "functions" of disengagement are applicable to all industrialized societies.

Code	Backing elements (B), i.e., On account of . . .
8	= . . . D8
201	. . . common knowledge.
202	. . . mechanisms for maintaining social continuity and development, such as training, promoting, and retiring.
203	. . . psychobiological mechanisms for maintaining personal adjustment, such as reducing exhausting activities and stressful responsibilities.
204	. . . the findings from the social and behavioral sciences.
204a	. . . 204, e.g., those relating to disengagement.
205	. . . convenience in word usage.
211	. . . cultural norms.
212	. . . the observed relationships between "interactions" and "ties."
230	. . . the relevance of these problems to the psychological and social aspects of adjustment to human aging.
262	. . . the distinction that has to be made between "form" and "function."
270a	. . . the apparent causal link between these prior conditions (D74, D75, D76) and society's subsequent reactions to older individuals.
270b	. . . the apparent causal link between these prior conditions (D70, D71, D72, D73) and society's subsequent reactions to older individuals.

TABLE 1–*Continued*

Code	Rebuttal or restriction elements (R), i.e., Unless . . . or Although . . .
62	= . . . D62.
13	= . . . D13.
18	= . . . C18.
301	. . . death and decrement of ability in late life are not inevitable.
302	. . . natural death becomes highly predictable and not preceded by decrements of ability, e.g., as in Huxley's *Brave New World*.
303	. . . the individual is engaged through a different set of skills (central roles).
304	. . . the individual may disengage "prematurely" and society may subsequently attempt to reengage him.
305	. . . different roles, suitable to the disengaged state, are available.
307a	. . . there are countervailing influences which restrict the individual's choice of relational rewards; e.g., if the central interactions implicate peripheral interactions and rewards, the individual may have a narrower choice of relational rewards.
307b	. . . there are countervailing influences which hinder the shift from vertical to horizontal solidarities, e.g., social class attitudes.
307c	. . . there are countervailing influences within the individual, e.g., ego defensiveness.
307d	. . . there are countervailing influences within the society, e.g., social positions held for life.
307e	. . . there are countervailing influences, in the person or in society, which work against mutual readiness for disengagement, e.g., discrepancies between the person and others in society regarding the conditions of his retirement.
308a	. . . there are compensating factors which also create and/or reaffirm norms.
308b	. . . there are compensating factors which help to sustain interactions and ties.
308c	. . . there are compensating factors which help to sustain membership in a peer group.
308d	. . . there are compensating factors which affect sociable skills or the mediation of social relationships.
308e	. . . there are compensating factors which affect status identity, e.g., unless there is some carry-over of status through the long-term consequences of instrumental actions in the preretirement period.
308f	. . . there are compensating factors which affect the nature of adjustment during disengagement.
308g	. . . there are compensating factors which affect the widow's cathexes, e.g., close dependants.
308h	. . . there are compensating factors which affect the widow's social relationships, e.g., a special status during widowhood with obligatory relationships.
308i	. . . there are compensating factors which eliminate or reduce the expected variability.
308j	. . . there are compensating factors which neutralize or override the effects of those ecological factors thought to be important determinants of disengagement.
308k	. . . there are compensating factors which affect the rate and kind of adjustment the individual has to make.

TABLE 1—*Continued*

Code	Rebuttal or restriction elements (R), i.e., Unless . . . or Although . . .
320	. . . exceptional cases are considered.
322	. . . equally satisfying substitutes can be found.
323	. . . such individuals, i.e., those having high prestige and considerable power, prepare for and compensate for the change.
330	. . . cathexis can perhaps be distributed among a group of kin.
333	. . . these problems are not independent of one another, e.g., if they are simply aspects of one problem.
335	. . . W130f constitutes a contradiction in terms.
336	. . . there are special, local, or temporary, circumstances which militate against these normal outcomes.
353	. . . the term "initiate" does not imply "ready."
354	. . . the term "ready" is ambiguous, e.g., it cannot have precisely the same meaning for both the person and society, although the meanings may be coordinated.
369	. . . exceptions to W169 can be found.

In the presentation of the "disengagement argument" which follows, an attempt is made to make explicit a sufficient number of the statements to spell out the minimum requirements and implications of Damianopoulos's account of the theory. As far as possible, the form of words used by Damianopoulos has been retained; but it proved impossible to make the theory explicit and coherent without introducing a variety of changes. So, in some respects at least, the "disengagement argument" presented here reflects the author's understanding of it; some other person might very well have presented the argument rather differently. But this is precisely what is needed, for the constructive comparison of such differences should lead eventually to the construction of a more satisfactory theory of disengagement. For example, the notion of "ego energy" is not satisfactory by modern psychological standards, and the statements describing the central roles of men and women are not very satisfactory by sociological standards. But the intention here is not to propose extensions to and improvements in disengagement theory; rather, the intention is the preliminary one of making explicit what seems to be already implicit in the theory. It will be obvious that disengagement theory depends heavily upon commonsense, and no attempt will be made here to refer to raw observational data. Although the 42 basic arguments assimilate all of the postulates and corrollaries in the formal statement by Damianopoulos and are interconnected in a variety of ways (as indicated by equal signs in Table 1 or by suitable connecting lines if the networks are set out in diagrammatic form), little attempt has been made to go beyond the interrelationships implicit in the formal statement. Perusal of Tables 1 and 2, however, reveals several possibilities for the reconstruction and

TABLE 2

*The Internal Logical Networks of the Disengagement Argument as Related
to the Postulates (P) and Corollaries (C) Formulated by
Damianopoulos*

Network 1

P.2	D8, so Q1, C1 (= D1); since Wd101c, on account of B204 and B212.
P.2	(C1 =) D1, so Q2, C10 (= D10); since W11 (= D11), on account of B204; unless R308a.
P.2	(C10 =) D10, so Q2, C1 (= D1); since W12 (= D12), on account of B204 and B212; unless R308b.
P.6	(C1 =) D1, so Q3, C9 (= D9); since W109, on account of B201 and B204; unless R308k.
P.1	D2 and D3, so Q2, C1 (= D1); since W102 and W103, on account of B202 and B203; unless R301 and R302; although R13 (= D13 = C13).
P.2	D11 and D12, so Q3, C1c; since W1 (= D1 = C1), on account of B8 (= D8).
C.1.1	D4, D5, D6 and D7, so Q1, C13 (= D13); since Wd101a, on account of B205.
C.1.2	(C13 =) D13, so Q3, C26; since W106 and W107, on account of B204; unless R308i.
C.1.1	(C13 =) D13, so Q3, C16; since W104, on account of B204; unless R308i.
C.1.1	(C13 =) D13, so Q3, C24 and C25; since W105 and W106, on account of B204; unless R308i.
P.8	D8, so Q3, C16 (= D16) and C17 (= D17); since W116 and W117, on account of B201 and B204; unless R307a (e.g.); although R307b.
P.8	D16 and D17, so Q1, C21; since Wd 101i.
C.8.1	D23, so Q3, C22; since W123, on account of B201 and B204; unless R322 and R323.

Network 2

P.3	D19m, so Q1, C20m (= D20m); since Wd101j, on account of B205.
P.3	D19f, so Q1, C20f (= D20f); since Wd101k, on account of B205.
P.3	(C20m =) D20m and (C20f =) D20f, so Q3, C1d; since W120, on account of B201 and B204.

Network 3

C.6.1A	D33m (see also D1m), so Q3, (i) C30m (= D30m); since W127m, on account of B201 and B204; unless R320 and R308c.
C.6.1A	D33m (see also D1m), so Q3, (ii) C31m (= D31m); since W128m and W129m, on account of B201 and B204; unless R320 and R308d.
C.6.1A	D33m (see also D1m), so Q3, (iii) C32m (= D32m); since W20m (= D20m), on account of B201 and B204; unless R320 and R308e (e.g.).
C.6.1A	(C30m =) D30m, (C31m =) D31m and (C32m =) D32m, so Q1, C34m; since Wd101e, on account of B230; unless R308f and R333 (e.g.).
C.6.1B	D41 and D42, so Q3, C35m (= D35m); since W143, on account of B201 and B204; unless R320.
C.6.1B	(C35m =) D35m, so Q3, C36m; since (i) W130m, (ii) W131m and (iii) W132m, on account of B201 and B204; unless R320 and R336.

TABLE 2—*Continued*

Network 4

C.6.2A	D33f (see also D1f), so Q3, (i) C30f (= D30f); since W127f, on account of B211; unless R320 and R308g (e.g.); although R330.
C.6.2A	D33f (see also D1f), so Q3, (ii) C31f (= D31f); since W128f, on account of B211; unless R320 and R308g.
C.6.2A	D33f (see also D1f), so Q3, (iii) C32f (= D32f); since W129f, W136 and W137, on account of B204, B211 and B205; unless R320 and R308h (e.g.).
C.6.2A	(C30f =) D30f, (C31f =) D31f and (C32f =) D32f, so Q1, C34f; since Wd101f, on account of B230; unless R308f and R333 (e.g.).
C.6.2B	D41 and D42, so Q3, C35f (= D35f); since W143, on account of B201 and B204; unless R320.
C.6.2B	(C35f =) D35f, so Q3, C36f: since (i) W130f, (ii) W131f and (iii) W132f, on account of B201 and B204; unless R335, R320 and R336.

Network 5

P.9	D64, D65, D66 and D67, so Q1, C63 (= D63); since Wd101b, on account of B205.
P.9	(C63 =) D63, so Q2, C68 (= D68); since W161 and W163, on account of B 204; unless R308j.
P.9	D69, so Q2, C62, (= R62); since W169, on account of B204a; unless R369.
P.9	(C68 =) D68, so Q1, C61; since Wd101d, on account of B262; although R62 (= C62).

Network 6

P.4	D46 and D49, so Q3, C53 (= D53); since W152 (= W146 × W147), on account of B204; unless R307c and R307d.
P.4	(C53 =) D53, so Q3, C54 (= D54); since W153, on account of B201 and B204; unless R307e (e.g.).
P.5	(C54 =) D54, so Q3, C1a; since W153 and W154, on account of B201 and B204; unless R354.
P.5	not D55 and not D56, so Q3, not C1a; since W156 and W157, on account of B201 and B204; unless R354.
P.5 C.5.1 C.5.3	D55 and not D56, so Q2, not C1a and C57; since W158, on account of B201 and B204; although R18 and R304.
P.5 C.5.1 C.5.2	D56 and not D55, so Q2, C1a and C57; since W158, on account of B201 and B204; unless R303; although R18 (= C18).
P.4	D46, so Q3, C55 (= D55); since W146, on account of B204; unless R307c and R353.
P.7A	D70, D71, D72, and D73, so Q1, C55 (= D55); since Wd101g, on account of B270b.
P.4	D47 and D48, so Q3, C56 (= D56); since W147, on account of B204; unless R307d and R353.
P.7B	D74, D75 and D76, so Q1, C56 (= D56); since Wd101h, on account of B270a.

improvement of disengagement theory. For example: (a) The network of argument actually consists of six independent subsidiary networks, so that additional basic arguments are needed to interconnect them. (b) At least one chain of arguments seems to be circular, so that improvements are needed to eliminate such circularity without, however, destroying the internal consistencies (the overdetermination of claims) and the corroboration characteristic of a good scientific argument. The analogy of a "web" of argument is apt, since a web requires anchorage points, a focal point, and a balanced or consistent structure. (c) Most of the definitions could probably be improved, and additional definitions introduced. (d) Empirical support is assumed, especially in the class of B statements; but such support needs to be made explicit, and all empirical findings and generalizations are open to question, thus generating more subsidiary arguments.

B. Notation

The statements in the different classes have been allocated code numbers as follows:

Class	Numbers	Type of statement
D	1 to 99	Observation or empirical generalization
Q	1 to 3	Confidence in or probability of confirmation
C	1 to 99	Claim or conclusion
W	101 to 199	Warrant or principle of inference
B	201 to 299	Backing or justification for warrant
R	301 to 399	Reservation and condition of rebuttal

Some code numbers have been left blank in the interests of ease of association and symmetry, and to allow additional statements to be introduced with convenient code numbers. Statements in class D and class C are parallel and each pair has the same code number, e.g., D14 = C14. In practice, however, the same statement may not occur in both classes, e.g., Di may be a starting point, with no corresponding Ci. Some statements occur in more than two classes, in which case the same statement has the same number in each class. The letters m and f can be attached, e.g. D31m and D31f, to indicate a reference to males and females respectively. The letters a, b, c, etc., are attached, as in R7a and R7b, to indicate some similarity in the function of the statements or, as in Wd1a, Wd1b, etc., to indicate definitions of terms. In these and possibly other ways, each class of statement can be subdivided, thus revealing patterns and relationships which clarify the structure of the overall argument. It is conceivable that studies in the comparative logic of the social and behavioral sciences, using this kind of analysis, would reveal similarities of structure and content that are not apparent

at present because of the inadequacies of theory construction and notation in
these disciplines.

VII. THE ROLE OF MODELS AND ANALOGIES
IN THEORY CONSTRUCTION

One aspect of theorizing concerns the role of models or analogies, which can be
used heuristically by means of imagery and creative thinking, to establish
possible bridges or links with other theories and to deduce or predict
consequences. Thus, the model or analogy provides an interesting pattern which
bears some resemblance to the pattern of the explicandum (the facts or
observations and relationships which have to be explained). But, whereas a
theoretical account of the facts attempts to show that they are logically implied
by some set of prior postulates, treatment of the same facts by means of an
analogy or model simply attempts to show that they can conveniently be
thought of "as if" they were characterized by roughly the same internal logic.

Hesse (1963) has presented a concise account of the logic of reasoning by
analogy, and her treatment of the topic provides the basis for the present
section. She distinguishes between the positive, neutral, and negative parts of the
analogy. The positive parts are those which resemble parts of the internal logic
of the explicandum. The negative parts are those which contradict or differ from
the corresponding parts of the explicandum. The neutral parts are those which
are either irrelevant or unknown. The unknown parts are of considerable
importance because they provide suggestions for further inquiry; on
examination, these previously unknown parts of the analogy turn out to be
either positive, negative, or irrelevant. The theory then comprises the positive
and unknown parts of the total original analogy.

While the theory is being constructed, naturally, its internal logic is not well
developed and there may be no way of knowing, from the explicandum itself,
how this internal logic is to be extended, as we saw in connection with the
theory of the serial production of creative responses. Now a model is any system
of ideas which permits further deductions (predictions) to be made from the
theory; in the first place it helps to generate implications by making available a
ready-made internal logic for the explicandum; and in the second place it helps
to assign research priorities among all the implications that might be considered.
Furthermore, the finding of a suitable model or analogy gives at least some kind
of meaning to the hitherto "inexplicable" explicandum. And this insight may, if
it is valid, lead to productive theorizing and empirical research. Eventually,
however, it should be possible to develop an internal logic for the explicandum
which contains its own theoretical terms, and is independent of the model.

An analogy has the general form: A : B as C : D. Some analogies are fairly straightforward comparisons of critical similarities and differences between two configurations of facts. Other analogies, however, are more complicated and it becomes necessary to define terms and clarify relationships. The aim of "drawing an analogy" is to find some clues to the internal logic of the explicandum, so that one is in a better position to explain the existing facts and to extend and simplify one's range of understanding by accounting for further facts. The analogy or model is an approximation to a rational account of the observations that need to be explained. It should be understood that more than one analogy may be drawn, and that some analogies may be better than others; some analogies may be positively misleading. The assumption is, however, that the analogy or model on the one hand and the explicandum on the other have roughly equivalent—or isomorphic—causal systems. An explanation is a set of postulates implying a variety of causal or functional relationships among variables for which observational evidence is available. An analogy or model is a sort of template whereby the configuration of elements in one explanatory set, which is fairly well articulated, is used to establish a configuration of elements in another explanatory set, in the hope that the elements in the second set will become more meaningful and more productive of implications for empirical research.

Only one model or analogy need be presented in detail as an example. It is based on material by Rabbitt (1968). Rabbitt draws an analogy between human beings and computers in the processing of information. For example, if we use the notation AM to refer to the analogy or model, and EX to refer to the explicandum, and a, b, c, etc., to refer to corresponding elements in each, then we can draw an analogy between three elements in computer engineering, namely, (a) cycle and other times, (b) programs, and (c) logical size, and three elements in human performance, namely, (a) decision times, (b) problem solving strategies, and (c) intellectual capacity. So that:

AMa : computer engineering   as EXa : human performance
AMb : computer engineering   as EXb : human performance
AMc : computer engineering   as EXc : human performance

The relations which are known to hold between AMa, AMb and AMc are imposed, by analogy, upon EXa, EXb, and EXc. For example, (a) computers with longer cycle times compute more slowly, just as people with longer decision times solve problems more slowly; (b) computers using inefficient programs take longer and carry out more operations (and are therefore working closer to capacity) than computers using efficient programs, just as older people using inefficient problem solving strategies take longer and carry out more operations (and are therefore working closer to, or at the limit of, their capacity) than younger people using efficient strategies; (c) computers with greater logical capacity do not have to deal with computations in piecemeal fashion and can carry out sets of operations in parallel rather than in series, just as people with greater cognitive capacity do not have to deal with a problem bit by bit and can coordinate several ongoing mental functions, e.g., through the processes of short-term memory.

Rabbitt's explicandum consists of the results of experiments in human performance dealing with such things as redundancy, concept formation, and short-term memory with particular reference to adverse age changes in these aspects of human performance. The analogy so far consists of three positive parts, and the question is whether the analogy can be further developed so as to generate more insights into the effects of aging on human performance. It should be mentioned in passing that the central nervous system (CNS) is generally regarded as being the most interesting and important determinant of human performance; so that we might consider a sort of triangular analogy between CNS functions, human performance, and computer engineering. It should also be mentioned in passing that it is not good enough simply to develop the analogy, it is also necessary to translate the terms of an analogy into appropriate terms in the explicandum and to test, by empirical research, the implications of reasoning by analogy; otherwise there is a risk that models and analogies will be developed for their own sake, as it were, rather than for the sake of the explicandum.

For reasons which are not yet clear, human cognitive performance in later life becomes slower. This might come about because of some intrinsic slowing in the CNS processes underlying human performance, or it might come about because of a reduction in CNS capacity (loss of neurons) making necessary some rerouting of CNS processes. Human cognitive performance is also less efficient in later life, in the sense that older people are less able to ignore irrelevant information, less able to profit from the structure in transmitted information, less able to modulate their performance, less able to work out the implications of information, i.e., to solve problems. This might come about because of some intrinsic slowing in the CNS processes, which reduces the overall capacity of the cognitive system because of limitations imposed by STM; or it might come about because of a direct reduction in CNS capacity brought about by the cumulative effects of the loss of neurons. Either way, the older person has to compensate for the reduction in capacity by adopting strategies still within his means; but, in comparison with the strategies possible using a faster system with a larger capacity and memory store, these compensatory strategies are relatively time-consuming and inefficient. They require more operations because of the overlap between the piecemeal components of the strategy, and because of the need to double-check elements, which are now relatively remote in time, to minimize the risk of error in a relatively cumbersome procedure. The older person prefers to have more information than is strictly necessary to reach a decision. This too seems to be linked with his inclination to minimize the risk of error, and with the difficulty he seems to have in focusing sharply on the critical issues in the problem and in defining sharply the boundaries of the problem.

The confidence we have in expectations derived from reasoning by analogy arises from the knowledge that the processes we are hypothesizing have already been demonstrated in another context. It is wrong, however, to suppose that essentially new models cannot be invented; and, in the long run, the validity of the model depends upon its own internal logic and not upon its origin. Where the model or analogy seems to be useful, it will not be rejected, even if some parts of the analogy are negative, unless a more satisfactory alternative model is forthcoming. The degree of correspondence revealed by an analogy is not measured simply by counting the similarities and differences, but rather by the extent to which it is possible to equate the internal logic of one system with that of the other, i.e., it is the grammar rather than the vocabulary of the two languages that is of interest.

The dangers of reasoning by analogy are too well known to be mentioned here. Our only concern is to show that different explicanda may be accounted for by the same explanation, and the explanation, i.e., theory, for any one explicandum can be constructed either by the invention of new theoretical notions or by analogy with existing notions. Whatever the origin of the explanatory concepts, the intent is the same—to develop an internal logic for the explicandum and to show how the facts of observation can be deduced from a set of primitive notions, postulates, definitions, and bridge principles.

VIII. COMMENTARY ON BIRREN'S COUNTERPART THEORY OF AGING

Birren (1960) provides a useful commentary on the general problem of theory construction in life-span developmental psychology. Birren reminds us that theories are needed to account for the apparently orderly progression with age of some behavioral characteristics—a progression which is unidirectional, and to some extent cumulative and organic; a progression, moreover, which seems to be under the partial control of one or more pacemakers, probably having important effects on the CNS. But it is difficult to see how such control, e.g., over longevity and rates of physical deterioration, could have evolved *directly* among organisms in the postreproductive (aging) period of their life, since there seem to be no evolutionary selection pressures affecting the reproduction of favorable or unfavorable characteristics. Hence Birren's (1960), "counterpart theory" of aging: "If . . . longevity [is] inherited . . . longevity must be a correlate or counterpart of a characteristic which is subject to selection [p. 308]." The "characteristic," presumably, might be plural. Birren's justification for proposing this theory is that in their normal competitive surroundings animals do not survive long enough to become senescent. But when they are reared in captive or domesticated circumstances they do survive. Hence, ". . . the individuals have the *potential* for senescence whether or not there is the opportunity for expression [p. 308] ."

Birren seems to argue that, if the process of aging arises from "counterpart" characteristics subject to selection pressures only during development, then (a) aging is no simpler or more orderly than development (in fact, it seems much *less* orderly in that there is greater diversity between individuals in the onset, rate, and pattern of age changes as compared with changes during earlier development), and (b) the mechanisms of aging will be different for different species (because, presumably, different species are exposed to different selection pressures). Thus, the effects of aging would be the long term consequences of characteristics which were operative in the developmental period, but the working out of these consequences is affected and made more variable by individual differences in many intrinsic and extrinsic factors. If selection pressures are less marked or absent in the postdevelopmental period, then, because selection restricts the range of individual variation by tending to eliminate individuals with adverse psychobiological characteristics, late-appearing psychobiological characteristics would tend to show more variation among individuals than would early-appearing characteristics. Empirical evidence seems to confirm this conclusion, and Birren's counterpart theory is supported, though indirectly, by this argument.

Empirical evidence directly relevant to the counterpart theory of aging would relate to the possibility of showing, for example, that, within a species, strains which can be bred for differential longevity exhibit differential developmental characteristics, and, by further demonstrating that if strains are bred for these differential developmental characteristics they also exhibit differential longevity. This is the kind of cross-validation required to eliminate the possibility that the supposedly differential developmental characteristics are accidental correlates of longevity. The further development of the theory would seem to consist in proposing functional relationships and causal connections between developmental characteristics and age changes, and testing these hypotheses against the evidence. Hopefully, in the long run, the theory should describe a system of psychobiological factors, their interrelationships, their ontogeny, and their short- and long-term effects on behavior. These effects would be difficult to predict.

The theory does not require that the biologically adaptive developmental characteristics be positively correlated with a *long* life expectation. For example, the psychobiological basis of social dominance during development may, for all we know, be negatively correlated with physical and mental health in late life and with longevity. Again, there is evidence that (whatever the reasons) selection pressures are operating against intelligence in that less intelligent parents are having rather more children than more intelligent parents. Yet people with higher intelligence tend to live a little longer than people with lower intelligence. Similarly, for all we know, some characteristics which are adaptive (and positively selected) during development may be uncorrelated with any characteristics in the postdevelopmental period.

Birren (1960) is of the opinion that the behavioral capacities—effective mechanisms for remembering and anticipating, language, for example—directly resulting from a highly evolved CNS are biologically adaptive, having been subject to strong selection pressures during development; moreover, because "... the neurons of the central nervous system are fixed post mitotic cells ... [p. 314]," the CNS provides that element of irreversibility in development, i.e., makes psychological development unidirectional; and, because of the gradual but cumulative loss of cells, possibly acts as one of the more important pacemakers determining the rate of aging. Genetically speaking, as we have seen, the development of the CNS seems to be programmed up to the end of the period of reproduction. What happens afterwards is that the organization of biological elements which it governs runs on, but becomes degraded and less capable of self-repair and self-correction, until eventually the system becomes critically inadequate and breaks down completely.

But is it possible that there are selection pressures operating on late life characteristics? In complex societies particularly, it is conceivable that adverse psychobiological changes in the postreproductive period could militate against survival and reproduction among offspring, e.g., because of inadequate parental care and guidance. Human society and culture are aspects of biological evolution, and aging has cultural features which react upon biological processes, e.g., delaying marriage, caring for grandchildren; so possibly bringing about postreproductive selection effects. Human social history, however, is brief in comparison with evolutionary history, and it seems unlikely that postreproductive selection effects would be discernible in the short run, even if the effects existed.

One line of evidence which might be relevant to Birren's counterpart theory of aging is that relating to sex differences in longevity. It could be argued that women have been more rigorously selected than men, because of the mortality associated with childbearing, and that the set of biological characteristics so selected provides the "counterpart" for the greater life expectancy of women. Birren's counterpart theory (plus the extensions proposed by this section) has a logical structure. Readers are invited to work out the anatomy of the argument using the method of dissection recommended here. This exercise should create a better understanding of the method and greater appreciation of the distinction between "analytic" and "substantial" logic. And, who knows? It might even stimulate some useful advances in theory construction in life-span psychology.

IX. CONCLUSIONS

Most of the philosophical issues raised by attempts to construct theories and to use scientific methods in life-span psychology have been settled; the philosophy of behavioral and social science as presently developed seems to be well able to deal with them. Thus, we should look elsewhere for reasons as to why developmental psychology seems scientifically or theoretically inadequate. One reason is that the impression may be mistaken; it is impossible to say whether a scientific discipline is making satisfactory progress—there are no norms of development to be derived from a study of the history of science. Another reason is that developmental psychology is hampered (distorted and limited) by administrative obstacles such as the time, cost and manpower needed for longitudinal studies and adequate samples, and by value judgments which dictate research priorities independently of their theoretical importance, and forbid, or at least retard, research which looks harmful to individuals or to society generally. Hence, the restrictions on the experimental study of psychoanalytic theory, sexual development, and social isolation. Many additional reasons for the apparent lack of progress can be found.

What passes for "theory construction" is often the discovery of a rule, relationship, or classification which seems to bring order into otherwise disorderly data, and permits inferences that previously could not be made. We have been concerned with the problems associated with tracing out and evaluating the implications of such creative conjectures. These problems are basically the same as those in other scientific disciplines.

ACKNOWLEDGMENT

This chapter was written during the author's appointment as Visiting Scientist at the Philadelphia Geriatric Center. The author wishes to express his thanks to that organization and especially to Mr. Arthur Waldman and Dr. M. Powell Lawton who arranged the appointment, and to Miss M. Gilligan who coped with the typing.

CHAPTER 5

Models of Development and Theories of Development[1]

HAYNE W. REESE

UNIVERSITY OF KANSAS
LAWRENCE, KANSAS

WILLIS F. OVERTON

STATE UNIVERSITY OF NEW YORK
BUFFALO, NEW YORK

ABSTRACT

Models, which originate in metaphor, exist on several levels ranging from all inclusive metaphysical models to narrowly circumscribed models of specific features of theories. Models at the more general levels form the determining logical context for models at lower levels. This categorical determinism stretches from metaphysical levels through scientific theories, to the manner in which we analyze, interpret, and make inferences from empirical evidence. Two radically different models which have had a pervasive effect upon the nature of

[1] The first listed author wishes to emphasize that this paper represents a collaborative effort, and not a senior-junior relation between the authors.

*psychology generally and developmental psychology specifically are the organ-
ismic and mechanistic world views. The history and nature of those models are
discussed and the manner in which they become transformed into corrolary
issues which form the metatheoretical basis for theory construction is analyzed.
Theories built upon different world views are logically independent and cannot
be assimilated to each other. They reflect different ways of looking at the world
and, as such, are incompatible in their implications.*

I. INTRODUCTION

Many psychologists appear to believe that the operationalists and logical
positivists had given them a categorical imperative demanding, among other
things, that their concepts have a certain form of definition and that the truth or
falsity of propositions be determined in certain specified ways. However, as
Bridgman himself pointed out, "... there need be no qualms that the
operational point of view will ever place the slightest restriction on the freedom
of the theoretical physicist to explore the consequences of any free mental
construction that he is ingenious enough to make. It must be remembered that
the operational point of view suggested itself from observation of physicists in
action [Bridgman, 1954 (in P. G. Frank, 1961, pp. 79-80)] ." (Also, see P. G.
Frank, 1954, in 1961, pp. 25-26.) The point is that operationalism is not a guide
but rather a history; as a history it may serve a guiding function, but no better
than any kind of history can serve as a guide. (It is perhaps worth noting
explicitly that operationalism is not a philosophy of science, but, in Bergmann's
1954 terms, only a footnote in the logical analysis of the formation of scientific
concepts.)

The operational analysis fits the activities of some psychologists, but not the
activities of others. It describes what behaviorists try to do, but not what
"cognitive" psychologists such as Piaget and Werner try to do. The purpose of
this paper is to examine the differences between these approaches. We will see
that the crucial difference is so fundamental and broad in its implications that
syncretism is impossible, and the only rapprochement possible is like the parallel
play of preschoolers in that the protagonists are separate, but equal and
mutually tolerant. We will see that the frequently discussed search for a
"common language" in psychology can reasonably occur only within models.
Across models there can never be a common language because the very nature of
different models dictates different language. We will first consider models and
theories in general, then the concept of development, and finally the mechanistic
(reactive organism) and organismic (active organism) models in the study of
development.

II. MODELS AND THEORIES

A. Models

1. *Levels of Models*

In science, a "theory" is a set of statements, including (a) general laws and principles that serve as axioms, (b) other laws, or theorems, that are deducible from the axioms, and (c) definitions of concepts. A "model" is structurally separate from a theory, but is functionally part of its axioms (see Lachman, 1960; Toulmin, 1962). According to A. Kaplan (1964), "The proper concepts are needed to formulate a good theory, but we need a good theory to arrive at proper concepts [p. 53]." As with other paradoxes, this "paradox of conceptualization" is resolved when it is recognized that there are levels of concepts, models, and theories. Any theory presupposes a more general model according to which the theoretical concepts are formulated. At the more general levels, the concepts are generally less explicitly formulated, but they nonetheless necessarily determine the concepts at lower levels. This categorical determinism stretches from metaphysical and epistemological levels "downward" through scientific theories, to the manner in which we analyze, interpret, and make inferences from empirical evidence.

The most general models, variously designated as "paradigms" (Kuhn, 1962), "presuppositions" (Pap, 1949), "world views" (Kuhn, 1962; Seeger, 1954), and "world hypotheses" (Pepper, 1942), have a pervasive influence throughout the more and more specific levels, as noted by Kessen (1966) and others before him (Black, 1962; Pepper, 1942; Toulmin, 1962). The different levels of models are characterized by different degrees of generality, openness, and vagueness. At one extreme are implicit and psychologically submerged models of such generality as to be capable of incorporating *every* phenomenon. These metaphysical systems are the world hypotheses referred to above. They are basic models of the essential characteristics of man and indeed of the nature of reality. Examples, which will be considered in detail in Section IV, are the mechanistic and organismic world hypotheses. In the mechanistic world view, the model for all phenomena is the machine; in the organismic world view, the model is the biological organism and its activities.

Less general, more specific, and more explicit are the models that have been called "ideals of nature" or "principles" (Toulmin, 1962), "paradigms of science" (Kuhn, 1962), and "suppositions" (A. Kaplan, 1964). They are not "philosophical" models, that is, they are not part of the logic of science, but rather are part of the psychology or pragmatics of science (see Bergmann, 1954; Grünbaum, 1954; Margenau, 1954; Pap, 1949). These might be called "pragmatic models." We will have little further to say about them in this paper.

At the other extreme are the relatively specific and precise models that in the past have most commonly been connoted by the term "model." These can be called "theoretical" models, provided it is kept in mind that this designation is meant only to distinguish them from the more general metaphysical and "pragmatic" models. The "theoretical" models include, on a scale from general and abstract to specific and concrete, (a) conceptual models formulated solely in verbal language, (b) analogue models, and (c) scale models.

2. Theoretical Models

a. *The Nature of Theoretical Models.* It is generally agreed among philosophers of science and scientists that general theoretical models are metaphorical (e.g., Black, 1962; Braithwaite, 1953; Chapanis, 1961; Ferré, 1963; Lachman, 1960; Rashevsky, 1955; Schon, 1963; Seeger, 1954; Toulmin, 1962). In Braithwaite's words, for example, "Thinking of scientific theories by means of models is always *as-if* thinking [Braithwaite, 1953, p. 93]."

Model terms are not the same as theoretical terms. According to Margenau (1954), nonempirical criteria establish concepts as an internally consistent set or theory, but cannot validate the concepts. The validation of concepts is an empirical matter. However, he was asserting that every valid concept, which by definition must belong to a satisfactory theory, must have two definitions, one formal or "constitutive" and one instrumental or operational.[2] The situation actually appears to be more complex than that, in a way, yet in another way more simple. A concept can have only one definition, and two definitions must define two different concepts (e.g., Bergmann, 1957). Therefore, the concept defined formally and the concept defined operationally are not necessarily collapsible, and are certainly not identical on any logical argument. Hence the simplification. The complexity is that there are not two, but three kinds of concepts that must be considered. There are the formally or rationally defined theoretical concepts, the operationally defined descriptive concepts, *and* the concepts that describe characteristics of the model. It is not necessary to assert that the three kinds of concept have the same referent, especially if "referent" is

Early training trials	Stimulus 1 $\rightarrow$ Approach Response $\frown$ Reward
	Stimulus 2 $\rightarrow$ Approach Response $\frown$ Nonreward
Later training trials	Stimulus 1 $\rightarrow$ Approach Response $(_SH_R)$
	Stimulus 2 $\rightarrow$ Inhibitory Response $(_SI_R)$

Figure 1. A model of inhibition in discriminative learning.

[2] Bergmann (1957) has pointed out that strictly speaking a concept cannot be "valid" or "invalid," only arguments can be. However, it seems clear enough that Margenau meant something like "establish the probable truth value of statements containing a concept" when he spoke of "validating a concept."

interpreted as immediate sensation, or directly observed data. Rather, it is meaningful to assert that certain concepts, one of each kind, are correlated. Thus, "inhibition" is a theoretical concept in Hullian theory related to the empirical concept of inhibition, or reduction in response frequency. The concrete model that illustrates the correlation might take the form shown in Figure 1. How well the model works is not our present concern; essentially, the model says that an approach response is conditioned to the stimulus that is associated with reward and an inhibitory response is conditioned to the stimulus that is associated with nonreward.

b. *Functions of Theoretical Models.* (1) *Representation.* Chapanis said, "Recently . . . I noted a title about a model of hypothesis behavior in discrimination learning (Levine, 1959). When I read the article, however, I was disappointed to find that the author's 'model' was primarily an empirical method for solving a set of simultaneous equations [Chapanis, 1961, p. 118]." Actually, Levine did describe a model, which represents behavior as describable by "hypotheses" (in the sense used by Krechevsky, 1932); the equations referred to by Chapanis are not part of this model, but only tell how to put it to use.

Scale and analogue models represent phenomena, but only in the sense of simile. Scale models represent elements and their relations; analogue models represent only the relations among the elements. The representation is almost descriptive, as opposed to metaphorical; and it can be argued that such models are useful to the extent that the simile is accurate, that is, to the extent that the representation approximates true description. (We are using the term "description" to mean a catalog of observed or measured properties; see Alexander, 1963.) If the scale and analogue models are accurate, in the sense just specified, these kinds of models can be useful to scientists. An example is the practical value of model airplanes in a wind tunnel for testing engineering or even more basic principles.

Other, more general theoretical models represent in the sense of metaphor; such models are to be interpreted as assertions that "*X* behaves *as if* it were *Y.*" This point is not always clear. For example, the machine is frequently used as a model in psychology, but W. S. McCulloch (1955) has asserted that "Everything we learn of organisms leads us to conclude not merely that they are analogous to machines but that they are machines [p. 39]," and ". . . organisms, even brains, are machines [p. 39]." It is this kind of assertion, among other dangers of using models, against which "eternal vigilance" is required when models are used (e.g., Braithwaite, 1953).

(2) *Deployment.* It has been argued (for reviews see Black, 1962; Ferré, 1963) that any model limits the world of experience and presents the person with a tunnel vision. Being committed to a particular model may make a person blind to its faults, and may dissipate his empirical efforts into fruitless channels.

However, a good model increases the horizon, since one of its functions is to aid in the deployment or extension of a theory (see Lachman, 1960; Toulmin, 1962). A good model acts like a pair of binoculars. This function is related to the metaphorical function. Models provide rules of inference through which new relations are discovered, and provide suggestions about how the scope of the theory can be increased. It is this function that makes a good model more than a simple analogy.

Models, as implied above, can also serve as a shortcut to deduction. They show *how* the theory is to be applied. This function has been called a prop (e.g., Black, 1962); but it is not only a prop for the obtuse or lazy, it is also a prop for the busy.

The characteristic of models that permits their utilization in the deployment of theories, and increase in their scope, is that they have "excess meaning." Since they are analogues, they contain elements or relations that are only "accidentally" present. The presence of excess meaning can be useful; for example, the excess meaning of the Copernican model provided the basis from which Kepler and later Newton made their discoveries. However, the presence of excess meaning has a serious disadvantage when the model is erroneously interpreted as description.

c. *Evaluation.* The use of models has its pitfalls, as well as its advantages. Some of the dangers have already been mentioned—reifying the model and attributing its properties to the phenomenon modeled. Another pitfall is attributing to the model properties that are meaningful only when predicated about the phenomena that were supposed to be explained by reference to the model. The question of consciousness in automata is an example (Lachman, 1961). Other dangers have been listed by Chapanis (1961).

Models cannot be assessed as true or false if it is accepted that they are based on metaphors, but only as more or less useful. Hence, their evaluation is pragmatic (Lachman, 1960; Toulmin, 1962): How well does the model fulfill its functions? Nevertheless, some philosophers have spoken of the "validity" of a model (e.g., Black, 1962; Pepper, 1942). If they mean the extent to which it faithfully *describes* reality, they are not really talking about the validity of a model, but about the accuracy or adequacy of a description. Notice that it is not at all necessary in principle that the metaphor be valid or accurate. It is not being asserted that the real world *is* thus and so, only that the real world behaves *as if* it were thus and so. It may well be true that only accurate metaphors are useful, but that is an empirical problem; it is not a self-evident or necessary truth.

3. *Metaphysical Models*

a. *Characteristics.* Pap (1949) has argued, "It is one thing to say that the firm belief in a 'deterministic universe,' let us say, motivated Laplace to perfect astronomy with mathematical tools. It is different to contend that the propositions of astronomy depend on the validity of such sweeping beliefs [p. 407] ." However, Pap missed the point that is properly to be made, that the mathematical theory of astronomy developed by Laplace makes sense only in a deterministic universe. The deterministic universe is a model of reality, not a description of reality. As a model, it cannot be true or false, only more or less useful. Whether or not the universe is "really" deterministic is beside the point. Thus, Laplace's activities depended upon a belief in, or at least acceptance of or assumption of, a deterministic universe, a belief or assumption that not only motivated the activities but also made possible the success.

It might be argued that Laplace's success inductively justifies the conclusion that the universe is deterministic, and that therefore the matter is empirical and not metaphysical. The argument is persuasive, but not compelling, because there are, in principle at least, other assumptions that might lead to systems that are equally successful. All world views that are adequate have this kind of inductive support. If one does not, it is eventually abandoned.

According to Kuhn (1962) and Pepper (1942), differences between world views are irreconcilable, and even prevent full communication. From this point of view, pleas for a synthesis of such approaches as Piaget's on the one hand and American behaviorism on the other are futile (see B. Kaplan, 1966). According to Pepper this kind of synthesis or eclecticism must lead to confusion because it involves mixing different world hypotheses. Different world views have different criteria for determining the truth of propositions, and therefore a synthesis that mixes world views also mixes truth criteria. It is important to note, however, that *translation* of a theory from one model to another is not the same as synthesis or assimilation. Translation involves taking the terms and propositions from one theory (and from its model), redefining them consistently with the new model, and relating them to the other terms in the new theory. Translation, in other words, is actually the construction of a brand-new theory with an unmixed model.

Kuhn (1962) is particularly clear on the impossibility of communication when different world hypotheses are involved:

To the extent, as significant as it is incomplete, that two scientific schools disagree about what is a problem and what a solution, they will inevitably talk through each other when debating the relative merits of their respective paradigms. In the partially circular arguments that regularly result, each paradigm will be shown to satisfy more or less the criteria that it dictates for itself and to fall short of a few of those dictated by its opponent. There are other reasons, too, for the incompleteness of logical contact that consistently characterizes paradigm debates. For example, since no paradigm ever solves all the problems it defines and since no two paradigms leave all the same problems unsolved, paradigm debates always involve the question: Which problems is it more significant to have solved? Like the issue of competing standards, that question of values can be answered only in terms of criteria that lie outside of normal science altogether, and it is that recourse to external criteria that most obviously makes paradigm debates revolutionary [pp. 108-109]. . . . the proponents of competing paradigms will often disagree about the list of problems that any candidate for paradigm must resolve. Their standards or their definitions of science are not the same [p. 147] . . . . Since new paradigms are born from old ones, they ordinarily incorporate much of the vocabulary and apparatus, both conceptual and manipulative, that the traditional paradigm had previously employed. But they seldom employ these borrowed elements in the same way [p. 148] . . . . most fundamental . . . the proponents of competing paradigms practice their trades in different worlds . . . . Both are looking at the world, and what they look at has not changed. But in some areas they see different things, and they see them in different relations one to another. That is why a law that cannot even be demonstrated to one group of scientists may occasionally seem intuitively obvious to another [p. 149]. [Quoted by permission.]

Pepper (1942) has made much the same point in his analysis.

A particularly good example of revolutionary paradigm debates is in the field of language development, in the controversy between, on the one hand, behaviorists such as Staats (1968), C. E. Osgood (1968), and Jenkins and Palermo (1964) and on the other hand the psycholinguists (see Palermo, 1970a). The paradigm of the behaviorists is, of course, mechanistic; the paradigm of the generative-grammar theorists is "contextualistic," in which the fundamental presuppositions are change and novelty (Pepper, 1942). [It might help promote an intuitive grasp of contextualism to note that Gestalt theory is also contextualistic, although Pepper (1942, p. 219) identified its root metaphor as mechanistic. Apparently, he was taken in by its pseudophysical analysis of *Gestalten.*]

b. *Evaluation.* Different world hypotheses cannot be compared evaluatively with one another, because of the basic lack of communication, the partial overlap in subject matter, and the difference in truth criteria. Each must be evaluated separately, and in obedience to its own ground rules. Only "internal" evaluation is possible. The adequacy of a world hypothesis is determined by its precision and its scope. Precision is the ability to produce an adequate or compelling interpretation of a fact, and the ability to produce only one such interpretation (or at most a few such interpretations). A world hypothesis that produces vague interpretations of facts or that produces an overabundance of interpretations of a single fact lacks precision. Scope refers to the range of facts that can be interpreted. ". . . a world hypothesis may have apparent precision in the interpretation of many fields of fact, but lack world-wide scope through its inability to offer any interpretation of some field or fields [Pepper, 1942, p. 118]."

One final point about paradigm debates needs to be emphasized in this section. It is obvious that communication is not *necessarily* impossible; otherwise, Kuhn and Pepper could not have understood and written about the differences between paradigms. Therefore, students should probably be given eclectic training, in which they become familiar with more than one paradigm, unlike the monotypic training that has been customary. This kind of eclecticism is not the kind that Pepper warned against, in which world views are mixed. There is another kind of eclecticism that is not undesirable and that may, in fact, be necessary, giving further force to the argument for eclectic training. There are eclectic theories which include more than one world view, but if such a theory always keeps the paradigms separate and specifies when each is to be applied, it completely avoids the undesirable eclecticism in which world views are mixed and hence truth criteria are confused.

It seems likely that current examples of this "good" kind of eclecticism have been accidental, in that there appear to have been no deliberate attempts to avoid the undesirable kind of eclecticism. Consider four examples. (a) One is S. H. White's (1965) analysis of the transitions that occur between about five and seven years of age in children. Before the transition, a mechanistic, associative model accounts for behavior; after the transition, a cognitive model seems to be needed. (b) Another example is Kohlberg's (1968) analysis of various cognitive developments, in which he argues that the development of certain abilities, such as reading and writing, can be accounted for by a learning (mechanistic) model, while others, such as the logical operations in Piaget's theory, must be explained with a cognitive (organismic) model.[3] (c) A third example is the less formalized practice of many text writers and research workers of implicitly assuming one model—the mechanistic one—in accounting for at least prenatal and infant behavior, and often child behavior in general, and assuming another model—often organismic but sometimes contextualistic (e.g., generative grammar) or formistic (e.g., the mathematical models)—in accounting for adolescent and adult behavior. A circle is completed by many of the accounts of behavior in old age, which again become mechanistic. (d) Our final example is Uznadze's (1966) theory of mental activity. According to Uznadze, human behavior is mechanical or habitual until an obstacle or a problem occurs (or, as American psychologists might say, until the habitual behavior is frustrated or comes in conflict with other habitual behaviors that also tend to be aroused). When that occurs, man shifts to another level of operation, a "plane of objectivization" or cognitive level. The theory, which is similar to Claparède's (1951) *prix de conscience*, thus explicitly includes a mechanical model and implicitly includes an organismic model, and, further, specifies when each is applicable.

At our present stage of knowledge, these kinds of eclectic theories seem to be necessary to account for the whole range of human behaviors throughout the life-span. Whether or not a single, one-model theory can ever be constructed,

---

[3] Kohlberg (1968) seems to invoke a model that improperly mixes world views when he says that the developments of certain concepts "represent an organic mixture of structural and informational changes [p. 1035]." Structural changes can occur only in the organismic model, and by informational change, Kohlberg was referring to the mechanistic, learning model.

especially one using a mechanistic model, is not a question that is worth debating. It is an empirical question, to which only the future can provide an answer.

B. Theories

1. *The Functions of Theories*

Theories in science are used to explain and to predict phenomena. "Explanation" and "prediction" cannot, unfortunately, be given noncontroversial meanings. In the logical positivist analysis, the terms are almost synonymous, since they differ only with respect to the time of occurrence of the phenomenon under consideration. If the phenomenon has already occurred when it is considered, it is to be *explained*. If it has not yet occurred, it is to be *predicted*. The process is the same in both cases; the explanandum (the description of the phenomenon) or the prediction is derived by *deduction* from a set of premises including (a) statements of antecedent conditions, (b) a set of sentences which represent general laws or theoretical principles, and (c) usually implicitly, a set of definitions of the terms involved in the laws or principles (see Frank, 1954, in 1961, p. 13; Hempel & Oppenheim, 1948; Lindsay, 1954). Toulmin, however, has argued that deduction is not always involved, and indeed, that it is usually not involved. According to Toulmin (1962), "It is the *terms* appearing in the statements at one level, not the statements themselves, which are logically linked to the statements in the level below [p. 85]." A prediction is not deduced from laws; it is obtained from an *application* of the laws. These different conceptions are not contradictory because they are applicable in different paradigms.

"Understanding" has been taken by some to mean ability to predict or explain, but this usage is controversial. It has been argued that "true" understanding in psychology requires reduction of explanations to a physicochemical or at least physiological basis, although logically one might insist on reduction to a subatomic basis. We can perhaps come close to a noncontroversial meaning if we take "understanding" to refer to the integration of knowledge; and we might then say that the functions of a theory are to organize and integrate knowledge and to direct research.

2. *Families of Theories*

Even within a single field of knowledge, theories can be classified into "families." A family is a set of theories that are based upon the same model, although not necessarily the same specific content area. Examples include Piaget (1960) and Erikson (1950), in a family of theories formulated within the contexts of the organismic world hypothesis and the active organism model, and Mowrer (1960), Bijou and Baer (1961), and Sears (Sears, Rau, & Alpert, 1965) in a family of theories formulated within the contexts of the mechanistic world hypothesis and the reactive organism model. Controversies about theories from different families involve paradigm debates, which are, as we have seen, futile. Controversies about theories within the same family can involve no metaphysical, epistemological, or theoretical-model issues, only theoretical and empirical issues. We will consider this point further in Section IV.

3. *Evaluation of Theories*

As Chapanis (1961) has aptly said, "Models . . . are judged by criteria of usefulness; theories, by criteria of truthfulness [p. 113]." More precisely, except for evaluation of the logical consistency of the statements it contains, a theory must be evaluated pragmatically.[4] How adequate are its explanations and predictions (Hempel & Oppenheim, 1948)? Does it produce understanding (Toulmin, 1962)? It is by now presumably accepted by all scientists that theories cannot be proved to be true, but only supported by empirical evidence.

P. G. Frank (1954) has suggested the following criteria for acceptance of a scientific theory: (a) "agreement with the observable facts that can be logically derived from the theory [in P. G. Frank, 1961, p. 13]." A "fact" is a sense impression (P. G. Frank, p. vii), presumably the same as a *datum* in Pepper's (1942) sense. (b) Simplicity: The theory should contain few and simple principles, especially when "simple" is understood in the mathematical sense. (c) Fertility: ". . . the fitness of a theory to be generalized, to be the basis of a new theory that does not logically follow from the original one, and to allow prediction of more observable facts [P. G. Frank, 1961, p. 16]." (d) Agreement with common sense and with the "self-evident" laws of nature (but see Pepper, 1942, on "self-evident" laws). (e) Interpretation of the theory as support for moral rules. This last criterion is trivial because although value judgments of two kinds are valid, value judgments of this kind are not. The valid kinds are the ones that Kuhn (1962) mentioned, in connection with decisions as to which problems it is more significant to have solved, and the kind involved in statistical significance decisions.

In a discussion of value judgments in science, Rudner (1954) noted that all sciences involve the validation (acceptance or rejection) of hypotheses, and argued that the validation necessarily involves value judgments. In psychology, for example, validation usually depends upon obtaining a .05 value of probability. The argument is trivial, because it misses the objection to value judgments of the third kind. The objectionable value judgments take the form, "*X* is true because it *should* be true." There is nothing culpable in requiring greater statistical confidence for more important decisions than for lesser decisions, whether the importance is assessed as theoretical or social. The

---

[4] The method suggested by Bromley in the preceding chapter can be used for the logical analysis and perhaps for the pragmatic analysis.

psychologist is making no value judgment when he cites research showing that typical school systems are middle-class in orientation and that lower-class children do more poorly in them than do middle-class children. He is, however, making a value judgment when he asserts that the evidence shows that the orientation should be changed.

III. THE CONCEPT OF DEVELOPMENT

A. Uses of the Term Development

There has been controversy about how to define the term *development*. To Heinz Werner, the term meant "increasing differentiation and hierarchic integration"; it was not even limited to processes unfolding over time (B. Kaplan, 1966, p. 662). Since "increasing differentiation and hierarchic integration" of the kinds of structures Werner was interested in cannot be directly observed, it is clear that for him "development" was not an empirical term.

According to Nagel (1957), the term often connotes ". . . the notion of a system possessing a definite structure and a definite set of pre-existing capacities; and the notion of a sequential set of changes in the system, yielding relatively permanent but novel increments not only in its structure but in its modes of operation as well [p. 17]." The notion is that there is an organized structure, exhibiting certain functions, and that the structure changes in organization or form, with consequent changes in function. To many psychologists, especially those who have been called "developmental psychologists" (see, e.g., Reese, 1970), it is also implied that the changes are unidirectional, irreversible, and directed toward certain end states or goals.

As an alternative to this organismic definition, Spiker (1966) has presented a conception of the term as used by the psychologists who have been called "experimental child psychologists" (see Reese, 1970). According to this conception, the connotative meanings of the term are both unnecessary and undesirable. Instead of implying an organization of some kind and instead of the teleological implication, the term is taken to refer to the two kinds of change identified technically as ontogenesis and phylogenesis, but specifically with respect to *behavior*. That is, functions change during the life-span, and they have changed during the course of evolution. From this position, it is no more necessary to assume that ontogeny is directed toward some goal than it is to assume that evolution has been directed toward the emergence of man.

Within the behavioral definition of development, as opposed to the organismic definition, theories of development have generally been refinements or extensions of more general behavioristic theories. For example, as an extension of a learning theory, the major difference would be a quantitative one, the duration of time involved. Developmental psychology from this perspective is concerned with changes in behavior over periods of weeks, months, or years; learning psychology is concerned with changes over periods of seconds, minutes, or days (Zigler, 1963). A characteristic of this approach is that age is not seen as a psychological variable; it reduces to time and time per se causes nothing. Changes may be correlated with time or age, but not caused by it; age is an index variable and not a causal variable. Thus, the approach requires identification of other variables that are correlated with age and that may be causal with respect to the observed behavioral change. However, since many of the "causal" variables so identified prove to be recalcitrant to experimental manipulation, and indeed recalcitrant even to direct observation, the explanations of the behavioral changes that are correlated with age are likely to refer to inferred processes that are assumed to change with age.

The organismic definition has the advantage that it can be applied to more than behavioral change with age, for example, the development of music, art, literature, science, philosophy, and history. It shares, however, a disadvantage with the behavioral definition: Changes in the organization of a structure, in the sense referred to in the organismic definition, cannot be directly observed. They must be inferred from behaviors (or products, in the other kinds of development mentioned).

This last point is crucial for an understanding of the opposing points of view. Although for both groups the meaning of the term development is determined by the context of the models they accept, behaviorists view the term as descriptive and organicists view it as theoretical. For behaviorists, the term labels the phenomena that are to be explained, and for organicists it occurs in explanations of observed behavioral changes. The consequences of this distinction will be considered in Section IV.

It should be admitted, however, that the behaviorist—organicist issue is sometimes not as clear-cut as we have stated it, because some behaviorists have defined development in such a way that it is a model concept and not a descriptive term. Baer (1966), for example, said, ". . . development is behavior change which requires programming . . . ." He added that ". . . programming requires time, but not enough of it to call it age." Programming means presenting a sequence of experiences in optimal order. The approach emphasizes the study of developmental *processes*, not merely their outcome or "typical calendar schedule." The study of behavioral changes as a function of age is the study of outcomes of an apparently inefficient programming that occurs in the natural environment (see also Bijou & Baer, 1963, p. 198). An earlier definition was given by Bijou and Baer (1961): "By 'psychological development' we mean progressive changes in the way an organism's behavior interacts with the environment. An *interaction* between behavior and environment means simply that a given response may be expected to occur or not, depending on the stimulation the environment provides [p. 1]." The progressive changes "occur with the passage of time between conception and death [p. 2]." These definitions clearly refer to a model of development.

B. The Concept of Stages of Development

Spiker (1966) examined "two common prototypes" of developmental law. One is egg-caterpillar-cocoon-butterfly, a special instance of the general sequence embryo-larva-pupa-imago. This is a *stage* law, and may or may not specify the exact age at which the stages occur. The other prototype is exemplified by the weight, height, or volume of a plant as a function of the time since planting, or the number of different phonemic sounds typically produced by infants at different ages. This type of developmental law is more specific with respect to age. However, the essential difference is not how specific the law is with respect to age, but whether it refers to stages or to a continuity of development.

Stage, within one world view, is a feature of certain models. From this point of view, it is not ever asserted that development actually proceeds through stages, only that it can be represented by reference to stages (Reese, 1970). Whether this representation is convenient or useful is one question; whether it tends to be misunderstood as descriptive is another; and whether it is accurate is irrelevant. Realization that stage in this sense is a model concept would have prevented much needless controversy about whether development "really" progresses through stages. The controversy arose because of misapplication or inappropriate generalization of model issues to empirical questions and theoretical issues.

From the viewpoint of another world hypothesis, stage is not a model concept but a theoretical concept. From this point of view, it is equally irrelevant to ask whether statements about stages are accurate. The relevant question remains pragmatic: Is the theoretical stage concept fruitful, that is, does it enter into adequate explanatory and predictive statements?

We will consider these two approaches to the concept of stage in more detail in Section IV.

C. Issues about the Concept of Development

There are a number of issues that have arisen with respect to developmental models and theories. Some are relevant and some irrelevant.

1. *Development as a Descriptive Term*

There are no relevant issues about "development" as a descriptive term referring to change. It might be objected that the continuity—discontinuity issue is an important empirical issue about the nature of the change, but we have just seen that this issue is about models and theories and is therefore not empirical but pragmatic. That is, the proper question is not whether development is continuous or stage-wise, but which conception is more fruitful. It is therefore only when one begins to specify or interpret developmental changes that issues begin to emerge; but when specification or interpretation begins, we are immediately confronted with model or theoretical meanings of development. An example of this problem is demonstrated in the specification presented by behaviorists as opposed to that presented by organicists. For example, Spiker (1966) appealed to psychologists to restrict the term development to applications involving ". . . changes in behavior that normally occur with an increase in the chronological age of the child [p. 41]." Organismic psychologists, in contrast, tend to restrict the application to changes in the form or organization of a system, such changes being directed toward certain end states or goals. In each case, development has changed from a term having purely descriptive status to one that implicitly involves model and theoretical meanings, that is, principles for ordering the world. At the most general level, the changes involve the mechanistic and organismic models. The nature of this involvement will be described in Section IV.

2. Development as a Theoretical Concept

If it is accepted that there are no issues about development as a descriptive term, then the obvious controversy about it has to do with its other guises. As suggested previously, it appears that the theoretical controversy is a reflection of the adherence of the two groups of psychologists—the behaviorists and the organicists—to radically different world hypotheses. This radical split determines not only the definition of development, but also other controversies that pervade the field of psychology generally and developmental psychology specifically.

If two theorists adopt different basic models, there can be no fruitful debate between them; their views will be irreconcilable. Between theories in the same family, however, there may be debate or disagreement; but even so there can be no issues of theory construction—no metatheoretical issues. One example of a theoretical issue is that between McNeill (1966) and Slobin (1966a), who disagree on the extent to which inherent structure must be assumed. Another example is the disagreement as to whether language structures are basic to more general cognitive structures (the psycholinguists and Bruner) or the general cognitive structures are basic (Piaget).

It follows from the above discussion that there are no theoretical issues of philosophical import. This is not to say that there are no theoretical issues; rather, these issues are pragmatic matters, involving, for example, the psychology of the scientist who adopts one specific theoretical formulation over another, or the adequacy with which a theory encompasses the phenomena that are within its scope. What look like issues that are not empirical disappear when it becomes clear that terms are being used with different referents, and therefore that there is no common ground for communication.

3. *Irrelevant Issues*

Certain issues dividing behavioristically oriented developmental psychologists from organismic developmental psychologists have been proposed, but they are irrelevant to the issues about models. These irrelevant issues include (a) applied versus basic research, (b) experimental versus nonexperimental methods, and (c) child as subject versus child per se. The last is not only irrelevant but also trivial, since it is based upon the intent or interests of the researcher rather than on the outcome of his research (see Reese, 1970, for review).

IV. THE MECHANISTIC AND ORGANISMIC MODELS OF DEVELOPMENT

A. Introduction

The aim of this section is to introduce those models, and the corollary positions implied by those models, which are most influential in the study of psychology generally, and of developmental psychology specifically. To accomplish this aim we may begin by briefly reviewing the nature and origin of models. As mentioned in an earlier section, the origin of models lies in metaphor. The process of understanding begins with a problematic area of inquiry in which there exist some observed facts and regularities. In an effort to understand and explain this area of inquiry, one turns to another area of knowledge which presents fewer problems or is better organized. This second area will then become the model for the first, and the investigator is faced with the riddle-like task of discovering and formulating the formal properties of the model area which are appropriate to the original area of inquiry, and rejecting those which are not. As Black (1962) pointed out, the model when formed becomes a lens through which we look at our subject matter in a new way.

For our present purposes it is important to recognize that the establishment of the most circumscribed and concrete models is dependent upon the availability of more general models, and these upon more general models yet, in an ever-widening series terminated only by the most general and hence most basic models—metaphysical models. It is in this sense that we are not today, nor can we ever expect to be, free of basic philosophical presuppositions. The specification of mediating responses (r_m), for example, is based on the S-R model, which requires that all behavior, whether internal or external, have the same logical status (Fodor, 1965). The S-R model in turn reflects a model of man as a reactive organism and its epistemological correlate of *naïve realism.* Ultimately this model finds its source in the model of the universe as the great Newtonian machine. In contrast, Piaget's specification of "operation" is based on a biological model (Furth, 1969) which accepts a fundamental difference between behavior and operation. The biological model is in turn rooted in a model of man as spontaneously active and its corollary epistemological position of *constructivism.* Finally, this model finds its context in the metaphysical system of Leibnitz, in which activity is viewed as the essential characteristic of all substance.

Thus, the more general models form the determining logical context within which more specific models are formulated and elaborated.

B. The Mechanistic Model in Psychology and Development

The basic metaphor employed for the mechanistic model is that of the machine. As Pepper (1942) pointed out, the species of mechanistic model that develops depends on the type of machine considered, for example, the watch or computer, but the fundamental categories remain constant, and hence, ultimately result in the same theoretical attitudes. This model has been analyzed in depth elsewhere (Matson, 1964; Pepper, 1942; Schon, 1963) and we need only mention some of its most salient and pertinent features.

As a cosmology, the model represents the universe as a machine, composed of discrete pieces operating in a spatio-temporal field. The pieces—elementary particles in motion—and their relations form the basic reality to which all other more complex phenomena are ultimately reducible. In the operation of the machine, forces are applied and there results a discrete chain-like sequence of events. These forces are the only efficient or immediate causes; purpose is seen as a mediate or derived cause. Given this, it is only a short step to the recognition that complete prediction is *in principle* possible, since complete knowledge of the state of the machine at one point in time allows inference of the state at the next, given a knowledge of the forces to be applied. A further characteristic of the machine, and consequently of the universe represented in this way, is that it is eminently susceptible to quantification. Functional equations may be constructed that exhibit the relationship between the pieces in their operation.

Since its construction, the mechanistic model of the universe has in turn been elaborated and employed for further model construction in the most diverse areas of inquiry, including science, history, religion, aesthetics, epistemology, and psychology (Cassirer, 1951). When displaced to the sphere of epistemology and psychology, the transformation has resulted in what has variously been termed the *reactive,* passive, robot, or empty organism *model of man.* In its ideal form this model characterizes the organism, like other parts of the universal machine, as inherently at rest. Activity is viewed as a resultant of external or peripheral forces. Related to this is the representation of psychological functions, such as thinking, willing, wishing, and perceiving, as complex phenomena that are reducible to more simple phenomena governed by efficient causes (and the history of the machine).

A most significant characteristic of this model for developmental psychology is that change in the products of the machine or behaviors of the organism is not seen as resulting from change in the structure of the organism itself. The appearance of qualitative changes is considered either as epiphenomenal or as reducible to quantitative change, since the organism, like the elementary particles of classical physics, does not exhibit basic qualitative changes. As implied by the other characteristics of this model, the quantitative change is strictly determined by efficient causes. However, there exists in the model the possibility of qualitatively different *operations*, switched on or off depending upon the history, level, or kind of stimulation applied. The assumption of such mechanisms, in fact, provides the major explanations of developmental change in behavior.

The epistemological position that derives from this model is that of *naive realism*, a copy theory of knowledge according to which the knower plays no active role in the known, and inevitably apprehends the world in a pre-determined way.

In closing this section it should be noted that, although the model of the human organism as a reactive or passive receptacle of stimuli has evolved through history, its basic categories have remained the same. The relatively recent move to mediating reponses or r_m, while admittedly more powerful than the basic S-R conception, in no way changes the basic ideal model. The history of this model stems from the time of John Locke, who reacted against the seventeenth century procedure of solving problems on the basis of appeals to phenomena that were even less well known (e.g., Descartes' solution to the problems of epistemology by making an ultimate recourse to God as the source of all knowledge) and accepted the Newtonian ideal as a model by proclaiming his famous dictum of the blank slate or *tabula rasa*: "nothing is in the intellect which is not first in the senses." Even Locke, however, did not go as far as the logic of this model dictated, but rather left man with the inherent psychological function of reflection, which was composed of the processes of comparing, distinguishing, judging, and willing (Cassirer, 1951). From this point forward, the empiricist movement in philosophy and psychology from Bishop Berkeley and Hume, through the Mills, and down to the twentieth century behaviorists, can be viewed as an attempt to bring the reactive organism model progressively closer and closer to the logic of the mechanistic model of the universe. The most recent changes in neobehaviorism are directed toward maintaining the general model and extending its scope.

C. The Organismic Model in Psychology and Development

The basic metaphor employed for the organismic model is the organism, the living, organized system presented to experience in multiple forms.

As a cosmology this model was first systematically elaborated by Leibnitz. In his monadology, Leibnitz began from an organic base with the assertion that the essence of substance is activity rather than the static elementary particle proposed by the mechanistic model. This activity was viewed as consisting "in a continuous transition from one state to another as it produces these states out of itself in unceasing succession [Cassirer, 1951, p. 29]." (Also see Allport, 1955.) From such a point of view, one element can never be like another, and as a consequence, the logic of discovering reality according to the analytic ideal of reducing the many qualitative differences to the one is repudiated. In its place is substituted a search for unity among the many; that is, a pluralistic universe is substituted for a monistic one, and it is the diversity which constitutes unity. This unity is found in discovering the rules of transition from one form to another and in establishing the system in which the transition occurs. Thus, unity is found in multiplicity, being is found in becoming, and constancy is found in change.

In this representation, then, the *whole* is organic rather than mechanical in nature. The nature of the whole, rather than being the sum of its parts, is presupposed by the parts and the whole constitutes the condition of the meaning and existence of the parts (Cassirer, 1951, p. 31).

A final aspect of this organismic model of the universe relevant for our purposes concerns the nature of cause. According to the principle of the activity of the monad, through progressive acts of differentiation or individuation, the monad is in continuous transition from one state to another. This notion of progressive development does not involve the mechanical connection of efficient cause leading to additive effect, but rather involves a teleological relationship. For Leibnitz, the specific nature of this relationship is preformistic or vitalistic rather than epigenetic. Regardless of the specific details, the important point here is that efficient cause is replaced by formal cause (i.e., cause by the essential nature of a form). This and the earlier mentioned fact of acceptance of qualitative differences preclude the possibility of a strictly predictive and quantifiable universe.

Like the mechanistic model, the organismic model of the universe has been elaborated and employed for further model construction in a number of diverse areas. In epistemology and psychology the transformation has resulted in the *active organism model of man.*

A primary characteristic of this model is its representation of the organism as inherently and spontaneously active, a view of the organism as the source of acts, rather than as the collection of acts initiated by external (peripheral) force.

A second basic characteristic of this model is the representation of man as an organized entity, a configuration of parts which gain their meaning, their function, from the whole in which they are embedded. Here the category of form (see Merleau-Ponty, 1963) enters as a basic category for the analysis and understanding of behavior. From this point of view, the concepts of psychological structure and function, or means and ends, become central rather than derived. Inquiry is directed toward the discovery of principles of organization, toward the explanation of the nature and relation of parts and wholes, structures and functions, rather than toward the derivation of these from elementary processes.

For developmental psychology the nature of the representation of change is most critical. In this model, as in its cosmological referent, change itself is accepted as given. This means that change is not itself explainable by efficient, material cause; while efficient causes may inhibit or facilitate change, it is formal, rather than efficient, cause that is basic. Such a position results in a denial of the complete predictability of man's behavior. Furthermore, the nature of change is qualitative as well as quantitative. Just as substance in the cosmological view is in constant transition from one state to another, so also, the active organism model represents man as a system in which the basic configuration of parts changes, as well as the parts themselves. At each new level of psychological organization, new system properties emerge which are irreducible to lower levels, and which are therefore qualitatively different from them.

The epistemological position which derives from the active organism model of man is that of *constructivism*. It asserts that the knower, on the basis of his inherent activity and organization, actively participates in the construction of the known reality. Although this position denies that a copy theory of knowledge or knowledge of things-in-themselves is possible, it does not deny the existence of an external reality as a strictly idealistic position would. Rather, it affirms that the world, as known, is a product of the interaction between the active knower and things-in-themselves. The organism can know the world only through the structures that mediate his behavior. Developmentally considered, as psychological structures change, there is a qualitative change in the mode of knowing the world.

The acceptance of the active organism model has implications for the acceptance of various theories and techniques. The individual who accepts this model will tend to emphasize the significance of processes over products, and qualitative change over quantitative change. Products (behavior) or achievements will be employed to infer the necessary conditions for their occurrence, that is, to infer psychological structures. Changes in psychological structures will be the basic referents of developmental interest, and these changes will reflect basic qualitative changes conceptualized as changes in levels of organization or stages. In addition, he will tend to emphasize the significance of the role of experience in facilitating or inhibiting the course of development, rather than the effect of training as the source of development. In general he will emphasize a structural or structure-function analysis of behavior, rather than a functional analysis. The basic outline of this type of analysis is the description of structures at a given period, the ordering of such periods, the discovery of rules of transition from one period to another, and the determination of experimental conditions that facilitate or inhibit the structural change.

Like the reactive organism model, the active organism model has evolved through history while maintaining its basic categories. Thus, for example, today a true epigenesis replaces the earlier preformism and vitalism (see von Bertalanffy, 1962), but within this context the basic category of formal rather than efficient cause is maintained. The elaboration and evolution of the model began with Leibnitz's psychological and epistemological speculations. Following his cosmology, Leibnitz maintained that the fundamental nature of mind consists in its activity. He viewed mind as a whole composed of formative forces, and this idea set the stage for the future task of the eighteenth century German Enlightenment, the task of specifying these forces in their specific structures, and of understanding their reciprocal relations (Cassirer, 1951, p. 124). Later, Kant built upon this base his critical idealism, which provided an empirical dimension so well captured in his famous aphorism, "Concepts without percepts are empty, percepts without concepts are blind"; and Hegel elaborated his own developmental concept of the dialectic. Today, the model is best exemplified in the philosophy of Ernst Cassirer (1953). The model also evolved in psychology itself, and is manifested historically in the "act" psychology of Brentano and the Würzburg school. Currently it is represented in such theories as von Bertalanffy's general systems theory (1967, 1968), Werner's and Piaget's theories of development, and the ego psychologists such as Erikson (1950).

D. Corollary Model Issues

With these models in mind we may look more closely at some of the prescriptive implications that arise from accepting one or the other. We shall call these implications corollary model issues in order to underscore our position that the issues that exist at this level are model-like or pretheoretical in character, and hence are not open to empirical test. This is not to deny that these issues themselves have further prescriptive value for theory and empirical work. Indeed, one of our primary aims is to demonstrate what is open to empirical test and what is not. It is our hope that such a demonstration will allow the developmental psychologist to identify more clearly that which is testable, and to avoid pointless polemics based on a failure to recognize that different models result in different types of theories and in different definitions of what is to be considered meaningful.

In this section, then, we will describe some of these corollary model issues, point out how they affect the analysis and understanding of development, and describe some of the confusions that have resulted from a misunderstanding of their status. Since the mechanistic corollaries are relatively well known, and since most of the confusion of past polemics has arisen from a lack of understanding of the organismic corollaries, we shall focus our primary attention on these latter, and use the former for points of contrast.

1. *Holism versus Elementarism*

The assumption of holism derives from the active organism model. More particularly, it derives from the representation of the organism as an *organized* totality, a system of parts in interaction with each other, such that the part derives its meaning from the whole. While the notion of holism has been specified in many contexts, in psychology it finds its most articulate formulation in Werner and Kaplan (1963). The holistic assumption

maintains that any local organ or activity is dependent upon the context, field or whole of which it is a constitutive part: its properties and functional significance [meaning] are, in a large measure, determined by this larger whole or context [p. 3].

This assumption has the status of a regulative principle for the general analysis of behavior. If accepted, it prescribes certain procedures and prohibits others. Negatively characterized, it prohibits the assumption that two behaviors have identical meanings solely because they are physically identical. Thus, for example, in the study of social development it would be considered illegitimate from a holistic viewpoint to equate initially the upturned lips of the infant, the preschool child, and the adult as a reflection of the establishment of positive social contact. The "smiling response" may find its meaningful context in terms of gastrointestinal disturbance, positive social contact, or nervousness. Similarly, from this viewpoint the verbal behavior of certain animals, of human children, and of human adults cannot be initially equated.

Failure to understand the nature and status of the holistic assumption has often led to misapplication. First, the assumption is not an admonishment to study the whole child, or study the whole *anything*. There is no opposition here to analysis or to the study of part processes. Indeed Werner (1948), in his discussion of the role of holism, called for a "creative analysis," that is, an analysis in which part processes are investigated, but in the context of the whole of which they are a part. Second, the assumption is not a statement of the "individuation" (mass or global to specific) developmental trend. Initial motor movements and percepts may or may not be global in nature, but they certainly are not *holistic*.

Thus far we have dealt only with the negative characteristics of holism, what it prohibits, and not what it prescribes. In a more positive vein we may ask what acceptance of the holistic assumption does prescribe for the analysis of behavior. Before doing this, however, we will first point out the value of understanding the holistic assumption in theory construction and interpretation.

Any theory built upon the active organism model will in some way translate the holistic assumption into its theoretical concepts, just as a theory built upon the reactive organism model will translate the elementaristic assumption into its concepts. Recognition of this leads to recognition that theories built on independent models cannot be assimilated to each other without violent rupture of the logical framework of one. Failure to recognize this leads to faulty overgeneralizations and confusion.

An aspect of Piaget's theory may be taken as illustrative. Piaget accepts the assumption of holism and translates it into his theory in the concept of "organization," one of the two basic functional invariants. "Organization" functions as the basic logical distinction between internal cognitive structures (schemata and operations) and external responses. This logical distinction does not, of course, exist in theories which hold an elementaristic assumption, for in such theories—including those which accept internal mediators—responses are physical processes regardless of whether they are observed or inferred. Here, then, is a most basic and important distinction between the two types of theories. Recently, however, a number of mechanistically oriented psychologists have come to view Piaget's theory as quite compatible with the reactive organism model in "general behavior theory." This unwarranted view requires ignoring the basic concept of organization, and emphasizing other subsidiary aspects of the theory.

Let us then turn to the positive characterization of the holistic assumption. Rather than assessing behavior in terms of material identity, this assumption directs assessment in terms of the function of the behavior in the whole or context in which it is embedded, that is, according to the function, or ends, or goals of the organism or part processes which are being investigated. This leads to the next corollary model issues of structure-function.

2. *Structure-Function versus Antecedent-Consequent*

It follows from what has been said thus far that the active organism model results in the view that the organism as a whole, and part processes of the organism, have definable functions. The task set forth, then, is to define these functions or goals and to investigate the structures or means which serve them. The paradigm is familiar in biology. The biologist acts *as if* each organ or structure has a function. He defines the function and inquires into the operation of the structure in serving this function. For psychology, the paradigm is similar but the structures are psychological and not physical or physiological. Psychological structures refer to the relatively stable organizational properties or patterns of specific behavioral systems.

As with holism, the notion of structure-function will be incorporated into any theory based on the active organism model. Piaget does this explicitly. He defines the general function of intelligent behavior in terms of biological adaptation, and conceptualizes the structures that serve this function as sensorimotor schemata and logical operations. This serves as the basis for the evaluation of the operation of the structures, as exhibited in various behavioral achievements. It also provides the basis for a process-achievement distinction since qualitatively different types of structures, processes, or modes of operation may result in the same behavioral achievement. For example, Piaget (Inhelder & Piaget, 1964) has speculated that incomplete matrix problems may be solved according to perceptual schemata, or logical operations. [By manipulating task variables Overton and Brodzinsky (1969) have empirically investigated this hypothesis.]

From a reactive organism model, analysis proceeds in terms of antecedent-consequent relations (e.g., Bijou & Baer, 1963). Recently, there have been various modifications of this model from its original single-stage, specific model of $S \rightarrow R$ to a two stage model of $S \rightarrow r_m\text{-}s_m \rightarrow R$, where r_m is conceptualized as an intervening variable or hypothetical construct. This modification has permitted a distinction like the process-achievement distinction, and allows for incorporation of a great deal of data that would otherwise be explicable only in terms of structure-function (Berlyne, 1966). It should be recognized, however, that this modification does not make the two approaches compatible. Most generally, as mentioned earlier, this modification maintains the basic categories of the reactive organism model. As a consequence, both the source and nature of "structure" and "r_m" are radically different (Fodor, 1965).

Kohlberg (1968) has recently analyzed various positions concerning the source of structure, and we may briefly note that within the active organism model two different views have been, and are currently, held. (These views reflect within-model theoretical issues.) The *nativistic* view, as currently represented by Chomsky and his colleagues (McNeill, 1966), maintains that psychological structures are present as complete structures from birth; the *interactionist* view represented by Piaget (1968) maintains that although some structure (organization) exists at birth, structures develop through a complex interaction between the present organization and the ongoing activity of the individual. In contrast, the reactive organism model maintains that the functioning of r_m originates solely on the basis of environmental determinants. Thus we again encounter the between-models issue of formal versus efficient cause.

A final consideration in the analysis of structure-function is that such a proposition is clearly teleological, in that it involves the attribution of purpose, goal, or function to the organism. This is not, however, a subjective purposivism, nor is any ontological assertion made (Taylor, 1964). It is, as was the case with holism, a regulative principle which directs one to act *as if* there are inherent functions, in the same way that the elementaristic position directs one to act as if there are no inherent functions. Given this status, purpose (or more generally, form) is a basic category for a theory constructed on the active organism model, but a theory constructed on the reactive organism model will treat purpose as derived. Spiker (1966) pointed out that general behavior theory introduces terms such as "drive," goal," and "anticipatory goal response" to account for (derive) behavior that appears to involve purpose. Treating purpose as derived maintains the possibility of a complete behavioral determinism. In contrast, Piaget and Werner introduce purpose as a basic theoretical category, which is employed to account for the operation of structures. Here, then, the possibility of a complete determinism is denied.

This analysis leads to the primary area of concern for developmental psychology, the nature and direction of developmental change.

3. Structural versus Behavioral Change

Up to now, we have said nothing in this section about the primary referent for developmental psychology. Neither holism nor structure-function in themselves make any reference to change, and it is consequently possible to construct theories based upon these implications without considering development (e.g., G. Kelly, 1963, in the area of personality). The situation is similar for theories built upon the implications of elementarism and antecedent-consequent relations, which also make, in themselves, no reference to change.

We may formulate the corollary model issues here in terms of two questions: What is it that changes in development, and what is the nature and direction of this change? The answer to the first question is given through the focus of each model discussed above. That is, for the active organism model the focus is upon changes in structures and functions, while for the reactive organism model it is upon response changes (including implicit responses). Here, as a matter of fact, we come to the basic rationale for the divergent primary clauses in the definitions of development discussed earlier in this paper: Within the active organism model, development refers to changes in the form, structure, or organization of a system, *such changes being directed toward end states or goals*; in the reactive organism model, development refers to changes in behavior *with increasing chronological age*. It is the italicized clause of each of these definitions which we must now explore in order to explicate the nature and direction of developmental change.

It will be recalled that in the active organism model, like its cosmological referent, change is determined by the form of the organization. In terms of structure-function this means that the nature and direction of change are given by the postulation of a general functional prerequisite. In this sense, development is an *a priori* concept. A general end state or goal is stated and this acts as a principle for ordering change. Again, here, as earlier, the teleological aspect is regulative, not ontological. As Kessen (1966) pointed out, "to understand a developmental progression one must ... state the developmental end point [p. 63]."

The developmental end point or functional prerequisite will be formulated in a different manner, depending on the level of analysis considered. At a most general level, deriving directly from the active organism model, there will be total acceptance of H. Werner and Kaplan's (1963) directiveness assumption, which in part states that organisms develop "toward a relatively mature state [p. 5]." Once maturity is defined, we cross from the level of metatheoretical propositions to theory itself. Thus, both Werner and Piaget define maturity in terms of intellectual or cognitive functioning, and psychoanalytic theory defines maturity in terms of sexual or genital functioning. These functions then become the general focus and end point of development for each theory. Within this context, Werner formulates the specific theoretical end state of differentiation and hierarchic integration (orthogenetic principle) which serves to order "analogous processes" (structures). Piaget employs the concept of equilibration process to order variable structures (schemata and operations). Psychoanalytic theory introduces the reality principle to order the structures of id, ego, and superego.

From this perspective, then, change and direction of change are given. This should, however, in no way be taken to mean that such an orientation precludes the possibility of empirical investigation. While there is a denial that a search for environmental *determinants* is useful, there is no question of the importance of isolating the types of experiences which facilitate or inhibit the change as given. In addition, as discussed by Wohlwill (1963a), empirical investigations play a significant role in determining whether the sequence of structural changes is that given by the specific theory, and whether diverse behaviors have a sufficient degree of interrelatedness to be considered to reflect the same underlying structure.

According to the reactive organism model, change is determined by efficient cause. In terms of the response focus of the model, this means that response changes, whether within the context of several trials or several years, occur as the result of external stimulation or on the basis of stimulation present after a response is made (reinforcement contingency). From this point of view, developmental psychology becomes an arbitrary subdivision of general behavior theory (Zigler, 1963). It represents to some an area which

> . . . specializes in studying the progressions in interactions between behavior and environmental events. In other words, it is concerned with the historical variables influencing behavior, that is with past interactions on present interactions [Bijou & Baer, 1961, p. 14].

Establishing the interactions takes time, and furthermore, previously established interactions influence the later establishment of others, producing directionality (i.e., correlation with age). Others, such as Berlyne (1966), have proposed to account for direction as a derived category by considering age as an intervening variable, differing from other intervening variables in that it is independent of stimulus conditions and is unidirectional and linear with time. Age, then, becomes a concept like "drive," "reinforcement," and "r_m" and it is employed to account for (derive) direction in the way these other concepts are introduced to account for (derive) purpose.

In our analysis of the nature of change we have not considered a frequently discussed major feature. This is the question of whether change is to be represented as completely continuous or as discontinuous. Although this concerns the nature of change, we will treat it as a separate corollary model issue because of the amount of attention it has received.

4. Discontinuity versus Continuity

The essential model issue here is whether successive behavioral forms are reducible (continuity) or irreducible (discontinuity) to prior forms (H. Werner, 1957). As a model issue, it is completely irrelevant whether change is gradual or abrupt, small or large, whether it is assessed according to one type of methodology or another. These considerations become relevant only when we turn away from models, and to empirical dimensions.

According to the active organism model and its holistic corollary, an organization has systemic properties which are characteristic of that organization as a whole, and not of any of the individual parts. For example, vision is a property of the visual system in interaction with other systems and not a property of the cornea, retina, optic nerve, or occipital cortex. This is the core meaning of the often stated phrase, the whole is different from the sum of its parts. When the parts and organization change, the resulting organization will have new or novel systemic properties. This is exemplified in the physical case where hydrogen is combined with oxygen to form water. Water has properties, such as wetness, which are not characteristic of its components. The new properties are *emergent* in the sense that they are not analyzable into simpler components, and hence cannot be derived or predicted from them. Thus, from this perspective, there is a basic discontinuity between various levels of organization.

Nagel translated this point of view into a developmental context (see Section III,A), and Langer (1969) translated it into a specifically human developmental context:

Formally, they [humans] are organizations of organs or systems of action . . . . they are endowed with (a) the necessary systems for initial interaction with the milieu . . . . and (b) the self-generative characteristics that insure their own development . . . . Of course, the *various systems emerge* at different times of life. Developmentally, humans are actors or operators who function to keep themselves adaptively interacting with the environment, thereby *conserving* their own *organization at the same time as they transform it* . . . . A new stage of development arises when a new or transformed system becomes dominant and functionally subordinates or incorporates previously existing systems [p. 87 (italics added)]. [Quoted by permission.]

When translated into specific theories, the discontinuity position forms the basic rationale for the assertion of qualitative differences between levels of organization and modes of operation. Thus, for example, in Piaget's theory the child operating at the level of sensorimotor schemata knows his world in a qualitatively different manner from the child operating on the basis of logical operations because these latter structures have systemic properties which are not present in the former, for example, properties of associativity, composition, identity, and reversibility.

As a model issue, discontinuity and qualitative change is not open to empirical test. In the past, failure to recognize this has led investigators to assert support or nonsupport for discontinuity, according to whether they found or did not find gaps or abrupt shifts in the phenomena under study, such as saltatory versus gradual development of locomotion. Such findings may be relevant to the question of whether the concepts of a specific theory are useful, but they have no relevance to *model* discontinuity. As H. Werner (1957) pointed out, qualitative changes may become distinct gradually.

In a similar vein, model discontinuity is not a denial of continuity at all levels. At the theoretical level, where general functions are introduced, the specification of such functions as principles of ordering change will impose a type of continuity. For example, all structures and functions will form a continuous series leading toward hierarchic integration, equilibration, or genital maturity. Or, at empirical levels, we may find a continuity in the sense of a gradual transition from one behavior to another without any observed gaps in this transition. In either case, from this model position it is continuity in the context of discontinuity, that is, in the context of the assertion that later forms are not reducible to earlier forms.

From the reactive organism model, and its corollary elementarism, all change is strictly continuous in the sense of being reducible to (i.e., predictable from) earlier states. Apparently novel behavioral forms turn out upon analysis to be results of antecedent events. In the case of motivation, for example, when this position is translated into theory, adult goals can be viewed as secondary or learned drives, which upon analysis are seen to "serve as a facade behind which the functions of underlying innate drives are hidden [Dollard & Miller, 1950, p. 32]." Developmental change, then, can involve only *apparently* emergent qualitative differences, such as that distinguishing the behavior of a mediating child from the behavior of a nonmediating child in the discriminative-shift problems. What looks like emergence is actually predictable from the history of the child, that is, from knowledge of his interactions with the environment and his basic response (operating) characteristics. Furthermore, the same theoretical principles remain applicable throughout the developmental period.

The concepts of "level of organization" (discontinuity) and "continuity" introduced in this section provide the model rationale according to which various theories either do or do not incorporate a concept of stages as a basic theoretical category. We may turn to this issue as our final corollary model issue.

5. *The Issue of Stages*

Kessen (1962) has suggested several uses of the term "stage," from its literary-evocative usage (e.g., "The child is in the chimpanzee stage."), to stage as a paraphrase for age and for observations (e.g., "Johnny is in the negativistic stage."), to its use as a theoretical construct. While recognizing these various usages, we are here concerned with whether the model which one accepts requires that his theory introduce stage as a basic theoretical concept or whether the accepted model leads to rejection of the introduction of stage as basic.

Within the active organism model, change is in structure-function relationships or in organization. As organization changes to the extent that new system properties emerge (new structures and functions) and become operational, we speak of a new level of organization which exhibits a basic discontinuity with the previous level.

Theories which accept the active organism model will logically begin with an acceptance of levels of organization. This will then be translated into a theoretical concept of stage. Stage will then derive its specific meaning from other theoretical terms in the particular theory. Thus, for example, H. Werner, Erikson, and Piaget all logically begin with an acceptance of levels of organization and each translates this into a specific theoretical concept of stage in accordance with the particular aims and content of the rest of his theory.

There is, then, within the context of the active organism model, a necessary relationship between model "level of organization" and theoretical "stage." Recognition of this clarifies several problems concerning the application and understanding of theory. One example is the problem of the relevance of empirical data to the theoretical concept of stage. B. Kaplan (1966) has suggested that stages as theoretical concepts have value independently of whether or not they define empirical sequences of behavior. Kohlberg (1968) noted Kaplan's position but suggested that "it is extremely important to test whether a set of theoretical stages does meet . . . empirical criteria [p. 1022]." The apparent conflict between these two positions is resolved when it is recognized that while both are employing the active organism model, Kaplan is making a model statement concerning levels of organization which is not open to empirical assessment, and Kohlberg is referencing a specific set of stages defined by a particular theory (i.e., Piaget's stages). We may empirically question whether Piaget's specific stages are the appropriate representations of the development of intellectual functioning, but we cannot empirically question that there are some stages as defined by model levels of organization.

A second example of the value of understanding the relationship between levels of organization and stages concerns the independence of theories which accept such a distinction from those which do not, that is, the independence of active organism based theories and reactive organism based theories. This problem was also discussed earlier with reference to holism. In the present context, it must be recognized that the translation of levels of organization into theory as stages means that "stage" is a central and basic category for the theory. To ignore this status and treat stage as subsidiary or unimportant is to do violence to the logical basis and logical independency of the theory. Thus, for example, when Berlyne (1966) stated that it is "a serious misunderstanding to think that existence of stages is an essential part of what Piaget has to tell us [p. 73]," he was committing what may be termed an "error of assimilation." That is, he was attempting to assimilate Piaget's theory into general behavior theory by displacing a concept from its central position in one model to a derived status appropriate to another model.

Turning generally to the reactive organism model, it should be obvious that given the position of strict continuity there is no logically necessary basis for the introduction of a concept of "stage" into theory. When stage has been introduced at all, it has been conceptualized as ancillary to the basic theory. Thus, for example, stage is viewed as a convenient and conventional summary description, or as an empirical law, or most recently (Bijou, 1968) as naturalistic-empirical phenomena based on "empirically defined biological, physical and social interactions [p. 423]." Regardless of the specific formulation, stage defined from the reactive organism model has a different status and value from stage defined from the active organism model.

V. SUMMARY AND CONCLUSIONS

Our basic aim in this paper has been to demonstrate that pretheoretical models have a pervasive effect upon theory construction. Theories built upon radically different models are logically independent and cannot be assimilated to each other. They reflect representations of different ways of looking at the world and as such are incompatible in their implications. Different world views involve different understanding of what is *knowledge* and hence of the meaning of *truth*. Therefore, synthesis is, at best, confusing.

Theories built upon the same model may be considered a *family of theories*. They may differ in content (e.g., Piaget's focus on intellectual development and Erikson's focus on social-personality development) or on specific theoretical issues (e.g., Chomsky vs. Piaget concerning how much structure is to be initially assumed), but these differences will either be compatible or resolvable. This will not be the case *across* different families of theories, because of their different presuppositions.

Our analysis of "corollary model issues" could and, for a complete picture of categorical determination, should be extended to include model implications for specific research strategies. Some of these implications have been hinted at, but a complete elaboration would go beyond the scope of the present paper.

We may conclude with the point made at the beginning of this paper. The search for a common language in psychology is a search for common models, not a case of assimilating different theoretical concepts to each other.

GENERAL
METHODOLOGY

CHAPTER 6

Methodology and Research Strategy in the Study of Developmental Change

JOACHIM F. WOHLWILL

CLARK UNIVERSITY
WORCESTER, MASSACHUSETTS

ABSTRACT

This paper treats selected methodological issues arising in developmental research, starting from the premise that the analysis of the characteristics of the function relating variation in response to age belongs at the focus of developmental research. It examines the possibilities for utilizing selected aspects of such functions as dependent variables, and shows the dependence of this type of analysis on the level of measurement utilized in assessing the behavioral variable. Scalogram-analytic approaches to constructing developmental scales are reviewed. The distinction between qualitative and quantitative change is given particular emphasis, and the limitations of attempts to translate the former into the latter are pointed out. The paper proceeds to a consideration of the place of the longitudinal method in developmental research, and to the problems of design involved in separating out effects of chronological age from secular shifts associated with historical time.

The latter half of the paper is devoted to an examination of modes of descriptive analysis of developmental change, to a treatment of general problems arising in the correlational study of the patterning of developmental change for two or more variables, and to a discussion of the assessment of stability of behavior over the course of development, as part of the more general problem of the study of individual differences in development.

I. INTRODUCTION:
THE AGE VARIABLE IN DEVELOPMENTAL RESEARCH

Treatments of methodological problems in developmental psychology abound, yet systematic attempts to examine the methodological implications of the questions and issues which are the concern of developmental investigators are comparatively rare. The reason for this anomalous state of affairs is not difficult to find. Comprehensive discussions of methodological techniques and approaches by developmental psychologists have, for the most part, been undertaken from an eclectic orientation, with little if any attempt made to define or delimit the province of the developmentalist, much less to formulate a coherent theory or point of view that might give direction to the treatment of methodological issues. On the other hand, developmental theorists who have presented the most clearly articulated points of view *vis-à-vis* developmental problems—notably Piaget and Werner and their associates—have given little thought to the implications for methodology of their theoretical positions and the issues of research design arising in the investigation of developmental problems.

The present review will not attempt to duplicate or even supplement the coverage of general problems of methodology and technique in child-psychological or aging research that are already available (e.g., J. E. Anderson, 1954; Birren, 1959b; Mussen, 1960). Rather it will focus on a selected set of general issues of research strategy arising in developmental research, starting not from a specific theory about development, but from a particular, possibly idiosyncratic, point of view about the nature of the age variable and the major paradigms of research which make up the developmental enterprise.

The central thesis which underlies the treatment of these questions which is to be presented in this chapter is that the investigation of changes in behavior with age, which constitute the main province of the developmental psychologist, is analogous to the study of other changes in behavior taking place along a temporal dimension, such as sensory or perceptual adaptation and forgetting. Accordingly, the age variable is not to be construed as an independent variable at all, but rather as a dimension along which change is to be studied. This view leads us to conceive of age as forming part of the dependent variable, that is, the subject matter of developmental studies is defined as behavior *change* taking place as the individual grows from birth to old age, or more particularly the properties and characteristics of these changes and the variables governing them.

The rationale for this conception of the age variable is presented in greater detail in a paper being published separately (Wohlwill, 1970). Let us point out three major consequences of this definition of the age variable which are of interest for discussion of methodology and research design.

a. Since age is not an independent variable (no more than time is in studies of forgetting), questions of causation do not arise with respect to it, nor is it to be construed as a shorthand for other variables supposedly determining the behavior changes observed to occur "as a function of age."

b. The basic data of the developmental psychologist relate, explicitly or implicitly, to the *developmental function* which characterizes or describes the changes taking place with age for any particular behavioral dimension. This means that the focus should be not on absolute amounts or types of behavior at a single point in time, but on the form and properties of this function, whether qualitatively or quantitatively defined.

c. Longitudinal analysis is the method par excellence of the developmental psychologist, and, in many cases, the only one that will permit the requisite detailed analysis of developmental functions.

Rather than elaborating further on the points just stated, let us proceed to apply the approach which we have suggested to the present review of methodology, in the expectation that these points will become clearer and more compelling when seen in the context of the problems to which they are pertinent.

II. THE FORMULATION AND ASSESSMENT OF THE DEPENDENT VARIABLE IN DEVELOPMENTAL STUDIES

A. The Concept of the Developmental Function

The term "developmental function" is intended to refer to the form or mode of the relationship between an individual's age and the changes occurring in his responses on some specified dimension of behavior over the course of his life. As just noted, it is the specification of this function, and the variables affecting it, that is considered to be the primary task of the developmental psychologist.

The definition just stated, however simple-minded and preformal, needs elaboration in at least three respects. First, what is meant by *form or mode* of the relationship? These represent the basic, generalizable characteristics of the function, varying from statements of order or sequence, for purely qualitative variables, through statements concerning direction of change, or general shape of the function, to specifications of the form of the function in terms of a mathematical equation. Thus, with respect to the motor sequence of development, the developmental function would consist of the determination of the discrete steps which make up this sequence, in their appropriate order, coupled with at least approximate indications of the points or intervals on the age continuum corresponding to the appearance of each step. For most quantitative dimensions, the function would refer to the overall pattern of change (e.g., monotonically increasing; inverted U-shaped, etc.), together with an indication of the approximate age periods within which each differentiable phase of the function is contained. Finally, for certain limited kinds of dimensions, notably those of physical growth, and conceivably certain psychological ones such as intelligence or vocabulary, it may be possible to specify more precisely, in mathematical or graphic form, the exact shape of the function, or at least the particular family of curves (Gompertz, logistic, polynomial of the nth degree, etc.) to which it belongs.

A second point requiring comment is that the definition of the function is *specific to a given individual.* Much of the criticism leveled at the use of the age variable in psychological research (e.g., Kessen, 1960) has centered on the failure of age to predict level of response on behavioral dimensions, due to the ubiquitous individual differences in behavior found at any given age level. This objection ceases to apply once we agree to treat age, not as an independent variable, but simply as a temporal dimension along which change in behavior occurs; for any given individual, furthermore, we may postulate that there is a determinate function describing the particular changes occurring over the course of his development. The assumption is that corresponding functions for different individuals will have some overall communality, but they need not be identical in every detail; more important, even the general characteristics may not become apparent without reference to the individual functions. It is interesting to note that this focus on the individual is common in other realms of psychological investigation, in which, however nomothetic in conception and intent, the research involves detailed analysis of functional relationship between behavior and such dimensions as time (adaptation), trials (learning curves) or stimulus magnitude (psychophysics).

A third question raised by the definition of "developmental function" relates to the expression *on some specified dimension.* In effect, the definition presupposes that the task of dimensionalizing behavioral development has been carried out and that a limited number of dimensions have been isolated which are, to some degree, situationally independent and generalizable and which lend themselves to the study of developmental change in the manner being suggested here. Verbal fluency, conservation ability, and selective attention may be suggested as possibly viable instances of such dimensions; on the other hand, dependency, susceptibility to the Poggendorff illusion, and scores on the Seashore musical abilities test would presumably not qualify, being either too clearly multidimensional or too stimulus- or task-specific to be usefully approached in this manner.

B. Problems of Measurement

A concern with the specification of developmental functions further presupposes that certain conditions have been met with regard to the measurement of the behavior changes in question, these conditions varying according to the degree of specificity desired for the statement of the function. Perhaps the most critical aspect of this problem relates to the need for scales that are indifferently applicable to the total portion of the life cycle over which changes are to be recorded. For instance, there is a basic discontinuity in our information about the course of the development of the constancies in infancy and that from early childhood onwards. The reason is obvious: The psychophysical methods on which we have relied for our data on developmental changes in constancy are not readily applicable with preverbal children, and even if some method could be devised to quantify nonverbal indices of constancy, as in some of the animal research, the results obtained would of necessity have little comparability to those obtained at older ages.

The "applicability" of a scale has to be understood, of course, to be a joint function of the attributes of the task utilized—e.g., its suitability for eliciting meaningful responses across the age spectrum—and of the measuring instrument employed—particularly its power to discriminate among individuals over all portions of the age spectrum. Take the case of the Stroop test, for instance, which measures the degree to which the meaning of a word which is incongruous with one of its salient stimulus characteristics (e.g., the word "blue" printed in red) interferes with the naming of that attribute (e.g., the response "red"). Here the scale of measurement is the time variable; it is, in the literal sense, applicable at all ages, and it would be easy to obtain measurable responses from 4-year-old children on this task—assuming they had mastered the vocabulary of color words. But since they would (presumably) be unable to read, the resulting measure would not be a measure of interference for them. On the other hand, there are cases where the measuring scale itself presents a problem, by failing to discriminate between individuals who fall outside of a certain range of ages. This would be the case particularly when a task becomes either so difficult or so easy that the measures obtained from it fail to yield information in regard to age changes. For instance, a measure of the number of errors made in discriminating up-down reversals would quickly approach an asymptote of 100% correct beyond the age of about six years; conversely, a measure of the number of indirect questions asked in playing a game of twenty questions would be unlikely to differentiate below that age.

One strategy for dealing with this problem consists, basically, in using *a varying set* of tasks, constructed so as to reveal differential amounts of the variable whose developmental function is under investigation. For instance, in the example just referred to, it might be possible to obtain sensitive indices of up-down reversal discrimination all the way up to adulthood by using stimuli sufficiently complex—e.g., random nonsense shapes of increasing numbers of sides. (Or consider certain works of nonrepresentational modern art!) The problem now becomes one of scaling or measurement, in that we are no longer dealing with responses to a single constant stimulus or task, but rather to a series of stimuli or tasks presumably varying in difficulty; more generally, both stimuli and criterial responses are made to vary according to the subject's position on the behavioral dimension. The best example of this approach is provided, of course, by the field of standardized tests, such as the Raven matrices, for instance.

Curiously, the measurement considerations entailed in arriving at a single score as a measure of an individual's ability on such a test, by taking the number of correct responses he gives to such a set of items, have rarely been made explicit. Since any given score may represent varying combinations of items passed, each of which may be presumed to measure different amounts of the ability, such a score cannot be treated as isomorphically related to any determinate value on the dimension of ability, or whatever, assumed to underlie the items. The result is, of course, that the particular quantitative characteristics of a developmental function (or any other function) obtained from its use have to be interpreted with great caution, though in a purely pragmatic sense it may well be of value in revealing gross amount of change along a dimension.

Eventually we may look forward to the application of more sophisticated scaling methods to allow us to assess an individual's status on a developmental dimension in a manner such as to ensure not only comparability of content for the different parts of the dimension, but at the same time a continuous scale along which developmental change can be charted. Workers in the field of cross-cultural research have had to face up to the same problem. Berrien (1968) and L. V. Gordon (1968) in particular have concerned themselves with the place of construct-validity principles in constructing measuring instruments that would provide comparability in the assessment of a variable across different cultures. Their discussion is certainly pertinent to our problem, but in developmental psychology the comparability question becomes confounded with the continuity question. Postulating a unitary dimension across the age span under investigation presupposes that there are no major discontinuities in the development of the behavior in question, such as there obviously are in the assessment of intelligence when we move from infancy to childhood. Ways of checking on this assumption, and of determining the stability of dimensions over age, are discussed from a factor-analytic standpoint in Chapter 7 by Nesselroade. At the same time we may anticipate the discussion of developmental scaling to follow, by citing Bentler's (1969b) method of monotonicity analysis, which promises to be particularly valuable for the purpose of arriving at unidimensional developmental scales.

C. Level of Measurement as a Determinant of Developmental-Functional Statements

It is apparent that both in degree and in kind, statements of developmental function will vary according to the measurement characteristics of the response scale utilized. In this respect, four types may be distinguished, involving, respectively, (1) equal-interval scales, (2) ordinal scales obtained through stimulus-scaling procedures, (3) response-derived ordinal scales, and (4) nominal scales.

1. *Equal-Interval Scales*

This category is intended to include ratio scales, i.e., those for which an absolute zero exists. There are, in fact, very few cases in psychology of equal-interval scales lacking an absolute zero—with the possible exception of some scales of sensory magnitudes, or errors of illusion, which may extend to either side of the zero point. Where equal-interval scales are available, the possibility exists in principle of specifying the form of the developmental function in mathematical terms; how useful or meaningful such attempts will prove in practice is another question, which depends on a variety of factors, such as the reliability of the measures, the "robustness" of the function under variations in task-related variables (stimuli, wording of instructions, etc.), and of course the magnitude of the changes in response associated with age.

2. *Ordinal Scales Based on Stimulus-Scaling Methods*

Scales made up of a set of response categories which are either intrinsically ordinal (as in the case of a rating scale, or responses to stimuli or tests constructed to represent differing amounts of complexity, abstraction, etc.) or have been scaled by application of one of the stimulus-scaling methods (i.e., those falling into Quadrants III and IV, in Coombs's (1960) schema) permit the specification of the form of developmental functions in gross terms, i.e., direction of change, monotonicity, etc. An example of the use of this type of scale in developmental research is found in an investigation by H. P. Lewis (1963), who on the basis of drawings made by children between kindergarten and grade VIII to represent various three-dimensional objects or configurations constructed a set of five prototypes to represent five levels of adequacy in the representation of depth. Data were then collected to indicate the same children's *preferences*, that is, choices of the prototype which they thought to be "best." This enabled the author to compare the level of spatial representation present in the children's own drawings with their preferred level as shown in their choices of the prototypes.

The developmental use of this type of scale is much less common than one might suppose. Its rarity probably is attributable to the difficulty of finding sets of responses which can be scaled along a dimension conceptually independent of age and which is still applicable along a reasonably large segment of the age spectrum. A particular problem with most rating scales, limiting their usefulness in this latter sense, is the lack of any absolute anchoring of the points on the scale—e.g., the behavioral referent for a response judged as "somewhat independent," or "displays marked leadership qualities," is apt to vary both in amount and, equally important, in kind from one age level to another.

3. Ordinal Scales Based on Response-Scaling Methods or Empirically Determined Developmental Sequences

Where scales are constructed by application of scalogram-analysis methods, utilizing individuals who themselves vary along an age dimension, it is apparent that we can no longer speak of a developmental function, since the order among the responses is not independently defined, that is, is itself derived from the response patterns of the respondents, which in turn are determined by their position on the developmental continuum. Accordingly, the only datum of interest is whether the items and the subjects jointly define some underlying continuum. The response scale itself remains an essentially nominal one, becoming ordered only by virtue of the order of the respondents along the age dimension. Consequently no function relating an individual's position on the scale to age can be determined; to the extent that the term "developmental function" is applicable here at all, it would consist of the specification of the order of appearance of the individual responses, combined with the age of their appearance in an individual, or the mean age in a group. The basic difference between this case and the preceding one is illustrated in Figure 1, representing the motor sequence, as given by Shirley (1933b), juxtaposed to data from the aforementioned study by Lewis, indicating the level of spatial representation preferred by a plurality of the children at each age (i.e., grade). To what extent this latter graph presents an accurate picture of the form of the age changes actually occurring for this type of judgment (in the sense of corresponding to the shifts which the choices of any given child would show if studied longitudinally) is an open question, but at least the question is meaningful and empirically answerable. In the case of Shirley's data, on the other hand, the inverted S-shaped pattern in which the sequence is shown is, of course, purely

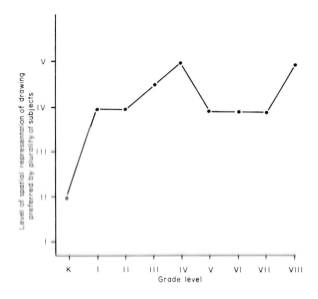

Figure 1a. Example of developmental changes along independently scaled ordinal scale. (Data from H. P. Lewis, 1963.)

Figure 1b. Examples of developmental sequence without independent scaling: Shirley's motor sequence. (From Shirley, 1933b, Frontispiece. Reproduced by permission of University of Minnesota Press.)

arbitrary—a straight line, or any topologically equivalent configuration, would have done equally well.

4. *Nominal Scales*

Where the points on a behavioral variable consist of a set of nominally scaled responses which do not conform to a developmental sequence, the term "developmental function" ceases to have any determinate meaning. This can be seen easily by noting the impossibility of defining an individual's movement along this variable in such a way that one could meaningfully talk, for instance, of the time taken to change from one point on the scale to another (as one can in the previous instance). About all that one could do with this type of data would be to tabulate incidence figures, showing the frequency with which any given type of response appears at any given age level.

Developmental psychology is replete with data of this kind, such as those on developmental changes in children's fears, types of humor, causal reasoning, preference for games, etc. In some of these instances there is a tacit assumption that these categories do in fact represent an ordered set, but a priori criteria for ordering them are rarely made explicit. One exception to this rule is provided by Kohlberg's (1964) scale of moral reasoning, which provides a good example of a shift from a nominal scale to a stimulus-scaled ordinal one, since the levels on this scale were defined by Kohlberg in terms independent of age or development. They have, in fact, been effectively applied to adult populations.

D. The Scaling of Qualitative Developmental Data

1. *Scalogram Analysis and Its Limitations*

The application of scalogram methods to the study of developmental sequences has gained considerable popularity, notably in the investigation of the development of concepts and abilities. This research conforms to the cumulative model of scaling, epitomized by Guttman's scalogram analysis technique and its derivatives (cf. Torgerson, 1958). Although employed to seeming advantage in a number of instances the approach has definite limitations, some of which have been brought out in a perceptive discussion of the problem by Kofsky (1963; cf. also Wohlwill, 1960b). These are basically of three types.

First, there is a statistical problem, owing to the fact that in any set of items varying in difficulty level or popularity, a considerable degree of scalability will be built in on a pure chance basis. This is brought out by the typical size of the chance-reproducibility coefficient, as calculated by a procedure such as B. F. Green's (1956); where this coefficient is as high as .85, as it often is (cf. Wohlwill, 1960b), the fact that the observed reproducibility is significantly higher, or that the index of consistency (which is a function of both; cf. B. F.

Green, 1956) may attain to the somewhat arbitrary standard of .50 stipulated by Green to indicate scalability, ceases to loom very impressive. The problem could be alleviated by resort to more stringent measures of scalability, such as that of the proportion of subjects exhibiting perfect scale types, or possibly the proportion of perfect scale types to total number of different response patterns (cf. Milholland, 1955), but these have not been employed in the developmental literature, at least.

Second, the determinate, unidimensional model of development which is implied when Guttman-type scalogram methods are applied to developmental data requires that we make two very strong assumptions whose validity is frequently questionable: (a) that all systematic variance among the set of responses under study is attributable to a single dimension, and (b) that to each individual corresponds a determinate position on the scale defined by the responses, such that those responses falling below his position will have a 100% probability of emission, and those above will have a 0% probability of emission.

Where, as almost invariably happens, an empirical set of data fails to conform to this ideal any of three conclusions may be warranted: (1) The model does fit the data, but errors of measurement give rise to error patterns and thus account for the deviation from perfect scalability. This conclusion can never be proven, but may be warranted, as long as reproducibility is high. (2) The model is deficient in its determinacy assumption. As brought out in the section on measurement, developmental change during a transition period between stages is best conceived of as a probabilistic affair; thus where a fine-grained analysis of the steps of a developmental sequence is desired, some considerable departure from perfect scalability is probably to be expected. (3) The model is deficient in its unidimensionality assumption. This has probably been the most typical conclusion drawn from lack of scalability of a set of responses, and techniques of multidimensional scaling have prospered as a result. They have, however, found little application thus far to the study of developmental problems, possibly because the developmental-sequence notion was not congenial to it; furthermore, the problem of conceptualizing developmental change simultaneously along two independent dimensions has not been faced up to.

The third of the limitations of scalogram technique has to do with the problem of identifying the behavioral dimension underlying a set of items that has been found to be scalable. A purely empirically determined scalable set of items which does not have some face validity as representing a homogeneous scale is not particularly useful—a scale, for instance, made up of the following items which would undoubtedly scale to a highly satisfactory approximation: crawling, saying "mama," walking down a set of stairs, riding a tricycle, counting backwards, playing checkers, doing long division, driving a car. If the latent continuum recovered by a set of scalable response patterns is to represent anything more than age itself, in other words, the scale must have some internal validity as a measure of some definable dimension. The most effective way of providing for such validity is to construct the scale to represent some postulated dimension of development, and to employ scalogram analysis mainly for purposes of verification of scalability. This point ties in with the arguments made in the discussion on measurement in favor of response-independent as opposed to response-inferred scaling methods.

2. *Disjunctive versus Cumulative Models in the Developmental Scaling of Items*

The discussion thus far has concerned itself exclusively with applications of the cumulative model of scaling, which is predicated on the assumption that an individual will respond to (or pass) all items whose scale position is below his own. This model fits the case of the development of responses which measure abilities, skills, concepts, and the like, where it is reasonable to assume that previously mastered responses are retained in the individual's repertoire of available skills as he moves up the developmental scale.

This model is to be contrasted to the disjunctive one (also variously designated as *point*, or *nonmonotonic*; cf. Torgerson, 1958), in which the assumption is made that any individual responds only to items which are at or near his own position on the scale. The classical Thurstone attitude scale, in which the subject is asked to pick out those statements which he agrees with most, is a good illustration of the application of this model, though Thurstone himself does not seem to have concerned himself with the scalability question as such. The model is of interest for developmental psychologists in at least two kinds of situations: in the scaling or dimensionalizing of data on interests, preference, and the like, and in the scaling of observational data, in which typical or dominant modes of response are recorded, rather than all of the responses that the individual might be capable of giving. (For instance, creeping, crawling, standing erect with support, and walking would be an example of a series of items which would conform to the disjunctive model if studied observationally, while it would represent a cumulative scale if the investigator were to determine which of these responses the infant or child was capable of giving.)

There has been very little work on the problems of scaling and of measurement of reproducibility which arise in the application of this model. Wohlwill (1963b) and Leik and Mathews (1968) have considered approaches to the determination of item order and the derivation of indices of scalability for data conforming to this model. The former is based on an unpublished paper by Mosteller, in which a scalar value on the latent dimension is attributed to each item, and an analytic, iterative procedure is outlined, yielding an item order and set of values which satisfies the criterion of minimizing the intra-S response variance, i.e., the spread of the scale values of the items endorsed by each S. Leik and Mathews adopt a less formal approach to the derivation of item order, which should, however, prove satisfactory for practical purposes, though it only yields an ordinal scale, as opposed to the equal-interval scaling made possible by Mosteller's procedure. Note that either method may run into difficulties in finding a determinate order among the items where scalability is low; for this and other more substantive reasons, the model would be more useful— particularly in application to developmental research—if an independently derived a priori order among the items can be stipulated. Once an order among the items has been established, the measurement of reproducibility is quite straightforward; an index for this purpose is given in Wohlwill (1963b), while Leik and Mathews (1968) further provide an index of scalability which takes chance-reproducibility into account. Their procedure, incidentally, does not require the number of items endorsed or responded to by each S to be constant (provided it is greater than one); this can be a notable advantage in applications of the method to observational data, where different children may exhibit differing numbers of the behaviors comprising the scale.

How useful this model will prove in practice in application to developmental data remains to be seen. Paradoxically, it is most likely to prove successful where it is least needed, i.e., in situations where the alternative, that of direct determination or verification of the developmental sequencing of the responses through longitudinal study is most easily applied, namely in the study of psychomotor development in infancy. As a matter of fact, the closest approach to data conforming to this model known to this writer comes from McGraw's (1943) observational data in this area, as illustrated in the developmental record of *one* of her subjects reproduced in Figure 2.[1]

3. Variants of Scalogram-Analytic Methods

Two further scaling methods, closely related to scalogram techniques, may be mentioned in passing, since they appear to have some relevance to the analysis of developmental data, and possibly to the construction of unidimensional scales. The first is Loevinger's (1947) method of homogeneous tests. It assesses the homogeneity, or unidimensionality, of a test as a composite of the homo-geneities of the associations of the responses to all pairs of items (i.e., the prevalence of +— over —+ patterns, when items are arranged in order of increasing difficulty). The procedure has the advantage of permitting the

---

[1] For illustrative purposes, we may cite the value of the reproducibility coefficient for the data given in Figure 2, determined from the 18 observation times at which more than one response was exhibited, by means of Wohlwill's (1963a) formula. (In the case of the patterns with three responses, the lowest was arbitrarily omitted.) This value was .947. For the same set of 18 patterns, Leik and Mathews' (1968) scalability index is .871. The writer knows of no other application of these indices to data on ontogenetic development; a pilot attempt to use it with data on age changes in preference for games, over the range from 8 to 14 years, yielded a reproducibility coefficient of only .37.

Prone   Progression

Name	Age in Days Observation	Movies	A	B	C	D	E	F	G	H	I
Briggs, James		2	+	−	−	−	−	−	−	−	−
	11		+	−	−	−	−	−	−	−	−
	18		+	−	−	−	−	−	−	−	−
	24		+	−	−	−	−	−	−	−	−
		30	+	+	−	−	−	−	−	−	−
	38		+	−	−	−	−	−	−	−	−
	44		+	−	−	−	−	−	−	−	−
	52		+	−	−	−	−	−	−	−	−
		62	+	+	−	−	−	−	−	−	−
	65		+	+	−	−	−	−	−	−	−
	74		−	+	−	−	−	−·	−	−	−
	81		−	+	−	−	−	−	−	−	−
	89		+	+	−	−	−	−	−	−	−
		95	−	+	+	−	−	−	−	−	−
	102		−	+	−	−	−	−	−	−	−
	107		−	−	+	−	−	−	−	−	−
	118		−	+	+	+	−	−	−	−	−
		124	−	−	+	−	−	−	−	−	−
	128		−	−	+	−	−	−	−	−	−
	135		−	−	+	−	−	−	−	−	−
	142		−	−	+	−	−	−	−	−	−
	153		−	−	+	−	+	−	−	−	−
		156	−	−	−	+	−	−	−	−	−
	167		−	−	+	−	+	−	−	−	−
	170		−	−	+	−	+	−	−	−	−
	177		−	−	+	−	+	−	−	−	−
		186	−	−	−	+	+	+	−	−	−
	191		−	−	−	+	+	−	+	−	−
	193		−	−	−	−	−	+	−	−	−
	199		−	−	−	+	+	−	+	−	−
		202	−	−	−	+	+	+	−	−	−
		205	−	−	−	−	−	+	−	−	−
	213		−	−	−	−	−	+	+	−	−
	220		−	−	−	−	−	+	+	+	−
		221	−	−	−	−	−	+	+	−	−
	227		−	−	−	−	−	−	−	+	−
		229	−	−	−	−	−	−	+	−	−
		230	−	−	−	−	−	−	−	+	−
	235		−	−	−	−	−	−	+	+	−
	237		−	−	−	−	−	−	−	+	−
	243		−	−	−	−	−	−	−	+	−
		250	−	−	−	−	−	−	−	+	−

Figure 2. Record of response types exhibited by one child at different ages in the development of prone progression. (From McGraw-Hill, 1943, p. 32. Reproduced by permission of Hafner Publishing Co.)

calculation of homogeneity values for individual items, thus affording a sound criterion for eliminating items from a scale; it further avoids the problem of chance reproducibility which arises with Guttman scales. In all other respects, however, it shares in the limitations and drawbacks of the latter.

Finally, brief mention may be made of Bentler's (1969b) method of monotonicity analysis, which represents an extension of the methods of Guttman and Loevinger to the case of relationships among responses to items which are assumed to represent a space of n latent ordinal dimensions. It is a close cousin of factor analysis, but without requiring any assumptions about linearity of relationships or making use of metric information. The coefficient of monotonicity is, in effect, a rank-order correlation coefficient; applied to binary-choice (e.g., pass-fail, agree-disagree) data, it is closely related to *phi*. The unit of analysis is not, however, a pattern of responses for a given S (such as those which constitute the usual contingency table or scalogram matrix), but rather the pattern of *differences* within all possible pairs of Ss, considered over two or more items.

More particularly, Bentler's coefficient of monotonicity is a function of the ratio of the probability of concordant relationships to the probability of discordant relationships, where "concordance" refers to like-signed differences between pairs of observations (i.e., Ss) on two ordinally-scaled variables or items, and "discordance" refers to differences that are opposite in sign. (As an example, given two individuals, A and B, responding to two binary-choice items, X and Y, a concordant relationship would mean that for both items, either A passed while B failed or vice versa; a discordant relationship means that A passed and B failed on item X, and the reverse held true for item Y.) What this means is that Bentler's model does not scale individuals directly, but rather searches for the minimal number of dimensions which can reproduce the differences among his Ss in their responses to a given set of items.

Monotonicity analysis, though not as yet applied to concrete data, developmental or otherwise, avoids the deterministic feature of Guttman's scalogram technique; it is neutral, furthermore, in regard to the existence of any particular functional relationship among a set of items. It is thus less appropriate to the determination of sequential invariance for some postulated developmental sequence than to the verification of dimensional homogeneity (or departure from it) of responses to a set of stimuli or tasks assumed to represent a developmental continuum.

E. Qualitative versus Quantitative Change as a Problem in the Measurement of Developmental Functions

From the standpoint of methodology, the still hotly debated issue of the qualitative as opposed to quantitative character of development can be looked at as a measurement question, i.e., whether or not behavior is measurable along a quantitative scale. This is an oversimplification, however, to the extent that it ignores the appropriateness of the measuring instrument as a measure of the developmental variable. In particular, one frequently finds attempts to apply quantitative measures to variables which are by definition qualitative, and the results will generally reflect the artificiality of this procedure.

The measurement of conservation (Piaget, 1950) provides a good illustration of this point. It is a qualitative variable, by definition—i.e., the categories of nonconservation, transitional, and conservation represent discrete categories or modes of response, as much as do crawling, standing erect, and walking. Attempts to place them on a quantitative scale have usually taken one of three forms: (a) Shifting from the individual to the group, incidence data are obtained, indicating the proportion of subjects in a given group falling into each category. (b) By constructing a set of items to measure the behavior in question, number of correct responses are totaled, or a scoring system is devised to take account of intermediate level responses. (c) Occasionally an attempt is made to shift to a completely different quantitative index, such as latency.

Each of the above approaches runs into difficulties. The first is the most frequently used, and the least controversial, but the results obtained refer to attributes of a sample, rather than of an individual. Since the psychological changes reflected in the acquisition of conservation take place within individuals, and presumably at different rates and times in different individuals, group incidence data cannot be used to provide a picture of the developmental function, notably as regards the abruptness or smoothness of the acquisition process—as the qualitative-quantitative question is so frequently, though inappropriately, formulated. Even less valid is the use of such group-incidence data to answer questions concerning differential *rates* of the acquisition of different concepts, in terms of the interval within which there is a change from 0% to 100% (e.g., Vinh-Bang, 1959).

The second approach has the virtue of retaining the individual as a focus; however, the assumption that by sampling from a universe of responses of a given type, such as conservation, a more quantitative, i.e., continuous, picture of development will be obtained is unwarranted. This is apparent already from a scrutiny of the *distribution* of the responses obtained. Few present-day investigators are in the habit of examining their data carefully to get an accurate picture of the form of frequency distributions; the result, at least in this instance, can be quite revealing, however. In the case of conservation responses, the distribution is quite generally strongly bimodal, or highly skewed, depending on whether a sufficiently large range of developmental levels is sampled to include subjects at all levels. This has been found, not only by the present author (Wohlwill, 1960b; Wohlwill, Fusaro, & Devoe, 1969) but even more dramatically by Bentler (1969a), who finds that distributions of scores on 12-item tests of conservation take the form of Figure 3.

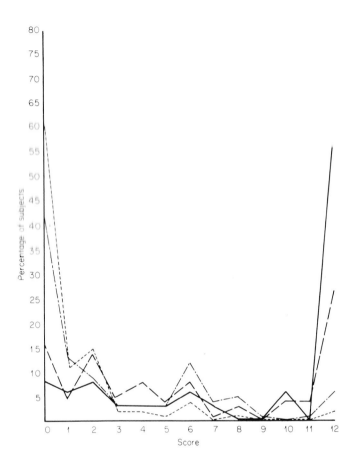

$(--)\ 7\frac{1}{2}$ - 8 $(N = 36)$; $(-\ -)\ 6\frac{1}{2}$ - 7 $(N = 73)$; $(---)\ 5\frac{1}{2}$ - 6
$(N = 78)$; $(---)\ 4\frac{1}{2}$ - 5 $(N = 8)$.

Figure 3. Frequency distribution of scores on 12-item test of conservation. (From Bentler, 1969a. Reprinted with author's permission.)

Bentler interprets these data to indicate continuity of development from nonconservation to conservation, based on the even distribution of transitional subjects all along the scale from 1 to 11 correct responses. This argument is debatable; there is no a priori reason why transitional subjects should fall in any particular portion of the scale. But the essential finding remains the marked tendency for cases to pile up at the extremes of the scale, even in groups representing a very limited span of ages. It should be apparent that with distributions such as these, the use of quantitative procedures taken from psychometrics and test theory—e.g., calculation of reliability coefficients, and intercorrelating scores with other measures such as achievement test scores, IQ, and the like—is suspect (cf. Carroll, 1961). Thus Goldschmid and Bentler's (1968) attempt to apply such psychometric techniques to their scale of conservation, utilizing the same data whose distribution is shown in Figure 3, must be viewed with skepticism.

Finally, we may simply refer in passing to the possibility of imposing a quantitative scale on development falling into qualitative categories, by turning to indicators of the strength of response that might be devised. Thus, in the case of a Piagetian concept, Charlesworth and Zahn (1966) have argued for the use of latency of a surprise reaction in the face of an apparent violation of the principle. Similarly, one might be able to use number of trials to extinction (i.e., subject's abandoning the principle upon repeated confrontation with its apparent violation) as a measure of the strength of a concept or principle.

The question of the relative merits of these alternative approaches ultimately must be decided in terms of their respective value in uncovering information about the processes underlying the qualitative changes under investigation. For instance, while it would be easy to quantify the study of the development of locomotion by measuring the speed with which the infant moves through a given space, it is unlikely that we would be helped in our understanding of the way in which this development takes place by adopting such a measure. From this point of view, a variant of the second approach may be suggested, involving an attempt to measure a given individual's *probability* of making a response falling into a particular category and charting the mode of changes in these probability values over the course of the acquisition and consolidation of the response. An attempt to apply such a probability model to the transition process from the preoperational to the operational child (using Piaget's terminology) in the acquisition of conservation concepts has been presented by Flavell and Wohlwill (1969) and applied with some success to data previously reported by Uzgiris (1964). This approach clearly presumes that the response of interest is sampled under a variety of tasks or conditions, so that a probability estimate can be obtained; in contrast to the formally similar test score approach, however, it does not presuppose any continuity in the transition process, nor make any assumption about the nature of the distribution of responses, since probability distributions, in contrast to test score distributions, may take highly nonnormal and even discontinuous forms. Furthermore, conceptually, the probabilistic formulation is more consistent with a basically qualitative phenomenon, and its application is consequently less likely to do violence to the essential nature of the data than other quantitative procedures.

III. THE LONGITUDINAL METHOD:
ITS VALUE AND LIMITATIONS AND SOME COMPROMISE SOLUTIONS

A. The Information Carried by Longitudinal Data

The pros and cons of the longitudinal versus the cross-sectional method, and the problems to be faced in the planning, execution, and administration of longitudinal research, have been discussed at great length in the literature (e.g., J. E. Anderson, 1954; Baltes, 1968b; Dearborn & Rothney, 1941; N. Goldfarb, 1960; H. E. Jones, 1958b; Kessen, 1960; Kodlin & Thompson, 1958). Since many of the arguments on this subject are undoubtedly overly familiar by now, no comprehensive review of them will be presented here. Instead, we will look at this question from the particular point of view of the analysis of developmental functions which is at the core of this chapter.

As long as age is looked at as an ordinary differential variable, and the study of age-related differences in behavior defined as the subject matter of developmental psychology, no particular advantage accrues to the longitudinal method, except for that deriving from the use of a repeated-measurement, as opposed to an independent-groups design, namely greater sensitivity for tests of significance, and opportunity for analyzing individual trends (Baltes, 1968b). Baltes' point in regard to the former of these advantages is worth noting: He points out that the gain in sensitivity from repeated-measurement designs is worthwhile only where age differences are so small as not to be detected from comparisons of independent age groups. For certain purposes, however, the advantage of longitudinal data will be found to be actually proportional to the magnitude of age differences; for instance, where the characteristics of the developmental function are of interest, rather than statistical reliability of age differences, a clear-cut age trend must be presupposed for the benefits of the longitudinal information to be fully realized.

The advantages, as well as the limitations, of the longitudinal method will be considered throughout the remainder of this chapter, in the contexts of the particular questions studied in longitudinal research. In generic terms, there are three types of information which are preserved by longitudinal data. These are, respectively, information as to (a) individual identity, (b) temporal patterning of the developmental changes occurring in a given individual on a particular variable, and (c) patterning of the relationships between variables changing over time in a given individual.

Of these, the first is the least important. It merely indicates the fact that longitudinal data are dependent measures, that is, that they allow us to place individual measurements obtained at time t_1 into one-to-one correspondence with those at time t_2. This dependence has an effect, of course, on tests of

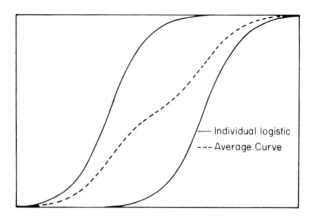

Figure 4. Two logistic curves and their average. In this case, two symmetrical logistics (solid lines), average to give a mean curve (broken line) which has two skew cycles. (From Merrill, 1931, p. 40. Reprinted by permission of Wayne State University Press.)

significance for age differences and on the power of these tests in particular.[2] However, retention of individual-identity information has a further important advantage in age-level comparisons besides decreasing the error estimates in tests of significance: It ensures identity of the population at the various age levels, whereas cross-sectional comparisons not only typically involve cohort differences (cf. Section III, B), but frequently differences in other respects, e.g., between the populations represented by a particular grade school and a particular high school in the same town, or between a sample of college students and a sample of older persons present at a single institution. These are, of course, matters subject to some control, but the practical difficulties in the way of obtaining comparable samples in different age groups over an extended age span are not to be minimized.

The second type of longitudinal information referred to above concerns aspects of the temporal patterning of responses for a given individual—information which is apt to become obscured when group-average data are relied on. Rate of change and, above all, shape of the developmental function are examples of such temporal-pattern data subject to distortion through group averaging. Let us note, first the demonstrations by Estes (1956), Merrill (1931), and Sidman

---

[2] For instance, if we were to analyze a longitudinal set of data covering two points on the age variable, with measures at the two ages correlated only to the extent of .50, and equal variances at the two ages, the standard error of the difference would be reduced by a factor of .7 by taking the repeated measurement information into account. Thus, against an alternate hypothesis of a true difference $= 1.96\sigma_{\bar{x}_1 - \bar{x}_2}$, and for $\alpha = .05$, the power would be increased from .50 to .65. (If the two measures are correlated to the extent of .9, the gain in power would be from .50 to .89.)

(1952) that information with respect to the shape of a growth curve is *not* preserved under averaging, as long as the curve is exponential in form—such as the function common in learning-theoretical work, $y = M(1 - e^{-kx})$, and other similar or more complex functions developed in the study of biological growth (Shock, 1951; von Bertalanffy, 1960). Merrill presents a particularly convincing illustration of such distortion in the case of the logistic curve $y = k/(1 + e^{a+bx})$, which is reproduced in Figure 4. Note that in this instance the composite averaged curve appears more complex than the component individual curves; a more typical result, however, is that averaged curves result in the smoothing out, not only of random irregularities in the data, but of systematic departures from simple form—notably those occasioned by discontinuities in the process represented—so as to lead to a spuriously simple form. This point is shown most convincingly in Shuttleworth's (1939) classical study of the physical growth spurt (cf. Figure 5) (see Van der Vaart, 1953, for a generalized treatment of this question).

In the study of behavioral development this particular problem is probably less serious than it has been considered to be either in the study of learning (e.g., Sidman, 1952) or physical growth (e.g., Tanner, 1951). The data of the developmental psychologist will almost inevitably retain such a considerable amount of error, or indeterminacy, that other types of functions, which may have less rational appeal, but are less susceptible to distortion through averaging will prove fully satisfactory. The general class of polynomial functions of the form $y = a + bx + cx^2 + \ldots + kx^n$ is a case in point. For functions of this type, it has been shown (Estes, 1956; Merrill, 1931) that the mean curve (that drawn through the mean y value corresponding to any given value of x, i.e., to any given age group in a cross-sectional study) is not only equivalent in form to the mean-constant curve (that obtained by fitting the individual records to a set of such polynomials and averaging the corresponding constants thus obtained), but that the actual values of the constants of these two curves are identical.

Finally, turning to the third type of information, concerning intra-individual patterning of relationships among variables over time, we note that there is in this case no substitute for the longitudinal method at all. Wherever we are concerned with relationships between amount or direction of change for two or more variables, or between such change and any other information about the individual, we are necessarily forced to resort to the longitudinal method.

B. The Confounding of Age and Secular Time

A major shortcoming of *cross-sectional* data in regard to age differences, which has been emphasized increasingly in recent writings (Baltes, 1968b; Baltes & Reinert, 1969; Damon, 1965; Kuhlen, 1963; Schaie, 1967) is the confounding of the chronological age variable with the cohort or generation variable. That is,

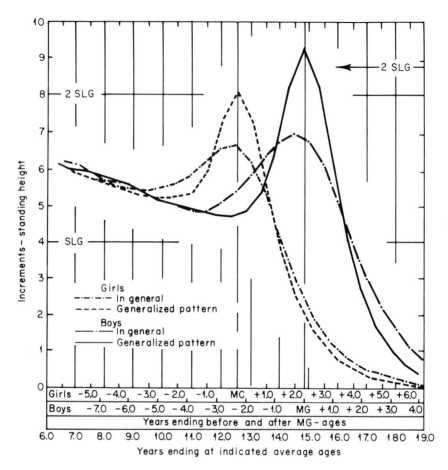

Figure 5. Average annual increments in standing height of children in general contrasted with generalized patterns based on nine groups of girls and ten groups of boys, grouped by age of maximum growth. (From Shuttleworth, 1939, p. 39. Reprinted by permission of Society for Research in Child Development.)

when a group of 60-year-olds is compared with a group of 20-year-olds, they differ not only in their respective ages, but they come from populations representing very different histories—e.g., present-day 60-year-olds lived through two world wars and a depression, whereas 20-year-olds have had no such experience. Similarly, the former group grew up under vastly different circumstances in regard to education, technology, diffusion of knowledge through mass media, etc., than the latter. The repeated finding of substantial discrepancies between longitudinal and cross-sectional data, both for biological variables such as height and vital capacity (Damon, 1965) and psychological variables such as performance on various cognitive and psychomotor tasks (Kallmann & Jarvik, 1959; Schaie & Strother, 1968a,b) points to the important role which the cohort factor may play. While the examples just given come from studies of changes over the years of adulthood and old age, equally convincing evidence comes from comparisons of the growth of children, sometimes over a very narrow span of cohorts. Thus Wolff (cited by B. S. Sanders, 1934, p. 187) reported yearly increases in the mean heights and weights of children of the *same* age, over the period from 1924 to 1928, which approached (and in the interval 1926 to 1927 actually exceeded) the mean difference in any given year between age groups separated by a year. [See Wolff (1940) and Tanner (1961) for other similar evidence on secular changes in physical growth.] Baltes and Reinert (1969) report similarly impressive cohort-differences in intelligence-test data, over a 12-month period.

In an attempt at a systematic treatment of this question, Schaie (1965) has proposed a trifactorial model, which aims to isolate the contribution to developmental data of the three factors of chronological age, cohort (the set of individuals born at a given time, e.g., in a given calendar year) and time of measurement, e.g., the calendar year in which a given set of data are obtained. Schaie's "general developmental model" is illustrated in Table 1 which allows us to distinguish among the three prototype designs which he has proposed.

The specifics of these three designs and of their uses, as well as the controversy that has arisen in regard to the interpretation of data obtained from them (Baltes, 1968b) are more fully discussed in the chapter by Schaie in this volume. It is nevertheless worthwhile to dwell briefly on the conceptual distinction among the three factors specified in Schaie's model, particularly in view of their obvious interdependence (i.e., given an individual's age and cohort, time-of-measurement is determined). To do so, let us turn to a prior analysis of this same question by Kodlin and Thompson (1958) and in particular to a graphic representation of the three variables of Schaie's model.

In Figure 6 we see cohort differences (*C*) represented by the relative heights of the four vertical planes drawn perpendicular to the time axis, while time of measurement (*T*) would be represented by the relative heights of the shaded vertical planes and similar planes parallel to it erected at lower points along the time dimension. Finally, age differences (*A*) are represented by planes that could be drawn parallel to the time axis, i.e., intersecting the cohort planes at right angles.

Looking at this problem from the point of view of developmental-function analysis, the conceptual distinction among the three factors of age, cohort, and time of testing becomes apparent. First, let us note that age, cohort, and time of testing represent conceptually very different types of variables. We have already indicated the sense in which age is optimally viewed as an aspect of the dependent variable. Cohort, on the other hand, is clearly a differential variable,

TABLE 1

*Schema for Research Designs Corresponding to Schaie's (1965)
Trifactorial Model of Developmental Studies[a,b]*

Cohort (year of birth)	Time of measurement														
	'56	'57	'58	'59	'60	'61	'62	'63	'64	'65	'66	'67	'68	'69	'70
1946						15									
1947						14	15								
1948						13	14	15							
1949						12	13	14	15						
1950	6	7	8	9	10	11	12	13	14	15					
1951		6	7	8	9	10	11	12	13	14	15				
1952			6	7	8	9	10	11	12	13	14	15			
1953				6	7	8	9	10	11	12	13	14	15		
1954					6	7	8	9	10	11	12	13	14	15	
1955						6	7	8	9	10	11	12	13	14	15
1956						6	7	8	9						
1957							6	7	8						
1958								6	7						
1959									6						

[a] Entries represent ages corresponding to each combination of cohort and time of measurement.

[b] In this table, *cohort-sequential* design is represented by the cells included within the horizontal parallelogram; *time-sequential* design is represented by the cells included within the vertical parallelogram; *cross-sequential* design is represented by the cells included within the square.

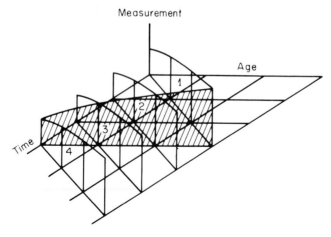

Figure 6. Longitudinal mean growth (unshaded planes) for cohorts 1 to 4 in the age-time diagram. Cross-sectional growth indicated by striped plane. (From Kodlin & Thompson, 1958, p. 25. Reprinted by permission of Society for Research in Child Development.)

analogous to sex and race, and the basis for differences related to it are just as difficult to pin down. Time of testing, finally, to the extent that it represents a factor conceptually separable from the cohort factor, is best regarded as a variable of a situational kind, i.e., relating to conditions operating at particular points in time which may affect behavior.

More precisely, we may attempt to differentiate between age, time, and cohort effects in the following terms: Cohort effects represent systematic alterations in the shape or course of the developmental function, while time effects represent temporary variations or aberrations superimposed on the developmental function. Age effects, finally, are those embodied in the generalized developmental function as such, once cohort and/or time effects have been extracted. This situation is best shown graphically, as in Figure 7. (The prototype curves there illustrated admittedly represent ideal cases; in any real set of data the difference between the two models is apt to become blurred.)

C. Shortcuts to the Study of Long-Term Longitudinal Change

Apart from the possible role of cohort and time-of-testing effects, Schaie's cross-sequential and time-sequential designs share one overriding advantage over the cohort-sequential design (as well as over the traditional longitudinal design), in collapsing the total age period covered into a much reduced span, while still permitting the collection of partially longitudinal information. In fact, Schaie's cross-sequential method (represented by the measures within the square in Table I) corresponds formally to Bell's (1953, 1954) "accelerated longitudinal" method, which provides coverage over a total period of $n(k - r)$ years by testing n cohorts over only k years, with r years overlap between successive cohorts.

As Schaie (1965) notes, the cross-sequential method is in fact intended for use where age differences can be assumed to be *absent*. If applied to study age changes, it reveals an important limitation: The sampling of the various ages is markedly uneven, being sparsest at the extremes of the continuum (e.g., in the square of Table 1, one sample each at ages 6 and 15) and densest in the middle (five samples each at ages 10 and 11). For this reason, the time-sequential design, corresponding to the vertically oriented parallelogram of Table 1, is preferable. This design provides an immediate cross-sectional picture of the changes occurring over the total age span, allowing for suitable modifications of the age sampling that may be indicated on the basis of these results. Even more important, it provides the most complete information on effects of prior testing: measures of each age between 10 and 15 are available for all values of number of prior tests from 0 to 4. The information in this respect below the square only duplicates that for the 6- to 9-year period contained within the square, but for that same reason can provide a basis for differentiating test-retest effects from changes due to cohort or time of testing.

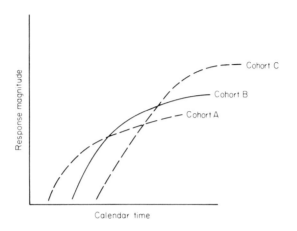

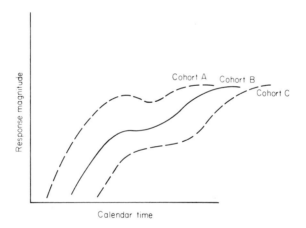

Figure 7. (a) Prototype curves to illustrate cohort differences in developmental functions. (b) Prototype curves to illustrate time-of-measurement effects on developmental functions.

Finally, let us note that, for many practical purposes, a more limited subset of the above may prove sufficient, such as would be provided by the design of Table 2, in which the overlap has been reduced from four to two years, with a sharp reduction in the number of cohorts required.

Bell's Convergence Method. Bell (1953, 1954) has suggested a particular mode of treatment of data obtained in the manner just described, that is, by utilizing successive partially overlapping longitudinal measurements. His proposal is to attempt matching of individual subjects in adjoining longitudinal groups on

TABLE 2

Abbreviated Time-Sequential Design

Cohort (year of birth)	Time of measurement				
	1961	1962	1963	1964	1965
A (1947)	14				
B (1949)	12	13	14		
C (1951)	10	11	12	13	14
D (1953)	8	9	10	11	12
E (1955)	6	7	8	9	10
F (1957)			6	7	8
G (1959)					6

the basis of the information in the overlapping periods, so as to construct a synthetic record of individual growth over the total period. In an application of this approach to data from the Harvard Growth Study (Dearborn, Rothney, & Shuttleworth, 1938), Bell arrived at a set of synthetic growth curves which allowed him to recover the information in the original individual records showing the relationship between age of puberty and period of maximum growth in height: Groups of these composite records corresponding to individuals reaching puberty before 12½ years showed a downward trend of height increment over this three-year-old span; records for individuals reaching puberty between 12½ and 13½ showed an increase followed by a decrease in increment, and those for individuals reaching puberty after 13½ showed a monotonic increase in height-increment.

The method does not appear to have been more widely applied, most probably because with most behavioral measures the task of matching individuals to obtain synthetic longitudinal curves is apt to prove extremely difficult. Test-retest effects would be particularly damaging, unless sufficient information concerning them was available to permit calculation of regressed scores adjusted for them. Nevertheless, the obstacles to the construction of such composite curves on an individual basis need not detract from the usefulness of this type of design to extract information concerning grosser patterns of change. Provided that determinate criteria can be specified for grouping individuals characterized by divergent patterns of growth, it may turn out to be feasible to generalize Bell's methodology to the study of homogeneous sub-groups of individuals.

D. Concluding Comment

In conclusion, it is clear that where phenomena or processes unfolding over time run their course over a time period approaching or even exceeding the span of the scientific career of the investigator, compromises need to be made with the ideal of following the changes as they take place. Different strategies have been evolved by different sciences for this purpose. In certain fields, changes charted over a very limited period can be extrapolated to cover the whole span over which the problem under study runs its course. Astronomy—e.g., Halley's work on the orbits of comets—comes to mind as one example. More frequently, a purely retrospective approach is taken, utilizing an essentially historical method. Geology and paleontology are prime examples of this case. Its application to the study of human development is frought with difficulties, but as increasingly complete records of the biological and behavioral development accumulate (cf. the Aberdeen Child Development Project), such a retrospective approach may become formally equivalent to a prospective one, and therefore increasingly feasible and profitable. The most incisive evidence on particular aspects of behavioral development, however, is apt to come from relatively short-term longitudinal research, of the kind discussed in this section, in which the major changes occurring over the course of development to maturity, and even beyond, can be telescoped to bring them within the scope of a limited term project, without sacrificing entirely the longitudinal focus required to reveal clearly the major processes and dimensions of change.

IV. THE DESCRIPTIVE ANALYSIS OF DEVELOPMENTAL FUNCTIONS

A. The Major Attributes of Developmental Functions

In developmental psychology, as in any area concerned with the study of change, the place of descriptive study looms particularly large, since a complete picture of the course of change will frequently convey some direct information concerning the processes which govern that change. Let us turn, then, to the major parameters or attributes in terms of which developmental functions can be usefully described.

1. *Form of the Developmental Function*

Statements of the form of the developmental function may vary all the way from simple indications of increase or decrease to elaborate attempts to specify the nature of the function in mathematical terms. Broadly speaking, we may distinguish three main levels of analysis:

a. *Assessment of Overall Direction of Change.* Here description of the change is limited to determination of increasing and decreasing phases in the amount of some variable over age. For this purpose, ordinal data suffice, and, providing that interindividual variation in the overall form of the function is not too great, cross-sectional data will probably yield as adequate information as longitudinal.

Indeed, most of our cross-sectionally based information as to age changes (e.g., with respect to perceptual functions) is of this type.

b. *Determination of Components of Trend.* Where the data permit application of trend analysis procedures, a determination of the best-fitting orthogonal polynomial function to describe the data can be made. At the simplest level, this permits differentiating between linear and curvilinear trends, even though both may be monotonically increasing, thus providing some indication of acceleration and deceleration as well as direction of change. More generally, it provides a more systematic, analytic approach to the isolation of the main components or phases of the developmental function considered both in terms of direction and of rate of change. Furthermore, it provides a convenient and useful basis for comparing individuals or groups in these respects, in terms of the overall form, as well as the more specific aspects such as slope of the function. It requires, however, equal-interval (though not necessarily ratio-scale) data, and a large enough number of points on the age continuum to reveal the details of the developmental function.

c. *Mathematical Specification of the Developmental Function.* In principle, in any situation permitting the application of trend analysis, the polynomial equation describing the data, with the actual values of the constants contained in it, may be specified (cf. D. Lewis, 1960, p. 416 ff., for details). This would rarely seem to be a profitable undertaking, unless one had considerable faith in the reliability of the measures, and their sensitivity to detect with precision any amount of quantitative variation along the dimension being measured. This situation is most nearly met in the study of physical growth, where we not only find frequent calculations of the constants of growth curves, but considerable effort to determine the particular types of exponential equations most adequate to the representation of some given aspect of growth (e.g., Shock, 1951; von Bertalanffy, 1960). Work in this field suggests, in fact, the possibility of deriving mathematical growth curves on a priori grounds, starting with a given model of the growth curve, i.e., a particular set of assumptions about the mechanisms of cell proliferation, etc., governing the growth process and its limitation or eventual reversal. Such rationally derived curves are generally exponential in form, such as the Gompertz,

$$y = exp\,(be^{cx})$$

or the logistic

$$y = k/(1 + e^{a+bx})$$

Although mathematical functions of this kind are well-known to psychologists in the study of learning, little use has been found for them thus far in work on behavioral development (see H. G. Birch & Lefford, 1963, for a rare and non-too-convincing exception).

As noted earlier, for the developmental psychologist polynomial functions (of the form, $y = a + bx + cx^2 + \ldots + kx^n$) are apt to be fully as satisfactory for descriptive purposes and more convenient. As a matter of fact, even in the study of height they may be applied to advantage in some situations, as demonstrated by Vandenberg and Falkner's (1965) success in distinguishing between fraternal and identical pairs of twins by fitting simple parabolic arcs (polynomials of the second degree) to their growth curves for height and comparing the within-pair variance of the values of the constants obtained for the two classes of curves.

2. Rate of Change of the Developmental Function

While rate of change is but one particular aspect of a developmental function, it is of special interest in at least two respects. First, comparison of rates of change (or simply increments) at different portions of the age scale provides a particularly useful basis for spotting major discontinuities in the operation of developmental processes (cf. the preadolescent growth spurt), or the apparent sudden improvement in performance in adjustment to distortion of sensory feedback in early adolescence (K. U. Smith & Greene, 1963). Second, it is frequently fruitful to translate differences in absolute standing between two groups (or individuals) at some point during their course of development into differences in *rates* of development, provided that more than one point on the age variable is available, or that a common origin with respect to the behavioral variable in the two groups can be assumed (cf. Wohlwill, 1970).

Where it is possible to express a developmental function by means of a mathematical equation, rate of change can of course be determined by differentiating the equation. More generally, $\Delta X / \Delta t$, i.e., the amount of change per unit of age, can be employed as a measure of rate; it has, in fact, found wide application in the study of physical growth (Dearborn & Rothney, 1941; Tanner, 1963), but its use assumes that the variable being measured has been satisfactorily scaled so that differences in amount can be equated for different portions of the scale.

3. Age Corresponding to Specified Points of the Developmental Function

Under certain circumstances the question at what age a specified point of the function is reached becomes of interest. This is true particularly with respect to the age at which growth ceases, i.e., the age corresponding to the asymptotic level or maximum of the function. This question has been extensively debated in connection with the variable of intelligence, dating back at least to the early days of Thurstone (1925), who on the basis of his artificially constructed curve of intelligence decided there was no evidence of a slow-down of intellectual development even by late adolescence; Freeman and Flory (1937) came to a similar conclusion on the basis of their scale of mental ability.[3] Thurstone likewise raised the question of the origin of intelligence, i.e., the age at which the function reaches the value of zero; this he found to correspond roughly to the age of conception! In the same vein, we may be interested in determining ages for the attainment of maximum growth, for the start of acceleration of growth (e.g., at adolescence), for the onset of decline (e.g., in old age, etc.).

4. Values of Maxima, Minima, and Terminal Level of Response

At any of the determinate points of the developmental function mentioned in the previous paragraph, the level or magnitude of the response attained may become a useful parameter in terms of which to characterize an individual or group. This is true in particular with respect to terminal level of the response, which, representing the endpoint of the developmental function, can be interpreted without reference to the age level of the individual in whom it originated. For functions subject to aging effects, on the other hand, the maxima (or minima, as the case may be) reached at maturity would be the datum of major interest.

The usefulness of these parameters is brought out to particular advantage when applied to assess group differences relating to experiential histories, conditions of rearing and the like. Here expressing the effects of such variables in terms of diffential attainment at maturity, rather than in terms of mean differences at some arbitrary point of the individual's development (as is the most typical practice in studies of the effects of experience), would greatly enhance the significance of the findings from such studies.

B. Descriptive Analysis with Respect to Qualitative Change

The consideration of qualitative changes demands some modification in the set of developmental-function parameters just outlined for quantitative dimensions of behavior. Thus, the *form* of the function ceases to be a valid concern; by the same token, rate of change loses its original mathematical reference, reducing to the amount of time taken to advance from one step or level of behavior to another. Comparisons of rates in this sense for different parts of the sequence have little meaning (e.g., one would not deduce from the fact that the period of Piaget's sensorimotor intelligence runs its course in roughly half the time, or even less, of that of concrete operations, that cognitive development slows down following infancy). But such time values represent useful indices to compare speed of development in different individuals or groups.

[3] It is interesting to note that the question of the termination of development has preoccupied not only psychologists, but biologists as well. An interesting general treatment of the problem of determining whether a given organism has reached the "adult" phase is given by Van der Vaart (1953).

Similarly, age of appearance of particular types of behavior can represent a datum of interest, as in Fantz and Nevis's (1967) comparison of institutionalized versus home-raised infants in terms of the age at which a preference for the more complex of two stimuli is first exhibited. Longeot (1967) has, in fact, argued for the construction of absolute age scales to replace those current in the field of intelligence testing, by taking definable points on a continuum formed by a set of standardized tasks derived from the work of Piaget, and measuring cognitive development in terms of the age at which these points are attained. As for terminal level, it could be invested with informative value, where there was substantial variation among groups or individuals in the extent of some developmental sequence actually traversed (e.g., certain cultures or groups lacking formal schooling beyond childhood do not reach the stage of formal operations, in Piaget's sense).

V. THE STUDY OF FUNCTIONAL RELATIONS AMONG DEVELOPMENTAL VARIABLES

A. General Issues

The study of the interrelations among variables in process of development, and more particularly of the changes in these interrelationships during the course of development remains at present at a rather primitive stage. Since Chapter 7 by Nesselroade presents a more detailed discussion of techniques of correlational and factor-analytic research as applied to developmental problems, we will content ourselves with pointing out the main uses to which such research has been or could be put, the kinds of questions which it can answer, and the difficulties and issues of design which have to be faced.

Basically, research in this field has been designed to answer one of two quite different questions. The first is: What are the changes in the interrelationships among behavioral variables at different ages or levels of development? This may be taken as an extension of the description of developmental change, with the dependent measure taking the form of measures of correlation, factorial structure, and the like. The second question is: What are the interrelationships among developmental changes taking place with respect to two or more behavioral dimensions? While this, too, could be taken to represent an essentially descriptive approach, it is generally viewed as transcending that level of research. Frequently the intent is to reduce age changes on two or more variables to a common factor or process, or a more limited set of such processes. Alternatively, the aim may be to subsume the change on one variable under that of the other, i.e., a direct functional relationship between them is postulated.

We will restrict ourselves to a consideration of the second of these concerns, since it rasies the most interesting, as well as the most difficult, issues of methodology. Indeed, one of the major difficulties is that traditional approaches dealing with this latter type of problem have been prone to lapse into methodologies appropriate for handling the former.

Consider, for instance, a study such as that of Feffer and Gourevich (1960). These authors wished to examine the hypothesis that changes in social-role perception with age could be accounted for in terms of changes on dimensions of cognitive development derived from Piagetian theory. They obtained measures of these two types of behaviors at several different ages—and immediately found themselves confronted with the inevitable dilemma: What to do about the role of age. Leaving age in the correlation would obviously lead to a spuriously inflated value, so they opted for the alternative of partialing it out, by recourse to a "roving median" technique (subjects were split into above and below the median for their age groups, and these dichotomized groups were then combined). They found a substantial residual relationship between their role-taking task measures and the children's performance on the Piagetian tasks. The obvious question arises: What is the *developmental* significance of such a finding? In the process of partialing out age, has the baby not been thrown out with the bathwater?

It can be argued, with some surface plausibility, that a demonstration of an association between two or more variables over several different age levels is presumptive evidence that the changes taking place with respect to these variables are related. [In this respect the evidence would be more convincing if given separately for each age group, as Wolfe (1963) has done in a closely related study.] Yet such data do not really provide any direct evidence of the functional relatedness of the changes taking place on the variables being intercorrelated. In fact, there are reasons of both a statistical and a logical nature for distinguishing between correlation within age levels and correlation of changes between age levels. Thus, if two sets of variables were to be found highly correlated at times t_1 and t_2, the correlation between the difference scores might still be relatively low.[4]

Logically, too, it is quite conceivable that a different set of determinants may enter into *change* in behavior as compared to absolute levels of the behavior at a given time. For instance, a substantial correlation between verbal and mathematical intelligence measures may exist over different age levels, reflecting their shared "g" (overall "native" ability) environmental factors operating on both, etc. Yet the amount of change in the two realms over a given period may show a

---

[4] At the extreme, if the two variables were scores on alternate versions of the same test, the intercorrelation between them would be equal to the reliability of the test. If we suppose further that there was no mean change in performance from the first to the second testing, the changes on the two forms would reflect error of measurement exclusively, and would presumably show little, if any, intercorrelation.

much lower correlation, for instance, if experiential factors (e.g., schooling) were more strongly influential in one realm than the other. (Compare R. B. Cattell, 1966d, p. 370 ff., for a more comprehensive discussion of the relationship between change factors and initial and final factors.)

B. Intercorrelation of Change Measures and Developmental-Function Parameters

The way out of the predicament alluded to in reference to Feffer and Gourevich's study is obviously to get direct measures of change, through longitudinal data, and intercorrelate these. Yet we are still well short of having solved the problems that arise here. First, there are the myriad of problems besetting change-score analysis (cf. Bereiter, 1963), which arise from the spurious negative correlation between initial and difference scores due to uncorrelated error variance present in both initial and final scores, as well as from the linear model imposed upon the data when difference scores are used as the basis for analysis.

Measures of absolute change between two occasions, furthermore, provide only a coarse indication of the course of development. For what we are ultimately interested in is the interrelationship among the total developmental functions for a set of variables. To date, virtually the only attempts to deal with this type of question have taken the form of the factor analysis of measures over a series of occasions, via P-technique (restricted to a single individual, with measures on a number of tests). The major shortcoming of this technique is that occasions are treated as a random variate (as subjects are in traditional factor analysis); no provision is made for the order built into the age variable. The result is that age is apt to emerge as a primary factor, with the danger that it may overdetermine the resulting factorial structure (cf. Cattell, 1963a). Since these techniques are discussed more fully by Nesselroade, suffice it to call attention to F. T. Tyler's (1954) use of incremental P-technique (which, dealing with increment rather than raw data, partially alleviates the problem just mentioned), as well as to the possible use of analysis of variance approaches to test for homogeneity of growth on two or more dimensions. The one attempt to apply this approach by Kerlinger (1954) makes use of incremental data representing various dimensions of physical growth, which are very similar to Tyler's. Both of these, incidentally, are limited to the analysis of one individual at a time, and it is not apparent how one might be able to pool the results of separate analyses carried out on several different individuals.

Whatever the merits of these approaches, they are fundamentally inadequate for bringing out temporally patterned interrelationships among variables over the course of development, since none of them "searches" the data for evidence of this kind. The major problem, in other words, is that the form of the developmental function is left out of account; furthermore, relationships that might operate across a time gap are not given a chance to emerge.

One approach that represents, in principle, a notable advance over the preceding in this respect is that of time-series analysis, which provides for the determination of time-lagged correlations, e.g., variable X at time t_i may be correlated successively with variable Y at times t_i, t_{i+1}, t_{i+2}, etc. (cf. Holtzman, 1963). The method requires, however, an inordinately large number of repeated measures on each variable; furthermore, it is basically designed to handle cyclical- rather than directional-change data.

A very different approach to the teasing out of functional relationships among developing variables would be to take given parameters of the developmental function of each and to intercorrelate these. To take a rather idealized case, given two variables (e.g., vocabulary growth and verbal fluency) which are thought to conform to the Gompertz function

$$y = vg^{h^x}$$

it would be perfectly feasible in principle to intercorrelate the values of the constants from the two sets of curves (obtained for a sample of individuals). It might be found, for instance, that v, representing asymptotic level, was rather highly correlated for the two functions, but that g and h, representing, respectively, initial level and rate of growth, were not; this would indicate that the two functions developed largely independently of one another. If, on the other hand, h showed a substantially larger correlation than g and v, this might point to interdependence of the developmental aspects of the two functions, with an additional component defining base and asymptotic level (possibly genetic in origin) being unrelated between the two functions.

Such methods, it would seem, are required to bring out to the fullest extent the dynamic interrelationships existing among developmental processes, since these interrelationships may well operate across a gap in time, thus partaking as much of sequential patterning as of interdependence among processes at a given point in time. This approach, it may be noted, provides a further example of the potential value of the specification of developmental functions, and the treatment of the parameters of the latter as dependent variables.

C. Functional Relationships Among Qualitative Variables

Where the nature of the variables under study does not permit the determination of quantitative parameters of the developmental function—notably in the study of stage-type phenomena—a different set of issues arise, and different approaches are required to deal with them. Some of these have been foreshadowed already in the preceding treatment of the assessment of scalability of a set of items, which can be looked at either as a problem in the construction of an ordinal scale, or as a problem in the determination of sequentially patterned relationships among a set of behaviors.

In an earlier paper (Wohlwill, 1963a), the author distinguished among two parallel questions of concern to the investigator of developmental stages. The first relates to the approach of a set of responses to sequential invariance, and can be approached through tests of scalability or homogeneity; the second concerns the extent to which two behaviors supposed to be related via a stage-determined structural network do indeed appear in synchrony, and thus involve tests for degree of association among response frequencies as indexed by *phi* and similar measures.

Further analysis (cf. Flavell & Wohlwill, 1969) has shown this to be a vastly oversimplified view of the problem, however. The basic difficulty, particularly with regard to the latter question, is that during the period which is of chief interest for the question of the interrelationship among stage-related behaviors, i.e., the transition period between stages, there are both empirical and logical reasons for not expecting a very high association between formally related behaviors. The very notion of a transitional period, in which new behaviors or concepts are in process of emerging, is one which favors inconsistency rather than determinate patterning of behavior.

Here again we are in need of methods for teasing out functional relationships among variables changing over time which transcend the model of simple correlational analysis. One approach, given longitudinal data, may be termed *change-pattern analysis*. It consists in relating differential amounts of change taking place with respect to one variable from one occasion to another to differences in another variable on each occasion. In this manner various types of mutual relationships between two variables undergoing development can be detected, as shown in Table 3. In this table, three types of situations are contrasted: type A, representing sequential patterning; type B, representing reciprocal sequencing; and type C, representing parallel development.

The essential information in these fictitious data resides in the comparison of data for variable X at time T_1 for groups which are equated on Y, but differ in their subsequent change from time t_1 to time t_2 (e.g., rows 1 vs. 2 vs. 3; row 4 vs. 5). (In the case of sequential patterning, if Y preceded X, the analysis would need to be rotated $90°$, with shift-patterns on X being correlated with initial level on Y.) The values for t_2 are of interest mainly to check on the internal consistency of the data. In the reciprocal sequencing case, however, these values also serve to indicate the differences with respect to Y of groups equated for terminal level on X on occasion t_2, but representing differential amounts of shift from t_1 to t_2.

TABLE 3

Three Models of Change-Pattern Analysis[a]

ΔY pattern		Time 1 Level of X			Time 2 Level of X		
		I	II	III	I	II	III
Sequential	I- I	20	10	0	10	15	5
model	I- II	10	20	10	0	20	20
	I-III	0	10	10	0	0	20
	II-III	0	15	25	0	0	40
	II- II	0	20	10	0	10	20
	III-III	0	0	30	0	0	30
Reciprocal	I- I	20	10	0	15	10	5
model	I- II	10	30	0	0	40	0
	I-III	0	20	0	0	10	10
	II-III	0	40	0	0	20	20
	II- II	0	30	0	0	30	0
	III-III	0	15	15	0	5	25
Parallel	I- I	30	0	0	25	5	0
model	I- II	35	5	0	5	30	5
	I-III	15	5	0	0	5	15
	II-III	5	30	5	0	5	35
	II- II	5	25	0	0	25	5
	III-III	0	5	25	0	0	30

[a] Entries represent frequencies; data shown are hypothetical.

In the case of data of this kind, where both variables are measured in equivalent categories (the presumption being that types I, II, and III mean equivalent things for the two variables), essentially the same information could be derived from the cross-sectional examination of the patterns at each occasion separately. This is shown in Table 4, which is derived from the data in Table 3 simply by summing the frequencies for each response type on X on each occasion, and tabulating these as a function of the response-type frequencies on Y. In this case attention would focus on the relative frequencies in particular cells, as indicated by the arrows in the table which show relative advance of one variable over the other at a given time. The direct analysis of change patterns, however, provides not only more compelling evidence of functional mediation of changes in one variable by another, but may be applied where the categories of the two variables are not comparable, so that one cannot speak of advance of one over the other, or where X is a continuous variable, as in the case of the study of relationships between measurement of conservation by Wohlwill *et al.* (1969).

TABLE 4

Contingency Tables for Association between Variables X and Y Corresponding to Change-Pattern Analysis of Table 4[a]

	Level of Y	Time 1 Level of X			Time 2 Level of X		
		I	II	III	I	II	III
Sequential	I	30	40	20	10	15	5
	II	0	35	35	0	30	40
	III	0	0	30	0	0	90
Reciprocal	I	30	60	0	15	10	5
model	II	0	70	0	0	70	0
	III	0	15	15	0	35	55
Parallel	I	80	10	0	25	5	0
model	II	10	55	5	5	55	10
	III	0	5	25	0	10	80

[a]Arrows point to comparisons between cases of advances of X over Y and vice versa; these contain the information differentiating the models. Analysis assumes that levels of X and Y are commensurate.

VI. THE STUDY OF INDIVIDUAL DIFFERENCES WITHIN THE DEVELOPMENTAL-FUNCTIONAL FRAMEWORK

A. The Problem of Stability of Development

A great deal of study has been devoted to the question of the stability of behavior over the course of development; notably with reference to the variable of intelligence, but more recently also with reference to dimensions of personality development (Emmerich, 1964; Kagan & Moss, 1962), and more general aspects of development (Escalona & Heider, 1959; A. Thomas, Birch, Chess, Hertzog, & Korn, 1963). With very few exceptions, stability has been identified with predictability, in a very specific sense: the magnitude of the correlation between measures of the same variable (or variables presumed to be linked across age) at two different ages. This approach, which is most familiar through the work on the constancy of the IQ, has three immediate consequences. First, stability is assessed as a characteristic of a *variable*, within a particular reference group, rather than of a given individual's development with respect to that

Second, stability is measured in purely relative, i.e., group-referent ctual changes taking place along the variable in question do not enter into consideration. Third, stability measures are specific to the particular interval of age over which the correlation is determined.

Is there any other way of conceiving of stability such that it could be looked at as a characteristic of the development of an individual, and more particularly as a parameter of his developmental function? If it is possible to specify some idealized function for the development of a particular variable, stability might be interpreted in terms of the correspondence of the actual function to the ideal one. The question now becomes one of specifying this function. Three approaches may be suggested.

The first is the *idealized function* approach. It presupposes that an idealized latent function can be specified as a prototype of an individual's development along a given variable. The measure of stability might then be the average deviation of the observed points from this ideal function, which can serve as a measure of the predictability of the individual's growth, just as the standard error of estimate does in a regression situation.

A variant of the above approach may be called the *developmental-channel* approach. It would consist in determining in advance the major differentiable types or patterns of developmental functions, selecting the one most nearly corresponding to that of the individual under study, and measuring deviations from that pattern. This is best illustrated by reference to the Wetzel (1941) grid (cf. also Stott, 1967, p. 47 ff.), which plots the individual's combinations of height and weight at each age, starting from the assumption of a simple logarithmic progression for each variable, along a set of parallel channels; thus stability could be indexed by the extent of movement of the individual's graph from one channel to another.

The third approach, by far the most widely applicable, is the *normative* one. It requires only that a set of measures obtained from an individual at successive ages be translated into relative units, by relating them to the mean value of his age group; stability may then be expressed in terms of the consistency (i.e., lack of variance) of these relativized values across age. This can be done by resort to any of the developmental indices familiar to those in the field (cf. Bayley, 1956): notably standard scores or developmental quotients (such as IQ).

How do such measures of individual stability relate to the correlational measures of stability determined from groups of subjects heretofore? Let us consider this question separately for the two contrasting cases of relatively high and relatively low stability in the classical sense. First, if this stability is high (though presumably still well short of unity, which would mean perfect equivalence among the developmental functions for all individuals in the group), individual stability may still be relatively low. This is because the classical stability measures may be in part produced by the overlap between the content of the tests at the two times being intercorrelated, as J. E. Anderson (1939) has suggested. This is confirmed by Roff's (1941) finding that intelligence-test measures at one age were uncorrelated with measures of amount of gain from that age to a later one. Thus rate of change of intelligence need not be constant, and individual stability, in the sense considered here, may be low.

If stability of the variable (in the classical sense) is low, individual stability or regularity cannot be expected to be very high. This is because, in general, instability with respect to a variable points to developmental changes in the dimensionality or factorial composition of the variable, i.e., discontinuity with respect to the definition of the variable itself. Thus the low stability of intelligence measures, when measured from infancy to adolescence, has generally been traced to the lack of comparability of the components of intelligence when traced over such an extended period of age. While Emmerich (1964) has shown that instability and discontinuity are conceptually separable, and that under special circumstances the former may occur without the latter, such cases are in fact quite exceptional, and basically artifactual, arising mainly where ceiling effects bring everyone to the same level on a variable on later testing, thus depressing stability coefficients, or where there are "sleeper" effects which cause stability to be lowered at a particular age (e.g., adolescence), only to increase again subsequently.

Let us note, finally, that all of the previous discussions of stability conceive of invariance in a purely relative sense, whether in terms of the preservation of individual differences along a dimension for a group as a whole, or of the consistency of a given individual relative to the group or to some actual or hypothetical norm. There are other types of stability which have been much less frequently discussed, let alone investigated. First of all, stability may be conceived of as absolute invariance, in situations where there are no mean changes in level with respect to the variable in question. Something approaching this type of stability is assessed in the investigation by Thomas *et al.* (1963), in which infants' dominant level of response at two ages were measured (on rating scales) and compared directly in terms of amount of shift. Generally speaking, however, such absolute invariance has rarely been of interest to developmentalists. Second, stability may be looked at in an ipsative sense, as referring to invariance in the patterning of responses or traits within a given individual. W. E. Martin (1964) investigated stability of this sort, with reference to the personality profiles of nursery school children over a period of time (cf. also Emmerich, 1967). This too has been only rarely employed as a focus of interest, just as the ipsative study of development generally has lagged far behind either the classical-developmental or the differential (cf. Emmerich, 1968). Finally, the problem of *continuity*, which Emmerich contrasts to that of stability, can itself be thought of as concerning stability, in the sense of constancy in the patterning across individuals of the responses on a set of variables. Thus we may propose Table 5 as a guide to the conceptualizing of the stability problem.

TABLE 5

Schema for Conceptualizing Types of Stability[a]

	Individuals	Groups
	Absolute invariance *No developmental change*	Absolute invariance *No developmental change*
Univariate	Regularity of developmental function *Developmental changes in level*	Preservation of individual differences *Developmental changes in level or measuring instrument*
Multivariate	Patterning of responses or traits within individual *Developmental changes in level or measuring instrument*	Intercorrelations among variables (continuity) *Developmental changes in level or measuring instrument*

[a]Nonitalicized material refers to the referent of the stability concept. Italicized material indicates developmental changes from which invariance would be abstracted.

The implications of the distinctions made in this table, and the interrelationships among the various types, require much more thorough treatment than it is possible to give them here, but the classificatory schema presented in Table 5 should aid in enlarging our consideration of this problem beyond the confines of the intercorrelating of measures over a pair of occasions, as it has almost exclusively been considered heretofore.

B. The Problem of Individual Differences in Development

Given a developmental-function framework, one aspect of the individual-difference question which soon becomes apparent is that of specifying inter-individual variation among the parameters of this function. This question has been alluded to at various earlier points of this chapter; one of the primary reasons indicated for the desirability of longitudinal data, in fact, relates precisely to the need to preserve information about individual differences in rate, in the form of the function, etc. Clearly this information can become of interest in its own right, as a basis for differentiating individuals over the course of their development, along given dimensions, or parameters of their developmental function, while individual differences at a particular age, or in terminal level, may be much less informative—indeed, with respect to terminal level, they may well vanish (as in the case of variables such as walking ability, correctness of speech, etc.).

The approach to obtaining this kind of individual-difference information is straightforward enough when dealing with quantitative variables for which parameters of the developmental function are readily determinable. At least implicitly it is utilized in research in which children have been categorized as early versus late maturing, for instance; the work of Tanner (1963), comparing the growth of children suffering from illness interfering with growth, and their response to the elimination of this interference, affords a particularly good example of the interpretation of differences in rate and pattern of growth.

When we turn to qualitative measures, the two main types of questions about individual differences concern variations in the sequence of responses as they emerge during the course of development and variations in the age of attainment of any given response. The latter is an expression of rate of development and needs little further comment. As to the former, it raises the question whether there are variations among individuals in the path taken towards the end point of some developmental sequence. This notion has had considerable appeal, but evidence concerning it is very scant. It presupposes, first, that we have either determined a reliable modal developmental sequence or that we are dealing with a sequence conforming to the disjunctive rather than the cumulative model, which in turn requires that we obtain observational data on actual, spontaneously occurring, rather than potential elicited behaviors; furthermore, it almost certainly requires that we obtain longitudinal data, in order to be able to separate out a limited number of differentiated sequential patterns from a general *lack* of sequential patterning.

Finally, let us cite the all too sketchy but nevertheless useful set of models which Loevinger (1966) has provided to distinguish among different types of developmental patterns. Of particular interest is her differentiation between two cases: in the first, all individuals arrive at a common end point, but vary in their speed of attaining it (e.g., learning to walk); in the second, individuals develop at different rates, as well as attaining different end points but with a constant terminal age of their development (e.g., growth in intelligence, as assumed for standard intelligence tests). Loevinger's models are too imperfectly worked through and discussed to be very helpful as presented, but they point the way to a systematic treatment of individual differences in a developmental-change context, which furthermore has important implications for the assessment of stability, in the traditional sense of the preservation of individual differences.

VII. CONCLUSION

Those who might have looked to this chapter for a comprehensive treatment of analytic methods and techniques for the study of child behavior and developmental changes in behavior will undoubtedly have come away disappointed. The aim has been rather to confront the major types of questions which arise from a concern for developmental change and to indicate general approaches and research strategies required for answering them. In some cases the requisite analytic techniques have been developed, and reference has been made to them; more frequently, they remain to be worked out. Hopefully, the asking of the questions themselves will promote efforts to attack these analytic problems.

In order to keep the length of this chapter within reasonable bounds, it has been necessary to omit the consideration of several major areas of developmental study, which might have brought into clearer focus the benefits to be derived from the developmental-function analysis approach advocated here. In particular, the implications of this approach for the study of behavioral development as a function of particular conditions of experience should be noted. This question has been dealt with, albeit in only the most sketchy fashion, in the paper referred to in the introduction to this chapter (Wohlwill, 1970). A more extended treatment of it is currently in progress, as part of a more systematic overview of the problems of methodology and research design arising in developmental research.

Let us reiterate, in closing, the central thesis which has inspired this chapter. The study of developmental problems requires a focus on the study of change, that is, on the description and analysis of the characteristics of behavioral change, and its correlates and determinants. If change is to be made the object of study, it follows that our measures must have direct reference to relevant aspects of change—whence the emphasis on the analysis of developmental functions. A further consequence of this focus on change is the insistence on longitudinal data, not only to take account of individual variations in rate and patterning of development, but to provide direct measures of the parameters of the developmental functions stipulated as the units of analysis, and of their relationship to other relevant variables.

Acceptance of these ideas will impose considerable burdens on the resourcefulness, as well as the patience, of the developmental investigator—not to mention his sources of support. In particular, the insistence on the need for longitudinal data would undoubtedly result in a substantial deceleration of the rate of progress in our field. However, if we agree that the rate at which developmental research is proliferating at present is outstripping our ability to assimilate it, such a deceleration may not be without its benefits for the progress of our discipline.

ACKNOWLEDGMENT

This paper was written while the author was a Research Fellow at Educational Testing Service in Princeton, New Jersey, with partial support from a Faculty Research Grant from the Social Science Research Council.

CHAPTER 7

Application of Multivariate Strategies to Problems of Measuring and Structuring Long-Term Change

JOHN R. NESSELROADE

WEST VIRGINIA UNIVERSITY
MORGANTOWN, WEST VIRGINIA

ABSTRACT

Developmental psychology, as a scientific discipline, has not paid sufficient attention to methodological techniques that permit the examination of change in a multivariate setting. Multivariate analysis techniques and procedures are discussed which are relevant to the investigation of qualitative (structural) and quantitative change—two crucial aspects of the study of long-term change in a life-span developmental context. More specifically, the strategy of comparative factor analysis attempts to disentangle qualitative and quantitative changes as distinct sources of variability evidenced by the empirically determined characteristics of factor loading patterns and factor scores. Suggestions are discussed for assessing the degree of structural invariance in a set of measures, a necessary prerequisite for the examination of quantitative change. Implications of Cattell's "covariation chart," which defines six covariation techniques (R, Q, P, O, S, T), for the study of developmental change are discussed. It is suggested that the typical, cross-sectional, factor analysis procedure (R technique) may not be the most useful for studying developmental phenomena. Attention is drawn to alternative covariation techniques and some discussion is given of their application to particular developmental issues.

I. INTRODUCTION

The development and use of models and methods for attacking the complex, pervasive problems associated with the study of behavioral change has become more and more a focal point for the creative activities of researchers who recognize the value and power of multivariate analytical techniques. Numerous methodologies are currently available (e.g., R. B. Cattell, 1966d; Corballis & Traub, 1970; C. W. Harris, 1963; Horn & Little, 1966) which blend together sophisticated analytical procedures and the capability of simultaneously dealing with a number of measurement variables across time. It seems fair to state that behavioral scientists are gradually becoming more aware of the fact that solutions to seemingly intractable problems do require the use of complex, intricate, analytical tools. The chief advantage of being able to examine a set of response measures simultaneously is that patterns of responses rather than isolated behaviors can be subjected to systematic investigation.

It has often been pointed out (e.g., Coan, 1966) that the central issues facing developmental psychology are among the most complicated addressed by psychologists. Unfortunately, as Wohlwill (Chapter 6) indicates, developmental psychology as a discipline has yet to face up to the task of erecting a strong, concise foundation for its own development either in terms of formulating basic testable concepts, or designing its own potent methodological approach.

As the title suggests, the general concern of the present discussion is that of indicating some areas of application of multivariate analysis to the problems of structuring behavioral change. It is the writer's intent to keep the discussion relatively brief, reasonably nontechnical, and selective rather than comprehensive. We will emphasize primarily the notion of structuring change rather than measuring it, although the two obviously cannot be cleanly separated. The two central themes this paper will focus on are those of quantitative versus qualitative change and intraindividual stability versus intraindividual variability.

II. IMPLICATIONS OF MULTIVARIATE TECHNIQUES FOR STUDYING PATTERNS OF CHANGE

It is unfortunate that the immediate association which many researchers make to the term multivariate analysis is, "Oh, yes, correlational techniques— nonexperimental." Somehow it is seemingly impossible to lay this fallacy to rest although a number of writers have made the attempt. One apparent reason for its wretched longevity is the lack of discrimination made between the simplest kind of one-occasion, cross-sectional correlational analyses and a large class of other multivariate techniques and designs. First, the reader should be reminded that most of the more cherished analytical methods of classical bivariate experimental psychology have generalized counterparts in the realm of multivariate techniques. For example, there is the generalized T test (Hotelling, 1931) for comparing two groups for differences in means on several response variables simultaneously. In a similar vein multivariate analysis of variance (MANOVA) and discriminant function analysis permit one to examine differences between several groups or treatment conditions on a number of dependent variables with the unique advantage of doing so within the context of a single analysis. One highly pertinent advantage accruing to these multivariate procedures is the removal of ambiguity such as is often found when several dependent variables are analyzed in traditional univariate analyses of variance, either as separate variables or as arbitrarily constructed composite variables (L. V. Jones, 1966).

A second related point is that increasingly successful rapprochements are being achieved between what traditionally have been labeled *experimental* and *correlational* approaches (J. Cohen, 1968; Corballis & Traub, 1970; Fruchter, 1966; Tucker, 1966). Even Cattell (1966b), who can scarcely be regarded as an enthusiastic advocate of bivariate methodology, recognizes the value of the traditional, manipulative experiment, given that the dependent variables incorporated be of known factorial composition. He has offered a thorough discussion of the parameters characterizing *experimental designs* and *analytical methods* and argues that the somewhat narrow definitions usually given the two approaches—correlational and classical experimental—cover only a small number of the viable procedural possibilities. The chapter by Fruchter (1966) in the *Handbook of Multivariate Experimental Psychology* explores in detail the use of factor analysis in manipulative and hypothesis testing designs.

Without involving ourselves in fruitless debate over such issues as the status of derived variables, such as factors, as psychological constructs, let us admit that there are advantages to being able to examine and, possibly, even to manipulate not single variables but complexes or patterned relationships among many variables in concert. This necessarily involves some degree of abstraction, although one may choose not to move too far from hard data.

It is basic to the "multivariate ethic," however, that the abstractions, concepts, or constructs, with which segments of behavioral science must ultimately deal, are not adequately indexed by single, observable responses (R. B. Cattell, 1946, 1968a; Cronbach, 1957). To the extent that one is willing to operate in terms of abstractions or concepts derived from data there are two related and well-recognized aspects involved in making such identifications; both of which can be efficiently treated within a multivariate framework. The first is that of finding out what measures "belong" to the concept; the second is that of determining what measures do not "belong."

Techniques such as factor analysis enable one to systematically explore the interrelationships of a number of variables, all potentially of interest to the investigator, in such a way as to detect how subsets of such variables may behave as a coherent unity over different situations or conditions. Bereiter (1963) has argued that, to the extent that a set of variables covary over different situations, they are measuring the same thing. Nunnally proposes that "the test of how well different supposed measures of a construct 'go together' is the extent to which they have similar curves of relationship with a variety of treatment variables (Nunnally, 1967, p. 90)." Although the latter remark is made with reference to the role of controlled experiment there is a distinct conceptual similarity between it and Bereiter's assertion when we map "covary" to "go together" and "situation" to "treatment variables."

One often finds when utilizing multivariate techniques such as factor or components analysis that particular observables, however operationally sacred they may be, are not unidimensional in nature. Thus while a single observable may not in itself be sufficient to define a construct neither can we guarantee, a priori, that it will reflect only the one construct it has been selected to represent. This is why writers such as R. B. Cattell (1968a) have repeatedly argued that one of our first concerns should be that of identifying the concepts, units, or entities with which we are eventually to deal, by means of techniques which afford knowledge of the structural properties of, and relationships among relevant variables.

One hastens to add that the term *structural relationships* is not meant to apply only to characteristic relationships among variables measured in the context of studying stable individual differences, but also to the more complex domain of dynamics and change. This seems to be another aspect of the lack of appreciation for multivariate techniques in developmental research. That is, many people see these techniques as being relevant only to the study of interindividual differences at specific points in time. Methods will be discussed later which indicate that this is clearly not so.

III. IMPLICATIONS OF FACTOR ANALYSIS FOR STRUCTURING QUALITATIVE AND QUANTITATIVE CHANGE: FACTOR LOADING PATTERNS AND FACTOR SCORES

Factor analytic techniques, and it must be recognized that this term subsumes a rich variety of analytical procedures, constitute some of the most powerful tools now available for efficiently examining relationships among observables. Various derivatives of the basic model permit the application of these methods to data representing changes over time. To aid subsequent discussion let us briefly consider a statement of the basic model or specification equation (Cattell, 1966c) as given in Equation 1.

$$a_{ji} = b_{j1}F_{1i} + b_{j2}F_{2i} + \cdots + b_{jk}F_{ki} + S_{ji} \tag{1}$$

Equation 1 states that measured response, a_j, of individual i is a weighted sum of his (person i) factor endowments (or scores). The b_j's are the weights (factor loadings) indicating the contribution of each factor to performance a_j, and the F's are individual i's factor scores. S_{ji} is a part which is specific to individual i's a_j response. Note that the b's are subscripted without reference to particular individuals, that is, the b's convey the relationships between observables and factors, while the F's are subscripted without reference to particular variables. They indicate the individual's amount, so to speak, of the various factors. Thus, by weighting and combining a given individual's factor scores, using the weights appropriate for a particular a_j, one arrives at an estimate, if you will, of the individual's score on a_j.

Obviously this model is an additive one, linear in the relationships between the F's and a_j's. While Equation 1 states the model as a predictive one, in practice, of course, one begins with the observables, the a_j's, and solves for the b_j's and F's. In examining the implications of this model for the study of qualitative and quantitative change Nesselroade (1970), has elaborated on its use in the case where one has data obtained from the same individuals at different points in time. Although this will be discussed more fully later on, an important point can be made here regarding differences in qualitative and quantitative change with respect to the specification equation. Consider a second equation, say,

$$a_{ji'} = b_{j1}F_{1i'} + b_{j2}F_{2i'} + \cdots + b_{jk}F_{ki'} + S_{ji'} \tag{2}$$

where the subscript i', indicates that individual i has been remeasured at another point in time, distinct from that implied in Equation 1. Note that the factor loadings (b_j) are the same in both Equations 1 and 2 but that no such restriction is placed on the factor scores $(F_{i'})$. But suppose there is a difference in the measured performance (a_j) from one time to the next. If we subtract (1) from (2) to obtain (3) we may write the difference as:

$$a_{ji'} - a_{ji} = b_{j1}(F_{1i'} - F_{1i})$$
$$+ b_{j2}(F_{2i'} - F_{2i}) + \cdots + b_{jk}(F_{ki'} - F_{ki}) + (S_{ji'} - S_{ji}) \tag{3}$$

If the left hand side of (3) is some nonzero value then one or more of the terms in parentheses on the right hand side must also be nonzero. If the differences in parentheses on the right hand side are interpreted as quantitative shifts on the factor continuua from one time to another we are suggesting that, under the condition of invariant factor loadings, one kind of quantitative change (observable) may be accounted for by quantitative change of another type, i.e., changes in factor scores. At a theoretical level it may be pointed out that similar arguments apply to group comparison data. Suppose we let $a_{ji'}$ represent the mean a_j score for age group 1 and a_{ji} the mean a_j score for age group 2. If the $b_j{'}s$ are the same for both groups (same factor loading patterns) then a difference in group means on the observable is reflective of differences in group means on one or more factors. In terms of factorial composition of the observables, in this situation there is no necessity for invoking notions of qualitative change or difference.

Let us note, on the other hand, that (3) also suggests another interesting possibility. Because of the compensatory nature of the additive model under discussion, hypothetical changes in several factor scores could be such as to cancel each other, and thus show up as no change in terms of the observables. That is to say, that changes in the terms in parentheses on the right-hand side of (3) could effectively summate to give zero or near zero values for the left-hand side. Such effects could not be "teased out" by paying attention only to single response measures.

Some implications for the detection and examination of qualitative change may also be drawn from this elementary statement of the factor analytic model. In Equation 4 we have rewritten (2) in such a way as to recognize both different factor loadings and factor scores, as well as the possibility of a different number of factors.

$$a_{ji'} = b_{j1}^* \, F_{1i'}^* + b_{j2}^* \, F_{2i'}^* + \cdots + b_{jq}^* \, F_{qi'}^* + S_{ji'}^* \qquad (4)$$

Subtracting (1) from (4) to obtain (5)

$$a_{ji'} - a_{ji} = b_{j1}^* \, F_{1i'}^* + b_{j2}^* \, F_{2i'}^* + \cdots S_{ji'}^* - b_{j1} \, F_{1i} - \cdots - S_{ji} \qquad (5)$$

we see that there is no simple reduction[1] of terms analogous to that in (3). The right-hand side of (5) is an additive function of both sets of parameters. The question which the writer finds compelling in this: Given this state of affairs, how meaningful is it to subtract a_{ji} from a_{ji}', even though a_{ji} may represent John Brown's score on form A of the Peerless Intelligence Inventory at age 18, and $a_{ji'}$ his score on the same instrument at age 22? More generally it may be argued that, within the framework of the linear model under discussion, a_{ji} and

---

[1] A reduction of terms is possible under certain conditions. Given the same number of factors on both occasions of measurement and no change in factor scores the observed changes can be expressed as

$$a_{ji'} - a_{ji} = (b_{j1}^* - b_{j1}) F_{1i} + (b_{j2}^* - b_{j2}) F_{2i} + \cdots + (S_{ji}^* - S_{ji})$$

(see C. W. Harris, 1963; Nesselroade, 1970).

$a_{ji'}$ in this situation differ qualitatively and do not lend themselves to quantitative comparisons.

Realize that for expository purposes we have dealt with the specification equation for only one variable, a_j, when in actual practice, one would typically have a specification equation for each variable. As derived by a factor analysis, for example, these specification equations would differ in the b's since each observed variable would be represented as an unique combination of factors.

Baltes and Nesselroade (1970) have suggested that in order to make quantitative comparisons between say, different age levels, one should first establish qualitative equivalence of the behavioral dimensions on which the comparisons are to be made. Their argument is that identification of qualitatively (structurally) equivalent dimensions should rest on demonstrated invariance of factor loading patterns—the b_j's of the specification equation—and that quantitative comparisons are then justifiably made on the factor scores. In brief, the crux of the argument is that for factors from, say, two different age levels, which have the same loadings, we have evidence that the factors relate to observables in the same way, thus providing support for the inference that the factor scores represent measures of the same derived concept. Figure 1 illustrates these points by comparing hypothesized factor solutions for two age levels. Associated with each of the five factors is a continuum of factor scores. For factor B, however, drawn here to indicate the same loading pattern for both age levels, the factor scores have been located on one continuum to suggest that quantitative comparisons might be appropriately made.

Let us note in passing that considerable emphasis in this discussion is being placed on the factor scores—the often "forgotten member" of factor analysis. It is well known that when one factors a correlation or covariance matrix into common and unique factors by standard methods, one obtains the matrix of factor loadings but not the matrix of factor scores. The latter, if desired, can only be estimated, and the methods of estimation available (Harman, 1960; McDonald & Burr, 1967) are unsavory to some. R. B. Cattell (1968a) has recently discussed some problems and possible lines of attack in connection with these issues, including estimation in such a way as to preserve mean differences between groups involved in separate analyses. Developments such as those of Horst (1965) and Tucker (1966) which emphasize factoring the data matrix itself, rather than the covariance matrix derivable from it, further underscore the role of factor and component scores.

Returning to the use of factor analysis in the detection of qualitative and quantitative change, let us consider two major possible research approaches which relate to the honored distinction between cross-sectional and longitudinal studies. Coan (1966) has suggested that the comparison of factor loading patterns for different age groups in an attempt to establish ontogenetic continuity must face up to two issues. One is that the universe of behaviors is

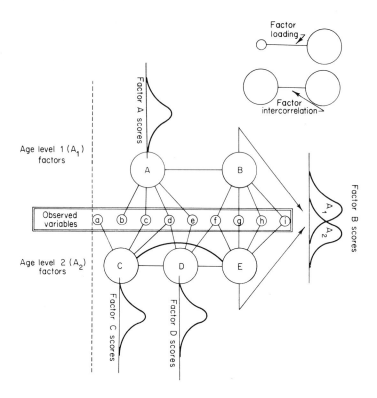

Figure 1. Hypothetical comparison of factor solutions for two age levels.

not constant for different age levels and therefore the manifest nature of the
factor in behavioral measures will change. Second, he defines members of a class
of qualitative changes such as "factor metamorphosis," in which the factor
gradually changes its loadings and "factor emergence," in which a new factor
arises from previously uncorrelated behaviors, an opposite process—"factor
disintegration," etc. Empirical verification of these events, it should be noted,
would have to rest on much more stringent tests for the number of factors, and
more powerful rotational procedures than are typically employed by factor
analysts (Nesselroade & Baltes, 1970).

    One can distinguish between studies involving comparisons of factors at
different age levels for: (a) different samples of subjects at each age level, and (b)
the same sample of subjects measured at each age level. The respective
weaknesses and virtues of cross-sectional and longitudinal studies as discussed for
example by Baltes (1968b), and commented on by Wohlwill (see Chapter 6)
would apply here as well. Appropriate use of multivariate strategies, however,

would permit one to sort out generational and ontogenetic differences in terms of factors rather than variables (Baltes & Nesselroade, 1970).

A feature of interest in the longitudinal approach is that one is not only able to compare factor loading patterns at different points in time, but, where appropriate, one can also determine factor score stability coefficients. The latter are sensitive to differential changes in individual's factor scores with the passage of time. In another context the writer (Nesselroade, 1967, 1970) has stressed the use of models which permit invariance of factor loading pattern over time and stability of factor scores to be regarded as independent events. Corballis and Traub (1970) have developed a model—longitudinal factor analysis—which does permit both factor loadings and factor scores to vary between occasions of measurement while still yielding a unique factorial solution.

IV. CORRELATIONAL TECHNIQUES WHICH BEAR DIRECTLY ON THE PROBLEMS OF STRUCTURING CHANGE

R. B. Cattell (1966a) has presented a systematic framework for classifying factor analytic and other multivariate techniques in terms of the types of data relational systems available to a discipline. His original "covariation chart" (R. B. Cattell, 1946) defined six primary factor analytic techniques in terms of data classifiable in a three-dimensional space defined by persons, tests, and occasions of measurement. Figure 2 indicates the essential features of such a three dimensional scheme using age levels, measurement variables, and persons to define the dimensions. Cattell's generalization of the covariation chart—the Basic Data Relation Matrix (BDRM)—incorporates some ten dimensions, including the original three of the covariation chart, and permits the logical definition of a much greater number of covariation techniques, depending upon which parameters one permits to vary. Coan (1966), with special reference to the needs of developmental psychology, has defined twenty-four such covariation techniques in terms of four design components or dimensions: variables, external stimuli, occasions, and subjects.

Let us confine our attention here to briefly outlining the techniques specified by the three-dimensional covariation chart. Readers wishing a more thorough discussion are referred to the papers by R. B. Cattell (1966a) and Coan (1966).

R technique is the well-known cross-sectional analysis in which one factors variables correlated over people measured at one point in time. It is to be noted that such an analysis may incorporate persons from more than one age level. The main point is that this technique utilizes a two dimensional matrix of data bordered by persons and measurement variables as shown by the (R, Q) facet in Figure 2. The alternative method of analysis for this type of data, in which one factors people correlated over variables, has been labeled Q technique. J. Ross

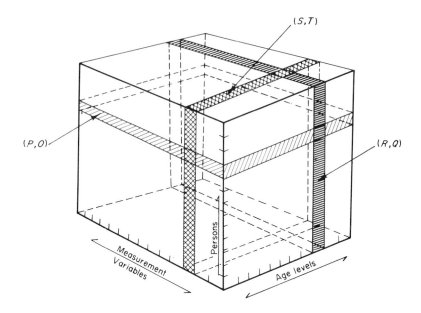

Figure 2. A modification of Cattell's covariation chart stressing its developmental implications.

(1963) has offered some reconciliation of the difference between these two techniques, long a controversial issue. Neither, it should be recognized, offers any direct evidence concerning intraindividual variability and/or stability.

P technique analyses, of which there are now eight or so in the literature (R. B. Cattell, 1963a, 1966d), involves the factor analysis of variables correlated over occasions of measurement or age levels, all measures obtained on one individual. Bereiter (1963, p. 15) has suggested that "*P*-technique is the logical technique for studying the interdependencies of measures" which vary together over time. This methodology has been specifically criticized (Holtzman, 1962; Horn & Little, 1966) but the writer maintains that in principle it is highly germane to the province of developmental psychology.

As indicated by Figure 2, *P* technique aims directly at the problem of defining dimensions of covariation among variables across time, age levels, or situations. The criticism that its generalizability is severely limited since all measurements are based on a single subject is plausible on the surface, but one may argue that what is needed is for more researchers to commit the time and effort to run an entire sample of such analyses to see whether or not the factors are generalizable. There are no necessary logical reasons why one should expect, a priori, that the factor loading patterns for different studies will not replicate each other. On the other hand, it may be that for some research purposes, generalizability across subjects is not important. One may be more interested in generalizing over measurement occasions (e.g., age levels) for a single person.

A second advantage of P technique analysis is recognized when the information inherent in the factor scores is considered. Whereas the factor loading pattern defines dimensions of intraindividual variation in terms of response variables, the factor scores indicate the relative level of score on each factor for each time of measurement. Since these scores are explicitly tied to time of measurement one can order an individual's factor scores with respect to the time continuum to get a fuller description of the mechanisms of change. Indeed, if one has exerted some controlled manipulation of environmental aspects during the course of data collection he is in a position to map fluctuations in factor scores to stimulus variation. R. B. Cattell (1963a, 1966d) has more fully discussed this latter approach—stimulus controlled P technique— and other potentially valuable variations of the basic analytical method.

One last point with regard to using P technique is that in long-term studies one should be sensitive to the fact that blocks of occasions, i.e., subsets out of the total number of occasions, can create their own factors which would appear in the factor matrix as though they were general to all occasions of measurement. By examining factor scores, or perhaps better, by "blocking" occasions and doing several P-technique analyses, each over a subset of measurement occasions, one could detect qualitative changes (in factor loading patterns) over the span of measurement. This procedure could be used, for example, to test hypotheses concerning ontogenetic discontinuities.

The transpose of P technique—O technique—involves the same type of data matrix but begins by correlating occasions over response measures and analyzes for dimensions of occasions rather than response dimensions. Coan (1966) has suggested that O and related techniques may offer a means for the identification of stages, trends, cycles, points of transition, etc. It should be noted that the work of Horst (1965), J. Ross (1963), Tucker (1966), and others suggests that for a given type of data matrix, with certain scaling solutions and adaptations of the model, one gets the same basic factorial solution by doing either member of the pairs of solutions R and Q, P and O, or S and T techniques (to be discussed next).

S and T techniques, the one being the transpose of the other, constitute the remainder of the basic six approaches definable in terms of the covariation chart. Here the basic data consist of scores obtained by measuring a set of subjects with *one* instrument over a number of age levels or occasions. One can covary individuals over occasions (S technique), or he can covary occasions over persons (T technique). The former identifies person dimensions and the latter, occasion dimensions. Hofstätter (1954), for example, used the T technique in an attempt to isolate components of change in intelligence test scores.

One of the most striking applications of factor analytic methods to data of this type has been with a model developed by Tucker (1958, 1966) for purposes of analyzing learning data. The data matrix is composed of learning performance scores for each subject on each trial. Use of this model isolates generalized (reference) learning curves but it also yields a set of scores, analogous to factor scores, which may be unique for each person. By weighting and combining the reference learning curves by means of a given individual's unique weights that individual's learning curve can be reproduced. Two critical aspects of this approach are: (a) it determines the number and shape of reference learning curves necessary to account for the given data, and (b) it permits the recognition and quantification of individual differences in performance. In one sense it offers a test of the reasonableness of averaging individuals' learning curves to describe the learning function but it will no doubt be put to more positive uses. It has strong implications for developmental psychology not only as a highly sophisticated model for analyzing learning data but, more generally, for examining long-term, temporally related, changes.

V. OVERVIEW OF MORE GENERALIZED CORRELATIONAL TECHNIQUES

There is one final aspect to be discussed concerning the application of multivariate procedures to data sets specifiable within the covariation chart. The techniques discussed thus far were defined for primarily two-dimensional score matrices, or facets, only. In many cases an investigator may have data which are classifiable in three or more dimensions, e.g., a battery of test scores for a sample of individuals measured on each of several occasions or age levels. Rather than performing separate analyses for various two-dimensional subsets it may be advantageous to bring all data into a single analysis. Cattell (1966d) has discussed one method—grid designs—for "unrolling," as it were, three dimensional data into a two-dimensional configuration for more traditional analysis. Horn and Little (1966) have described a procedure, based on the multiple discriminant function model, for isolating dimensions of change and stability in data classifiable in three dimensions. The longitudinal factor model (Corballis & Traub, 1970) mentioned earlier, utilizes subjects x tests x occasions data but has yet to be generalized to more than two times of measurement. C. W. Harris (1963) also has discussed the application of factor analysis to two-occasion sets of data.

Tucker (1963) has generalized the basic factor analytic model to simultaneously handle data involving more than two modes of classification. Termed

3-mode, or, more generally, n-mode factor analysis, use of this technique permits the decomposition of an n-dimensional data matrix into a set of factor matrices, one for each mode of data classification, plus a core matrix linking them together. Although the algebra involved in explicating the structure of the model is demanding, the possibilities for developmental psychology become obvious when one considers that one mode or classification dimension may be time of measurement.

One last factor analytic technique to be mentioned deals directly with change scores—differential-R (dR) analysis (R. B. Cattell, 1963a, 1966d). Here the attempt is made to get directly at the structure of change by intercorrelating and factoring difference score data. That is, one subtracts each subject's score on each variable on one occasion from the corresponding score on the other occasion and uses these algebraic differences as basic data. Use of this technique has tended to produce factors similar in loading pattern to usual R-technique factors. The writer has discussed the relationships between dR and R-technique factors elsewhere (Nesselroade, 1967, 1970), indicating under what conditions differences and similarities should appear in the factor loading patterns.

VI. AREAS OF CONVERGENCE BETWEEN MULTIVARIATE TECHNIQUES AND DEVELOPMENTAL CONCEPTS

For those who are sold on the virtues of experimentation using a single observable as the operational expression of a concept, most of the analytical tools discussed in the preceding sections, admittedly, will offer little excitement. What these techniques do provide is an analytical substrate for the design and conduct of research studies, either as the outgrowth of theory or in preparation for theory development, which attempt to examine simultaneously a variety of response measures. They offer, in addition, a great amount of lattitude in choice of inference levels in moving from empirical data to abstract concepts. Patterns of covariation among response measures, once convincingly replicated across age levels, subpopulations, conditions, or occasions of measurement may be difficult to resist "naming," even if an investigator is basically disinclined to do so, but that is another issue.

At various points in this discussion the writer has alluded to particular developmental issues and the implications of covariation techniques for their study. Let us briefly focus more clearly on a few major points. One of these is the concept of developmental stages (Beilin, 1969; Emmerich, 1968; Kessen, 1962; Van den Daele, 1969) and qualitative versus quantitative differences in behavior. Beilin, for example, suggests that empirical support for the stage concept requires, at the very least, evidence that differences in behavior are qualitative. The use of factor analytic techniques has been mentioned (also see

Baltes & Nesselroade, 1970) as a first step in determining whether various dimensions of behavior are qualitatively the same or different. The point is that use of these methods to structure behavior as it changes over time will either provide evidence for the necessity of invoking the concept of qualitative variation or else suggest that the observed differences in behavior can be cast into quantitative comparisons. For example, either different factors or a different number of factors at two age levels would not only be indicative of qualitative change but they would also provide a description of: (a) its dimensionality, and (b) the particular subsets of variables involved.

Investigations of the differentiation hypothesis in the abilities area (see Reinert, Chapter 17) represents one of the early attempts to utilize multivariate techniques to isolate qualitative change. These early studies were somewhat unsuccessful as a function, in the main, of the lack of powerful factor analytic techniques, especially rotational solutions, to test for invariance of loadings—a deficiency which has been virtually eliminated. A similar approach could be used in areas other than intelligence, e.g., developmental learning and perception using various differentiation hypotheses other than age differentiation.

Differentiation studies in general represent a class of R-technique (and, by implication, Q-technique) analyses in which the basic data are scores for samples of subjects measured on a set of variables at particular points in time. Comparisons are then drawn between factor loading patterns derived from say, different age levels. It also seems worthwhile to consider more fully the implications of the other basic covariation techniques for classifying developmental phenomena.

P and O techniques, for example, fall clearly into the category of ipsative approaches (Emmerich, 1968). These techniques deal with the structuring of intraindividual variability over time and offer not only a means for determining dimensions of covariation among observables but also indicate groupings of measurement occasions, e.g., age levels, in terms of continuity or discontinuity of intraindividual change, as discussed earlier. Thus far, these models simply have not been explored in a long-term developmental context.

For those favoring the use of one "dependent" variable at a time S and T techniques hold the promise of a powerful set of methods for looking at issues of change. In S and T techniques, it will be recalled, only one response measure is used but the sample of subjects is measured repeatedly. These measurements could be as frequent as trials in a paired-associates learning task or as infrequent say, as annual measurements of ability. One may then examine patterns of covariation among persons (across time) or patterns of covariation of measurement occasions (across persons). For example, a sample composed of subjects of different initial ages, each person measured at regular intervals, might be analyzed by S technique to reveal that in terms of measured performance over time 10-year-old Billy is more similar to 8-year-old Freddie than he is to other

10-year-olds on a particular factor. Recourse to the factor scores, which, in this instance, would relate occasions of measurement to factors, would indicate for which occasions of measurement the classification of Billy with Freddie was relevant. The transpose type of analysis—T technique—would provide factor loadings indicating clusterings of occasions of measurement and the corresponding factor scores would indicate the rank order of persons on these dimensions.

Another point of convergence between multivariate analysis procedures and developmental concepts can be seen in the discussion by Emmerich (1968) of the issues of "continuity-discontinuity" and "stability-instability." The present writer (Nesselroade, 1970) has discussed techniques for isolating four types of factors, each cross-classified on the basis of: (a) the constancy or inconstancy of its loading pattern, and (b) the stability or instability of the factor scores. As pointed out by Baltes and Nesselroade (1970) these seem to provide an operational definition for Emmerich's four types of structural development. Basically, the strategy is that the determination of factor score stability coefficients is an appropriate, meaningful operation providing one accepts a factor as being the same at two points in time. Thus, for example, one may determine factors which show a high degree of similarity of loading pattern across occasions of measurement but, for some of these invariant factors, the rank order of individuals' scores may alter considerably while for other factors, the individuals may remain highly stable in their ordering. In personality description these two types of factors have been identified as states and traits, respectively (R. B. Cattell, 1966d), but the implications of these concepts and allied analysis procedures for the study of long term change must be more fully explored.

VII. CONCLUSION

This paper has not attempted to describe in great detail multivariate analysis procedures nor has it focused on highly technical and specific applications of multivariate techniques to the study of behavioral change. Rather it has aimed to provide a brief overview of the logic and methods of a class of analytic procedures developed to systematically deal with comprehensive sets of data. The writer has tried to point out the capabilities of these methods for dealing with general problems of behavior change and it is hoped that their implications for developmental psychology have been sufficiently emphasized.

It seems fair to point out that the development of complex methods and models for dealing with change has far outstripped their systematic application to empirical data. It may also be that it has outrun solutions to some questions regarding very basic topics such as scaling. Hopefully these issues will be resolved as more researchers, both substantively oriented ones and statistically oriented ones, begin attending to them.

PERCEPTION
AND
COGNITION

Life-Span Changes in Visual Perception

PETER E. COMALLI, Jr.

TEMPLE UNIVERSITY
PHILADELPHIA, PENNSYLVANIA

ABSTRACT

Empirical evidence, graphically illustrated and discussed, is presented to demonstrate life-span changes in perceptual achievements. The studies cited show perceptual performance between children and the aged to be more similar than between young adults over the course of the life-span. A plea is made for developmental theory to be more cognizant of such progressive-regressive changes in order to have a truly life-span developmental psychology.

I. INTRODUCTION

Walter R. Miles (1933), in a presidential address to the American Psychological Association, made a strong plea for psychologists to turn their experimental searchlight clear across the length as well as the breadth of man's life-span. Despite the background support of his own research, Miles' plea went largely unheeded; nevertheless, he was instrumental in creating a separate area of psychological interest in gerontology. Interestingly enough, another presidential address, this time delivered by Bayley (1963) to Division 20 (Maturity and Old Age) of the APA on August 29, 1958, called for the life-span as a frame of reference in psychological research. Now, finally, in 1969 this conference is attempting to give serious attention to a life-span developmental psychology.

My intent in this paper is merely to present in a cursory fashion some of the empirical evidence for life-span changes in perception with the hope that future research and theory will make the goals of this conference a concrete reality. I will not attempt to review even partially the vast amount of experimental literature on sensory functioning since excellent reviews are available from infancy to maturity (Kidd & Kidd, 1966; Munn, 1965; Rivoire & Kidd, 1966) and from maturity to old age (McFarland, 1968; A. D. Weiss, 1959).

II. VISUAL ILLUSION

Among studies with geometric optical illusions, the Muller-Lyer illusion pattern still remains the most popular for investigation at all ages. As a point of departure for further comparisons a series of extended studies by Wapner and Werner (1957), Wapner, Werner, and Comalli (1960), and Comalli (1965b) demonstrated age changes in susceptibility to the Muller-Lyer illusion over the life-span. A Brentano version of the pattern was used and the method of adjustment employed. Figure 1 presents the developmental course from 6 to 90 years of age. The graph indicates that, in general, there is a decrease in illusory effect from 6 to 12 and, after a rise at 15-19, susceptibility to the illusion remains fairly constant between 20 to 39, beyond which there is an increase in

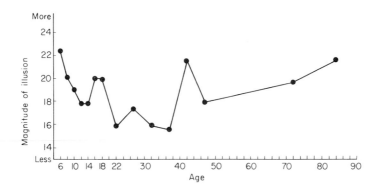

Figure 1. Age changes to Muller-Lyer Illusion (Comalli, 1965b; Wapner & Werner, 1957; Wapner *et al.*, 1960).

illusion effect with advancing age. Of the several studies cited by Wohlwill (1960a), all are in agreement with regards to the decrease of this illusion from ages 6 to 10 (Binet, 1895; Piaget, Maire, & Privat, 1954; Pintner & Anderson, 1916; Walters, 1942). More recent studies in this age range provide additional confirmation (Comalli, 1969; Hanley & Zerbolio, 1965; Pollack, 1964; Segall, Campbell, & Herskovitz, 1966).

Empirical studies bearing on the age range from young adulthood to old age are less numerous than those concerned with the early phase of development. Gajo (1966) criticized the general increase in susceptibility to the Muller-Lyer illusion from maturity to old age as being due to an artifact of method rather than a function of regression as hypothesized by Wapner et al. (1960). In his experiment, Gajo utilized two psychophysical methods, method of adjustment and method of limits, counterbalanced the position of the standard and controlled for visual acuity and for discrimination of length. Using three age groups, 30-44 years, 45-59 years, and 60-77 years, his findings showed that the oldest group was more susceptible to the illusion than the two younger groups and held for both psychophysical methods used. Eisner (1968), in contrasting the regression notion with the accuracy notion of Gajo, and in an attempt to clarify age trends in aging Ss to the Muller-Lyer, utilized the cross-sequential design (Schaie, 1965) and in addition provided for analysis of variables of verbal intelligence and length of institutionalization. Ss were selected from two VA domiciliaries and consisted of 133 Ss ranging in age from 55 to 75 years and devoid of psychiatric diagnoses or acute medical problems. All Ss were retested after a six month interval. Both cross-sectional and longitudinal analysis showed increased illusion effects with age. Thus, there is general confirmation among

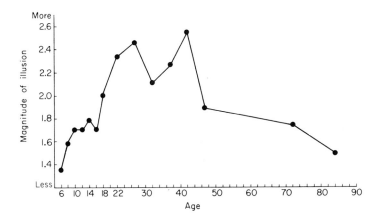

Figure 2. Age changes to Titchener circles illusion (Comalli, 1965b; Wapner & Werner, 1957; Wapner et al., 1960).

various studies that from childhood to old age there is first a decrease in susceptibility to the Muller-Lyer illusion, followed by a stable period of no change, and finally an increase in the illusory effect in old age.

In contrast to the Muller-Lyer illusion, life-span changes to the Titchener circles illusion pattern (Figure 2) shows illusory effects to increase with increasing age in early development followed by a decrease in the old age period (Comalli, 1965b; Wapner *et al.*, 1960). Confirmation of this age trend is unclear, however, as the studies by Gajo (1966), Eisner (1968), and Comalli (1969) with this pattern found little change between middle and old age groups, although the trend for the latter two investigators indicated a decrease in the illusion effect in old age.

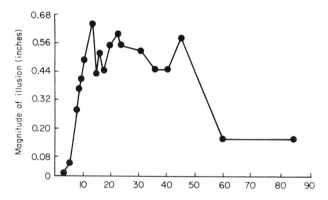

Figure 3. Age changes to Ponzo illusion (Leibowitz & Judisch, 1967).

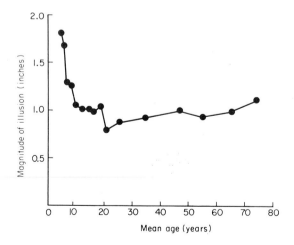

Figure 4. Age changes to Poggendorff illusion (Leibowitz & Gwozdecki, 1967).

Two other illusions covering the life-span have been reported: one with the Ponzo illusion (Leibowitz & Judisch, 1967), and the other with the Poggendorff illusion (Leibowitz & Gwozdecki, 1967). With the Ponzo illusion, at the youngest age level, susceptibility was minimum and increased with increasing age to 13, leveled off through age 50, and then decreased in magnitude for the two oldest groups tested (Figure 3). On the other hand, the Poggendorff illusion was greatest among the youngest age group, decreased with age until approximately ten years and then levels off with the trend to increase again in old age (Figure 4). Thus through the life-span, age-related changes in susceptibility to Muller-Lyer, Titchener Circles, Ponzo, and Poggendorff illusion patterns are consistent with the developmental notion of showing progression followed by regression (Wapner et al. 1960). The life-span findings with these illusion patterns, furthermore, have important implications for the theoretical formulations of Piaget (1961), Pollack (1969), and Gregory (1966) who have proposed developmental explanations of illusions (Over, 1968) for the early part of development, but without consideration of subsequent changes during the latter part of the life cycle.

III. SPATIAL ORIENTATION

Experimental studies dealing with perception of spatial orientation encompass a variety of variables and are quite numerous. Fortunately, this area has been well summarized and critically evaluated by Howard and Templeton (1966). On the other hand, developmental studies are less numerous (Rivoire & Kidd, 1966; Wohlwill, 1960a), and life-span data rare. The early work of Wapner and Werner (1957) provides one of the few examples of where the empirical research carried out in early development was later extended to cover the area of maturity and old age.

In the monograph study of 1957, Wapner and Werner found two significant developmental trends in the perception of verticality from ages 6 to 20 years. One concerns the effect of body tilt: Within the younger age levels, a luminescent rod in a darkroom is perceived as vertical when tilted to the side at which the body is tilted; this is in contrast to older age levels where it is perceived as vertical when tilted opposite the side of body tilt.

In two extensions of this study (Comalli, Wapner, & Werner, 1959; Comalli, 1965b) it was found that perception of the apparent vertical remains opposite the tilt of the body until the beginning of the sixth decade when perception of the vertical reverts toward the body tilt. These results may be seen in Figure 5. Thus, the developmental shift in the direction of overcompensation for the effect of body tilt during adolescence is reversed during senescence.

A second developmental trend relates to the effects of starting position. This effect is observed in the displacement of the apparent vertical to the side at

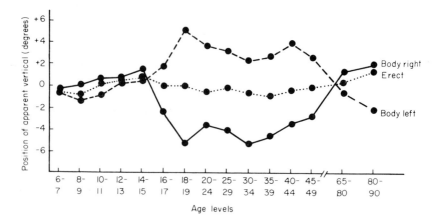

Figure 5. Age changes in effect of body tilt on perception of verticality (Comalli, 1965b; Comalli et al., 1959; Wapner & Werner, 1957).

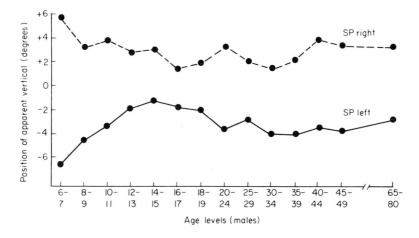

Figure 6. Age changes in effect of starting position on perception of verticality (Comalli *et al.*, 1959; Wapner & Werner, 1957).

which the rod is initially placed at the beginning of a trial. The developmental trend here is a steady decrease in starting position effect up to late adolescence, followed by no further change from maturity into old age. (See Figure 6). The developmental changes with respect to the effect of body tilt and starting position effects were interpreted as being consistent with the general developmental principle that with increase in age there is increasing differentiation of self and object. It was assumed that this lack of differentiation at the early age level is manifested in two ways: (a) by egocentricity, that is, the formation of a frame of reference whereby the stimuli are interpreted in terms of body position and (b) by stimulus boundedness, which refers to the inordinate impact of object stimuli. The reversal in the tilt relation of body and rod in old age was taken to indicate the reverting to a more egocentric organization of space. The relative absence of large starting positions effects in the old was taken to characterize an important difference between children and the aged in that the older person still maintains a relatively stable spatial frame of reference not as easily disturbed by every change in stimulation.

A study by Davies and Laytham (1964) using eight men and eight women matched for distribution of intelligence in each of six age decades from twenties to seventies failed to substantiate the findings of Comalli et al. (1959) with respect to regression. In the Davies study, all age groups located the vertical to the side opposite to the body tilt. Since it has been found that in early development the tendency to overcompensate for effects of body tilt appears much earlier in females than in males, by roughly four years (Wapner & Werner, 1957), the possibility exists that in senescence, the developmental changes in females may occur later than in males.

In old age, systematic studies bearing on this point have not yet been carried out. However, the Davies study points out the importance of using smaller age intervals than is customarily employed in assessing age changes in the latter half of the life-cycle. This is borne out by a further replication by Comalli (unpublished). Data from this study is presented in Figure 7. The age range covers decades from the 20s to the 80s and with a larger sample of Ss, all males. It can be seen that the results are consistent with the earlier findings of Comalli et al. (1959) and Comalli (1965a). It is apparent, however, that reversals for the effect of body tilt on apparent vertical are not clearly manifested for males until the 70s while starting position effects remain normal in the 70s (See Figure 8). In this connection, it is important to note that the 80-year-old group is distinguished from the 70-year-old group by the manifestation of larger starting position effects. In an earlier paper, Comalli et al. (1959) argued that the absence of increased starting position effects in old age, coupled with egocentric position of the apparent vertical, defined changes in spatial organization occuring in old age as part of normal ontogenetic development, while pathological changes could be evidenced by the presence of large starting position effects. It still remains for future studies to determine whether such a distinction can be usefully made.

The development toward increasing compensation for effects of body tilt have also been observed with respect to auditory localization. Liebert and Rudel (1959) tested the midline localization of sound under conditions of left and right body tilt from 5 to 17 years of age. With increasing age they found an increasing displacement of the estimated auditory midline toward the side

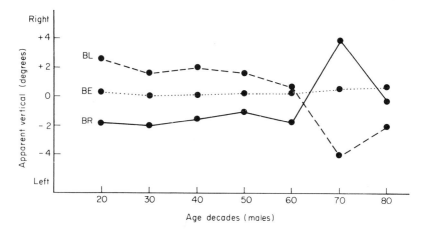

Figure 7. Age changes in effect of body tilt on perception of verticality (Comalli, unpublished data).

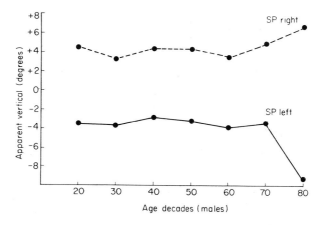

Figure 8. Age changes in effect of starting position on perception of verticality (Comalli, unpublished data).

opposite body tilt and decreasing starting position error. In a following study, Rudel, Teuber, Liebert, and Halpern (1960) performed the same test on brain damaged children over the same age range from 5 to 17. Differences between the two groups in setting the auditory midline under body tilt emerged only in late childhood. On the other hand, from the earliest age tested, brain damaged Ss had larger starting position effects and this difference was maintained throughout subsequent years. The extension of these two studies into the old-age period would appear to be very promising.

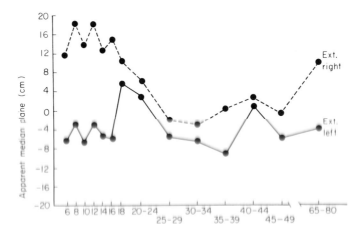

Figure 9. Age changes in effect of asymmetrical extent on position of the apparent median plane (Wapner & Comalli, unpublished data; Wapner & Werner, 1957).

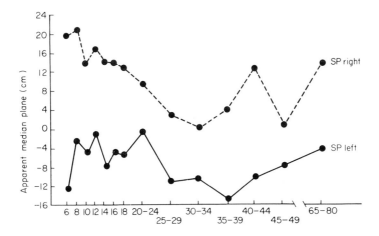

Figure 10. Age changes in effect of starting position of apparent median plane (Wapner & Comalli, unpublished data; Wapner & Werner, 1957).

Life-span data on two other perceptual characteristics of spatial localization, (apparent median plane; apparent horizon) first studied in the early period of development by Wapner and Werner (1957) and later extended into adult maturity by Wapner and Comalli (unpublished) may also be mentioned here. In one experimental situation the *S*'s task was to adjust in a darkroom the right or left edge of a luminous square so that it appeared straight ahead (apparent median plane). The test conditions involved variations of two factors: asymmetrical extent (i.e., the placement of the square extending to the left or right of the point of fixation), and starting position, (i.e., the initial location of the fixated part of the luminous square with respect to the objective median plane). The developmental effects of asymmetrical extent and starting position on the location of the apparent median plane, in terms of deviation from the S's objective straight ahead, are shown in Figures 9 and 10.

It may be noted that the large effects of asymmetrical extent found through most of the early developmental phase, and greatly diminished in the adult phase, begins to emerge again in the aged; while the large starting position effects demonstrated in childhood show decreasing effects to young adulthood, no reversal is suggested with advancing years. This bears a striking parallel to the findings with apparent verticality previously discussed.

Another set of experiments dealt with changes in the localization of the apparent horizon, a term referring to the physical position of an object in space *perceived* as at the horizon or eye level. The task of the S was to adjust in a darkroom a luminous stimulus object so that it appeared at his eye level. In one experiment the stimulus was a pictured object of hands pointing upwards and of hands pointing downwards. In the other experiment the stimulus material consisted of four words; two had an upward connotation, ("climbing" and "higher"), and two had a downward connotation ("dropping" and "falling").

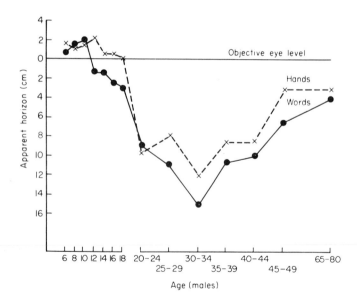

Figure 11. Age changes to presented words and to pictured objects on the poisition of the apparent horizon (Comalli & Wapner, unpublished data; Wapner and Werner, 1957).

The design of the experiments was intended to investigate the developmental changes in the effect of directional dynamics inherent in pictorial material and words. No consistent developmental effects of induced directional sets were found, but what did emerge from the data was a systematic change with age of the overall position of the apparent horizon, independent of directional dynamics. Figure 11 shows a developmental shift of the apparent horizon from a relatively high position at early ages to progressively lower levels with increasing age and then reverting to higher levels again with continuing increase in age. Interpretation of this life-span developmental trend is unclear, and could possibly profit from the additional study of changes to meaningless stimuli, e.g., a horizontal line, as well as to meaningful stimuli.

IV. PART-WHOLE DIFFERENTIATION

Witkin, Lewis, Hertman, Machover, Meisser, and Wapner (1954) in their earlier work conducted a series of developmental studies on what they termed perceptual field dependency. Of relevance to this paper were three tests of field dependency, the Rod-and-Frame, Body-Adjustment, and Embedded-Figures Tests. Each required the S to separate an item—a rod, his own body, or a simple geometric figure—from its background or context. Results from these studies indicated a general course of development from childhood to early adulthood of decreasing field dependency, i.e., less reliance on irrelevant contextual cues, with increased age. These test situations have been extended into advanced age by Comalli (1962, 1965a) and Schwartz and Karp (1967). In the Rod-and-Frame Test (RFT) situation a tilted luminous square frame surrounds a luminous

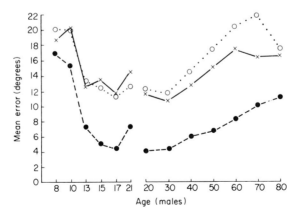

Figure 12. Age changes to Rod-and-Frame Test (Comalli, 1962, 1965a; Witkin *et al.*, 1954). Dashed lines for body erect and frame tilted, solid line for body and frame tilted to opposite side, dotted lines for body and frame tilted to same side.

rod in an otherwise completely dark room. With the frame tilted, S is required to bring the rod to plumb line position under conditions of erect and tilted body positions. Figure 12 presents life-span data on the RFT by combining studies from Witkin and Comalli. It can be seen that the steady decrease in the influence of a tilted luminous frame on the perception of the rod as vertical during childhood and adolescence is followed by a steady increase with advancing old age.

In the Body-Adjustment Test (BAT) S is seated in a chair in a small room with the room tilted; S is required to bring his body-in-the-chair to a vertical position. Figure 13 combines the data from Witkin *et al.* (1954) and from

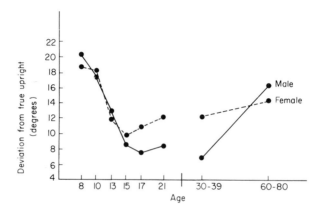

Figure 13. Age changes in adjustment of body to upright position under conditions of a Tilted-Room (Schwartz & Karp, 1967; Witkin *et al.*, 1954).

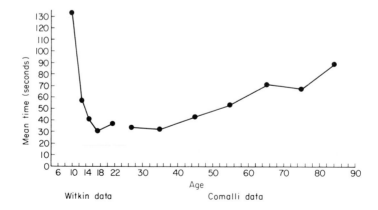

Figure 14. Age changes to Embedded-Figures Test (Comalli, 1965a; Witkin *et al.*, 1954).

Schwartz and Karp (1967). Again, as in the RFT, the tilted condition of the room has the greatest effect on children's perception of body position, decreases in its effect to adolescence, and finally reverts to an increased effect in old age. The Embedded-Figures Test (EFT), although not involving orientation toward the upright, does require the *S* to separate an item (a simple geometric figure) from the field in which it is embedded (a complex figure), the task being easy or difficult depending on the structure of the complex figure. Again, the life-span trend may be seen by combining the data from Witkin *et al.* (1954) for the early period in development with that of Comalli (1965b) for the later part of development. Figure 14 shows the average time taken to find the simple forms in the more complex figures. Difficulty in this performance rapidly decreases to midadolescence and after a period of no change, performance difficulty begins a steady increase with advancing age.

The capacity of the individual to maintain directed sequential activity independent of intruding stimuli was assessed with the Stroop Color Word Test in another life-span study by Comalli, Wapner, and Werner (1962). The test consisted of three tasks: (a) the reading of 100 randomly arranged color words (red, blue, and green) printed in black ink; (b) the naming of 100 randomly arranged patches of color (red, blue, and green); and (c) naming the *color of the ink* in which 100 color words are printed where color of the ink and the color designated by the word are incongrous; e.g., the word "blue" printed in red ink, the word "green" printed in blue ink, etc. All three tasks were to be performed as rapidly as possible with time serving as the measure. Figure 15 shows the obtained findings: Interference, i.e., susceptibility to intrusions of word reading on color naming, is greatest with young children, decreases with increasing age to adulthood and increases again with older age.

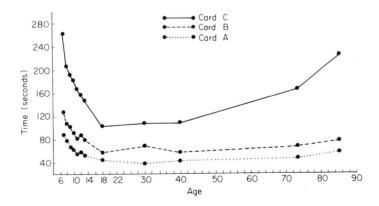

Figure 15. Age changes to Stroop Color Word Interference Test (Comalli, 1965b; Comalli *et al.*, 1962).

V. PERCEPTUAL CLOSURE

The developmental data bearing on whole versus part perception has many facets, well summarized and detailed by Wohlwill (1960a) for early development but minimally represented in studies of aging (Comalli, 1967).

Studies of closure have suggested in general that the adult is more capable of recognizing an incomplete form than either children or the aged. Street (1931) for his Gestalt Completion Test failed to find age differences between elementary and high school children. On the other hand, Mooney (1957) and Brenner (1957), using incomplete black and white representations of the heads and faces of particular categories of persons (sex and age) found perceptual competence, in terms of number of correct identification, to significantly increase with age. Using the technique of presenting Ss with incomplete pictures consisting of disconnected patches, which when viewed as a whole with the gaps filled in, could be seen as familiar objects, Verville and Cameron (1946), Basowitz and Korchin (1957), and Comalli (1963) all found that older Ss had a more difficult time than younger adults in recognizing incomplete pictures of familiar objects. In the study by Comalli (see Figure 16) the four perceptual closure tests used by Thurstone (1944), i.e., the Street Gestalt Completion Test, the Mutilated-Word Test, the Dotted-Outline Test, and the Hidden Digit Test, all showed similar age differences occuring primarily in the oldest age group. However, because time is used as a measure, it is difficult to know whether achieving perceptual closure is due to a lessened integrative ability or more a function of other factors such as, greater cautiousness in the aged to respond, their giving up sooner, or a tendency to become fixated to isolated parts of the

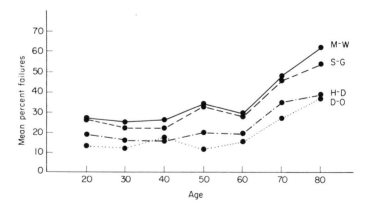

Figure 16. Age changes to four perceptual closure tests: Street Gestalt, Mutilated-Words, Hidden Digits and Dotted-Outlines (Comalli, 1963).

stimulus array. J. P. Thomas and Charles (1964), using partially erased words, similar to the Mutilated-Word Test, varied the stimulus size to double and triple the standard size. In comparing older versus younger adults, they found that with an increase in stimulus size, performance improved with both groups but still remained relatively poorer for the older Ss at all sizes.

A different and very interesting technique was used by Wallace (1956), which can be considered a study of temporal closure. Complete designs and pictures were mounted upon a band moving downward behind a narrow horizontal slit, so that only part of the picture was visible at any given time. The figures used varied from outlines of geometric figures to more complex pictorial representations. No age differences were found for simple figures, but with increasing complexity of designs older Ss showed poorer performance in correct identification—the greater difficulty of older Ss with complex material seemed to be due mainly to the greater amount of temporal integration required.

VI. SPEED OF RECOGNITION

In an early study reported by W. R. Miles (1942) from the Stanford Maturity Study, 684 Ss aged 6 to 89 were tested on six varieties of perceptual-test materials. Letters, numbers, short sentences, colors, groups of lines, and common expressions faultily written made up the printed material. Presentation of each of the stimuli was initiated tachistoscopically by the S for 0.1 second and for only one trial. Immediately after viewing, the S recorded what he had seen. Figure 17, obtained from a mean table, shows the number of items

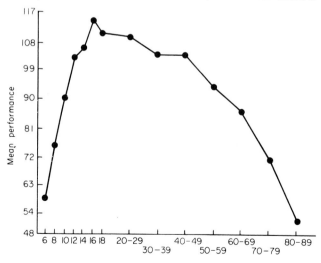

Figure 17. Influence of age on visual perception span and speed (W. R. Miles, 1942).

correctly seen and recorded. The graph shows perceptual efficiency and speed to rise rapidly from early age to midadolescence after which it begins a slow and then rapid decline into advanced old age. Unfortunately, evidence was not presented concerning the relative contribution made by the various kinds of materials to the overall score.

A somewhat clearer study was performed by Rajalakshmi and Jeeves (1963) on perceptual speed as measured by tachistoscopic form discrimination, and covered an age range from $5\frac{1}{2}$ to 75 years. The experimental task consisted of the identification of one odd figure in a set of five stimulus figures presented simultaneously. The stimulus figures were taken from reading readiness books

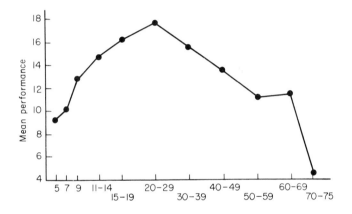

Figure 18. Performance in tachistoscopic form discrimination at different age levels (Rajalakshmi & Jeeves, 1963).

used in kindergarten classes and caused no difficulty to subjects when given unlimited exposure time. However, when four successive exposures of one second each with a dark interval of one second between exposures was given, systematic age changes were found. Figure 18 indicates the direction of the changes: Under limited time conditions, speed in form discrimination progressively improves up to maturity and declines rapidly thereafter.

VII. CONCLUSION

The empirical evidence presented in this paper show changes to occur in a systematic manner over the entire life-span. Developmental theory, presently focused primarily on progressive changes found in the early part of the life cycle, needs also to address itself to the regressive changes found in the latter part of life. It is only then that we will have a truly life-span developmental psychology.

CHAPTER **9**

Light Detection and Pattern Recognition: Some Comments on the Growth of Visual Sensation and Perception

HARRY MUNSINGER

UNIVERSITY OF CALIFORNIA,
SAN DIEGO, CALIFORNIA

ABSTRACT

The point of this paper is to distinguish energy detection from pattern recognition; I believe neonates capable only of energy detection. Early structuralists viewed perception as the connection of elementary sensations and memories. Gestalt psychology assumed we see structure by innate organization. I think we begin with energy detection and painfully program our pattern recognition device. The mechanisms required to detect energy are simple: a set of counters and a criterion for separating signal and noise. However, pattern recognition is more difficult: We need many counters to accumulate information, we need smoothing and sharpening processes; we need template matching; and we need networks which extract distinctive features for analysis and categorization. Two conceptions or detection and recognition exist: Some see detection as a byproduct of recognition; however, I believe detection develops first and feeds the recognition device. Evidence from neonatal and infant studies shows the human newborn is not sensitive to brightness changes and his visual acuity is comparable to adults' rod vision. Also, anatomical evidence suggests the neonate's fovea does not work. I propose a simultaneous detection and recognition paradigm, a signal detection analysis, and a way to avoid muddy or cloudy developmental data to study energy detection and pattern recognition.

I. INTRODUCTION

Our ability to handle visual input can be structured variously; I propose to distinguish visual *energy detection* (a simple decision that something is there and where it is in the field) from *pattern recognition* (a more complex decision about what it is). First, some early history of sensation and perception is reviewed for perspective. Then, the paper defines detection and recognition, proposes mechanisms required for their operation, and suggests a developmental course. A little anatomy follows; it concerns the structure of the eye, lateral geniculate, and visual cortex. Major findings about adult and neonatal visual perception are consistent with the proposed detection-recognition mechanisms. A simultaneous detection-recognition paradigm is proposed to explore sensation and perception.

Various methodological problems occur when we study infants, children, and adults simultaneously: Children and adults may use different decision processes. Judgment and sensitivity need to be separated; their unconfounding leads us to the theory of signal detection (D. T. Green & Swets, 1966). A final section covers some design problems unique to muddy or cloudy developmental data and explores the relation between origin and slope of psychophysical functions and detection or recognition.

II. SOME HISTORY OF SENSATION AND PERCEPTION

Early structuralists (Helmholtz, Wundt, & Titchener, in Boring, 1953) differentiated two components of perception: sensations (innate, visual, and meaningless) and images (past memories associated with sensations). They were impressed by developments in chemistry (elements and combination laws for these elements). The structuralists searched for the perceptual periodic table and for laws to join simple elements into complex perceptions. However, if we assume that detection and recognition are different processes, then sensations may not be the elements of perception. The question changes: Instead of searching for basic sensations, we should seek the distinctive features of patterns.

Gestalt psychology (Wertheimer, 1923) bypassed this question by assuming that perceptual objects are given immediately. However, many studies show that learning to see form requires experience; pattern recognition is not innate (Hebb, 1949). Object perception is a complex function of distinctive feature extraction, selective attention, and meaning; it requires sophisticated information handling mechanisms.

III. THE MECHANISMS OF DETECTION AND RECOGNITION

Specification of visual mechanisms remains a central problem in psychology; speculation has ranged from sensory processes alone, perceptual processes alone, to various combinations of sensory and perceptual systems (Hershenson, 1967). Clear criteria for differentiating sensation and perception are scarce. The list might include: (a) complexity of relations between inputs and responses, (b) locus of processing, (c) number of transformations performed on the input before presentation to the central processor, (d) time of appearance in the developmental sequence, and (e) mechanisms involved in processing.

Different mechanisms, complexity of relation, and developmental variation are used to differentiate the visual processes in this paper. My central theme is that *sensory* systems (a) are sensitive to energy, (b) are attention directing, and (c) develop early; on the other hand, *perceptual* systems (a) are sensitive to information, (b) are pattern analyzing mechanisms, and (c) develop throughout the child's life. I assume that energy detection occurs in the neonate while pattern recognition develops during childhood.

What mechanisms are required to detect energy changes compared to those involved in pattern recognition? Detection devices need a set of counters to accumulate neural impulses over some specified interval and a criterion to decide whether the neural counters registered noise or light. A criterion could be the average count over the last N intervals. If any counter exceeds this average during an interval, we assume the input was a signal; if all counters remain below this average we assume the input was noise. The detection device must also remember which counter was above criterion so it can align the fovea.

A more sophisticated criterion (for deciding signal from noise) can be achieved by giving the detection device feedback and a means of adjustment. For example, suppose the device can raise its criterion—require a higher count— following a false alarm (saying something happened when in fact nothing was there) and can lower its criterion when it misses (says nothing happened when in fact something was there). Of course, the criterion is unchanged following a hit and a correct rejection. Feedback would adjust the detection criterion to match current energy levels and background noise. The system's stability is regulated by the size of criterial changes following a miss or false alarm (large changes bring quick adjustment and instability).

Pattern recognition is a much more complex process. We need many counters, each related to energy changes in a small area of the retina. In addition to many counters, we need smoothing and sharpening processes; these mechanisms might rotate the image, fill in errors, smooth the outline, emphasize contours, and transform the input into a common size. Following these initial transformations, we can either compare the input directly with an image stored in memory (template matching) or extract features from the input (lines, angles, slopes, patterns) and make a series of decisions on the basis of these features, thus classifying it (unconscious inference). A distinctive feature analysis requires networks of bipolar cells to fire when particular combinations of retinal cells are stimulated.

Some process of judgment may intervene between detection or recognition and overt responses. For detection, I assume the decision is automatic—the newborn *must* orient his fovea toward energy. Recognition eventually comes under a more voluntary control. The judgment process evaluates a percept, combines it with a priori probabilities of occurrence and payoffs for various outcomes to decide upon a response. Relations between judgment and sensitivity are outlined later.

My developmental assumptions are three: First, the detection process is available early (at birth). Second, the detection device automatically orients the pattern recognition system toward information. Third, following repeated stimulation the perceptual system begins to function. Pattern recognition may grow, as Hebb (1949) suggested, by tracing contours; on the other hand, it may develop through maturation, or it may require neural maturation and stimulation to develop. *In any case, the detection system guarantees information input to the pattern recognizer.* The pattern recognition device may be prewired so that it is sensitive to certain features of environmental information; input could then activate these feature extracting mechanisms and repeated experience could coordinate their signals to form object percepts.

Figure 1 shows the proposed developmental stages of detection and recognition; I assume the detection device (Figure 1a) functions at birth. Energy changes produce sensations which trigger an orienting mechanism designed to align the fovea (pattern recognition device) with information. Since the pattern recognition device is not functional at birth, the fovea should drift. The result would be repeated eye movements between the detection device and the fovea. In the next stage (Figure 1b), the pattern recognition system begins to store images of the input. The final stage (Figure 1c) includes a detection device, a functional pattern recognition process, and a judgment system which coordinates perception and response. How judgment develops is hypothetical at best; its growth must account for the infant's shift from stimulus capture to active information searching. Piaget (Flavell, 1963) speculates on the process; it is not crucial to my argument, so I move on.

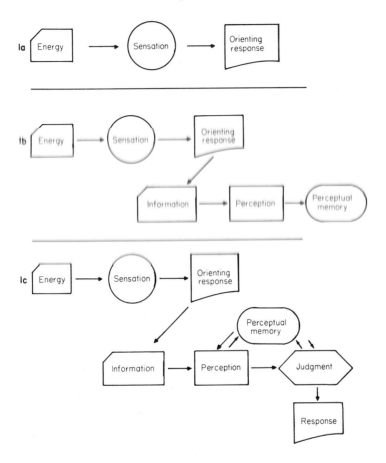

Figure 1.

A Little Anatomy

The vertebrate visual system is quite complex; the optical apparatus (cornea and accommodating lens) focuses an image on the retinal mosaic at the back of the eye. The distribution of rods and cones in the retina varies (Figure 2): This systematic variation has strong functional implications; it represents a compromise between wide-angle vision and sharp visual acuity.

Between the eye and the brain there are at least six types of cells: Three types are located in the retina itself (an embryonic outgrowth of the brain); the geniculate body and two layers in the visual cortex complete the differentiation. Processing begins in the retina, is then elaborated in the geniculate body, and

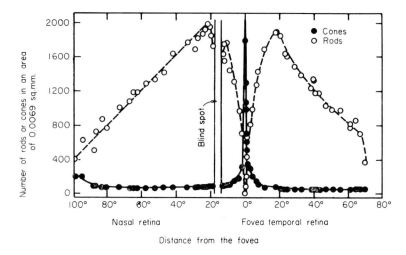

Figure 2. Rod-cone density.

final computations occur in the visual cortex. Preprocessing makes good sense—the transmission of raw input along the optic nerve would require many paths; to relieve this burden, the retina filters and transforms information before sending it on to the lateral geniculate and the visual cortex. Retinal preprocessing might include image smoothing, contour extracting, noise filtering, and the coding of distinctive features. The lateral geniculate enhances differences between on and off regions of the retina; it is primarily a contour differentiator and noise suppressor. The cortex contains at least two functionally different cell types. some respond to lines of varying slant while others signal movement in the visual field (Hubel & Wiesel, 1962).

There must be at least two levels of organization in the retina: One concerns connections between receptors and bipolar cells, another level of organization occurs between bipolar and ganglion cells. I believe receptor-bipolar cells simply summate energy (sensitivity is increased by linking several receptors to one bipolar cell); on the other hand, I think ganglion cells are related to feature extraction networks. Thus, the eye's grain and sensitivity is controlled by receptor-bipolar mapping, while recognition is related to bipolar-ganglion cell relations. Ganglion cells extract information from wide areas of the retina to feed feature extraction networks. Bipolar cells link receptors to increase sensitivity.

B. Why Detect and Recognize?

As eyes evolve, their acuity and differentiation generally increase. Evolution can either distribute this acuity over the entire eye, or it can concentrate resources in a small area. Concentration yields increased acuity (ability to differentiate patterns of information); however, it also produces tunnel vision (see Figure 3). There is a middle ground that evolution might find—a compromise: We can produce a highly differentiated central fovea, and around that small center spread another device to detect energy changes. The detection system is a light-sensitive alarm to signal and guide ocular orientations. A dual eye produces fine acuity *and* wide-angle sensitivity. The detection device can monitor large visual areas using few bipolar cells; once energy is detected, the eye aligns its more sophisticated pattern recognition device (fovea) with the information. The

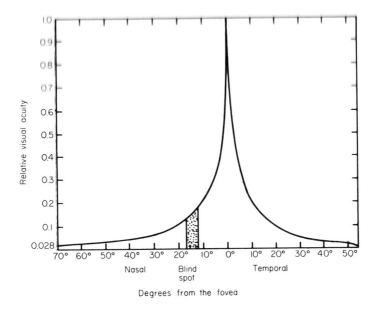

Figure 3. Visual acuity at different retinal positions.

periphery of our retina is served by relatively few neural fibres while the fovea receives many neural connections. Our networks of rods (where a single neural fiber serves approximately one hundred receptors) is primarily an energy summation system designed to maximize sensitivity; however, during summation, *information* is lost. To offset this peripheral information loss we have a central area to differentiate patterns. The rods monitor a wide field and are more sensitive; the fovea is less sensitive but assesses information more easily. Together they constitute a sophisticated perceptual instrument. The fovea can detect brightness, but detection is secondary to pattern recognition. This is a complex problem; only careful study will determine the developmental relations of detection and recognition in rods and cones.

C. The Relation between Detection and Recognition

There are two popular views of energy detection and pattern recognition: One position assumes they reflect a single perceptual process; however, I believe energy detection and pattern recognition are related occasionally by accident.

Proponents of a single mechanism for detection and recognition assume the visual system contains only feature analyzers sensitive to patterned input. To detect, the observer must be aware that some feature analysing network is firing. However, to recognize, the observer must know the *particular* feature analyzer or set of analyzers fired. For detection, information is lost; the device summates over many receptors. For recognition, information is differentiated; the system makes its decision on the basis of which feature analyzing networks are active. J. P. Thomas (1965) showed that the contour gradient of a small patch of light is related to its brightness when exposed foveally at relatively long durations. These data suggest the fovea is primarily a pattern recognition device; even for brightness judgments, the fovea differentiates. Lateral inhibition is proposed to account for differences in perceived brightness as a function of contour diffraction. Blackwell and Smith (1959) reported differences in detection accuracy as a function of form (a circle was easier to detect than other forms presented foveally).

The assumption of two processes implies that energy detection follows different rules than pattern recognition. Detection is a primitive process complemented later by recognition; recognition represents the final stage of perceptual development. Developmental and experimental evidence suggests that detection and recognition are different. Although pattern perception is affected by some of the same variables which determine energy detection (i. e., intensity and duration of stimulation), form recognition and energy detection are differentially related to other variables (e. g., size of detail, similarity of shape). Energy detection and form recognition thresholds are not correlated (Ives & Shilling, 1941). Marshall and Day (1951) noted that in detection one need not keep bars of light separate; however, to recognize two bars their separation must be preserved. At higher levels of illumination the recognition system retains discrete information. The opposite occurs at low levels of illumination; peripheral receptor fields (many rods connected to a single bipolar cell) summate

E. Wolf and Zigler (1950) reported that when crude measures are used, detection and recognition are related. However, when the discrimination of form is made difficult, detection accuracy is unrelated to recognition difficulty (in stimuli equated for area).

Kleitman and Blier (1928) demonstrated that the ability to recognize forms in the periphery of our visual field is closely related to size; larger forms are easier to recognize over more of the visual field. Also, they found that detection ability is invariant over changes in form, while recognition ability varies with shape similarity.

Krauskopf, Duryea, and Bitterman (1954) showed that sensitivity to light (detection) varies with exposure duration and area of the stimulus, but is *unaffected* by extensive changes in configuration. By contrast, recognition accuracy varies with exposure duration, area of the stimulus, *and* configuration. In a related study (Harcum, 1967) eight forms were used to determine detection and recognition thresholds; detection ability was invariant over the several forms, while recognition accuracy varied with shape.

Zeidner, Goldstein, and Johnson (1954) factor analyzed various measures of visual accuracy collected during dark adaptation. They found four major factors:

	Percent variance
Resolution of fine detail, rod vision	20
Resolution of fine detail, cone vision	20
Brightness differences, adapted cone	20
Brightness differences, adapted rod	19

Measures at low illuminance (the ability to detect energy) show no relation to measures taken at higher levels of illumination (pattern recognition)—further support for different mechanisms of detection and recognition.

Studies of visual masking sometimes find that the detection of light (Sperling, 1965) is related monotonically to the interval between stimulus and mask (ISI). However, when the observer must recognize form, accuracy is often a nonmonotonic function of ISI (Weisstein & Haber, 1965). Although there are problems in comparing the masking of light and form, the studies show different functions. Alpern (1953), however, found a nonmonotonic relation between brightness detection and masking ISI. In a recent review of the field, Kahneman (1969) noted: "It appears likely at this time that different masking effects may be involved in brightness reduction and in contour inhibition . . . ."

IV. DETECTION AND RECOGNITION IN NEONATES

The ERG *b*-wave (associated with rod functioning) is easily measured in neonates; however, *a*-waves (associated with cone vision) require sophisticated selective amplification. This implies that rods function at birth, but cones do not—at least not well.

Anatomical evidence (Mann, 1964) shows that the neonate's retina is less differentiated than the older infant's; the fovea is not clearly defined until two months following birth; there are relatively few cones present in the neonate's retina. These data strongly suggest the detection device is available before pattern recognition develops. In fact, the detection device may guide the recognition system to information for growth.

A recent study by Doris, Felzen, and Poresky (1969) supports the notion that neonates detect only energy. Doris *et al.* showed that increased brightness does *not* enhance neonatal visual acuity—a result consistent with scotopic vision, but not at all what one would expect if cones were functioning. They showed earlier (Poresky & Doris, 1967) that increased brightness enhances the visual acuity of 2-4-month-old infants. Between birth and 2-4 months the infant shifts from detection alone to a detection-recognition system.

Hershenson (1964) reported that neonates are not sensitive to variations in the pattern of human faces but are sensitive to variations in brightness. In fact, neonates are sensitive to a dimension of brightness; Hershenson found significant differences in looking time between each of three levels of brightness. He also found that neonates look longer at a simple checkerboard than at more complex arrays of black and white squares. This finding is in direct contrast to studies by Munsinger and Wier (1967); they showed that older infants look longer at more complex forms. Quite possibly simple checkerboards are more attractive to neonates because only their detection device works; it may be attracted to large uninterrupted areas of brightness or simple contours. On the other hand, older infants spend their time exploring more complex shapes, since they have a functioning pattern recognition system.

Acuity measures (using looking time as a response) show the neonate is able to resolve line separations of around 1/8 in. at 10 inches viewing distance (Fantz, 1965). This is equivalent to 20/200 vision. If we assume that only his detection device functions, then the neonate's acuity should be related to the maximal sensitivity of his rods. The maximum density of rods in the adult eye occurs $20°$ from the center of the fovea (see Figure 2). Assume this represents the point of maximum rod sensitivity (Figure 4); then measures of adult acuity taken $20°$ from the fovea should be roughly comparable to neonate acuity. Estimates of adult visual acuity $20°$ from the fovea may be found in Figure 3; relative acuity at that point is .10. This is precisely equivalent to measures of newborn visual acuity (20/200). I am persuaded that neonatal visual acuity reflects only rod vision (energy detection), and foveal pattern perception is nonfunctional.

Other relevant data on neonatal perception are found in studies by Salapatek and Kessen (1966). They measured neonates' ocular orientation to an 8-inch triangle placed 9 inches from the babies' eyes. Measurements of their data show that neonates shift their eyes about 3.5 inches (on the average) in scanning lines and angles of the triangle. If we convert the babies' 3.5-inch scans into degrees of visual angle we find their eyes are moving about $21°$; this figure is remarkably close to the distance between maximal rod density (detection system) and the center of the fovea (recognition system). The neonate has a detection device and an automatic orienting reflex which bring his fovea into contact with inform-

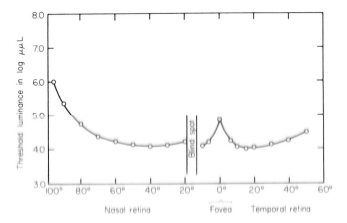

Figure 4. Detection threshold at different retinal positions.

ation. The detection system is available at birth to orient the fovea toward parts of the visual field which contain information. The infant must learn to recognize through exposure; the detection device provides this information.

V. SIMULTANEOUS DETECTION AND RECOGNITION

How may we study the relation between energy detection and pattern recognition? With a simultaneous detection and recognition paradigm in which we present either S_a, S_b, or nothing (see Table 1). In this design, the observer is asked (in a counterbalanced order, at some a priori probability) whether there was something there (detection); independent of his first response, he is asked what was there (recognition). We require four classes of response:

  i. I detect it and it is *a*
 ii. I detect it and it is *b*
iii. I did not detect it but I think it is *a*
 iv. I did not detect it but I think it is *b*

Few simultaneous visual detection-recognition studies exist (Munsinger & Gummerman, 1968).

Experiments in audition ("critical-band" experiments) suggest auditory detection and recognition are related. For example, in audition, detection is affected by prior information about the tones to be presented. Suppose we perform a simple yes-no detection under one condition and define the stimuli clearly for him in a second condition. His detection accuracy should be

TABLE 1
The Detection-Recognition Task

Observer's responses

Stimulus conditions	S_a Y S_b	S_a N S_b
S_a		
S_b		
n		

independent of prior information about the stimulus if detection and recognition are different mechanisms. However, we know it is harder to detect an unknown auditory signal than to detect one which is known. Why should this be so? Some theorists suggest that the child can tune his auditory system to detect tones of known frequency. However, there exist no studies in vision; therefore, it is an open question. The visual analogy could be either different hues or various forms. The experiment would include prior knowledge of the stimulus set for some trials and no knowledge of the stimulus set on others. If detection and recognition are different processes, detection accuracy should be identical under conditions of prior knowledge or uncertainty of the stimulus. These experiments exist for recognition alone, of course (e. g., Lawrence & Coles, 1954), but we badly need data on detection of known and unknown visual stimuli to test these speculations.

VI. DETECTION, RECOGNITION, AND METHOD

What is the relevance of various experimental techniques to sensation or perception? It should be clear that studies of brightness are irrelevant to pattern perception. Also, studies of brightness which concentrate their measures within the fovea are of dubious value. We need appropriate methods to study energy detection *and* pattern processing. Sensation (including detection, scaling of elementary sensations and characteristics of hue) should be differentiated from the more complex processes of perception (pattern recognition). Table 2 shows some proposed relations between common experimental techniques (classified by whether they require relative or absolute judgment) and detection-recognition processes. Relative judgments are typically more stable (less error variance) than absolute judgments. Absolute judgments require a stored image

TABLE 2

A Matrix of Recognition-Detection Experiments

	Relative judgment	Absolute judgment
Energy detection	Two alternatives forced choice	Yes-no detection
Pattern recognition	Discrimination of sameness	Identification
	Discrimination of difference	Novel stimulus—either mismatch or form a new category

for comparison, so the increased variability may be attributed to memory processes. Detection paradigms include the two-alternative forced-choice situation (relative judgment) and the yes-no detection experiment (absolute judgment). Recognition studies require either discrimination (in which the subject makes the relative judgment of sameness or difference) or identification (in which he can absolutely recognize the input or say it is novel). Identification studies require a stored memory trace for comparison. If the input is novel, the observer must learn a new category before he can identify it. This last condition is perceptual development.

VII. PERCEPTION AND JUDGMENT

Relations between perception and judgment may be introduced under the older title of stimulus error and introspection. Titchener insisted that his subjects attend only to the contents of perception; they were to avoid the stimulus error (the a priori probability of stimulus occurrence, varying payoff for responses). They were not to guess about what they saw. Classic procedures assumed the introspectionist maintains a stable criterion (a proper attitude). It made no sense that the observer could be wrong; introspection cannot lie. However, the stimulus-error still exists; observers use extraperceptual data in their judgments. Our solution cannot be to train the child for introspection. Instead, procedures for separating sensitivity and judgment must be applied. To study sensation and perception we need a model which will help us separate perceptual abilities from decision processes.

Early conceptions of sensitivity centered on the notion of threshold; the observer was assumed to be aware of stimuli above threshold and unaware of stimuli below it. This classic view assumed that a stimulus initiates neural impulses which produce an effect in the cortex (Bartley, 1958). Clarity of the central effect changed with stimulus intensity, receptor state, neural adaptation, and noise level in the nervous system. If the effect was large enough the visual center would discharge, yielding a response (e. g., "I see it."). The stimulus intensity necessary to produce this effect was the threshold. Since many factors (e. g., stimulus intensity, receptor sensitivity, neural efficiency and noise level) varied randomly from trial to trial, producing an approximately normal distribution of values, the average of this distribution was taken as the "typical" threshold.

Newer notions emphasize the ration of signal to background noise rather than absolute physical energy of the stimulus in defining sensitivity. Conceptions of signal, noise, and decision criterion are used to measure perceptual ability. In addition to receptor sensitivity, the observer's criterion (how he separates those trials on which to say "yes" from those on which to say "no") also affects behavior. There is good reason to believe children have difficulty maintaining a stable criterion. Variable criteria produce underestimates of sensitivity; children with variable criteria would appear insensitive when compared with observers who maintain a more stable criterion (even though both have equal sensitivity). Many reported differences between children and adults may reflect this criterial variation and not sensory development.

VIII. DETECTION THEORY

Signal detection theory (Green & Swets, 1966) provides a convenient analysis of the process that generates signals (stimuli to which the child responds) and noise (stimuli to which he does not respond). An example may help introduce those notions of decision theory relevant to our discussion, and can serve as a convenient referent. The problem can be understood through a set of questions: Given a particular sensation, which response should the child make? What is a good choice? How may we analyze his responses? In presenting this example, we need to understand three concepts: *likelihood ratio, decision rule,* and *criterion.*

Consider the following game: Three tetrahedral dice are thrown. Two of the dice have one, two, three, or four spots appearing on their sides (noise). The third (odd) die has nothing on two sides and two spots on the remaining two sides. You do not see the individual dice, but you are aware of the total number of spots which appear. You must decide (on the basis of the total number of spots) whether the odd die showed zero spots (no signal) or two spots (signal). What strategy should you use? You could choose randomly; however, if you want to be correct, you need a rule. How can you make intelligent decisions about the number of dots on the odd die, given only the total of all three dice and some statistical information about the frequencies of the possible combinations? (See Table 3 for the possible combinations of spots and their resultant totals.) Assuming your aim is to maximize the number of correct decisions, the best policy (for our particular example) is to say "zero" for those totals *below*

TABLE 3

Statistical Information about the Possible Combinations of Three Dice

Total spots	Possible combinations Die 1	Die 2	Odd die	Probability odd die is "2"	Probability odd die is "0"	Likelihood ratio $L(T) = \dfrac{p(T \mid 2)}{p(T \mid 0)}$
2	1	1	0	0/16	1/16	0
3	1	2	0	0/16	2/16	
	2	1	0			0
4	1	1	2	1/16		
	2	2	0		3/16	
	3	1	0			1/3
	1	3	0			
5	1	2	2	2/16		
	2	1	2			
	1	4	0			
	4	1	0		4/16	
	2	3	0			2/4
	3	2	0			
6	2	2	2	3/16		(criterion)
	3	1	2			
	1	3	2			
	2	4	0			
	4	2	0		3/16	3/3
	3	3	0			
7	3	2	2	4/16		
	2	3	2			
	1	4	2			
	4	1	2			4/2
		3	0		2/16	
	3	4	0			
8	3	3	2	3/16		
	4	2	2			
	2	4	2			3/1
	4	4	0		1/16	
9	4	3	2	2/16	0/16	∞
	3	4	2			
10	4	4	2	1/16	0/16	∞

six, and to say "two" for those totals *above* six. Six is ambiguous; you should randomly guess "zero" and "two." This is because the likelihood of the total being six is the same, given either zero or two spots on the odd die. For the totals seven through ten, the probability of that number given two spots is higher than the probability of that number given zero spots. Similarly, for the totals less than six, their probability is greater given zero than the probability of that same number given two. The ratio of the probability of a particular total given that the odd die is two, and the probability of that same total given that the odd die is zero, is called a likelihood ratio. (Probabilities are called likelihoods, and this is the ratio of two probabilities.) To maximize correct decisions we must say "two" when the likelihood ratio exceeds one, and "zero" otherwise. When the likelihood ratio is one, you decide some other way.

There are three parts to a typical experiment: (a) some states of the world (stimuli), (b) input about these states (sensations), and (c) a decision (response). In a detection situation, states of the world are the presence or absence of energy. The observer looks at a display to obtain the input he will use in his decision, then makes a differential response (e. g., yes-no; A-B) to tell us what it is. The observer makes mistakes; some of his decisions are not related to states of the world. We assume that the state of the world "signal plus noise" and the state of the world "noise" produce different sensations; to the observer, these sensations are analogous to the total number of spots in our earlier example. Given a sensation, an observer must decide which state occurred: One way to do this is to compare the sensations with hypothetical statistical estimates of which state is more likely to produce the particular sensation he experienced. When a particular sensation occurs on a given trial, he compares its value with his own statistical estimates to decide whether signal or noise produced the sensation.

Several factors affect the outcome of an experiment: the a priori probability of stimulus presentation, the physical values of the signal, and the payoff matrix. In a typical experiment, signal energy is held constant (or varied systematically) while the observer's sensitivity is estimated at various criteria. Response criteria may be varied by changing the payoff matrix (rewards and punishments), by verbal instructions, or by varying the a priori probability of occurrence of signal or noise.

The responses an observer may use are determined by the experimenter. Usually they are in 1 : 1 association with possible states of the world, and it is easy to score them as correct or incorrect. There are at least two types of correct decisions (hits and correct rejections) he can make and two types of errors (false alarms and misses, see Table 4). In general, when we decrease the probability of one type error, we increase the chance of others; it is impossible to increase both kinds of correct decisions simultaneously.

Signal detection theory lets us unconfound sensitivity estimations and judgment criteria. Measures of sensitivity (derived from both hit *and* false alarm rates) are independent of the particular criterion a child uses to decide the presence or absence of a stimulus (although criterial variability may still present a problem). Unfortunately, most studies of children have not used the methods of signal detection. Age changes may be due either to development, or to differing criteria between age groups. Only by considering both hits *and* false alarms can we separate judgment and sensitivity to obtain reliable developmental variation.

TABLE 4

Response Matrix of Detection Experiments

	S	N
s	$p(S\|s)$ Hit	$p(N\|s)$ Miss
n	$p(S\|n)$ False alarm	$p(N\|n)$ Correct rejection

$$p(S|s) + p(N|s) = 1$$
$$p(S|n) + p(N|n) = 1$$

To compare detection and recognition results, we must convert the yes-no detection data into percent correct (the form of our recognition data). Happily, the area under an ROC curve (a plot of hits versus false alarms; Green & Swets, 1966, p. 51) is exactly equal to percent correct in the two-alternative forced-choice situation (our recognition task). There are simple formulas for converting ROC curves into percent correct for more than two alternatives (Green & Swets, 1966, p. 50). Following translation to percent correct we can easily compare detection and recognition studies. To collect an ROC curve we must shift the subject's criterion (change his false alarm rate). We can vary his criterion by giving different instructions (e. g., "say yes more often when you are not sure"), by changing the a priori probabilities of signal and noise, or by varying the payoff for hits and false alarms. By changing the observer's false alarm rate we obtain several points on an ROC curve; by connecting these points we can obtain the area under it. This area easily converts to percent correct. The recognition task uses a two-alternative forced-choice situation in which the data are percent correct recognition.

IX. MUDDY AND CLOUDY DEVELOPMENTAL DATA

Recurring problems in developmental data are the constraints of chance (the mud) and perfect accuracy (the clouds). Ceiling and floor effects occur in developmental studies because often tasks are too easy for adults (clouds) and too difficult for young children (mud). As a result, interactions may reflect floor and ceiling constraints instead of developmental differences. As a solution to this problem, I propose the following tactic: Rather than measure children and adults over the same restricted range of a variable, expose all subjects to a range of task difficulty sufficient to move their performance from the mud to the clouds (chance to perfect accuracy). Examine your results from time to time while you are collecting them; when a particular group enters the mud or the clouds, simply fill in the remaining values (between their particular floor and ceiling) and move on to another group. Counterbalancing should pose no particular problem. This procedure gains maximum information, since you expose each group only to those levels of difficulty which contribute systematic variation. Finally, rather than entering the data into an analysis of variance, simply compute confidence limits[1] for the various curves, and look at them. You will immediately know whether the origins and slopes are the same or different.

With the entire range available, we can look at infants', children's, and adults' psychophysical functions for differences in slope, origin, or both. Figure 5 shows some possible functions. (The example lists exposure duration as the independent variable—it might be similarity or size of stimuli.) If we measured infants, children, and adults (over a restricted range) under any of these outcomes we would find an interaction in the analysis of variance. However, I believe most of you will agree that the slopes in Figure 5a are parallel, but displaced along the abscissa. On the other hand, Figures 5b and 5c show interactions of slope.

What can different slopes and origins mean? I believe the origin (where the function begins to climb out of the mud) is related to signal and background noise; if the origins are identical, then the levels of background neural noise are comparable. Different origins (as in Figure 5a) suggest that infants have a higher background noise level than children, who in turn have a higher neural noise

---

[1] Confidence limits for a single subject may be computed by:

$$\frac{N}{N + z^2} \left[p + \frac{z^2}{2N} \pm z \left(\frac{p(1 - p)}{N} + \frac{z^2}{4N^2} \right)^{1/2} \right]$$

where z is the standard score in a normal distribution cutting off the upper .025 proportion of cases, P is the observed proportion x/N (P is used synonymously with "probability"), and $N = x/P =$ the number of cases P is based upon (see Hayes, 1963, p. 291, for derivation.)

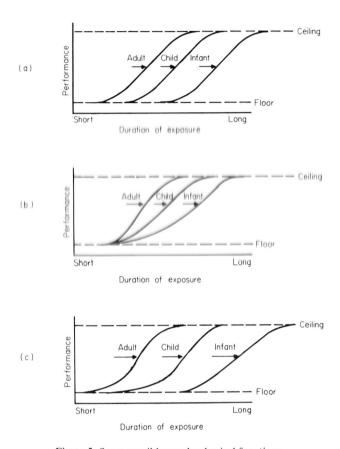

Figure 5. Some possible psychophysical functions.

level than adults. On the other hand, slope is related to discrimination power of the system. A steeper slope reflects greater discrimination ability. For example, the hypothetical results in Figure 5a show adults, children, and infants have the same discrimination ability but different neural noise levels. The results in Figures 5b and 5c show adults are more sensitive to differences than infants. The implications of these notions are three: First, instead of merely collecting data in a restricted range, extend the variable from floor to ceiling to obtain origin and slope for the function. Second, where a function climbs from the mud is important information about the observer's detection ability. Finally, the slope of a function is related to an observer's discrimination ability (recognition accuracy).

The combination of signal detection theory (to separate perception and judgment) and extended psychophysical functions allows measurement of detection and pattern recognition over age. Based on my earlier speculation, the origin of psychophysical functions (detection) should be invariant over age— because detection is assumed to function adequately at birth; however, the slope of psychophysical functions should vary systematically with development, since pattern recognition is assumed to grow with experience. Variations in detection ability may be the result of criterial variability; only by separating judgment from perception and by collecting both the slope and origin of functions can we determine the course of seeing. Finally, we need to apply these methods in a simultaneous detection-recognition paradigm (varying such conditions as masking, knowledge of stimulus set, place on the retina, and interfering stimuli) to clarify the developmental course of sensing and seeing.

CHAPTER 10

Cognitive Changes in Adulthood

JOHN H. FLAVELL

UNIVERSITY OF MINNESOTA,
MINNEAPOLIS, MINNESOTA

ABSTRACT

Cognitive changes during childhood have a specific set of formal "morpho-genetic" properties that presumably stem from the biological-maturational growth process underlying these changes: Thus, childhood cognitive modifica-tions are largely inevitable, momentous, directional, uniform, and irreversible. No such underlying process constrains and directs adult cognitive changes, and hence their morphogenetic properties should be quite different from those that obtain during childhood. The most important adult cognitive changes are probably the result of life experiences, and would for the most part be expected to lack the across-subjects uniformity that characterizes the child's intellectual growth. It is possible that there might be some experience-based adult changes that do meet the uniformity criterion, but the identification of such changes has scarcely begun.

The aim of this paper is to speculate about a topic which unfortunately lies well outside my own field of specialization, namely, the nature of cognitive change, not during childhood, but during the adult years. The anchoring point for these speculations is the cognitive development of the child. We think we have learned something about cognitive changes during this particular portion of the life-span, and it may be that what we have learned can illuminate the state of things in adulthood.

I. DIFFERENCES BETWEEN CHILD AND ADULT COGNITIVE CHANGES

In my view, much of what is interesting and distinctive about preadulthood intellectual changes results from their being guaranteed in fact and significantly constrained in form by biological-maturational factors. This is not of course to deny or underplay the role of experience or environmental inputs in the growth process. There are, however, certain characteristic properties of childhood intellectual changes which I believe no theory that considers only environmental inputs could ever satisfactorily explain. One is the very fact that cognitive change is inevitable—guaranteed to occur—in neurologically-intact growing children the world over. Another is that the changes we witness between birth and maturity are of immense scope and significance; they are truly *big* changes, both quantitatively and qualitatively. Furthermore, the evidence suggests that at least the major landmarks in the child's cognitive evolution emerge in a fixed order; there is, in other words, considerable intrinsic directionality and inter-individual uniformity in the developmental progression. And finally, the changes that occur are largely irreversible; that is, the cognitive structures and operations that eventually emerge are essentially permanent, essentially unextinguishable.

This view of the nature of childhood changes is obviously not original to me. For example, Piaget (1967) and Lenneberg (1967) have recently offered similar, strongly biologically oriented accounts of intellectual and linguistic development respectively. Nonetheless, many may disagree with this view on the grounds that it neglects milieu effects, individual variation, and the like. At the risk of accentuating the disagreement, one further speculation will be suggested: As we come to learn more and more about the deeper-lying, essential aspects of childhood cognitive change, this feeling of within-species developmental homogeneity and uniformity will actually increase rather than diminish. This is precisely what appears to be happening already in the psychology of language (Chomsky, 1967), and it will probably also happen in the area of cognitive growth in general.

The picture with respect to adult cognitive changes is at least superficially quite different because it is the underlying presence of a biological growth process that lends to childhood changes their inevitability, magnitude, directionality, within-species uniformity, and irreversibility. It is not immediately obvious, however, that there is any biological process indigenous to the adult portion of the life-span that could impose such definite and strong constraints on intellectual change. This does not imply that there may be no interesting biological changes during the adult years, and the claim is not made that adult cognitive changes cannot and do not occur. What is suggested is that these biological changes are different from their childhood counterparts, and because they are different they would be unlikely, on the face of it, to dictate a set of cognitive changes with the very same "morphogenetic features," so to speak, as the childhood ones have. To put it another way: if we should restrict the meaning of "developmental" to refer to those changes with age that have childhood-type morphogenetic features, then the application of the term to the adult years reflects a hypothesis rather than a statement of established fact. Correspondingly, appellations like "life-span developmental psychology," if meant to be more than metaphors, would need explicit defense.

If one actually looks at reported data on adult cognitive changes (e. g., Botwinick, 1967; H. E. Jones, 1959), one does not find much support for such an extension of the concept "developmental" (it may be revealing that the word does not even appear in the index of Botwinick's book). There seems to be no compelling and consistent evidence that at least the sorts of intellectual changes commonly studied are inevitable, of striking magnitude, or uniform across adulthoods; it could be conceded perhaps that they are irreversible and directional, although the directionality does not seem to manifest itself in a fixed sequence of well-demarcated stages or developmental landmarks. The typical finding seems instead to be a cognitive change with roughly the following sorts of properties: (a) it appears to be more quantitative than qualitative in nature and of considerably less magnitude or moment than the typical infant-to-adulthood change; (b) it does not occur in all adults. My impression, then, is that the physiological changes that occur in normal adulthood do not lead to or support cognitive changes of the consistency, size, and kind that are mediated by the childhood growth process.[1] That a number of findings reported in the literature on aging (e. g., Botwinick, 1967) are of considerable interest to developmental psychologists of Genevan persuasion probably is true because we are psychologists, rather than because we are developmentalists. If we cannot look to biological processes as a basis for any very interesting (i. e., to a Piagetian) cognitive changes during the adult years, what about the process of experience or environmental stimulation?

---

[1] A recent paper by Kohlberg and Kramer (1969) makes a similar point regarding adult changes in moral thinking, namely, that they are not "developmental" in the abovementioned narrow sense.

II. THE ROLE OF EXPERIENCE IN ADULT
COGNITIVE CHANGE

Like the child, the adult may experience an enormous number of important and potentially change-inducing encounters with the world of people and things; moreover, if accorded a normal life-span, he will have a longer period of time in which to experience them. If one could discount the nature of the organisms involved (for instance, that young children might be regarded as intrinsically more environmentally malleable than adults), one could argue that adulthood is the nearest thing we have to a pure experiment-in-nature for assessing the change-making power of experience alone, that is, relatively unconfounded by significant and directional biological changes. The suggestion here is that experience is in fact a far more promising source of interesting adult cognitive changes than are biological events, and that the changes so wrought might also prove to be more similar to the childhood prototypes in their morphogenetic features.

One can imagine some of the major categories of experimental settings which could provide occasions for really significant and enduring changes in an adult's cognition. There are programmed ones, like psychotherapy and adult education, which some adults encounter. There are also unprogrammed ones, such as marriage, child rearing, occupational activities, grandparenthood, retirement, widowhood, and so on, that many or most adults encounter. The important experiental nutrients for the child's cognitive growth are both human and nonhuman-inanimate in nature, and he accordingly constructs implicit mental models of both the logical-natural world and the social-interpersonal one. Most adult cognitive changes probably concern the latter, that is, they consist of changes in the individual's implicit theories regarding the self, others, and the human condition generally.

Notice that the types of cognitions one would think of here are not of the psychometric or learning task variety, not of the sort so prominently featured in the studies Botwinick (1967) reviews. They have to do with judgments, attitudes, and beliefs rather than skills and you therefore could, if you prefer, categorize them as personality rather than cognitive phenomena. They do, however, most decidedly entail genuine cognitive activity (probably at the developmental level of Piaget's concrete operations, at least for most adults).

Cognitive changes of this ilk, brought about through significant and impactful life experiences, have apparently been little studied by psychologists. There is, however, some interesting recent evidence concerning one of the above mentioned sectors of unprogrammed experience, namely that of rearing one's own children. Stolz and her colleagues (Stolz, 1967) gathered extensive interview data from a group of mothers and fathers on the perceived determinants of their cognitions and behaviors regarding child rearing. It is apparent that tacit conceptual models about the nature and management of children develop and change as a consequence of a wide variety of experiential influences. One such influence is the parent's repeated interactions with the child himself. The following passage provides one illustration of how an adult's experiences can significantly modify and change his thinking in a particular area:

> A parent learns by experience, not only with his spouse, but also with his children. As shown in the previous section, parents are continually responding to children's behavior, and children are responding to their parents'. By this interaction parents gradually build up generalizations concerning children and attitudes concerning specific methods of child-rearing. A mother or father acts in a certain way with his child; if the method used is successful in bringing about what the parent wants, then such behavior is reinforced, and the parent is likely to use this method again, not only with the child with whom it was successful but with other children in the family, especially those born later. If, on the other hand, the parent's method fails, he is less likely to try it on other children in the family. In the process of experience, parents learn not only about the usefulness of their method, but they also gain insight into why it succeeds or fails. It is through interaction with a child that a parent often learns what to expect of a child and what behavior is appropriate for his stage of development. [Stolz, 1967, pp. 196-197].

What sorts of morphogenetic features could such experience-based changes be expected to have, again using childhood development as the yardstick? It was suggested earlier that adult changes of the skill or ability variety are not likely to be either momentous or uniform from adult to adult. In contrast, at least some of the experienced-based changes in attitudes, beliefs, etc., might accurately be characterized as momentous. Although the changes in one's thinking resulting from having lived in a concentration camp, or having raised a family, or having experienced occupational success or failure, etc., are doubtless qualitatively different from the changes defined by say, the child's transition from pre-operational to concrete-operational thought, they need not be much less consequential for the individual concerned.

On the other hand, like the above-mentioned skill changes, they ought in general to lack the uniformity feature. While many of the major occasions and settings for change-making experiences are encountered by the vast majority of adults (marriage and parenthood, for example), the actual psychologically defined *experiences* undergone in these "normative" settings must vary widely from individual to individual. Experiential variation could be expected to result in a relative uniformity of change only if operating in concert with a constraining process of biological growth, as suggested to be the case during childhood. In the absence of a maturational "governor," uniformity of changes should be positively correlated with uniformity of experiences—but there simply may not be much uniformity of experiences across adulthoods, even within the same subculture. Parenthetically, a similar state of affairs probably obtains during childhood for those psychological characteristics which are not tied to a direction-giving biological process, that is, which are not "developmental" in the narrow sense. Disregarding initial constitutional differences and other complications in order to make the point, it could be said that some experiences might lead a child to become increasingly aggressive with age, and that others might make him increasingly nonaggressive with age. In both cases there is genuine change over time as a function of experience; however, both the experiences and the ensuing changes differ in the two cases, a fact that need not bother the student of the antecedents of aggressiveness-nonaggressiveness. I think Erikson's (1959) model of life-span changes well illustrates the point I am trying to make. While he does indeed assume a universal sequence of change-inducing problems to be coped with, he definitely does not assume that all people have the same concrete experiences while coping with these problems, nor that they all change in the same way as a result. Likewise, Stolz (1967) never for a moment suggests that the emerging and changing schemas regarding children and their upbringing have the same content from one parent to the next. To be sure, it is at least possible that there might be some uniformity and sequential orderliness for certain very general ego processes. There might, for example, be uniform shifts with age in the distribution of one's identification with, and investment in, the growth and life fortunes of various other egos. The egos in question could include an adult peer who ages with one (one's spouse or intimate friend), an older person whom one sees pass from middle to old age (one's parent), a younger person whose childhood, young adulthood, and perhaps middle adulthood fortunes become objects of concern (one's child, nephew, etc.), a much younger reduplicate of the latter, of whom at least the childhood years may also be available for cathexes (one's grandchild, grandnephew, etc.).[2]

This last point suggests that perhaps we should not be too hasty in giving up the search for universal or near-universal cognitive changes in adulthood, changes presumably based on subtle and hard-to-identify commonalities of adult experience. There might for example, exist common experiences associated simply with the fact that one is now at a particular point in the life stream—with having lived this much of life already and having that much more expected to be lived. Neugarten (1966a, 1966b, 1968, 1969) has nicely elaborated this and other seminal ideas about adult changes in a recent series of papers. While not all of the interesting changes she discusses could plausibly be regarded as uniform across human adulthoods, some of them might approach universality. For instance, she has evidence from interview data that there is a gradual reversal across adulthood in the way biological time is perceived, namely, from time-since-birth to time-left-to-live. Similarly, as people pass from middle to old

---

[2] I am grateful to Harold W. Stevenson and Bernice L. Neugarten for ideas leading to this suggestion. Neugarten nicely captured the essence of the suggestion in saying: "Once a child is born, and perhaps for both men and women, the self concept is never again limited to that which goes on within one's own skin (personal communication)."

age there appears to be a shift from an active-assimilatory to a passive-accommodatory model of how best to cope with the environment. Moreover, the cognitions associated with being of a specific age may only be part of the story. That is, it is possible that one's implicit schema of "the X-aged person" undergoes systematic and possibly uniform changes as age period X is first anticipated in prospect, later lived through and experienced, and finally reviewed in retrospect. In other words, there may be important modifications in a person's image of any adulthood period as a function of his own gradually but inexorably changing relationship to that period, modifications which may, furthermore, be much the same from one aging individual to another. Like the most interesting of childhood cognitive processes, the images in question are probably quite deep lying and hard to articulate—not of the sort that would be readily elicitable by questionnaires and other objective tests. In fact, really extensive, almost psychotherapy-like depth interviewing may be necessary, at least for the preliminary identification of putative universal changes (less time-consuming procedures may suffice later on, once we know exactly what we are trying to measure). If the search for uniform changes, however carried out, should prove successful, we would finally have the adulthood version of something dear to any Piagetian's heart: namely, the Development of Man as contrasted with the developments of men.

LEARNING
AND
RETENTION

Learning in Children and in Older Adults

JACK BOTWINICK

WASHINGTON UNIVERSITY,
ST. LOUIS, MISSOURI

ABSTRACT

Learning studies based on children were integrated with comparable studies based on older adults. Classical conditioning studies were represented primarily by the eyeblink response with the processes of habituation and extinction receiving special attention. Learning based upon prior experience, including pretraining studies, was discussed giving emphasis to the distinction between learning (process) and performance (act). The problem of speed of response was examined in the context of paired-associate and serial learning; and finally, studies on incidental learning were reviewed indicating that typical growth and decline curves do not always apply to abilities across the life-span.

An effort was made to integrate learning studies based on children with comparable studies based on older adults. When a single study involved subjects of extreme, diverse age, such as children and old people, it was regarded as specially noteworthy for the present purposes and reviewed in some detail. These studies tended to be reported more in the recent aging literature than in the child literature. When it seemed relevant, problems prominent in one literature but not in the other were given brief review. This was to make up for important omissions caused by the emphasis of integrating the two literatures.

In a very general way, the present chapter begins with a consideration of the simpler forms of learning and builds up to the more complex forms. To anyone who has worked with the simpler forms of learning, however, it is clear that even these are complicated and often beyond our complete understanding.

I. CONDITIONING

All types of conditioning studies have been prominent in the child literature, with, perhaps, instrumental and operant conditioning being of more current interest to American psychologists, and classical conditioning of more current interest to Soviet and Czechoslovakian investigators. Operant conditioning studies have not been prominent in the aging literature, only classical conditioning with human subjects and instrumental conditioning with animals.

A. Classical Conditioning

Although there are many classical conditioning studies with subjects both of very young and very old age, the studies in most instances are not, strictly speaking, comparable. They have been carried out with different purposes in mind, they have involved different specific methodological operations, and, as a result, relate to different factors. On what basis, then, are studies to be integrated?

Conditioning studies involving various age groups may be compared on the basis of the CS, UCS, or the CR. According to Brackbill (1962), Soviet investigators emphasize the CS. In fact, she indicated that for the Soviets it is only the CS, not the UCS or CR, which is the "really influential member." She wrote, "The age at which a simple conditioned connection can be developed *is* a function of the type of CS used. It is *not* a function of the type of UCS-R combination used. . ." (p. 110).

The prescription then is to compare data of different studies dealing with various age groups, where the CS employed is the same. This makes for problems. Would it be meaningful to compare data based on GSR responses of the aged (J. Botwinick & Kornetsky, 1960) and eyeblinks of infants (Lintz, Fitzgerald, & Brackbill, 1967) when the UCS in the former case was shock and in the latter an air puff, because the CSs in both cases were auditory signals? If "yes," would the complex CS tones in the latter case be functionally the same as the CS pure tones of 450 Hz in the latter case? There is no clear direction to follow—probably no integration would be totally adequate.

An effort was made here to circumvent these considerations by simply comparing studies on the basis of the CR, and not the CS. Since the eyeblink seems to be, by far, the most studied CR across the life-span, and in fact seems to be the only CR investigated sufficiently often in a variety of age studies to make generalizations possible, the discussion here will be limited to the eyeblink. This limitation may not be as severe as it may first appear since the eyeblink CR studies seem to reflect what other conditioning studies do.

1. Eyeblink Response.

Braun and Geiselhart (1959) carried out one of the very few studies in which both children and aged subjects were conditioned. These investigators conditioned and extinguished the eyeblink response, when the CS was an increase in the brightness of a disc, and the UCS was a puff of air delivered to the eye. Braun and Geiselhart compared subjects of three age groups on the basis of 80 conditioning and 20 extinction trials. The age groups were: boys aged 8-10 years, and men aged 18-25 years, and 62-84 years.

Through 60 conditioning trials, the percent CRs was higher for the children than for young adults, and throughout the entire 80 trials, higher for the children than for the old adults. The two adult groups were similar through the first 20 trials, but at that point the young adult group improved markedly and the elderly group only slightly. At the start, the rate of conditioning was relatively high for the children, and low for both adult groups. Extinction rates were related to conditioning rates, that is, the higher the percentage CRs, the higher the resistance to extinction.

Although the percentage of the children's CRs was higher than that of both groups of adults during the first 60 trials, the latency of these CRs was longer. Braun and Geiselhart (1959) did not accentuate these latency data, and their meaning is not at all clear. It would seem, however, that when considered in relation to the high conditioning rate of the children, a problem of neural responsivity may be indicated. It may turn out, for example, that these results can be framed as an extension of certain facts known about neonates.

Neonates appear so responsive to their environments that many types of stimuli can elicit CR-type-behavior. This can give the impression of conditioning when it is not necessarily occurring. Wickens and Wickens (1940) demonstrated the need to distinguish between true conditioning and a reactivity which resembles it. They paired a buzzer (CS) with a shock (UCS) with one group of neonates, presented only the CS with another group, and only the UCS with a third neonate group. Conditioning was found in the first group, but similar performance was also seen in the third group. Considering these results in conjunction with data of subsequent studies, Stevenson (1970) suggested that when the UCS has aversive properties, there is the danger of incorrectly labeling the responses of neonates' CRs. Neonates are so sensitive that any aversive changes in environment might elicit CR-appearing behavior.

Accepting this line of thinking, if the air puff (UCS) in Braun and Geiselhart's study can be considered aversive, and if we think of the properties of the response processes as having some continuity from infancy to childhood, then aspects of Braun and Geiselhart's data may be suggestive of a special sensitivity on the part of the children. Very early during the conditioning, the CR rates for the 8-10 year olds were high, but of long latency. Following conditioning, the children's responses were very resistant to extinction. The children, therefore, were responding at high rates throughout. Can it be that, confounded with a true conditioning, there was, as with the infants of Wickens and Wickens (1940), a high level of responsivity which was to an extent independent of the CS-UCS contingencies? This hypothesis is negated to some extent by the fact that the overall age trends were substantiated by tests of statistical significance only to the extent that the oldest group was different from the two younger ones.

This study by Braun and Geiselhart (1959) is the only one involving such varied age periods of life. And even in this study the emphasis was on one end of the age continuum. While the data of the children have been emphasized here, it was the data of the older subjects that were emphasized in their report. The emphasis was that the aged subjects were less modifiable by the CS-UCS pairings than either group of younger subjects.

Kimble and Pennypacker (1963) reported similar results when subjects aged about 20 and 67 years were compared. The CS was one or the other of two neon lights, remaining on through the presentation of an air puff UCS to the eye. The subject was led to believe that the experiment was one of RT, with the air puff serving as a stressor. The subject had to depress one of two keys (indicated by the position of CS light) in response to a buzzer which sounded one-half second after the air puff UCS.

Kimble and Pennypacker, in finding that the aged subjects did not condition as readily as did their younger adult counterparts, reported that many of the old subjects showed rapid habituation to the UCR. In fact, the habituation was so prominent that they suggested that the lowered conditionability of the older subjects could be accounted for by their increased tendencies of habituation. The problem of habituation is important and it will be discussed more fully in a later section.

Still keeping with the aging literature, but more briefly, there are other conditioned eyeblink studies. Solyom and Barik (1965) carried out an eyeblink conditioning study very similar to that of Braun and Geiselhart (1959) and of Kimble and Pennypacker (1963), but they extended the study to include examination of two elderly samples along with a young adult sample. One of the two elderly samples was chosen to be free from known brain damage, and the other was chosen as institutionalized and with brain damage. The elderly subjects of both groups were of similar age, 70-84 years. The young subjects were aged 20-43. Again it was reported that the elderly subjects showed an overall lower percentage of conditioned CRs than the younger subjects. The two elderly groups were different from each other in the rate of acquisition of the CR; the demented group conditioned at a slower rate. The demented subjects "only dimly recognized" the connection between CS and UCS, even after 60 trials. Solyom and Barik (1965) concluded that senile decline is associated with decreased excitability and retarded awareness of sensory cues.

Overall, then, it would seem that, with the eyeblink at least, advancing adult age makes one less reactive, and therefore, less conditionable. Brain pathology on top of this accentuates the problem. What does the conditioned eyeblink literature on infants and children tell us? "In the United States, the eyeblink as a CR has been used extensively in research with adult human beings but has rarely been used with younger Ss and never successfully with infants." So began a study on conditioning the eyeblink in infants (Lintz et al., 1967). When this position is considered next to the one put forth previously, that is, the conditioned eyeblink response appears to be more represented in the data of subjects across the life-span than any other, we get some idea of the extent to which the life-span data truly exist.

We will return to the study by Linz et al. but first earlier studies will be discussed. In an interesting but less than completely well-controlled study, Irzhanskaia and Felberbaum (1967) studied 33 children born 1-2.5 months prematurely and tested 1.5-2.5 months after birth. For two weeks prior to conditioning, the children sucked their only food, milk, through nipples which had been stored in mint and had a mint odor. On the first conditioning trial either mint or anise, the CS, and the air puff UCS were presented simultaneously. Thereafter the UCS followed the CS. The olfactory CS was presented by holding a glass slide of appropriate solution under the infant's nose. At each session half the subjects first received mint and air and then anise and air; for the other half, the order was reversed. A conditioned blinking reflex was developed to both odors in all infants. However, it developed more rapidly to mint, the odor of pretraining, than to anise. It was concluded that the eyeblink could be conditioned in infants, even in those born prematurely.

In another very interesting Soviet study, Koltsova (1967) used classical conditioning procedures in the investigation of the acquisition of language of children aged 24-26 months. The data involved the eyeblink and thus are pertinent for the present purposes. For those children conditioned by traditional methods, CRs soon extinguished, even in the face of an increased number of reinforcements. This habituation pattern with children referred to by Koltsova both as inhibition during monotonous stimulation and extinction during reinforcement, appears similar to the pattern of Kimble and Pennypacker's aged subjects.

This pattern may be conceived as different, perhaps opposite to that reported by Wickens and Wickens (1940), already discussed. Possibly Stevenson's (1970) idea of UCS aversiveness is the key. When the stimulus is clearly aversive, the infant may be found highly sensitive and responsive; so much so, in fact, that he will maintain high rates of CR-type responses even in the absence of CSs. However, when the stimulus is mild, but not especially positive, the infant seems to adapt out or to become sated very quickly.

If the question whether the eyeblink could be conditioned in infants remained open, it was closed by a positive demonstration in what was probably the best controlled of all infant studies on eyeblink conditioning. What made the study of Linz et al. (1967) superior to many was the concern with problems of extinction during reinforcement, and the control "for spontaneous blinking, for effects of presentations of CS alone, and for effects of unpaired presentations of CS and UCS. . . ."

Linz et al. tested 20 infants aged 33-133 days; there were 8 subjects in an experimental group and 4 in each of three control groups. The CS was a 65 dB complex sound and the UCS was a mild air puff to the eye.

For the experimental group, CS alone was randomly interspersed among CS-UCS pairings in a 1 : 3 ratio, making for a partial reinforcement procedure. One of the reasons for this was to guard against the extinction during reinforcement found by Koltsova. Only 25 trials per day were given because with infants it had been found that this is about the limit of the period of their cooperation. Conditioning continued to a criterion of 9 CRs out of 10 successive trials. Lintz et al. indicated that this represents a more stringent criterion than is usually employed in adult conditioning studies.

There were 3 control groups: In one, the most important one, the subjects received the same total number of CSs and UCSs as the four slowest conditioners of the experimental group, but the CSs and UCSs were unpaired. A second control group received random-interval presentations of CS only, and a third control group received neither CSs or UCSs—this was to test for spontaneous blinking.

The results of Lintz et al. were clear. Eyeblinking was successfully conditioned to sound CS. None of the three control groups made CR type of responses at anywhere near the frequency of the experimental group. The authors concluded from the data of the three control groups that "administration of the UCS is the most important pseudo-conditioning control component for the conditioning situation."

Considering these infant conditioning studies together with the adult studies discussed earlier, the following generalizations seem appropriate. To the extent that the data reflect neurophysiological development, and to the extent that the various studies may be compared, it could be said that newborn or at least near newborn babies have nervous systems sufficiently intact for at least simple learning such as the conditioned eyeblink. There is a concentration or cooperation factor, and there is a habituation factor with which to contend, but by and large, infants are conditionable. If the neural mechanisms are not fully developed this early in life, they certainly seem to be by age 8-10 years. They are maintained with perhaps some lowering of function into young adulthood, but at the end of life there is clear change. The old person seems to be relatively insensitive to his environment and relatively unmodifiable. Again note the precaution: The procedures, purposes, and controls have been extremely varied from study to study, and as a result the comparisons are at best approximate.

For the sake of more completeness, it ought to be indicated that much of the infant literature, particularly the recent literature, involves appetitional UCSs such as milk. According to Stevenson (1970)[1] these studies "have given much more clear-cut demonstrations of neonatal conditioning than had previously been available." Not only have neonates been conditioned, but they have learned to differentiate between stimuli and to reverse responses with respect to them. Similarly, in old age, the conditioning patterns have been found consistent in a wide variety of situations. Slowness in the acquisition of the CR has been seen with the GSR, hand retraction, and other types of responses. It would seem that most of the generalizations regarding conditionability and age based upon the eyeblink CR hold for other types of CRs as well.

2. *Habituation.*

If habituation is to be regarded as a type of learning, it seems to be a most simple type. Habituation is operationally simpler than conditioning in that it involves only one stimulus and conditioning involves two, the CS and UCS. Also, unlike conditioning, association is not involved in habituation unless it is an association of the stimulus with the absence of any other environmental event. Habituation seems to be primary to conditioning, or at least involved in it. It was already seen in both the studies of Koltsova (1967) with infants, and Kimble and Pennypacker (1963) with aged people, that poor conditioning resulted when their subjects stopped or diminished responding to the air puff UCSs. As indicated, Kimble and Pennypacker concluded that the apparent age change in conditionability is attributable to this fact.

These are not the only studies demonstrating such age patterns. Habituation was seen in a simple conditioning study of the GSR (J. Botwinick & Kornetsky, 1960). In this study three groups were compared: a young adult group (20 years of age), an elderly group (71 years) selected on the basis of very stringent health criteria, and another elderly group (73 years) characterized by more "normal" good health, having a variety of typical noninterfering ailments. The general procedure involved habituating each subject's GSR to the CS alone *before* the

---

[1] Quotations from Stevenson (1970) are from a prepublication copy of the paper.

conditioning trials. The CS (a 65-70 dB tone of 450 Hz) was presented until there was no response in 4 out of 5 consecutive trials. Following this, the CS was paired with a shock UCS for 15 trials. The very healthy older subjects conditioned less readily than did the young controls, but, more importantly for the present purpose, they also habituated more readily prior to conditioning than did the young subjects. The less healthy older subjects also showed less CRs than did the young subjects but not significantly less. They did, however, habituate more readily to a statistically significant extent. Habituation scores and conditioning scores were correlated: The correlation ratio was .71.

There was an important aspect to these data which might best be discussed in the forthcoming section on "extinction," but will be discussed here because of its relevance to habituation. Following conditioning, the other attempts to increase conditioning rates, extinction was carried out to the same criterion of 4 out of 5 consecutive trials. When elderly and young subjects were equated on their measures of habituation, conditioning, or extinction, and then tested on one or the other of the two measures, age differences were no longer found. It can be concluded from these data that rate of habituation determines both rate of conditioning and rate of extinction. The tendency to habituate may be an inverse aspect of general responsiveness.

It will be recalled that while in Koltsova's study (1967) the infants habituated to the air puff UCSs during conditioning, in Wickens and Wickens' study (1940) the aversive shock UCSs during unpaired training was sufficient to cause pseudoconditioning. In this latter study, the neonates were so generally responsive that they failed to make specific discriminations between stimuli. The data of Koltsova and Wickens and Wickens considered together may indicate that the very subjects who habituate readily with mild stimuli (low responsiveness) may be the ones who maintain high response levels to stimuli perceived as aversive. In this manner the same subject can appear, paradoxically, insensitive and overly responsive.

Age comparisons across the total life-span in habituation tendencies are lacking. All we know at present is that elderly subjects, at least in two contexts, habituated more readily than young adults, and that habituation was found in the earliest periods of life. It would be interesting to know the developmental patterns of habituation across the life-span with both mild and not-so-mild stimuli.

3. Extinction.

There is a cogent argument that extinction is not simply a corollary of conditioning but is a new learning process. It is simply a new adjustment to a new environmental context, and not a negative or opposite function of conditioning. As such, extinction becomes a habituation process, but a special kind of habituation in that it operationally follows a previously reliable association in which the CS was involved.

In the conditioning studies of Braun and Geiselhart (1959) with the eyeblink, and J. Botwinick and Kornetsky (1960) with the GSR, extinction rates were seen to be functions of age; high resistance to extinction in childhood, decreasing in adulthood and lowest in old age was observed. However, the extinction rates were so much a function of the conditioning rates that when the latter were controlled for in relation to age, statistically significant age differences in extinction were no longer seen.

Some aging studies seem to point to an independence between extinction and conditioning. In some studies there is the general idea that resistance to extinction is reflective of a type of behavioral rigidity, a type of maladaptive perseveration of response which no longer serves a useful function. Marinesco and Kreindler (1934) conditioned a reflex retraction of the subject's hand pairing a UCS shock with either a CS bell or colored light. As found in the eyeblink studies, the hand retraction CR was achieved more slowly by aged men than by younger adults. However, unlike the data of Braun and Geiselhart (1959) and of J. Botwinick and Kornetsky (1960), extinction was achieved more slowly by the aged subjects. Since the data of Marinesco and Kreindler (1934) were not reported in quantitative fashion it is difficult to evaluate their results. Nevertheless, it may be worthwhile to speculate about them. The hand-withdrawal response is normally a completely voluntary response, the eyeblink is normally only partially voluntary, and the GSR is involuntary. It is possible that the relationship among age, conditioning, and extinction is different for voluntary and involuntary behavior. There are no appropriate data available to test this hypothesis, except perhaps data of instrumental avoidance conditioning of animals. These will be discussed in a later section.

B. Operant and Instrumental Conditioning.

Operant and instrumental conditioning are not always considered in a single context. Operant conditioning usually refers to the continuous measurement of the rates of simple responses emitted under very well controlled reinforcement contingencies. Instrumental conditioning usually refers to the measurement of a variety of response characteristics, frequently under less controlled reinforcement contingencies. Both are differentiated from classical conditioning in that in the latter, reinforcement is automatically administered independent of the response.

It is regrettable that there are so few aging studies of human operant conditioning, since it would seem that there is a wealth of potential in such studies. Among the reasons for studying operant conditioning in the elderly would be to answer questions such as what are effective reinforcers, what stimulus conditions appear interesting, how can we shape and control behavior. Clearly, answers to these questions would be most valuable. Also of importance are questions relating to differences between normal aged and the impaired aged. There are practical implications here, but the relevant basic data are not available. Until they are, there will be much guess work in the planning of programs for both the healthy and deteriorated aged.

Although there do not seem to be studies available in the human aging literature which systematically investigate the age factor in operant conditioning, there is at least one study in which data were presented on individual psychotic subjects of different ages. In a series of six experiments using mixed-age groups, 24-74 years, Ayllon and Azrin (1965) attempted to increase the rate of occurrence of certain adaptive behaviors by rewarding hospitalized mental patients with tokens which could later be exchanged for rewards of their choice. The authors state that age set no discernible limit on the effectiveness of the reinforcement procedure, which was, in general, quite successful.

In the child literature, on the other hand, human operant studies are more frequent. Many of the operant studies with children involve social behaviors and social reinforcers. Infants' social behavior, such as vocalization and smiling, has been successfully reinforced, and with older children verbal behavior has been "shaped." However, such operants are subject to the influences of a wide variety of variables. "The sex of the subject, sex of the experimenter, sex role preferences, and previous opportunities for social interaction. . " are important in determining the operant learning rates (Stevenson, 1970).

While the basic data of operant conditioning across the life-span are not available, there are data on instrumental conditioning. Unfortunately these data are based upon research with only rats as subjects.

1. *Animal Studies*

Perhaps the earliest animal age studies were carried out by Stone (1929a). In the first experiment in his series, he placed rats aged 20, 50, 100, 240 and 730 days into a box from which escape could be made by stepping on a platform. As an approximate guide to the age periods of rats, it may be estimated that pubescence is achieved by 3-4 months, adulthood by 6-8 months, middle age by 10-14 months, and old age by 20-26 months. Rarely does a laboratory rat live beyond 3 years. Thus, Stone's rats ranged in age from infancy to advanced senescence.

Stone reported that during approximately the first 10 trials there was a consistent pattern of longer escape times with increasing age. By the end of the experiment the time taken to escape was similar for all age groups. Thus, it would seem that infant rats may learn more quickly than the more mature ones. However, in Stone's studies the general activity levels of his subjects and the nature in which he differentially motivated them may have accounted for some of his results. To motivate the rats Stone (1929a, 1929b) used a method of differential starvation, based upon age.

In contrast, Verzár-McDougall (1957) tried to use a uniform method of maintaining animals on 80% of their normal body weight. Rats aged 2-3, 8-9, 12-18, 20-27 and 30 months were compared in the learning of multiple T maze. The rats aged 2-3 months were considered to have learned the maze as well as the next older age group, but there was difficulty keeping these youngest rats on the uniform deprivation schedule. Despite the differences in the methods of motivating the animals used by Stone and Verzár-McDougall, the results of the two studies were similar. Learning scores became progressively poorer with increasing age of the rat.

Denenberg and Kline (1958) carried out a study in which better control of the performances may have been maintained. Female hooded rats were trained to avoid an electric shock by responding to a buzzer within five seconds after it sounded. The response was one of pressing upon a door and going through it. There were three age groups of rats: 30, 60, and 225 days. The 60-day rats tended to be the quickest learners and the 30-day rats the slowest, but the differences among the three groups in the number of avoidance responses only approached statistical significance. When it came to extinguishing this response, the three groups were significantly different with the youngest group being the most difficult to extinguish.

It may be recalled that under the subhead "extinction" it was hypothesized that resistance to extinction of voluntary responses may change with age independently of acquisition scores. This resistance to extinction was conceptualized as a type of behavioral rigidity. The data of Denenberg and Kline (1958) support the hypothesis of independence.

In a study similar to that of Denenberg and Kline, K. Battig and Grandjean (1959) studied albino male rats aged 1, 3, 5, 7, 9, 13, 19, and 25 months. The three youngest groups conditioned more readily than the older groups. The oldest group was the slowest to condition and the 3-month group was the quickest.

Taken together these animal studies indicated that, with the type of tasks used, very young rats appear to learn as well as mature rats, perhaps they learn more quickly. Very old rats perform less well. To the extent that motivation factors were properly controlled, these results may be analogous to those of classical conditioning.

2. *Human Studies.*

Although the terms operant and instrumental conditioning refer to a wide variety of learning situations, more often than not the terms refer to relatively simple situations. If we compare these simple situations in the child literature with those in the aging literature, we find so very little correspondence that, with perhaps only one exception, integration of the studies become meaningless, if not impossible. The one exception is the problem of stimulus generalization.

Stimulus generalization is a process by which different stimuli become functionally equivalent, at least to an extent. When a subject is trained to respond to one stimulus, he will tend to respond to a different one also if it is similar to the first one in some way. The likelihood of response to the different stimulus increases in relation to the degree of similarity between the two stimuli. By these functions organisms can respond to a variety of stimuli or stimuli contexts, even when experience with them has been totally lacking. Extreme stimulus generalization, however, may be totally inappropriate and unrewarding.

R. I. Watson (1954) contended that older people narrow their range of interests and concentrate on essential features while ignoring the rest. From this he hypothesized that, in a test of stimulus generalization, older subjects, as compared to younger ones, would tend to generalize less, that is, differentiate more among the stimuli presented to them. Arnhoff (1959) put this hypothesis to a test by measuring the speed of response to visual stimuli varied in the space dimension. Seven lights were mounted horizontally on a plywood panel and any one of these could be made to turn on. Subjects aged 19-27 years and 60-82 years were instructed to respond as quickly as possible only when the center light of the seven was on.

In the main, Arnhoff confirmed Watson's hypothesis, but the nature of the problem was more complicated than at first may be envisioned. The older subjects tended to make relatively fewer responses to the lights off center. In fact 9 of the 54 subjects never did respond to the peripheral (off center) lights. Arnhoff (1959) considered the possibility that the performance of these subjects may have represented an attitude or task orientation which resulted in their slowing down in order to maintain accuracy. He reasoned that errorless stimulus generalization performances on the part of these elderly subjects may not have permitted a fair test of the generalization notion. Accordingly, he eliminated those elderly subjects who made errorless scores and compared the remaining elderly subjects with the younger ones. Having done this the differences between age groups in the generalization functions, as measured by the speed scores, were no longer significant.

It is fortunate for the present purposes that the stimulus generalization task used by Arnhoff was a popular one. In somewhat different form this same task was used by several child investigators. Stevenson suggested that, "From a developmental point of view, it might be expected that mature Ss will show more restricted gradients of stimulus generalization than will younger Ss. Several studies have found this the case." Thus, with respect to decreased stimulus generalization, Stevenson's expectation for increasing age of children was similar to Watson's for increasing age of adults. This is an example of where predictions and age data appear similar at both ends of the age spectrum, but where the mechanisms or reasons for these predictions may be quite different.

Mednick and Lehtinen (1957) reported a flatter gradient of generalization for children aged 7-9 years than for children aged 10-12. Jeffrey and Skager (1962) considered the idea that the greater generalization by the younger *S*s may have reflected a lack of interest in the task. They attempted to heighten motivation by a training condition in which children of two age groups received poker chips when correct responses were made, but lost chips when incorrect responses were made. Later the children were able to cash in the chips to see a movie cartoon. The procedure was identical for control groups of both ages except that chips were not given and not required for the movie. It was found that for children aged 6-7 years the added incentive often made for less generalization; their performances were similar to those of the older children aged 9-12 years. For these older children, performances did not differ between the two conditions of motivation. This study, then, points to one important interaction between age and motivation with respect to stimulus generalization. Age changes in stimulus generalization may be lessened when younger children are highly motivated.

It is seen from all these stimulus generalization studies that across the life-span, motivation or task orientation can be important in determining how well or poorly stimuli will be generalized. Sensory and motor abilities, even when correlated with age, are not sufficient to determine stimulus generalization performances.

II. DISCRIMINATION LEARNING

The interest and research effort in discrimination learning has been appreciable in the child literature, but not in the aging literature. In what follows, examples from the two literatures are more or less equally discussed, thus representing the child literature to a relatively much smaller extent.

A. Stimulus Pretraining.

In making discriminations between two stimuli it is necessary first to compare them in order to determine their distinctive features. Then, once these are noted, it is necessary to learn which of the distinctive features are relevant. The relevance of the distinctive features is determined by the investigator in his conditions of reinforcement. Not surprisingly, the learning of stimulus discriminations has been hastened by pretraining which obliges the subject to attend to the discriminative stimuli and which points him to their relevant features. There has been controversy over whether attention to the stimuli or having information about their distinctiveness is more crucial, but this controversy need not involve us here.

With verbal children and with adults, stimulus distinctiveness is made easier by attaching verbal lables to the discriminative stimuli. This was demonstrated in a study with elderly subjects by Crovitz (1966). Her study started with the well-known fact that elderly people, particularly deteriorated elderly people, find the Wisconsin Card Sort Test very difficult. This test involves a deck of cards on each of which one or more stimuli are drawn; the stimuli are varied on the basis of shape, number, and color. The subject goes through the deck, one card at a time, making a discrimination on the basis of one of these features. The experimenter gives information which enables the subject to learn which of these distinctive stimulus features is the relevant one.

Crovitz made the task simpler by requiring a discrimination based upon number only and by eliminating some of the irrelevant features of the stimuli. She compared two groups of elderly people. One group watched her sort the cards (discriminate between stimuli on the basis of number), and then verbalized the basis of her sorts. The control group did not have this pretraining. In the subsequent test for discrimination learning, the results were dramatic. All the subjects of the experimental group learned the discrimination while only just more than half of the control group were able to do this.

This study suggests the practical benefits to the elderly which may result from appropriate training. More aging studies of this type are needed, but these should include control groups receiving an equal amount of pretraining, but of another kind. If an experimental group has pretraining and a control group does not, a superiority in discrimination learning by the experimental group may be the result of prior experience in the experiment, rather than the result of the experimental manipulation. In other words, pretraining may be nothing other than a condition which permits a learning to learn phenomenon.

Norcross and Spiker (1957) carried out a study in which there were two pretrained control groups as well as an experimental group. In addition, two age groups of children were compared. Children aged 3-6 and 5-6 years were divided into three groups such that: (a) the experimental group was pretrained to attach discrete names to pictures of female faces. Each time one member of the pair was presented, the subjects were trained to say "Jean;" each time the other member was presented the subjects said "Peg." (b) One control group was pretrained with pictures of male faces and, in similar fashion, taught to attach male names. (c) A second control group was presented with the female faces and simply identified the pairs as different or the same.

It is very important in such a study that the actual amount of experience with the pretraining materials be similar from one group to the next so that the learning to learn factors be similar. In this Norcross-Spiker study the groups were similar in terms of statistical significance, but were different in the actual number of training trials to the pretraining criteria. The younger experimental group needed approximately twice the number of trials as did the controls. To a lesser extent the pattern of the older children was similar. However, if we accept the statistical results, that is, experimental and control groups were similar in the extent of their pretraining experience, the difference between groups was in the type of pretraining only, not in the amount.

The discrimination learning tests were two-choice problems of the female faces. The experimental group, pretrained with the female faces, performed significantly better than either of the two control groups. Differences between the two control groups were not significant. The older children performed better than the younger children, but the results of the pretraining were similar for both age groups.

The problem of equating experimental and control groups was handled in what seemed to be a more adequate fashion in a subsequent study by Norcross (1958). She used a within-subjects design in which subjects were pretrained with distinctive names to one pair of stimuli and with similar names to a second pair. In the test for discrimination learning, the pretraining experience with distinctive naming made for better performance than did the pretraining with similar naming. These experiments together demonstrate the benefit of proper pretraining.

B. Learning from Prior Experience.

In considering the effects of pretraining on subsequent learning, we have already become involved in one aspect of the effects of prior experience. What distinguishes this section from the previous one is that here the prior experience is not one of special priming for more effective performance, but simply one of carrying out a task.

There are at least two types of problems which, while operationally different, share conceptual similarities: learning set and transfer of training. The question asked in the learning set experiment is, what effect does the learning of a series of problems have on the learning of subsequent problems? Is there a learning to learn effect which makes the subsequent series a simple task only because it was not presented first in the experiment? In the transfer of training experiment the question asked is, what effect does the learning of a first problem have on the learning of a second problem?

1. *Learning Set.*

This important problem was first demonstrated with animals. Later, as Stevenson (1970) indicated "The first studies of learning set with children as *S*s were aimed at determining whether children could form learning sets (they could) and whether brighter children formed learning sets more rapidly than duller children (they did)."

For example, Reese (1965a) reported data of 37 nursery school children, aged 38-66 months. Each child was presented with a tray with two reward wells that were covered by the stimuli during each trial. The stimuli were 60 pairs of objects with multiple characteristics; each problem involving one pair of stimulus objects. Training was given on each problem to a criterion of five consecutive correct responses, rewarded by chocolate candies. New problems were given until the subject developed the learning set as determined by a stringent criterion involving five consecutive problems. While the children clearly formed learning sets, the rate of formation was not related to age. When the subjects were divided at the median age of the total group and both halves compared, the two halves were found similar in their performances.

A failure to find age differences in the acquisition of learning sets was also reported by Harter (1965). However, she did find differences associated with both IQ and MA. Using a factorial design of three IQ levels (70, 100, 130) and three MA levels (5, 7, 9), 81 children of wide age range were examined with a procedure similar to that used by Reese. The rewards in this case were marbles, rather than candies. Each child was given ten 4-trial problems daily until a criterion involving five successive problems was reached. Harter found that learning sets were developed more quickly with increasing IQ and increasing MA. There was an interaction effect such that the largest differences were found between MA groups at the 70-IQ level, or, if the emphasis is on IQ, the smallest learning set differences were found between IQ groups at the 9-year MA level.

Except for one possible factor, it would be possible to conclude from Harter's data that it is not age per se that determines learning set ability, but intellectual functioning and rate of intellectual growth. The one factor is that in Harter's study chronological age was confounded with IQ and MA. The youngest children (mean age = 3.5 years) were found in the 130-IQ and 5-MA group, while the oldest children (mean age = 13.0 years) were found in the 70-IQ and 9-MA group. A more pure test of the developmental patterns would have involved age variations while keeping constant intellectual ability categories.

Only one study of learning set was found that involved aged subjects, possibly because a greater ingenuity is required for testing learning sets in adults. Levinson and Reese (1967) compared four age groups with respect to learning set: 53 nursery school children, 53 fifth-graders, 57 college freshmen, and 209 people aged 61-97 years. A standard discrimination learning set procedure was used; each subject was given a number of two-stimulus simultaneous discrimination problems each using a different pair of stimuli. Four trials were given on each problem. Training continued to a criterion of 93% correct choices on Trials 2-4 of five consecutive problems, or until a predetermined fixed number of problems had been given. Learning performance improved with age up through the college group, and was markedly inferior for the aged group. The aged group required six times as many trials to criterion as did the preschool group. Within the aged sample, there were some retired professionals, and these subjects did much better than did the other aged. Position habits were strongest in the aged group and weakest in the fifth-grade and college groups, as were the variety and persistence of incorrect response patterns.

2. *Transfer of Training.*

While only the child and not the aging literature seems to include a substantial body of learning set studies, both literatures include studies of transfer of training. Once again, however, the purposes of these studies and the procedures tend to be different in the two literatures.

Gladis and Braun (1958) examined subjects in three age groups: 20-29, 40-49, and 60-72 years. Subjects in each group had to learn the association of eight response words with eight two-letter consonants, e.g., the word INSANE and TL. After this original learning (which may be described by the paradigm, *A-B*), each subject had to learn one other list of eight new response words which were paired with the same stimulus consonants of the original list (paradigmactically, *A-C*). There were other parts to this study but they need not be discussed here.

Gladis and Braun concluded from their results that the youngest group (20-29 years) showed the most transfer effect, that is, their performance was more greatly improved in *A-C* over *A-B* as compared to the two older groups. The two older groups showed only slight transfer, indicating that the middle aged and elderly subjects did not benefit much from their previous *A-B* learning experience.

There is an interesting feature to the study, which, it will be seen, may mitigate such a conclusion. Positive transfer (improvement) resulted, but it was negative transfer (interference and poorer performance) that was expected. It was expected because a second response word had to be associated with a stimulus which had already been associated with a first response word. Gladis and Braun attributed the positive transfer to a "learning how to learn."

As if in comment to this study, White, Spiker, and Holton (1960) suggested that positive transfer and negative transfer may be confounded in one set of results. If both effects were confounded in Gladis and Braun's data, the performances of the two older groups may have been more a matter of appreciable negative transfer than a matter of slight positive transfer.

White *et al.* hypothesized that human subjects are able to inhibit an *A-B* association when an *A-C* is known to be correct. This would minimize negative transfer effects when there is ample time to inhibit the association and make the correct *A-C* response. However, when there is not ample time, negative transfer effects may be maximized. The inhibition of the incorrect responses takes time and may take the form of a long latency correct response, or of an omission error if the time available for response is too brief.

White *et al.* put this hypothesis to a test. Fifth-grade children were trained on a paired-associate motor task which involved the association of a different button with each of six stimulus lights (*A-B*). Subjects received either 5 or 20 training trials. The transfer task for each subject comprised three *A-C* problems (interference), and three *D-C* problems (new associations as a control for positive transfer).

White *et al.* reported that there were significantly more correct responses in the *D-C* condition than in the *A-C* condition, supporting the idea of confounded negative and positive transfer in *A-C*. More important, perhaps, was the tendency for a greater number of omission errors to occur in the *A-C* condition than in the *D-C* condition. This tendency was not significant but was more pronounced for the more highly trained group. For the 20-trial group omission errors were 27 and 18 for *A-C* and *D-C* conditions, respectively. For the 5-trial group the pattern was reversed, 9 and 12 respectively. These patterns were highlighted when the response measure was speed of correct responses rather than the number correct. For the 20-trial group, but not the 5-trial group, the subjects responded more rapidly in the *D-C* condition than in the *A-C* condition.

These data clearly demonstrated the importance of the interval of time permitted for response. This interval sets the limits of opportunity within which the correct response may be made. Arenberg (1967) may not have known about the study of White *et al.* (1960), but he did know about the importance of the interval, especially as it affects learning performance by aged subjects. Using the same word lists that Gladis and Braun (1958) used in one part of their study, Arenberg varied the interval in two ways; subjects in two age groups were permitted 1.9 seconds or 3.7 seconds to respond in the *A-B* and *A-C* conditions.

When the interval was short (1.9 seconds) the older group (about 70 years of age) was significantly poorer in *A-C* list performance than the younger group (about 35 years). When the interval was long the two age groups were not significantly different. This suggests that the older people needed the extra time provided in the longer interval to demonstrate their learning, perhaps (taking the lead from White *et al.*, 1960) because they needed more time to inhibit the inappropriate *A-B* associations.

There is one complicating feature in Arenberg's study. The older group was poorer than the younger group in learning the original *A-B* list when the anticipation interval was long. They required a mean of 19.3 trials to learn it, while the younger subjects required 11.0 trials. The older group, therefore, had more general learning experience prior to the learning of the transfer *A-C* list. The over-all literature suggests two contradictory possibilities with regard to this. On one hand, the extra experience of the older subjects, rather than their need for extra time in the *A-C* condition, may have been the crucial factor accounting for their relatively good performance in the *A-C* condition. In other words, there may have been more opportunity for learning how to learn with the extra experience. On the other hand, subjects performing poorly on original learning tasks may perform particularly poorly on the subsequent tasks of transfer. This would suggest that Arenberg's results may be even more impressive than at first supposed.

There is a specialized literature of transfer of training dealing with the problem of reversal and nonreversal shifts. In the reversal shift problem the subject is trained to choose black over white, for example, and then is tested for relearning a white over black choice. The nonreversal shift problem involves a relearning on the basis of a different quality, as for example, large over small (after having just learned black over white). In this problem the two discriminative stimuli would each be of two distinctive qualities, brightness and size.

From a strict S-R formulation, the reversal shift should be the more difficult of the two. From a formulation based upon mediation concepts such as verbal labeling, the reversal shift should be less difficult. There has been considerable interest in the implications of these theoretical formulations in the child literature, but not in the aging literature. In reviewing the literature on reversal and nonreversal shift problems, Stevenson (1970) indicated that the earlier research had demonstrated that reversal shifts are more difficult for lower animals, but nonreversal shifts more difficult for human adults. This would tend to confirm the mediation view; however, after examining a variety of these studies, Stevenson concluded that, ". . .none of the theories is capable of handling the essential results. Each can incorporate a part. . .".

Despite this less than satisfactory conclusion the reversal-nonreversal shift problem could be useful in aging research. It might give a clue as to the type of learning strategies older people tend to use, or learning habits by which older people tend to be governed. While the aging literature does not seem to include the problem of reversal-nonreversal shift, there is a body of information on the reversal shift itself.

One such study covering a wide age range was carried out with animal subjects by J. Botwinick, Brinley, and Robbin (1962). Pubescent, adult, and aged Sprague Dawley female rats (ages: 3-4, 8-12, and 22-27 months, respectively) were trained to go either to the right or to the left in a single choice Y maze in order to obtain food. The alternate position response was not rewarded. After the original learning, the position responses were reversed. The non-rewarded direction became the rewarded one, and the rewarded position response became no longer rewarding. After this reversal shift was learned (R_1), the animals were retrained on the originally learned position (R_2). Following this there were two further reversals $(R_3$ and $R_4)$.

It was found that the old age rats were particularly poor in the first and second reversals $(R_1$ and $R_2)$, as compared to the middle and younger aged rats. However, when subjects in each of the three age groups were matched on the basis of their scores on the original learning task, the differences among age groups in their reversal performances diminished and were no longer statistically significant.

In the second part of this study the results were different. An effort was made in this second part to reduce the variability of performance scores by increasing the size of the food pellet reward, and by decreasing the time the rat was left in the maze after making the position response. In this part the three age groups were not found significantly different in any of the experimental sequences, not in original learning nor in any of the reversals. Thus, any generality of a difficulty in reversal shifting in later life, or in general learning performance for that matter, was brought into question by this second part of the study.

It is interesting in this context that in referring to a study by Jeffrey (1965), Stevenson wrote that it "shows how a modest change in the testing procedure can produce results that have a destructive effect on any theory that postulates changes with age in the ease of reversal learning." Jeffrey trained college students and children aged 4, 6 and 8 years to make a color discrimination. Instead of simply reversing the reinforcement contingencies, he also changed the stimuli from circles to squares. In so doing he failed to find the expected age differences in making the reversal shifts. Age differences could have been expected in Jeffrey's study on the basis of several previous studies, as well as on the basis of results in an earlier part of his own study.

3. Response Bias.

We close this section with a very brief discussion of response bias in order to highlight an area of research which seems to be totally lacking in the aging literature. Such research seems to be greatly needed. There may be response biases in the discrimination learning of old people, in the data from which clinical assessments are made (e.g. Wisconsin Card Sorting type of tests), and in questionnaire studies involving alternative choice. These biases can distort the results in ways that we presently do not know.

Ther are many types of data suggesting that older people tend to perseverate responses and this could certainly be viewed as a response bias. However, there is good evidence that the perseveration may not be the primary factor. It may be secondary to an ability factor, that is, how difficult the task is found and how available alternate choices seem to be. Facts about response bias in later life are unknown and the relevant studies are yet to be carried out.

In the child literature several studies on response bias have been carried out and, according to Stevenson, the results of these studies were not to be anticipated from any prior theory. In two-choice situations 3-year-olds tend to repeat their particular position responses. However, "a preference for alternation is present at age 4, persists through age 8, and drops out by age 10 [Stevenson 1970]."

III. PAIRED-ASSOCIATE AND SERIAL LEARNING

Some of the studies of paired-associate learning have already been discussed in the context of transfer of training problems. In pointing out that the time interval permitted for response is an important factor, a major focus in the aging literature has already been highlighted. The emphasis upon time relations has been for the purpose of determining whether the deficit typically seen in old age is one of performance or of learning. Again, the literature with children is seen carried out for different purposes and with different goals. There are, however, overlapping concepts and these will be reviewed.

The literature of the 1930s and 1940s pointed to a diminution in the ability to learn paired associates with advanced adult age. In the 1960s this notion was tested in a series of studies which contended that at least part of the age deficit may be an inability to respond quickly enough, rather than inability to acquire information. Canestrari (1963) and Arenberg (1965) tested this contention in paired associate learning; and Eisdorfer, Axelrod, and Wilkie (1963), and Eisdorfer (1965) tested this in serial learning. In each of these studies some aspect of pacing of stimulus presentations was varied.

Canestrari had three pacing schedules in his paired associate learning study. He had a fast pace where the word pairs were exposed for 1.5 seconds with the same amount of time allowed between word pairs, a medium pace where 3.0 seconds were allowed for stimulus exposure and intertrial durations, and a condition in which the subject paced himself. In this self-paced condition the subject controlled the apparatus so that he could get as much time between word pairs as he desired. Male subjects aged 60-69 years were compared to younger subjects aged 17-35 years, with the finding that the largest differences between age groups occurred with the condition of fastest pacing, and the smallest differences with the condition of self-pacing. These results indicated that some proportion of the age deficit may be accounted for by the nonlearning factor of the loss of speed with age. Not all the age deficit was accounted for by the speed factor since the performances of the elderly group were poorer than those of the younger group in all three conditions of learning, including the condition of self-pacing. These results were corroborated by Arenberg (1965) in a very similar experiment.

In a different part of the study by Arenberg, older subjects (60-77 years) and younger subjects (18-21 years) learned the paired words by a procedure in which paced and self-paced trials were alternated. One subgroup of each age experienced fast pacing trials (1.9 seconds) alternated with self-pacing trials, and a second subgroup of each age experienced slow pacing trials (3.7 seconds) alternated with the self-pacing trials.

The crucial test in this study involved the comparison of error scores during the self-paced trials which followed the experimenter-paced trials. The thinking behind this crucial test was that if the older subjects learned the task during the fast paced trials, but did not have enough time to respond, they would make poor scores during this fast pacing but good scores during self-pacing. However, if the older people did not learn well during the fast paced trials, then their performances would be poor during self-pacing. It was found that the older group was disproportionately poorer than the younger group during the self-paced trials when these followed fast pacing than when these followed the slow pacing. The conclusion, therefore, was that the poor performance of the old group during the fast pacing could not "be attributed to insufficient time to emit a correctly learned response" (Arenberg, 1965, p. 424).

Instead of varying the pacing schedule in paired-associate learning, Eisdorfer et al. (1963) varied the stimulus exposure interval in a serial learning experiment. Their purpose was similar to that of Canestrari and Arenberg in that they were interested in determining the effects on performance of the time period during which response was possible. One group of elderly subjects was given a long stimulus exposure period (8 seconds) and another group was given a short one (4 seconds). At a point of a crucial test, the exposure intervals were reversed for the two groups. The test involved the comparisons of the performance during the long exposure periods which followed brief ones, with the performances during brief exposure periods which followed long ones. It was found that performance scores of the elderly subjects were more a function of the time permitted for response during the crucial test trial than the time permitted during the trials preceding this test.

This type of result was demonstrated with children as well as the elderly. Price (1963) carried out a paired-associate verbal procedure in which one group of children (aged 49-66 months) performed with a relatively short, 2-second anticipation interval and another group of similar age performed with a long, 6-second interval. On the second half of the task both groups performed with the long interval. If both groups performed equally in the second half, when in the first half performance was worse with the short interval, then it could not be reasoned that learning was poor during the short interval. The results were in accord with this formulation, suggesting that only performance was impaired during the short anticipation period.

There is a general assumption running through the aging literature that the relatively poor performances of the elderly subjects were due to either learning difficulties or to slowness in response. It is possible that other factors influenced the performances. For example, on the basis of similar data, Eisdorfer (1965) suggested that anxiety may be responsible for the poor performances of older subjects. He suggested that rapid pacing may be stressful to the aged subjects; it may increase their anxiety levels. Heightened anxiety, he indicated, may result in withdrawal, and consequently, poorer performance.

Affective factors in paired-associate learning have not been investigated in the aging literature but they have in the child literature. These factors have been more complicated than Eisdorfer's anxiety hypothesis might suggest, but they have not contradicted it. Castaneda and Lipsitt (1959), studying fifth-grade children, manipulated drive level, inducing stress by a time pressure for response in a paired-associate motor task. It would seem that this study has direct bearing on the aging studies since time pressure has been thought so important in the performances of the aged. They found that high stress led to improved performance when habit strength of the associates was high, and disrupted performance when it was low. In a different study (Castaneda, Palermo, and McCandless, 1956) anxiety was measured, not induced, and the concept task difficulty was used rather than habit strength. The results of this study were compatible with those of Castaneda and Lipsitt (1959): A statistically significant interaction was found between anxiety and task difficulty. The high anxiety children, as compared to low anxiety, tended to perform more poorly on the difficult parts of the task and better on the easier parts.

If we are to relate these data to the aging studies, two hypotheses present themselves. The older subjects performed more poorly than the younger subjects because: First, as suggested by Eisdorfer (1965), the rapid pacing stressed or made the older subjects more anxious than the younger ones. The learning materials were difficult (low habit strength) for both age groups, but equally so. Second, young and aged subjects were equally stressed but the learning task was more difficult (lower habit strength) for the older subjects than for the younger ones. This second hypothesis throws the problem back to an explanation of learning deficit. It is possible, of course, that both these hypotheses are partially correct: The older subjects in the studies discussed were more stressed by the rapid pacing, but independent of this, the tasks were also more difficult for them.

It would be amiss to end the present discussion without mentioning that some studies did not demonstrate this interaction between anxiety and habit strength or test difficulty, as for example, the study by Lipsitt and Spears (1965). Regardless of results, however, these studies concerned with motivational factors indicate that to better understand performance deficits in later life, benefit may be gained from greater attention to affective and experiential or task variables than has heretofore been manifested.

IV. INCIDENTAL LEARNING

Incidental learning refers to the acquisition of information or skill which is not relevant to the main purpose in a learning task. The literature dealing with incidental learning and age is not vast, but unlike other research problems there seems to be a near equal interest in the developmental changes at both ends of the age spectrum. This may be because predictions of quite a contradictory nature can be made on the basis of seemingly rational considerations. It can be reasoned that as children develop they become more generally able, and so they should be better incidental learners. Similarly, on the other end of the age scale, if in later life learning ability is poor then it may be predicted that incidental learning will be poor. This reasoning is based on the notion that incidental learning is part of general learning, or at least that incidental and intentional learning are related. Alternate predictions can also be made. These are based on the idea that it is wasteful to attend to vast amounts of meaningless information. With experience and maturity the subject learns to ignore these irrelevant factors and in so doing, becomes poorer in performance when it involves incidental learning. We will return to these concepts later.

Willoughby (1929, 1930) reported one of the earliest studies on incidental learning. He gave a test, not unlike the Digit Symbol substitution subtest of the Wechsler Intelligence Scale, to male and female subjects age 6-68 years. When the subjects completed the test, he asked them to recall the associations between number and symbol. This was a surprise task since he had not announced previously that he would require this. Willoughby reported that the recall of the digit-symbol associations increased to about the age of 17 years and then declined gradually thereafter. This age pattern of incidental learning was very similar to that pattern of actual performance on the Digit Symbol test. Thus, it would seem that the two functions may be related to some degree. This study was the only one in which most of the life-span was covered. In a similar study, dealing with adult aging, Bromley (1958) tested subjects in their 20s, 40s, and 60s with the complete Wechsler-Bellevue Test, and then without forewarning asked them to recall the eleven subtests. Small age decrements in recall scores were found.

These two studies, and the next one by Kausler and Lair (1965) are not typical incidental learning studies in that it may be argued that the incidental cues were not really irrelevant. They were part of the central task and at least partially relevant to it. In Kausler and Lair's study two groups of subjects of approximate mean ages 35 and 56 years were compared on paired-associate learning performance. The two groups were not significantly different in supplying the response word when the stimulus word was presented. In the test of incidental learning the subject was asked to supply the stimulus word when the response word was presented. This task has been described as a "variant of incidental learning." In this situation, the young group displayed significantly greater recall than did the older group.

These three studies may be taken as evidence of decline, although a small decline, in incidental learning with increasing adult age. There are two studies which do not indicate such a decline. The procedures of these two studies are in some ways more typical of those seen in usual incidental learning studies. In the first study, Wimer (1960) compared adults over 65 years of age with adults under 30 years in their recognition of incidentally learned word-color associations. Each of six words was printed in a different color on a separate card. All subjects were asked to read each word as rapidly as possible, being informed that they were partaking in a speed reading experiment. Half the subjects of each age group were informed they would be tested afterward for knowledge of the specific color in which each word was printed; half were not informed. Later, both halves (intentional and incidental learners) were tested for *recognition* of the word-color associations.

The subject viewed a complex array of words and colors and had to identify the color in which each word had appeared previously. The array was so complex that perhaps for this reason scores of the older subjects were the same in the intentional and incidental conditions. The array may have been less difficult for the young in that their performances were more superior in the intentional learning than in the incidental learning. However, they were not different from the elderly subjects in the incidental condition.

The second study in which incidental learning was not found to change with age was reported by Hulicka (1965). Subjects aged 30-39, 60-75, and 76-89 years were shown pictures of seven male faces each paired with a name (e.g., Joe) and a city (e.g., Chicago). The subjects were told to learn the associations between the faces and the names. Each subject was then tested for this learning, but also tested for the incidentally learned associations of faces and cities. The recall tests took place 20 minutes and one week after acquisition. Statistically significant age differences were not found in either intentional or incidental learning. There were, however, statistically nonsignificant age decrements.

These five studies when taken together raise questions, rather than answer the one of whether advanced age brings decline in incidental learning ability. When decline was found it appeared to be slight, and the investigators tended to view the decline as reflecting a useful process. These studies tended to suggest that, if general intellectual decline is part of old age, it would be adaptive for the elderly to rely only upon cues that are important for the task at hand, and pay less attention to irrelevant cues. In finding a task more difficult than younger people, the elderly may focus upon what is expected and relevant rather than upon what is not, and thus maximize the probability of optimum performance with intentional tasks.

Based upon very similar reasoning, Stevenson (1970) pointed out that a prediction could be made that incidental learning would decline with the increasing age and ability of children. In the aging literature poor incidental learning is explained on the basis of failing ability; in the child literature poor incidental learning tends to be explained on the basis of increasing efficiency. Both explanations, or predictions, presuppose the protective mechanism provided in ignoring irrelevant cues so that attention may be better given to the relevant ones.

The studies of children and incidental learning suggest that the relationship may be more complicated than typically presented. In the first of these studies, Stevenson (1954) had children aged 3, 4, 5, and 6 years learn a V-shaped maze. He had three experimental conditions, but for the present purposes differences in these conditions need not be considered. The starting point of the maze was the apex of the "V" and this was 20 feet from each of the goal boxes located at the ends. The two goal boxes were 10 feet apart. One box was locked with a padlock and contained a reward object, and the other box contained the key necessary to open the lock. The box with the key also contained the irrelevant objects used in assessing incidental learning.

After appropriate preliminary training the subjects were given six trials to find the key and to use it in obtaining a reward. Following this, the tests of incidental learning were made. Subjects were shown objects identical to the ones in the goal box with the key, and then told they were to find the goal box objects. Successful performance of incidental learning was indicated by going to the appropriate goal box. Stevenson found that, in general, incidental learning performance improved with increasing age from 3 to 6 years. (In one of the three experimental conditions the 3-year-olds were second only to the 6-year-olds in performance but this was the only major exception).

In a later study Maccoby and Hagen (1965) tested children in grades 1, 3, 5 and 7. The children were shown picture cards, each with a distinctively colored background, and their task was to indicate when this background color matched a color chip which was displayed. Following a series of trials on this intentional task, the incidental task was presented. This task involved identifying the foreground pictures which appeared on each background color. Half the children were tested with a distraction condition and half without it, but this variation need not concern us here.

Recall scores of intentional learning increased systematically with increasing age from grades 1 through 7. However, while recall scores of incidental learning increased slightly from grade 1 to 5, they decreased from grade 5 to 7. In finding no significant correlation between incidental and intentional learning scores, Maccoby and Hagen (1965, p. 289) suggested that the subjects did "not 'trade' efficiency on one (type of learning) for efficiency in the other. The findings are difficult to interpret in terms of a single limited information-processing 'capacity' characterizing each individual."

If it is possible to form an integrated concept from Stevenson's and Maccoby and Hagen's studies, it would be that incidental learning performance improves from 3 to approximately 11 years of age and then declines to approximately 13 years of age. This age range is extended in the next and last study to be described in this chapter. The study compares children and young adults and it may be fitting that we end the discussion by describing a pattern not at all in keeping with preconceived notions of continuity from one period of life to another.

A. W. Siegel and Stevenson (1966) tested children aged 7 through 14 years, and adults aged 19 through 35 years (mean age = 22.5 years). The adults comprised one age group and the children were combined into successive age groups (7-8, 9-10, 11-12, and 13-14) in the analysis of incidental learning. There were three tasks, and in each the stimuli were drawings of objects projected from slides. In the first task, three successive objects were presented to which the subject responded by pressing one of three response buttons. Correct choice was rewarded by marbles which later could be exchanged for a prize. In the second task the objects were embedded in a complex including three other objects. The third task was of incidental learning. Objects of the embedded complex were individually presented along with other objects, and the task was to identify the objects of the embedded complex as seen in the second task.

The results of this study as it involved the children were similar to those of Maccoby and Hagen. Siegel and Stevenson found a significant increase in incidental learning from 7-8 to 11-12 years. From 11-12 to 13-14 years there was a significant decrease. Thus, the presumed maturity and greater ability of the older children was detrimental to incidental learning. However, the greater maturity of the adults was not detrimental. Adults performed better than any of the children.

In general, performances on the initial, intentional task were similar among the children of all ages, but the performances of the adults were superior to those of the children. It is tempting to explain the incidental learning age patterns as a reflection of intentional learning ability, but this is not permitted by the data. Coefficients of correlation between intentional and incidental learning scores were not significant for children. However, there was significant correlation for adults ($r = .41$). The nature of the correlation does not clarify matters though, it confuses them. Among adults, the slower learners in the original task showed a higher degree of incidental learning than did the faster learners. One advantage to life-span research is that it provides a greater variance to demonstrate relationships. It would have been interesting had Siegel and Stevenson been able to combine data of all their subjects and plot the relationship between the two types of learning.

A. W. Siegel and Stevenson (1966, p. 817) indicated that "it might have been expected that the adults would show a low level of incidental learning. This was not found, probably because the task was so extremely simple for adults. It is likely that as tasks become increasingly simple for Ss involved, greater incidental learning will be found." Yet, in explanation of the finding that the slower learners among the adults had better incidental learning scores than the faster learners, they hypothesized, "that the slower learners had to pay closer attention to the stimuli during the second part of the task to maintain the correct response and thereby learned more about the incidental stimuli."

This seems to be the problem with the post hoc explanations of developmental patterns in incidental learning. Both relatively good and relatively poor performances, age decrements and age increments, monotonic and non-monotonic functions within limited age ranges are all explained in terms of either the efficiency of not learning irrelevant factors or the ease with which such learning takes place. If the adults used by Siegel and Stevenson found the test easy, and therefore had high incidental learning scores, this should be even more true for the better learners. This would seem to be the case unless the task is considered to be qualitatively different for adults than for children, or for one age group of children than for another. This, of course, would not permit age comparisons. However, if we maintain that the same task is qualitatively similar for age groups across the life-span, and that we can consider all the studies together, the data seem to show a continuing rise in incidental learning until adulthood, with the exception of a dip in late childhood or early adolescence. In late life there may be a dip once again.

This is a complex function, not to be understood unless we have total life-span studies explicating the relationships between incidental learning and a host of important factors. Among these are ability in intentional learning, brightness levels of subjects, difficulty levels of intentional and incidental problems, and variations in different types of problems. It might also be meaningful to investigate experiential factors such as richness of the normal environment (that is, amounts of relevant and irrelevant information to which the subject is habitually exposed) and the past record of rewards and punishments for attending to irrelevant cues. Clearly, it is much more difficult to investigate such factors than to vary task or subject characteristics. But, if we want to explain developmental patterns in incidental learning, it may be necessary to attempt such investigation.

ACKNOWLEDGMENT

This paper was supported in part by Public Health Service Research Grant HD-04524 and Training Grant HD-00047 from the National Institute of Child Health and Human Development.

CHAPTER 12

The Experiential Origins of Human Behavior

LEWIS P. LIPSITT

BROWN UNIVERSITY
PROVIDENCE, RHODE ISLAND

ABSTRACT

Studies of learning processes in infants and young children are reviewed, and it is concluded that human infants, including newborns, are capable of learning under both classical and instrumental procedures, as well as some procedures combining features of both of these. Learning capacity seems most enhanced when experiential circumstances capitalize upon the congenital and sometimes idiosyncratic response repertoire of the infant. Individual differences, reflected through measures of chronological age and physiological dispositions, set limiting conditions upon capacity for learning, but those limiting conditions must always be determined empirically rather than merely presumed.

I. INTRODUCTION

I judge and hope that by now the old controversies concerning the relative contributions to human development of genetic predispositions and environmental determinants have been laid to rest sufficiently securely that I need not explain at length or even defend the title of my presentation. That there are experiential origins of human behavior should be self-evident; indeed, a large portion of my own research on infant behavior processes deals with some of these. In studying the plasticity of infant behavior, however, one can neither ignore nor denigrate the role of physiological dispositions, temporary states, or individual differences among members of the species; clearly, there are species differences that produce limitations on the capabilities of the organism, even under learning conditions or other experiential circumstances most conducive to change in human behavior. Nevertheless, concern with the uniquely *experiential* origins of human behavior strikes a number of us child developmentalists as a reasonable preoccupation in that the control of infant behavior is so obviously related to the consequences of environmental variations, under both naturalistic and laboratory conditions. It is not the aim of those researchers among us, as I understand our scientific concerns, to establish that experiential determinants of behavior are more important in any way than constitutional, hereditary, or age-generated determinants. I doubt that many of us are even interested in trying to tabulate the relative amounts of variance attributable to one or another of these classes of variables, for most of us are by now in agreement with Anastasi (1958) that such an approach leads truly to a dead end.

We should all be convinced by now that any assessment of the relative contributions of hereditary versus environmental factors will be necessarily limited in generality to the boundaries of experiential input arranged within the study from which those assessments have been made. It would be easy to demonstrate a large contribution of experience to human development simply by allowing the range of experience to operate fully—such as by rearing one member of an identical twin pair under conditions of extreme isolation from social learning experience, while rearing the alternate sibling in a situation generally conducive to the development of, for example, talking and problem solving. Any competent geneticist can easily invent the counterpart study which would show that hereditary predisposition is really more important. It is probably impossible to teach a chimpanzee plane geometry, even under the best of educational circumstances. By the same token, however, it is impossible to teach a human to hang by his tail from a tree. Genetic predispositions and limitations are obvious, and age-imposed limitations are a special type of genetic disposition. The general *principle* of such limitations on the plasticity of the human organism should need no further rehearsal or debate. The task for the learning psychologist is, just as Anastasi (1958) implies, one of pursuing the mechanisms or processes by which experiential conditions work their wonders in altering human behavior, the tissue limitations notwithstanding.

Having thus stated at the outset that my present mission needs no defense, and having now demonstrated by my own behavior that perhaps it does, let me indicate the remaining scope of the task before me. I should like to deal here with the question of what infants learn, with the mechanisms by which these learned changes in behavior presumably come about, and with the possible differences that these learned behavior changes make in the later, if not ultimate, history of the human organism. Questions relating to the potentialities of humans throughout the life-span must begin with empirical studies of infant learning capacities, and the processes underlying these. The origins of human behavior are undoubtedly orderly (lawful), but knowledge of these matters still remains largely a "blooming, buzzing confusion" pending the further systematic exploration of the behavioral consequences of early stimulation. We are, however, making modest progress and I shall try to report succinctly some recent advances made in the study of infant behavior, effects of specific stimulating conditions, and individual differences.

The burgeoning literature in the area of infant learning processes, particularly over the past ten or so years, has overwhelmed us all, and it has become a real challenge for infant researchers to remain abreast of all of the most recent findings. Coverage here is restricted to relatively few issues relating to the understanding of behavior modification in infants and to a limited amount of data bearing upon these concerns.

II. UNCONDITIONED AND CONDITIONED BEHAVIOR

It is easy, and a rather frequent occurrence, for persons who do not understand fully the nature of conditioning processes to assume that the course of conditioning, and the manner in which conditioning is implemented, are independent of the physiological repertoire of the organism under study. Appreciable numbers of undergraduates remark on their final examinations, for example, that John B. Watson believed that all behavior is conditioned. Nothing, of course, is farther from the truth, although some of Watson's most popularly cited remarks do little to dispell this misunderstanding. The facts of the matter are that J. B. Watson (1919) was a respectable physiologist for his time and that he was quite clear concerning the importance of the unconditioned response repertoire of the human infant in enabling conditioning.

Indeed, it was Watson who made one of the first systematic attempts to catalog the physiological or unconditioned reflex dispositions of the newborn, on the basis of which he suggested that all subsequent learning depends. Watson told us about the response systems of fear, rage, and love, and he attempted to demonstrate (although rather poorly, I think) the stimulus conditions under which these response classes could be observed. He even tipped his hat to individual differences in the elicitability of these responses, and he suggested that to a large degree their elicitation is state-dependent. While it remained for later researchers to demonstrate how very soon after birth such learned alterations in behavior might be effected, Watson did provide a prototypic demonstration of the manner in which learning, and hence human development, capitalizes upon the prior presence of unconditioned responsivity in generating new behavior. This was accomplished through the J. B. Watson and Rayner (1920) study, in which the infant's fear and crying responses to noise served as the "congenital given" on the basis of which a conditioned reaction to the presentation of a white animal (which previously elicited no such emotional response) could be established. Conditioning phenomena always depend for their occurrence upon the initial availability in the organism's repertoire of a response which either may be attached to a new or previously neutral stimulus (as in the case of classical conditioning) or which may be enhanced in frequency or intensity of emission through reinforcement consequences (as in the case of operant learning).

Interestingly, the Watson and Rayner experiment can have several implications for us in the present context. One relates to the nature of the conditioning processes actually involved in that demonstration. Another has to do with the ethological sensitivity the researchers showed in selecting the particular response system and stimuli which they chose for their demonstration of learned fear. A final implication relates to the occasional scientific usefulness of violating traditional models, particularly in areas of exploration which are rather poorly understood.

While it has been generally accepted that the study of Albert, the 11-month-old subject in the conditioned fear experiment, is of the typical classically conditioned sort, a reinterpretation of the procedures (Church, 1966) gives one pause to reconsider the real nature of the learning process underlying this as well as, perhaps, some other historic studies persistently referenced as of the classical conditioning variety. Church suggests that because the aversive stimulus used in the study, noise, was not presented contingent upon the occurrence of the conditioned stimulus (the white rat) but instead was presented contingent upon the child's response of touching the animal, the paradigm is that of an instrumental punishment procedure, rather than of classical aversive conditioning. The Church observations on the Watson and Rayner experiment should serve as a caution that our distinctions among classical and operant paradigms may not be honored as much in experimental practice as they are in our conceptualizations. However, the experimental successes of child psychologists in documenting infant learning phenomena seem to have been enhanced on a number of occasions in which researchers departed from traditional conditioning models to capitalize on the response repertoire peculiar to the young organism. Watson and Rayner must be credited with a keen sensitivity to the behavioral topography of the 11-month-old in order to accomplish the study of Albert. It is nevertheless of more than passing interest that Watson made his point about the learning capacities of infants by demonstrating an instance of instrumental rather than of classical conditioning.

Research progress relating to infant learning has often been aided by the adoption of experimental manipulative techniques related to but not dictated entirely by traditional styles for the study of such processes. Usually the departures from the classic models or paradigms represent accomodations on the part of the researcher to the special response attributes of the organism whose behavior is being manipulated. Such special characteristics may be attributable to species membership, age, class, or even to prior learning; some special attributes are due simply to individual variability within species or age groups. In the field of infant studies, birth weight, and sucking style on first contact with the nipple, are such variables.

Papousek (1961) found that the changing topography of the sucking response with increases in age made difficult the longitudinal study of classically conditioned sucking behavior. Papousek's solution to the problem was to focus upon a different but ethologically or functionally related response system, that of head-turning, and to utilize a modified classical conditioning procedure. Briefly, a tone was used as the conditioning stimulus, while for the unconditioned stimulus a sequence of events was used; first the baby's cheek was stimulated with the bottle nipple near the mouth, and if this did not result in an ipsilateral head-turn, the experimenter gently turned the head in the appropriate direction and placed the nipple in the baby's mouth to provide reinforcement. The paradigm was such as to provide the opportunity for classically conditioned anticipatory head-turning to occur in response to the tone and prior to the presentation of the unconditioned sequence of stimuli. In this instance, it may be noted that the conditioning paradigm is rather unique. Because the touch to the infant's cheek did not unfailingly elicit an unconditioned head-turn, the unconditioned stimulus was embellished to produce a "forced" unconditioned response that would consistently occur following the presentation of the auditory conditioning stimulus.

The adoption of this rather unique procedure enabled Papousek to establish classical appetitional conditioning in neonatal infants and under conditions in which the obtained effect could be noted to transfer reliably over successive days of training (Papousek, 1961, 1967). According to Papousek (1967), p. 258): "The mean number of 177 trials for [the neonatal group] represented approximately three weeks of conditioning, and shows that during the 28 days of the neonatal period most newborns can achieve even a relatively severe criterion of conditioning (five consecutive positive responses, i.e., ipsilateral head-turns of 30 degrees, in the 10 trials of one day). But wide individual differences in the newborns were apparent; the fastest conditioners needed only 7, 10 11, or 12 days, the slowest ones, more than a month." It is quite apparent that Papousek's elaboration of basic classical conditioning methodology was responsible for the early-conditioning effect obtained in the newborn child. This constituted a considerable advance in knowledge about the neonatal human, for infants of that age had not been traditionally celebrated in the child development literature for their precocity. Moreover, the documentation of very early learning in the human opens the way for the further exploration of the importance of cumulative learning experiences and individual learning differences in the determination of later behavior, especially later learning proficiency.

In a series of experiments which elaborated upon the technique developed by Papousek, Siqueland and Lipsitt (1966) found it possible to draw upon some features of both classical and operant conditioning while conforming fully to neither of these models. In three experiments they demonstrated learning in the first two to four days of life, the conditioning session for each child lasting no longer than one hour. To accomplish this, they used techniques involving the strengthening of a head-turning response through "operant" reinforcement contingencies.

Siqueland and Lipsitt noted that the head-turning response prior to conditioning tended to occur, ipsilaterally, about 25% of the time when the baby's cheek was stimulated next to the mouth. It was therefore decided that experimental subjects would receive a dextrose solution *contingent upon* the occurrence of the ipsilateral head-turn when the tactile stimulus was provided. Unlike Papousek's technique, the infants in the Siqueland and Lipsitt studies did not receive induced head-turns on any trial in which the response failed to occur. Thus the response of concern was an unconditioned or congenital "rooting" reflex, but one which occurred only about one-fourth of the time prior to conditioning experience. The administration of dextrose solution upon the occurrence of this response, however, superimposes an operant or instrumental learning condition on the behavior, which might be regarded initially as a low-level respondent. One can classify these procedures as neither purely respondent nor strictly operant, for the measured behavior throughout the experiment remained respondent (that is, controlled by the eliciting tactile stimulus), although that respondent was manipulated through response-contingencies. Further complicating the distinction between classical and operant methodologies, these studies involved the presentation of a 6-second auditory stimulus whose onset was prior to but overlapped in the last three seconds with the administration of the tactile stimulus. In the first of the three studies, then, 30 trials of conditioning were administered to an experimental group of 18 subjects, under a 30-second intertrial interval condition. The tactile stimulus for all subjects occurred at the left cheek. Subjects in the experimental group rose from a level of about 30% responding at the beginning of training to over 80% responding at the end of the 30 trials, relative to a control group which received the same auditory-tactile stimulations and reinforcement but under conditions in which the dextrose was delivered about ten seconds after the tactile stimulus. Reinforcement occurred in this group *not* contingent upon the control subject's behavior, but rather on a schedule dictated by the behavior and reinforcement history of matched experimental subjects, and only after a delay of 10 seconds following the tactile stimulus. This group showed no increase in response.

A second study was instituted in which the tactile stimulus was presented on opposite cheeks on alternate trials, with two different auditory stimuli accompanying the left- and right-sided stimulation. Reinforcement here was given differentially for ipsilateral responding to the two "eliciting" stimuli, and learning was shown through increased responding to the reinforced side, relative to frequency of responding to the nonreinforced side. Once again a learning effect was obtained in the experimental group, as evidenced by the acquisition of differential response to the two sides, relative to a control group which received the same tone-tactile stimulations and the same reinforcements but not under conditions dictated by the subjects' own response propensities.

A third experiment in the Siqueland and Lipsitt series turned to the use of a within-subjects discrimination learning procedure which sought to demonstrate reversal learning following the initial learning phase. Tactile stimulation was delivered only on one side, but two auditory stimuli served as positive and negative cues. Turns to right-sided stimulation in the presence of one auditory cue were reinforced with dextrose, while such turns to the other cue were not. The discrimination was acquired readily within a half-hour period and, moreover, reversal behavior occurred reliably when the cue-reinforcement contingencies were reversed in a second half-hour of training. These data are presented in Figure 1.

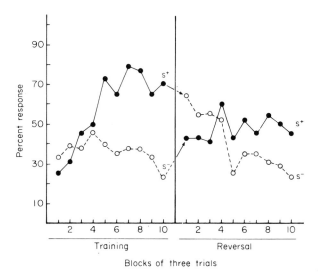

Figure 1. Comparison of percentage responses to positive and negative stimuli during original training and reversal trials. (Reproduced with permission of authors and publisher, Siqueland & Lipsitt, 1966.)

Attention should perhaps be called to the fact that in none of the foregoing three studies was there evidence for the occurrence of classically conditioned anticipatory responses, that is, an increase in response over trials to the tone prior to the presentation of the tactile stimulation. Yet it is apparent that the tones had a determining effect on learning behavior, at least in the third study where only the tones could provide the appropriate differential cues for reinforced and nonreinforced head-turning. It would appear that, if this series of studies were to be viewed as a contest between classical and operant conditioning, the operant aspects of the methodology won over the classical. Given the conditions under which the anticipatory tone stimulation seemed to affect behavior, this stimulation might be better conceptualized as a discriminative or setting stimulus (for operant behavior) than as a conditioning stimulus. The news will probably be received with dismay in some quarters if it turns out that operant conditioning has a certain ontogenetic primacy over classical conditioning. Perhaps better, we are dealing here with a gray area of methodology in which the distinction between classical and operant learning becomes academic.

To return to our consideration of life-span developmental implications, it is apparent from the preceding Botwinick review that there has been a relatively small investment of scientific resources in the comparative study of different age groups in operant conditioning situations. If one looks only at reaction-time and classical conditioning data on humans as they age, one might get a somewhat distorted picture of developmental functions—the organism starts off rather badly, gets better, then deteriorates. Recent data on newborn condioning, on the other hand, suggest that in the first few days of life we may be as proficient in learning as we ever will be again! Similarly, it can be presumed that somewhere there is an operant reinforcer that may increase monotonically in incentive value with increasing age, and that a rather different kind of learning organism will some day be revealed through the judicious application of this incentive in an appropriate performance task. All of this is simply to say again that it does not make much sense merely to study age effects in the absence of the study of interacting variables, such as learning technique, performance requirements, incentives employed, and so on.

Further implications of recent findings with infants include considerations of the fact that a primary objective of developmental studies is to assess the effects of early experience on later behavior (Caldwell, 1964), while another is to document long-range consistencies in styles of behavior (Kagan & Moss, 1962). It is a statistical imperative that both types of studies will increase in scientific usefulness only as the earlier measures of behavior (for example, of learning, or the impact of experience) reach a high degree of refinement. By refinement is meant objectivity and repeatability.

III. A BRIEF REVIEW OF SELECTED FACTS ABOUT
INFANT BEHAVIOR PLASTICITY

As implied previously, one approach to the understanding of life-span developmental psychology would be to first seek as much knowledge as is possible to obtain about the origins of infant behavior. In line with this view I should like to use the present opportunity to set forth, perhaps too succinctly, a series of general propositions, all of which probably have enough supportive data now to warrant accepting them as essentially correct, concerning the plasticity of infant behavior. (In line with the previous discussion, it will be apparent that the first of these propositions must be that newborn infants are capable of learning.) These several assertions all have considerable promise of yielding life-span information of significance in understanding the development of intelligence and affective expression.

A. Newborns Learn

Data from a number of laboratories, in the United States and elsewhere, now indicate rather decisively that conditioning procedures may be implemented whereby the human neonate will display conditioned behavior (Lipsitt, 1963, 1966; Papousek, 1961, 1967). By this is meant that the human infant within the first few days of life can be demonstrated capable of developing a new association based upon stimulus and reinforcement circumstances in the environment impinging upon his receptors. The learning may take the form of the acquisition of a new disposition to respond to a previously neutral stimulus, or it may involve the potentiation of a response already occurring with low incidence (Lipsitt, 1963). That is, the process must involve the acquisition of an association not previously present; this can be between either a response and its associated reinforcer or a previously neutral (or relatively ineffective) stimulus and an initially effective stimulus. In either event, the process must be established as independent of maturational and sensitization effects (an absolute requirement for the learning argument). Research has already been described in which it has been shown that within the first few days of life, infants will enhance their head-turning responding in the presence of a tone-tactile stimulus compound under conditions in which such responses are systematically reinforced (Siqueland & Lipsitt, 1966). Moreover, Siqueland (1968) has shown significant free-operant enhancement of head-turning responding under conditions in which such head-turns in either direction are operantly reinforced. Sameroff (1968) has shown that differential reinforcement of specific components of sucking behavior will selectively enhance the reinforced component relative to other nonreinforced aspects of the response. Papousek

(1967) has reported that repetitive practice over a succession of days gradually enhances the strength and durability of head-turn conditioning. Lipsitt and Kaye (1964) paired a 15-second tone with insertion of the nipple in the baby's mouth. For the experimental group, the nipple was inserted into the infant's mouth one second after onset of the tone, while for the control group, the tone and nipple were not administered contiguously; the nipple for the control group was inserted for a 15-second period 30 seconds following offset of the tone, to control for possible sensitization effects. Measures of response strength on tone-alone trials obtained during extinction indicated a highly reliable difference between the experimental and control groups. Lipsitt, Kaye, and Bosack (1966) have demonstrated that the anticipatory sucking response of newborns to a feeding tube may be enhanced through the administration of dextrose solution through the tube, relative to a control group which receives the same stimulus and reinforcement conditions but with the dextrose delivered under noncontiguous conditions.

B. Newborns Habituate.

The habituation process involves the gradual diminution of response to an initially effective stimulus under conditions of repetitive presentation of that stimulus and under conditions in which response decrement due to sensory or motor fatigue can be ruled out (Bartoshuk, 1962a; Bridger, 1961, 1962). Habituation can be demonstrated in human newborns, very likely in all sensory modalities. It has been shown that various responses, such as respiration, heart rate, bodily motility, sucking interruption, and so on, are subject to progressive response decrement under the habituation procedure (Bartoshuk, 1962b; Bridger, 1961; Engen & Lipsitt, 1965; Engen, Lipsitt, & Kaye, 1963; Keen, Chase, & Graham, 1965; Lipsitt, 1966), and frequently several response systems simultaneously habituate. Recovery of the habituated response is demonstrable with the passage of time since last stimulation and under conditions involving the introduction of stimuli discrepant from the habituating stimulus, or stimuli relatively novel to the organism (Bartoshuk, 1962a; Bridger, 1961; Engen & Lipsitt, 1965). Some laboratories have had difficulty in confirming habituation phenomena (Haith, 1966; Hutt, Lenard & Prechtl, 1969), however, and further research must be directed toward the understanding of the conditions under which habituation limitations of the newborn prevail. It is likely that the relative novelty of stimuli is pertinent to the elaboration of conditioning, and it will therefore be of some importance for life-span developmental psychology to explore the effects of stimulus familiarization (habituation training) on subsequent conditioning processes.

C. Individual Differences in Response Exist at Birth and Some Endure

Those who are well-practiced in circumspection will recognize that this proposition is rather guarded. It admits only that some individual differences exist reliably at birth, and no commitment is made as to the extended durability of these. Research is so lacking in this area that no bolder statement can be made at the present time (Horowitz, 1969). However, we do know that newborns vary at birth with respect to sensory thresholds (Bridger, 1961; Graham, Matarazzo, & Caldwell, 1956; Karelitz & Fisichelli, 1962; Korner, Chuck & Dontschos, 1968; Lipsitt & Levy, 1959; Lipton, Steinschneider, & Richmond, 1966), in general activity or muscular tension (Irwin, 1930), in disposition toward crying (Gordon & Foss, 1966; Karelitz, Karelitz, & Rosenfeld, 1960), in respiratory regularity (Apgar, 1953), in heart rate (Bridger, 1961; Graham & Jackson, 1970), in sucking rate (Haith, 1966; P. H. Wolff, 1968), and even in heart rate deceleration response to external stimulation (Lipsitt & Jacklin, 1969). While a number of such studies have demonstrated within-session reliability of response measurement, or repeatability of measures over a two-day period, few longitudinal studies are available beginning with the newborn period and carrying on for many months. One study over the first two years of life, however, suggested that some general and other specific behavioral characteristics as activity level, tendency to approach or withdraw, general adaptability, attention span, distractibility, and persistence tend to be stable over this period of time (H. G. Birch, Thomas, Chess, & Hertzog, 1962).

Individual differences are likely to have numerous environmental consequences—for the mother's behavior toward the infant in various respects such as frequency of feeding, amount of cuddling provided, attention gained in response to crying, and the like. Such individual differences unquestionably have pertinence for the infant's capacity for learning, depending upon the sensory modalities involved in the response requirements necessitated for the learning experience to be "appreciated" by the infant organism. In most conditioning experiments, and in many habituation studies as well, individual differences are frequently ignored or minimized (for example, through swaddling or selection of only quiet babies for study) for convenience in response assessment. Little information is currently available relating to the durability of such individual variations at birth, or as to the ease with which such "congenital" differences may be altered through experiential manipulations.

D. Cardiac Deceleration Is a Developmental Process

Graham and her colleagues (see Graham & Clifton, 1966; Graham & Jackson, 1970) have recently summarized a large amount of heartrate response data from infants under various conditions of stimulation and have suggested that most studies with newborns have documented only a heartrate acceleration phenomenon and that instances of heartrate deceleration in response to external stimulation of the newborn are very rare indeed. However, numerous experimenters, including the Graham group and, for example, W. J. Meyers and Cantor (1967), and Clifton and Meyers (1969), have found heartrate deceleration to be a very frequent, if not typical, response of the *older* infant to such stimuli. This has led Graham and her co-workers to suggest that cardiac acceleration represents a defensive response (perhaps similar to a startle reflex), while cardiac deceleration represents orienting behavior (or a set to assimilate information rather than a maneuver to ward it off).

The data, it is suggested, indicate that the newborn is primarily a defensive responder and that only with increasing age does the orienting or stimulus-assimilating set become operative. Most of the data relevant to this line of argument are from studies in which auditory and visual stimuli have been utilized. Recently it has been possible for Lipsitt and Jacklin (1969) to document a reliable cardiac deceleration phenomenon in newborns under conditions in which the infants were provided with olfactory stimulants. It was shown that an experimental group receiving a 50% solution of asafetida showed more cardiac deceleration in the first few seconds following stimulation than a control group which received a mock (odorless) stimulant in exactly the same manner and for the same number of trials as the experimental group. These data are provided in Figure 2. Furthermore, the day-to-day consistency of newborns with respect to cardiac deceleration in response to stimulation was reflected in a correlation coefficient greater than .60 between first and second days of testing.

Early indications from this line of studies are, then, that some sensory systems may mature physiologically more rapidly or sooner than others, permitting orienting behavior to occur in some sensory modalities while other modalities may still be operating on a "defensive" basis. As Graham suggests, too, stimulus intensity and other properties of stimuli may be pertinent factors in the determination of whether defensive or orienting behavior will occur at any given age.

An interesting implication of these data is that the type of heartrate response elicited by a given set of stimuli from individual infants may provide a basic indicant of physiological maturity and hence, possibly, the conditioning capacity of the individual organism. The study of the heartrate response system has exciting ramifications for other aspects of infant behavior as well, for it may become possible eventually, utilizing computer techniques, to study simultaneously the magnitude of the accelerative and decelerative components of the heart-rate response and the relative habituation rates of these with successive presentations of stimuli. Similarly, individual differences among infants with respect to the dominance of each of the components must be investigated as well

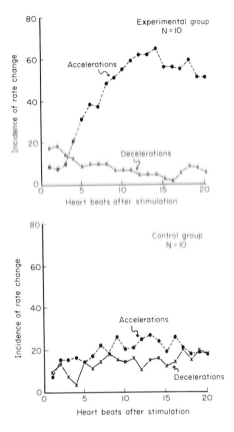

Figure 2. Accelerative and decelerative changes in response following stimulation for an experimental and control group of newborns. The experimental subjects were administered an asafetida odorant on 10 successive trials. (Reproduced with permission of authors, Lipsitt and Jacklin, 1969.)

as the conditioned "weighting" of the components. With respect to the latter possibility, it is conceivable that onset of orienting behavior in infants may be facilitated through stimulus exposure, stimulus differentiation training, and reinforcement of attentional behavior.

E. Conjugate Reinforcement Produces Rapid Learning

As was said previously, it is not unlikely that a number of recent advances made in the understanding of infant behavior have been due to experimenters engaging in novel departures from old techniques. Some of these departures have profitably involved the discovery of behaviors in which infants can be observed to engage persistently. For example, we have all observed an infant of about one month of age to lie quietly on the floor in the supine position turning his head to and fro, fixating various objects above and at his side, cocking his head this way and that and, in general, engaging with fascination in the panorama of stimulus events which he thus administers to himself. That the infant is assimilating and remembering the stimulus inputs under such conditions is readily confirmed, I think, through the introduction of a poignant novel stimulus which the baby quickly fixates and concentrates upon with great curiosity. While the importance of novelty stimulation has been emphasized by a number of experimenters (e.g., Hunt, 1965; Kagan, Henker, Hen-Tov, Levine & Lewis, 1966; McCall & Kagan, 1967; Uzgiris & Hunt, 1965), it is equally important to appreciate that under such conditions the human infant *administers to himself* successive and uninterrupted episodes of different kinds of stimulation.

It so happens that stimulation in the visual modality is the easiest for humans to instrument for themselves, by engaging in specific and deliberate sense-orienting behaviors—through turning the head, moving the eyes, manipulating visual objects into different perspectives, and so on. This may be critically important as experimenters seek to find "curiosity reinforcers" that are particularly appealing to the infant. It is perhaps no accident that visual attention behavior of the young infant is now studied so extensively. Ever since Fantz (1958, 1967), most of the infant studies involving the documentation of response preferences under conditions in which multiple opportunities are presented have utilized visual stimulation. Curiously, many of the visual fixation methods bear great similarity to operant conditioning procedures, although few of the visual researchers in this area seem to conceptualize their endeavors in such terminology or with historic reference to the operant conditioning literature. I would not want to push this analogy too far, for the visual attention researchers are also entitled to their new departures and to the privilege of selecting their own theoretical and methodological forebears, but it is worth noting that the method frequently involves the tallying of cumulative responses (for example, frequency of fixation, time of fixation) in the presence of differential discriminative stimuli, the end result of which is the opportunity to tabulate which of these stimuli seems most "reinforcing" and therefore attracts the greatest incidence of operant responding. One exception of the tendency of visual researchers with infants to abhor the operant methodology (or at least its terminology) is J. S. Watson (1965, 1967) who has sought to study the progressive *changes* in the investment of attention in different visual stimuli.

Interest in the possibility of using continuously changing visual stimulation in my infant laboratory as a reinforcer for operant behavior dates from acquaintanceship with Uzgiris and J. McV. Hunt's observations (1965) that young infants are inordinately fascinated by the opportunity to manipulate their own visual environment through the shaking of mobiles hanging above their cribs. At about the same time, we heard of the work of Ogden Lindsley showing that infants would operate a kicking manipulandum when this was instrumented to produce a steady and changing visual stimulus contingent upon that kicking behavior (Lindsley, 1962; Lindsley, Hobika, & Etsten, 1961). The Lindsley procedure is one in which the visual reinforcer is presented contingent upon the subject's operant behavior, but in which the reinforcer occurs immediately and continuously, rather than discretely or episodically as in the case of the delivery of a food pellet or a candy. An important feature of this type of reinforcement is that it occurs in amounts commensurate with the level of operant activity in which the subject engages. Thus the subject can maintain a high and continuous rate of stimulus input through the maintenance of high-rate responding. When the response level wanes, in intensity or rate depending upon the instrumentation employed, the reinforcer progressively wanes, and vice versa. When one stops to think about it, as one should, this is perhaps more like real life than most other laboratory situations in which the effects on exploratory behavior of novel stimulus presentation are studied.

Our first utilization of the Lindsley procedure (Lipsitt, Pederson, & DeLucia, 1966), called a "conjugate reinforcement method," involved the study of 44 twelve-month-old infants in a special situation that enabled the subjects to control the clarity of their own visual stimulation. The infants were seated in a chair before a box with a plexiglass panel on the surface facing the infant. Behind the panel was a colorful clown rotating continuously on a motor driven shaft The clown could not be seen unless the inner box was lighted, and the light could be activated only by the subject pressing the panel at a minimum rate. Moreover, the light available in the box, and hence the visual intensity of the clown stimulus, was instrumented to be directly proportional to the infant's rate of response. The faster the panel was hit, the brighter the scene became. As response rate waned, the light diminished gradually and could be brought up again only by resumption of a more rapid response rate. The procedure resulted in modest but reliable conditioning effects, represented by increased response rates when the panel was "hot," and extinction behavior when the reinforcement contingency was withdrawn.

Several studies of conjugate reinforcement utilizing hanging mobiles have been instigated in the Brown infant laboratories (Rovee & Rovee, 1969; Wilcox, Appel, & Robbins, 1965). The Rovees began their experiment with their own son and later enlarged the sample to demonstrate that the operant response rate of foot-kicking in ten-week old children tripled within the first six minutes of conjugate reinforcement, while control subjects who received comparable but noncontingent mobile-shaking stimulation remained at the base level throughout a similar period of time. All six infants receiving the conjugate procedure, which involved the activation of a brightly colored mobile connected by string to the infant's leg, were responsive to the reinforcement operations, as evidenced by increasing rates during conditioning, and decreasing rates during extinction, over a 27-minute test period. Similar studies conducted by L. Smith and Lipsitt (in preparation) corroborate the Rovee findings over multiple sessions for a two-month period and suggest that the procedure may be utilized to document color preferences through comparison of relative rates of response under conditions in which differently colored mobiles are utilized in different sessions. Figure 3 shows an exemplary experimental session with an infant 76 days of age in the Smith and Lipsitt study. A further refinement of the procedure currently under investigation has involved the utilization of the sucking response (following Siqueland, 1969) to activate the mobile action.

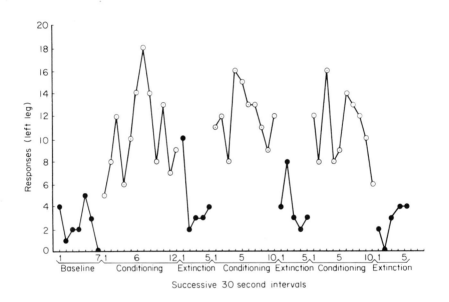

Figure 3. Total number of responses from 68-day-old subject in mobile conjugate reinforcement learning situation, over successive phases of testing. Number of responses increases during conditioning phases relative to baseline and extinction phases. (Reproduced with permission of authors, Smith and Lipsitt, in preparation.)

Data from these mobile studies suggest that the conjugate reinforcement procedure provides a powerful reinforcement condition. Again, the naturalistic analogs of such procedures are apparent. When infants suck, they obtain milk or other intraoral stimulation commensurate in amount with the intensity or rate of the behavior. When infants turn their heads in the presence of visual stimulus opportunities, the amount of stimulus input is commensurate with the behavior rate. It is likely that infants have different pacing standards or needs (as has been suggested by Kagan, 1969), and research might be profitably directed toward the study of optimizing behavior of infants with respect to the self-paced administration of sensory stimulation. "The pleasures of sensation," to borrow an apt phrase from Pfaffmann (1960), could most assuredly provide the infant researcher with some of his most potent reinforcers, if implemented in the conjugate style that seems so appropriate for the congenitally curious human infant. It is not so wild a suggestion that opportunities for self-administered conjugate reinforcement early in the lives of humans may well set in motion certain patterns of behavior found at later ages. At least it is an empirically testable assertion.

IV. COMMENTS ON THE CONCEPT OF "STATE"

Recent conceptualizations of infant "states" have tended to imply unduly that states are conditions of the organism which are independent of stimulus-response contingencies, or are refractory to environmental manipulation (Prechtl, 1969). While it is very likely that the condition of the organism is pertinent to the ease with which stimulus inputs may be effected, and while it is possible that the state of the human neonate is somewhat less plastic than that of the normal adult or older child, there is nevertheless no empirical basis for sanctifying the concept of state by attributing immutability to state conditions. The fact is that states are assessed through observation of various types of response, such as regularity of respiration, eyes open versus eyes closed, muscular twitching versus slow continuous limb movement, and other response attributes which are affected considerably by stimulating conditions which may exist at the moment of observation and measurement. That one can devise a graded scale involving a continuum running from little movement to much movement, or deep sleep to fully awake (or aroused) is undeniable; this has been done by numerous infant observers. That reliability of observation or ratings on such scales may be achieved, however, should not becloud the equally important fact that such response attributes of the newborn are quickly brought under the control of environmental factors. Food intake schedule (Irwin, 1930; Marquis, 1941) quickly begins to control the fluctuating state of the newborn, as do efforts to awaken the baby through the presentation of intense stimuli, such as mothers administer to their infants when they wish to feed their sleeping infants. Rocking is also a well-known and reliable method for altering the state condition of the infant (Brossard & Décarie, 1968; Gordon & Foss, 1966).

Evidence is available, then, to indicate that within the first few days of life, infants adapt to or lock in on a temporally dictated feeding schedule, they stop crying when subjected to a rocking experience, they delay crying when subjected to vestibular stimulation, and they go quickly from quiet sleep to boisterous crying when suddenly startled. While it is important to document the waxing and waning of "state" conditions under naturalistic or noninterfering laboratory conditions, it is equally necessary for the infant organism to be understood as a creature who is, even in his state fluctuations, responding to both intrinsic and extrinsic stimulation. The drums to which the newborn is listening, moreover, may not always coincide with the observer's idiosyncratic attention preferences; when the observer thinks the infant is merely lying quietly and without stimulation, his internal organs might be supplying stimulation which produces a "spontaneous" or "uninstigated" startle response.

Conceptually, states should perhaps be regarded as conditions of the organism not unlike those filed under the rubric of "drive" in some learning theories. They are fluctuating response attributes, dependent upon diverse stimulus circumstances, they may perhaps be acquired as well as indigenous to the organism, and they may be treated either as independent or dependent variables within an experimental paradigm.

The concept of state has special pertinence to considerations of life-span developmental psychology inasmuch as states are often regarded, erroneously or otherwise, as relatively stable attributes of the human organism. It is tempting to conceive of the child who is hyperactive at birth as the child who will become the overactive, obstreperous adolescent or hypersensitive adult. That there are such "life plans" congenitally given is a realistic possibility, but to date there are no data of which this writer is aware that would strongly support the contention. One as often hears of placid children becoming obstreperous, and of "acting-out" children who eventually "settled down." Examples of biographical flip-flops so abound in the psychological literature as, first, to make one dubious of the veracity of the supposition about such stabilities without decisive documentation, and second, to suggest that psychogenic or learning factors may effect striking alterations in behavior and emotional expression. Behavior scientists are perhaps as subject as any other occupational group to community delusions, and it is especially in this "life-span-life-plan" area that delusions are tempting. We will not truly have a life-span developmental psychology, and we will not definitively know about the longitudinal consistencies underlying human behavior, until proper developmental documentation has been made of some of these suppositions.

V. SUMMARY

It has been suggested that advances in life-span developmental psychology will be facilitated by the full exploration of the plasticity of infant behavior. This goal will necessitate the extensive study of unconditioned and conditioned behavior in the newborn and must involve the exploitation not only of classical and instrumental conditioning models but various innovative elaborations of these as well. It was agreed that individual differences unquestionably determine to some extent the receptivity of the infant organism to various learning experiences, that the state of the infant is a pertinent variable for study both as an independent and dependent measure, and that naturalistic observations of infants often provide clues in the search for and eventual discovery of experiential determinants of infant behavior. That there are definable and differentiable states of the infant organism that may be discerned and documented reliably was accepted, but the view was urged that the so-called states are always under stimulus control, either internal or external, and that states may be experientally manipulated (although, like most psychological attributes, within limits). It was suggested that sufficient evidence now exists to assert with confidence that conditioning and habituation processes are present in the newborn human, that individual differences with respect to a number of psychological attributes exist at birth and some of these endure, that cardiac deceleration reflecting orienting behavior to external stimulation is a developing process within the first few months of life, and that conjugate reinforcement techniques show considerable promise in the study of infant learning.

CHAPTER 13

Retention—Forgetting as a Nomological Network for Developmental Research

DONALD H. KAUSLER

ST. LOUIS UNIVERSITY
ST. LOUIS, MISSOURI

ABSTRACT

Developmental trends in long-term retention were examined within the rubric of contemporary verbal learning theory. The model employed was a revision of the conventional rote-conditioning model of classical verbal learning. The revised model emphasized generalized habits mediating such processes as a selector mechanism, stimulus selection, and mnemonic devices for associative learning. Special attention was given to hypotheses, and the related empirical evidence, regarding developmental trends across the age continuum in retroactive and proactive inhibition. The source for these hypotheses was interference theory as approached from the viewpoint of the revised model. In addition, a brief summary of the relevance of recognition learning models to retention-development relationships was given

I. INTRODUCTION

Retention and forgetting have been virtually the exclusive property of the psychology of verbal learning throughout the scientific history of memory. In his recent stimulating book on memory, Adams (1967) noted cogently that "Memory research is so strongly weighted toward verbal behavior that we sometimes forget how little we know about the forgetting of other response classes [p. 310]." That is, the processes of retention have been firmly ensconced within the context of a young-adult-based verbal learning theory, and research on retention has been characterized by its heavy reliance on the methodological paradigms and procedures of verbal learning. Consequently, the present review of research on developmental trends in retention and forgetting will focus on the nomologies of verbal learning and their capacity for incorporating developmentally relevant variables and processes. There is, however, a paucity of published research on long-term retention for populations other than young adults, and the present review will necessarily emphasize potentially viable research areas for developmental psychology.

More specifically, the nomological network identified with the interference theory of forgetting and related processes will serve as the focal point for our review. Until the past few years, interference theory in its classical form dominated research on forgetting without modification of its basic tenets. In fact, Postman (1961) aptly summarized in the following manner the stature of interference theory as it entered into the 1960s:

Interference theory occupies an unchallenged position as the major significant analysis of the process of forgetting. The only serious opposition has come from the trace theory of the Gestalt psychologists, but that point of view has thus far proved experimentally sterile and resistant to rigorous test. As a result, the recent years have seen little debate about the basic assumptions of interference theory. Developments in the study of forgetting have consisted largely of extensions and refinements of interference theory and of methodological advances in the measurement of retention [p. 152].

The steady state described above, however, is presently experiencing pressures for more radical changes. Some of these potential changes involve revisions of the basic assumptions of classical interference theory, with the thrust for change being led by interference theorists themselves. Other potential changes, motivated by recent analyses and experiments that depart significantly from the circumspect content of classical interference theory, require new processes, such as a perceptual feedback mechanism, mediational devices, rule behavior, and preexperimental linguistic habits, to be added to the overall theoretical structure. Finally, a theory considerably more formidable than gestalt trace theory is beginning to emerge as a serious opponent. This theory stems from such areas as information processing and computer analogs, and its processes include organization, storage, search, and retrieval. The impact of this theoretical orientation upon interference theory is uncertain, and is, moreover, largely beyond the scope of the present paper. However, the issues raised by the "opponent" will be briefly touched upon later.

II. VERBAL LEARNING: MODELS, PROCESSES, AND PARADIGMS

A. Models

1. The Conventional Model: Rote Processes

The placement of interference theory squarely within the context of verbal learning makes a preliminary discussion of the contemporary state of verbal learning a prerequisite for the consideration of the retention-development relationship. The conventional theoretical model (a term borrowed from Adams, 1967) for verbal learning is a composite of classical associationism, a Hullian S-R learning theory, and a functionalism traced to Robinson, Carr, and McGeoch—a composite somehow blended together and identified as the end product of what started with Ebbinghaus. The model portrays verbal learning as the acquisition of first-order habits between stimulus (S) and response (R) units (nonsense syllables, adjectives, etc.) contained within a list. Acquisition of any one habit is a passive, rote process that is promoted by the contiguous presentation of the S unit and the R unit and by the reinforcement provided by informative feedback as to the correctness of subject's response. Each habit is, with the exception of the potential involvement of stimulus and/or response generalization effects, acquired independently of every other habit, and each is acquired via a *direct* (i.e., without mediation) connection between the S and R units. A given habit gains associative strength incrementally until the strength exceeds a threshold value. Further contiguous presentation-reinforcement sequences continue to add increments to the habit; eventually, associative strength is sufficiently above threshold to assure that oscillation effects will not depress excitation of the habit momentarily below threshold value (cf. Underwood & Keppel, 1962, for the contrast between this view and that of an all-or-none model). When all of the habits connecting the S and R units within the list reach superthreshold values, the list has been learned.

Further evidence for the model's obvious bias toward a conditioning concept-ualization is the central role played by the habit-family hierarchy concept. On early learning trials a given S unit elicits, either implicitly or explicitly as an intrusion error, responses learned preexperimentally to that unit. Initially such responses are the highest strength members of the hierarchy, and the R unit assigned arbitrarily to S is ranked well below the preexperimental members in terms of associative strength and probability of elicitation. Reinforcement of R as it occurs contiguously with S increases the strength of the first-order habit, whereas nonreinforcement of the preexperimental responses to S extinguishes their underlying habits and diminishes their potency as competitors for the elicitation of R. The consequence is a gradual shift, with trials, in the composition of the hierarchy. The R component eventually displaces the other responses and becomes the dominant, highest strength member of the hierarchy. As noted above, manifestation in performance follows the attainment of superthreshold strength by the new monarch of the hierarchy.

2. *A Revised Model: Generalized Habits and Mediation*

The difficulty of simple conditioning concepts in serving as sole ingredients a model designed to explain verbal learning, certainly one of the more complex variants of human learning, is well attested to by Grant's (1964) comments:

> I do believe, however, that in our thinking about learning phenomena we may have adopted in the past a somewhat zoocentric bias as opposed to a more valid anthropocentric approach to learning. If so, freeing ourselves of this zoocentric bias may prove helpful. The human *S* is capable of more than the animal *S*. He learns with great ease things that are difficult or impossible for the animal—and then he goes on to greater complexities of behavior. We can present our human *S* with learning problems in conditioning experiments, for example, where he is not particularly efficient and does not far surpass the performance of lower forms, but this is not "typical" human learning. I conclude that a valid psychology of human learning is vastly more complicated than a valid psychology of animal learning, because vastly more numerous, more diversified, and more complicated processes are involved [p. 28].

Fortunately, the most singular attribute of the past decade's activity in verbal learning is the extensive refurbishing of the conventional model along dimensions consonant with Grant's position. The most striking change involves the model's conception of the subject as a passive, rote participant in the learning of a list of verbal units. Current views accept as commonplace frequent transformations of any one of the primary elements of the learning process—S units, R units, and first-order S-R habits—by an active, cognitive subject. In keeping with the S-R framework of the conventional model, transformations are viewed here as being mediated by *generalized* habits, habits which transfer from the subject's extensive (at least in young adults) preexperimental behavioral repertory. Generalized habits, unlike first-order habits, are not specific to any one association within the list. That is, the activation of a generalized habit affects more than one S-R association in the list, the number ranging from a limited subset to the entire set of associations. The transition in perspective from a passive to an active subject is beautifully accentuated by Underwood's (1964a) remarks:

The image of a subject in a verbal-learning experiment as being a *tabula rasa* upon which the investigator simply chisels associations, and quite against the *S*'s wishes, is archaic. The *S* is far from passive and the tablet has already impressed upon it an immense network of verbal habits. Some of these habits are simple and direct and some are conceptual in their inclusiveness, i.e., they are second-order habits. A more accurate description of the verbal-learning experiment is one in which the *S* actively "calls upon" all the repertoire of habits and skills to outwit the investigator [p. 52].

Several generalized habits relevant to the retention-development relationship will be discussed briefly here, and others will be discussed later in the context of retention processes per se. Stimulus selection is a generalized habit that applies specifically to the S units of a verbal list (Underwood, 1963). Postulating a selection process has led to the important distinction in contemporary verbal learning between the nominal stimulus, the formal S unit as it is presented to the subject by the experimenter, and the functional stimulus, the element of the formal S unit that serves as the subject's "personalized" cue for eliciting the paired R unit. When the S units are highly meaningful terms, such as familiar words or nonsense syllables, there is likely to be little, if any, disparity between nominal and functional stimuli (Kausler, 1966, pp. 66-68; Leicht & Kausler, 1965). However, when the S units are low meaningful terms, such as paralogs or unfamiliar nonsense syllables, the probability increases greatly that subjects will select less than entire units as functional stimuli, and the nominal-functional disparity increases. For example, the initial letter of a low meaningful nonsense syllable serves as the functional stimulus for many young adult subjects (Postman & Greenbloom, 1967).

The selector mechanism is another generalized habit, one that applies to the R units of a verbal list (Underwood & Schulz, 1960). The mechanism operates to reduce interference from response units that are not included within the list, including associates of the R units themselves. In the learning of a single list it is a rare event to have extralist responses (that is, units not contained in the list) occur as errors. The selector's function is to scan the subject's store of latent responses (for example, words in his vocabulary if words are the intralist R units) and to reject members of the total population that are inappropriate to the list content. Postulating a selector mechanism, of course, greatly reduces the relevance of the habit-family hierarchy in the conventional model. That is, a selector mechanism may short circuit the rote demotion of competing responses within the hierarchy through their nonreinforcement, coupled with the reinforcement of the correct response. It should be noted that the selector mechanism is somewhat similar to the perceptual trace mechanism introduced by Adams (1967) as a supplementary mechanism to the memory trace, or habit as used in the conventional model. In addition, list conditions exist for which the operation of a selector-like mechanism is directed toward the inclusion of a class of responses, rather than toward the exclusion of a broad class (that is, responses not included in the list). This kind of mechanism is especially relevant to lists containing multiple instances of a taxonomic category. For example, all of the R units may be names of animals; the concept of "animal" may then function as a rule which restricts the pool of responses to animal names only.

Generalized habits may also enhance the short circuiting of S-R associative learning by promoting the use of mediational devices, such as verbal chains composed of associates to S and/or R units that bridge the gap between S and R (Underwood & Schulz, 1960) and images that link S and R units into a perceptual compound (e.g., Yuille & Paivio, 1968). Mediation may reduce markedly the amount of practice that would otherwise be needed to nudge an association above threshold strength via a rote, contiguity-reinforcement sequence. Hypotheses about mediation in human learning have been entertained for many years (W. C. Shipley, 1933, 1935), but the emphasis has been on mediation as an extension of rote conditioning processes. By contrast, current verbal learning theory largely accepts mediation as the consequence of a generalized habit to construct some kind of rule, plan, or strategy for learning associations. That is, the young adult subject actively adopts the use of mediational devices for many of the pairings within a list.

A revision in the conventional model that incorporates generalized habits is presented summarily in Figure 1. The revised model is the one that will generally be followed in the remainder of this paper. However, the emphasis on an active subject and on generalized habits in no way abrogates the importance of rote processes in verbal learning and retention. The ubiquitous nature of rote processes in young adult subjects is well illustrated by recent research on verbal discrimination (VD) learning and transfer. In VD learning the subject's task is to establish discriminations between paired wrong and right items, a task that does not demand associative connections between the paired items as S-R counterparts. Nevertheless, Spear, Ekstrand, and Underwood (1964) demonstrated that such associative learning does take place as an incidental by-product of the intentional task (that is, establishing intrapair discriminations regarding item functions). Moreover, extensive associative learning occurs even when the VD list permits the complete application of a generalized habit or rule that enables the subject to ignore the wrong items (Eschenbrenner & Kausler, 1968). The implications of these rote processes for the retention-development relationship will be explored later.

B. Multiple Processes in Verbal Learning

The preceding discussion makes it clear that verbal learning phenomena cannot be squeezed into a single process model that accommodates only S-R associative learning. Instead a multitude of processes enters into even the simplest of verbal

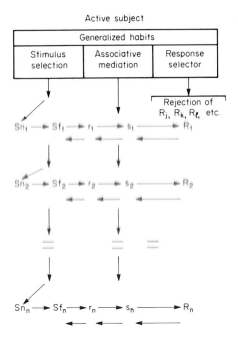

Figure 1. A revised model for learning multiple verbal associations. The emphasis is on an "active" subject who selects functional units (S_f) from nominal stimuli (S_n), mediates via verbal or visual devices between S and R units, and rejects extralist R units (R_J, R_K, R_L, etc.). In addition, the direction of the association is bidirectional—that is, it may lead from R to S as well as from S to R.

learning tasks. As described above, these processes involve S units and R units separately, and together as S-R associations. Underwood, Runquist, and Schulz (1959) stimulated an early multiple process view of verbal learning by their identification, in operationally defined terms, of two broad stages, response learning and S-R associative learning. One process entering into response learning is the previously noted selector mechanism. However, when unfamiliar letter sequences, as in low meaningful nonsense syllables, serve as R units, the process underlying the response learning stage is more likely to be the integration of the separate letters within the unit. Response integration is basically a rote associative process encompassing a chained sequence of S-R associations, with the individual letters doubling as both S and R units. The original version of stage analysis grouped stimulus-related processes under the S-R associative stage. However, more recent versions seemingly call for a separate stage devoted to S units, and for such processes as stimulus selection as underlying mechanisms. The operational reality of this extension of stage analysis has been greatly enhanced by refinements in methodology (e.g., Postman & Greenbloom, 1967; Underwood, Ham, & Ekstrand, 1962). In addition, analyses of the S-R associative stage have been extended to include "backward" or R-S associative learning, either as incidentally learned components of S-R practice or as symmetrical manifestations of S-R associations, as an important process in the phenomena of verbal learning (Ekstrand, 1966; Kausler, 1966, pp. 68-70).

C. Methodological Paradigms for Learning, Transfer, and Retention

1. *Paired Associates*

Any one methodological paradigm is unlikely to offer a complete representation of the rich array of processes spanned by verbal learning phenomena, and the use of multiple paradigms in verbal learning research is certainly desirable. Nevertheless, one particular methodological paradigm, paired-associate (PA) learning, is especially amenable to tests of the interference theory of forgetting, including extensions for retention-development relationships. More specifically, the PA paradigm translates readily into the operational procedures flowing from the interference theory of forgetting. A PA list for which retention is to be measured is composed of clearly designated nominal S and R units, arranged into multiple S-R pairs and symbolized collectively as an *A-B* list (*A* and *B* representing S units and R units, respectively). Propaedeutic to an interference theory analysis of retention is practice on a second list bearing an *A-C* (identical S units, different R units) relationship to the *A-B* list, thereby generating competition between *B* and *C* responses to *A* stimuli, the *sine qua non* of interference theory. Retroactive inhibition (RI) is then defined in terms of an *A-B, A-C* practice sequence followed by recall of the *A-B* list, and proactive inhibition (PI) is defined in terms of an *A-C, A-B* list sequence followed by recall of the *A-B* list. The PA paradigm also translates into other RI and PI list sequences which maintain the functional identity of the *A-B, A-C* and *A-C, A-B* interference relationships and are therefore germane to interference theory. Thus list sequences of *A-B, C-D* (different S units and different R units in the two lists) and *C-D, A-B* for RI and PI, respectively, are viewed as introducing competition-interference for the response learning stage of List 2, even though the *A-B* and *C-D* associations themselves are free of interference. This analysis assumes that response learning per se occurs in the context of the total list, the memory drum, the experimental environs, etc. These contextual cues function as *"A"* stimuli for both sets of R units, and the response learning stages of the two lists enter into either *"A'-"B," "A'-"C"* (RI) or *"A'-"C," "A'-"B"* (PI) relationships (McGovern, 1964). List sequences of *A-B, C-B* (different S units and identical R units in the two lists) and *C-B, A-B* for RI and PI, respectively, are also viewed as introducing competition-interference, with R-S learning serving as the locus. For example, for RI, acquisition of A-B and C-B "forward" associations is presumed to be accompanied by the simultaneous aquisition of at least some B-A and B-C "backward" associations. Converting B terms to "A" equivalents and A and C terms to "B" and "C" equivalents, respectively, the R-S associations of the two lists may be seen to enter into the "A"-"B," "A"-"C" relationship indigenous to interference theory (cf. Kausler, 1966, pp. 364-371, and E. Martin, 1965, for further elaboration).

2. Serial Learning and Free Recall

Serial learning, a popular methodological paradigm for interference theory during the 1930s and early 1940s, has lost favor in recent years, primarily through preoccupation with the problem of identifying the source of functional stimuli employed by subjects in learning a serial list (R. K. Young, 1968). There are signs (e.g., Keppel & Zavortink, 1968) that serial learning may be ready for a return to the retention-forgetting fold, but the still limited interest in serial learning seems sufficient cause for its exclusion from the remainder of this paper. In contrast, free recall learning is a currently "hot" methodological paradigm, with most of the heat being kindled by the paradigm's ready translation into the organizational, storage, and retrieval processes of information processing approaches to retention. Research with this paradigm will not be reviewed systematically in this paper. It should be noted here though that retention phenomena relating to free recall learning have also been interpreted within the framework of interference theory (e.g., Postman & Keppel, 1967). Finally, a number of specific paradigms fit into the general rubric of short-term memory, with each paradigm having a common recall of single items (R units either with or without S units as cues for recall) after a relatively brief retention interval (cf. Postman, 1964a, for an overview of the various specific paradigms). However, the emphasis on long-term retention in this paper necessarily limits our later coverage of this important research area to the relevance of interference theory for short-term memory research on both children and aging subjects.

3. Recognition Tasks

In each of the previous paradigms retention measures follow acquisition stages for which the subject's task is to recall R units, and acquisition in each paradigm is therefore determined in part upon the availability for recall of the R units. In addition, other methodological paradigms, such as the previously described VD paradigm, stress recognition of R units during acquisition stages, rather than recall. Recognition of R units has been treated commonly within the conventional model of verbal learning as simply requiring a lower threshold for performance than does recall of the same units (Adams, 1967). However, there have been a number of recent theoretical and empirical developments in the general area of recognition learning that fall outside of the models described earlier, but still fall within a general S-R framework. These developments have considerable importance for the retention-development relationship, and the final section of this paper will be devoted to recognition paradigms.

III. A NOMOLOGICAL NETWORK FOR RETENTION-DEVELOPMENT RELATIONSHIPS

A. Verbal Learning and Age-Sensitive Processes

In an important review of research on verbal learning in children, Goulet (1968b) argued effectively for the use of "the highly developed methodology as methodology in verbal learning to study developmental learning processes" [p. 359]. He added further that the "versatility of the verbal learning tasks, especially those using paired associates, is emphasized in regard to the ease with which they can be modified to study learning in a developmental manner while still circumventing sources of confounding which plague developmental psychologists [pp. 359-360]." Developmental learning processes in this context refer to those learning processes that interact with chronological age over the years of childhood. A number of the learning processes suggested by Goulet to be age sensitive, such as stimulus selection and R-S learning were introduced earlier in this paper as components of models, processes, and paradigms entering into a general theory and methodology of verbal learning. In the present section an attempt will be made to identify the likely role of these age-sensitive processes in retention as well, an objective that was largely beyond the scope of Goulet's review. Moreover, the concept of age-sensitivity will be broadened to include elderly populations as well as children. Verbal learning methodologies have been gaining in importance in contemporary gerontological research, just as they have in research with children, and empirical evidence relating to retention processes has been emanating from laboratories at a fairly steady rate (Botwinick, 1967).

The emphasis in this section will be on variations with age in those processes of generic verbal learning theory that are seemingly relevant to any theory of verbal retention-forgetting. Discussion regarding the specific phenomena of RI and PI and the implications of traditional interference theory for age-related changes in RI and PI will be delayed until the next section. It must be noted here, however, that the mere presence of RI and PI in developmentally apposite populations is of no special theoretical significance to either verbal learning or developmental psychology, or to their hybrid. What is of interest is evidence for variations in RI and PI with variation along the age continuum.

B. Testing Developmentally Oriented Hypotheses Within a Nomological Network

The utilization of a verbal retention-forgetting model as a nomological network that anchors processes to both independent and dependent variables is patterned after the methodological procedure advanced by Cronbach and Meehl (1955) for testing the construct validity of psychological tests. Somewhat similar uses of the procedure were made by Kausler and Trapp (1959) in contrasting experimentally manipulated drive with scale-inferred drive and by Russell (1961) in contrasting verbal habits acquired in the laboratory with those acquired via natural language experiences. As adapted here, the procedure calls for developmentally oriented hypotheses concerning those processes ("constructs" in the language of Cronbach and Meehl) in the generic theory that have been substantially anchored at both ends of the network through systematic research with young adult populations. The hypotheses themselves flow from extant developmental theories and/or extensions of already well-documented developmental learning phenomena, and the procedural strategy closely resembles that described by Underwood (1957a, pp. 235-247) as a form of operational identification. Some process, P, of concern to developmental theory is presumed to be tied adequately to an independent (I)-dependent (D) variable functional relationship in the young adult populations. The independent variables for these functional relationships are typically task or procedural dimensions, such as meaningfulness of the units, interunit similarity, rate of presenting units for study, etc., and the dependent variables are typically trials to criterion, transfer scores, recall scores, etc. As the level of I is varied from I_1 to I_2 to I_3, etc., statistically reliable and replicable changes in D are observed, that is, $I_1 \rightarrow D_1$, $I_2 \rightarrow D_2$, $I_3 \rightarrow D_3$, etc., with the arrows simply signifying the presence of I-D correlations. The verbal learning theorist infers that the trend in the $I \rightarrow D$ correlations reflects an underlying trend in P from P_1 to P_2 to P_3, etc., and the complete sequence becomes $I_1 \rightarrow [P_1] \rightarrow D_1$, $I_2 \rightarrow [P_2] \rightarrow D_2$, etc. A developmental theory then enters the scene via some hypothesis that the process in question varies from P_1 to P_2 to P_3, etc. as age (A) increases from A_1 to A_2 to A_3, etc., with I remaining constant at a fixed level, say I_1. Empirical evidence for a set of $A_1 \rightarrow D_1$, $A_2 \rightarrow D_2$, $A_3 \rightarrow D_3$, etc. correlations that fits the trend for the reliably demonstrated $I_1 \rightarrow D_1$, etc. correlations supports the hypothesis that $A_1 \rightarrow P_1$, etc. Corroborating evidence for the age-sensitivity of the process accumulates when similar correlations can be demonstrated for other dependent variables deduced to be affected by variations in the underlying process.

One detailed example of the above procedure will be given here, and summarized in Figure 2 as well, before we turn to applications intrinsic to retention phenomena. Interlist similarity of R units in verbal transfer tasks, defined, for example, in terms of associative relatedness, may be varied along a

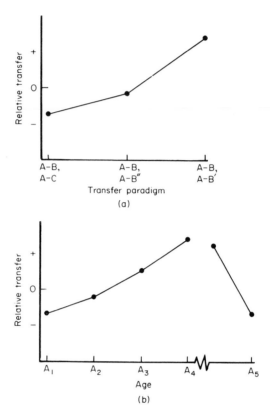

Figure 2. (a) Transfer in young adults as a function of the similarity between List 1 and List 2 R units, from dissimilarity (the *A-B, A-C* paradigm), to moderate similarity (the *A-B, A-B″* paradigm), to high similarity (the *A-B, A-B′* paradigm). (b) Predicted transfer in the *A-B, A-B′* paradigm for young children (A_1), intermediate age children (A_2), older children (A_3), young adults (A_4), and elderly subjects (A_5) as the transfer mechanism changes from interference to mediation and back to interference.

continuum ranging from dissimilarity to complete identity. If we identify the R units of List 1 as *B* terms, we discover that the List 2 counterparts range along a *C* (dissimilar) to *B* (identical) dimension. Furthermore, intermediate points of similarity may be identified by the symbol *B′*. When identical S units, symbolized here as *A* terms, are employed in the two lists, two critical transfer paradigms are engendered for purposes of testing hypotheses regarding processes underlying the effects of interlist R similarity on transfer; *A-B, A-C* and *A-B, A-B′*. We have already encountered the *A-B, A-C* paradigm as representing a prototype for analyzing competition-interference phenomena. Negative transfer for this paradigm, relative to an *A-B, C-D* control paradigm (that is, control for nonspecific transfer effects, such as learning-to-learn; cf. Kausler, 1966, Chapter 8, for a general discussion of transfer effects), is the highly reliable outcome for young adults. On the other hand, the A-B, A-B' paradigm, which technically conforms to the competition-interference prerequisite of learning two different R units to the same S unit, yields either zero transfer or moderate amounts of positive transfer for young adult subjects (e.g., Postman, 1964b). Presumably, whatever competition-interference is present during List 2 practice is at least partially compensated for by an additional mediational process that enhances the response learning stage of List 2. An immediately relevant developmental hypothesis is that of a "mediational deficiency" in both young children (Reese, 1962) and elderly individuals (Canestrari, 1968a). If the hypothesis is valid, the A-B, A-B' paradigm reverts to the A-B, A-C paradigm at both ends of the age spectrum, and pronounced negative transfer, rather than positive transfer, is the expected outcome. The developmental hypothesis thus leads to the intriguing prediction of a curvilinear relationship between amount of transfer and age, as shown in Figure 2. Unfortunately, reviews of the literature (Botwinick, 1967; Goulet, 1968b; Keppel, 1964) reveal that there is virtually no reported research on the A-B, A-B' paradigm that involves other than young adult subjects. The neglect of this research problem area is especially important in light of contemporary developments in the interference theory of forgetting (see Section IV).

C. Age-Sensitive Variables and Processes

1. Degree of Original Learning and Associative Strength

A serious problem that threatens any cross-age research on retention processes is the potential confounding created by age differences in the rate of learning of the to-be-retained material, be it a single list or a list in a RI-PI paradigm. Differential rates of learning generally yield different terminal degrees of habit strength prior to the start of the retention interval, and, of all the variables related to forgetting, degree of original learning is by far the most potent (Underwood, 1954). Other independent variables, such as meaningfulness, may exert much of their effect on retention indirectly through their effect on degree of learning. In order to ascertain the effects of such variables on retention processes per se, it must first be made certain that the groups of subjects representing the levels of the independent variable have all attained the same level of learning. To the extent that different age groups learn verbal tasks at different rates, an assurance of equal learning must be made before meaningful age contrasts in retention can be made.

Underwood (1954, 1964b) has provided several very useful and straightforward methods for projecting the degree of learning at the end of any given trial to what habit strength has become as the consequence of the increment contributed by that trial. By appropriate pilot research the investigator determines the number of trials required at each age level to yield identical projected degrees of learning. In the retention experiment proper the predetermined number of trials would then be administered to the appropriate age group. As a general rule, the number of trials should be somewhat less than the number required to reach full mastery of the list (Underwood, 1964b). Unfortunately, the usual procedure in developmentally oriented research on retention is to take all groups to a common criterion of mastery, such as to one perfect recitation of the entire list, on the assumption that this criterion guarantees equal original learning for all groups. As illustrated in Figure 3, an

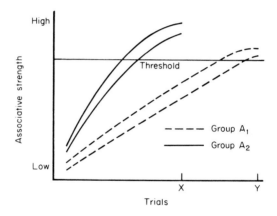

Figure 3. Hypothetical learning curves for two "easy" S-R pairs at two different age levels (A_1 and A_2). X and Y represent trials at which the most difficult pair in the list is mastered and practice terminated (at X for A_2 and Y for A_1). Easy pairs have higher terminal associative strengths in A_2 than in A_1, even though both groups are "equated" by having them attain the same criterion of mastery.

incremental theory (see Section II, A 1) implies a threshold value for correct anticipations that is below asymptotic strength for a given S-R association. Assume that two age groups, A_1 and A_2, practice a list of six paired associates to one perfect recitation, with Group A_2 reaching this criterion in fewer trials than Group A_1. The number of trials required in each group is directly dependent on the number required to learn the most difficult of the six pairs. The five easiest pairs in the list are likely to reach threshold values sufficiently early to receive postthreshold practice during the trials needed to push the remaining pair above its threshold. The fact that the five easiest pairs for Group A_2 are learned at a faster rate than the five easiest pairs for Group A_1 suggests, as illustrated in

Figure 3 for two such pairs, differential final habit strengths in the two groups, with differential susceptibility to forgetting as a consequence.

This important source of confounding is intrinsic to retention-development relationships only if learning rates do indeed vary markedly across that segment of the age spectrum being investigated. It does seem to be understood implicitly that learning rate for paired associates does improve progressively across the years of childhood. For example, Goulet (1968b), in reviewing the learning literature for this age period, stated that "On a gross level, it has been demonstrated that the speed of PA learning increases with age [p. 360]." The evidence for a regular step-by-step progression, however, is equivocal. For kindergarten and second grade groups both Loomis and Hall (1968) and Kausler and Gotway (1969) found faster PA learning for the second graders, the former study with aural presentation and the latter with visual. Jensen and Rohwer (1965) also found superior learning for second graders, but only when the procedure involved a mediational technique. When rote practice prevailed, Jensen and Rohwer found, surprisingly, slightly faster learning for the kindergarten group. Reese (1965b) reported faster PA learning for a group ranging in age from 63 to 96 months than for a group ranging in age 56 to 60 months, with the latter group in turn being superior to a third group ranging in age from 36 to 48 months. Faster PA learning by fourth graders than by second graders was obtained by Kausler and Gotway (1969) and also by Jensen and Rohwer (1965), but only in the rote condition of the latter study. Using a modified PA task, Cole, Sharp, Glick, and Kessen (1968) found faster learning in fifth than in third graders. Lack of a difference in learning rates between fourth and six graders was obtained by Palermo (1961), Jensen and Rohwer (1965) (in both their rote and mediational conditions), and Kausler and Gotway (1969). Faster learning in eighth graders than in fourth graders (Gallagher, 1968), fifth graders (Shapiro, 1966, aural presentation), and sixth graders (Jensen & Rohwer, 1965, in their rote condition only) has also been observed. The inconsistency in demonstrating a steady progression in PA proficiency from the preschool period through the eighth grade level undoubtedly reflects the "noise" created by the wide variation in materials learned, presentation rate, type of instructions, etc. Nevertheless, the evidence is sufficient, in light of the seriousness of the consequences, to warrant the inexorable practice of equating degree of learning in cross-age studies on children's retention processes.

The opposite assumption, namely, a steady decrement in learning rate with age, is equally implicit in gerontological research. However, here again, the evidence is far from being unequivocal. Restricting our sample of research to fairly recent PA studies, we find slower learning rates for "elderly" subjects (usually averaging in their fifties or beyond) than for "young" subjects (often, more appropriately, "middle age," averaging in their late thirties or forties) reported by Canestrari (1963, 1968) and Arenberg (1965), but not by Kausler and Lair (1965, 1966) and Lair, Moon, and Kausler (1969). As with children, the inconsistency undoubtedly reflects the "noise" created by the use of varying exposure intervals, varying kinds of materials, etc. At any rate, the seriousness of the learning rate problem should be enough to assure attention to the need for equal learning in any research on retention in aging populations.

2. *Rote versus Mediated Learning*

Degree of learning, as used in the previous context, is a quantitative dimension that considers only the superthreshold strength of to-be-retained associations. A second, qualitative, dimension may also be of considerable importance in developmental research on retention. This dimension broadly dichotomizes associative learning into rote versus mediated learning, with the latter category, in turn, being further dichotomized into verbal versus visual mnemonic devices (see Section II). A recent spurt of research activity on mnemonics is beginning to fill the earlier unfortunate void precipitated by an all too rigid adherence to the conventional model (see Section II). Most importantly, evidence is accumulating with young adult subjects which indicates that forgetting is markedly reduced when either verbal (e.g., Adams & Montague, 1967) or visual (e.g., Bugelski, 1968) mediators are employed during the original learning of the to-be-retained associations, relative to the purported rote learning of the same associations. The question may be raised as to whether or not mediation per se accounts for the disparity in retention. One way of viewing the underlying mechanism for the efficacy of mediation on retention is in terms of the formation of a stable organization (or "gestalt") that is highly resistant to the disruptive influence of interfering activities. However, an alternative interpretation is to resort to the quantitative dimension and assume that mediated associations have simply reached a higher level of terminal strength than have rote associations (cf. Adams & Montague, 1967, for a thorough discussion of these alternatives and their methodological consequences). This second alternative implies that mediated versus rote learning is only an interesting side issue, that degree of learning by one process could be equated with the degree attained by the other. Evidence for this alternative view was provided by Olton (1969). Retention of paired associates learned with and without a verbal mnemonic did not differ for fifth graders when degree of original learning was carefully equated for the two conditions. Replication of this study at other age levels is highly desirable.

The mediation-rote distinction is of special significance to retention-development relationships during childhood in light of both the previously noted mediational deficit hypothesis (Kendler & Kendler, 1962; Reese, 1962) and its reasonable alternative, the production-deficiency hypothesis (Flavell, Beach, & Chinsky, 1966; Keeney, Cannizzo, & Flavell, 1967). The mediational deficit hypothesis postulates an absence of relevant verbal mediational activity during the preschool years, followed by a transitional period during the five to seven years of age period. Consequently, PA learning during these years is more likely to be rote in nature than is PA learning during the middle to late years of childhood. On the other hand, the production-deficiency hypothesis posits the presence in young children of latent verbal skills that are capable of mediating learning experiences; however, the spontaneous activation of these skills is unlikely to occur at early ages, and utilization of the skills becomes contingent upon extrinsic prodding in the form of special instructions and examples, guidance, controlled rehearsal procedures, etc. Flavell and other investigators have gathered an impressive amount of evidence in support of a production deficiency as it manifests itself in short-term memory (e.g., Kingsley & Hagen, 1969) and free recall (e.g., Moely, Olson, Halwes, & Flavell, 1969), and a comparable involvement of a production deficiency in verbally mediated PA learning seems reasonable.

Even if a verbal mediational deficit could be reliably demonstrated in young children, a comparable deficit in visual imagery (or iconic imagery) as a source of mediation would seem unlikely (Bruner, 1964). The production-deficiency hypothesis, however, remains equally viable when applied to visual mediators, in the sense that their spontaneous activation during PA learning may be inversely related to age during childhood. The concept of production-deficiency is an example of what we earlier called a generalized habit (Section II). Older children are more likely to show spontaneous transfer of preexisting habits (here referring to mediational strategies) to a novel PA task than are younger children, and such transfer, when activated, affects many, if not all, of the pairs within the list.

A number of recent PA studies with children touch upon the mediational deficit versus production-deficiency issue. Considering first those studies dealing with verbal mediators, Jensen and Rohwer (1965) found that requiring subjects to construct simple sentences (a mediating activity) incorporating each pair of S and R units (pictures) on the first trial only yielded greatly superior PA acquisition than a simple naming of the objects depicted in the S and R units (a rote activity) from the second through twelfth grades. However, for kindergarten subjects in the same study, the sentence construction and naming objects procedures yielded virtually identical performances. This outcome could be interpreted as either a mediational deficit at the five-year-old level, with the five-year-old being irresponsive to what is otherwise an effective mediational procedure, or a production deficiency which at that age level requires a prolonged mnemonic activity before mediation can be primed. In an elaboration of the sentence construction procedure Rohwer, Lynch, Suzuki, and Levin (1967) provided sentences incorporating S and R units, rather than having subjects (first, third, and sixth graders) construct their own sentences, and contrasted sentence-mediated PA learning with learning under the naming (rote) condition. In addition, they varied the type of sentence in terms of the key word connecting the S and R units, with verbs, conjunctions, and prepositions representing the three levels. They discovered that verbs as the connectors served effectively in promoting mediated learning, whereas neither the conjunction nor the preposition condition differed significantly from the naming condition. Although the main effect for grade level was significant, and each higher grade performed significantly better than the grade below it, the interaction between sentence condition and grade level was negligible. The lack of an interaction is surprising in that the mediational facilitator (verb sentences) would be expected to diminish grade differences, especially between third and sixth graders, whereas the rote condition would be expected to enhance grade differences, especially between first and sixth graders. Briefly, other investigators (e.g., Milgram, 1967; Reese, 1965b) have found that verbal mediators are at least as effective as visual mediators, even for four-year-old children. In fact, contrary to the mediational deficit hypothesis, Milgram (1967) reported that four-year-old children "apparently strengthen initially weak associations in PAL more effectively by repeating a sentence than by gazing upon its equivalent pictorial form [p. 602]." The implications for developmental research on retention are important, but thus far there has been, with the exception of the Reese study (1965b), no empirical attempt to relate mediational activity to subsequent retention across age levels. Reese did administer a retention test after two weeks, but the unequal attrition of subjects across age levels and the likely confounding of mediated learning with overall degree of learning make the data somewhat nebulous.

An identical set of problems must be faced in research on retention processes with gerontological populations. Younger adult subjects are considerably more likely to report the use of mediational devices in learning a PA list under standard instructions (that is, no attempt is made to prime a generalized habit for mediation) than are elderly subjects (Hulicka & Grossman, 1967). Granted the usual suspicion of subject reports, the disparity in percentages of subjects reporting mediation is nevertheless convincing (68% versus 36%; Hulicka & Grossman, 1967). As is true with children, differential retention between young and elderly adult subjects can be attributed to either an overall difference in terminal degree of associative strength or to a difference in mode of learning (rote versus mediated), or to a combination of both. Furthermore, the question of a true mediational deficit in elderly subjects is also subject to a reexamination in light of the production-deficiency hypothesis. Hulicka and Grossman (1967) found that elderly subjects increased their reported mediational activity considerably when they were primed by appropriate instructions for either verbal or visual mediators, and that this increase was accompanied by a corresponding increase in PA learning proficiency. Their conclusion, one closely paralleling conclusions stemming from research on young children, was that "It would seem that the relative infrequency of the spontaneous use of mediators by old Ss, along with an unwillingness or inability to use 'odd' mediators, might account for some of the well-documented age-related deficit in paired-associate learning [p. 50] "—a conclusion extended here to include the possibility of PA retention as well. Corroborating evidence for the Hulicka and Grossman findings has since been given by Canestrari (1968).

3. The Selector Mechanism and Interference Proneness

A popular hypothesis among theorists working with populations other than the young adult reference population is that of a heightened susceptibility to interference in a variety of verbal tasks and situations. Schizophrenics have been the leading candidate for consideration (e.g., Lang & Buss, 1965), but both children and the elderly have received their share of attention. Young children are perceived as being more prone to interference than older children, with the age range from five to seven years being a transition period (White, 1965), and elderly individuals are perceived as being more prone than young or middle-age adults (Jerome, 1959).

Interference in the present context refers to the competition between two responses, B and C, to the stimulus A, when both B and C are learned as successive and independent R units to A the S unit. For example, if B is learned initially as the response to A, then B may intrude and block the learning or performance of C as a new response to A. In an entire list of A-C pairs the B responses form a general class of "old and no longer appropriate" responses, and, as described in Section II, the inhibition of an inappropriate class of responses is accomplished by the selector mechanism. Age correlated changes in "interference proneness" therefore imply age related changes in the efficacy of the selector mechanism.

For both RI and PI, interference is dually involved, once during the learning of List 2 (A-C in RI and A-B in PI), with unlearning of List 1 responses and associations as the consequence, and again during the recall of A-B (List 1 in RI and List 2 in PI), with competition-at-recall as the consequence (see Section IV). Thus the concept of interference proneness takes on special significance in retention-development relationships. However, it is important that tests of the age-interference relationship be conducted independently of RI and PI measurements if we hope to assess interference effects that are not confounded by other processes. Both RI and PI are complex phenomena that represent resultants of multiple determiners, and the components stemming from interference may be masked by other determiners (Section IV). The test recommended here is the standard A-B, A-C negative transfer paradigm as contrasted with the A-B, C-D control paradigm.

Negative transfer in the A-B, A-C paradigm, as reflected in the retarded learning of A-C pairs, presumably results from the covert arousal of B terms from List 1 as competitors of C terms during List 2 practice (or vice versa if the two lists form a PI rather than RI sequence). However, the negative effect of interference is partially balanced by two other effects which contribute positively to the learning of, or the performance of, new A-C associations. One is the nonspecific transfer of warm-up and learning-to-learn which occurs whenever subjects have had practice on a prior list, regardless of the prior list's relationship to the critical transfer list (Kausler, 1966, pp. 360-361). The second is the transfer of stimulus differentiation which occurs whenever the S units of List 2 are identical to the S units of List 1, a contingency certainly found in the A-B, A-C paradigm (Kausler, 1966, pp. 368-369). That is, the process of identifying functional S units as discriminable cues for eliciting R units has already been accomplished during List 1 practice, and the process does not need repetition during List 2 practice. Valid tests of interference that are uncontaminated by these two sources of positive transfer have two basic requirements. First, the A-B, C-D paradigm, the standard control for nonspecific transfer, must be included within the test, thereby permitting performance on the C-D list to serve as the baseline for estimating the direction and magnitude of transfer on the A-C list. Second, the S units (both A and C terms) must be simple elements that have already been clearly differentiated preexperimentally by the subject population being tested, elements such as single digits or letters, or highly familiar words or pictures. With the use of these kinds of elements, the added task of differentiating between the S units of List 2 for C-D pairs, but not for A-C pairs, will not greatly alter the estimate of transfer on the A-C list.

The transfer method is effective whenever interference is to be measured at any one age level. However, a complication is introduced whenever the method is employed to test developmental trends in interference. Degree of learning on List 1 (A-B) pairs bears an important, but only vaguely understood, relationship to the magnitude of negative transfer on List 2 (A-C pairs) (Mandler, 1962). Variation in rate of learning across age levels is again an important issue to the extent that rate and degree of associative strength covary. The problems and potential solutions discussed earlier in terms of direct retention phenomena apply equally well here and should be given serious consideration by investigators testing age-related changes in interference proneness.

When age is the independent variable in A-B, A-C transfer research, negative transfer is expected at each age level. The question raised here is the interaction between age and List 2 content (A-C pairs versus C-D pairs). Four- and five-year-old children are expected to display more negative transfer (that is, a greater differential between A-C and C-D pairs) than seven- and eight-year-old children (White, 1965), but the amount of negative transfer should remain relatively invariant during the remaining years of childhood. Similarly, elderly individuals are expected to display more negative transfer than young or middle-age adults (Jerome, 1959).

Adequate tests of age-related trends in interference are rare. Transfer studies on children have usually included factors that confound pure tests of age-related proneness to interference. The most serious problem is created by the use of mixed lists as List 2 to evaluate the amount of negative transfer (e.g., Price, Cobb, & Morin, 1968; Spiker, 1960). A mixed list is one in which each of the transfer paradigms included in the experiment is equally represented. For example, a six pair List 2 would have three A-C pairs and three C-D pairs, relative to the A-B pairs of List 1. Each subject would then serve as his own control for measuring transfer by comparing his A-C score with his C-D score. In contrast, an unmixed list procedure requires separate groups for A-C pairs and C-D pairs at each age level. For a given experimental subject all six pairs in List 2 would be A-C in content, and for a given control subject all six pairs in List 2 would be C-D in content. Generalized habits regulating the selector mechanism are likely to differ between mixed and unmixed list conditions (W. F. Battig, 1966; Postman, 1966; Wickens & Cermak, 1967), and children's performance on a mixed list is likely to give a different estimate of interference per se than is performance on an unmixed list (Johnson & Penney, 1965). The interaction between age and the nature of generalized habits related to the mixed-unmixed list distinction poses an interesting question for future research in developmental verbal learning, but the interaction is irrelevant to the question of age-related interference proneness. Unmixed lists give a more valid test of the proneness hypothesis than do mixed lists, and the former should be used exclusively for such tests.

The only study that is apropos to the age-interference relationship in children is by Loomis and Hall (1968). Negative transfer was found with unmixed lists for both kindergarten and second-grade groups, but, contrary to the expectation of decreasing interference with increasing age, negative transfer was greater for the second-grade group than for the kindergarten group. It is obvious that considerably more transfer research over a wider span of grade levels is sorely needed before any conclusion can be reached regarding a trend in interference proneness across childhood.

The concept of interference proneness is even more widely held for the elderly than it is for young children, and yet the generation-of-data gap is as great for this population as it is for children. The well known study by Gladis and Braun (1958) is purported to demonstrate greater interference in A-B, A-C transfer for elderly than for young adult subjects. However, the study was really designed to test the effects of age-related interference on RI, and the control condition employed, a single list group characteristic of RI research, is inappropriate for evaluating interference independent of retention itself. Other studies with the A-B, A-C paradigm (Arenberg, 1967; Hulicka, 1967) are similarly inappropriate for testing the interference proneness hypothesis, and there remains a great need for systematic research across the adult age continuum that tests the age-interference relationship with appropriate transfer methodology.

There is an alternative procedure for testing developmental trends in interference proneness. The procedure conforms to transfer methodology in principle, but, in contrast to the usual transfer test, only a single list is learned in the laboratory. Briefly, the single list is composed of "cross associates" and is constructed by re-pairing S and R units that are preexperimentally related to one another. For example, stimulus words and their primary associates from word association norms, such as, *table-chair, king-queen,* and *loud-soft,* may be re-paired to form *table-soft, king-chair,* and *loud-queen* as S-R pairs within the list. The single list is functionally equivalent to the List 2 of a transfer sequence in which "List 1" is actually the preexperimental learning of the to-be-re-paired S-R units. Although pairs like *table-chair* and *table-soft* function as *A-B, A-C* (sequential) associations, the paradigm itself is considerably more complex than the *A-B, A-C* paradigm created by the learning of two laboratory-based lists. In fact, the cross associates paradigm is more appropriately an example of the *A-B, A-Br* (S and R units identical for Lists 1 and 2, but the units are paired differently in List 2 than in List 1) paradigm of classical transfer research. The *A-B, A-Br* paradigm has in common with the more traditional *A-B, A-C* paradigm interference from competing S-R associations during List 2 practice, but, in addition, it has the added interference resulting from competing R-S associations (Kausler, 1966, pp. 365-366). Thus, in some respects, the cross associates method permits a more sensitive assessment of interference proneness than the standard *A-B, A-C* method. The complete application of the method demands a control condition learning a single list bearing a *C-D* relationship to the *A-B,* or preexperimental, pairs.

The difficulty in applying the cross associates method to age-related trends in interference proneness rests in the experimenter's inability to estimate the degree of "List 1" learning extant prior to practice on the laboratory list. There is evidence that highly associated words, as revealed by normative data, may be learned at unequal rates by children of different ages when the words serve as S-R pairs in a PA list (Klinger & Palermo, 1967; Wicklund, Palermo, & Jenkins, 1964). Apparently, word associates have different absolute S-R strengths at different age levels, even though they may have equal relative or normative strength. This is a problem of general importance to developmental learning psychologists, but the problem enters here only as a source of confounding age-related trends in interference. It is true that for any given age level in childhood the method of cross associates provides an effective means of testing other hypotheses, such as ones derived from motivational theory (Castaneda, 1965; McCullers, 1967). A differential absolute strength between elderly and middle-aged subjects is less likely (Kausler & Lair, 1966), and the method of cross associates seems to be more satisfactory at this end of the age continuum. In fact, Lair *et al.* (1969) have recently provided convincing evidence of interference proneness in the elderly by means of the cross associates method. Earlier use of the method by Ruch (1934) and Korchin and Basowitz (1958) also supported the concept of heightened interference in the elderly, but the choice of S and R units in the two studies necessarily makes their results ambiguous. The cross associates in both studies consisted of false equations, with terms like 3 X 4 = as the S unit and 2 as the R unit for one pair, 2 X 4 = as the S unit and 9 as the R unit of a second pair, etc. The nominal stimuli were therefore multiple digit units with overlapping interunit content. Stimulus selection is undoubtedly a major component of the total learning required by such lists, and the interaction between age and task dimensions related to stimulus selection in the elderly is an unknown factor.

4. Stimulus Selection

The importance of stimulus selection was noted above in prescribing a test of interference proneness that is unconfounded by compensatory positive processes. The emphasis at that point was on the methodological advantage of using S units for which the nominal-functional stimulus disparity (see Section II, A, 2) is minimal. The present emphasis is on the effect of increases in the nominal-functional disparity on retention phenomena, and the probable course of the retention-development relationship with increasing disparity. The underlying mechanism for any disparity-retention-development relationship is again interference encountered during List 2 practice of an *A-B, A-C* transfer sequence. With nominal S units of high meaningfulness, there is likely to be little, if any, disparity between nominal S units and functional components selected by subjects as cues for eliciting R units during the acquisition of List 1 (*A-B* pairs). The identical functional stimuli are likely to be selected during List 2 practice, and the basic *A-B, A-C* interference relationship is therefore present at the onset of List 2 practice. On the other hand, with nominal S units of low meaningfulness, subjects may select one element of a given S unit as their functional stimulus during acquisition of List 1 and a different element of the unit during acquisition of List 2. The *A-B, A-C* list relationship then reduces itself to the functional equivalence of an *A-B, C-D* list sequence, and associative interference should be less pronounced during List 2 practice than under the high meaningfulness condition. Support for this conceptualization has been found with young adult subjects by Bryk and Kausler (1966) and E. Martin (1968).

It is conceivable that a similar selection process is involved when meaningfulness is kept constant and age is varied (Goulet, 1968b). The meaningfulness of various S units (for example, nonsense syllables, unfamiliar words, etc.) is likely to be lower for young children than for older children, and the nominal-functional disparity for such units is correspondingly likely to be greater for young than for older children. Consequently, interference during List 2 practice may well be positively covaried with age when there is some degree of nominal-functional disparity. Surprisingly, this concept leads to the prediction that RI and PI effects should be less pronounced for young children than for older children, given nominal S units for which preexperimental familiarity (or meaningfulness) covaries positively with age. An obvious initial step in testing the validity of this hypothesis is to conduct preliminary tests of age sensitivity in stimulus selection itself, independent of retention measurements.

One of the few studies relevant to tests of age sensitivity in stimulus selection is by Gaeth and Allen (1966). Among the conditions included in their study were two in which nominal S units were formed by altering the letter order of three letter words containing the same middle and third letters, but different initial letters (e.g., *fan, pan,* and *can*). In one condition (their Condition C) the alteration followed the consistent order of the middle letter first, then the first and third letters (e.g., AFN, APN, and ACN). In the second condition (their Condition D) the alteration did not follow a consistent sequence for all S units (e.g., AFN, PNA, and CNA). The first condition permits the application of the generalized habit of always selecting the reliably different middle letter of nominal S units to serve as functional stimuli. A similar generalized habit is ineffective in the second condition where letter redundancy occurs at each ordinal position. Gaeth and Allen found that fourth, fifth, and sixth graders did not differ in their learning rates for a PA list containing the redundant S units. However, the sixth graders were significantly more proficient than the fourth and fifth graders in learning a PA list containing the nonredundant S units, suggesting an age-related change in a generalized habit closely associated with the selection process. A complication in interpreting this study follows from the fact that in each condition the nominal S units were actually anagrams. It is conceivable that the underlying dimension being tapped with such materials is a developmental trend in the ability to solve simple anagrams, rather than a generalized habit related to stimulus selection. Further research on developmental trends in the use of generalized habits in stimulus selection is highly desirable, especially with nominal S units that are not scrambled versions of meaningful words (e.g., AXN, ALN, and AQN). Replication on children of the transfer methods employed to test hypotheses about stimulus selection in young adult populations (e.g., Postman & Greenbloom, 1967; Underwood *et al.*, 1962) would also have great pragmatic value for charting developmental trends in stimulus selection.

The elderly represent a further intriguing, but unexplored, population for testing the concept of age-sensitivity in stimulus selection. Of special significance is the likely decrement in applying generalized habits as aids in stimulus selection, with the hypothesized decrement following from the previously discussed mediational (or production) deficit in the elderly. Tasks comparable to those of the Gaeth and Allen study should provide effective tests of this hypothesis.

5. R-S learning

The final age-sensitive process considered in this section is that of R-S learning during PA practice (see Section II,B). This process, like others analyzed above, enters initially into retention-development relationships through its influence on the degree of interference occurring during the transfer stages of RI and PI list sequences. Earlier (Section II,C,1) we noted that an *A-B, A-C* list sequence symbolizes both phenotypical and genotypical transfer paradigms. The phenotype is the traditional *A-B, A-C* (identical stimuli, different reponses) paradigm of classical transfer research in which associative interference is traced to competing "forward" or S-R associations. The genotype, however, stretches the paradigmatic boundaries to ensnare any other source of interference that fits the *"A"-"B," "A"-"C"* sequence. Of special interest here is the traditional *A-B, C-B* (different stimuli, identical responses) paradigm of classical transfer research. This paradigm meets the genotype's *"A"-"B," "A"-"C"* prerequisite by virtue of the *B-A, B-C* sequence formed by the R-S associations of the two lists (Section II,C,1). The close connection between the *A-B, C-B* paradigm and the general problem area of concept learning (Underwood, 1966) greatly enhances the paradigm's importance to developmental psychologists, and an understanding of developmental trends in RI and PI effects for the paradigm should be a high priority project for future investigators. The assignment of interference to R-S sources, however, suggests the strong need for preliminary assessment of developmental trends in R-S learning per se, again in a context that is independent of specific retention measurements.

The obvious starting point is to look for measurements of R-S learning on developmentally relevant populations that follow the same operational procedures used with young adults. But, once more, we find a data deficit for populations other than young adults. With young adult subjects the amount of R-S learning is estimated to be 80% or more of S-R learning, provided the nominal S units are highly meaningful words (e.g., Dron & Boe, 1964). When less familiar nominal stimuli are employed, estimates of the amount of R-S learning, both in absolute amounts and in amounts relative to the degree of S-R learning, become complicated by the question of nominal-functional stimulus disparity (Kausler, 1966, pp. 68-70). In one of the few R-S learning studies with children as subjects, Palermo (1961) found that R-S learning averaged only 57% of S-R learning in fourth and sixth graders (with no difference in R-S learning between grade levels), even though highly familiar terms served as nominal S units. Reduced R-S learning in children, if reliably demonstrated, implies that interference for the A-B, C-B paradigm may be less for children than it is for young adults. However, the incorporation of developmental trends in R-S learning into projections regarding correlated trends in RI and PI effects could evolve into an extremely complicated problem. R-S learning is viewed by many verbal learning psychologists as being a form of Type II incidental learning (Kausler & Trapp, 1960) in which incidental (R-S) and intentional (S-R) learning take place simultaneously. Type II incidental learning for other learning tasks has all the characteristics of being the knuckle ball of developmental learning, an area already having enough difficulty handling a simpler assortment of curves. That is, Type II incidental learning seems to show a peculiar cubic curve when plotted against age from the preschool through young adulthood period (cf. Botwinick's paper in the present volume), and a similar trend for R-S learning would add horrendous dimensions to an understanding of RI and PI effects.

There is reason, however, to question the validity of the complex age-degree relationship predicted for R-S learning by the Type II incidental learning analogy. Recent data by Kausler and Gotway (1969) suggest that the degree of R-S learning may actually be invariant with respect to age for a wide band of the age continuum. Their six-pair PA list, composed of familiar pictures as S and R units [in common with the earlier Palermo (1961) study], was learned to the criterion of one perfect S-R trial. A paced R-S recall was then given by presenting R units individually and requesting S unit recall, a procedure commonly used to measure the degree of R-S learning in young adults. The number of R-S pairs correctly recalled averaged 5.06, 4.75, 5.25, and 4.81 for kindergarten, second, fourth, and sixth grade groups, respectively. The between-groups effect clearly did not reach statistical significance. Similarly, the groups did not differ in relative (to S-R) amounts of R-S learning, averaging 84%, 79%, 87%, and 80% for kindergarten through sixth grade. As described earlier (Section III,C,1), the groups employed by Kausler and Gotway did differ significantly in the number of trials required to attain the S-R criterion. Although the greater number of trials at the younger age levels may have provided a sufficient number of extra practice trials to compensate for an overall R-S learning deficit at these ages, supplementary correlational analyses by Kausler and Gotway indicated that this was an unlikely source of bias. The equality in R-S learning between fourth and sixth graders is in agreement with Palermo's (1961) earlier study. The discrepancy between the two studies rests in their separate estimates of the amount of R-S learning in children—57% (Palermo), an amount well below that of young adults, versus 80% (Kausler and Gotway), an amount quite comparable to that of young adults. The deficit reported by Palermo could well be the product of the transfer procedure he used to test the amount of R-S learning, rather than the product of a true deficit in children. His procedure called for a mixed transfer list containing two R-S (i.e., B-A) pairs from List 1, together with two continuing S-R (i.e., A-B) pairs from List 1 and two new S-R (i.e., C-D) pairs. Inferior performance on the R-S pairs probably resulted from a selection process mediated by generalized habits, a process akin to that described earlier in conjunction with mixed lists in the *A-B, A-C* paradigm. Unfortunately, acceptance of the equality of R-S learning across childhood is plagued by the nasty problem of "proving" the null hypothesis. One resolution of the null problem is through repeated demonstration of the absence of an age deficit, both with the standard R-S recall method and with other methods, such as the method recommended by Goulet (1968b) for measuring R-S learning in children.

Even if we could assume the validity of the invariance-with-age hypothesis for children's R-S learning, there is reason to expect an overall covariation between amount of negative transfer in the *A-B, C-B* paradigm (relative to the *A-B, C-D* paradigm) and developmental level. Some limited empirical support for this prediction is available (Gladis, 1960). As is true for the *A-B, A-C* paradigm, net transfer for the *A-B, C-B* transfer is also the resultant of several component processes (Kausler, 1966, p. 371). One of these processes is the positive transfer of response learning from List 1 to List 2, a process absent in the control paradigm. The masking effect of developmental trends in this process must be cast aside before developmental trends in interference proneness can be tested. Response learning transfer may be effectively minimized by employing highly familiar R units for *C-B* and *C-D* pairs, thereby reducing the advantage of having already learned *B* units during List 1 practice. Variations in transfer amounts across age levels could then be traced primarily to a selector mechanism serving to inhibit intrusions of S units from List 1, a mechanism analogous to the one inhibiting R units from List 1 as intrusions during List 2 practice in the *A-B, A-C* paradigm. It is the age sensitivity of this R-S interference mechanism that needs careful and systematic investigation with children of varying ages. However, support for the age sensitivity of this mechanism can be given only if we know more about the raw nature of R-S learning in children. Age variation in *C-B* learning could be attributable to age variation in absolute amount of the R-S associations acquired or in the ability to inhibit interference from a constant amount of R-S associations, or to a combination of both. Explanations of any demonstrated age variation in RI and PI for the *A-B, C-B* paradigm must be at least partly contingent upon the answers to these essential preliminary questions.

IV. INTERFERENCE THEORY AND
RETENTION-DEVELOPMENT RELATIONSHIPS

A. Component Processes of RI and PI

Operationally, RI is defined by the contrast in recall between an experimental group learning an *A-B, A-C* list sequence and a control group learning only the

A-B list. (It should be noted that in this section an *A-B, A-C* sequence refers to the specific paradigm of "identical stimuli, different responses" for the two lists. This classical transfer paradigm has served effectively as the prototype for research on interference processes in RI and PI. However, interference theory also applies to other paradigms that fit the *"A-"B," "A"-"C"* genotype, and the implications of interference theory for these other paradigms will be discussed at a later point.) Lower recall of the *A-B* list by the experimental group (i.e., recall of List 1) than by the control group (i.e., recall of the only list), with length of the retention interval equated between groups, completes the operational definition of RI. Similarly, PI is defined by an *A-C, A-B* list sequence for the experimental group and an *A-B* only list for the control group. Lower recall of the *A-B* list by the experimental group than by the control group (i.e., recall of the only list), with retention interval again equated, completes the operational definition of PI.

Although the immediate objective of interference theory is the explanation of laboratory demonstrated RI and PI, it is clear that the theory views RI and PI phenomena as prototypes for a broader range of forgetting, both inside and outside of the laboratory. Consequently, forgetting in the general sense is to be explained by the same processes that account for RI and PI. The classical interference theory of McGeoch (1942) and Melton (Melton & Irwin, 1940) is a direct extension of the conventional model of verbal learning (Section II,A,1), and it is therefore not surprising to discover that the component processes are conditioning-like concepts. The two primary processes of the theory are unlearning and competition-at-recall. In addition, there are two supplementary processes, spontaneous recovery and list differentiation, that may interact with the primary processes at varying points along retention intervals. An excellent analysis of these component processes, together with a systematic review of the related research with young adult subjects, appeared recently (Keppel, 1968), and only a cursory overview of classical interference theory will be attempted here.

Unlearning for the experimental subjects of RI and PI list sequences is, like negative transfer, the product of interference generated by *B-C* competition during List 2 practice. Unlearning is defined as the unavailability of List 1 R units (*B* terms in RI and *C* terms in PI) on a recall session that follows the cessation of List 2 practice. The baseline for establishing the amount of unlearning directly attributable to *B-C* interference is provided by the recall scores of the control subjects (the only list condition for both RI and PI). Lower recall scores for experimental than for control subjects, however, may reflect competition-at-recall in addition to, or even instead of, unlearning qua unlearning. Competition-at-recall, as the name indicates, refers to the restoration of *B-C* competition at the time recall is tested. List 1 R units may be latently available for recall, but the competition between *B* and *C* terms blocks their overt evocation during a paced recall test. Even on an unpaced recall test, a subject's measured availability of R units may be reduced by his inability to differentiate between lists when the instructions request the recall of only one specific set of R units (either List 1 or List 2). Methodologically, the problem of separating true unlearning from the "noise" created by competition-at-recall and the failure to differentiate between lists was largely solved by the introduction of the "modified modified" free recall (MMFR) task (Barnes & Underwood, 1959; cf. Melton, 1961, for the origin of the term). Both competition-at-recall and difficulty of differentiating between lists are presumed to be eliminated in the MMFR task by having subjects recall, without time limit, both R units (i.e., both B and C) that had been paired with each S unit (i.e., A term).

By means of the MMFR procedure Barnes and Underwood (1959) were able to give seemingly unconfounded evidence for the unlearning of List 1 R units in young adult subjects. Furthermore, the comparison between MMFR scores and paced recall scores for the same set of R units provides an indirect measure of the amount of forgetting (either RI or PI) that is attributable to the composite processes of competition-at-recall and failure to differentiate between lists. Paced recall scores measure the effects of both unlearning and the competition-differentiation composite, and subtracting from these scores the estimate of unlearning provided by MMFR scores should yield a remainder stemming only from the competition-differentiation composite. Recent studies by Houston (1966, 1967, 1968) that have employed this comparison between MMFR and paced recall scores have led to the conclusion that the effects of the competition-differentiation composite process in young adult subjects may be negligible for both RI and PI.

These recent studies by Houston support the notion that RI in young adults is exclusively the consequence of unlearning and spontaneous recovery. Within the context of interference theory, the amount of RI is expected to be greatest immediately after List 2 practice and then decrease with time over the retention interval. Improved retention in the experimental group after a period of time follows from the expected spontaneous recovery of at least some of the unlearned A-B associations. Although the evidence for spontaneous recovery over long-term retention intervals is equivocal (Keppel, 1968), a recent study by Postman, Stark, and Fraser (1968) does offer convincing evidence for the reality of spontaneous recovery over briefer time intervals (30 minutes or less). Unlearning linked to interference from laboratory-acquired A-C associations is not the only source of unlearning to be considered. Additional unlearning produced by uncontrolled encounters with verbal materials during the retention interval should occur in roughly equal amounts for the experimental group and the control group. This extralaboratory unlearning accounts in part for the decrease in recall scores commonly found for the control group as the length of the retention interval increases, and it may also account for the failure to find spontaneous recovery of unlearned List 1 associations over longer time intervals (that is, the added unlearning cancels out any gain in recall from spontaneous recovery). Finally, contemporary interference theory also places considerable emphasis on preexperimental linguistic habits as a source of interference and unlearning for both experimental and control groups (see Section IV,C,2).

PI is generally found to be zero immediately after List 2 practice (Keppel, 1968). Absence of PI here means equal *A-B* recall scores for the experimental group (List 2 recall) and the control group (only list recall), whether recall is measured by the MMFR test or by a paced recall test. Equality of recall is to be expected in that the recall measure follows immediately after the experimental and control groups have attained the same criterion of *A-B* acquisition. However, this criterion is reached by experimental subjects after overcoming the effects of competition from *A-C* (List 1) associations during List 2 practice, and some degree of unlearning of these competing *A-C* associations, accompanies mastery of the new *A-B* pairs. At the time of immediate recall, the *A-B* associations for experimental subjects have achieved dominance over the now weaker *A-C* associations, and competition-at-recall should be minimal. Classical interference theory explains subsequent increases in PI as the retention interval increases by the spontaneous recovery of these unlearned *A-C* associations and the restoration of competition at the time of a delayed recall test. Unlearning therefore plays only an indirect role in PI, rather than a direct role as in RI, and competition-at-recall is clearly the primary process identified by classical interference theory as the causal mechanism for PI after long-term retention intervals. In theory then, long-term PI should not exist when List 2 recall is measured by the "competition-free" MMFR task. And yet long-term PI has been clearly demonstrated with MMFR tasks (Houston, 1967), and, in fact, in amounts comparable to the amounts found with paced recall tests. One solution to the dilemma facing interference theorists is to question the widely held assumption that the MMFR task is truly competition-free and then return to the drawing board for further methodological innovations (Keppel, 1968). A second, and more plausible solution is to accept the notion, alluded to earlier, that *young adult subjects* are largely free of interference from competing associations during recall at any point along the retention interval. This is tantamount to accepting the hypothesis that the selector mechanism of young adults readily permits rejection of intruding associations from List 1 in terms of identifying these associations as being inappropriate for the recall task at hand.

Acceptance of the above hypothesis necessarily reduces the nomological network for PI, at least as it applies to young adults, to a single process—unlearning. Of course, with other, more interference prone, populations, competition-at-recall may take on much greater significance as a causal mechanism for PI. At any rate, a complete reliance on unlearning forces the addition of a new dimension to the concept of unlearning as it enters into PI effects (Houston, 1967, 1968). This new dimension is the uncontrolled rehearsal during the retention interval of those *A-C* associations that resisted unlearning during List 2 practice. Having resisted unlearning, these *A-C* associations are likely to represent a homogeneous class of strong associations. On the other hand, the to-be-retained *A-B* associations are likely to be more heterogeneous with regard to associative strength. Weak *A-B* assocations that happen to have strong *A-C* counterparts are the ones likely to be unlearned via uncontrolled rehearsal of List 1 associations. The net result is an increase in PI across the retention interval, an increase that is, of course, commonly reported in the research literature (Keppel, 1968). The temporal variations in RI and PI described above are presented graphically in Figure 4.

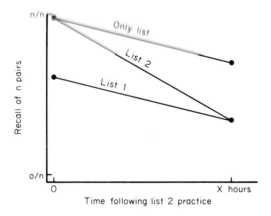

Figure 4. Recall of List 1, List 2, and the only list in retroactive inhibition (RI) and proactive inhibition (PI). RI equals the difference in recall between List 1 and the only list; PI equals the difference in recall between List 2 and the only list.

B. Developmental Trends in RI and PI

1. *Relevance of Interference Theory to Age Variations in RI and PI*

In Section III the concept of interference proneness as an age-sensitive process related to the efficacy of the selector mechanism during response competition was introduced, and suggestions were given for testing the concept independently of RI and PI effects. To the extent that such tests reliably demonstrate age variations in proneness and, moreover, demonstrate significant interactions between age and other processes (e.g., stimulus selection) related to proneness, interference theory takes on added importance for explaining developmental trends in RI and PI. As noted earlier, there is little direct research bearing on the important question of age-sensitivity to interference. In this section we will discover that there has also been little research directed toward developmentally correlated changes in either RI or PI. The present discussion will therefore concentrate on predicted trends in RI and PI that follow from the implicit assumption of an age-interference covariation. The mere presence of RI and PI, like the mere presence of negative transfer, in other-than-young-adult populations is of little interest; what is of concern is variation with age in amount of RI and/or PI. Where possible, relevant research will, or course, be cited.

2. *Further Consideration of the Degree of Learning Problem*

Before extending the network of interference theory to include RI and PI phenomena in children and the elderly, we need to return briefly to the critical methodological problem of assuring equal degrees of learning at each age for the to-be-retained list (List 1 in RI and List 2 in PI). Increasing degrees of List 1 learning have been found to yield increasing resistance to *A-B* unlearning as measured by the MMFR task for young adult subjects (e.g., Birnbaum, 1965), and a similar degree—unlearning relationship is to be expected for populations of any given age. For any given age level, the most direct test of this expectancy is to contrast MMFR scores taken immediately after List 2 practice for experimental groups differing in degree of List 1 practice (e.g., to criterion only versus varying degrees of overlearning beyond criterion) with MMFR scores taken after equal-time neutral activity for only list control groups. In one of the few studies employing the MMFR task on children, Loomis and Hall (1968) found, for both kindergarten and second grade groups, a significantly positive relationship between degree of List 1 practice and MMFR scores for List 1. The absence in this study of only list control groups prohibits a firm conclusion that *A-B* unlearning itself was caused by interference from the competing *A-C* associations of List 2. Nevertheless, the inference that increased degrees of List 1 learning led to increased resistance to unlearning at both age levels seems reasonable. Loomis and Hall also found significantly higher MMFR scores at each degree of List 1 learning for second graders than for kindergarten subjects, a superiority they attributed to the faster rate of learning, hence greater associative strength, in the former group. Thus age and amount of unlearning are likely to be correlated through their common correlation with degree of learning. If the primary interest of the researcher is age-sensitive processes in RI other than degree of learning, it will greatly behoove him to equalize List 1 learning for each age level employed.

At first glance the problem of an age-degree-of-learning bias seems less serious for PI research than for RI research. The bias, when present, operates from correlated changes in *unlearning*, and classical interference theory postulates that unlearning has only an indirect effect on PI (Section IV,A). However, a current view of PI cited earlier (Houston, 1967, 1968) suggests that PI may be more directly contingent upon unlearning (via uncontrolled rehearsal of List 1 associations during the retention interval) than had been previously assumed. Consequently, the assurance of equal degrees of learning for List 2 across age levels in PI research seems to be just as important as the same assurance for List 1 in RI research. Postman and Stark (1964) have discussed the issues involved when groups differ in their rates of learning on List 2 and have offered several alternatives for solving the problem.

3. RI in Children and Elderly Subjects

Interference theory identifies unlearning to be the primary process responsible for whatever RI is found immediately after List 2 practice. Even with equal degrees of List 1 learning, different age groups should vary in amount of immediate RI—if the groups also vary in interference proneness. Unlearning, as an extinction-like process, is the product of the nonreinforced evocation of List 1 R units during practice on List 2. Control over the evocation of these incorrect R units is a major function of the selector mechanism, a mechanism defined as the ability to inhibit an inappropriate class of responses (see Section III,C,3). Variability in the inhibition of inappropriate responses then represents the dimension of interference proneness. The potency of variation in interference proneness on RI has been demonstrated in a number of studies, but all of these studies have been on young adults. For example, Postman, Keppel, and Stark (1965) found that RI was greater when the R units of the two lists came from the same form class (e.g., adjectives) than when the units came from different classes (e.g., adjectives and letters). The selector mechanism is presumed to be more proficient in the latter case where the change in form class permits a readily discriminable cue for inhibiting List 1 R units. With task materials kept constant, age-sensitive interference proneness implies that a similar change in the proficiency of the selector mechanism accompanies changes in chronological age. Increasing proficiency of the selector mechanism should, in turn, lead to decreasing amounts of RI found immediately after the termination of List 2 practice.

If young children are less proficient than older children in inhibiting competing responses (White, 1965), then the amount of evocation, and concomitant unlearning, of A-B (List 1) associations should be inversely related to age for at least the four- to eight-years segment of the age continuum. Loomis and Hall (1968) did find less List 1 recall immediately after List 2 practice for their kindergarten group than for their second grade group, in agreement with the inverse relationship hypothesis, but, as already noted, the difference in rates of learning between the two groups obscured the interpretation of their finding. More importantly, their transfer findings in the same study indicated greater negative transfer in the second grade than in the kindergarten group, the antithesis of what is to be expected if kindergarten children are indeed less proficient than older children in inhibiting competing responses. However, there is evidence with young adult subjects which indicates that the amount of A-B unlearning and the amount of A-C negative transfer do not always correlate. Goulet and Bone (1968), in an extension of the Postman *et al.* (1965) study, again found less RI for a change in form class of B and C terms than for a continuation of the same form class, but they also found that the amount of negative transfer was invariant with respect to the nature of the form class relationship. It is conceivable that a similar lack of correlation may be found when the proficiency of the selector mechanism is altered by developmental level rather than by task variables, like that of form class. Second-grade children may have the capacity for inhibiting competing A-B associations, but the operation of the mechanism may require an amount of time that is large enough to cut drastically into the total time available for rehearsing the new A-C pairs. Kindergarten children, on the other hand, may not be inhibiting the competing A-B associations at all, and they may continue to evoke, overtly or covertly, the A-B associations during List 2 practice until they are gradually unlearned by rote nonreinforcement. The net result would be nearly equal amounts of negative transfer at the two age levels, but much less RI at the second grade than at the kindergarten level.

Tests of the above hypothesis require an extension of the Loomis and Hall study that follows the basic design of the Goulet and Bone study, and also assures equal degrees of A-B learning for each age level. The design calls for the inclusion of both transfer control groups (i.e., A-B, C-D Groups) and RI control groups (i.e., A-B only list groups). RI and negative transfer may be simultaneously measured with this design, and valid comparisons may be made between age levels on both measures of response inhibition.

The presence of developmental trends in RI beyond the initial post-List-2-recall period is a function of several factors. The first factor, spontaneous recovery of unlearned A-B associations over time should reduce the amount of RI, and it should also yield an absolute increase in A-B recall in the experimental group of the RI paradigm, contingent upon the extent of interference produced by extralaboratory sources (see Section IV,A). As far as this reviewer can determine, there has been no research directed toward tests of spontaneous recovery in either children or elderly subjects. Such tests require measurements of A-B recall at various temporal intervals, beginning with the initial post-List-2 measurement as the baseline. However, spontaneous recovery in young adults after periods of hours and days is doubtful, and there is no reason to suspect that other age groups would be either more or less "spontaneous recovery prone" than young adults. The second factor is the degree of extralaboratory interference unlearning encountered by experimental and control groups at any given age level. Although the degree of extralaboratory interference may well vary as a function of age, there is no reason to suspect that unlearning due to these sources would differ for the experimental and control groups at any one age level. Consequently, this factor should not contribute to developmental trends in RI when RI is defined in terms of the usual experimental-control group contrast. The remaining factor is that of competition-at-recall and the resultant competition-differentiation composite process discussed earlier. Research on young adults has consistently shown that B (List 1) and C (List 2) availablilty converge after a sufficiently long retention interval, thereby confronting subjects with two responses of equal strength to each *A* stimulus (Keppel, 1968). Although this situation seems ideal for activating the competition-differentiation composite process, young adults are, nevertheless, free of interference from this source. However, a similar freedom does not necessarily apply to other age levels where the concept of increased interference proneness remains a viable issue. What is obviously needed in developmental-retention research is a systematic test of age differences in competition-at-recall by the same method that has served effectively as the test for its presence in young adults, namely, contrasting recall obtained by the MMFR task (measuring unlearning only) with recall obtained by the paced task (measuring unlearning and competition).

An important study by Koppenaal, Krull, and Katz (1964) provides partial answers to questions about the relative effects of the above factors in determining long-term RI trends for children ranging in age from four to eight years. Specifically, three age groups (four, five, and eight years old) were tested for *A-B* recall (List 1 for the experimental group and the only list for the control group at each age level) after a retention interval of twenty-four hours by means of both the MMFR and paced recall tasks. In addition, the age groups differed only slightly on trials to criterion in the original learning of the to-be-retained list. Even this slight difference was corrected for a potential bias by an appropriate technique (Underwood, 1964b), and the study is one of the few in the developmental-retention area that is free of the differential degree of learning problem.

Their data revealed significant amounts of RI for the eight- and five-year-old groups, but not for the four-year-old group, when recall was measured by a paced task. In fact, the mean *A-B* recall for the four-year-old group exceeded slightly the comparable means for both the five- and eight-year-old groups (with the latter two means being identical). Unfortunately, the study did not include a condition in which recall was measured at each age level immediately after termination of List 2 practice (or after an equal period of neutral activity in the control groups). It is therefore difficult to interpret precisely the source of the peculiar finding of no RI at the youngest age level. One possible interpretation is that the amount of unlearning during List 2 practice was greatest in the youngest group and least in the oldest group, in agreement with the hypothesized positive relationship between age and the proficiency of the selector mechanism. Acceptance of this position requires the inference that B terms were less available for recall immediately after List 2 practice in their four-year-old than in their eight-year-old group, an inference that is supported by the recall data of the Loomis and Hall (1968) study reported earlier. The difference in recall after twenty-four hours could then be explained by postulating a maximum amount of spontaneous recovery of unlearned A-B associations at the youngest age level, with the amount of recovery being progressively less with increasing age. As noted earlier, a developmental trend in spontaneous recovery is unlikely, and the first interpretation is unlikely to receive empirical support.

A second interpretation is that the amount of unlearning during List 2 practice was equal across age levels, but the amount of extralaboratory interference unlearning was unequal across age levels. Specifically, this interpretation postulates less extralaboratory interference unlearning in four-year-old subjects than in older subjects, and, moreover, less interference-unlearning for four-year-old subjects in the experimental condition than in the control condition. Again, we have already indicated the unlikelihood of this kind of interaction, and the second interpretation needs to be rejected.

A third interpretation has in common with the second the postulation of equal amounts of RI immediately after List 2 practice for all age levels. The difference in interpretation rests in the locus of inequality between age levels. The locus here becomes competition-at-recall, a process of minor importance in determining RI effects for young adults. The process as applied here calls for a relationship between age and interference proneness that is the reverse of the usual proneness hypothesis. Young children would be viewed as being less prone to competition-at-recall than older children. The hypothesis is in agreement with the Loomis and Hall (1968) study in which negative transfer, a general index of interference proneness, was found to be greater for second grade subjects than for kindergarten subjects. The present reviewer, however, feels that this explanation is untenable. It is tantamount to viewing the selector mechanism as deteriorating with age, a trend that seems inconsistent with other evidence regarding the development of cognitive processes. In addition, the MMFR data provided by Koppenaal *et al.* (1964) obviate the reliance on the competition-at-recall process. They found that their MMFR means were not greatly superior to their paced recall means, a finding that strongly suggests that unlearning accounted for most, if not all, of the RI reported.

A fourth, and final, interpretation is the one strongly preferred here. It accepts the concept of a production deficiency in the verbal mediation of young children (see Section III,C2), and therefore accepts the concept that young children are unlikely, unless specifically guided otherwise, to employ verbal mediators to bridge the gap between S and R units of PA tasks. The B terms of List 1 for experimental subjects are therefore unlikely to persist during List 2 practice in vain attempts to employ them as links between A and C terms. Older children, however, should display self-produced attempts at mediating the A to C associative gap. The just learned B terms from List 1 are likely to be high priority choices for mediators, but the deliberate selection of B terms that are unrelated to C terms negates the effectiveness of their mediating capacity. Flavell (1970) has noted that the development of mnemonic-mediational activity is partly a function of the child's ability to "home in" on an effective activity for a given task. Six- to eight-year-old children may well attempt to mediate A-C learning, but the mnemonic selected is simply not effective for the task at hand. Four-year-old children should make better use of their selector mechanism than eight-year-old children in the sense of permitting an earlier inhibition of B terms during List 2 practice and, coincidentally, a greater protection of the B terms from unlearning. This principle may be operative even though the optimal proficiency of the selector mechanism may well be greater in the older group. The pattern calls for less RI in four-year-old than in six- to eight-year-old children at both immediate (post-List 2) and delayed recall (e.g., after one day) periods. With still older children the irrelevance of B terms to mediate A-C associations should become more apparent, and the overall increment in the proficiency of the selector mechanism should now manifest itself by improved inhibition of B terms and the concomitant improved protection of B terms from unlearning.

There is an important supplementary process that adds to the predicted drop in RI amounts beyond the age range of six to eight years. Older children, with their more elaborate preexperimental associative networks, are likely to form more stable mediating chains during List 1 learning than are six- to eight-year-old children. In Section III,C,2 it was pointed out that research on young adult subjects revealed strikingly less forgetting for associations learned via mediators than for associations learned rotely (although the effect may be attributable to differential degrees of original learning rather than to a direct mediation-retention relationship). Specifically, stable mediators between A and B terms of List 1 increase markedly resistance to unlearning during practice on the interfering A-C pairs of List 2 in RI designs, and this positive attribute of retention should become of increasingly greater importance during the later years of childhood. The overall developmental pattern suggests a curvilinear trend between age and amounts of RI across the years of childhood. The developmental trend in unlearning and the resultant developmental trend in amount of RI over retention intervals are illustrated in Figure 5. The one bit of conflicting evidence for the hypothesis is the finding of Loomis and Hall (1968) that immediate recall of experimental A-B pairs was greater for second grade than for kindergarten subjects. The discrepancy, however, is the likely consequence of the greater associative strength of A-B pairs for the former group at the onset of List 2 practice. Tests of the hypothesis will require guidance techniques that overcome the production-deficiency for mediating List 2 learning present at the young age levels.

The raw frequency of studies contrasting amounts of RI for young and

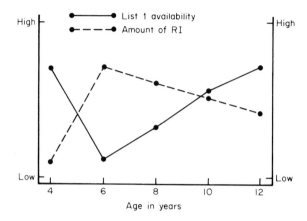

Figure 5. Hypothetical relationship between age and List 1 availability (unlearning effect) and between age and amount of RI. Unlearning of List 1 pairs during practice on List 2 is viewed as being the primary mechanism of RI.

elderly adults is greater than that of studies making similar contrasts for varying ages of childhood. However, the gerontological studies have characteristically employed methodologies that prohibit an effective analysis of the processes contributing to age differences, if any, in RI. The main thrust of these studies has been the simple objective of demonstrating whether or not RI for elderly populations does exceed that for younger populations. Some studies (e.g., Arenberg, 1967) have found greater RI in elderly subjects, whereas other studies (e.g., Gladis & Braun, 1958; Hulicka, 1967) have found no difference in RI between elderly and younger subjects. Undoubtedly, an insidious factor in these studies is the degree of success attained in equating groups on associative strength during List 1 learning. The methods employed, analysis of covariance (Gladis & Braun, 1958) and trials to a common criterion for all groups (Hulicka, 1967), are not entirely satisfactory, and much of the work in this area needs repetition with associative strength being equated by the methods recommended by Underwood (1964b). Another methodological problem is the absence of the MMFR task in gerontological research, despite the advisability of including both MMFR and paced recall measures of RI in the same study. Consequently, when RI is found to be greater in elderly than in young adults on paced recall measures only, it is impossible to determine if the outcome represents greater unlearning or greater competition-at-recall, or both, in the elderly. Similarly the common use of only one retention interval in each experiment, usually an interval in which the paced recall task follows shortly after List 2 practice in the experimental groups, makes it impossible to determine age differences in spontaneous recovery, delayed competition-at-recall, and susceptibility to extralaboratory interference and unlearning.

Thus there are virtually no data available that permit analyses of contrasts between elderly and younger adults in the amount of RI over varying retention intervals, nor are there data that permit analyses of the processes which would account for any observed disparity in RI patterns for elderly and younger adults. In view of the self-produced mediational deficit in the elderly (see Section III,C,2), it would not be surprising to discover that the course of RI over retention intervals follows closely the course charted above for six- to eight-year-old children. That is, RI is expected to be greater in the elderly than in younger adults, starting with the post-List-2 recall period and continuing until that point in time where recall for the experimental and control groups converge. The culprits leading to greater amounts of RI in the elderly are again hypothesized to be the unstable mediators used during the original learning of List 1 A-B associations, with decreased resistance to A-B unlearning during A-C practice as the consequence, and the crude attempts to insert the irrelevant B terms as intermediate links in the learning of the new A-C associations. Given the inadequacy of past research on RI phenomena in elderly populations, evidence in support of this hypothesis can be gleaned only from future investigations which manipulate mediational variables like instructions and guidance, in combination with the effective use of the methodological factors cited earlier.

4. PI in Children and Elderly Subjects

Interference theory has been gradually abandoning its classical positions that PI is the direct consequence of the competition-differentiation composite of processes and that the unlearning-spontaneous recovery composite of processes contributes to PI only indirectly through variation in strength of the competing A-C (List 1 in the PI design) associations at the time of A-B (List 2) recall. The prima facie evidence for this excision of competition-at-recall comes from the failure to find differences in A-B recall as measured by MMFR and paced recall tests (see Section IV,A). There is some evidence for accepting the generalization that competition-at-recall is similarly ineffectual for instigating PI over retention intervals in children as well. Koppenaal *et al.* (1964) included tests of age differences in PI, along with their tests of age difference in RI. They failed to find pronounced differences at any age level studied between A-B recall as measured by MMFR and A-B recall as measured by a paced recall trial. The lack of simultaneously gathered MMFR and paced recall scores for post-college-age subjects limits further developmental generalization of the demise of the competition process. However, there is no a priori reason for viewing the senescent end of the age continuum as introducing either a qualitative or a quantitative difference in inhibitory mechanisms that would distinguish them from the inhibitory mechanisms of, say, four- or five-year-old children. Consequently, the present view accepts the notion that competition-at-recall is a negligible factor in determining age-related changes in PI effects across the entire developmental continuum (but it would be comforting to see future research supporting the conjecture).

The burden for explaining PI changes over retention intervals has fallen on the ever-broadening shoulders of the unlearning process. Here the process has been broadened to place the responsibility for PI on the unlearning of *A-B* (List 2 associations) by the spontaneous and uncontrolled rehearsal of those *A-C* (List 1 associations) that were strong enough to resist unlearning during List 2 practice. An account of age-related trends in PI across retention intervals must then be based entirely on this revised version of the unlearning process.

Assuming that both List 2 for the experimental group and the only list for the control group have been learned to the same criterion, PI should be zero immediately after List 2 (or only list) practice, regardless of the age level being investigated. Moreover, the absolute amount of immediate recall should be invariant with respect to age, again assuming that the list has been learned to the same degree at each age level. After a retention interval, the amount of PI is contingent upon the number and strength of *A-C* associations that have resisted unlearning during List 2 practice and the extent of spontaneous rehearsal of these associations during the retention interval. Young children (four or five years old), for reasons cited earlier, should have more *A-C* associations available for spontaneous rehearsal than slightly older children (six to eight years old, or thereabouts), but the availability dimension should swing upwards again for still older children. Similarly, young to middle-aged adults should have more *A-C* associations available for rehearsal than elderly adults. The real obstacle to formulating predictions about developmental trends in PI over retention intervals occurs in the admittedly vague concept of spontaneous or uncontrolled rehearsal. An attempt to measure the amount of rehearsal within the context of a long-term retention interval presents a recalcitrant, if not hopeless, methodological problem. An effective alternative may be to bypass the long-term paradigm completely and to rely instead on the method introduced by Flavell and his associates (e.g., Keeney *et al.*, 1967) for assessing spontaneous rehearsal in serial short-term memory. The experimenter simply counts the amount of spontaneous rehearsal as indexed by lip movements, etc. occurring during the brief retention interval and then partitions subjects into categories of "producers" and "nonproducers" of spontaneous rehearsal on the basis of the counts. The method seems especially adaptable to long-term retention research over the four- to eight-year-old age range, and perhaps the sensecent period as well. Older children and younger adults are unlikely to give such "lip service," and their spontaneous rehearsal activity should occur at the covert level only. The extension to long-term PI research calls for prior identification of "producers" and "nonproducers" at each age level investigated by means of the serial short-term memory task, and then the introduction of the traditional long-term PI design. Of primary concern is the interaction between age and category on the course of RI over the retention interval.

Evidence from research on production deficiency (see Section III,C,2) clearly indicates that the preponderance of four- and five-year-old children are nonproducers of spontaneous rehearsal. Consequently, subjects at this age level are expected to display little PI at delayed retention tests, even though the number of *A-C* associations latently available for rehearsal may be high. On the other hand, the preponderance of six- to eight-year-old subjects are producers of spontaneous rehearsal, and significant amount of delayed PI should be evident at these age levels, despite the expected decrement in the number of *A-C* associations that are latently available for rehearsal. This pattern of age-related changes in PI is in agreement with the PI component of the study by Koppenaal *et al.* (1964). After twenty-four hours, significant PI was found for their eight-year-old group, but not for their five- and four-year-old groups. Unlike RI, the amount of PI should show a further increment for still older children through the expected increase in the availability of *A-C* associations (as protected from unlearning during List 2 practice by their more stable mediated learning) for spontaneous rehearsal. Moreover, the expected decline in spontaneous rehearsal by the elderly leads to the surprising conclusion that PI, unlike RI, should be less pronounced after retention intervals in the elderly than in younger adults. Empirical tests of PI in the elderly seem to be nonexistent, and it is impossible to cite evidence either for or against any hypothesis that could be made concerning PI trends during senescence.

Developmental trends in the processes hypothesized to determine age variation in PI over retention intervals are summarized in Figure 6, together with the expected pattern in age-related changes in amount of PI. As described above,

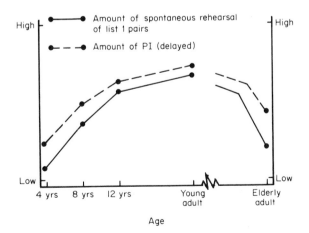

Figure 6. Hypothetical relationship between age and spontaneous rehearsal of List 1 pairs during the retention interval and between age and amount of PI on a delayed retention test. The unlearning of List 2 pairs by the uncontrolled rehearsal of List 1 pairs during the retention interval is viewed as being the primary mechanism of PI.

effective tests of the hypothesized trends consist of isolating in advance producers of spontaneous rehearsal at those age levels, namely early childhood and late adulthood, where the preponderance of individuals consists of nonproducers. Subgroups identified to be producers should conform to the PI profile characteristic of other age levels, namely older children and younger adults, in which spontaneous rehearsal is a dominant attribute.

C. Extensions of Interference Theory and Their Developmental Implications

1. Further Analysis of the Unlearning Process

The preceding discussion of interference theory made it very clear that the contemporary version of the theory is far from being static. Thinking regarding the basic processes of the theory has kept pace with the challenging demands of new experimental evidence. Through such evidence, the unlearning process has attained its present status of being the primary process in the theory's account of both RI and PI phenomena. However, questions have been raised by theorists regarding the basic nature of the unlearning process. One of these questions is "What is it that is unlearned during practice on an interfering list?" At times we have referred to the unlearning of associations, and at other times we have referred to the unavailability of responses. The dual use of the unlearning concept is derived from McGovern's (1964) analysis of associative interference into separable list-based and context-based components (see Section II,C,1). For example, unlearning for List 1 of an *A-B, A-C* sequence consists of both the unlearning of the specific *A-B* associations and the unlearning of the context-*B* associations. The latter form of unlearning amounts to the unavailability of List 1 R units.

Recent studies (e.g., Postman *et al.*, 1968; Sandak & Garskof, 1967) with college-age subjects which have measured unlearning by means of associative matching tasks have suggested that List 1 associations per se are relatively untouched by interference during List 2 practice and are highly resistant to unlearning. Thus the so-called *A-B* unlearning demonstrated by the standard MMFR and paced recall tasks is mainly the decreased availability of the *B* response units. The distinction between associative unlearning and response availability closely parallels the distinction made in information processing theory between the storage and the retrieval of information. Information that remains stored in memory may, nevertheless, be lost from recall by the unavailability of appropriate retrieval channels. Translated to an *A-B, A-C* interference-unlearning relationship, the *B* terms remain stored in memory to a considerable degree following List 2 practice, but access to the terms is blocked. The associative matching task is apparently an effective means of retrieving this stored information.

Postman *et al.* (1968) have contributed substantially to the identification of the process blocking the retrieval of *B* immediately after the cessation of List 2 practice. This blocking is considered to be a major source of the *A-B* "unlearning" that is observed on the MMFR test. Their experimental analysis provides strong support for the presence of inertia in the subject's selector mechanism. The inertia is in the form of a response set, established during List 2 learning, to inhibit the occurrence of List 1 R units. The inhibitory set continues into the period immediately following List 2 practice, and performance on an immediate recall test tends to overestimate the amount of List 1 unlearning, conceived in terms of loss from storage. Postman *et al.* also found that the inhibitory response set dissipates over the first twenty to thirty minutes following List 2 practice, thus allowing for the "spontaneous recovery" of those *B* terms that remained available for recall (i.e., in storage) but were blocked (i.e., not retrieved) by the generalized set to inhibit List 1 R units. Their findings suggest that the gradient of RI for young adults over retention intervals is likely to be greater if the "immediate" measure of List 1 recall is taken after the inhibitory set has been dissipated.

The study by Postman *et al.* deserves careful replication at various age levels. Conceivably the inertia quality of the selector mechanism may be age-sensitive, and developmental trends in RI may, in part, be influenced by an age-inertia covariation. For example, it is possible that the greater post-List-2 recall of *A-B* associations for second grade than for kindergarten subjects (Loomis & Hall, 1968 see Section IV,B,3) is the consequence of greater inertia in the latter group. This interpretation posits a positive correlation between the amount of inertia and age from the kindergarten through young adult period, and future research on retention-development relationships should be cognizant of this possibility. Similarly, future developmental research should make effective use of the associative matching task as an important supplement to the MMFR and paced recall tasks. There are no available data which have teased apart the unavailability of *B* terms from the actual unlearning of *A-B* associations in other than young adult subjects. The existence of age-related differences in the relative contributions of these sources of unlearning remains an important question for future research.

A second question about the unlearning process concerns its contribution to RI and PI effects in paradigms other than the specific *A-B, A-C* phenotype. Of special significance is the concept of unlearning as it applies to the *A-B, C-B* paradigm, the prototype for disjunctive concept learning. We have earlier identified the source of interference-unlearning for this paradigm to be in the competition, during List 2 practice, between the R-S associations of the two lists. There is ample evidence with young adults to indicate the unlearning of List 1 R-S (i.e., *B-A*) associations during practice on *C-B* pairs (Ellington & Kausler, 1965; Keppel & Underwood, 1962b). In fact, the course of unlearning over varying numbers of List 2 trials for R-S associations closely parallels that found for S-R unlearning by Barnes and Underwood (1959; cf. Ellington & Kausler, 1965), thus suggesting the comparability of R-S unlearning processes to S-R unlearning processes. The key question, however, is the dependency of S-R associations upon the fate of their R-S counterparts. Does unlearning of *B-A* (*R-S*) associations mean that *A-B* (S-R) associations have also been unlearned— and to the same extent? If the answer is in the affirmative, RI and PI phenomena for the *A-B, C-B* list sequence should be much like those found for the standard *A-B, A-C* sequence. The question of the mutual dependency of the fates of S-R and R-S associations remains a largely unresolved problem with young adult subjects (e.g., Johnston, 1967, 1968). Eventually, researchers in the area of retention-development will have to grope with the complicated dependency issue as a possible age-sensitive phenomenon. That is, the degree of independence between S-R and R-S associations may well vary with age, even if the absolute amount of R-S learning remains invariant with age.

2. *Extraexperimental Interference*

The forgetting of a single list is considered by classical interference theory to be a special case of RI. Here the single list functions as an experimental *A-B* List 1, and extralaboratory experience during the retention interval is the functional equivalent of an *A-C* List 2. The retention loss for the single list is explained by the same generic classes of processes that enter into explanations of completely laboratory-bound RI phenomena. An understanding of forgetting for a single list is, of course, essential for interference theory in that a single list serves as the baseline for evaluating experimentally produced RI and PI phenomena. Interference theory's affinity toward the forgetting of a single list is greatly accentuated by the fact that it epitomizes the general kind of forgetting that takes place in everyday living. Most everyday learning consists of learning single sets of materials. These sets are not ordinarily succeeded immediately by the learning of new sets that conform to the contrived interference lists of experimental RI paradigms. However, other similar materials are likely to be encountered eventually during the hours or days that pass before recall of the original material is called for, and these are the naturally occurring counterparts of an *A-C* list.

The adequacy of the RI analogy for explaining single list forgetting has been seriously questioned during the past decade by interference theorists themselves. The questioning began with Underwood's (1957b) insightful reexamination of the data from past experiments on the forgetting of single lists. Underwood's analysis of these data revealed a striking positive covariation between the amount of observed forgetting and the number of lists the subject had learned in the laboratory prior to the to-be-retained list. The covariation strongly suggested the inference that PI, rather than RI, is the major factor to be considered in explaining single list forgetting. That is, single list forgetting is propagated more by prior *A-C* experience than by interpolated *A-C* experiences. The significance of this inference is apparent in Postman's (1961) statement that:

Perhaps the single most important recent development in interference theory is the increasing recognition of proactive inhibition as a mechanism of interference. The major value of this development lies in the fact that it has provided us with a new purchase on the analysis of long-term forgetting outside the laboratory [p. 166].

The recognition of PI's importance in single list forgetting for sophisticated subjects does not absolve interference theory from identifying the sources of interference in the forgetting, usually around 20% after twenty-four hours, of single lists by naïve subjects. Underwood and Postman (1960), in an innovative extension of classical interference theory, reasoned beautifully that the subject's own extraexperimental linguistic associations are the logical choices for such interference. Specifically, they identified two linguistic sources, letter-sequence interference and unit-sequence interference, which may compete with the new sequences of linguistic habits demanded by a set of new learning materials. Briefly, the extraexperimental sequences are "unlearned" during the learning of the new material, but the "unlearned" sequences recover over time (spontaneous recovery) and compete with the new sequences at the time of recall. The inability to find support for either spontaneous recovery or competition-at-recall independently of the extra experimental situation casts some doubt about certain aspects of the extraexperimental analysis (See Section IV,A,1). In addition, direct experimental attacks have not been very rewarding in their efforts to offer evidence for the operation of letter-sequence and unit-sequence interferences in young adult subjects (Underwood & Ekstrand, 1966). Nevertheless, the concepts are intuitively appealing, especially in terms of suggesting hypotheses about developmental trends in single list retention (and "outside of the laboratory" retention). Variation in linguistic experience along the age continuum offers a natural laboratory for tests of extraexperimental hypotheses, tests which should be of great interest to developmental and verbal learning psychologists alike. There has been surprisingly little, if any, attempt to take advantage of this natural laboratory opportunity. It should be noted, however, that the results of the Koppenaal *et al.* (1964) study were interpreted by the authors themselves as providing support for extra experimental sources as the medium for age-related differences in forgetting. As indicated earlier (Sections IV,B,3 and IV,B,4), the present reviewer prefers alternative explanations which seem to be more consistent with other available bits of information.

3. Short-Term Memory

The scope and intent of the present review has necessarily forced the exclusion of developmental trends in short-term memory. The general problem area of short-term memory is, of course, a "hot" topic in contemporary psychology, and developmental trends in short-term memory throughout the age continuum have received a healthy amount of both theoretical and empirical attention. Many of the phenomena found in short-term memory seem to be better understood within the rubric of either decay theory (e.g., J. Brown, 1958; Conrad, 1967) or limited capacity theory (e.g., Murdock, 1964) than within the rubric of interference theory. Nevertheless, there is an impressive amount of evidence for the presence of interference processes, akin to those found in long-term retention, in a wide range of short-term phenomena. An interference theory analysis has succeeded in identifying both RI (Corman & Wickens, 1968) and PI (Keppel & Underwood, 1962a; Wickens, Born, & Allen, 1963) for short-term memory. The present section closes with the recommendation that developmentally oriented researchers consider seriously the replication of these analyses on both children and aging populations. Such replications are likely to provide valuable insights into age-related changes in memory.

V. RETENTION-DEVELOPMENT RELATIONSHIPS FOR RECOGNITION LEARNING

A. Processes of Recognition Learning

The preceding sections of this review concentrated almost entirely on the PA methodological paradigm. This concentration is indicative of the paradigm's overwhelming dominance of theoretical and empirical activities within verbal learning. This dominance is not surprising in view of the basic associative nature of PA learning and the multitude of generic processes inferred to be operative during PA learning and retention. We have also stressed recall measures in this review because such measures are characteristic of PA retention research. Recognition when applied to PA retention is considered to be simply a more sensitive measure of "availability" of associations than is recall. That is, it is more sensitive in the sense of requiring a lower threshold for activating an association than does recall, a notion consistent with the incremental concept of verbal learning (see Section II).

An active movement in contemporary verbal learning has been the liberation of recognition from the constraint of its role in the PA paradigm and the "recognition" of recognition as an important variant of learning-retention in its own right. The recognition of words as being familiar or unfamiliar on the basis of past experience is undoubtedly an important everyday problem of retention. The question of age-related changes in the processes underlying recognition should be of great concern to developmental learning psychologists.

In its simplest form recognition is studied in the laboratory by exposing a series of items to subjects for successive study. Presumably, each individual item is "learned" during the study period, and the subsequent test of recognition is actually a retention test. A common retention test is to ask subjects to judge for each item whether or not it had been presented during the original study period. The method itself was introduced by Shepard and Teghtsoonian (1961) for the purpose of testing the retention of three digit numbers. An interesting variation of the method was employed by Underwood (1965) to study what he called "false" recognition. More generally, the false recognition method is designed to test a theory of recognition learning and retention that calls for processes that are relatively untapped in the PA paradigm and other standard methodological paradigms. The theory views recognition as being a discrimination process for which response frequency provides the discriminative cues. Briefly, exposure to a word elicits an implicit perceptual-like response called the representation response (RR), together with implicit associative responses (IARs) that are word associates of the studied word (Bousfield, Whitmarsh, & Danick, 1958). For example, *table* as an item included in the list is presumed to elicit words like *chair* as IARs. The RRs to the word *table* provide an experimentally produced increment to the total response frequency for this word, an increment which is not present for words excluded from the list. According to the theory, subjects employ this frequency differential as the cue for deciding the prior presence or absence of the word in the list. However, words like *chair* have received an increment in response frequency via the occurrence of an IAR during exposure to the original list, and utilization of the response frequency cue could well lead to a false recognition of that word. The theory thus accounts for an important distortion of a memory process.

Space limitations prohibit a detailed discussion of the developmental implications of the false recognition method. However, it should be noted that age-related changes in memory distortions are as interesting to developmental learning psychologists as are age-related changes in amount of normal forgetting. Young children are expected to have a lower production of IARs, and therefore a lower rate of false recognitions (or memory distortions), than older children. In a test of this hypothesis, J. W. Hall and Ware (1968) found exactly the opposite—kindergarten children had a significantly higher rate of false recognitions than did third grade children. Concluding that there is an inverse relationship between age and IAR production makes little theoretical sense. Consequently, Hall and Ware wisely concluded that the age differential is a manifestation of the increased proficiency in older children of a selector mechanism that is akin to the selector mechanism of PA learning and retention. That is, older children have an increased capacity to reject words that are not included in the orginal list, regardless of the associative characteristics of these words. The generality of recognition processes in human memory merits continued use of the false recognition method in testing developmental trends throughout the age continuum.

B. Verbal Discrimination Learning and Retention

Goulet (1968b) has argued compellingly for the advantages of including the VD paradigm in the methodological arsenal of developmental learning psychologists, and his arguments will not be repeated here. Moreover, the space limitation, and the by now exhausted patience of the reader, permits only a few additional comments on retention-development relationships for VD learning.

The general characteristics of the VD paradigm were described in Section II. As noted then, the VD situation offers an intriguing composite of recognition and associative processes. This is especially true when the VD situation is extended to become the equivalent of an *A-B, A-C* transfer-retention paradigm (Kanak & Dean, 1969; Kausler, Fulkerson, & Eschenbrenner, 1967). The recognition processes are those postulated by a frequency-of-responding theory (Ekstrand, Wallace, & Underwood, 1966), a theory that is largely an extension of Underwood's frequency theory for the recognition of individual items. The associative processes consist of learning associations between intrapair right and wrong items which are much like the S-R and R-S associations of PA learning. The associative learning in the VD context, however, is clearly a variant of Type II incidental learning, and as such is affected by the same variables that influence other variants of Type II incidental learning (Kausler & Sardello, 1967).

Both RI and PI for intentional VD learning (i.e., learning intrapair discriminations) were investigated with young adult subjects by Eschenbrenner (1969). The RI and PI paradigms were created by employing successive lists in which the wrong items of List 1 continued on as wrong items in List 2 but the right items of List 1 were replaced by new right items in List 2 (the functional equivalence of an *A-B, A-C* phenotype; cf. Kausler *et al.,* 1967). RI and PI were measured by the number of trials required to relearn Lists 1 and 2, respectively, relative to an appropriate control condition. RI, but not PI, was found for the intentional component of the VD task, and, interestingly, the amount of RI covaried positively with the amount of RI for the incidental associative component of the total VD task. Eschenbrenner viewed his findings in terms of an interaction between the intentional and incidental processes, an interaction of considerable interest to retention-development relationships in light of the peculiar developmental trend suspected for Type II incidental learning in children. (In fact, associative learning on single VD lists for children of varying ages should offer a firm test of this peculiar curvilinear trend when the units involved are clearly verbal in nature). Furthermore, there is evidence to suggest that the frequency of responses to wrong items differs between elderly and younger adults (Kausler & Lair, 1968), a difference that should yield contrasting amounts of intentional RI for these age groups. Finally, the retention of an intentional task for which the discriminative cues are presumed to be based on the frequency of responding to individual items should provide another age-sensitive test of the production-deficiency hypothesis.

VI. CONCLUDING COMMENTS

Verbal learning research with young adult subjects is presently in a state of rapid expansion, in terms of both sheer productivity and conceptual advancements. This expansion has been especially prevalent in the component area of retention and forgetting. Unfortunately, research with subjects of other ages has not kept pace. Moreover, the research that has been done with children and the elderly is often spawned by hypotheses that are only marginally related to verbal learning theory, and the methodology employed is often deficient with regard to permitting tests of hypotheses originating from verbal learning. Part of the problem rests in the still lingering stereotyped conception of verbal learning as an area of "rote" processes, a conception that is unattractive to many developmental psychologists. The present reviewer has tried to convey the current state of theory in verbal learning-retention. In many respects, theory has moved heavily in the cognitive direction, a movement consonant with much of the flavor of contemporary developmental psychology. The introduction of cognitive-like processes in verbal learning theory has not, of course, eliminated the important role of rote-like processes in verbal learning and retention. Nevertheless, there seems to be much commonality for concepts like mediation, stimulus selection, etc. as they are approached from the separate vantage points of verbal learning theory and developmental theory. Hopefully, much of the present data gap on developmental trends in retention processes will be filled in the near future by researchers attracted to these commonalities.

During the course of this review a number of hypotheses were offered for retention-development relationships. The intent was to suggest hypotheses that are consistent with the overlap in processes between current verbal learning theory and developmental theory. The further intent was to stimulate research on the content areas encompassed by the hypotheses. Undoubtedly, many, if not all, of the hypotheses will be proved wrong. Nevertheless, the present state of verbal developmental learning is such that even bad hypotheses of heuristic value are better than no hypotheses at all.

LANGUAGE

CHAPTER 14

The Language Acquisition Process:
A Reinterpretation of Selected Research Findings

KLAUS F. RIEGEL

THE UNIVERSITY OF MICHIGAN,
ANN ARBOR, MICHIGAN

ABSTRACT

In contrast to traditional interpretations, relations rather than elements were considered as the basic information in the language acquisition process. As relational information is acquired the child will engage simultaneously in two types of intellectual processes: (1) He will identify the elements (words) and abstract their meaning by intersecting various relations such as ZEBRA-ANIMAL; ZEBRA-STRIPEs; ZEBRA-AFRICA; ZEBRA-RUNs; etc. (2) He will recognize the free elements of relations intersecting at one or (more likely) several points as members of classes, such as "animals," "toys," "places," "animated actions," etc.

In the main body of the paper research findings on the identification of both the elements and classes of the natural language were reviewed.

A final section dealt with the more complex operations of combination and transformation: (1) Combinations either assemble several relations into long

357

strings or—more important—combine classes. In discussing different types of combinations, such as those implying logical, spatial, or temporal orders, we touched upon the topic of logical syntax, syllogistic and analogical reasoning. (2) Transformations imply the reversal in the direction of one or more of the relations combined. The generality of such a process in regard to psycholinguistic, cognitive, and social performances was emphasized.

Our interpretations need to be supplemented by discussions of extralingual and interlingual relations. The former relate objects, actions and emotions to labels. The latter connect terms across different language under bilingual conditions.

I. INTRODUCTION

This paper does not provide a comprehensive review of the research and theorizing on language development during the life-span. Since this field has grown at an exceedingly fast pace, such a task reaches beyond the technical means and capacity of single writers. It is not surprising, therefore, that most of the recent reviews have been restricted to subtopics. In particular they have overemphasized the acquisition of syntax. They have been limited to the most recent advances in the field of language development and, without exception, have excluded any discussion of changes in psycholinguistic behavior during adulthood and aging.

Aside from these limitations there are still large areas of related research and theorizing which have been altogether omitted from the discussions of language development. A vast body of information has been accumulated, for instance, on the topic of verbal learning. Parallel, though much retarded, an increasing amount of research is being done on cognitive processes. Not only is this field developing in almost complete independence from that of verbal learning but the relations to the psychology of language and language development have been frequently disregarded. It is the purpose of this paper to reconsider some of these trends and to reinterpret some of the older, and several recent, research findings.

A. Elements and Relations in the Study of Psycholinguistic Processes

1. *Sensory Psychology and Learning*

Since its very beginning psychology has been burdened with a conceptual model quite inappropriate for most of its areas of study. This model emphasizes the priority of smallest, indivisible particles and, secondarily, their random movement which produces accidental connections and leads to the development of more complex forms. The successful application of this model in physics and chemistry during modern times provided a strong impetus for the adaptation of similar psychological theories.

Wundt, especially, undertook the ambitious task of developing a comprehensive model of the mind based on the notion of smallest psychic elements and their connections by associative bonds. Almost all of the research activities in his laboratory were directed toward the goal of isolating and describing three sets of psychic elements—sensations, images, and simple feelings—which when charted like the chemical elements of the periodic system, eventually would allow the scientist to explain complex percepts, ideas, and emotions as compositions of these basic elements. Except for his specific findings and interpretations of sensory and perceptual processes, the major objectives of Wundt's endeavors have been forgotten or are regarded as futile.

While Wundt devoted most of his attention to the analysis of a system of psychic elements and hardly ever advanced to the study of their connectivity, Ebbinghaus, with the flash of a genius, avoided these cumbersome analytical explorations. Virtually by inventing the basic element of his studies, the nonsense syllable, he ventured right into the analysis of the laws of their connections. Latter day psychologists have taken great pains to show that true nonsense syllables lack any connections to other elements or, if this did not turn out to be the case, they determined empirically the degree of built-in connectivity for control purpose (Noble, 1952). While thus providing some methodological refinement, they neither questioned the role of these elements nor the basic feature of their connectivity, the random or free associative connection.

2. Cognitive Psychology

In comparison to the studies of verbal learning, relations rather than particles have been emphasized in theories and research on cognitive development. However, with the exception of Piaget's earlier interest in the social function of children's speech, these psychologists, by and large, have deemphasized or disregarded the connections between cognition and language. Piaget, in particular, considers language as a means of expression for the child and as a tool for the investigator to explicate the thoughts of the child. Contrary to most of his other interpretations, little is said about the fact that a well-structured linguistic system exists in the environment independently and prior to any thought of the child, and that, when exposed to it, the child's adaptations are partially determined by it.

Our statements are not intended to reduce the significance of intellectual achievements. They rather point to the intricate relationship between thought and language and, more generally, to the complexity of the problem of meaning which neither philosophers, linguists, or psychologists have been able to dissolve.

In our opinion, this failure has to be attributed to the atomistic view of language and language behavior. Indeed, if we emphasize psycholinguistic elements, such as syllables or words, we have to look for surplus features that characterize the concept, idea, or meaning of terms. If, on the other hand, we emphasize psycholinguistic relations, we imply a priority of meanings over words and subsequently have to interpret how words are recognized and categorized. In exploring these processes—though close to cognitive psychologists—we can rely on studies of verbal learning.

3. *Linguistics*

Many psychologists, in trying to come to grasp with the problem of structure in the language acquisition process, have assimilated recent interpretations of transformational linguistics, especially those proposed by Chomsky (1957, 1965, 1968). In dealing with structural properties, linguistic theories undoubtedly have been superior to the atomistic and associationistic models. This superiority was achieved by an early recognition of linguistic relations at the expense of linguistic elements. As expressed by Jesperson (1937), the purpose of a linguistic analysis is "to denote all the most important interrelations of words and parts of words in connected speech. . . . Forms as such have no place in the system [pp. 13, 104]."

While these ideas were further explicated by different linguists, Chomsky aims beyond such descriptions, toward an universal system of linguistic structure from which the expressions of the various languages would be generated through transformations. Instead of using simplicity as the main criterion for such a system and instead of relying on the organization of the linguistic environment for explaining the acquisition of the structural properties of the language, Chomsky returns to the rationalism of Descartes and to a notion of a priori or even innately given structural organization. Throughout the following discussion we will emphasize the concept of structure without accepting the notion of innate forms.

Another point of departure concerns the abstractness of linguistic formulations. Linguists in searching for the most consistent and stable rules have often been forced to go beyond the data given and to engage in metalanguages about abstract classes and their ordered arrangements—and for good reasons, because only when they consider such abstract organizations can they describe general rules rather than situations in which the exceptions outnumber the confirmations. On the other hand, the highly abstract character of linguistic descriptions (both phonetic and syntactic) might also be responsible for their failure to explain the language acquisition process (implying that the notion of "innate linguistic capacities" does not provide an explanation but rather indicates a lack of it) and to derive a system of semantic descriptions. It is on these two topics, language acquisition and semantics, that psychologists seem to be best prepared to pursue the goals of their own science rather than to follow the challenges of modern linguistics.

B. Psycholinguistic Relations: Definitions and Paradigms

1. *Basic Types of Relations*

Throughout our presentation we will argue for the priority of relations over elements. Whenever psycholinguistic information is provided, it consists of connected and never isolated terms. Thus, we say "(a) zebra (has) stripes" or "(a) zebra (is an) animal" and even if we were to use nothing but the word "zebra" we, most likely, point to a "real" zebra or to the picture of one. Thus we are invoking a special, extralingual relation between a label and the object, event, or quality denoted by it, which we will call an "ostensive relation."

At some occasions we may utter single words like "go" or "stop," expecting that the listener will perform the related actions. The role of demands or commands has received considerable attention in classical studies of conditioning and is basic to Skinner's interpretations of verbal behavior. However, these extralingual regulations which we will call "intensive relations" are rarely discussed in reviews on language development even though their significance is recognized to an increasing extent (D. Birch, 1966; Luria, 1961).

Finally, special extralingual relations are invoked if a person utters, usually in an idiosyncratic manner, some words or sounds such as "bravo," "ouch," etc., in order to indicate his emotions or feelings. Many theories on the origin of language, beginning with the one proposed by Darwin, have focused upon these expressive and connotative relations. However, with the exception of studies on sound productivity (DeLaguna, 1927; M. M. Lewis, 1951) and, in a remote sense, on phonetic symbolism, little attention has been given to this topic in studies of the language acquisition process.

All three extralingual relations (ostensive, intensive, expressive) are important for the initiation and control of psycholinguistic behavior but play an increasingly subordinate role during the later periods of the language acquisition process. The vast majority of information consists of intralingual relations, e.g., relations between words and, occasionally, of interlingual relations, i.e., relations between words of different languages. For this reason and because most of the research and theorizing has dealt with an analysis of word-word relations, the following discussion will be restricted to this topic.

2. *Intersection of Relations*

If relations are combined or intersected, two intellectual operations can take place. The meaning of the element at the intersection can be explored, i.e. a word can be identified, and/or the free elements of the intersecting relations can be recognized as members of a class. Both processes involve an abstraction from the information immediately given, the relations. Both processes may occur simultaneously and rather rapidly. However, if one of the elements or the particular types of relations implied are unfamiliar to Ss, considerable time might be required for completing either one or both of them.

Two relations can be combined in no more than four different ways. If we denote the left-hand element (stimulus) by X_1, the right-hand element (response) by X_2, and the relations by T_i, the first combination of two elements, indicating a trivial cycle, trivial loop, or reverberation, would read

$$X_1 \ T_i \ X_2; \qquad X_2 \ T_i \ X_1 \qquad (1)$$

If relations would combine in this manner only, for instance if in a word association study BLACK would always elicit WHITE and WHITE would always elicit BLACK, then no associative structure would exist (Deese, 1965). In analogy to the periodic system of chemistry we would deal with noble gases that do not combine with other elements and therefore, are *ideally* suited for studying the physical state of a system, i.e., the distribution of the molecules under varying conditions. Fortunately for our purpose, psycholinguistic relations never combine exclusively in such a trivial manner but always reveal sufficient variation in their arrangements.

Reverberations are exceptional forms of combinations and are significant for special conditions only, i.e., for the strengthening of classes. The three remaining combinations of two relations are of greater generality and are identical with the chaining paradigm, the response equivalence paradigm, and the stimulus equivalence paradigm as recently discussed by Jenkins and Palermo (1964). All three are shown in Figure 1. The chaining paradigm can be written as

$$X_1 \ T_i \ X_2; \qquad X_2 \ T_i \ X_3 \qquad (2)$$

If nothing but chaining paradigms were prevailing, a language would consist of idiosyncratic strings of elements. More likely, various chains will crisscross one another, thus lending transient strength to the complex network of relations of which a language is made up. The chaining paradigm might allow for the identification of the connecting (intersecting) element, such as of ROSE in the chain of SMELL-ROSE; ROSE-FLOWER, but it is unlikely that the free elements, SMELL and FLOWER, will be recognized as members of a class.

The remaining two paradigms allow both for the identification of the intersecting elements as well as of classes. The response equivalence paradigm can be written in the form

$$X_1 \ T_i \ X_2; \qquad X_1 \ T_i \ X_3 \qquad (3)$$

It represents the sets of relations diverging from a common stimulus as usually reported in word association norms (see Entwisle, 1965; Palermo & Jenkins,

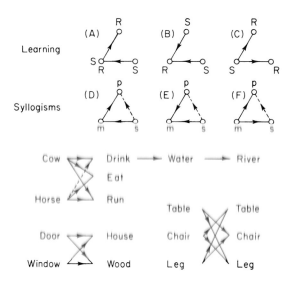

Figure 1. Samples of relational maps.

1964; Jenkins & Palermo, 1964; K. F. Riegel, 1965a, 1965b). The stimulus equivalence paradigm can be written in the form

$$X_1 \ T_i \ X_2; \qquad X_3 \ T_i \ X_2 \qquad\qquad (4)$$

Recordings of this type are much harder to obtain from associational data (see K. F. Riegel & Zivian, 1968) and consist of lists of stimulus terms that converge upon shared response terms.

3. Criteria for Classes

Students of verbal learning regard the last two paradigms as sufficient conditions for the acquisition of word classes. Undoubtedly these two paradigms represent a minimal requirement only because they imply that any two responses elicited by a common stimulus, such as the free associative responses CHAIR and EAT to the stimulus TABLE, would form a class. They are abstractions because in such simple forms they occur under laboratory conditions only. In concrete situations a multitude of combinations are embedded in one another, making up the complex network of the natural language and, thereby, strengthening the classes at varying degrees. But because of their abstractness, these paradigms, next to the simple relations, may also serve as the main building units into which this network can be partitioned.

The superposition of the paradigms can be demonstrated by the following example. If a child has learned that COWs DRINK, EAT, and RUN and that HORSEs EAT and RUN, he has formed a network of relations involving two semantic classes. As shown in Figure 1, COW is a stimulus for three response equivalence paradigms involving the terms: DRINK/EAT, EAT/RUN, DRINK/ RUN. HORSE is the stimulus for one response equivalence paradigm: EAT/RUN. Furthermore, both EAT and RUN are the responses for two stimulus equivalence paradigms both involving COW/HORSE.

Intuitively it is apparent that the classes of response and stimulus terms depicted in Figure 1 are more firmly established than when only a single

TABLE 1

Matrix of Selected Relations Shown in Figure 1

	Drink	Eat	Run	Water	River	House	Wood	Table	Chair	Leg
Cow	X	X	X							
Horse		X	X							
Drink				X						
Water					X					
Door						X	X			
Window						X	X			
Table									X	X
Chair								X		X
Leg								X	X	

response or stimulus equivalence paradigm were invoked. The strength of classes might, indeed, be determined by enumerating the number of stimulus or response paradigms embedded in the more complex display. For such an enumeration, it is convenient to rewrite the diagrams in matrix form as shown in Table 1.

If the rows are designated by the left-hand terms and the columns by the right-hand terms, then, the relations appear as cell entries of the matrix. For any stimulus, the distribution of equivalent response terms is now immediately accessible in the corresponding row; similarly for the distributions of equivalent stimuli. These are listed in the columns. Stimulus-response chains can be located by going back and forth between rows and columns of the matrix. Starting, for instance, with the stimulus COW we find the response DRINK. Entering the row for the stimulus DRINK we may find WATER as one of the responses; in the row for WATER, we find the response RIVER, etc. Finally, reverberations appear as entries in cells symmetrically located around the main diagonal of the matrix; thus, TABLE-CHAIR would appear in the upper right triangle, CHAIR-TABLE in the lower left.

In developing an empirical criterion of class strength, we compare the distributions of entries between the stimuli and responses, respectively. The responses EAT and RUN given to the stimulus COW are shared by HORSE. Since COW also elicits DRINK we might include this word as a member of the response class, thereby, weakening, however, the strength of the stimulus class. The same procedure is to be followed when we determine the response classes. The larger the number of shared entries, the greater is the class strength.

A detailed analysis of the strength of the word classes shown in Figure 1 will not be attempted here. Such an analysis will also have to account for the strengthening of classes through reverberations. If, thereby, we do not rely on the questionable assumption that all terms elicit themselves with maximum strength, i.e., CHAIR-CHAIR, TABLE-TABLE and LEG-LEG (Deese, 1962), the cells along the main diagonal of our matrix will have remained empty and thus can be used for locating the extralingual relations. In applying the traditional classification of content words into nouns, verbs, and modifiers, we place the ostensive relations into the cells on the main diagonal within the set of noun-noun relations. Since intensive relations represent verb labels for actions, and expressive relations, modifier labels for qualities, emotions, and feelings, we place them on the main diagonal within the sets of verb-verb and modifier-modifier relations, respectively.

With our last suggestions we have closed out the remaining cells of the matrix. A substantial extension is necessary, of course, if we consider other than monolingual conditions (K. F. Riegel, 1968b). Bilingual conditions imply three other matrices in addition to that of the first language A; one representing the intralingual relations of the second language B; and the other two interlingual relations A-B and B-A. The cells along the main diagonals of the intralingual matrix for B are filled again by extralingual relations whereas those of the interlingual matrices are filled by equivalence relations or translations. Types of compound and coordinated bilingualism (Ervin & Osgood, 1965) as well as developmental levels of bilingual proficiencies (K. F. Riegel, 1968b) differ in the degree to which interlingual relations are acquired.

4. *Types of Intralingual Relations*

Thus far we discussed the general procedures for determining word classes and for estimating their strength but have not given any thought to the types of relations involved. Apparently many types of relations are conceivable, and most importantly, will lead to different and only partially overlapping classifications. Thus, ZEBRA together with TIGER, CANDYSTICK, and BARBER SIGN are forming a class sharing STRIPES as a common part. On the other hand, ZEBRA will be categorized with COW and HORSE, because they perform the same actions. Furthermore, ZEBRA might be categorized with ELEPHANT, NEGRO, and NILE, all of which are located in AFRICA. There seems to be no unique way for deriving classifications and, in this writer's opinion, this is the only reason why philosophers, linguists, and psychologists have failed to develop and to operationalize comprehensive semantic interpretations.

Relying on some of Piaget's interpretations (Inhelder & Piaget, 1958), we have previously categorized relations into three groups: (1) logical relations based on the words (rather than objects, events, or qualities) and derived by verbal abstraction, such as synonymity, antonymity, superordination, coordination, and subordination; (2) infralogical or physical relations based on the denoted objects, events or qualities (rather than words) and derived by abstracting physical features of these items, such as parts, wholes, locations, preceding, contemporaneous, or succeeding events; (3) grammatical relations derived from the phenomenal structure of linguistic expressions and representing response terms which are nouns, verbs, adjectives, foregoing words, or following words to the stimuli.

The above list of general relations does not presume to be exhaustive or nonoverlapping. Both these properties will have to be empirically investigated if comprehensive semantic interpretations are to be derived. The list has been presented for further references and to emphasize that, thus far, we have dealt exclusively with builtin or implicit relations. These implicit relations are supplemented by explicit clues of the language.

If we receive the message: ZEBRA-ANIMAL or ZEBRA-STRIPEs and ZEBRA-RUNs, we do not only have four different words at our disposal but, more important, the implicit relational information of superordination, whole-part or actor-action. The relational information seems to be insufficiently safeguarded, however, if it were not supplemented in a partially redundant manner through the linguistic context. Thus, we usually receive phrases like, "The zebra is an animal" or "The stripes of the zebra" or "The zebra runs." In these examples the auxiliary "is" (used as a proper verb) plus the indefinite article "an" explicate the logical relation; the definite article "the" and the preposition "of" explicates the infralogical relation, whereas the grammatical relation does not receive any further explication except for the inflection "s" marking the verb. We call these explicit clues redundant because they do not occur in young children's "telegraphic" speech production. Apparently, implicit relational information is prior to its explicated form.

Recently the explicating clues of implicit relations, especially the prepositions, articles, pronouns, and conjunctions, have received little attention from linguists and psychologists. However, some pertinent evidence has been obtained in earlier studies of children's language. The role of conjunctions, in particular, opens further perspectives extending into the area of logical syntax (as distinguished from linguistic syntax) and redirecting us toward the analysis of cognitive developments as pursued by Piaget.

II. INTRALINGUAL RELATIONS

According to our interpretations, the immediate information given consists in relations. Once such information has been received, the language learner will engage in two intellectual activities: He identifies elements, and he abstracts classes. This holds for all types of relations: extralingual, intralingual, and interlingual. If we were to follow the natural course of development, we would have to start with a discussion of extralingual relations. Since these represent exceptional conditions, however, we limit our descriptions to intralingual relations.

A. The Identification of Psycholinguistic Elements

In the following two experiments, the accuracy and speed of identification of target words on the basis of intralingual relations were investigated. In both investigations, the traditional method of word associations was reversed by presenting response terms (clue words) selected from word association norms to *S*s and asking for the identification of the stimulus term (target word). Theoretically, single clue words, such as ANIMAL, STRIPEs, or RUN should not lead to the identification of the target word ZEBRA, except when both are connected exclusively or at very high associative frequencies. If several clue words are given at the same time, however, *S*s ought to succeed in their identification task by intersecting the various relations at the target word even if all the associative frequencies are relatively low.

1. *Word Identification during the Early Years*

(Quarterman and Riegel (1968) selected four types of relations from the Michigan restricted association norms (K. F. Riegel, 1965b) and presented them embedded in sentence frames, either singly or in all possible pair combinations. Subjects were 24 children each at the 1st, 3rd, 6th, and 9th grade levels. The task was described as a guessing game and the following instructions for the target word ZEBRA were used in the preparatory trial:

I am looking for something that

is an ANIMAL	(Superordinate)
is like a HORSE	(Similar)
has STRIPEs	(Part)
can be found in AFRICA	(Location)

The sentences for the clue combinations were derived by joining the dependent clauses of two single clue frames, for instance,

I am looking for something that is an ANIMAL and has STRIPEs.

As shown in Figure 2, there is an increase with age in the percentage of identifications of the target words both for single and double clue conditions. (The percentages for the latter represent averages over all those combinations of which the listed relation is a member.) However this increase is already halted at the 6th-grade level. Under all conditions and for all age levels double clues are more efficient (46%) than single clues (28%) except for single similars at the 1st grade level. This exception indicates either a lack of short-term retention which prevents young children from retaining the two bits of relational information sufficiently well and/or a lack in combinatory ability which prevents them from successfully intersecting the two relations.

In terms of utility, the infralogical relations of parts and locations are interspersed between the logical relations of similars and superordinates. This order is precisely the same for all age levels as well as for single and double clue conditions. Thus, there is no shift with age in the relative effectiveness of infralogical and logical relations. Similars (56%) are always the best single clues. Their effectiveness can be but little improved if a second clue is added (58%). The opposite is true for single superordinates and locations. Both are very poor single clues (15% and 14%, respectively) but are greatly improved when second clues are added (42% and 39% respectively). In particular, the classical generic definition by superordinates (class names) and parts (attributes) is about the worst strategy for word identifications (34%); only superordinates and locations (26%) and single clues (28%) are worse yet, but never single similars (56%).

2. Word Identification during the Later Years

When the age range was extended by including Ss above the age of 63 years (K. F. Riegel, 1968a), the slight downward trend beginning after the 6th grade was confirmed. The average decline in performance between the 6th graders and the aged Ss amounted to 10% for single and 12% for double clues, being most marked for similars, namely 26% for single and 18% for double clues. The smallest amount of decline occurred with superordinates when given singly (3%) and with parts when used in combination with any of the other three clues (6%), indicating perhaps the low performance ceiling of the former (the maximum is but 19%), and the high usefulness of the latter for all age levels (the maximum is 56%).

A more comprehensive interpretation of age changes in the identification of words can be obtained by comparing logical with infralogical clues. Both single and double logical clues (superordinates and similars) show larger age deficits (14 and 17%, respectively), than single and double infralogical clues (locations and

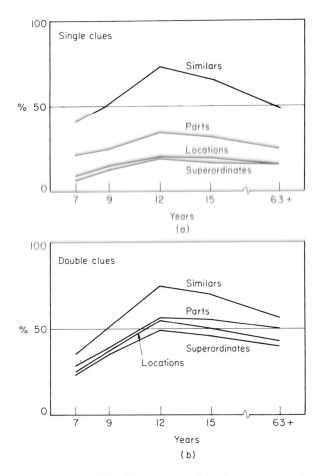

Figure 2. Average percentages of identified target words by five age groups when single clues (a) or double clues (b) were given.

parts; 6 and 4%, respectively). For the mixed clues the decline is 1% greater than the overall average, namely 12%. These results are congruent with the findings on language production, discussed in the following section, as well as with those by K. F.Riegel and Birren (1967) on verbal reaction times of aged *S*s. They imply a specific lack on the part of old *S*s to deal with the more abstract (logical) relations and a preference for concrete (infralogical) forms of conceptualization.

3. *Factors Influencing the Identification of Words*

Conceivably, the slight decline in performance from the 6th to the 9th grade could be due to sample biases and further increases during the late adolescence and adulthood may be expected. Unfortunately, supplementary data are not available. The additional information on college students by Zivian and Riegel (1969) and by Lacher and Riegel (1970) has been obtained under modified testing conditions and thus is not directly comparable with that of the previous study.

In the study by Lacher and Riegel, target words were visually presented to Ss on a tachistoscope rather than to be identified by conceptually intersecting the clue word relations without any presentation of the target words. In the study by Zivian and Riegel, college students merely received the clue words and an indication of the type of relation involved, rather than relations embedded in sentence frames. Prior to the testing, general explanations of the types of relations were provided to the 36 undergraduate students of this study. By employing two additional types of relations (subordination and preceding events), the three logical and the three infralogical relations were given singly, in all double and in all triple combinations during three testing sessions.

The modified form of presentation led to a marked increase in task difficulty, so that even under triple clue conditions, the percentages of identifications fell below those obtained with the sentence frame procedure. While the percentages increased very systematically with the number of clues given the third one added but 8% to the total percentage. On the average, single, double, and triple clues produced 19, 36, and 44% of identifications, respectively, whereby infralogical clues were least (24%), logical clues intermediate (38%), and mixed clues (44%) most effective.

Of particular interest in this analysis is the negative correlation between the size of the sets of possible responses and the percentages of identifications. The former represents the number of other stimulus (target) words that, according to the Michigan norms, converge upon the response (clue) words. The greater the number of stimuli, such as ZEBRA, COW, HORSE, etc, that converge, for instance, upon the shared superordinate ANIMAL, the harder the identification of any of these stimuli as target words will be. As indicated in our introduction, the divergence or convergence upon shared right- or left-hand terms are basic conditions for the establishment of semantic classes. Thus, our results point to the close interdependency between the tasks of word identification and of class recognition.

In particular the reaction times for correct identifications were longer for multiple and logical clues than for the other conditions. On first consideration, this seems to contradict our predictions concerning the class of possible responses. One would expect that when this class is small and well defined (perhaps by logical relations), Ss will respond quickly. However, when the class of possible responses is large and ill defined, almost any word in one's vocabulary will do and, therefore, the response should also be emitted quickly. If the decision about what is the appropriate class of responses is made more complex by adding more clues or by specifying a more strictly defined relationship then reaction time will be lengthened.

These statements suggest that the identification process consists of two subprocesses, the first of which is a search for an appropriate class and the second for a particular response. For multiple and logical clues the initial subprocess is lengthened and the second is shortened. For those clues which do not delimit well-defined classes of responses, the initial subprocess is virtually eliminated and the length of time taken by the second subprocess will be determined primarily by free associative relations. These subprocesses are closely related to the two factors, emergence time and selection time, proposed by K. F. Riegel and Birren (1966) to predict the speed of associative reactions. In this study both old and young Ss were found to have longer latencies when either too many or too few responses were available.

4. Operational Definition of Meaning

The studies and results reported touch upon a small section of a complex problem. Only a few relations and very few elements of a complicated network that changes with. age have been taken into consideration. Moreover, both investigations were limited to situations in which all words and relations were expected to be well within the repertoire of the Ss tested. The identification of unknown terms, a problem of greatest importance for the acquisition of new meanings, was excluded from consideration.

According to our exploration, the identification of elements, such as words, depends both on the specificity of the different types of relations involved and on the size of the total repertoire of relations. If the specificity of different types of relations is not recognized by the child, he will be limited to a random search in his comprehension and production processes. However, a person lacking such a skill is also unlikely to have an extended vocabulary and, thus, both factors are closely interdependent. Ideally, we ought to derive separate estimates of the changes in ability to operate with specific relations and in the size of the repertoire of relations available. Such attempts will be made in the analysis of language production tasks for which more data are available. Without exception, we expect an increase with age in the size of the repertoire coupled with finer differentiations of the relations which, subsequently, allow for more precise delineation of word classes.

Aside from specific inferences on developmental differences, some general conclusions concerning the study of meaning and its operationalization can be derived from our investigations. In emphasizing relations rather than elements as units of our analysis, we provided a semantic basis for our interpretations. The combination of different relations leads to the identification of the meaning of the intersecting term. The greater the number of intersecting relations, the more complete the explication will be. Subsequently, we might consider the meaning of a term as sufficiently explicated, i.e., operationally defined, if for a given set of relations, let us say, 90 out of 100 persons successfully identify the intersecting term. Further research would have to tell us what types of relations are important for what kind of stimuli and how the meaning of one term is blended through its usage in connected discourse, i.e., under the additional constraints of logical and linguistic syntax.

5. *Growth of the Vocabulary*

The identification or comprehension process may be visualized as consisting of two or more left-hand items that are relationally converging upon the target item at the right. In the production process usually, a single left-hand item is given and relationally divergent items are sought. This representation makes us aware of the large body of research on developmental changes in verbal production, namely the studies on vocabulary growth.

The literature on vocabulary growth and the methodologies applied have been comprehensively reviewed by McCarthy (1954). For the analysis of the vocabulary during the very first years of life, a great number of complete and some quite old biographical records are available (see C. Stern & Stern, 1920). One of the difficulties in these explorations concerns the criteria by which particular sound sequences produced by a child are judged as being meaningful or not. Congruent with our interpretations, such a judgment will have to be based upon relational interpretations. If the child, for instance, utters a sound sequence resembling the word MILK and if at the same time he is pointing ostensively at the object, we would consider his utterance as a word even though it might be phonetically quite at variance to the proper pronunciation and even though we might interpret his statement in a much further reaching manner by giving the child something to drink. If the child produces sound sequences which cannot be consistently related to certain objects, events, or qualities then we would have to reject these utterances as meaningless.

At the age of about three or four years, the attempt to obtain complete records of children's vocabulary becomes a very difficult task and investigators usually switch to time samples of children's speech. Increasing with age, greater use will also be made of vocabulary tests. For the youngest age levels, such vocabulary tests consist of the naming of pictures or objects and, thus, rely on extralingual, ostensive relations. Tests of instructions, such as used in the Stanford Binet, also imply extralingual relations. However, even their simplest items involve rather complex logical and linguistic confoundings. For instance, when we test a child's understanding of the instruction "pick up the key" or "go to the door," he has not only to recognize an intensive and an ostensive relation but he has to connect these relations according to specific semantic rules.

The intralingual relations which represent the focal point for our discussion also received the most extensive consideration in the literature. When vocabulary tests are used for the exploration of the acquisition and deterioration of these relations, two methods have been distinguished: the recognition or quantitative vocabulary tests and the definition or qualitative vocabulary tests. Generally, the former consists of multiple choice items, so that out of sets of four or five relations intersecting at the stimulus term, S has to pick one which is closest in meaning.

Recognition vocabulary tests are based upon similarity relations. In good test items, also the wrong alternatives will be related to the left-hand terms, for instance by denoting parts, locations, or more likely, superordinates, subordinates, and coordinates. Hard rules about the selection of the correct (as well as of the incorrect) responses have not been provided in any of the test descriptions. Most test designers seem to realize however, that perfect synonymity does not exist in the language but that there are always more or less marked deviations in meaning between any two terms.

6. Qualitative Changes in the Vocabulary

The second major form of a vocabulary test includes open-ended terms that are to be defined by Ss. If qualifying scores are assigned to the different types of relations produced the evaluation of the performance can provide more comprehensive insights into the individual's abilities than the pass-or-fail scores of the recognition vocabulary.

One of the most comprehensive analyses on age differences in qualitative vocabulary responses has been prepared by Feifel and Lorge (1950), covering the age range from 6 to 14 years, and by Feifel (1949) covering that from 15 to 79 years. In both studies, the Stanford Binet Vocabulary was applied to large groups of Ss but like all attempts to categorize a rich variety of expressions, Feifel's classification is hampered by ambiguities. Thus, his first class of "synonyms" includes generic definitions, e.g., "eyelash = hair over the eye that protects you" as well as functional relations, e.g., "straw = hay that cattle eat." This is disturbing, since the next category includes responses denoting the use and description of items, e.g., "banana = yellow and you eat it." The third class includes explanations e.g., "priceless = worth a lot of money" and the fourth illustrations, inferior explanations, repetitions, demonstrations, e.g., "priceless = gem," "puddle = puddle of water."

The most dramatic results were observed for the young Ss. The frequency of the use of "synonyms" increases from about 1 to 11 for the 45 test items. During the adult age span, the changes are small. A less marked increase from $\frac{1}{2}$ to 4 occurs in the use of "explanations," a development which is again halted during the adult age span. The category of "use and description" loses its significance early in life but regains importance during the late years of adulthood. The last category of "illustrations, etc." is only rarely used by Ss and shows slight and unsystematic changes over the age span. Errors decline very markedly during the early years and remain about constant throughout adulthood.

Feifel's findings are congruent with those obtained with the Wechsler (1958) tests (see also Fox, 1947; Fox & Birren, 1950) and with the interpretations of Yakorcynsky (1941). Generalizing across the different methods used we conclude: (a) There is a qualitative increase and decline in vocabulary ability with age which cannot be identified with recognition vocabulary or with pass-and-fail scores. These changes imply cognitive reorganizations on the part of the Ss. (b) Also increasing with age, Ss apply multiple rather than single relations in their responses. During old age this trend is reversed. (c) Although not clearly revealed by these data, increasing with age, Ss avoid redundant or overlapping multiple relations. Thus, they do not say: Zebra = animal, like a horse, that lives.

7. Differential Decline in Vocabulary Abilities

The interest among psychological gerontologists in the differential decline of qualitative vocabulary scores can be traced back to their attempts of estimating intellectual deterioration on a quasi intraindividual basis. As shown by Babcock (1930) and J. G. Gilbert (1935), quantitative recognition tests are not only highly predictive of a person's general intelligence but also remain virtually stable throughout the whole adult lifespan. Subsequently, these scores may serve as estimates of the original level of intellectual functioning with which other test scores can be compared in order to obtain percentage deficiency scores or deficiency ratios.

In an exploration of intellectual deterioration, the present author combined the advantages of the definition tests, i.e., their qualifying evaluations, with those of the recognition tests, i.e., the "objectivity" and simplicity of the evaluations, by developing a battery of five recognition tests, SASKA (K. F. Riegel, 1967). These tests were expected to show in the following order an increasingly greater decline with advancing age: *synonyms* (slight increase), *antonyms* (stability), *selections* of attributes or parts (slight decline), *classification* of coordinates (greater decline), *analogies* (greatest decline). These predictions have been confirmed in several studies (K. F. Riegel, 1968c) and were based on the notion that over and above a general word recognition ability (assumed to be stable or slightly increasing with age), the various relations invoked by the tests require specific selections (assumed to make the responding increasingly more difficult for older Ss). If the classes of possible alternative responses increase in size in the above order of the tests, an explanation of the differential decline in performance could be based on older Ss' difficulties to make selections within large sets of responses.

In order to substantiate such an explanation, the same stimuli and instructions as used in the verbal test battery were given to college students in open-ended versions of the tests. Thus, Ss were asked to name as many synonyms, atonyms, parts or attributes and coordinates, respectively, as they could think of within a period of one minute per stimulus and relation. Since the number of different responses produced was found to increase in the predicted order of the relations, the explanation of the differential decline was supported, i.e., the explanation that this decline is a function of the class size of competitive responses. The more potential responses there are, the more the performance of aged *Ss* will be negatively affected.

8. Developmental Differences in Associative Behavior

In further extension of this exploration, the 120 test words of the verbal battery were also applied as stimuli of a free word association test to 120 young persons between 16 and 20 years of age and 76 *Ss* each of the age levels 55-59, 60-64, 65-69, 70-74, and over 75 years of age (K. F. Riegel & Riegel, 1964). Five year retest data on the old *Ss* are also available (K. F. Riegel, 1968a). Since changes with age in the preference for particular relations were at the center of our interests, extensive criterion lists were developed for the classification of the free associative responses. For this purpose, nine judges gave two restricted associations each to the same 120 stimuli applying five different relations. They were asked to name either synonyms, antonyms, coordinates, superordinates, or parts (attributes).

According to the results produced by the judges, different relations given to the same stimuli quite often converge upon the same responses. While this finding is promising for a successful identification of word classes, it raises the more immediate question on the independence of the different types of relations and, in general, on the major dimension of a semantic-syntactic space. A comprehensive analysis of this problem has not yet been completed, but our data (K. F. Riegel & Riegel, 1963) allow us to determine such a structure on a preliminary basis as shown for noun stimuli in Figure 3.

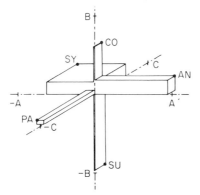

Figure 3. Factor loadings for five types of restricted associations given to noun stimuli. SU = Superordinates; CO = Coordinates; SY = Synonyms; AN = Antonyms; PA = Parts.

The results confirm the independence of the five relations and justify their use as criterion lists for the classification of the free associative responses of our old *S*s. A continuous even though slight increase with age in the preference for superordination and synonym relations was observed. However, the production of such responses seems to become increasingly harder for the aging *S*s, since there was also a continuous increase in reaction times. Indeed, by an age of about 65 years, a large number of *S*s turns toward idiosyncratic and subjective evaluations of the stimuli if not of the test and the testing situation. This shift in implicit preference from logical to subjective-connotative relations was also revealed by the negative attitude of most older *S*s toward the free association tests which they seem to regard as too ambiguous and without sufficiently precise directions and structure. Thus, the decline in performance with age seems to be at least in part determined by an implicit reorientation producing inappropriate response tendencies.

9. *Developmental Differences in Semantic Structure*

During the past few years this author has collected a considerable amount of information on restricted associations. In comparison to the definition or qualitative vocabulary tests where the choice of relations is left to the *S*s (even though it is expected to be meaningful), the method of restricted associations directs *S*s to find a response bearing a specified relation to the stimulus. Thus, *S*s do not only have to search their repertoire for any response available (as in free associations), but they have to recognize first the relationship involved and then they have to apply it in their selection of an appropriate response. Subsequently, the records reveal more specific differences between age levels than either available through free word association or vocabulary tests.

In the following study (K. F. Riegel, Riegel, Quarterman, & Smith, 1968), free associations and seven types of restricted associations were obtained from 48 *S*s each at the 3rd grade, the 6th grade, and the undergraduate levels. The following results were obtained. First, there is a continuous even though slight increase with age in the total number of different responses given. Only under exceptional conditions, such as for the superordinates, a decline in response variability with age was noted indicating an increasing restriction to the most appropriate response terms. Second, increasing with age, the responses given under different instructions to the same stimuli begin to deviate from one another and are less overlapping, indicating greater differentiation of the relations imposed by the instructions. Third, comparisons between free and restricted associations indicate a shift in mutual dependence. Free associative responses at the higher age levels are predominantly made up of primary or high ranking restricted associations, especially coordinates, similars, and contrasts. At the lower age levels, all types of restricted associations and also low ranking responses appear among free associates. This result—partially shown in Figure

4—confirms the findings with definition vocabulary tests as well as our interpretations of the semantic-cognitive operations of mature speakers.

The psycholinguistic repertoire of a mature person consists of response classes defined by particular relations such as common locations, parts, functions, qualities, etc., of the items assembled. When responding within meaningful context, the individual's choice will first consist in a selection of an appropriate class. Second, he will make his choice among the co-occurring class members.

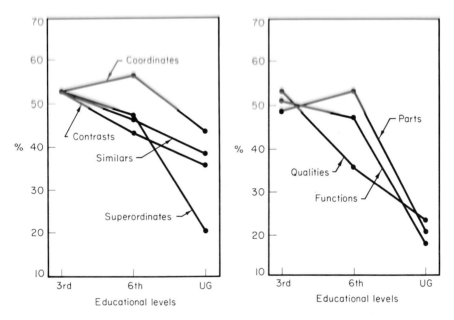

Figure 4. Average percentages of free associations that occur also as restricted associations at three age levels.

When he reacts in a meaningless task, such as under free associative conditions, he will brush aside or skim over all classes and his choice of a response will be primarily determined by the item most often represented in the repertoire and most strongly connected with the stimulus. But whatever a psychologist asks him to do, his responses will bear a meaningful relation to the stimuli, simply because completely meaningless relations are inconceivable for natural languages. Moreover, most persons will have developed their preference for particular relations as indicated by the preference among older Ss for logical responses, and thus, they never approximate sufficiently well a state of random responding as envisaged if their associations were "free."

10. *Developmental Differences in the Input-Output Ratio*

The preference for certain relations in the responding of some people does not necessarily match the preference of some other people for whom these responses may serve as stimuli. Stated more generally, the amount and form of the relational input might not be congruent with that of the relational output. In particular, the input-output balance may change with age and our educational procedures may not match the semantic-syntactic standards of children at various ages. In exploring these questions and in attempting to check the laboratory methods of the restricted associations against the linguistic behavior or children exhibited in everyday situations, we selected some 30 stimuli from the Michigan norms and asked 24 3rd and 24 6th graders to incorporate these words into written sentences. In order to obtain information on the relational input, we searched through the two readers used by the same children for the occurrence of the same 30 stimuli and when located, copied the whole sentences of which the stimuli were a part.

Aside from comparing the input and output as well as the 3rd and 6th grade level in terms of sentence length and sentence parts, particular attention was given to the degree to which terms (responses) related to the stimuli according to any of the 16 tasks of the restricted association norms would be picked up by the writers or readers and incorporated into the sentence in addition to the stimuli that elicited these responses. In the left-hand part of Figure 5, the percentages are given per word written by the children or in the readers. It is not

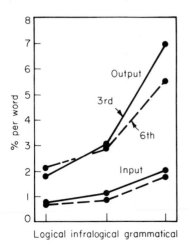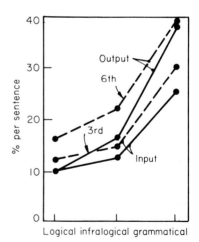

Figure 5. Average percentages of words related in three ways to 30 stimuli of the Michigan restricted association norms and used in sentences written by 3rd and 6th graders (output) or in 3rd and 6th grade readers (input) given per word (a) or per sentence (b).

surprising that grammatical relations are most often incorporated into the sentences followed by infralogical and logical relations. While the latter seems to gain relative in importance in the 6th graders' output, it is surprising that the age differences are rather slight. More surprising yet, the children incorporate many more relations taken from the adult norms than the writers of the readers.

The last result receives a further modification when the variation in sentence length is taken into account. On the average, 3rd graders produced sentences with 5.5 words, 6th graders with 7.6 words. The average sentence length in the 3rd grade reader was 13.0 and in the 6th grade reader 17.5 words. When we computed the percentages of related words (as determined by the norms) per sentence rather than per word, the differences between input and output are much diminished (see right-hand part of Figure 5). On the assumption that the Michigan norms represent the most important relations of the language, we have to conclude that the short sentences written by the 3rd graders incorporate this information in a more efficient and compact manner than either the 6th graders or the readers. The very long sentences of these books seem to be burdened with decorative details whereas the children are brief and to the point.

From a very practical point of view, the study of the input-output ratio has attracted considerable attention among educators concerned with problems of sociocultural deprivation. Such investigations need to be extended to the study of the aging process. Retirement, loss of a partner or friend, undoubtedly, produce severe reductions in a person's communication potential. Decline in vision, hearing, and mobility increase the significance of these deprivations even further. As the chances for communication decrease, the older person may, of course, turn to new channels. Thus, as the information exchange at his job site is eliminated, he might devote more attention to his family or, perhaps, turn to reading and writing. In doing the latter, he increases his input rate about ten times but, at the same time, his output is slowed down in a ratio of about 3 to 1. Subsequently, his former input-output balance is disturbed without taking, as yet, sensory and motor losses into account. Of course, few elderly persons may, indeed, succeed in switching from spoken to written communication channels, but may be forced to withdraw altogether or to become passive recipients of information through radio and television. Even though intuitively convincing as powerful determinants of an intellectual and social breakdown during the later years, none of these factors has received any noteable empirical or theoretical attention.

B. The Identification of Classes

As a child accumulates relational information and apprehends the meaning of words by intersecting these relations, he also acquires implicit knowledge about classes. As outlined in our introduction, minimal criteria for the formation of classes in terms of stimulus and response equivalence paradigms have been proposed and applied in learning research. Maximal criteria are met if the free ends of intersecting relations are symmetrically connected with one another. In the context of natural languages intermediate conditions prevail. These are characterized by numerous crisscrossing relations. The enumeration of embedded stimulus and equivalence paradigms, it has been suggested, could serve to detect these classes and to estimate their strength. In the following sections we will apply this method to the study of the language acquisition process.

If a linguist explores an unknown language, he first needs to rely on ostensive relations. Except for the rare condition of unequivocal proper names there will always be a large range of objects denoted by a common label but varying in many features. If this were not so, the language would be nonreductionistic. Only when several items are labeled by a common name does a language become an efficient means for communication. Consequently, for any term, the linguist needs relational information under numerous conditions in order to obtain an understanding of the full range of its meaning.

The linguist's task becomes more difficult if the words do not designate concrete objects, but events, qualities, or abstract ideas. For their analysis, the linguists might compile a list of all the contexts in which these words occur. For instance, if he were interested in the term ENTELECHY as used by Aristotle, he would extract and compare all the sentences which include this word and, thereby, determine classes of related items that "define" this term. In analyzing another term, such as APEIRON he will detect some contextual overlap which indicates not only that both ENTELECHY and APEIRON, but also other related terms form a class. His records also imply that certain concatenations of classes are permissible and interpretable. Thus, primitive, semantic-syntactic rules can be abstracted by the linguist.

1. Distributional Analysis of English Words

In applying this methodology to psychological data, we imply that an individual proceeds exactly as the linguist in acquiring knowledge about his language and communicative skills. We asked four graduate students in psycholinguistics to judge the permissible concatenations among the 200 stimuli of the Michigan norms (K. F. Riegel, 1965a, 1965b) given in three sets of 124 nouns, 40 verbs, and 36 modifiers. The classification of the stimuli was empirically derived by the three judges. The percentage agreements for the classifications were 93, 89, and 91%, respectively. For further analysis by the computer, the nouns had to be reduced to 90 items.

The main task for the students consisted in making "yes" or "no" judgments on the possible concatenation of any two items belonging to the following class combinations: noun-verb (whereby the noun was to be considered as a subject of a sentence), verb-noun (whereby the noun was to be considered as an object of a sentence) modifier-noun, verb-modifier. The five other form-class combinations were excluded because they would be made up of identical form classes (paradigmatic combinations), or because they represent unlikely or unpermissible syntactic sequences, i.e., the sequences noun-modifier and modifier-verb. All stimuli were printed on cards and handed to Ss in separate pairs of decks. The data were summed over Ss and yielded four matrices of the sizes 90 × 40, 40 × 90, 36 × 90, and 40 × 36, respectively.

In line with our relational interpretation, we determined which set of left-hand terms would combine with the same right-hand terms and vice versa; we determined which set of nouns, for instance, could function as subjects for which set of verbs. Without going into the technical details, the results shown in Table 2 provide information on the overlapping classifications of nouns based on the verb-noun (rows) and noun-verb (columns) combinations.

As shown in Table 3, the first class (A and A'), equally clearly identified by both sets of combinations, denotes "persons." The only exception is BABY which in the N-V analysis is included in the class of "animals." All other classes are more clearly delineated by the N-V than the V-N analysis, i.e., B: body parts, C: animals, D: food items, E: municipal organizations (and some food items), F: abstract processes, G: utensils (and places). The items in the last row of Table 2 have been omitted because their ties to the V-N classes are much weaker than those of the items listed in the main body of the table. They are given in the last section of Table 3 together with the single entries of Table 2.

While, in general, the N-V analysis leads to less ambiguous results, class G (utensils) is more clearly delineated (as class E'_i) in the V-N analysis. This is not surprising since "utensils" are more likely to function as objects than as subjects of a sentence. It is also not difficult to understand that the two types of data lead to somewhat different classifications. After all, items functioning as subjects of a sentence play a different role than when they are functioning as objects. This suggests that not only different types of relations produce different classifications, but also that the reversal of a relation, for instance, from N-V to V-N will modify the system. As indicated in our introduction, the multiplicity and ambiguity of the classification systems seem to be the main, if not the only reason, for the lack of progress in the analysis of the semantic structures.

2. Paradigmatic and Syntagmatic Classes

At the present time, neither all of the methodological problems of our analysis have been resolved, nor have similar data been obtained from age groups other than college students. However, an extension of the methodology to the study of restricted associations—for which developmental data are available—seems possible. Before we discuss such an application, we review some findings derived from free association tests which have attracted much interest among developmental psychologists.

TABLE 2

Number of Words per Category Derived from Noun-Verb Relations (columns) and from Verb Noun Relations (rows) and Average Interword Correlations (r) within Categories

V-N	Nouns-Verbs (N-V)							$\bar{r}$
	A	B	C	D	E	F	G	
A'	15		1					.87
B'		8	5	1	1			.76
C'			5	12	3			.76
D'		1			3	4	3	.68
E'							11	.75
Omitted	0	1	0	4	3	5	4	
$\bar{r}$	.74	.66	.72	.72	.67	.67	.70	

TABLE 3

Word Categories Derived from Noun-Verb Relations (first columns of letters) and from Verb-Noun Relations (second columns of letters) [a]

Adult	AA'	Body	BB'	Food	DC'	Anger	FD'
Boy	AA'	Arm	BB'	Crust	DC'	Controversy	FD'
Girl	AA'	Foot	BB'	Bread	DC'	Justice	FD'
Man	AA'	Leg	BB'	Cheese	DC'	Leadership	FD'
King	AA'	Hand	BB'	Mutton	DC'	Crater	GD'
Nurse	AA'	Brain	BB'	Fruit	DC'	Building	GD'
People	AA'	Stomach	BB'	Vegetable	DC'	Barn	GD'
Patriot	AA'	Intestine	BB'	Cabbage	DC'	Light	GE'
Civilian	AA'	Bird	CB'	Whiskey	DC'	Candle	GE'
Child	AA'	Eagle	CB'	Milk	DC'	Lamp	GE'
Doctor	AA'	Hawk	CB'	Glue	DC'	Bulb	GE'
Foreigner	AA'	Butterfly	CB'	Butter	DC'	Blade	GE'
Woman	AA'	Moth	CB'	Tobacco	EC'	Door	GE'
Soldier	AA'	Insect	CC'	Lettuce	EC'	Tool	GE'
Thief	AA'	Tiger	CC'	Leaf	EC'	Top	GE'
		Sparrow	CC'	Community	ED'	Knife	GE'
		Sheep	CC'	Country	ED'	Bed	GE'
		Spider	CC'	City	ED'	Covering	GE'

[a] Single entries between distant categories are CA' Baby, DB' Wing, EB' Head, BD' Abortion. Words not entering the five V-N categories are: B: Sickness; D: Ocean, River, Stream, Water; E: Town, Metropolis, Organ; F: Music, Dream, Memory, Religion, Mouth; G: Sun, Moon, Satellite, Cottage.

In her paper of 1961 on free word associations of children, Ervin proposed a distinction between paradigmatic and syntagmatic responses. In the narrower sense, the former can be regarded as substitutes for the stimulus in a sentence slot or, more generally, as members of the form class of the stimuli, such as nouns, verbs, or modifiers. Syntagmatic responses belong to a form class other than that of the stimulus; the stimulus-response sequences resemble telegraphic versions of sentences. According to Ervin's findings, which have been confirmed in several other studies (Entwisle, Forsyth, & Muus, 1964), young children show a relatively strong tendency to respond syntagmatically, but, increasingly with age, paradigmatic responses begin to dominate. As the present author has shown (K. F. Riegel & Riegel, 1964), there is slight, but consistent, reversal in this shift during late adulthood. Especially, verb responses to noun stimuli occur to an increasing extent, a result which is congruent with Feifel's observation on the increasing preference of old *S*s to denote the usage of items in definition vocabulary tests.

The class of syntagmatic responses includes six different relations (noun-verb, verb-noun, noun-modifier, modifier-noun, verb-modifier, and modifier-verb). In the preceding section, nouns were categorized on the basis of shared verbs (predicates), but when the relation was applied in the reverse order, i e., when verb-nouns instead of noun-verbs relations were considered, only partially overlapping results were obtained.

The categorization is still more confounded when relations within the set of paradigmatic responses are analyzed. For the stimulus TABLE, for instance, the class of paradigmatic responses might include FURNITURE (superordinate), CHAIR (coordinate), WOOD (substance), LEG (part), KITCHEN (location), etc. Each of these responses implies a specific subrelation (indicated in parentheses) within the general paradigmatic relation. These subrelations can serve to determine meaningful subclasses within the larger class of nouns. As our results have shown (K. F. Riegel & Riegel, 1964) changes in the preference of these specific response classes and the relations on which they rely are more important indicators of developmental and aging processes than the gross, grammatical classification into paradigmatic and syntagmatic responses.

Representing simple relations as cell entries of the matrix, shown in Figure 6,

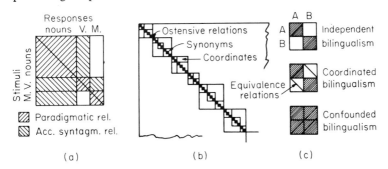

Figure 6. Matrices of word relations. (*a*) Paradigmatic and syntagmatic relation. (*b*) Subsets of paradigmatic relations. (*c*) Relations within and between first (A) and second (B) languages shown for three types of bilingualism.

the stimuli will appear as rows and the responses as columns. Using, provisionally, the grammatical classification into nouns, verbs, and modifiers we find the paradigmatic associations within the three large squares around the main diagonal of the matrix. The syntagmatic associations appear in rectangulars off the main diagonal. Those representing acceptable sequences of English sentences have been shaded, i.e., the noun-verb, verb-noun, modifier-noun, and verb-modifier relations. According to Ervin, the child, increasingly with age, progresses toward the main diagonal of the matrix. Of course, he associates within a limited set of vocabulary items only, such as within the sets of terms denoting animals, persons, toys, food items, and manipulative and animated actions, etc. Subsequently large blocks of the matrix will remain empty, relating, for instance, to abstract terms, ideas, tools, cognitive actions, intellectual qualities, etc.

The delineation of these subclasses suggests that the blocks of paradigmatic and syntagmatic relations can be further subdivided than on the basis of form-class combinations. As much as the blocks of syntagmatic relations have to be considered as the product of the different form classes, so have the sets of these subrelations to be regarded as the product of various subclasses. If these subclasses and subrelations are sufficiently well analyzed we will, ultimately, be able to formulate a system of semantic rules. While traditional grammar and syntax consist of rules about general classes such as the concatenation rule subject-predicate-object, a system of semantics will consist of rules about the more specific subclasses such as the rule that actors (A) perform actions (B) at locations (C) with things (D). It is surprising that it could have ever been seriously suggested that the acquisition of the semantic rules follows rather than precedes those of syntax in the developmental process.

Reserving the cells right on the main diagonal for the extralingual relations (ostensive relations for the noun block, intensive relations for the verb block and expressive relations for the modifier block), we find close to the diagonal small squares of synonyms and symmetrically related terms, i.e. those that can clearly function as substitutes for one another. These blocks are embedded in the larger sets of coordinated terms. Further off the main diagonal we find blocks of asymetric relations such as object-superordinate, part-whole, object-location, etc.

Since children will get acquainted with infralogical relations such as part-whole or object-location, etc. before they learn the logical relations of superordination or similarity, etc. a continuing progression toward the main diagonal may be expected. Aging, on the other hand (K. F. Riegel & Riegel, 1964), is characterized by—almost obsessional—attempts to cling to the main diagonal (by responding with synonyms, antonyms, and superordinates) and—if unsuccessful—in an uncontrolled drift toward syntagmatic denotations of functions and usages or in subjective expressions and connotations.

3. *Developmental Differences in Word Classes*

Aside from the evidence presented by Ervin (1961), there is a large body of research literature on free associative responses in which various categorization systems, mainly of semantic, logical types have been applied. However, with few exceptions (e.g., Woodrow & Lowell, 1917), no evidence is available on developmental changes. Since the classification of free word associations moreover, is hampered by arbitrariness, shift in relevance and lack of reliability, the present author has preferred methods that leave these categorizations to the *S*s themselves.

In the following study (Zivian, Riegel, & Zeiher, 1967), restricted associations of three groups of 48 German *S*s each, aged 12, 15, and 18 years, to 40 noun stimuli were collected in West Berlin. The following eight types of relations were applied: superordinates, similars, verbs, adjectives, foregoing words, following words, locations, and parts. (Comparable data are available on American, Italian, and Spanish *S*s.)

The data were analyzed for clusters of stimuli connected through shared responses. An example for the part relations connected with the German stimulus KÄSE (cheese) is given in Figure 7. This figure lists the relations

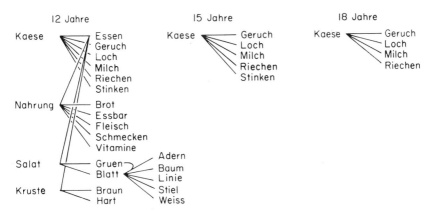

Figure 7. Sample maps for three groups of 48 German students each, aged 12, 15, and 18 years, derived from the part relations diverging from the stimulus KÄSE (cheese) and converging upon any of the responses.

diverging from KÄSE as well as those for NAHRUNG (food), SALAT (lettuce), and KRUSTE (crust) for which some relations converge upon responses shared by KÄSE. Since SALAT elicits the stimulus BLATT (leaf) another response distribution is hooked up to the map. In comparison to the map of the 12-year-olds, those for the older *S*s are much smaller in magnitude. For systematic comparisons of these maps, the statistics of Table 4 have been derived (see K. F. Riegel & Zivian, 1968). In the first column, the number of separate maps, such as those shown in Figure 7, are listed. Except for verbs, the total net of relations connected to the 40 stimuli are broken into an increasingly larger number of subclasses (maps). There are also large differences in the number of maps between the eight types of relations, being lowest for locations and highest for the symmetric relation of similars. The second column lists the total number of different words embedded in the nets. While there is some increase in the number of types with age and differences between the eight relations, these numbers need to be compared with the total numbers of relations embedded in the nets and given in the third column. If each stimulus would elicit a unique response, the number of types could be twice as large as the number of relations.

TABLE 4

Number of Maps, Types, Relations, and Chains for Relational Nets of 12-, 15-, and 18-Year Old German Subjects

Relation	Age	Maps	Types	Relations	Chains
Superordinates	12	9	141	87	66
	15	13	149	106	57
	18	17	154	108	57
Similars	12	24	168	102	24
	15	29	188	132	5
	18	32	193	132	13
Locations	12	5	125	130	45
	15	5	135	130	40
	18	7	133	120	39
Parts	12	10	150	109	58
	15	18	159	123	29
	18	16	172	131	36
Verbs	12	14	118	110	3
	15	10	131	127	0
	18	11	139	128	4
Adjectives	12	3	132	149	0
	15	9	141	140	0
	18	9	141	140	0
Foregoing words	12	7	126	132	4
	15	13	130	120	2
	18	24	124	102	1
Following words	12	11	127	122	3
	15	17	143	116	12
	18	22	149	120	7

The more relations that diverge or converge from points of intersects, the smaller the ratio between types and relations and the tighter the maps will be.

As shown in the last column of Table 4, the number of chains, i.e., strings of two or more relations, differs markedly between the different types of relations. Numerous chains are embedded in the maps of the logical and infralogical relations, whereas the grammatical relations seldom have a depth of greater than two elements. However, this does not necessarily imply that the network of the latter consists of many small maps. On the contrary, the grammatical relation of adjectives, for example, forms a few large maps only. Apparently the response distributions are parallel and overlapping but do not include other stimuli that would elicit new sets of responses. As the maps decrease in size with advancing age, also the chains become shorter.

Older children give more different and more distinct responses, i.e., responses that connect only with one or a few stimuli. Younger children are often using general responses to several different stimuli and, thus, knit them into one general network. For example GROSS (large) and KLEIN (small) occur in 12-year-olds as a response to twelve stimuli; in 15- and 18-year olds they occur to four and five words, respectively. Older children replace these general connectors by more specific ones, but not necessarily the longer strings by simple relations (see last column of Table 4). Since most of these problems can not be thoroughly reviewed at this place, it may be sufficient to summarize some of the implications by means of a diagram. Figure 8 shows the decrease in class size with advancing age for the relation of superordination.

4. Implicit and Explicit Relations

Thus far our discussion has dealt with relations implied in meaningful combinations of words. Such an implicit relation is unique for the words which it connects. An implicit relation is general if many words are combined in the same manner, i.e., if their left- as well as their right-hand elements form classes. Thus, the same general relation is involved, if we compare the pairs COW-DRINK, COW-EAT, COW-RUN, HORSE-DRINK, HORSE-RUN, namely that of actor-action. The transmission of relational information in natural languages seems to be insufficiently safeguarded if no other, and partially redundant clues, were built into the messages.

For infralogical or physical relations, additional clues are provided by function words, especially the prepositions. Prepositions in the narrower sense explicate spatial relations (such as in our restricted association tasks of locations) temporal relations, (such as in our tasks of precedings contemporaneities, and succeedings) as well as more general relations (expressed by our tasks of parts and wholes). Logical relations rely less frequently on prepositions but on special syntactic constructions of identity statements like "... is a ..." (superordination and subordination), "... is like a ..." (similarity), "... is not like a ..."

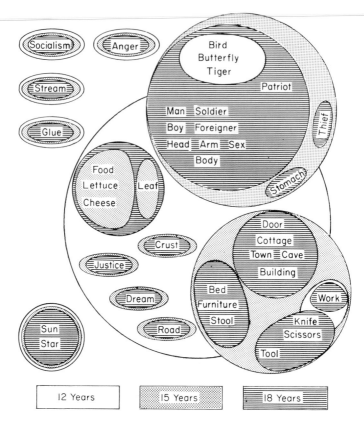

Figure 8. Classes of stimuli (translated) determined by converging (shared) responses for three groups of 48 German students each, aged 12 15, and 18 years.

(antonymity) and conjunctions "...and...." (coordination). Finally grammatical relations rely directly upon combinations of elements from distinct form classes such as noun-verb, noun-modifier, verb-modifier, or rely upon the linguistic contexts, like in our tasks foregoing and following words.

Since prepositions explicate relations, their study ought to further our understanding of semantic structures even though, as commonly emphasized prepositions, as all function words, do not carry meaning. Of course, this holds for an elementaristic viewpoint only. From a relational viewpoint, prepositions are carriers of explicit semantic information. Because of this important role, it is unfortunate that there seems to have been only one recent attempt in psychology to study prepositional relations, i.e., a multidimensional analysis of the prepositional space by H. H. Clark (1966). However, there is a considerable amount of older, descriptive information on the usage of different parts of speech (including prepositions) by children which ought to be reevaluated (see E. A. Davis, 1937, 1938; Grisby, 1932; Heider & Heider, 1940; Zyve, 1927).

In linguistics extensive studies of prepositional relations have recently been made by Lamb (1966), whereas in the interdisciplinary area of mechanical translations von Glasersfeld (1965) and Burns (1965) have approached these problems from a more pragmatic viewpoint. The latter authors made extensive studies on the existence and equivalence of prepositions in several European languages. Since there is considerable variability across languages (even between those closely akin to one another) their records provide information on the generality with which prepositions explicate relations. Thus, they deal with the question of linguistic-cognitive universals; a problem of considerable interest not only for cross-linguistic but also developmental studies.

Much as in our interpretations, von Glasersfeld and Burns speak of implicit relations or correlations which connect two terms or correlata such as the verb and indirect object of GIVE-JOHN and the categorizer and noun of the direct object SOME-BREAD. Implicit correlations are elaborated and at times modified by explicit correlations often involving prepositions, such as in the example GLASS OF MILK. In interlingual comparisons, prepositions often do not have equivalents at all, or have to be chosen from sets of alternatives. Thus, TO in English expresses both temporal as well as spatial relations as in "five minutes to three" and "they went to London," whereas in German two different prepositions are available, i.e., VOR and NACH (which, moreover, are opposites when used in the temporal sense). By searching through various languages it ought to be theoretically possible to determine a universal set of relational terms, i.e., prepositions, that are found in all languages, as well as supplementary sets representing the unique additions of particular languages.

With our discussion of prepositions we have approached most closely areas of inquiries traditionally assigned to linguistics. In the following sections we shall establish closer approximations yet. Throughout our discussion, the order of topics corresponded to the natural order in which a language is acquired. After relational information is provided, the child may derive and interpret elements as well as classes. Next, explicit relational clues, such as the prepositions, will be recognized and utilized. At the same time, the child will increasingly obey the proper sequential order of semantic classes, i.e., will apply semantic concatenation rules. At this moment the child is still not working within a syntax proper because he has not yet a sufficient grasp of the grammatical classes nor of the rules of their combinations and transformations. He will be ready for these operations when the classes and class relations available to him have become sufficiently general. Without exception, semantic classes are subsets of grammatical classes and semantics is prior to syntax.

III. PSYCHOLINGUISTIC OPERATIONS

Two types of psycholinguistic operations will be of concern to us: combinations and transformations. The former represent the operation of logical addition; the latter represent their inverse by which combinations are partially or completely reversed. Unfortunately, only remotely related evidence on the language acquisition process is available and, thus, we will be limited to a discussion of the general properties of these processes and of their logical rather than empirical, genetic order of appearance.

The operation of combination is involved in the most basic processes discussed, namely the identification of elements and the acquisition of classes. These performances are achieved by intersecting relations, i.e., by ordinal combinations. If linguistic skills would imply nothing but ordinal combinations of relations they could be described as Markov processes or as finite state grammars (Chomsky, 1957). We know that this is inconceivable because such models would not explain the well-documented (R. W. Brown & Fraser, 1963; C. Stern & Stern, 1920) productive and generative psycholinguistic skills of children and—as Chomsky and Miller (1963) argued—there is neither enough time nor space to store all the information necessary.

However, nothing prevents us from considering such a system as an early form of children's grammar. Even though it might be more parsimonious to propose just one universal system, such as transformational grammar, it is well conceivable that there is a succession of different grammars increasing in comprehensiveness (as well as, perhaps, in simplicity) which explain the acquisition of linguistic skills at different developmental levels. Such an interpretation is particularly tempting if it can be shown that the earlier grammars are successively embedded in the later ones.

If we accept this possibility, our previous discussion on the acquisition of word classes leads us directly to the next more complex grammar, the phrase structure grammar (Chomsky, 1957). This grammar is written in terms of classes and class concatenations. Conceivably, these classes are either general, like the grammatical form classes or—in line with our own discussion—are specific semantic subclasses. As much as relations differ in types, so do the class combinations. This point is not necessarily realized in phrase structure grammars.

In discussing the next more complex system, transformational grammar, it is pertinent to refer briefly to mathematical systems in which the concept of transformation has been first and most rigorously applied. Mathematical systems consist of sets of axioms defining possible operations with symbolic elements, such as numbers. The simplest number system defines nominal scales which allow for the categorization of items in distinct classes to which labels such as letters or numerals may be assigned. Since there exists no ordered relation between the classes, the degree of manipulation of transformation is almost unlimited and amounts to a relabeling of the classes and their members. Unlike the case in linguistics, logical or mathematical transformations keep the scales invariant, i.e., the classes remain the same even though their labels have changed. Without exception, transformations, as used by linguists, produce changes. When additional axioms on the transitivity of the operations are imposed, ordinal scales are generated. Subsequently, logical transformations, in keeping the order invariant, are more restricted than those applicable to nominal systems. Ordinal scales might be monotonically stretched, but the order of any two items may not be altered.

It is unfortunate that linguists have used the term transformation in precisely the opposite manner to mathematicians and logicians. For this reason, we shall speak of either mathematical, logical transformations or of linguistic transformations. Linguistic transformations, in producing variance, gain importance the more complex the system to which they are applied. In the case of categorical systems, they lead to the identification of the inverse of a class. If order is implied, such as in the syntactic rule: subject-predicate-object, they also imply rearrangements of these classes which either will make the transformed string unacceptable or will require a change in interpretation. In general, linguistic transformations deal with the reordering of sequences of classes or, at a lower level of class elements, by which, for instance, declarative statements are changed into questions, passive statements, negative statements, and vice versa. After discussing first the operations of combinations, we will attempt to show that the notion of transformations has an exceedingly wide applicability in the area of language acquisition as well as in the area of linguistic and psychological performances in general.

A. Combinations

As discussed in Section I,B,2, two relations can be combined in four different ways, of which the symmetrical combination or reverberation serves the strengthening of classes. Among the remaining three combinations, those of the convergent and divergent relations, i.e., the stimulus and response equivalence paradigms function for the identification of elements and, when superimposed, that of classes. The chaining paradigm represents a sequential hook-up of relations as occurring in more complex linguistic expressions, such as in sentences.

1. Syllogistic Reasoning

In spite of the limitations of the resulting grammar, the three paradigms allow, under some circumstances, for generative inferences, which, moreover, make-up the oldest topic of logical analysis, that of syllogistic reasoning. The basic three syllogisms—as described by Aristotle—correspond precisely to the three major paradigms of Figure 1. However, syllogisms require transitivity between the relations, as in the following example:

$$\frac{\begin{array}{l} \text{Socrates} - \text{man} \\ \quad\text{man} - \text{mortal} \end{array}}{\text{Socrates} - \text{mortal}}$$

The inference about the subject-predicate relations is possible because of the common, intersecting terminus medius. The inference connects the free ends of the intersecting relations with one another.

If symmetrical relations are combined as syllogisms the solution becomes trivial. However, for all practical purposes, perfect symmetry or synonymity does not exist in the natural language and thus, the inference becomes questionable as in the following example:

$$\frac{\begin{array}{l} \text{difficult} - \text{hard} \\ \quad\text{hard} - \text{firm} \end{array}}{\text{difficult} - \text{firm}}$$

If different types of relations, such as subordination and whole-parts, are combined, the inference becomes faulty and no systematic attempts seem to have been made to explicate the conditions for these inferences. (Aristotle has analyzed, however, the effect of negation, a problem related to that of transformations.) The false inferences drawn from the combination of different types of relations, such as:

$$\frac{\begin{array}{l} \text{animal} - \text{zebra} \\ \quad\text{zebra} - \text{stripes} \end{array}}{\text{animal} - \text{stripes}}$$

can be avoided if word classes and class relations rather than single words and simple relations are considered. However, this is but a different way of establishing transitivity. While we shall pay some attention to this possibility in Section III, A, 5, we first discuss more complex combinations than those depicted by the three paradigms.

2. Compounding of Relations

When two or more elements co-occur regularly, the relations involved may begin to function as elements of higher order. Such a stratification occurs for instance, when words are compounded such as, yellow-bird, store-keeper, window-pane, etc. Extending our symbolic representation, the condition can be depicted by bracketing the compounded terms:

$$(YELLOW - BIRD) = (X_1 T_1 X_2)$$

Subsequently, the problem raised would be expressed by the formula

$$(X_1 T_1 X_2) T_2 X_3$$

for instance,

$$(YELLOW - BIRD) - SINGS$$

in contrast to the original formula:

$$X_1 T_1 X_2 ; X_2 T_2 X_3$$
$$YELLOW - BIRD; BIRD - SINGS$$

The problems are not limited to word compoundings but lead us directly into questions of semantic and syntactic levels, strata, and hierarchies. The above example represents, indeed, the combination of a noun phrase NP, i.e. YELLOW - BIRD, with the verb SING. Instead of bracketing, Chomsky has preferred to depict the hierarchical organization by tree diagrams:

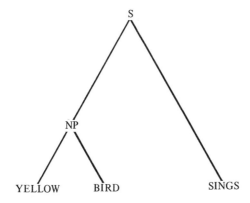

Thus, our example provides the important connection with the extensive discussions of syntactic structures and its acquisition (see McNeill, 1970a).

3. *Relations of Relations*

In spite of their concern about organization and structure, psycholinguists have paid little attention to what we might call relations of relations. Since logicians and mathematicians have more extensively discussed this question, we ought to translate, eventually, their idealized descriptions into the common language with which we are dealing.

Two relations, such as RABBIT-RUNS, EAGLE-FLIES, can be monotonically combined with one another and with other relations, thus, providing for the development of such classes as "animals" and "animated actions." These relations also can become a part of more complex expressions but, for this purpose, connectors need to be introduced. Two types of function words serve such connective purposes: conjunctions and relative pronouns. In particular, symmetric conjunctions like AND, TOO, ALSO, AS WELL AS, etc., the comma in enumerations, and relative pronouns like WHICH, WHO, and THAT, express—in analogy to our former distinction—logical relations of coordination and superordination-subordination between relations as in the following examples.

Superordination-Subordination: (RABBIT-RUNS) which (EAGLE-HAUNTS)
or RABBIT which (EAGLE-HAUNTS)-RUNS
Coordination: (EAGLE-FLIES) and (RABBIT-RUNS)

Asymmetric conjunctions like, IF . . . THEN, BECAUSE, BEFORE, AFTER, etc. and relative adverbs like WHERE, WHEN, WHY, etc. generate infralogical relations between relations and represent spatial, temporal causal, and other conditions as in the following examples:

Spatial: (HOUSE-BURNS) where (JOHN-LIVES)
Temporal-Causal: (CORN-GROWS) after (SUN-SHINES)
if (EAGLE-FLIES) then (RABBIT-RUNS) etc.

It is neither possible for us to provide a comprehensive analysis of the logical and infralogical connections of simple relations and other subunits of sentences nor is any substantial literature on the language acquisition process available. Perhaps some of the earlier descriptive studies on the usage of various parts of speech in children's language will be pertinent (see especially, E. A. Davis, 1937, 1938, Heider & Heider, 1940; Zyve, 1927). In spite of the lack of evidence, there can be no doubt that these logical and infralogical relations of relations are prior and of greater importance in the language acquisition process than any syntactic structure reflecting formal linguistic conventions. Since permutations of terms in logical syntax produce, in most cases, changes in interpretation, logical syntax is more basic and universal than the syntactic features of languages. Therefore, the child will first learn to operate with logical and infralogical combinations; as a by-product he generates sentences that incorporate words in their proper syntactic order.

4. Analogical Inferences

Thus far we have discussed verbal utterances as if they were nothing but strings of simple relations. While this is certainly true for their surface appearance, we also realize that underneath there are numerous interconnections allowing for specific interpretations as well as for the analysis of classes which, in turn, suggest a more comprehensive and more economic description. Subsequently, the relations appearing overtly in an utterance have to be thought of as selected from more general classes and systems of class relations. The possibility for such an extension has been given early in our paper when we described how an individual derives knowledge about classes and class relations. If we take these operations for granted, we can account for analogical inferences and make our interpretation of sentence production both more general and more flexible.

If two relations are combined and if there is transitivity between them, logical inferences can be drawn by connecting the free ends of the intersecting relations. If there is no transitivity, the inference is complex and ambiguous. However, an exception exists if the elements of one of the two relations are members of a class, i.e., if they either elicit each other mutually (reverberation), and/or if they are connected through various indirect pathways (stimulus and equivalence paradigms). Such cases provide the basis for analogical inferences through which a specific relation connected with one of the class members, such as the relations of whole-part, superordination, antonymity, etc., is transferred to other class members as in the following example. Class: BARN-STABLE; STABLE-BARN; relation: BARN-HAY; inference: STABLE-COW.

Our example lists only the most essential prerequisites for analogical inferences. Realistic inferences have to rely on well-developed relational structures in which the inferred term, COW, is already firmly embedded. Even though most important for generating information, analogical inferences—to this author's knowledge—have not been treated in a systematic and formal manner. For this reason, we can only suggest their exploration within a relational system but are not able to pursue this topic in a satisfactory manner.

5. Class Relations

If, instead of elements and simple relations we discuss classes and relations between classes, we shift to what Chomsky has called phrase structure grammar. Such an extension is not limited, of course, to syntax but holds for semantic systems as well. Instead of proposing simple relations such as RABBIT-RUNS, EAGLE-FLIES, and explicating the types of their combinations, we speak in terms of semantic classes such as "animals," "foods," "toys," "tools," "animated actions," etc. and in terms of general relations which do not only link but also define these classes. (Tentatively, we propose that the tasks of our restricted association norms represent such general relations.) Since there is no unique and nonoverlapping set of semantic classes, only the most formal and abstract features of the language, namely those of syntax, have been described in a less than ambiguous manner. But even here, multiple classifications of words often outweigh one-to-one assignments. These ambiguities might seem disturbing, but they also guarantee the richness of linguistic expressions and the creative potential of the language.

Rules of concatenations of semantic or syntactic classes are more general and abstract than rules about the chaining of simple relations and the concatenations of elements. Thus while the resulting semantic and syntactic systems are more powerful, Chomsky regards them as almost equally insuffient because they do not account for transformational operations. Transformation systems are more comprehensive but it is well conceivable, that these grammars "coexist" and that large portions of children's language skills might be sufficiently explained by systems of classes and class relations, without evoking more complex operations.

B. Transformations

Linguistic transformation, in contrast to mathematical transformations, introduce a change or rearrangement of ordered events, i.e., they imply the reversal of one or more relations. While we do not need to discuss at length the syntactic transformations and their acquisition [this topic has received thorough attention; see McNeill, (1970a)] it is of interest to demonstrate how widely applicable the concept of transformation is and how much it permeates various areas of psychology.

A first example of linguistic transformations has been presented by Lenneberg (1967). In the acquisition of speech patterns, the sequence of sounds produced is not necessarily related in an invariant manner to the sequence in which the motor nerves need to be fired. Thus, the production of a speech sound late in the sequence may need to be initiated prior to some other sounds earlier in the sequence. The crisscrossing of events of the two time sequences is primarily determined by differences in the length of the nerve fibers, the nerves and the muscles of the speech apparatus activated. Thus, the two time sequences are transformed in a nonmonotonic manner.

Second, in his attempt to explain the differential decline in semantic-cognitive functioning during the aging process, the present writer (K. F. Riegel, 1957) proposed two intellectual operations: one of combining or relating features such as of identifying essential parts, coordinated terms, class names, etc. and the other of finding their inverse, such as separating out the nonessential parts, reversing the relation of superordination, identifying nonsimilar, i.e., antonym items, etc. Each of these operations would increase the conceptual difficulties in solving the items and would, in particular, affect the performance of aged Ss in a negative manner such that with an increase in the number of operations, the decline in performance would be more marked. These propositions were successfully tested except for those involving the operation of reversals. Most likely, because our task relied too heavily on overlearned antonym relations like BLACK-WHITE, TOP-BOTTOM, etc. rather than on spontaneous reversal operations, the decline in performance was negligible (see K. F. Riegel, 1959b, 1968c). If the reversal operation had been applied under more complex conditions, perhaps in conjunction with several other operations, different results might have been obtained.

A third example has been discussed in the literature on language development (see E. A. Davis, 1938; Goodenough, 1930; F. M. Young, 1942) as well as in interpretations of personality changes, namely the acquisition of the ostensive relations and the active use of the personal pronouns. All parents are aware of the difficulty in, if not impossibility of instructing a young child on when to use "I" and when to use "you." Precise information is much too abstract and will not be understood by the child, such as "whenever you speak of or about yourself, use I, whenever you address another person, use you, etc." Moreover, this example at the beginning implies the use of the address "you" which it purports to explain. Nevertheless, at an age between two and four years, the child, all of a sudden, seems to perform some kind of an internal switch between what he hears and how he says things. Prior to this moment, he will be restricted to using proper names for other persons as well as for himself, a method which frequently is reinforced by well-meaning parents.

Fourth, researchers of personality development have regarded the switch to an active use of personal pronouns as an indication of much deeper rooted changes in the child, changes which essentially indicate his growing awareness of himself and the differentiation of his own wishes, emotions, and thoughts. Also the early Piaget (1959) in his studies of egocentric and socialized speech has devoted much attention to these changes. At an age at which a child is well able to apply personal pronouns, he still may fail to switch flexibly from restricted self-concern (perhaps in form of monologue without social interactions) to a concern about others (be it through directions, questions, or transmission of information). Whether we view this development with Piaget as progressing toward a socialized state or with Vygotsky (1962) as an internalization of overt speech culminating in speechless thought, it indicates the child's increasing ability to put himself into different positions (Sarbin, 1954) and thus implies conceptual, emotional transformations.

Fifth, our last remarks imply that social behavior, in general, requires transformation, namely the interacting person's ability to switch roles. That such role switching behavior is of greatest importance not only for language development but for the emotional and intellectual development of children has not only been confirmed by clinical observers, but has been proposed since the earliest investigations and interpretations of children's games (Groos, 1896, 1899). More recently, Weir (1962) emphasized the significance of games, in particular, with imaginary instruction-giving partners for language development. Livant (personal communication) has made the concrete proposal to apply mathematical game theory to the study of linguistic activities of children. In a game like "Simple Simon Says," for instance, particular ostensive relations of pointing at body parts are brought into conflict with (are negated by) intralingual relations. Thus, the game does not only provide an exercise in labeling but also in transformations.

Sixth, our attempts to consider children's games, their role behavior and certain aspects of their personality development as exercises or expressions of transformations seem to have us far removed from the original form in which transformations have been discussed in linguistic theories. We approach this topic more closely again when we consider some of Piaget's recent interpretations. The concept of transformations in Piaget's work is linked to the notions of reversibility and equilibrium. The child's ability to reverse a cognitive operation either by overt manipulations or, at a later stage, conceptually, represents one of the most important criterions for equilibrium. Piaget provides numerous examples of how children at certain ages are able to reverse a series of items or to derive judgements about conservation by realizing the reversibility of the process of pouring water from one container into another. Bruner (1964) gives a somewhat more complex example of a two-dimensional display of 16 beakers, defined in height and width, (four instances each) which after two examples are placed onto a second display board, are to be arranged by the child in inverse orders.

Seventh, as in linguistics, Bruner's task of transformation, while keeping the structure of the arrangement invariant, nevertheless asks for a flip-over of the two dimensions. In linguistic transformations such a reversal is rarely extended over the whole string of relations but over a selected subset only, such as between the verb and subject (see Beilin & Kagan, 1969). Partial reversals of this type are crucial for translations, especially between inflected and noninflected languages. Noninflected languages generally rely on one or a few fixed word orders, whereas inflected languages use word order as a means of expressing information about different sentence types and thus, produce greater variability. Undoubtedly, the need to transform the word order between languages places a heavy burden upon the translator but also makes the study of translation and bilingualism an exceedingly rich source of information.

According to Piaget's, as well as to our own, view the ability to reverse intellectual operations can only be developed after the operation itself is performed and, perhaps, has been organized into a well-developed cognitive skill. For this reason it might not be too disappointing that a young field like psychology—as most clearly stated by Stevens (1951)—has been exclusively concerned with the identification of features that remain invariant during the processes under investigation. On the other hand, Piaget and modern linguists encourage us to go beyond the analysis of invariant features and to study those as in pattern perception processes that reverse or transform intellectual operations in the sense of the linguists. Of course it would be much too ambitious to expect that a formal and systematic treatment of these "variant" transformations could succeed in the near future and, thus, it was but the purpose of our discussion to call attention to the wide-spread evidence that could substantiate or advance some of these interpretations.

ACKNOWLEDGMENT

The preparation of this manuscript has been supported by grant 5 PO1 HD 01368–04 from the National Institute of Child Health and Human Development. The author gratefully acknowledges the assistance of Dr. Ruth M. Riegel.

CHAPTER 15

Research on Language Acquisition: Do We Know Where We Are Going?

DAVID S. PALERMO

PENNSYLVANIA STATE UNIVERSITY,
UNIVERSITY PARK, PENNSYLVANIA

ABSTRACT

A brief historical review and critical evaluation of research approaches to the problem of language acquisition is presented. Major attention is focused upon current psycholinguistic research and the linguistic as well as psychological environment from which it has grown. Research results are summarized which seem to be incompatible with current learning theories. It is concluded that a reorientation toward the field is required to include the mentalistic and rationalistic concepts currently found to be useful in linguistics.

I. HISTORICAL INTRODUCTION

I have long been amazed by the lack of attention which psychologists have given to language and the processes by which man acquires that unique behavior which distinguishes him from all other animals. Some psychologists have naïvely assumed that they were progressing toward an understanding of language in their

401

research on verbal learning but, as Glanzer (1967) has recently pointed out, the investigator in this field has done his best to force language out of the verbal learning laboratory. Child psychologists have shown little more interest than others in the problem of language. I recently contributed to a rather massive book on child psychology (Reese & Lipsitt, 1970) which devoted considerably more space to the discussion of discrimination learning than to language. This imbalance has been symptomatic of the entire field of psychology for the past fifty years. Before considering that issue, however, I should like to point out the characteristics of some of the research which has been done by child psychologists in an effort to understand the development and functions of language in the human organism.

A. Baby Biographies

As with most other aspects of child behavior, the history of the study of language acquisition began with biographies of babies. Numerous such observations of individual children are available for study. They range from general observations on the development of the semantic systems (e.g., Taine, 1876), syntactic development (e.g., W. G. Bateman, 1914), and phonological-development (e.g., Velten, 1943) in English as well as development in languages other than English (e.g., Gregoire, 1937), to language development of bilingual children (e.g., Leopold, 1939-1949) and even the language development of chimpanzees (Kellogg & Kellog, 1933).

The standard criticisms of baby biography studies apply to these reports as well. The observations lack objectivity, the observations are not always regular, the sample of children is unusually select, and the observer is biased. In addition, such data on language often suffer from the observer's lack of linguistic skills. Recording the language of the child in the usual alphabet, for example, tells little about the phonological development and some aspects of syntax of the child although it may not have a serious effect upon the interpretation of semantic development. One of the prerequisites for psychologists doing research in this area is some minimal knowledge of linguistics, i.e., it is essential to understand the structure of the behavior in order to study the nature of its development.

B. Developmental Research

During the 1920s through the 1940s psychologists began to direct a good deal of attention to a more objective description of the development of the human. Language was not neglected during this era and we find a rather large number of reports in the literature describing the sound and speech development of children. These studies were primarily concerned with describing the naturally occurring developmental patterns as a function of age, sex, socioeconomic status, rural and urban environments, race, size of family, and other related variables.

The classic series of reports from the longitudinal study on infant vocal development by O. C. Irwin (e.g., H. P. Chen & Irwin, 1946; Irwin & Chen, 1941) is a typical example of the research of this time. Another classic study in the same tradition is the cross-sectional study by Templin (1957) which was concerned with the development of articulation, speech sound discrimination, syntax, and vocabulary, as well as the interrelations among these aspects of language development. A large number of other developmental studies, most of which are less extensive, have been conducted and the results have been carefully summarized by McCarthy (1954).

The criticisms of these studies focus upon the failure to test experimentally any of the hypotheses generated to account for the apparent developmental trends. The characteristic methodological concerns were with the representativeness of the sample and the reliability of the measures used. Numerous inductive generalizations about children's development were advanced on the basis of the observations made but no effort was devoted to the manipulation of variables under the control of the experimenter to determine the functional relationships between such variables and the language behaviors of interest. In general, the research of this period also lacked any theoretical underpinning, i.e., the basic orientation was to find the descriptive facts and leave the theory construction to others.

C. Experimental Research

In the 1950s the child field took on a much more experimental orientation and research concerned with language turned to an exploration of the function which words have in affecting performance in various learning tasks. Considerable effort was devoted to the investigation of acquired distinctiveness and acquired equivalence of cues. The theoretical motivation for these studies came from the Hullian notion of secondary generalization (Hull, 1939) expanded by Dollard and Miller (1950). The basic idea, in the case of acquired distinctiveness, was that attaching distinctive verbal labels to physical stimuli which were similar would make the subsequent stimulus pattern of response produced stimuli associated with the verbal label, along with the actual physical stimulus, more distinctive than the physical stimulus alone. The resultant decrease in generalization of habit tendencies to the two stimulus pattern would allow subsequent learning of new responses to those physical stimuli to proceed more rapidly. The acquired equivalence of cues hypothesis follows the same theoretical lines of reasoning. It is argued that attaching the same or similar names to physically distinctive stimuli leads to an increased tendency for a response learned to one stimulus to generalize to the other. The Norcross

(1958), Jeffrey (1953), and W. O. Shepard (1956) studies are examples of research which has been interpreted as support for these theoretical hypotheses.

A large number of other studies grew out of this general theoretical framework as extensions of the acquired distinctiveness and equivalence hypotheses. It was reasoned that since a response could produce stimuli it should follow that other responses could be learned to those stimuli in new situations. Thus, any number of relatively more complicated learning situations could be accounted for in terms of responses learned to mediators consisting of an overt or covert verbal response and the stimuli associated with that verbal response. This particular area of research became of considerable interest when it was discovered that children below some critical age, variously set between five and seven years, were obviously able to talk, but did not seem to use the available language to mediate responses while children above that age did seem to make use of language to mediate new responses (e.g., Kendler & Kendler, 1962; Kuenne, 1946). Reese (1962) has reviewed the literature on the problem of what he has called the mediational deficiency of young children in a variety of tasks. White (1965) has discussed the same general issue within a broader context.

The research of the experimental child psychologist certainly met the objections raised earlier with respect to the developmental research. The research reflects rigorous methodological control and the goal has been the establishment of lawful relationships between independent and dependent variables. The major criticism of this research is that it has very little to do with language. Most of the investigators are primarily interested in the mechanisms of learning and only secondarily, if at all, interested in language. There is no evidence that the researchers in this group have any knowledge of linguistics, and for the most part, this is unnecessary to the research which they are pursuing because the research does have so little to do with language.

D. Verbal Learning

One other line of research should be mentioned here since it is often suggested that it has something to do with language, although child psychologists have contributed relatively little to the factual knowledge in the area. I refer to the field of verbal learning which has had a long and relatively uninterrupted history despite major changes in other aspects of the field of psychology. I think it is safe to say that most psychologists interested in traditional verbal learning problems are interested in the learning process and not the language which happens to be used in the learning task. In fact, the language is a nuisance which researchers in this field have unsuccessfully attempted to eliminate by the use of nonsense materials.

On the other hand, I do think that many of those interested in word associations and verbal mediation within the verbal learning tradition have considered that they are using a sound experimental approach to the complicated problem of language and that the results of their research may have some relatively direct bearing upon the understanding of language acquisition and language function. The theory of how words become associated which was advanced by Ervin (1961) is one example of how the relationship between verbal learning and language might be conceived as related. The R. W. Brown and Berko study (1960) has lent further credence to the idea that word associations and grammar are related phenomena. Those studying the phenomena of mediation in the verbal learning laboratory have also felt that their work is related to thinking, and therefore language, in the sense that it was conceived as an experimental examination of how ideas become associated (e.g., Horton & Kjeldergaard, 1961, p. 1). Three basic paradigms have been studied: the A-B, B-C, A-C chaining paradigm, the A-B, C-B, A-C stimulus equivalence paradigm and the B-A, B-C, A-C response equivalence paradigm. Strong experimental evidence for all of these mediation paradigms was provided with adult subjects by Horton and Kjeldergaard (1961). In addition, there is evidence to support the mediation interpretation when larger numbers of associative links play a part prior to the mediation test (Russell & Storms, 1955). The literature on mediation with adults is quite extensive but the experiments with children have in many ways been much more impressive largely because the mediation effects are not limited to the early trials of the transfer task as is typically the case in the adult studies. Studies of chaining (e.g., Nikkel & Palermo, 1965; Norcross & Spiker, 1958), stimulus equivalence (e.g., Palermo, 1962; Shapiro & Palermo, 1968), and response equivalence (e.g., Palermo, 1966) have all shown clear mediation effects with children.

The underlying assumption that this work deriving from the verbal learning laboratory was germane to language was made explicit when Jenkins and Palermo (1964; see also Palermo, 1970b) attempted to account for the acquistion of syntax by children using mediation theory as the major explanatory tool. The basic argument was that sentential sequencing involved the chaining paradigm and that grammatical classes are gradually differentiated through the processes of mediation of the stimulus and response equivalence type. It was argued that words used in the same syntactic positions tend to form equivalences and that once equivalences are formed, the use of one word from the class in a sentence allows generation of new sentences by substitution of other members of the class in the same syntactic position. New sentences can be devised through mediation by chaining.

A critical evaluation of this research and the theoretical efforts to account for language which the research has generated center primarily upon the naïvety of most of the psychologists involved with respect to the characteristics of the language they have attempted to explain. Some critics have argued that the theory is inadequate in principle (e.g., Chomsky, 1959; Fodor, 1965) but whether or not this is the case, there is no question of the linguistic ignorance of many of the persons working in the verbal learning area and, unfortunately, this includes most of those researchers who have indicated that they think that their work is related to language. Unlike those working with acquired distinctiveness of cues and the mediational deficiency hypothesis, a knowledge of the structure of language which linguistics provides is essential to those who do wish to relate their work directly to language behavior rather than limit research to the effects of words in relatively restricted contexts.

II. PSYCHOLINGUISTICS

This brief review of the research of child psychologists concerned with language behavior has been sketchy and certainly does not do justice to many who have contributed to the field, but it does give the flavor of some of the historical trends within the child area which have preceded the rise of the new specialty which has come to be known as psycholinguistics. The study of the process by which a child acquires his native language forms a part of the field of psycholinguistics.

While the term psycholinguistics has a history which dates at least back to 1935 (Kantor, 1935), it has only come to be widely used since the publication of a survey of theory and research in this area which grew out of a conference of psychologists, linguists, and anthropologists interested in bringing about a multidisciplinary attack upon the problems encountered in understanding the nature and function of human language (C. E. Osgood & Sebeok, 1954). While that book attempted to present the goals, techniques, and possible contributions to the study of language which could be made by the disciplines represented, it did not have an important impact upon any of the three fields concerned because the orientation toward the study of language began to undergo some dramatic changes very shortly after the volume was published. Those changes were initiated in 1957 by the publication of a thin volume written by Chomsky (1957) entitled, *Syntactic Structures.* Chomsky's book precipitated a scientific revolution within the field of linguistics which may well spill over into psychology via psycholinguistics.

A. Bloomfieldian Linguistics

Prior to the publication of *Syntactic Structures,* the science of linguistics in this country had been dominated by Leonard Bloomfield whose book *Introduction to the Study of Language* (1914) and a subsequent revised and extended version entitled simply *Language* (1933) had prescribed the subject matter and methodology of the field for the preceding four decades. Bloomfield is the father of what has been called the "American school" of linguistics and he tried particularly hard to establish linguistics as an autonomous and a scientific field.

His concern about autonomy apparently was directed toward psychology from which he wished to remain separate. In his 1914 book Bloomfield had tried to relate linguistics to psychology but the psychology to which he related it was that of Wundt. Unfortunately for Bloomfield, he had pinned his linguistics to a psychology which had just been rejected by J. B. Watson (1913) the year before. Between the time of his first book and his second, Bloomfield himself was converted from the psychology of Wundt to that of Watson. While Bloomfield adopted the behavioristic approach for his science, he rejected any affiliation with that changeable science of psychology and maintained that linguistics would stand on its own feet as an independent science.

Bloomfield also focused on the characteristics of science which he felt linguistics should strive to meet. He was evidently influenced strongly in this area by A. P. Weiss, one of the most exacting behaviorists in psychology. Weiss dispensed with the mind by reducing it to biological and socially observable events which could account for all behavior. Bloomfield extended his general notion to linguistics by adopting the same antimentalistic position. Bloomfield felt that mechanism was the necessary form of scientific discourse and he interpreted this to mean that the facts were to be observed and reported without any additional assumptions about other factors playing a part. In essence he took the same antitheoretical orientation toward his field which was taken by O. C. Irwin who was also markedly influenced by A. P. Weiss.

Bloomfield was reacting to the dualistic conceptions of language such as the "inner form" and "outer form" of von Humboldt and the "langue-parole" distinction of de Saussure which played an important part in the traditional linguistics of Europe. The Watsonian reaction of psychology to the study of consciousness and the introspective method seemed just the right solution to Bloomfield and he led linguistics down the same path. Bloomfield's descriptive fact collecting approach to the field was scientifically exact and unprejudiced by theory because he assumed that inductive generalizations would emerge from the descriptive data when enough of it was known. The approach taken was very similar to that approach which so long dominated the field of child psychology. The major difference between the two fields in terms of scientific approach was that child developmentalists were much more willing to study the child from a multidisciplinary point of view while Bloomfield wished to establish linguistics as independent of other disciplines.

B. Difficulties with the American School Approach

The descriptive, fact-accumulating, atheoretical approach to linguistics ran into difficulties, however, because it was unable to handle many of the interesting problems of language. For example, it was assumed by Fries (1940) that it would be possible to define grammatical classes by showing that one class fit into a slot in a standard sentence frame and other classes fit into other slots within a sentence frame. This substitution in frames technique, however, failed because it turns out that you have to know something about the grammatical structure of the sentences in advance in order to know whether a particular constituent will fit in the frame. For example, the slot in the frame "———— was good" can be filled by "The concert" and by "He was bad or he" but these two parts of sentences are clearly not comparable although both form perfectly grammatical sentences.

A related problem which poses difficulties for this group of linguists arises in connection with ambiguous sentences. Consider the sentence

You can't imagine how good oysters taste

which can have several meanings including the meanings that oysters taste good to someone, good oysters as opposed to bad oysters have a particular taste, and oysters themselves have a good sense of taste. The words in the sentence have different grammatical functions depending upon which reading is given to the sentence. One more example may make the point clear, The sentence

They were fascinating girls

is ambiguous and difficult to handle because the slot filled by the word "fascinating" may be used to define a verb or an adjective depending upon the meaning of the sentence. Only by recognizing this fact can the sentence be disambiguated.

While not wishing to give up the behavioristic and mechanistic orientation to the field, some linguists attempted to avoid the difficulties of the substitution in frames analysis of sentences by postulating a hierarchical analysis of the relation of the parts within sentences. Such an approach becomes more abstract, but it does solve some of the problems which the analysis of sentences as a series of slots arranged from left to right cannot handle. The phrase structure, or constituent structure, analyses of language were attempts to show that there are two structures to the last sentence discussed above and that one structure relates "fascinating" more closely to "were" in one interpretation and to "girls" in the other interpretation. This type of analysis shows that a sentence is composed of phrases or constituents and those constituents are composed of constituents. The constituents are related to each other in a hierarchical fashion. The relationships of the constituents may be represented by tree diagrams or by the use of brackets. The two interpretations the sentence mentioned above may be distinguished by the following bracketing of the constituents:

((They) ((were fascinating) (girls)))
((They) ((were) (fascinating girls)))

While introducing the phrase structure analysis solved some kinds of problems, it left others still unsolved. The sentence

He was killed by the falling bridge

does not have two different phrase structures to differentiate the two meanings which any native speaker of the language can recognize, i.e. one describing *where* he was killed and the other *how* he was killed. Putting different labels on parts of the phrase structure description might help but even that will not solve the problem posed by a sentence such as

Bill likes Jill more than Will

where the ambiguity of the sentence results from the lack of an overt manifestation of parts of the sentence which would disambiguate the sentence.

There are still other problems with a phrase structure grammar. Such a grammar cannot express the relation between the following two sentences:

I gave the key back.
I gave back the key.

The sentences are clearly related but the phrase structure analyses of the two sentences are quite different. Phrase structure grammar does not allow one to show the relation between a sentence and the paraphrase of a sentence or between two paraphrases of a sentence. Finally, there is no way for phrase structure grammars to handle the problem of the difference between the sentences

John is easy to please
John is eager to please

which have the same phrase structure but in which "John" is the subject of the sentence in one case and the object of the sentence in the other case, a point which is clear as soon as you attempt to paraphrase the two sentences.

C. Chomsky's Linguistics

Adherence to the type of science which Bloomfield outlined for the field of linguistics seems inadequate to account for aspects of language which are intuitively clear to any native speaker of the language despite the fact that the data have pushed linguists of this persuasion to the postulation of abstract structures which are not observable in the data. The language user seems to know more about his language than the descriptive linguist, restricted by the type of acceptable scientific procedures allowed by Bloomfield's perscription, is able to capture. Chomsky's contribution in *Syntactic Structures* was to convincingly point out some of the inadequacies of the Bloomfieldian approach and, more importantly, to offer a solution in the form of transformational generative grammar. The solution involved a redefinition of the field of linguistics and the methodology to be used. It prescribed an end to the radical empiricism of the Bloomfieldian era and an adoption of a mentalistic and rationalistic approach to the science of linguistics. In short, it precipitated a scientific revolution within the field of linguistics.

The goal of linguistics, according to Chomsky, is to construct a theory of language, i.e., to construct a grammar made up of a finite set of rules capable of generating all of the infinite set of grammatically correct utterances possible in any language and none of the grammatically incorrect utterances which might be possible. Such a set of rules would describe the knowledge which a native speaker of a language has about his language. This knowledge is referred to as the linguistic *competence* of the language user, i.e., the set of rules which allow the user to speak and understand the language by relating the sound system to the meaning system, the phonetic representation to the semantic representation. Competence is one of the factors which determines performance, i.e., competence is an abstraction which describes the prerequisite part of the mental equipment of the language user. It is in this sense that linguistics is mentalistic. It attempts to discover "a mental reality underlying actual behavior [Chomsky, 1965, p. 4]." Performance, of course, is the actual behavior which may be affected by any number of other variables and from which competence is inferred. Thus, a clear distinction is made between competence and performance, between the knowledge in the mind and the overt behavior. The overt behavior may be influenced by all kinds of other factors including such things as memory, fatigue, distraction, and a host of other variables. The grammar of a language, which is the goal the linguist seeks to attain, is a model for the idealized competence. The idealized competence may be distorted in various ways in performance because of the other nonlinguistic factors which can affect its expression. In order to understand performance, however, it is clear that the structure of competence or the grammars which characterize it, must be understood. In this sense linguistics is a part of psychology and not independent of it as Bloomfield attempted to establish.

The grammar of a language, according to Chomsky (1965), consists of a tripartite system of rules pertaining to semantics, syntax, and phonology. How these subsets of rules are interrelated is a matter of current linguistic controversy (e.g., J. R. Ross, 1967) but Chomsky argues that the syntactic component relates the deep structure of the semantic component to the surface structure of the phonological component. Thus, the semantic component consists of the rules pertaining to the underlying meaning to be expressed, the syntactic component consists of the rules for converting the deep structure to a surface structure form which can be interpreted by the phonological rules. There are, therefore, rules for interpreting meaning, rules for interpreting the sounds, and rules for pairing the appropriate meanings with the appropriate sounds.

The rationalist aspect of the new approach proposed by Chomsky is concerned primarily with the conception of the mind as being structured in such a way as to determine the form which language will take. The form which mental processes take is determined by the nature of the organism. It is argued that there is an innate latent mental structure which is characteristically human and which becomes active as a function of sensory experience, i.e., when appropriate environmental conditions are presented so that the latent structures may manifest themselves.

Applied specifically to language, Chomsky argues that all languages have common or universal constraints. The general form and even some of the substantive features of the grammar for particular languages overlap with those of all other languages, i.e., they are determined by the nature of the mental structures and processes which characterize man. Chomsky argues that there are substantive universal aspects of language and formal universal aspects. Neither has been well specified as yet but both have been characterized. The substantive universals refer to the nature of the phonological, syntactic, and semantic units of which language is composed. It has been suggested, for example, that all languages have a particular set of syntactic classes such as noun and verb or subject and predicate. It has also been argued that the phonological component can be characterized with a small number of features defined in terms of articulatory and acoustic properties which are independent of any particular language. Formal universals, on the other hand, refer to the form of the rules which will appear in the grammar. Transformational rules, for example, may be required to handle the syntactic component of the grammar satisfactorily.

The notion of language universals is particularly important to those researchers interested in going beyond linguistics per se to the study of language performance because it pertains directly to the processes of language acquisition. It suggests that the child is constrained in certain ways by his biological constitution. The child receives a limited amount of language from those who speak to him but he treats that data at the phonological, syntactic, and semantic levels in a restricted manner, i.e., the hypotheses about the input will be limited, and he will be able to determine the specific grammar which is appropriate to his language from the minimal input he does receive. It takes only a small amount of environmental support to permit the child to select the correct grammar for his language community and thus enable him to generate and comprehend utterances which are unique to him, i.e., to know or be creative with the language. It should be specifically noted, however, that the study of language acquisition involves the question of how the linguistic competence is brought into play, i.e., how a grammar is selected from among the many possible grammars as well as how performance may be determined by that competence and the other factors which affect performance. The competence model is not a performance model but the performance model must incorporate the competence model.

D. Early Psycholinguistic Research

Without facing the implications which accepting this position about language may have for a present day psychologist interested in the language acquisition process, I would like to examine the findings of some of the more recent research which has appeared in the literature. The relevant research began with descriptive reports of the initial linguistic constructions of children made by R. W. Brown and his colleagues (Brown & Bellugi, 1964; Brown, Cazden, & Bellugi, 1969; Brown & Fraser, 1964; Brown, Fraser & Bellugi, 1964; Klima & Bellugi, 1966), W. R. Miller and Ervin (1964; W. R. Miller, 1964a, 1964b), and Braine (1963b). The general methodology of these studies involved the collection of verbatim samples of the speech of a small group of children beginning at about the age of 18 to 24 months when the children were expanding from one word utterances to two word utterances. The children studied by Brown have been followed longitudinally at least until the children have mastered many of the linguistic structures of adult language a year or two later (R. W. Brown *et al.*, 1969). These descriptive data and the analyses which have been made of them provide some very interesting facts about language acquisition.

The first impressive fact is the rapidity with which children do acquire their language. Children seem to have mastered many of the intricacies of the language system before they enter school. Their sentences are not as long or complexly embedded, not as well articulated, and the vocabulary is not as diverse but the basic structure of the utterances is the same as the child will use for the rest of his life (Menyuk, 1964), a fact which was noted earlier by Templin (1957). This is an unusually impressive accomplishment when you consider the complexity of the language. Consider the facts that the child has, during his short two to four year period, acquired a vocabulary of a couple thousand words (more than one a day on the average), acquired a set of rules for putting words together to form sentences of many syntactic types, and acquired an ability to comprehend and produce the sounds of the complex and variant speech code. All of this occurs in an environment in which there is a great deal of signal noise and no recognizable effort to teach the language to the child. The available evidence which we do have about the reinforcement patterns of parents suggests that parents pay relatively little attention to the syntactic form of the child's language and a great deal more attention to the truth value of the child's statements (R. W. Brown *et al.*, 1969). Not only is there no apparent effort to teach language to the child, but frequently the teaching connected with language is at cross purposes with acquiring the language.

There is, of course, an opportunity for children to hear language used by competent adult speakers and to imitate what is heard. Ervin (1964) has examined the grammatical differences between the imitated utterances and the spontaneous utterances of five children. Grammatical rules were written for the free utterances of the children and then the children's spontaneous imitations of adult utterances were tested against the grammar to see if they were at the same or a more advanced grammatical level. While not denying that imitation may play some part in language acquisition, Ervin (1964) concluded ". . . that there is not a shred of evidence supporting a view that progress toward adult norms of grammar arises merely from practice in overt imitation of adult sentences [p. 172] ."

Slobin (1965) attempted a finer grained analysis of children's responses to expansions to determine whether there might be some circumstances under which the child appears to advance his grammar through imitation of the parent. Specifically, he examined exchanges between parent and child when the parent expanded something the child said and then the child imitated the expansion. Slobin found that under these conditions the child did expand his own previous utterance about 50% of the time. It would seem that Ervin's conclusion was too strong and that the child-parent reduction-expansion-reduction exchanges may play some role in language acquisition. It should be noted, however, that exchanges such as those which Slobin found to advance the language of the child were relatively infrequent and even then only 50% of the opportunities showed the expansions which might be expected under such circumstances.

Cazden (1965) experimentally examined the influence of adult verbal responses on the development of children's language. The research focused on comparing the effectiveness of expanding the utterances of children as opposed to merely presenting a model of the language in the sense of providing samples of well formed sentences. The subjects were twelve Negro children between the ages of 28 and 38 months attending an urban day care center. The children were divided into three groups matched on the basis of age, talkativeness, and initial level of language development measured in terms of mean length of utterance during the orientation period.

The experimenter spent 40 minutes each school day for three months with each of the four children in the expansion group deliberately expanding the utterances of the children. The modeling group spent 30 minutes per day over the same period with the experimenter during which time an equal number of well formed sentences were spoken to the child but no expansions were included. In other words, the experimenter responded to the children in the first group by expanding what they said and responded to the second group with normal conversation. The control group received no special treatment during the three-month period.

Analysis of the results indicated that there was no evidence that expansion aids the acquisition of grammar. In contrast to the initial hypothesis the children in the model group, with whom normal conversations were conducted, showed the most advance in language development on the measures used. In accounting for these results, it has been suggested that normal conversation increases the richness of the verbal stimulation, expands the ideas initiated by the child, and introduces more words and grammatical elements to express those ideas and related ideas. Expansion, on the other hand, merely repeats the same idea expressed by the child and does little more than echo what the child says (R. W. Brown *et al.,* 1969; Cazden, 1966). The results of this experiment, along with the Slobin (1965) analysis of the effects of parental expansions upon children's utterances, suggests that perhaps the ideal environment for child language development is one in which the parents expand the child's utterances both grammatically and semantically and thus provide both of the kinds of concepts necessary to the development of language.

Turning our attention to an analysis of the composition of the early utterances of the child, some additional interesting observations may be made. The two word utterances of the children in the studies of Braine, Brown, and Miller and Ervin all seem to show a characteristic structure. The child is not randomly juxtaposing two words which he has heard. There is an apparent system to his constructions which accounts for about 70% of the utterances heard. Examining the entire corpus, or sample, of the children's speech, it turns out that in the speech of all of the children observed there is a small group of words which occur fairly consistently in the first position, another smaller group of words which occur fairly consistently in the second position, and a large group of words which can occur in either first or second position. Using Braine's terminology (Braine, 1963b), we may say that the first language constructions of the child take the pivot-open or open-pivot form. There are two small classes of pivot words, one occurs in the initial position and the other in the second position and a larger open class of words which appear in either position. When the child uses single word utterances the words tend to come from the open class. The pivot words which occur in the first position tend not to overlap with the pivot words which occur in the second position but there is a great deal of overlap of the open class words in the two positions. Efforts to classify the words in the pivot and open classes in terms of adult grammatical classes is not particularly revealing (McNeill, 1970) but a close examination of the pairs of words suggests that in these various two-word utterances we may see the beginnings of constructions which are the adult equivalents of demonstrative constructions (e.g., "that truck"), noun phrases (e.g., two men), verb phrases (e.g., "See boy") and complete sentences.

In fact, G. A. Miller and McNeill (1969) have reported some very convincing data that these are the only kinds of constructions which the child is producing. They have noted that if one considers the pivot words, the nouns and verbs which Adam, one of Brown's subjects, used during the stage when he was beginning to utter two- and three-word utterances, there are only a few combinations which would reflect basic grammatical relations when analyzed from a linguistic point of view. Of the nine possible combinations of the three types of words taken in pairs, only four reflect basic grammatical relations and of the 27 possible combinations of the three types of words taken three at a time, only eight are admissible combinations from the linguistics analysis. An examination of every two word utterance made by Adam at this stage of his development revealed 349 such two-word utterances and every single one of them fell into the four admissible categories. All four admissible categories were used by the child and not one inadmissible utterance occurred. There were only 49 three-word utterances but each one of the eight admissible categories was used and not one of the three-word utterances fell in an inadmissible category. These are rather remarkable data considering the large number of alternative possibilities and the fact that some of the language of the parents could easily be construed by the child to fall into the inadmissible categories. R. W. Brown and Bellugi (1964) make the same point with respect to the development of the noun phrase in the speech of the child. It would appear from these data that even the very first multiword utterances of the child reflect aspects of the grammatical system which will eventuate. The child at this stage shows evidence of being able to conceptualize the relations expressed by the adult but lacks the abilities (perhaps nonlinguistic performance limiting abilities) necessary to produce a linguistically complete expression of those relations.

One other kind of observation made with respect to these developmental data should be mentioned. It has been noted in connection with a number of aspects of language development that the child progressively acquires rules pertaining to various aspects of language and these rules seem to appear relatively suddenly. When this happens the whole system changes regardless of the form of language preceding the new rule and often despite the fact that the new rule may lead to errors not previously made. This phenomenon has been pointed out by Ervin (1964) in connection with the development of past tense inflection of verbs, Bellugi (1964) in connection with the development of the negation system and interrogative structures (Bellugi, 1965), and by Slobin (1966b) in connection with various aspects of the acquisition of Russian.

Perhaps the case of past tense inflection is the simplest example to present here. Ervin has reported that after an initial period when no inflection is used, the irregular, or strong, verbs are correctly inflected for tense. Subsequently, the child acquires the regularized form of the past tense and overgeneralizes the regular form to the irregular verbs. Thus, the child is first observed to use the correct past-tense forms *ran, came, broke, did,* etc., in the appropriate contexts and at a later time, he begins to use the incorrect forms **runned, *comed, *breaked, *doed,* etc. Such overgeneralization errors of the regular form of the past-tense inflection persist in the language of some children into the elementary school years. Thus, the acquisition of the regular rule leads to errors in performance which were not made prior to the rule acquisition. In the case of the acquisition of the rules for negation, the child at one stage negates sentences correctly, subsequently he acquires a rule which is appropriate to some types of sentences but leads to double negation of other sentences. The latter sentences are corrected at a later time by a new rule which, in turn, leads to double negation of another type of sentence which has been correctly formed earlier. For example, the sentence

I don't want some sugar

is replaced at a later stage of development by

I don't want no sugar

and not until later does the child finally eliminate the seemingly more devious double negative of the more advanced level of development. The acquisition of a principle seems to be applied across the board until the child progressively differentiates and integrates the various parts of the system.

E. Psychological Reality of Linguistic Structure

It seems that these data derived primarily from observations and analyses of natural language make Chomsky's form of linguistics appear very appealing. The analysis of the structure of language which he has advanced seems to fit unusually well with the data. More important, perhaps, are the convincing mentalistic and rationalistic concepts which he advances in presenting his analysis of language and the manner in which the child acquires his language. These data seem to support his conceptions of how language is acquired in a much more persuasive manner than any analysis, including my own (Jenkins & Palermo, 1964; Palermo, 1970b), which has derived from various learning theory models. I do not see any convincing way in which current learning theories can account for the rapidity of language acquisition, for the lack of apparent conditions for learning including appropriate reinforcement conditions or effects of imitation, for the apparent aid to language acquisition of presenting new language rather than rewarding old language, for the evidence for underlying adult structures and lack of evidence of other stuctural forms in the earliest utterances of the child, and for the sudden changes in performance associated with what seems to be the adoption of new rules as the child progresses through the stages of acquisition. These kinds of data are just not within the realm of current psychological learning theory. This does not deny the usefulness of these theories in accounting for other kinds of behavior, particularly the behavior of lower animals, but I do not see how they can work for human language. Language is a complicated form of behavior which cannot be accounted for by the simple principles of conditioning no matter how elaborated. This is probably true of many other kinds of human behavior but we are fortunate that the linguists have accepted the task of providing us with the underlying structure of language behavior which is something we don't have for motor skills, a kind of behavior Lashley (1961) has argued cannot be handled by traditional learning theories. Despite this help from the linguist, we are still left with the problem of accounting for language performance with a theory which incorporates the linguistic model of competence. If we accept the mentalism and the rationalism of current linguistics, there is still a monumental research job ahead. Taking a mentalistic and rationalistic position does not remove one from the laboratory; rather, it reorients one toward the field of psychology in terms of objectives, research questions of interest, interpretations placed upon the findings, and the kinds of theoretical models which might be developed. In short, it requires what Kuhn (1962) has called a scientific revolution within psychology as is already taking place within the field of linguistics. As I have indicated elsewhere (Palermo, 1969), psychology shows all the signs which Kuhn describes of a science ripe for such a revolution. It is not difficult to show that a number of other areas within psychology are coming across anomolies which traditional behavioristic approaches and analyses are unable to handle.

Suppose for the moment that we accept this thesis. Suppose that we take the position that J. B. Watson (1913) was correct for his time, that his approach led us away from one kind of problem but now it has served its purpose and the time has come for a fresh orientation to the field. Suppose, further, that we accept Chomsky's views about language and the implications which that has for the conceptualization of the nature of the human organism and the behavior of that organism. If we do take such a position, we are immediately faced with the question of what research can be conducted which is relevant to the new questions at hand.

The initial answer to that question was a research attempt to demonstrate the psychological reality of the linguistic structure postulated by the linguists. It was assumed that if there is an underlying structure to language and if there are rules which convert that deep structure to a surface structure form, then it should be possible to show performance differences as a function of the complexity or number of rules which need to be processed in order to convert deep structure to surface structure. Slobin (1966a), for example, examined the development of the comprehension of active, passive, negative, and passive-negative sentences. His technique was to read his subjects a sentence and then present them a picture relevant to the sentence. The subject's task was to make a judgment as to whether the sentence was true or false relative to the picture. For example, sentences such as "The cat chases the dog," "The cat doesn't chase the dog," ' The dog is chased by the cat," or "The dog isn't chased by the cat" were presented and the picture depicted either the cat chasing the dog or the dog chasing the cat.

The subjects used in the experiment were six, eight, ten, twelve, and twenty years old, drawn from the kindergarten, second, fourth, sixth, and college grade levels. The response measure in all cases was the amount of time taken between the exposure of the picture and the selection of one of two switches indicating congruence or incongruence between the sentence and the picture. The results indicated that if the sentences were true with respect to the pictures, the reaction times were shortest for the simple active sentences and increasingly longer for the passive, negative, and negative-passive sentences. It had been anticipated that the negative sentences would be easier to comprehend than the passive sentences since the grammatical derivation of the negative sentences is less complex than that of the passive sentences. It appeared, however, that the semantic problems associated with negative sentences were a more potent variable than the syntactic problems. Thus, the subjects had more difficulty in making a decision about the picture if the sentence contained a negative element than if the sentence was in the passive form. In general, these results were similar to those obtained with adults by Gough (1965). Contrary to the results of the latter author, however, Slobin found that the children in his study had great difficulty with true negative sentences. Some of the children would not accept any of the negative sentences as being true of the pictures.

All sentences in which the subject and object were not reversable (e.g., The boy watered the flowers.) were easier for the children but performance on the passive constructions was especially facilitated. In fact, the passive construction was as easy as the active construction when nonreversable sentences were involved. It would appear that a part of the difficulty with passive sentences is in keeping track of which noun is the actor. Finally, the age differences did not seem particularly important in the study. There was an improvement with age on the more complex sentence forms but performance on the simple forms appeared to be relatively stable by the age of six.

It is clear from the results of the Slobin study, as well as others (e.g., Fodor & Garrett, 1967) which have attempted to investigate the psychological reality of the competence model, that the matter is much more complicated than had been imagined. Furthermore, it is clear that Chomsky's (1967) admonition that it would be a serious mistake to take the competence model as a performance model leaves a great deal for the psychologist to do in developing a theory to account for performance even if the linguists could present us with a perfect competence model which they are a long way from being able to do.

F. Future Research

If the approach exemplified by Slobin's research takes too simple a view of the problem, we are still left with the same question of research approach. Leaving aside the analysis of the structure of the behavior, how do we get at the questions of what the principles are which underlie correct performance? What kind of input does the child require in order to formulate those principles? What happens to the mind of the child when he formulates a principle? How does the child translate a principle into appropriate performance? What are the factors which interfere with or facilitate the actual performance guided by those principals? These are fascinating questions which demand ingenious experiments. It seems impossible to me to predict how they will be solved because we are just beginning to think about the questions and a review of the literature in the child area reveals that the surface has hardly been scratched.

Anisfeld and his colleagues (e.g., Anisfeld, Barlow, & Frail, 1968; Anisfeld & Gordon, 1968) are working with phonological rules to determine the behavioral significance of the distinctive feature analysis of speech sounds. McNeill (McNeill & McNeill, 1968) is examining the developmental characteristics of Japanese, in the manner of Brown, Miller and Ervin, and Braine, in an effort to make some cross-linguistic analyses with English. Slobin (1966b) has reported on the acquisition of Russian. Both are looking for linguistic universals which may be revealed in the common linguistic development of different languages. Huttenlocher and others (e.g., Huttenlocher, Eisenberg, & Strauss 1968; Huttenlocher & Strauss, 1968; Katz & Brent, 1968) have attempted to study comprehension as a function of various grammatical relationships within sentences. Still others are attempting to experimentally manipulate the conditions which lead to the production of various kinds of sentences (e.g., Hayhurst, 1967; E. A. Turner & Rommetveit, 1968). Braine (1963a, 1966) has attempted to construct artificial languages and examine the manner in which children acquire such languages but this approach has been severely criticized because the languages constructed lack the crucial properties of real languages (Bever, Fodor, & Weksel, 1965). My own research has centered about the construction or rule learning situations which are designed to be analogous to the kinds of rules which are found in language (Palermo & Eberhart, 1968). I have been trying to determine some of the variables which affect the rate at which rules are acquired and the effects of introducing irregularities into the rule learning situation. This research, however, does not directly involve language but is an attempt to abstract some of the characteristics of language for study in analogous situations. It is, therefore, subject to all of the problems which analogies bring with them. Most serious, of course, is the problem that the analogy may be a poor one and, as a result, irrelevant to language.

This does not cover all of the research which is currently being done with children in an effort to understand language acquisition but it gives a fair sampling of what kind of work has been published by those who have attempted to take the new linguistics seriously. It is a disappointingly small base from which to make predictions about the future course of research in this area. It is, however, exciting research in the sense that the orientation is fresh and promising of new insights. There seems to be a greater appreciation of what language acquisition may involve although there is a serious concern about what research approaches may be relevant to breaking open the important problems to experimental scrutiny. What kinds of research will help to answer the questions of the capacities, processes, and products of the human mind?

In answer to the question posed by the title of this paper, I do not think we know where we are going at the moment. I am sure that we cannot ignore linguistics and the scientific conceptualizations which Chomsky's linguistics implies, but I am not at all clear as to where that will lead us. At present we can only experimentally chip away at the language block until some of the larger pieces fall away and expose the more interesting characteristics of the model within. At the moment there are many in the field who are discouraged, but I am optimistic that future research will bring us new and useful insights before long.

ACKNOWLEDGMENT

Preparation of this paper was partially supported by Grant GB–8024 from the National Science Foundation and Public Health Service Research Career Program Award HD–28,120 from the National Institute of Child Health and Human Development.

INTELLECTUAL
ABILITIES

Organization of Data on Life-Span
Development of Human Abilities

JOHN L. HORN

UNIVERSITY OF DENVER,
DENVER, COLORADO

ABSTRACT

Data pertaining to the development of intellectual abilities in childhood and adulthood are reviewed within the framework of a general theory in which the cohesion-producing influences associated with acculturation and neurophysiology are emphasized and contrasted. First, it is noted that a striking amount of interrelationship has been found among abilities which, on the face of it, could be quite different—and when abilities are measured at quite different points in development (excluding only the first two years of life wherein the measured abilities bear little resemblance to, and are not predictive of, intellectual abilities measured in later childhood and thereafter). This broad cohesiveness is seen to represent a fact of interdependence of acculturational and neurophysiological influences—the fact that, to some extent, one determines and is determined by the other. It is noted, next, that interwoven within this broad pattern of interdependence are subpatterns of varying degrees of generality.

423

Some of these are seen to result from relatively focused kinds of training, as this derives from selective exposures, fairly specific kinds of motivations and similar factors. Quite broad patterns are found, however, and the evidence suggests that these represent more pervasive influences in development, such as those of acculturation, as such, and those associated with neurophysiological structure, maturation and damage. Indeed, accumulations of these pervasive influences throughout development appear to produce two broad patterns of the abilities which are identified as indicating intelligence. These patterns are said to indicate two intelligences, symbolized as Gf and Gc. In later childhood and adulthood the predictive and construct validities for these two become quite distinct. The abilities of Gc tend to increase—or at least not noticably decrease—with age in adulthood, but the abilities of Gf tend to decrease consistently and to a noteworthy extent throughout most of adulthood. Evidence indicating the neurophysiological and experiential factors associated with these changes is outlined.

I. INTRODUCTION

I have before me, scattered hither and yon, summaries of over six hundred studies pertaining to the development and organization of human abilities. I had hoped that I could capture the essential truths of all these and present this in an orderly manner to the reader. However, I now sit in glum despair, poignantly aware that I have been going around in circles in my study, that I cannot see any relationships between the results from many quite adequate studies, that my hopes for integration lie dashed on the rocks of contradiction and remoteness. Yet in what follows I have attempted to hold to my original purpose to organize the data which is most relevant for an understanding of the birth-to-death development of human abilities. I have rationalized that although such a grandiose scheme would be doomed to failure under even the most auspicious conditions, and is surely doomed in the present effort, nevertheless the attempt itself can be instructive, constructive, and therefore worthwhile.

Since this is merely a chapter, not a book, and many books could be (and have been) written about the development of abilities, only some of the more salient findings and theories can be touched upon. Fortunately for the reader several of the topics which are skimmed over here are handled in greater detail in the other chapters of this book. In some ways the present chapter is a rather verbose outline of the entire book.

The chapter is divided into five basic sections, this being the first and the fifth being followed by a general summary. In the second section some basic data pertaining to the interrelationships among abilities are outlined. The third and fourth sections are mainly theoretical. In these an attempt is made to cull from intellectual-psycholinguistic theories some of the major kinds of constructs needed to describe the behaviors that are measured in putative tests of intelligence. The idea of stages of development is used to help organize this material and in the last part of Section IV there is an attempt to show that the many-times replicated findings on factorial structure among abilities are a necessary consequence of identifiable influences operating in development. The fifth section is given over entirely to a review of the evidence and theory pertaining to development in adulthood. An attempt is made to show that the essential character of performance differences and performance changes associated with aging is elucidated by considering the matters in terms of the findings on factorial structure. In the general summary the top points of what are already acknowledged to be surface-like findings are trimmed off and presented in review.

II. UNITY AND DIFFERENTIATION AMONG ABILITIES

There are two major facts which any theory of human abilities must recognize. One is the fact that by adulthood the human displays many somewhat distinct abilities—abilities which are distributed independently in even rather restricted samples of subjects. The other is the rather surprising fact that the distribution for quite different abilities are not uncorrelated—that a notable amount of dependence is found even in rather restricted samples of subjects.

On the side of independence there are the findings, recently summarized by French, Ekstrom, and Price (1963), Guilford (1967), Butcher (1968) and Horn (1971), showing that some 28-50 separate primary factors are needed to account for the linear dependence found among the literally thousands of ability tests which have been invented. Several of these primary factors—e.g., in some of Guilford's work—may not be very important or may represent little more than alternate forms of the same test, as Humphreys (1962) has emphasized. To talk about an ability factor as a noteworthy influence in personality probably means that it must be defined across several different kinds of variables; it should have the kind of breadth validity which D. T. Campbell and Fiske (1959) and Horn and Cattell (1965) have discussed. Some of what are called primary abilities are not valid in this sense. But although some of the established primary ability factors may not be of practical or theoretical importance, still any adequate theory about human intellect must take account of the evidence indicating that several distinct, somwhat independently distributed, abilities are involved in the intellectual performances of older children and adults.

It seems apparent to common sense that primary abilities become differentiated through maturation and learning, as this occurs throughout development but particularly in childhood. Yet it has proved difficult to ask questions about differentiation in ways that make the questions answerable by empirical research.[1] It has proved difficult, therefore, to demonstrate the fact of differentiation with research data. Vernon (1950) cites the early work of Balinsky (1941), M. P. Clark (1944), and Garrett (1946) to support the hypothesis that differentiation occurs in childhood. Burt (1954), after careful evaluation of the studies then available, concluded that the evidence generally supports a differentiation hypothesis (in childhood) insofar as it is testable. Vernon also reviewed several studies (Doppelt, 1949; McNemar, 1942; Swineford, 1947; Vernon & Parry, 1949; H. S. Williams, 1948) which suggest that by the age of adolescence most of the differentiation of basic abilities is completed and that what might appear to be differentiation thereafter is development of specialized abilities associated with particular educational or vocational training.

The evidence on differentiation of abilities is fully reviewed in Chapter 17 by Reinert. Here it is sufficient to recognize that the weight of the evidence indicates that influences operating in childhood produce a differentiation of abilities—differentiation in the sense that, with age increase until adolescence or early adulthood, there is increase in the number of measurable basic abilities and decrease in the intercorrelations among these abilities.

Guilford (1964, 1967) has emphasized his findings that among over 7000 intercorrelations for putative ability tests, about 18% were found to be less than +.11. However, perhaps the more striking finding indicated here is the obverse of what Guilford emphasized—that 82% of the intercorrelations were positive and larger than +.10. This finding of positive manifold among the intercorrelations for an extremely wide variety of ability tests is one of the most interesting in the psychological literature; it is also one of the most frequently replicated findings.

Related here is the finding—less well established—that, with one notable exception, test-retest correlations for ability tests of rather different content, and often over several years, usually are positive and often substantial (e.g., Bayley, 1949; Bradway, Thompson, & Cravens, 1958; B. S. Bloom, 1964; Hindley, 1965; Husen, 1951; Pinneau, 1961; Sontag, Baker, & Nelson, 1958). (The notable exception is the correlation between measurements taken in the first two years of life and measurements obtained at other ages, the evidence for which will be reviewed in the next section.)

The fact of positive test-retest correlations for ability measurements has been described by J. E. Anderson (1939, 1940) as indicating overlap in the increments to ability in successive years throughout development. An ability measurement at year zero may be represented by t_0; at year one by $t_0 + t_1$, at year two by

---

[1] That is, in such study there is a multitude of nearly unavoidable methodological difficulties—difficulties in obtaining representative samples, in obtaining comparable tests, in standardizing the units of measurement of tests, in test ceilings and cellars, etc.

$t_0 + t_1 + t_2$, etc., so that by year m it is represented as $t_0 + t_1 + t_2 + \ldots + t_m$. If this is a good representation of fact, then the intercorrelations among ability measurements can be expected to show a particular pattern; namely, correlation for measurements obtained in adjacent years should be large relative to other test-retest correlations, and the correlations should decrease systematically with increase in time between the two measurements involved. Evidence has been accumulated to show that the Anderson theory does fit rather well to a wide range of test-retest data (J. E. Anderson, 1939; 1940; B. S. Bloom, 1964; Humphreys, 1960; Roff, 1941).

Humphreys (1960) has shown that the model implied by Anderson's theory is that which Guttman (1955) has described in mathematical terms as a simplex. In applying this model to ability data, however, Guttman did not use test-retest data, but rather intercorrelations among abilities which can be said to be a similar along a transfer surface. That is, the overlap in this case represents the idea that an ability represented by $t_0 + t_1 + t_2 + t_3$ would have developed through learning that was facilitated by an ability represented by $t_0 + t_1 + t_2$. Hence, high correlations among abilities would represent many common elements in transfer learning. Guttman showed that the intercorrelations among tests of arithmetic ability—extending from simple addition, through multiplication and division of integers to multiplication and division with fractions and decimals—tended to show the predicted simplex pattern.

Ferguson (1954, 1956) has used the concept of transfer—positive and negative—to explain both the general positive manifold among ability test intercorrelations and the fact of separateness of the primary factors. According to this theory, in the earliest phases of development transfer is a general and not a very powerful determinant of learning. This is consistent with Stroud's (1940) early work showing that transfer is not very effective unless the new task to be learned is rather closely similar to previously learned material or unless the teacher makes special effort to develop a relationship between the two learnings. But according to Ferguson's theory the initial weak transfer among rather dissimilar tasks is sufficient (by virtue of the principle primacy) to create a positive manifold for the intercorrelations among performances on various tasks. Persons who learned more on any one task would gain some facilitation in learning other tasks. But the facilitation would be greatest for the learning of new tasks which were most similar to the old. Hence learning in one area would tend to promote particularly efficient learning of a similar kind. There would be a trend toward a limit in learning in a particular area and this, according to Ferguson, is what is represented by primary ability factors.

The work of Fleishman and Hempel (1954, 1955) on the learning of motor skills, as well as some of the early work of Anastasi (1936), Greene (1943), and Woodrow (1938, 1939) on the effects of practice, and the more recent work of Duncanson (1964) and A. M. Sullivan (1964) on transfer, as such, and on abilities of the kind measured in intelligence tests, has shown that with practice and learning in a particular area the factor composition of tests changes, intercorrelations are generated which yield independent factors (this representing the emergence of abilities similar to primary abilities), that some of this change can, indeed, be attributed to transfer in learning and that the effects of this can be relatively pronounced when learning continues for some time in areas where subjects are relatively naïve at the outset.

Perhaps it should be emphasized that transfer, as the concept is used here, can be either postive or negative and that it accounts for much of what is discussed under the heading of generalization in learning. This implies that just as particularly high ability represents, in part, positive facilitation and generalization in new learning, so particularly low ability may represent the interference of previously learned material. Also, transfer similarity, as an explantion for the emergence of primary factors, can be seen to be analogous to other kinds of experiential similarity. For example, Horn (1967, 1968) has suggested that generalized learning not to learn and learning in accordance with a label given by others may account, in part, for the patterns of the intercorrelations found among ability test performances. Boigon (1968), Hayes (1962), and R. B. Cattell (1950, 1969a), have conceptualized somewhat similar ideas in terms of the development of attitudes and motivations pertaining to learning.

The general principle indicated here is that the emergence of linear patterns among ability performances must indicate systematic influences in development.

III. PROCESSES BASIC TO INTELLECTUAL FUNCTIONING

If we adopt something like an overlap theory to help explain what is known about human abilities and their development, it is advisable to specify as clearly as we can the nature of the t_0 term (or terms) in the Anderson equations. That is, it is desirable to have some ideas about the core determinants of abilities. To refer to such determinants, Horn has resurrected the ancient term *anlage*, now Americanized (so the plural is anlages) and infused into discussions of primary abilities and second-order derivatives of these (Horn, 1965, 1967; 1968; Horn & Cattell, 1966a, 1966b, 1967). Thus anlage refers to very basic, unlearned central organizing functions in all behavior which can be said to involve intelligence, where intelligence in this context pertains to all of the abilities—in particular, the primary abilities—which psychologists refer to when they use the term intelligence, general aptitude, g, etc. In this use of the term, anlage refers not only to a t_0 which is the first term in a sequence of development, as for an Anderson overlap model, it is also a function which can operate in a performance at a late stage in development. That is, unlearned reactivities and capacities influence the performances of even mature adults. Hence an anlage function relates not only to conditions imposed on the *development* of abilities but also conditions which operate in the *immediate expression* of an ability.

Perhaps the most denotable of anlage functions is what is commonly designated as short-term memory. Spearman (1927) discussed this (and similar processes) under the heading of span of apprehension and mental competition. G. A. Miller (1956) has discussed this kind of function as a limit on the human's capacity for processing information. In the concept of temporal integration Hearnshaw (1964) has emphasized that such a limit pertains to our processing of time-based information.

In solving a problem in an abstract reasoning test, such as Matrices, it is necessary to hold several relations in mind at one time. If span of apprehension is limited, this cannot be done and one fails the problem: The span anlage underlies performance on the reasoning task. Welford (1958), Heron (1962), and Clay (1956, 1957) have shown that inability in performing even rather simple intellectual tasks relates to inability to hold several elements within the span of immediate awareness. In childhood, as span increases so does the complexity of the problems the child can solve, and so does the speed with which he can learn (Inglis, Ankus, & Sykes, 1968a). Some results suggest that span increases rapidly until preadolescence, levels off in this period, and then increases slowly in adolescence (Mishima & Inoue, 1966).

Span of apprehension and temporal integration are suggested merely as examples of a class of functions which seem to be integral to intellectual ability and yet which do not appear to depend upon learning and socialization. The class is, as yet, rather poorly designated. However, functions such as are referred to in the Goldstein and Scheerer (1955) work on concrete-versus-abstract capacity would fall under this rubric. Similarly the ability (versus inability) to change a set, discussed by Spearman as perseveration, would represent an anlage function, as would the ability to maintain attention and resist distraction. That is, although this latter is influenced by socialization, nevertheless it would appear to involve an unlearned component which pertains to a central intellective function. (Hyperactivity and lack of impulse control are among the more frequently cited concomitants of brain damage.) It is possible that the processes underlying incidental learning, as discussed by A. W. Siegel and Stevenson (1966), are anlage functions.

Perhaps some of the functions referred to here are better defined under the heading of perception, as discussed by Comalli and Munsinger (see Chapters 8 and 9). Interesting in this regard are the now rather well-established findings indicating that defective perceptual-motor integration (as in copying designs), reversals in seeing and/or reproducing what is seen (as in reading-writing reversals), difficulties in crossing the midline (touch left hand to right ear), inability to distinguish figure-ground relations and aphasias are among the most reliable indicants of learning-achievement difficulties in the early years of schooling (B. Bateman, 1964; Myklebust & Johnson, 1962; R. T. Strong, 1964). The suggestion is that measurements represented by these kinds of observations would be indirect measurements of anlage functions.

Among the principal problems in using a concept such as anlage to refer to supposedly central organizing factors is the problem of distinguishing this at the behavioral level[2] from peripheral sensory and motor organizations and from organizations in the pathways leading from peripheral to central functions. We are far from answering this question in a way that is at once precise and pertains to intelligence, but, as will be indicated in subsequent sections, evidence is accumulating to suggest that anlage functions are more or less accurately recorded in measurements of memory span and ability to deal with complex relations among novel elements or elements (but not the relations among them) that have been highly overlearned—i.e., measurements such as are represented by the Goldstein-Sheerer tests, Matrices and Analogies with familiar words (Horn, 1965), as well as, possibly, the perceptual-integration tasks often used to diagnose brain damage (e.g., Graham & Kendall, 1960; Halstead, 1947; Haynes & Sells, 1963; Reitan, 1966; R. T. Strong, 1964).

It is implied that measurements of anlage functions reflect hereditary potential for development of intelligence. That is, to the extent that intelligence can be said to be inherited (and the evidence of Burt, 1955, 1958; Erlenmeyer-Kimling & Jarvik, 1963; Jensen, 1967, 1968; and Vandenberg, 1966b, indicates that certainly much of the observed variation in human abilities reflects inherited differences), it is so because the capacities indicated by anlage functions are determined by instructions written into one's physiological structure in gene endowment. However, even the purest measurements of anlage functions would not indicate inherited potential, per se. For the evidence is clear in indicating that damage to the structures which support intellectual functioning can occur before birth and throughout development (for review of this evidence see Mussen, Conger, & Kagen, 1963, for the childhood period; Birren, 1959a, for the adulthood period). Before birth, and unrelated to heredity, structure can be affected by position in uterus, toxemia, intrapartum rupture, premature membrane rupture, and various other labor complications. At birth other injuries are common and after birth there are possibilities for injuries from falling, from carbon monoxide poisoning, from eating lead-based paint, etc. This suggests that all individuals would have suffered some such damage, there being

---

[2] That is, the principal concern throughout this paper is with overt behavioral measurements of intelligence, not with the neurological, cellular, chemical organizations which may underlie the behavioral observations. Certainly, it is permissible—and often useful—to treat intelligence as a concept which may be explicated in the terms of neurophysiology, or the like. But the job of a psychologist must be to specify test performances and other overt behaviors which are indicative of intelligence, whence it becomes possible to relate the resulting psychological variables to variables of other disciplines.

only individual differences in amount of damage (Kawi & Pasamanick, 1958; Pasamanick & Knobloch, 1960). It implies that if individual differences in anlage functions reflect structural differences, then they do not reflect differences in heredity alone, but must also indicate differences in the amount of structural damage that would have occurred prior to the time of measurement.

In this context it is important to recognize the evidence suggesting that structural damage at an early period in development has a very different effect on expressions of intelligence than does comparable damage occurring at late periods in development. If obvious brain damage is sustained at a young age, then many abilities are found to be impaired (L. Belmont & Birch, 1960; Braine, Heimer, Wortis, & Freedman, 1966; Doll, 1933; Hebb, 1942; Doll, Phelps & Melcher, 1932; G. Weiner, Radar, Oppel, & Harper, 1968; H. Werner & Strauss, 1939). Verbal comprehension and similar school-type abilities are as much retarded as are abilities similar to those indicated by the Performance score on the Wechsler tests. However, if obvious brain damage occurs in adulthood, there may be relatively little permanent change in verbal comprehension and similar activities but marked decreases in the abilities measured with such tasks as Kohs Blocks of the Wechsler scales, Matrices and Series (Hebb, 1942, 1949; L. Belmont & Birch, 1960). It appears that anlage functions are instrumental in the development of abilities which, once developed, can be maintained with diminished anlage capacity.

It is apparent that what we can say about anlage function must be closely related to what we can say about neurological-physiological-chemical functioning, perhaps particularly that of the brain. However, the principal purpose here is not to examine neurological physiological processes underlying anlage function, but to indicate that some abilities depend more upon this (in the immediate testing situation) than do other abilities and that, for this reason, different kinds of neurological-physiological organizations are reflected by different ability measurements.

IV. DEVELOPMENT OF ABILITIES IN CHILDHOOD

A. Stages of Development

In all things which develop it is tempting to think of them as developing by stages, there being a perceptible jump from one stage to another. Surely this is true of attempts to describe the development of abilities in childhood, as is exemplified by hypothesis such as those of Piaget (e.g., 1936, 1946; Elkind & Flavell, 1969; Flavell, 1963) and the numerous attempts to find support for these hypotheses in studies based upon broad samples of children. This viewpoint is also implicit in the factor-analytic studies by Hofstätter (1954) and

Kotásková (1967) of test-retest correlations for abilities and in the scalogram studies by Kohen-Raz (1967) based on a similar kind of data. Cronbach's (1967) incisive critique of Hofstätter's analyses reminds us, however, that it is difficult to demonstrate more than merely arbitrary points of demarcation between supposedly distinct activity levels in a discontinuity theory, and that if the lines and demarcation are not made clear, the skeptic is free to suppose that the phenomena in question are best described as change by imperceptibly small transformations or continuously. Also, if a stage theory of development is to be more than merely a convenience in communication, completion of one stage should be a necessary—at some points, a sufficient—condition for development at a later stage. As Nesselroade (Chapter 7), Beilin (1969), Emmerich (1968), Van den Daele (1969), and others elsewhere have pointed out, this also has proved to be a very difficult hypothesis to formulate in terms of clearcut operations and analyses and therefore has proved to be a very difficult kind of hypothesis to support.

Nevertheless, truly it is a literary, logical, and pedagogical convenience to treat development in terms of stages. For these reasons, it is desirable to organize some of the data of this paper in this way—in terms of quasi-stages, as they might be called. Thus, the childhood period will be regarded as broken into three principal periods, namely: (a) the development of sensorimotor alertness, (b) the acquisition of concepts and aids, (c) the period of intensive acculturation. These correspond to the periods identified by Hofstätter (1954) in analyses on the data of the Berkeley Growth Study and are similar in many respects to the major periods identified in Piagetian-type theories (Elkind & Flavell, 1969; Flavell, 1963; Hunt, 1961; Piaget, 1936, 1946).

B. The Development of Sensorimotor Alertness

Hofstätter's first factor was characterized by measurements obtained between the ages of two months and approximately two years. The tests used in this period were the California First Year Mental Scale and the California Preschool Scale. At this level the major proportion of variance recorded with these scales is represented by behaviors which Bayley (1943) has characterized as indicating sensorimotor alertness. Similarly Piaget (1936, 1946) has referred to intellectual development in the first two years of life as a sensorimotor period.

Piaget (1936, 1946; Hunt, 1961) and others have described this period as one in which primitive instinct-like patterns get tied together in reticular networks and the playing off of these "circular reactions," as they have frequently been called (e.g., J. M. Baldwin, 1906; E. B. Holt, 1931; Piaget, 1936), comes under the control of external stimulus patterns and/or inner activators. Transfer learning and even trial-and-error learning would appear to be unimportant in these early changes. Rather, classical conditioning and frequent repetition would seem to be the principal factors.

The normative data gathered in studies similar to those of Bayley (1933, 1949, 1956, 1965) and Gesell (1940), as well as that found in the standardizations for various infant test, indicates that most children reach a rather high level of sensorimotor alertness by the end of the second year of life. This development does not appear to be very closely related to socioeconomic factors (e.g., Pikler, 1968) and, indeed, if a relationship exists, there are suggestions that it may be negative (Bayley, 1965). Also, the evidence from many sources, including that of the studies cited above, indicates that the rate of development of sensorimotor alertness is, at best, only very lowly related to development of what is labeled as intelligence at later ages. Some of the measures of sensorimotor alertness obtained in the first five or six months of life have been found to correlate *negatively* with intelligence test scores obtained at later ages, although most such correlations have been near zero (Hofstätter, 1954).

It should be noted in this connection that the infant scales referred to above do contain some reliably-measured items pertaining to abilities such as verbal comprehension (E. E. Werner & Bayley, 1966). When these are clustered to form a separate scale, the correlation between measurements in the first two years of life and later measurements of intelligence are found to be significantly positive, although this relationship is more apparent for girls than for boys (Bayley, 1968a; Cameron, Livson & Bayley, 1967; T. Moore, 1967). This may reflect a fact that intelligence tends to become defined in terms of verbal ability in childhood tests and that early socialization promotes development of such ability (e.g., see Baumrind & Black, 1967; Honzik, 1967; Levenstein & Sunley, 1968; Pederson & Wender, 1968). The important point is that a common verbal comprehension factor may account for most of the small amount of correlation that has been found between measurements obtained with infant scales and those obtained with the scales which are said to measure intelligence in childhood.

The evidence overall indicates that the essential characteristics of what is measured as intelligence in childhood is not very closely related to the sensorimotor alertness measured with infant tests. On the other hand, we must not overlook the fact that if there is impairment of sensory functions, perhaps particularly those of hearing and vision (in this order of importance), there is likely to be some retardation in intellectual development, although this may not represent permanent impairment (see Anastasi, 1961; pp. 142-147 for review). In this sense the development of sensorimotor alertness may be seen to be a precursor of later intellectual development, although perhaps not a necessary precursor.

Somewhat in contrast to this position, Hunt (1961) has argued persuasively that lack of opportunity to exercise elementary sensorimotor schemata in this first period of development may have very crucial and far-reaching effects on all subsequent development of intelligence. The position taken here does not necessarily contradict this statement; it merely argues from the evidence that the rate of development in this period, as indexed by the ability tests presently in use, is largely unrelated to what is called intellectual development in childhood.[3] It should be noted, too, that there is considerable evidence indicating that enrichment experiences arranged for the first two years of life do not have much influence on sensorimotor development. The results from Pikler's (1968) recent study, for example, indicate that for normal, healthy infants reared in an institution, special instruction did not affect the sequence or the age of appearance of the kinds of skills measured in infant scales (see also Jensen, 1969; Schmidt, 1965).

It must be granted that in certain rather unusual cases, as when children are raised in quite "unnatural" environments—as perhaps (though not necessarily) those described by Skeels and Dye (1939), Spitz (1946), Dennis and Najarian (1957) and Dennis (1960)—there may result sensory deprivation analogous to that measured by Cruze (1935) and Reisen (1947) and this may have a deleterious effect on later intelligence test performance. Also, we must remain aware of evidence, such as that of Hurley (1967), showing that experiences resulting from maltreatment and neglect in early life may have profound influence on the child's motivational structure—what Hayes (1962) has described as experience-producing drives—and this, in turn, may greatly affect subsequent intellectual development. But the mechanism implied by this kind of evidence is quite different from that implied by Hunt's theory.

In sum, then, although the development of sensorimotor alertness precedes development of the abilities of which intelligence is comprised and this latter development is to a small extent dependent upon the former, the *rate* of development of sensorimotor alertness probably is not appreciably related to the *rate* of development of intellectual abilities, and may even be slightly negatively related. Also, the experiential factors which promote or inhibit development of sensorimotor alertness in the early period probably operate largely independently of the experiential factors which promote or inhibit the development of abilities at later periods.

C. The Acquisition of Aids and Concepts

Spearman (1927) described two essential characteristics of man-like intelligence as the perception of relations and the eduction of correlates. These functions are central to concept formation and concept attainment. To a large extent tests of intelligence are measures of concept awareness. The development of what R. B. Cattell (1963b) has described as generalized solution instruments, or

---

[3] This indicates, incidentally, that it is folly, if not unethical, to act as if present-day infant scales provide a basis for estimating the development of intelligence.

aids, is also dependent upon the perception of relations and the eduction of correlates. This, too, is involved in most tests of intelligence.

It would appear that these features of intellection begin to become prominent in a child's behavior sometime in the second year of life and that, in fact, the formation of category systems (concepts) and the development of generalized solution instruments is fairly characteristic of a developmental period extending from age two onward. The second factor in the Hofstätter analysis was defined by tests which are used primarily in an age range from two to six and thus may be said to represent a period of attainment of concepts and aids. This period corresponds to the first (preconceptual) phase of the second major period described by those who follow a Piagetian scheme.

In the earliest development of this period concepts are represented idiosyncratically in terms of what might be called *symbols*, or experiences which anticipate other experiences. The child becomes aware of the relations which define category systems of the universe—for example, the concept "animal"— before he associates this with a conventional referent, here referred to as a *sign*—for example, the word animal. That is, according to the observations summarized by Piaget (1936, 1947a), G. A. Miller (1951), Bruner, Goodnow, and Austin (1956), R. W. Brown (1959), Hunt (1961), Flavell (1963) and others, the formation of concepts proceeds somewhat independently of the acquisition of conventional signs with which to represent concepts. Yet, interestingly, until the child has gained sign representations for the concepts of which he is aware, it is a technically difficult matter to assess his awareness of concepts: Hence, it is technically difficult to measure his capacity for perception of relations and eduction of correlates—it is difficult to measure his intelligence. As the child learns to use language, however, it becomes a fairly easy matter to measure his concept awareness *indirectly* by determining his ability to use conventional signs. This indirect measurement is characteristic of ability measurements obtained in the period from age two onward.

It is worth emphasizing that a child—or any person—is aware of much more than he is able to express, or even understand, in the terms of conventional languages and that, therefore, measurement of his intelligence through this system is, indeed, indirect. It is worth emphasizing, also, that dependence upon measurement through this system represents, in part, a taking of the easiest approach and that this is not necessarily the best approach in the long run. Ideally, we should measure concept awareness in two ways—through symbol representation and separately through sign representation. These would be correlated but perhaps not highly so. Thus a child diagnosed as lacking in intelligence on the basis of his ability to use signs might be diagnosed as highly intelligent on the basis of the degree of concept awareness indicated by symbol representations and vice versa (Horn, 1967, 1968, 1971).

Intelligence must be seen to involve not only awareness of concepts, but also awareness of a number of techniques for inventing or discovering new concepts and for identifying exemplars of concepts already formed. The techniques referred to here would include what are described as *operations* in some theories (e.g., Piaget, 1947a; Hunt, 1961; Guilford, 1967) and what are treated as strategies in other developments (e.g., Bruner *et al.*, 1956; I. Sigel, 1962). Here, following Cattell they will be referred to as "generalized solution instruments" or "aids," i.e., skills "the acquisition of which becomes a key, opening the way to rapid advance in some general area of cognitive problem solving" (Catell, 1963a).

An aid may be viewed as an abstraction representing a class of phenomena having something in common. In this sense an aid is a kind of concept. However, whereas the term concept is used to refer to categories of the phenomena of the universe (i.e., represented by nouns), an aid is thought of as referring to a series of behaviors or thinking operations which might lead to the formation or attainment of a concept.

An aid can be thought of as existing at several levels of complexity, much as concept representations can be thought of as existing at several levels of abstraction (those extending from the simple cue to the complex sign). The "learning sets" which Harlow (1949) described are rather low-level aids, analogous to a simple cue concept. In the learning set the animal (at least one at, or above, the phylogenetic level of a monkey) discovers a way of forming hypotheses (representing anticipations for an entire class of possible outcomes), a way of evaluating a test of these and thus a way of eliminating whole blocks of trials and errors which he would otherwise take in solving a particular kind of problem. Once the "set" is acquired the animal makes more efficient use of learning trials and thereby cuts the number of trials to a criterion of learning by a noteworthy amount. In human behavior the similar phenomena is described as "becoming aware of principles," "learning the tricks of learning," "learning for transfer," etc. The transfer learning of which Ferguson (1954, 1956) speaks in his account of the acquisition of intelligence must be based to a very great extent on acquisition of aids.

Reversibility in conservation can be regarded as an aid. Many who have studied child behavior have remarked on the fact that the young child's problem-solving behavior often indicates a concrete, rigid, centered, stimulus-bound, irreversible conception of the problem situation. The child seems to perceive relations but not to internalize the procedures whereby he thus perceives. He focuses on observed events to the exclusion of any consideration of what might have gone before or might come after. His perception is said to be "centered," as Piaget terms it, and in thus centering he fails to take cognizance of the operations which lead to an event or which might revert a situation to what it was before. As he experiences transformations in several contexts, however, the child internalizes sequences or expectations for change. With continued experience in actually reversing a sequence, or seeing it reversed, the child learns to apply the idea of reversibility in a wide range of situations (in some of which it is inappropriate). The notion of reversibility thus becomes a generalized solution instrument or aid.

Besides reversibility (cf. Goldschmid, 1967), we may think of transitivity, associativity, nullifiability, and other of the operations which Piaget describes as indicating the formation of aids. Aids are represented, also, by the use of systematic exploration (Elkind & Weiss, 1967) hypothesis testing (Odom & Coon, 1966), analogizing (Ginsburg, 1967; Punfrey, 1968), logical problem-solving (Neimark & Lewis, 1967) and conjunctive and disjunctive reasoning (King, 1966).

Some aids are techniques for dealing with limitations in anlage capacities. Such techniques may be referred to as compensatory aids. For example, the common practice of coding a telephone number into a three-digit prefix followed by a four-digit number is a technique enabling one to deal with limitations in span of apprehension.

This technique for coding numbers is also an example of a discovery—a creation—which has become part of the intelligence of a culture. That is, it is useful to recognize that a collection of ideas and generalizations (concepts), rules and techniques (aids) exists independently of the individual and yet can be appropriated by him for use in coping with the complexities which he meets in his environment. The compensatory aid for coding telephone numbers is a technique which, in our society, one does not need to rediscover for himself. One can learn it as part of a general education provided in this culture. Perhaps in this case it is almost as easy for an individual to develop such an aid himself as it is for him to learn the particular technique used in our society. But it is probably much easier to learn to use some aids of the culture— e.g., differentiation in calculus—than it is to either rediscover them or to invent new aids to deal with the kinds of problems for which these aids are appropriate. As Hayes (1962) has noted, the culture may relieve us of much of the burden of creativity by giving us access, through acculturation, to the products of creative acts scattered thinly through the history of the species.

Before an aid or a concept becomes part of the intelligence of a culture it is presumably the property of a particular individual. This points up the fact that some aids and concepts are idiosyncratic, even as common observations (as those of Piaget) have indicated. A person forms concepts and uses aids which are exclusively his own. To some extent he deals effectively with complexities—i.e., is intelligent—by virtue of his development of such idiosyncratic concepts and aids.

Just as it is likely that noteworthy development in the formation of concepts occurs before the preschool period and continues well after the early school years, so it is likely that development in the acquisition of aids begins before and continues after ages two to six. But just as only a small proportion of the variance in infant tests represents the concept formation which later is integral to measurement definitions of intelligence, so it appears that there is little reliable measurement of the acquisition of aids prior to the age of two. Conversely, the studies cited above indicate that the use of aids becomes characteristic in the behavior of children in the preschool and early school years.

There are two important practical implications of the considerations of the last two sections. One derives from the idea that intelligence, measured as a *behavioral* variable (see footnote 2), is to a considerable extent indicated by concept awareness (implicitly the capacity to form concepts) and facility in the use of aids (implicitly the capacity to develop aids). This implies that until a requisite amount of development has occurred, it is impossible to measure behavioral intelligence and that, therefore, we should not expect to obtain substantial correlations between infant measurements and later measurements (see footnote 3). The major common variance between measurements obtained at these two periods will be associated with anlage function. Other small amounts of covariance can result if more ingenious techniques are devised for determining concept awareness, in particular techniques which are less dependent upon use of conventional signs. Similarly, the extent of covariance can be increased by developing preverbal techniques for assessing the use of aids.

A second practical implication derives from the likelihood that, even with improved techniques for determining concept awareness and the use of aids, most tests appropriate for general use will, for convenience in measuring the "typical child," continue to be based upon the conventional. It surely is a great practical convenience to have tests which assess mainly an awareness of conventional signs and ability to use conventional aids. For predicting further acculturation, such tests will perhaps usually be most useful. However, the important practical point to remain aware of in using such tests is that the child's level of behavioral intelligence—not just his physiological potential, as Hebb (1949) argued—can be considerably different from that which is typically measured and, in principle, can be measured by techniques which can be made to be appropriate for the individual child.

D. Intensive Acculturation and the Emergence of Structure

The third factor in Hofstätter's solution overlapped rather a great deal with the second factor in the age range from four to six, and thus involved variance provided by some of the Stanford-Binet subtests used in this age range. However, it was characterized chiefly by the Stanford-Binet and Terman-McNemar Group Test measures obtained at ages nine, twelve, and fifteen. The Stanford-Binet includes progressivley more school-oriented verbal items as the age-level of its subtests increase. In the four-to-eight age range, for example, the tests requiring use of conventional signs and verbal explanation—as in Comprehension, Verbal Analogies, Verbal Similarities and Differences—are allowed increasingly (as age increases) greater weight in determination of the IQ score, whereas the tasks requiring the immediate perception of spatial similarities and differences contribute progressively less variance in the total scores. The Terman—McNemar subtests are also greatly involved with school-type information and with relations that are specifically taught in this setting.

The influence of the dominant culture is felt throughout development. But as the Anderson overlap theory would imply, it is recorded with increasing reliability as development proceeds. In the preschool period it is recorded mainly in the acquisition of those concepts and aids which can be obtained by exploration of an immediate neighborhood and communicated within an immediate family (although the omnipresence of television is perhaps greatly expanding the experiential base of this period). In the school years in most societies, however, the impact of the dominant culture is considerably increased. In this period the major work of the child is seen to be that of acquiring the intelligence of his culture.

Thus, the third developmental period suggested by Hofstätter's analysis can be characterized as one in which progressively more pressure is put on the child to express his abilities in terms of the kinds of performances that are encouraged in the formal acculturational institutions of a society—in our society, mainly the school. In at least a rough way this kind of encouragement reflects the hierarchy of values of the society and, more generally, of the culture possessed by the society (Levinson, 1961, 1963). The period extending from about six into adulthood may thus be characterized as one in which, principally, the anlage, relation-perceiving, concept formation, aid-discovering capacities of the child come to be "harnessed," as it were, by the culture, for use in maintaining the culture and expanding it in accordance with its existing structure.

It is important to recognize the character of some of the major influences operating in this period, for these influences must underlie development of the patterns of abilities which have been found in the many-times replicated research showing primary mental abilities (see French, 1951; French et al., 1963; Guilford, 1967; Horn, 1971, for summaries) and in the somewhat less-frequently replicated studies of broader abilities (see Horn, 1965, 1968, 1971, for summaries).

The quality of the school is emphasized by some investigators as the major factor promoting the shaping of an individual's intelligence in the mold of the collective intelligence of a culture (e.g., Greenfield, & Bruner, 1966). Other observers are impressed with the evidence suggesting that it is the quality of the home which provides the major impetus for this development (e.g., Mackie, Maxwell, & Rafferty, 1967). No doubt both are important.

A great wealth of data has accumulated to show that parental and home conditions which promote the child's feelings of worth, belongingness, self-reliance and, in general, lack of neuroticism, psychoticism, and psychopathy also promote school achievement and development of the intelligence measured with widely-used tests (Bayley, 1968a; Crites & Semler, 1967). For example, Honzik (1967), although stressing sex differences, found that general concern for the child, concern for his achievement, closeness of mother-son relations and father's friendliness toward daughter were among several somewhat similar variables that correlated with longitudinal change in intelligence test scores. The results of Baumrind and Black (1967) replicated earlier findings in pointing to the importance of consistent discipline and the granting of independence. Other results stress parent-child sharing and social interaction (Hill, 1967; Pederson & Wender, 1968). On the negative side, variables such as parental abuse (Hurley, 1967), maternal employment (Rieber & Womack, 1968) and over-dependence on parents (Kagen & Freeman, 1963) have been found to be associated with loss of intelligence as development continues in childhood.

There are data indicating that the shaping of particular abilities is a result of influences associated with the home and with the subculture with which parents identify. For example, the studies of Levinson (1961, 1963), Lesser, Fifer, and Clark (1965) and Jensen (1967) indicate that development is accentuated for the abilities that are most valued and most used in the family of origin and the subculture of this family. In Jewish homes and communities development of the primary ability V (verbal comprehension) is emphasized relative to the development of primaries such as I (inductive reasoning), N (number facility) and S (space). In the homes and communities of American Chinese, this pattern is reversed.

Such factors as parent-child sharing, the quality of schools, and the values of a subculture can be viewed as mainly *external* influences which operate somewhat independently of the basic anlage, relation-perceiving capacities of an individual to promote or inhibit the individual's acquisition of the intelligence of a culture. Other similarly independent influences can be seen to be mainly *internal*—i.e., to stem from personal qualities which in themselves do not represent intellectual capacities but which can partially determine intellectual development. For example, a physical defect or poor health can reduce the possibilities for the kinds of interaction with the environment which are necessary for the development of some abilities. R. B. Cattell (1950, 1969a) has brought together evidence to suggest that the resolutions obtained for conflicts occurring at various cross-roads in development, and the extent of confluence achieved for different motives, have far-reaching influence on the acquisition of abilities.

The well-established findings on primary ability factors indicate the outcomes of some of the systematic influences which operate in development. Thus, the replicated finding of N (number facility) indicates the shaping of an ability through a school curriculum and the support for this which can come from the home and the development of particular motives. The results of Hill (1967) and Werts (1967), for example, indicate that boys develop in this ability to the extent that they identify with a father who values this ability. Similarly, the fact that V (verbal comprehension) emerges in almost any factoring of ability variables indicates a shaping influence operating in the school and in the home (Levinson, 1961, 1963). But perhaps the shaping which produces broader patterns of abilities is of most practical and theoretical interest at the present stage of study of human abilities.

Formal institutions for acculturation, such as a school system, tend to be selective. Individuals who demonstrate facility in accepting that which is transmitted are encouraged (in subtle and not-so-subtle ways) to remain in the system and are moved to higher levels—i.e., are selected—whereas individuals who do not demonstrate this facility are discouraged from continuing and tend to move (or be moved) out of the system—i.e., are deselected. Thus, in the period of intensive acculturation there is, at first vaguely and then with more certainty, a kind of shaping of abilities produced by successive selections and deselections within the formal institutions for acculturation, principally the school system. Anastasi (1961, 1968) and L. E. Tyler (1965) cite no less than thirty-five separate studies indicating that the more an individual is isolated from formal acculturation and the mainstream of the dominant culture—as are mountain folk, canal boat children, rural and small town dwellers, itinerants, people of minority ethnic groups, etc.—the less he tends to acquire the intelligence of the dominant culture, as represented in widely-accepted tests of intelligence. As children become older, for some the accumulation of the concepts and aids which are part of the intelligence of the culture becomes quite impressive, whereas for others this accumulation is much less pronounced.

Selection and deselection can impose correlation between abilities that are not related by a functional process such as transfer of training and that otherwise would not be correlated. For example, knowing algebra and knowing the conjugation of verbs may not be at all related in the sense that one knowledge facilitates acquisition of the other and yet a correlation between the two can be produced by the fact that both are taught in the college-preparatory curriculum of the ninth grade, for which some children are selected (perhaps self-selected) and others are not.

But the intelligent behavior seen and measured by psychologists is not simply that which is produced by intensive acculturation. Evidence such as that adduced in recent studies by Mermelstein and Shulman (1967), Goodnow and Bethon (1966), Irvine (1966), Bath (1967), and Jensen (1967, 1968, 1969), as well as evidence reviewed earlier by R. B. Cattell (1962), R. B. Cattell and Cattell (1959) and Horn (1965), indicates that the development and expression of some abilities which are accepted as indicants of intelligence is relatively little influenced by formal education and related influences. Jensen (1967), for example, putting together the data of Kennedy, Van de Riet, and White (1963) and Terman and Merrill (1960), showed that whereas differences between the means for black and white children raised in the United States are marked when calculated for Vocabulary tests, the means are close together when calculated for Digit Span tests (the mean for blacks being above the mean for whites in some comparisons). Similarly the early work of R. B. Cattell, Feingold, and Sarason (1941) with groups of immigrants to the United States showed that performance on tests measuring reasoning with figural materials (e.g., matrices) did not improve appreciably with length of residency in America, whereas performance on the Binet-type tests did thus improve. Taken together, results such as these indicate that although no test is completely culture fair,[4] some measure abilities that are less influenced by intensive acculturation than are the abilities measured by other tests.

It should be noted that the above is *not* an argument that the abilities measured by relatively culture-fair tests are unlearned, although some tests (such as digit span backwards) would appear to provide fairly good measurement of unlearned anlage function. Rather the argument is that much learning is inner-directed, or directed by other influences which are not associated with acculturation, and that this kind of learning—call it incidental learning—produces intelligence as surely as does that which is more formally designed to inculcate the intelligence of a culture. Piaget's observations indicate, for example, that through spontaneous explorations of his environment a child learns many things which are recognized as important aspects of intelligence, but which are not formally taught in either the home or the school. A larger proportion of the reliable variance of some tests is associated with these aspects of intelligence than is true for other tests.

Relatedly, it should be noted that much of what is produced by intensive acculturation is truly a capacity to behave intelligently, not merely achievement. The concepts and aids which become part of the collective intelligence of a culture often represent extremely useful ways of comprehending and dealing effectively with the complexities with which any person may be required to cope. This is one reason why they become part of the collective intelligence, for man is an adaptive, pragmatic beast that preserves what is useful. Through the process of acculturation a person attains many concepts and learns to use many aids which enable him to solve much more complex problems than had he not acquired these elements. Even in tests in which the items are not slanted toward assessment of the collective intelligence, as such, the complexities of the problems often will yield to formulation in terms of the concepts and aids of a culture.

----

[4] This represents a principle derivable from other considerations, namely: no test of intelligence can be completely free of the cultural elements defining intelligence.

Thus a person who appropriates a relatively large section of the intelligence of his culture will often be better able to cope in situations demanding intelligence than will the person who has appropriated a smaller section of his culture's intelligence. This can be true even when the former is not as intelligent as the latter when intelligence is conceived of as the ability to form concepts and develop aids entirely on one's own. Also, intelligence should not be confused with the ability to learn, as such. As Lashley (1949) noted several years ago:

Learning involves both the ability to form associations and also the ability to solve problems, to discover the significant relations in the situation... Under favorable conditions every animal, at least above the level of the worms, can form a simple association .... In this sense the capacity to learn was perfected early and has changed little in the course of evolution [p. 30].

To some extent one can learn, acquire the intelligence of a culture, and thus become intelligent in one sense of this term without being particularly insightful or intelligent in a second sense of the term, and, conversely, one can be highly intelligent in this second sense, but not learn very much that would make him intelligent in the first sense.

Thus adumbrated are some of the major points of the general theory of fluid and crystallized intelligence, as stated originally by R. B. Cattell (1957, 1963b, 1967, 1968b, 1969a) and elaborated by Horn (1965, 1966a, 1966b, 1967, 1968, 1971; Horn & Bramble, 1967; Horn & Cattell, 1966a, 1966b, 1967). This states that as development proceeds through childhood and into adulthood, two broad classes of abilities become distinguishable. Those abilities which are most dependent upon the influences which operate in concordance with the formal institutions for acculturation tend to become intercorrelated and thus form one class. This results partly as a function of such processes as transfer, as indicated by the Ferguson theory, but perhaps more as a function of the influences which promote differences in personal adjustment, motivation, and systematic selection and deselection. On the other hand, many influences operate somewhat independently of those of acculturation to affect neurological-physiological structure, anlage functioning, and incidental learning. For example, in the United States, the correlation between social class (representing intensive acculturation) and incidence of low birth weight, labor complications, toxemia and other indications of prenatal impairment of brain structure appears to be very close to zero (Braine et al., 1966; Weiner et al., 1968). Moreover, the evidence on the effects of early and late brain damage (Hebb, 1949) suggests that although injury at a particular point in development affects subsequent development, it may produce relatively little impairment to some of the abilities already developed. The implication is that the influences which most directly affect anlage functioning and incidental learning will tend to produce intercorrelation among the abilities that most sensitively reflect these influences and thus this class of abilities will come to stand somewhat apart from those that mainly reflect intensive acculturation.

A major implication of this theory is that at some order of analysis in factoring among ability performances two very broad factors, each having properties of what is putatively intelligence, should be distinguishable. One of

TABLE 1

Oblique Structure in a Broad Sample of Primary Mental Ability Factors[a]

Primary factor symbol and name		Second-order factors and loadings					
		Gf	Gc	Gv	Gs	C	F
I	Inductive reasoning	50		28			
CFR	Figural relations	46		43			
Ma	Associative memory	32					
ISp	Intellectual speed	40			−21		
IL	Intellectual level	51					
R	General reasoning	23	30				
CMR	Semantic relations	33	50				20
Rs	Formal reasoning	34	40				
N	Number facility	24	29			34	
V	Verbal comprehension		69				26
Mk	Mechanical knowledge		48	25			
EMS	Experiential evaluation		43		23		
Fi	Ideational fluency		25		25		42
Fa	Associational fluency		35				60
S	Spatial orientation			50			−20
Vz	Visualization			58			
Cs	Speed of closure	21		36			
Cf	Flexibility of closure			48			
DFT	Figural adaptive flexibility			40			
P	Perceptual speed				48		
Sc	Speed copying				63		
Pf	Productive flexibility		−23		46		
C	Carefulness					60	

[a] After Horn and Cattell, 1967.

these factors should be defined primarily by abilities which can be seen to be quite closely related to intensive acculturation, whereas the other should be defined primarily by abilities which are less closely linked to this.

Evidence bearing on this hypothesis was reviewed recently (Horn, 1968, 1971). Some of the major results of this review are summarized in Table 1 and in the following statements of conclusions.

1. In samples of older children and adults, the primary factors labeled Figural Relations (CFR), Memory Span (Ms), Associative Memory (Ma), and Induction (I), measured by such well-known tests as Matrices, Letter Series, Paired

Associates Memory For Nonsense Syllables and Digit Span Backwards, are relatively weak indicants of formal intensive acculturation, yet measure what is recognized as intelligence and thus provide reasonably good measures of fluid intelligence (Gf).

2. The primary factors labeled Verbal Comprehension (V) and Experiential Evaluation (EMS), measured by tests such as Vocabulary, General Information and Social Situations are clearly indicants of the extent of intensive acculturation and thus provide reasonably good measures of crystallized intelligence.

3. A number of primary abilities allow for the operation of alternative mechanisms, either Gf or Gc. In doing the problems of these factors an individual can, to a large extent, depend upon the rather esoteric aids and concepts of the collective intelligence or he can depend less on these and more on anlage capacity and the aids and concepts which derive from incidental learning. The primary abilities which seem to best represent possibilities for the use of alternative mechanisms are General Reasoning (R) and Semantic Relations (CMR), measured by tests such as Arithmetic Reasoning and Verbal Analogies.

V. DEVELOPMENT OF ABILITIES IN ADULTHOOD AND OLD AGE

A. Possible Phases of Development

It is worth noting that in adulthood, perhaps no less than in childhood, it is defensible and sometimes convenient to suppose that there might be distinct stages in development. It would seem, for example, that the phase of intensive acculturation which was described in previous sections extends into young adulthood. In this century in the United States the average number of years spent in formal education has increased for each successive generation (see Pressey & Kuhlen, 1957). This implies that what Schaie and Strother (1968b) identify as cohort differences in abilities may mainly reflect differences in the amount of time spent in a phase of intensive acculturation by younger as compared with older persons all measured in a given year. Cohort differences might be interpreted in terms of the determinants associated with a particular phase of development.

For men, at least, the principal activities of development in adulthood have to do with occupational adjustment (Pressey & Kuhlen, 1957). For men, then, the principal learning which occurs throughout a number of years of adulthood is that which seems to make sense in terms of the kind of job one has or hopes to get. To the extent that formal institutions for acculturation are structured to inculcate aids and concepts of relevance for occupational adjustment, a phase of intensive acculturation is coincident with a phase of occupational adjustment.

However, it would seem that even if the educational system contains an implicit assumption that the principal purpose of formal education is to provide a basis for building occupational competence, this purpose is only imperfectly realized. Certainly, some of what is emphasized in education explicitly designed to prepare one for an occupation is largely unrelated to the demands of the job, and what is emphasized in many occupations often is lacking in formal education. Hence, it may be wise to distinguish a phase of development based upon occupational adjustment from the phase of intensive acculturation in the school years. Similarly it may be wise to recognize that this phase of occupational adjustment can be quite different from a phase (again, mainly for men) that begins when occupation ceases to be the primary criterion by which different men are distinguished—when one is, or most of one's age are, retired.

However, possible phases in adulthood are mentioned here not so much because they are widely used by those who attempt to describe development in adulthood (Shakespeare excepted), but because to think in terms of phases may help to indicate some of the important kinds of determiners of the abilities which can now be measured, and which one day might be measured, in adults.

B. Two Prima Facie Cases

1. *The Bullish Case*

It is apparent to common sense that learning continues throughout an individual's lifetime. Thus, insofar as intelligence is a product of learning alone, it is expected to increase over the entire life-span, from infancy to old age. Hence one prima facie case is that the abilities which truly represent intelligence will be found to improve with age in adulthood. If the tests do not show this, the argument continues, something is wrong with the tests. In particular, to speak of tests which measure what an intelligent child can do as if they measure what an intelligent adult can do may be nonsense.

2. *The Bearish Case*

The viewpoint that intelligence does not increase in adulthood is commonly met. The suggestion often made is that the development of intelligence is analogous to growth in stature and so it developes to a maximum in the late teens or early twenties, whence either it remains about the same throughout the rest of life or else it declines. But perhaps the most compelling form of this argument is that which derives from physiological considerations.

Many investigations of physiological differences of older and younger adults have produced evidence which indicates either an age-related physiological breakdown or an accumulation of damage in sensory and central structures. Age-related differences in sensory receptor structures have been identified and associated with loss of sensitivity in all sensory modalities—i.e., visual, auditory, gustatory, olfactory, vestibular, pain, kinesthetic, touch, and vibration sensitivity (Schaie, Baltes, & Strother, 1964; Welford, 1958). No doubt these differences are reflected in performances on intellectual tests. However, Welford concluded his evaluation of this kind of evidence with the surmise that to a considerable extent the age-related differences in performance on even rather simple perceptual tasks reflect age-related differences in central nervous system structures (CNS).

Some of the major kinds of differences between the brains of older and younger persons—as determined from osteoplastic craniotomy, autopsy, and the like—are listed in Tables 2 and 3. In Table 3, particularly, some attempt has been made to indicate similarities between characteristics associated with aging and

TABLE 2

Actual and Relative Weight of Human Brain
Determined on Samples of People of Different Ages [a]

Age	Brain weight of males (grams)		Brain weight of females (grams)		Brain weight of males and females	
	Average	Range	Average	Range	Average (grams)	Relative (grams/kilogram)
0–7 days	230	70–370	247	90–100		
7–12 mo	830	550–1360	817	720–930		
3 yr	1208	1090–1310	1088	1000–1220		
1–5yr					1134	80
6–10 yr					1298	60
10–14 yr	1400	1270–1640	1215	1010–1340		
11–15 yr					1402	40
16–20 yr					1360	29
20–29 yr	1392	960–1650	1252	1000–1480		
21–30 yr					1397–1480	26
30–39 yr	1367	1110–1690	1246	1030–1476		
31–40 yr					1387	25
40–49 yr	1358	1000–1670	1247	980–1680		
41–50 yr					1361	24
50–59 yr	1357	1100–1620	1227	1032–1440		
51–60 yr					1338	23
60–69 yr	1326	1100–1630	1208	1020–1650		
61–70 yr					1306	24
70–79 yr	1282	1100–1490	1175	920–1470		
Over 70					1218	24
Over 80	1250	1080–1430	1128	1020–1310		

[a]After Kovenchevsky, 1961, who used several sources: Marchand (1902), Handmann (1906), Kovenschevsky (1942), Roessler & Roulet (1932), Burger (1957).

TABLE 3
Some Gross Central Nervous System Characteristics
Associated with Aging and Brain Damage [a]

Characteristic	Frequency higher in samples of	
	Older persons (relative to younger persons)	Brain-damaged persons (relative to uninjured)
Macroscopic (naked-eye) examination		
1. Atrophy, less gray and white matter, smaller brain	yes	yes
a. Low brain weight	yes	yes
b. Low brain volume relative skull capacity	yes	yes
c. "Empty" space in brain area	yes	yes
i. space between inner surface of cranium and outer surface of brain	yes	?
ii. wide and deep cerebral ventricles and sulci	yes	yes
iii. missing areas (missing lobes, or the like)	?	yes
d. Narrow, small gyri (convolutions)	yes	yes
e. Few nerve cells	yes	yes
2. Abnormalities of meninges and covering membranes	yes	yes
a. Thick dura and pia-arachnoid	yes	yes
b. Fibrous meninges	yes	yes
c. Adherence of meninges to brain tissue	?	yes
3. Accumulation of cerebro-spinal fluid in subarachnoid areas	yes	yes
4. Schlerosis	yes	yes
Microscopic histological examination		
1. Disintegrated nerve cells	yes	yes
a. Alzheimer's neurofibriller degeneration	yes	?
b. Lipofuscin pigment accumulation	yes	?
c. Fatty degeneration	yes	?
d. Neuronophogia, Satellitosis and similar disintegration	yes	?
e. Fewer Nissl granules	yes	?

TABLE 3 (Continued.)

Characteristic	Frequency higher in samples of	
	Older persons (relative to younger persons)	Brain-damaged persons, (relative to uninjured)
2. Abnormal cell appearance	yes	yes
a. Presence of Alzheimer's cells and plaques	yes	?
b. Presence of cells in white matter	?	yes
c. Unusual arrangement of cells in layers of brain	yes	yes
3. Vascularization inadequacies and abnormalities	yes	yes
4. Cellular atrophy	yes	?
a. Uneven cell outlines	yes	?
b. Small cellular nuclei	yes	?

[a]After Bondareff, 1959; Korenchevsky, 1961.

those associated with the kind of brain damage that results from known diseases or known assault on the central nervous system.

Most of the characteristics listed in the age-related column of Table 3 are not invariably associated with aging. That is, not all older brains necessarily show the characteristic in question. The same sort of proviso applies to the items listed in the "brain-damage" column of Table 3. Many of the listed characteristics have been found, at least occasionally, in young people who have not been classified as having suffered brain damage. Hence the tables indicate statistical facts, not necessarily functional facts, although at the cellular level, particularly, it seems likely that some of the characteristics would typify old brains, if not because of intrinsic aging degeneration, then because "normal" living produces some (irreversible) brain damage and this accumulates as one continues to live.

According to Bondareff (1959,) Magladery (1959), and Korenchevsky (1961), one of the most uniform findings in the literature on aging is the age-related decrease in brain size (although the scatter about the means has generally been found to be high, too). Many of the characteristics shown in Table 3 may indicate this change, but the most notable, easily observed signs of this are the decreases in brain weight and volume, as indicated in Table 2, and the increase of "empty" spaces in the brain area. A decrease in cerebral blood flow and a consequent decrease in oxygen consumption in brain cells is also frequently found in analyses of mean differences for groups of older as compared with younger persons. At the cellular level there is microscopic decrease in cell size and in the number of neural cells in a given area. There is some evidence

(Critchley, 1942) that decrease in total number of cells is most marked in the frontal cortex.

Bondareff (1959) reports that the accumulation of lipofuscin in neuron cells is one of the events most reliably associated with aging. According to Sosa (1952), the accumulation of lipofuscin in neuron cells causes a breaking apart of the neurofibrillar network. In the final stage this results in neurofibrillolysis and death of the cell.

In theory these changes could be the inevitable result of an intrinsic maturational process which is built into the organism at a very early age—at conception, or by heredity. Alternatively, the changes could result from a series of external events the frequency of which accumulates with age. This last would suggest that the changes are, in part, a function of individual living habits, some of which can be changed. The questions at issue here are still quite debatable. Depressingly, however, what is not at issue is that, for any individual, the probability is high that as he gets older in adulthood (and also, very likely, in childhood) there is decrease in the neurological base which (it is generally believed) supports intellectual functioning.

The upshot of these kinds of findings is to strengthen a prima facie case for the contention that abilities which depend most directly upon neurological-physiological functioning will decline with age in adulthood.

C. The Behavioral Evidence

1. *Findings Based on Omnibus Tests*

Many studies designed to answer questions about age changes in abilities have been based upon what can be called omnibus tests of intelligence (Cronbach, 1960)—i.e., tests in which a single score is obtained by adding together scores on several rather diverse kinds of subtests or items. The Stanford-Binet, Army Alpha, Otis, and Wechsler tests are examples of such devices. These tests are comprised of rather different primary factors (cf. J. Cohen, 1959; L. V. Jones, 1949) and thus have different relationships with fluid and crystallized abilities. The results obtained with such tests have often seemed to be contradictory (Anastasi, 1958, 1968; L. E. Tyler, 1965).

Most of the cross-sectional studies using well-known omnibus tests have shown that older adults obtain lower total scores (on the average) than do younger adults. Typical of such findings are those reported in early investigations by Beeson (1920), using the Stanford-Binet, Yerkes (1921), Willoughby (1927), and H. E. Jones and Conrad (1933), using the Army Alpha, and C. C. Miles (1934) and C. C. Miles and Miles (1932) using the Otis. More recently the standardizations of the Wechsler tests, both in this country (Doppelt & Wallace, 1955; Wechsler, 1955, 1958) and in Germany (K. F. Riegel, 1958) and

Italy (Maleci & Montonari, 1953; Maleci & Pessina, 1954), have shown a peak in overall performance occurring somewhere between the late teens and thirty years of age, a gradual drop in average scores beginning in the late twenties or in the thirties, followed by a more rapid decline beginning in the late fifties or early sixties.

The cross-sectional analyses of Schaie and Strother (1968b)[5] indicate that for a composite score comprised of V + S + I + N + Fw (where the symbols correspond to primary abilities, as summarized by French et al., 1963), there was a peak at ages 31-35 and decrement thereafter, gradual, and somewhat erratic until 46-50 and then steeper and more consistent. In an earlier cross-sectional study Schaie (1959) found that controlling for educational and socioeconomic differences did not noticeably affect results showing decline in composite PMA IQ with age.

Lorge (1936) argued that apparent decreases in intelligence with age may not be decreases in the attribute, per se, but rather may represent a change in preferred rate of working on tasks generally, and on intellectual tasks in particular. He matched subjects according to their performance on the CAVD, a power test, and then looked at their performances on the Army Alpha and Thorndike tests, both of which are speeded. As predicted, he found that older adults whose CAVD scores were equal to those for younger adults had lower scores on both the Army Alpha and Thorndike tests. Such results could represent differential regression resulting from drawing extreme CAVD cases from the population of older individuals. In support of Lorge's position, however, Ghiselli (1957) reported findings which are not subject to this criticism. Using a test comprised of Vocabulary (similarities and opposites), Number Series, Analogies, and Proverbs items and allowing 1423 subjects to work as long as they needed to complete all problems, he found no consistent trend—either upward or downward—in average for age groups extending from 20 to 65 years.

Results obtained in several longitudinal studies have also been interpreted as contradicting the results from cross-sectional studies. Owens (1953) analyzing the scores obtained on the Army Alpha in 1950 (age about 51) by 127 persons who had taken the same test as Freshmen at Iowa State in 1919 (age about 20), found an average gain in total scores amounting to .55 of a standard deviation (as determined on the younger sample). This gain was significant. In further follow-up on 96 subjects of this sample in 1961 (age about 62), Owens (1966) found the mean score to be somewhat lower than the mean obtained in 1950, but the differences were not significant. H. E. Jones (1958c), using the Terman

---

[5] This study involved careful longitudinal, cross-sectional, cross-sequential and time-sequential analyses not only of omnibus scores based upon the PMA battery, but also on the separate factors of this battery (V, S, I, N, and Fw), three rigidity measurements, one psychomotor speed test and one measure of social responsibility.

Group Test, found that his sample of 83 persons averaged higher scores when tested at age 33 than when tested at age 17. Bradway and Thompson (1962) gave the Stanford-Binet to 111 individuals once at an average age of 13.6 and again some 16 years later at an average age of 29.5 and found that the observed rise in mean IQ from 112.3 to 123.6 was significant. In the Bayley and Oden (1955) study, using the Concept Mastery test with the Stanford "gifted" sample, both men and women improved significantly over a twelve-year period extending from a time when they were in their 20s or early 30s to a time when they were in their late 30s or 40s. In a study by Burns (1966) a shortened version of the Simplex Group Intelligence Test (2 vocabulary, 2 verbal reasoning, 1 number series, 1 digit memory and 1 number relations subtests) was administered to 80 university graduates, first when they were about 22, then when they were about 47 and finally when they were 56 years old. There was significant rise in mean score over the first period (ages 22 to 47), significant decline over the last period (ages 47 to 59) but the mean at age 59 was significantly larger than the mean at age 22. More recently, Bayley (1966) found no decline in W-B (Form 1) full-scale raw score for a group of 55 subjects tested once at about 15 and again at about age 36. In the longitudinal analyses of the Schaie and Strother (1968b) study, the decline at 31-35 in the cross-sectional analyses was not noted, there being instead a plateau from 31-35 to 41-45 and no significant decrement until 51-55.

The inconsistencies in these results are perhaps more apparent than real. Putting together the longitudinal results with those from cross-sectional studies, the suggestion is that intelligence measured by omnibus tests becomes a maximum sometime in the 20s, that it is at a plateau through the 30s and 40s, and declines systematically thereafter. The longitudinal results and, in particular, the cross-sequential analyses of Schaie and Strother imply that what looks like decline in the cross-sectional analyses for ages 20 to about 50 is primarily cohort difference, reflecting, perhaps, differences in length of intensive acculturation for the older and younger generations. The Owens' results for comparisons at ages 20 to 50 are consistent with this, since by age 20 the peak would not have been reached and at age 50 decline would not yet have become noticeable. The Owens' results for comparisons at ages 50 and 60 are not fully consistent, but possibilities of death selection and selection in other ways (e.g., see Atchley, 1967; K. F. Riegel, Riegel, & Meyer, 1967) together with the fact that the change was in the downward direction (though not significant), cast doubt on an argument that this is an inconsistency. The results of Jones (1958c), Bradway and Thompson (1962), and Bayley (1966) are in each case consistent because the early test scores were obtained before the peak performance would be expected and the later test scores were obtained after the maximum but before the decline in ability would be expected.

If an omnibus test score reflects a mixture of two independent sets of determinants—those of acculturation and those of physiology, as suggested in previous sections— results such as have been outlined in this section could obtain even when both prima facie cases are sound. For if the abilities deriving from one set of determinants tend to increase with age and the abilities deriving from the other set of determinants tend to decrease with age, a composite of abilities of both kinds could well show neither rise nor decline with age. If the effects of physiological loss eventually outweigh the effects of acculturation, or perhaps systematically slow the rate of acculturation, or if a shift from occupational toward retirement phases of development were to slow the rate of acculturation, then decline could be expected even in an omnibus score. To look at these questions more carefully, however, it is desirable to examine the data for separate primary abilities.

2. Findings Based on the Primaries of Crystallized Intelligence

Score on the concept mastery test of the Bayley and Oden study (1955) is derived from two subtests: Analogies and Vocabulary-General Information. These subtests have been found to be good markers for crystallized intelligence (Horn, 1965, 1966a; Horn & Bramble, 1967; Horn & Cattell, 1966b). As noted above, the results based upon the Concept Mastery test have indicated that intelligence (as thus defined) increases with age in adulthood. This finding is consistent with the results from many other studies.

There are no less than 20 studies, cross-sectional as well as longitudinal, showing that for subtests such as Vocabulary, General Information, Similarities, and Judgment the average scores for older adults (up to an age of about 60) are either no lower, or else are higher, than the average scores for younger adults. For example, the studies of Jones and Conrad (1933), Corsini and Fasset (1953), Owens (1953), K. F. Riegel (1958), J. C. Foster and Taylor (1920), Doppelt and Wallace (1955), Horn and Cattell (1966a, 1967), Strother, Schaie, and Horst (1957), Schaie (1959), Schaie and Strother (1968b) and Beeson (1920) demonstrated just such a pattern. Similar results have been reported by Foulds (1949), Foulds and Raven (1948), Shakow and Goldman (1938), Heston and Cannell (1941), M. C. Jones (1967), and Demming and Pressey (1957; H. E. Jones, 1959, for review). Whiteman and Jastak (1957) found that WAIS comprehension improves with age. Scores on the Practical Judgment subtest of the Army Alpha have been found to improve with age (Owens, 1953; H. E. Jones, 1959). Welford (1958) found that older persons often do better than younger persons on tests requiring considerable preplanning and decisions concerning what is not worth doing. Several matched-group studies of older and younger individuals (matching being based on omnibus IQ scores) have suggested that older subjects score higher on tests such as Vocabulary, Information, and Similarities (see Fox & Birren, 1949; Kamin, 1957; Miner, 1956; Norman & Daley, 1959). Christian and Paterson (1936) found that although younger adults attempted significantly more vocabulary items than did older adults, the average number correct did not differ significantly and that, moreover, when only the number correct among the first 60 items was counted, the older subjects had the higher scores on the average. H. E. Jones (1959) similarly found that when the ratio of the number correct to the number attempted was taken on vocabulary and information subtests, the ratios were generally higher for older subjects. A study by D. P. Campbell (1965), based upon scholastic abilities, showed that subjects at about 50 years of age performed better than they had 25 years earlier, when they were freshmen in college, and better than freshmen tested at the same time as the last testing of the 50-year-olds. Several studies are in general agreement in showing that number facility (primary factor N) either rises throughout much of the age span from 20 to about 50 or is at a plateau in this period (Bilash & Zubek, 1960; Horn & Cattell, 1966a; Schaie, 1959; Schaie & Strother, 1968b).

With one notable exception—viz., the Schaie and Strother (1968b) study—most studies suggest that fluency primaries, such as Ideational Fluency, Expressional Fluency, Spontaneous Flexibility, Associational Fluency and Word Fluency, either increase or do not decrease over the ages from 20 to 55 or 60 (Chown, 1961; Horn & Cattell, 1966a; Schaie, 1959; Schaie, Rosenthal, & Perlman, 1953). In the Schaie and Strother (1968b) study, however, Word Fluency was found to decrease more, and more systematically, than any other primary factor in the study—and from the 20s onward. Perhaps this finding should be interpreted (in the context of the Lorge and Ghiselli results) as indicating decline in perceptual-motor speediness (Birren and Botwinick (1951) found that older adults write more slowly than younger adults.) or breakdown of an anlage capacity (see review, Section 5, of Welford's and other work on intellectual speediness). In any case, the fluency tasks, generally, have been found to be rather poor indicants of crystallized intelligence although they do have some variance in this dimension (Horn, 1965, 1966a; Horn & Bramble, 1967; Horn & Cattell, 1966a, 1966b, 1967).

In general, then, the results uphold the common sense notion that intelligence defined as knowledge—i.e., as one's awareness of the collective intelligence of his culture—tends either to increase or at least not to decrease in adulthood up to about age 60. Beyond this age, however, the question is considerably more clouded. Most of the studies referred to above suggested that there was some decline in the individual's sampling of the collective intelligence after about age 60, but this was by no means the finding in all studies.

In study of this question of decline of crystallized abilities after age 60 (in the retirement period) particular account should be taken of the person's occupational role and avocational activities. This is indicated by Sward's (1945) findings, for example. He compared 45 university professors aged 60-80 with 45 academic men aged 25-35 and found the former to be superior in vocabulary and general information. Relatedly, D. P. Campbell (1965) found that increment in scholastic abilities over a 25-year period was greatest for those subjects who, earlier, had continued their education the longest. Results similar to this have been reported by several other investigators (e.g., Strother *et al.*, 1957; M. Williams, 1960). The early studies of Sorenson (1938), J. G. Gilbert (1941), and Bayley and Oden (1955) suggest that people who get into what might be referred to as "intellectual" occupations, and/or who acquire what might be called "intellectual" interests, maintain and increase the abilities that relate most clearly to acculturation, whereas, these kinds of abilities tend to either not increase or decrease for people in other kinds of occupations and with other interests.

3. *Findings Based on Tests Allowing for Alternative Mechanisms, Gf or Gc*

The above-mentioned findings by D. P. Campbell (1965) showing improvement in academic ability from age 25 to age 50 may suggest too much. For example, in a cross-sectional study, Osborne and Sanders (1955) found that Graduate Record Examination scores in Social Science, Literature, and Fine Arts did not decrease or increase systematically over an age range from 19 to 65, but group means for scores in the Biological Sciences, Physics, Chemistry, and Mathematics were systematically lower for the older group. The differences for Mathematics were small, however, at least until about age 45.

Performance in college-level mathematics involves number facility, which, as noted previously, tends to improve with age, and the general reasoning primary, R, measured by arithmetic reasoning (among other tests). In Section C,3 it was mentioned that R is one of those primary abilities which seems to involve both fluid and crystallized intelligence—and to about the same extent! This may help us to understand some of the findings obtained with R and similar primaries in studies of age differences.

The Wechsler Arithmetic subtest—which consists largely of "real-life" problems of the "change-making, stamp-buying, paint-estimating, job-finishing" type—seems to hold up fairly well with age. Doppelt and Wallace (1955) found the peak in performance on this test to occur at about age 40, and the drop thereafter, if any, was slight and slow. In the Norman and Daley (1959) matched-group study, Wechsler-Bellevue Arithmetic was up slightly for the older subjects. Neither Corsini and Fassett (1953) nor Horn and Cattell (1966a) found noticeable drop in this performance. However, in the longitudinal study of Owens (1953), based on Army Alpha Arithmetic Reasoning, and in the cross-sectional studies of Beeson (1920), based on the arithmetical reasoning problems of the Stanford-Binet, and Willoughby (1927), based on the Army Alpha, there did seem to be some decline in arithmetic reasoning ability. The suggestion is that the arithmetic reasoning tasks employed in the Wechsler scales and by Horn and Cattell allow for use of crystallized abilities to a considerable extent (although they are not particularly pure measures of Gc), whereas the arithmetic reasoning tasks of the Army Alpha and Stanford-Binet are more demanding of the anlage, relation-perceiving capacities of the fluid abilities. It is possible that the last-mentioned tests are relatively highly speeded, that intellectual speediness represents an anlage function and that this declines with age, as suggested by the evidence reviewed in Section 5.

There is some suggestion that the rise in vocabulary scores with age reflects an increase in awareness of concepts and with the labels that are used to tag concepts, but not an increase in the level of complexity with which one can cope in forming concepts. For example, the results of Feifel (1949), Yacorzynski (1941) and Bromley (1956, 1957) suggest that if tests are scored for refinement in the use of vocabulary, average scores may go down with age. Bromley reported, for example, that older subjects showed lower ability at autocriticism and evaluation in the interpretation of proverbs. By contrast, however, Bradway and Thompson (1962) found that their subjects improved more on the Stanford-Binet proverbs items than on any other in the battery. Gorham (1956) has argued that proverbs tests contain the factor V (a crystallized ability), which improves with age, and a reasoning component (eduction of novel correlates, a fluid ability), which does not improve with age and may decline. Whether scores on a proverb test rise or fall with age would thus depend upon the proportion of test variance that can be attributed to crystallized intelligence and the proportion that must go to fluid intelligence.

A similar kind of interpretation seems to be called for to explain the results obtained with analogies tests *other* than the Concept Mastery device. In the latter, it is required that one perceive rather simple relations between rather esoteric elements (e.g., Zeus-Jupiter :: Artemis-?). But analogies tests can be made to involve words that are quite familiar to most people and yet contain relations that are relatively complex. For example, most adults probably know the words "flame," "heat," and "rose," but some find it difficult to solve the analogy "flame-heat :: rose-?. The interesting finding suggested by both the cross-sectional and longitudinal studies (J. G. Gilbert, 1935; Horn & Cattell, 1966a; Jones & Conrad, 1933; Owens, 1953; K. F. Riegel, 1959b; Willoughby, 1927) is that while vocabulary scores for older adults are generally somewhat higher than for younger adults, the scores obtained on "common-word" analogy tests (involving items similar to the one above) have been found to drop steadily throughout an age range extending from 30 onward. This suggests that while adults are gaining in familiarity with some of the more esoteric aspects of their culture, they may be losing some ability (which they formerly possessed) to perceive relations and form abstractions.

4. *Findings Based on Tests Which May Measure Peripheral Functions, Gv*

The evidence reviewed in Birren's (1959a) *Handbook of Aging* indicates that with increasing age there tends to be a reduction in visual acuity, sensitivity to light, breadth and width of the visual field, color discrimination, and the like. These changes may in turn be most directly related to peripheral receptor changes, such as the decrease in range between minimal and maximal pupillary diameters of the eye, the flattening of the eye lens, the decrease in permeability of the lens, etc. (Lansing, 1959; Magladery, 1959). Such changes could well produce changes in performance on any intelligence test which involved spatial visualization. In a strict sense these changes would not indicate any necessary decrease in the ability to educe and perceive relations, as such, even as they produced reduced performance on tests that were intended to measure these latter.

The results are *not* clear in indicating decrease in spatial visualization abilities with age, however. In Kamin's (1957) study and that by Schaie *et al.* (1953) spatial orientation was one of the abilities that declined most with age. Fox and Birren (1949), Doppelt and Wallace (1955), and Norman and Daley (1959) all found Block Designs, Picture Arrangements, and Picture Completions to be among the tests which most clearly showed aging effects. Bromley (1956) found that his blocks test correlated −.52 with age. Tests such as USES's Block Counting and Spatial Relations, Bechtold's Shape Constancy and Harrell's Tracing have been found to load negatively on factors that are prominently marked by chronological age (Bechtoldt, 1947; Harrell, 1940; USES, 1944-1945).

But opposing the results from these studies are findings by Bilash and Zubek (1960), Horn and Cattell (1966a, 1967), Schaie and Strother (1968b) suggesting that decline is at most only gradual and (if it occurs) becomes noticeable only at a late age. The Schaie-Strother study is a particularly revealing one in this regard. In their cross-sectional analyses they found a decline very similar to that found in the cross-sectional studies mentioned above, but the longitudinal and cross-sequential analyses revealed a flat plateau from age 20 to 70. On the basis of these results they concluded that "the cross-sectional age differences can be attributed to differences between cohorts."

Still another reason for doubting the results showing decline in spatial factors derives from the studies of Horn and Cattell (1966a, 1966b, 1967) in which it was shown that these factors contain some variance in the factor interpreted as fluid intelligence but mainly define a broad visualization function (Gv) on their own. This was defined primarily by the primaries Spatial Orientation (S), Visualization (Vz), Speed of Closure (Cs), Flexibility of Closure (Cf) and Figural Adaptive Flexibility (DFT). But it also had some variance on such established measures of intelligence as Matrices (CFR, Figural Relations), although a major proportion of variance on this latter went to define the fluid intelligence factor also identified in this study. In the early work of El Koussy (1936) it was found that tests such as Kohs Blocks indicate visualization processes, but also have rather high loadings on the general intellective factor then interpreted in accordance with Spearman's theory of G. These findings indicate that not all of the variance associated with aging in spatial tasks is to be accounted for in terms of changes in peripheral visual functions. Some of this is likely to be fluid intelligence.

5. *Findings Based on Reasoning, Memory, and Speediness Factors*

It would appear that measures of memory, particularly span memory, often represent anlage functions at a fairly elemental level. Also, it would appear that span of apprehension is rather intimately involved in perceiving complex relations and drawing appropriate consequences, processes which presumably are measured in reasoning tasks. As noted in Section IV,C to grasp the essential relation of a Matrices item one must hold the various relations suggested by the rows, columns, and diagonals of the matrix in the span of immediate awareness. Moreover, the capacity to remain thus aware may be, in part, related to, or a function of, the speed of central nervous system functioning, as is suggested by the recent findings and theory of Ertl (1968) and Shucard and Horn (1971) and, perhaps, Furneaux (1952, 1961). Thus, memory, intellectual speediness and reasoning tasks might be expected to represent somewhat similar processes—and processes which are rather closely related to anlage capacity. If the latter declines as a function of neural decrement which accompanies aging, then performance on memory, speediness, and reasoning primaries could be expected to decline with age. In a rough way, the evidence seems to support this position, although a number of provisos need to be added.

There is little or no aging loss of what can be called long-term memory. As already noted, many studies have demonstrated that overlearned information, vocabulary, and problem-solving aids are retained over many years in adulthood. This retention may be partly a function of at least sporadic practice over the aging period, as Kay (1959) has argued. But, the learning and recall studies of Clay (1956), Shakow, Dolkart, and Goldman (1941) and Speakman (1954) indicate that once the older adult learns something, he retains it over periods of several days, several weeks, and several months just about as well as does the younger adult; and this seems to be true whether or not the learned material was initially novel or unusual.

But Welford (1958) cites several studies indicating that impairment to short-term memory accompanies aging, and the data from studies using the Digit Span subtest of the Wechsler (or other similar tasks) further supports this finding (Bilash & Zubek, 1960; Doppett & Wallace, 1955; J. G. Gilbert, 1941; Horn & Cattell, 1966a; Pacaud, 1955; Wechsler, 1958; Willoughby, 1927). The studies of Welford and his co-workers show that the impairment is most pronounced when short-term memory is required under conditions in which the subject must store information as he carries on other activities. In the Kay (1959) and Kirchner (1958) experiments, for example, subjects were required to simultaneously detect signals and prepare responses for signals previously detected. The older subjects were less able to recall correct responses than were the younger subjects. Clay (1956, 1957) and Heron (1962) likewise found that older persons were particularly subject to distraction in a task requiring simultaneous use of both immediate memory and other behavioral processes. Bromley (1958) found that recall of digits in reverse order declined with age, although recall in the stated order did not.[6] In the studies of Ruch (1934), Gilbert (1941), Kubo (1938), Horn and Cattell (1966a), and Laurence (1967) measures of paired associates memory were obtained under a variety of conditions and in all cases decreased with age, although the decline was less marked for meaningful than for nonsense material[7] and when cues were given to help in recall. In the early studies of H. E. Jones, Conrad, and Horn (1928) and Willoughby (1927) age decrement was found in immediate incidental memory—i.e., recall when the subject was not previously instructed to try to remember.

Thus, although no one study is convincing by itself, the evidence overall suggests that there are, indeed, adult age decrements in the number of elements which can be simultaneously stored in what can be termed an immediate-access memory storage compartment.

Speed of performance on perceptual and motor tasks has been found to decline with age in adulthood (Birren, 1955; Birren & Botwinick, 1951; Braun, 1959; H. E. Jones, 1959; Welford, 1958), although there are noteworthy exceptions and restrictions which need to be recognized when making this generalization. A noteworthy exception may be simple reaction time, as such. If this increases at all with age, it does so only very slightly (Welford, 1958). Verbal fluency also is an exception, as noted previously (although with the provisos indicated by the Birren and Botwinick, 1951, and Schaie & Strother, 1968b results).

But with these exceptions the consistent finding is that speed of performance declines with age. This shows up in, for example, simple, clerical-visual-perception tasks. Variance of this kind is probably involved to some extent in almost all intellectual tests. Numerous studies have shown an age-related drop in performance on the Wechsler-type digit-symbol tests (Birren & Botwinick, 1951; Birren & Morrison, 1961; Doppelt & Wallace, 1955; Loranger & Misiak, 1959; Norman & Daley, 1959; Whiteman & Jastak, 1957; Willoughby, 1929). Crossman and Szafran (1956) have noted that the average time to sort playing cards or weights into different classes rises steadily with age. Pacaud (1955) found that complex reaction time,—i.e., complex in the sense that different kinds of responses were required for different kinds of signals—increased with age. In Tallard's (1962) study, older subjects were found to take longer to

---

[6] A general finding of my work is that reverse recall is the better measure of Gf—both as concerns reliability and as concerns validity (see also H. P. Kelley, 1964).

[7] Kelley's (1964) definitive study of memory processes indicates that meaningful memory, nonsense paired-associates memory and span memory are quite distinct factors.

manipulate a·mechanical counter and to select different colored beads with tweezers than did younger subjects.

It is possible that the slower responses of older persons in most psychological tests is due mainly to changes in peripheral organs, such as the muscles or receptors. After reviewing a considerable body of evidence on this point, however, Welford (1958) concluded that this probably is not the case, that the

> slowing of sensorimotor performance with age is due not to longer time required to execute movements, as such, but to longer time needed to initiate, guide and monitor them, owing to limitation in the capacity of central processes [p. 107].

Welford cites several of his studies in support of this conclusion. In one, subjects performed a grid-plotting task under unspeeded (unpaced) conditions and under speeded (paced) conditions. Older adults were slower but more accurate than younger adults on the first task, but both speed and accuracy dropped with age on the second task. Welford also cites the Crossman and Szafran (1956) and W. Goldfarb (1941) experiments suggesting that the slower speed displayed by adults is not primarily a function of reaction time, as such, but rather of complexity in the sense of having to do two or more things at once (make discriminations and otherwise behave). When subjects were required to (a) merely deal cards into two piles (no choice), (b) sort according to color (black or red), (c) sort according to the four units, and (d) sort according to the four units and according to whether a card was a court card or not, there were practically no age differences for the first condition, but there were noteworthy differences for the conditions in which decision was required. Birren, Allen, and Landau (1954), Clay (1954), and others (reviewed by these investigators) have presented other kinds of data suggesting that as task complexity increases, age differences in speed of performance become greater.

The "task complexity" referred to in these studies of speediness is not necessarily equivalent to "task complexity" as this term is used to describe tests demanding exercise of intelligence. The referent for this latter is the complexity of relations which the subject must perceive. It is what some investigators (e.g., Goldstein & Scheerer, 1955) refer to as the abstractness of a problem or relation. In the studies mentioned above, complexity is introduced by increasing the number of things a subject has to do, or the number of things he has to keep in mind at one time. But, as argued previously, although this speediness complexity is not equivalent to the complexity of a relation, it may not be entirely different either. For even when abstract reasoning tests are given under untimed conditions, persons may fail by virtue of an inability to keep the several relevant aspects of the problem in mind at one time. Thus, slowness on a speeded clerical task may indicate the same kind of breakdown in anlage function as poor performance on an unspeeded abstractive reasoning task. The recent findings of Shucard and Horn (1971) indicate that although fluid intelligence is defined by both speed and level tests (where speed and level are defined according to the principles developed by Furneaux, 1952, 1961,[8] but with a more expanded set of tests than Furneaux used) the speed tests have larger correlations with the Gf factor and in other respects appear to be the better measures of the essential anlage, relation-perceiving processes of fluid intelligence.

Cross-sectional studies with the Wechsler scales agree in showing that "performance IQ" declines with age and declines more steeply than "verbal IQ" (J. Cohen, 1959; Corsini & Fassett, 1953; Doppelt & Wallace, 1955; Fox & Birren, 1950; Heston & Cannell, 1941; K. F. Riegel, 1958; Wechsler, 1955, 1958). The performance score is rather widely accepted as a relatively culture-fair measure of intelligence. Of course, some of the performance subscales—the Digit-Symbol task, for example—have little logical or psychological claim to be regarded as measures of essential aspects of intelligence (i.e., capacity to perceive relations) and such tests have a large perceptual-motor speediness component; but Digit Symbols would also involve the intellectual speediness component referred to above. Scores on other performance subtests, such as Block Designs, may depend upon a peripheral visualization function which is not central to intelligence. Here again, however, as noted previously, substantial portions of the variance of such tests represent processes which appear to be integral to intelligence. The suggestion is that performance IQ, although confounded with Gv and motor-perceptual speediness, is measuring a noteworthy portion of fluid intelligence and this is mainly what declines in intelligence as age increases in adulthood.

A consistent finding has been that tests which load the inductive reasoning factor (French *et al.*, 1963) show consistent negative correlation with age (Bechtoldt, 1947; J. G. Gilbert, 1935; Kamin, 1957; Owens, 1953; Schaie *et al.*, 1953; USES, 1944-1945; Willoughby, 1927). Horn and Cattell (1966b) found that performances on both speed and level versions of inductive reasoning tasks (after Furneaux, 1952, 1961) declined systematically with age. The ability measured in matrices tasks, widely accepted as a good indicant of intelligence (see Vernon, 1961), drops off sharply with age (Bilash & Zubek, 1960; Foulds, 1949; Foulds & Raven, 1948; Horn & Cattell, 1966b; Nyssen & Delys, 1952; Raven, 1948, 1954) beginning perhaps in the teens and almost surely in evidence by the mid-twenties. With the Shaw Test of Logical Classifications, Bromley (1956) found that both the number of classifications (obtained without time limits) and the number of highly abstract classifications decreased regularly with age.

---

[8] Speed is calculated by determining the average rate at which problems of moderate difficulty (for the subject) are solved, whereas level is calculated as the average difficulty of the problems one solves (i.e., irrespective of how many problems are solved).

In general, then, the evidence is fairly compelling in suggesting that in performances in which a great deal of previous learning—particularly acculturation—is not clearly an asset but which nevertheless indicate capacity for perception of relations and eduction of correlates, the older the person, the less adequate is the performance. The performances which thus appear to be most hampered by conditions associated with aging in adulthood are also those which appear to be most affected by known damage to the central nervous system (see Hebb, 1949; Horn, 1965, 1966a, 1968).

6. Some Summarizing Findings

Using several tests to define most primaries, Horn and Cattell (1967) obtained scores for 20 of the replicated primary mental abilities identified by French *et al.* (1963) and then operationally defined two very broad measures of intelligence, one comprised of primary abilities in which formal education and general experience could more or less clearly be seen to be prominent and one comprised of primary abilities in which these acculturational influences were much less in evidence. They called the first of these composites crystallized intelligence (Gc), the second fluid intelligence (Gf). Gf was defined operationally by performances on tests such as matrices, figure classification, common word analogies, match arrangements, letter series, rote memory, and verbal reasoning with common materials. In verbal terms, fluid intelligence was said to be an ability to perceive complex relations, educe complex correlates, form concepts, develop aids, reason, abstract, and maintain span of immediate apprehension in solving novel problems in which advanced elements of the collective intelligence of the culture were not required for solution. Gc was defined operationally by performances on such tests as vocabulary (synonyms), general information, social situations, esoteric analogies, tool identification, mixed arithmetic problems, arithmetic reasoning, and controlled associations. The process definition of crystallized intelligence stressed perception of relations, eduction of correlates, abstraction, etc. (as with Gf), but in materials in which past appropriation of the collective intelligence of the culture would give one a distinct advantage in solving the problems involved. Clearly either composite, taken by itself, would be accepted by most psychologists as a good measure of intelligence. Also defined was a concept of intelligence based upon the sum of Gf and Gc. This, it was argued, would be comparable to (although broader and therefore more valid than) the measurement obtained with a typical omnibus test of intelligence—the measurement commonly referred to as general intelligence, general aptitude, or G. In cross-sectional study of these different definitions of intelligence, analyses of covariance were used to control (individually and in various combinations) the linear effects associated with differences in sex, education, perceptual-motor speediness, verbal fluency, and carefulness. The principal results of these analyses are summarized in Figure 1.

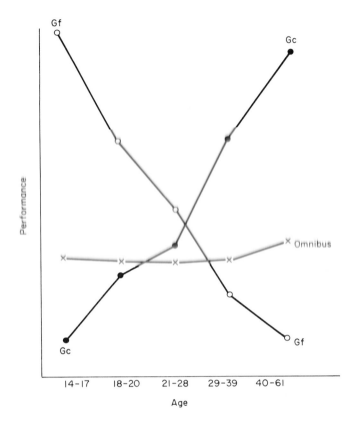

Figure 1. Performance as a function of age. Summary of covariance analysis results. Sex, education, visualization, fluency statistically controlled.

The general finding was that fluid intelligence declines steadily from the teen-ages onward, that crystallized intelligence rises steadily in adulthood from the teens through the fifties, that general intelligence, comprised of these two components, neither rises nor declines. The findings were most evident when controls were introduced by analysis of covariance, but with one exception they held up even when covariates were not introduced. The exception was that until sex and educational differences were controlled, the mean for fluid intelligence for the youngest group—age 14 to 17—was below the mean for the group with ages ranging between 18 and 20.

These results should not be given undue weight, of course, particularly since cohort differences are confounded with age changes in cross-sectional study. But the results are bulwarked by, and in fact summarize, much of the research on age changes and differences in abilities (both longitudinal and cross-sectional), as reviewed in previous sections. They are bulwarked, also, by the common observation that intelligence in some senses of this term both improves and declines with age in adulthood. At a practical level, they point the way toward further research and toward need for change in measurement of abilities in applied clinical, industrial, and educational settings.

VI. GENERAL SUMMARY

Tests designed to measure intellectual abilities generally have been found to intercorrelate positively, both on a given occasion and, excluding infancy, across different ages in childhood and adulthood. Thus some of the same determinants of ability performances apparently operate throughout life and over a wide range of kinds of tasks. It would appear that some of these determinants are written into the physiological structure of the organism in a genetic code, stated at conception and elaborated throughout development. Other determinants would appear to accumulate in modifications of structure produced by experiential factors, first perhaps mainly by the processes of classical conditioning, then by the processes of transfer of training, generalization, learning-to-learn and learning-not-to-learn and perhaps finally by processes involving the use of elaborated concepts and "generalized solution instruments." Still other determinants would appear to accumulate as deficits, so to speak, as a result of the war of attrition which the environment constantly wages against the individual and perhaps as a result of catabolic processes built into the genetic code.

But while unity is perhaps the most striking finding pertaining to intellectual processes, results showing distinct, operationally and statistically independent, primary, and more general abilities have been replicated in many researches. At the primary level, these adumbrate the character of more or less particular processes which are involved in general abilities and they point to the particular kinds of shapings of basic potential which are produced by curricula, by the values of cultures and subcultures and by a person's exposures, adjustments and motivations with respect to these. The more general abilities indicate the thrust of such overriding influences as those which accumulate as acculturation, those which are and which accumulate as determinants in the central nervous system (CNS) and those which are and which accumulate in more peripheral physiological structures.

Tests developed for assessment of the abilities of infants have produced mainly measurements of sensorimotor functions that are not indicative of the level of intellectual development reached at later ages. What correlation there is would appear to be due mainly to overlap in anlage functions.

What is measured as intelligence after age 5 or so involves identification of signs (this indirectly representing capacity to form concepts) and facility in use of generalized solution instruments (this representing capacity to develop such aids). Concepts and aids are, to some extent, idiosyncratic; but many, in what is referred to as the collective intelligence of a culture, are passed from one generation to the next. The extent to which one appropriates the intelligence of a culture represents his intelligence in one sense of this concept. This is referred to as crystallized intelligence, or Gc.

In development, a number of influences conspire, as it were, to enable some individuals to appropriate large sections of the collective intelligence of a culture, while curtailing this appropriation for others. The result is that individuals of equal potential can arrive at quite different levels of crystallized intelligence. But these influences operate relatively independently of those which initially and by a war of attrition influence physiological structure and the development and maintenance of those abilities which depend most directly upon this structure—the abilities of what is referred to as fluid intelligence. The result is that as development proceeds there is a separation of two broad patterns of performances putatively said to indicate intelligence.

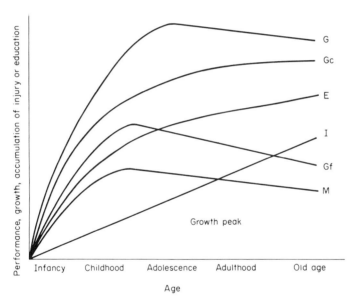

Figure 2. Development of fluid intelligence (Gf) and Crystallized intelligence (Gc) in relation to maturational growth and decline of neural structures (M), accumulation of injury to neural structures (I), accumulation of educational exposures (E), and overall ability (G).

In childhood, although there is an accumulation of injuries to the CNS structure which support intelligent behavior, attrition is masked by rapid development. In adulthood, however, irreversible injuries can be seen to accumulate to reduce the CNS base. But learning and acculturation also increase. Intelligence may thus both decrease and increase in adulthood; crystallized intelligence, if properly measured in samples of people who remain in the stream of acculturation, increases; fluid intelligence decreases. Some of the abilities which do not decline with age in adulthood include Verbal Comprehension, Experiential Evaluation, and General Reasoning (based upon problems of the kind found in everyday living), whereas abilities which do decline include Figural Relations and Classifications, Induction, and Associative Nonsense Memory. Decline in intellectual abilities seems to be associated with decrement in elementary processes indexed by capacity in keeping distinct elements in the span of immediate awareness and speed of thinking.

Age differences in perceptual-visualization abilities appear to represent mainly cohort differences, not changes intrinsic to aging. Perceptual motor speediness does not decline notably in adulthood.

Figure 2 provides a rough summary of the life-span development of intelligence. At first Gf and Gc are indistinguishable. As development proceeds, the two are drawn apart in a correlational sense. The accumulation of CNS injuries is masked by rapid development in childhood, but in adulthood the effects become more obvious. Fluid intelligence, based upon this, thus shows decline as soon as the rate of development of CNS structures is exceeded by the rate of CNS breakdown. Experience and learning accumulate throughout development. The influence of these is felt in the development of crystallized intelligence, which increases throughout much of adulthood. It, too, will decline after the rate of loss of structure supporting intelligent behavior exceeds the rate of acquisition of new aids to compensate for limited anlage function.

In this chapter many methodological difficulties have been sloughed off in order that the reader might obtain a general overview of what the evidence seems to be saying. However, these many methodological difficulties require that these overview generalizations be taken with caution. In the Chapter 18, Schaie will apprise the reader more pointedly of the kinds of cautions which he must heed.

ACNOWLEDGMENTS

I thank Mr. Lazar Stankov, Mr. Hal Bartlett, and the editors of this book for valuable help with the bibliographic research on which this paper is based.

CHAPTER 17

Comparative Factor Analytic Studies of Intelligence throughout The Human Life-Span

GUNTHER REINERT

UNIVERSITY OF MANNHEIM,
MANNHEIM, WEST GERMANY

ABSTRACT

Comparative factor analytic research related to the investigation of age-related changes in the pattern of intelligence is reviewed. Particular attention is paid to studies examining various forms of the differentiation hypothesis of intelligence as originally proposed by Garrett and Burt. While there appears sufficient evidence to indicate the existence of age-related changes in the factorial pattern of intelligence, the data are too contradictory to permit a clear-cut description of the nature of these changes. Attention is drawn to a number of methodological problems associated with comparative factor analytic research, and some implications for the construction of developmental curves are discussed. Finally, suggestions are made for the use of manipulative experiments in the exploration of the developmental conditions that might produce changes in the structural organization of intelligence.

467

I. INTRODUCTION

Scientific methods may be viewed as being similar to living organisms in that both may be said to "pass through developmental stages." If one were to examine the current status of factor analysis in light of this statement, it would certainly not be easy to determine which stage of development it has reached. Some colleagues hold that the "factorial study is not in its infancy" (C. E. Meyers & Dingman, 1960), while others such as Coombs (in Kallina, 1967) maintain that "factor analysis is dead." A review of the literature in developmental psychology might lead one to the impression that factor analysis has never been alive. For example, from the large number of textbooks in developmental psychology, I was able to locate only a few which reported factor analytic studies on the development of intelligence (e.g. Oerter, 1967; H. Werner, 1948). This is surprising, since there are a large number of factor analytic studies directly related to questions central to developmental psychology.

I will present a short summary of these studies to familiarize the reader with certain theoretical positions relevant to intellectual abilities and also point out certain of the methodological problems involved. In so doing, I will restrict my discussion to those comparative studies (a) which are relevant to life-span developmental psychology, (b) which use only items related to "intelligence" as the measurement variables, (c) which employ factor analysis as the method of data reduction, and (d) which make comparisons of the obtained factor patterns.

II. RELEVANT HYPOTHESES AND RESULTS

One can use either chronological age (CA) or other independent variables to classify the several publications collected. In so doing, two main groups can be distinguished: studies in which CA is handled directly or indirectly as the independent variable.

A. The Age-Differentiation Hypothesis

Studies using CA (or school grade respectively) as the independent variable form by far the largest group among all studies collected. For this reason, an overview regarding the distribution of these studies is necessary before presenting the developmental psychological hypotheses argued for in these studies.

My attempt to collect publications on comparative factor analytic studies of intelligence, in which samples of different age groups are compared, yielded some 60 publications. Considering the nationality of subjects used in these studies, approximately 60% of the studies were published in the United States, about 25% were published in England and Germany, whereas the remaining percentage came from Belgium, Canada, China, Finland, India, Japan, and Sweden. The majority of the studies used a cross-sectional design, while only a small number utilized longitudinal strategies. Figure 1 attempts to organize the studies found in this area. The age ranges which have been compared by the authors are shown first. It can be seen that most authors used subjects of preschool- and school-age and adolescents. There is only one author who worked exclusively with old-aged people, and only 8 authors can be said to have examined a broad age range.

Although the aims of the studies shown in Figure 1 differed from one another in detail, there is one common feature: Namely that instability or stability between compared factor patterns were interpreted with regard to the independent variable CA. In so doing, most of the authors referred more or less explicitly to the developmental process of intelligence. In this context a finding reported first by Burt (1919) and later by Spearman (1927) and Thurstone (1938) was usually mentioned. It was later labeled the differentiation hypothesis of intelligence (Garrett, 1946). At present its greatest opponent is perhaps Guilford (1967), while it has most strongly been supported by Burt (1954). According to a very often cited formulation by Garrett (1946, p. 373) the hypothesis can be stated as: "Abstract or symbol intelligence changes in its organization as age increases from a fairly unified and general ability to a loosely organized group of abilities or factors." Figure 2 illustrates the age-associated process of increasing differentiation as implied in the formulations of Burt and Garrett.

The age-differentiation hypothesis, as Anastasi (1958) appropriately has called the differentiation hypothesis, has been declared valid by Garrett (1946) for the age range 8-18 and by Burt (1954) for the age range between late childhood and early adolescence. Studies covering this age range partially supported, and partially failed to support, the hypothesis. Among studies using a longitudinal approach, the hypothesis was mainly supported by Asch (1936) and Burt (1954), but it was disproved by Swineford (1949) and Meyer and Bendig (1961). Among studies utilizing a cross-sectional strategy perhaps one-half yielded results which seem to verify the hypothesis (e.g., Dye & Very, 1968; Garrett, Bryan, & Perl, 1935; Mukherjee, 1962) whereas the other half seems to reject it (e.g., W. W. Clark, 1949; Gault, 1954; Hundal, 1966; McNemar, 1942). Somewhat diverse but, on the whole, unsatisfying results were reported by some Scandinavian authors (Heinonen, 1963; Lehtovaara, 1962; Stadius, 1964). Reanalysis of the Garrett et al. data (1935) and data of Chrysostome (1938) by Richards (1941) resulted in almost total agreement with the original studies. L. V. Jones (1949), on the other hand, in reanalyzing part of the data of McNemar (1942) could not support McNemar's interpretation. Some authors even found results within the school age range which seem directly opposed to a

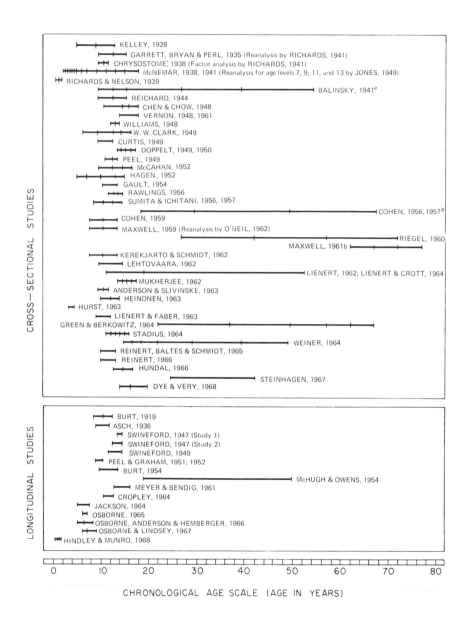

Figure 1. Factor analytic studies on the age-differentiation hypothesis of intelligence. Intersecting vertical lines indicate mean ages of age ranges investigated. [[a] Reanalysis by O'Neil, 1962; [b] reanalysis by Berger *et al.*, 1964 (all levels) and by Radcliffe, 1966 (first three levels).]

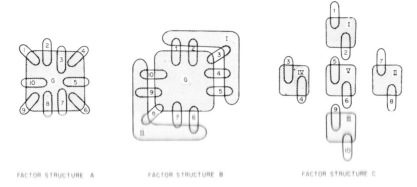

FACTOR STRUCTURE A   FACTOR STRUCTURE B   FACTOR STRUCTURE C

Figure 2. Factor structures A, B, and C show different levels of differentiation of intelligence structure according to the age-differentiation hypothesis of Burt and Garrett. Shaded areas represent different factors of intelligence: G indicates a general factor, whereas roman numbers (I, II, III, IV, and V) indicate independent group factors. Smaller oval areas in each structure represent the same 10 tests of intelligence. The shaded area of each test indicates the magnitude of saturation of this test by a given factor.

differentiation process, but rather seem to support a kind of integration with increasing age (T. Y. L. Chen & Chow, 1948; H. S. Williams, 1948).

Other authors found even more differing results. For instance, Reichard's data (1944) demonstrated integration within the age range 9-12 and differentiation between the ages of 12 and 15. In view of these and other developmental psychological findings, Reichard formulated an integration-disintegration hypothesis, which implies minimal integration at time of birth, gradually increasing integration during childhood till the age of 12, and from there on decreasing integration. Studies with infant and preschool subjects also revealed divergent results. Richards and Nelson (1939) tended toward a differentiation-integration-differentiation process in interpreting the results for the age group six months to one year, and from one year upward. On the other hand, Hindley and Munro (1968) claimed to have found a rather steady decline of the "g"-variance proportion for the same age ranges. Only in regard to the age span 3 to 4 do both McNemar (1938, 1942) and Hurst (1963) report no changes in the factor structures.

With regard to a life-span developmental psychology the most interesting group of studies, however, are those using and examining a much broader age range. Balinsky (1941) was the first author who studied the age-differentiation hypothesis within an age range from 9 to 59 years. He compared the factor patterns of six age groups, and found supporting evidence for the age-differentiation hypothesis looking at the first 4 age groups, i.e., the age range 9 to early adulthood (25-29). From that age onward a kind of dedifferentiation seemed to occur. In middle adulthood (ages 35-44) there appeared a strong, and in late adulthood (ages 50-59) a very strong first factor, with a concomitant decline in the relative variance proportions of the other factors. The results were interpreted by Balinsky (1941) as indicating a reorganization towards a "flexible complexity." Green and Berkowitz (1964) spoke of a general-to-specific-to-general hypothesis regarding the age range from childhood to late adulthood. Figure 3 summarizes the major hypotheses related to age-associated changes in factorial pattern of intelligence.

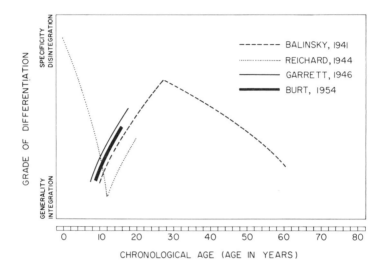

Figure 3. Direction and age levels for changes in factor structure according to the major age-differentiation hypotheses of intelligence.

The authors of the seven cross-sectional studies working with nearly the same age samples are partly in favor of Balinsky's view (Green & Berkowitz, 1964; Lienert, 1962; Lienert & Crott, 1964; Steinhagen, 1967), whereas others reject it in part (J. Cohen, 1956, 1957; R. M. Riegel, 1960; see also R. M. Riegel & Riegel, 1962) or reject it entirely (M. Weiner, 1964). Maxwell's (1961b) results neither contradicted nor supported Balinsky's results. O'Neil (1962) attempted to disprove the findings of Balinsky in a critical reanalysis, whereas Berger, Bernstein, Klein, Cohen, and Lucas (1964) and Radcliffe (1966), reanalyzing J. Cohen's data (1956, 1957), interpreted the outcome again as age-functional changes of factor structures. Finally, the findings of McHugh and Owens (1954), providing the only longitudinal study in the adult age range, largely supported the corresponding interpretations of Balinsky.

B. Studies Using "Secondary Age Parameters" as Independent Variables

A whole series of comparative factor analytic studies have used as independent variables parameters which at first glance show no intrinsic relationship to CA, but in which CA nevertheless seems to appear implicitly in the independent variables employed. These studies can be distinguished into four subgroups.

1. Ability-Differentiation Hypothesis

This class subsumes all those investigations which compare the factor structures of subjects at different ability levels. By different ability levels, one typically means different levels of IQ, a concept which expresses a relationship between intelligence and chronological age. To my knowledge, C. W. Thompson and Margaret (1947) were the first to give more intensive thought to the influence of the level of IQ on factor patterns of intelligence tests. A year later, this presumption was formalized as the following hypothesis by Segel (1948): "The organization of the mind is ... different for differing levels of brightness [p. 11]." This hypothesis appeared to be supported by means of a comparison of the average intercorrelation coefficients in high and low ability subjects. Contrary to Segel, in comparing high and low ability adolescents measured on the basis of their total score (IQ), Rawlings (1956) claimed to have found evidence that the factorial mental organization of adolescents is not a function of brightness.

Independently of these authors, Wewetzer (1958) formulated the divergence-hypothesis. This hypothesis maintains that the factor structures of intelligence for subjects with a higher IQ are more differentiated than those of age-matched subjects of lower IQs. This hypothesis has been named "ability-differentiation hypothesis" by Reinert, Baltes, and Schmidt (1965) in order to distinguish it from the age-differentiation hypothesis. When comparing groups (ages 10-14) of different intelligence, defined on the basis of grade in school (Lienert, 1960, 1961), total IQ score (Baumeister & Bartlett, 1962; Lienert & Faber, 1963), or teacher judgments (Amelang & Langer, 1968), the ability differentiation hypothesis has been confirmed in the studies by Lienert (1960, 1961) and Lienert and Faber (1963) and has been contradicted in the studies by Baumeister and Bartlett (1962) and Amelang and Langer (1968). Within the age range 8-10, I. Belmont, Birch, and Belmont (1967), comparing mentally subnormal children with normal children of the same age, found different factor structures, whereas studies comparing factor structures of mentally subnormal adults with normal adults disprove the general validity of the ability-differentiation hypothesis (Eyferth, 1963; Kebbon, 1965).

2. *Developmental Ability-Differentiation Hypothesis*

According to both the age-differentiation and the ability-differentiation hypotheses, parallel predictions are made with regard to changes of the factor structure of intelligence. This parallelism, known already to Spearman (1927) and later expressed very clearly by Segel (1948), induced Lienert (1961b) to conceptualize both hypotheses within one framework. Looking simultaneously at age and ability level, he stated that a low ability level corresponds to an ontogenetically earlier intelligence level and a high ability level corresponds to an ontogenetically later intelligence level. In other words, a low IQ is the consequence of an ontogenetically early fixation of the structural differentiation, whereas a high IQ is the consequence of an ontogenetically late fixation of the structural differentiation. Thus, Lienert postulated that there should be a high degree of similarity in the factor structure between older children and children of high IQ and between younger children and children of low IQ. Reinert *et al.* (1965) suggested naming this interpretation of Wewetzer's hypothesis "developmental ability-differentiation hypothesis."

3. *Performance-Differentiation Hypothesis.*

Finally, following Lienert's (1961b) argumentation, Reinert *et al.* (1965), have argued that average intellectual performance increases both as a function of chronological age and ability level, at least with regard to the first part of the life-span. Therefore, they have suggested that it might be most parsimonious to formulate a "performance-differentiation hypothesis" which maintains that "the degree of differentiation of the factor structure of intelligence is dependent upon the absolute level of intellectual performance." When taking the absolute overall performance on tests as a preliminary estimate of the absolute intellectual performance level, this hypothesis could also be called a "mental-age-differentiation hypothesis." First studies, aimed at testing the performance-differentiation hypothesis within the school age range, yielded positive results with boys (Reinert *et al.*, 1965) and partially positive results with girls (Reinert, 1965). Although additional data are clearly needed, it seems that the performance-differentiation hypothesis represents the most parsimonious framework presently available for the description of ontogenetic changes in the organizational pattern of intelligence.

4. *Developmental Personality-Differentiation Hypothesis*

A number of comparative factor analytic studies, taking personality variables as independent variables and the level of differentiation of the factor structure of intelligence as the dependent variable, could be subsumed under the name "developmental personality-differentiation hypothesis." In this context, the concepts of regression and fixation are of particular significance indicating a functional relationship between age and development. Altus and Clark (1949) have used the concept of fixation in order to explain the more undifferentiated factor structure of intelligence of maladjusted groups compared to well-adjusted groups. Subjects were adult illiterates and the grade of adjustment was tested by questionnaires. Similarly, Balzert (1966) used the concept of fixation in an attempt to explain more undifferentiated factor structures of extraverted versus introverted adults.

Simkin (1950) and Hover (1951) assumed that adult schizophrenics and neurotics, respectively, would show an undifferentiated factor structure of intelligence compared to normal adults because of regression toward develop mentally earlier behavior patterns. On the contrary, however, Simkin's study yielded a more differentiated factor structure with schizophrenics, and Hover's results also failed to confirm his hypothesis. Maxwell (1961a) reported more differentiated factor structures of neurotic children when compared with normal children of the same age. On the other hand, Lienert (1963) reported less differentiated factor structures for neurotic subjects, thus offering support to Simkin's and Hover's hypothesis. An additional hypothesis, stating a greater similarity between neurotic adults and adolescents than between neurotic adults and normal adults, could not be verified by Lienert (1963). Eysenck and White (1964) reanalyzing the data of Lienert, and an analogous study by R. Cohen and Wittemann (1967) did not find further evidence.

Finally, Lienert (1964), and Lienert and Crott (1967) did find less differentiated factor structures in students under the hallucinatory drug lysergic acid diethylamide (LSD) when compared with students under normal conditions. He explained this result by arguing for regression of personality, especially of intelligence, as a consequence of LSD.

III. METHODOLOGICAL ASPECTS AND PROBLEMS

If one is to estimate whether the studies regarding the differentiation hypothesis have increased our developmental psychological knowledge, one must first examine the methodological quality of the studies. Fairly extensive descriptions of the methodological viewpoints which these kinds of studies must take into account are summarized for instance by Burt (1954), Anastasi (1958), O'Neil (1962) and Reinert et al. (1965). Only those viewpoints necessary for familiarity with the most important problems and their solutions will be discussed.

A. General Research Strategy

The basic logic of the studies mentioned above can be described as follows: Two or more groups of subjects defined as different from each other with regard to an independent variable are compared with regard to the dependent variable, factor structure. If differences between factor structures of the compared groups are found and if the differences are significant, they are said to show a *developmental change* "caused" by the independent variable

In this context there are two main questions to ask: First, is it justified to interpret these differences as age changes? This question may be seen within the broader context of the studies and discussions concerning methodological strategies of developmental psychology (e.g., Baltes, 1968b; Schaie, 1965). Thus, when using a cross-sectional strategy, studies investigating the age-differentiation hypothesis would confound age differences with other possible differences (i.e., generation differences) associated with the comparison groups. The possibility of both an increasing and decreasing effect of such confounded differences between generations on the degree of differentiation in cross-sectional age samples would seem to obscure a clear interpretation of the findings as indicating ontogenetic change. On the other hand, when using a longitudinal approach, one has to deal with the confounding of age differences with selective dropout and practice effects.

The second question to be asked refers to the problem of whether developmental changes can be excluded when there are no differences in the factor structure. Besides the possibility that the test instruments have not been sensitive enough to measure possible existing differences effectively, the distance between the comparison groups on the continuum of the independent variable will also influence the result with regard to whether differences are found. If the distances are rather large (widely separated age levels, ability levels, etc.), then there may be changes for intermediate levels, since nonlinear trends of changes must not be excluded. Neither of these questions has received much consideration in the above mentioned studies. In support of the differentiation hypothesis, most authors tend to equate automatically existing differences with age-developmental changes in the mental organization. On the other hand, most authors contradicting the differentiation hypothesis tend to interpret the lack of differences as stability in the mental organization.

B. Special Design Components

Whether the inferences regarding the existence of differences are justified or not is also largely dependent upon the validity of the sampling procedures, the validity of the test samples, and the validity of the independent variables, that is, the validity of the criteria used to yield differences or similarities.

1. *Independent Variables*

Chronological age, ability level, performance level, and personality status are the parameters used as independent variables in these studies. They are justified as independent variables to the degree that the samples to be compared are homogeneous with respect to all characteristics relevant to intelligence performances but the independent variable itself.

Most authors used stratified samples, but also some random samples (e.g., Cropley, 1964) and incidental samples (e.g., T. Y. L. Chen & Chow, 1948; Kebbon, 1965) were investigated. Unfortunately, information required in order to make clear estimates as to the quality of the samples is missing. Here and there one can assume relatively high heterogeneity of the comparison samples (e.g., Balinsky, 1941; Garrett et al., 1935; Hurst, 1963), which in turn would imply differential expectations regarding the size of within-age correlations. Although this problem of the heterogeneity of samples poses a main problem to classical factor analysis, experiments aimed at clarification of this problem are rare (e.g., Kenny and Coltheart, 1960; Überla, 1968; Vukovich, 1965). Heterogeneity will yield a noticeable increase in the correlation size mainly when the sample contains subgroups which differ highly with respect to the mean of the variables to be correlated (e.g., males and females; subjects differing in length of schooling, etc.). Undoubtedly, heterogeneity more directly affects correlations than the factor structure, although heterogeneity itself may produce a distinct factor. Thus, T. L. Kelley (1928) argued that heterogeneity with regard to the characteristic "maturity" would result in a distinct factor in a factor analysis, a position attacked by Spearman (1927). Several authors, primarily Wright (1939) and Merz and Kalveram (1965) have proposed similar conclusions and applied them to the differentiation hypotheses. Burt and John (1942) have refuted the criticism raised by Wright, whereas Reinert, Baltes, and Schmidt (1966) examined some issues inherent in Merz and Kalveram's criticism of the age-differentiation hypothesis.

2. Measurement Variables

In selecting the test variables, there are three main points which have to be considered. The first point concerns the kind of test selected. If test results are to be generalized to "intelligence" as such, it follows necessarily that the test has to measure intelligence and not, e.g., school achievement. Moreover, the tests should represent as wide a range of intelligence as possible and should be appropriate for the problem to be measured. For example, test batteries aiming towards the measurement of general ability are obviously not suited for studying the differentiation hypothesis; this applies, e.g., to the Wechsler tests which have been used in one-third of all studies mentioned here—in most of the cases yielding results contradictory to differentiation. Test batteries with largely one-dimensional tests, such as the Primary Mental Abilities, are more suitable.

The second point refers to the question of whether the tests are subject-adequate. The tests must have, above all, a sufficiently wide range so that the intelligence levels of subjects can be measured properly; otherwise, asymmetrical distributions ("floor effects" versus "ceiling effects") may result, which question all prerequisites (homoscedasticity, linear regression) for computing product-moment correlations. In some of the studies this problem apparently has been neglected, while in other studies consideration of this problem resulted in dispensing with one or more of the tests originally incorporated. Another requirement stated very often and observed in many studies concerns the reliability of the tests which has to be of nearly the same value for the comparison samples. Kenny (1958), however, has shown this to be only of relative importance since the differences in test reliability do not affect the configuration of test vectors in common factor space.

Finally, the third point refers to the dilemma of the differentiation hypotheses concerning a more stringent, causative interpretation. The problem here is the difficulty of separating the relative influences of heredity and environment in the test instruments used thus far. It is hoped that studies concerning "fluid" and "crystallized" intelligence (R. B. Cattell, 1963b; Horn, 1968; Horn & Cattell; 1967) will approach a solution to this problem.

3. *Dependent Variables and Criteria for Evaluating Change*

The dependent variable "factor structure of intelligence" is an inclusive concept for several measures partly dependent upon each other. In the early studies on the differentiation hypothesis, factor structure meant primarily the structure of the unrotated factor loading matrix. In these studies, (a) increase in number of common factors, (b) decrease in communalities, (c) decrease of the variance proportions of the first factor, and (d) increase in the corresponding variance proportions of the remaining factors are seen to be indicators for the level of differentiation of factor structures. Moreover, the decrease in the average of the intercorrelations is usually taken as first indicator of a more differentiated factor structure.

In addition, since about 1940, *separately rotated* factor loading matrices have been compared qualitatively concerning their similarity. This was done most frequently by using simple structure as the criterion in addition to the ones previously mentioned. Since 1960, analytical rotations toward simple structure, mostly orthogonal, have been preferred. In the case of oblique rotation, a decrease of obliqueness is expected with increasing differentation. With both orthogonal and oblique rotations, a quantitative index for the degree of similarity of the factors can be obtained (Burt's "unadjusted correlation coefficient" or Tucker's "coefficient of congruence"). Several authors (e.g. Berger *et al.*, 1964; Mukherjee, 1962) have computed these coefficients.

Recently Sixtl and Fittkau (1969) summarized the fallacies and weaknesses of the above mentioned quantitative and qualitative criteria used for com parison. In fact, these criteria allow a great deal of subjective decision on the part of the experimenter, and perhaps some inconsistencies of the reported results are due to this lack of objectivity of the criteria. Sixtl and Fittkau advocate as a more adequate technique for comparison purposes the so-called similarity rotation. Using this procedure, the factor loading matrices to be compared are rotated in such a manner that they reach a maximum of numerical similarity.

Some studies on the differentiation hypotheses have already used such procedures, especially the transformation analysis by Ahmaavara (e.g., Heinonen, 1963; Hurst, 1963; Stadius, 1964). The latter procedure over-estimates, however, the similarity of test configurations. Recently, Steinhagen (1967) used a similarity rotation technique proposed by Fischer and Roppert (1964) which appears to be of superior power. A serious deficiency of the comparison methods, however, is that the sampling distribution of similarity coefficients is as yet largely unknown, which again opens the way to subjectivity of interpretations. Only very recently, the procedure of comparing real-data with random-data similarity coefficients (Gebhardt, 1968; Nesselroade & Baltes, 1970) appears to provide a strategy for coping with this problem.

IV. DISCUSSION AND CONCLUSIONS

In general, it seems fair to state that the available data do not allow for a clear-cut description of life-span changes in factor structure of intelligence. On the other hand, it is also apparent that the pessimistic statement by Coombs cited above does not seem justified. In contrast to Coombs characterization of factor analysis as being dead, factor analysis rather seems to be a vital living organism which, however, has to pass many labyrinths before reaching the intended goal. Before making any specific conclusions from the inconsistent body of data, it will be useful to elaborate on some difficulties inherent in the evaluation and comparative analysis of the existing research.

A. Difficulties in Evaluation

The preceding sections illustrate some of the difficulties in designing compara-tive factor analytical studies in such a manner that the influences of artificial parameters can be eliminated or at least be minimized. Thus, in view of the multiplicity of interacting variables, the diversity of the findings is not particularly surprising.

Unfortunately, many of the studies mentioned above do not offer sufficient information necessary to allow for a posteriori evaluation of the prerequisites needed for a proper comparison of factor structures. But even the more informative studies do not permit an unequivocal interpretation as to change versus invariance of factor structures. Moreover, in light of the complexity of the research object, the kind of global categorization into "strong" and "weak" studies as suggested, for example, by Guilford (1967) does not carry any conclusive evidence. Thus, as Pawlik (1968) has pointed out recently, unequivocal results might not be expected because of the wide differences in tests used at different age levels. Moreover, he has argued that existing research on the factorial invariance of intelligence runs the risk of confounding the effects of studying differential areas of intelligence at different levels of development with true ontogenetic changes in factor structure. The interaction between developmental level and the nature of tests used is indeed conspicuous (e.g., stage-developmental test systems at the preschool level, general test batteries at the adult and old-age level) and might preclude any comparative analysis throughout the entire life-span.

There is a whole series of additional factors which aggravate the comparison of the findings; for example, the fact that studies are conducted in different regions, different countries, and at different times of measurement. It appears very difficult to estimate the impact of associated differences in developmental conditions. In particular, effects of regionally and nationally different and over the years changing educational systems on the organizational pattern of intelligence deserve considerations. A further major hindrance in comparing the outcome of different studies refers to marked differences in preference for particular factor analytical methods and the type of criteria used in testing factorial changes. In view of such discrepancies in method, it appears most desirable to systematically reanalyze previous studies applying uniform methods of factor extraction and factor matching procedures. Such reanalyses, undoubtedly, should reduce the inconsistency of outcomes and might represent a very worthwhile strategy for further research in this area.

B. Indirect Evidence for Factor Change

It has to be noted that change in factor structure of intelligence is not necessarily a desirable goal for methodological and theoretical reasons. Vukovich (1967), for example, elaborates on some advantageous aspects of dealing with invariant structures only. Thus the expectation of some authors (e.g., Fischer & Roppert, 1965; Sixtl & Fittkau, 1969) that most of the differences in factor structures might be "rotated away" if appropriate matching procedures are used, is understandable. But the postulate of invariance looses its justification when it is in contradiction to already well-established scientific knowledge.

The conjecture that human behavior is changing with time is certainly more than well founded. There seems to be no reason to suppose that ontogenetic change should not be reflected in the structure of intelligence. It is conceded that numerical invariance of intelligence factors is a necessary postulate when comparing different samples of the *same* population, and configurationally invariant intelligence factors might be expected when comparing different samples from related populations. However, in the case where the comparison samples and populations differ significantly as to their developmental status, the requirement of invariance becomes less acceptable. Oléron (1957, p. 453) formulates this opinion rather definitively: *"Des facteurs qui resteraient stables d'un âge à l'autre seraient éminemment suspects."* In the framework of life-span research, when dealing with unselected samples from wide age ranges, factor invariance could be largely postulated. On the other hand, it appears reasonable to expect factor changes for the onset and offset of the chronological life-span.

This position, upon which most factor analysts would probably agree, has psychological plausibility and it is supported by the fact that individuals in different developmental stages attack the solutions of the same problem in different ways. Thurstone (1940), for example, mentions that solving a number problem can be mere routine for adults, whereas it can require inductive thinking in the child. Henrysson (1960) gives the example that the same test measuring intelligence factors in 10-year-olds might indicate perceptual speed in adults. Further evidence for plausibility of ontogenetic change in factor structure of intelligence is obtained also from studies comparing Ss of the same age and the same intelligence but different environmental conditions. These studies are of significance, since they also suggest what conditions might produce changes in factor structure of intelligence. Thus, the nature of intellectual training seems to play an important role in the development of mental organization. Anastasi (1958) has given an excellent review of such studies. Here, only such studies will be mentioned in which differences between factor structures have been interpreted in the sense of differentiation. A more differentiated factor structure of intelligence, for example, was found by Wewetzer (1968) for gifted adolescents in German high schools when comparing them with adolescents in vocational training schools and by Mitchell (1956) in a high status group when compared to a low status group. Furthermore, Very (1967) reported a more differentiated factor structure of mathematical ability in males when comparing male with female students and interpreted this as a function of cultural pressure dissimilar for the sexes.

In addition to research on such long-term experimental effects, there are some studies which suggest that short-term experience also leads to changes in intellectual factor structure. Thus, Anastasi (1936), Woodrow (1938), and Melametsä (1965) were able to induce experimentally changes in factor structure of intelligence by means of short-term training procedures. These studies are fundamentally in accordance with the explanation of ability development in the framework of learning theory as proposed by Ferguson (1954). Indeed, Ferguson's attempt to relate concepts of factor analysis and learning theory is a promising beginning for a process-oriented construct validation of factor concepts. The endeavor of Reuchlin (1964) to combine the age-differentiation hypothesis with Piaget's theory of cognitive development is another example of this type of approach.

C. Preliminary Conclusions

Despite the indirect evidence for changes in the factor structure of intelligence, the direct empirical evidence, based on comparing different age groups, does not allow for a clear answer. Consequently, reliable statements about changes in factor structure along the life-span are not yet possible. Optimistic conclusions, however, that the question should not be any longer oriented toward "whether" or "whether not" but rather "why" (R. F. Green & Berkowitz, 1964; Osborne & Lindsey, 1967) are not yet justified.

If one considers only those studies that reported differences in factor structure, then the majority give evidence for a trend toward increasing differentiation of the factor structure going from lower to higher developmental stages. This process seems to parallel the increase and/or decrease of the average test-scores in the sense of the performance-differentiation hypothesis discussed above. Referring to the life-span, this would mean that the factorial structure of intelligence, though not associated exclusively with chronological age as an antecedent, is becoming more differentiated during childhood and adolescence, is exhibiting invariance during early and middle adulthood, and might become less differentiated in late adulthood and old age. It should be emphasized again that this process has not been established yet with certainty. This is especially true for early childhood and old age, for which, on the other hand, such a process seems to be most plausible but also most difficult to assess. Moreover the statement made by Burt (1954, p. 85) with regard to the age-differentiation hypothesis seems to hold generally for all described differentiation hypotheses, namely that: ". . . it would be gross over-simplification to describe mental development exclusively in terms of a single sweeping principle whether of increasing differentiation or of increasing integration."

An interesting possibility for the "differentiation" of the usual differentiation-dedifferentiation model would be the attempt to transfer the factor change models, conceptualized by Coan (1966) for the area of personality development, to the area of intelligence development. Coan's notion of factor metamorphosis, in particular, seems to be a powerful candidate for the study of intelligence structure at the lower developmental stages, although one might run into difficulties regarding its operational clarity. In this context one might also explore the fruitfulness of some conceptions developed within the area of differential psychology (W. Stern, 1912, 1920), field-theory (Lewin, 1933; 1935; see also Schaie, 1962), or within the psychology of cognition (Piaget, 1947b) for a theory of factor change.

D. Implications of Factor Change

As long as the fact of factor change in intelligence structure is not clearly substantiated, all statements about theoretical and practical implications of such changes should not be understood as binding recommendations but rather as stimulating notions. Assuming the existence of changes in factor structure of intelligence, the following implications illustrate the significance of the question whether intelligence factors are ontogenetically changing or not.

From a theoretical viewpoint the most important implication of a changing intelligence structure refers to the conclusion that all demands for a general validity of intelligence structure models (e.g., Thurstone's model of primary abilities, Guilford's structure of intelligence model, Meili's gestalt-process model, Burt's and Vernon's hierarchical model) have to be abandoned. All these models would have to be modified and integrated into a developmental frame of reference. As a matter of fact, authors like Garrett (1946), Hsü (1948) and Bernreuter (1953), assuming that the age-differentiation hypothesis would lead to an approximation between Spearman's general factor model and Thurstone's multiple factor model, have in principle assigned different models to different sections of the age scale: the Spearman model to childhood and the Thurstone model to late adolescence and early adulthood, respectively.

The essential implications with regard to test construction (validity, reliability) cannot be dealt with in this paper. The interested reader is referred to papers by Garrett (1946), Anastasi (1961), Lienert (1961) and Lienert and Crott (1964). Important within this context, however, is the fact that age-variant measurement instruments necessarily would lead to a dissatisfaction with conventional age curves of intelligence. In the case of factorial change, these curves would not represent a common (identical) dimension of intelligence but different dimensions (factors) of intelligence in different segments of the age gradient. Nesselroade (Chapter 7) and Baltes and Nesselroade (1970) explicate the implications of structural change for such quantitative age comparisons and propose to either examine or construe factor invariance before quantitative age comparisons on factor scores are performed.

A final set of implications relates to future research which, in the opinion of this author, has not lost its attractiveness. What seems necessary in these studies is not so much a completely new set of hypotheses and new concepts nor a totally new set of statistical techniques. Regarding the theoretical basis, it appears necessary to clarify the existing concepts, for example, by means of more refined factor change models, which would permit a closer correspondence between theoretical concepts and associated data-reduction models. Regarding technical aspects, the utilization of existing factor-matching strategies (similarity rotations, comparison of empirical coefficients with random-data coefficients, comparison of "between" with "within" group coefficients) is of crucial significance.

Another important aspect relates to the systematic exploration of which developmental conditions might be responsible for changes in factor structures (see also Chapter 16 by Horn). What is clearly necessary here is an experimental approach (manipulation of such variables as amount of reinforcement, number of trials, interstimulus interval, etc.) in order to examine the processes underlying changes in patterns of intelligence. At this point, experimental research on learning and the classical multivariate research on intelligence structure may have a chance for a fruitful convergence. On the one hand, such a convergence would increase the awareness of learning research for problems associated with the multidimensionality of behavior. On the other hand, it would provide the factor analyst with new insights into the multiple antecedents for structural changes in behavior.

Finally it should be mentioned that research on factor changes in behavioral areas other than intelligence is rather scarce. Besides some experimental studies in the area of motor behavior (e.g., Fleishman & Hempel, 1954; Greene, 1943; Heinonen, 1962; Janke, 1965; Janke & Ritzmann, 1964), only some studies on psycholinguistic abilities (Quereshi, 1967a, 1967b), word association (J. P. Sullivan & Moran, 1967; Swartz & Moran, 1968) and perceptual abilities (Reinert & Tauscher, 1969) are available. The further exploration of factor changes in these and other related behavioral domains would significantly contribute also to the interpretation of comparative factor analytic research in the area of intellectual development.

CHAPTER 18

A Reinterpretation of Age Related Changes in Cognitive Structure and Functioning

K. WARNER SCHAIE

WEST VIRGINIA UNIVERSITY
MORGANTOWN, WEST VIRGINIA

ABSTRACT

Chronological aging as a frame of reference for the study of developmental phenomena is widely used but not very well understood. The three dimensions of age differences, age changes, and cultural change are often confused with one another and each in turn is at times erroneously taken as an estimate of developmental change. The general developmental model defining the interrelation between these dimensions is further explicated in this chapter. Particular attention is paid to the effect of generational differences and the literature is examined for examples where differentiation of generational effects from maturational change and environmental impact may properly be attempted. At the same time, attention is given to different classes of cognitive variables (i.e., crystallized and fluid intelligence) which by virtue of their presumed environmental or biogenic mediation are helpful in understanding the relationship between generational differences and common environmental impact at specified times of measurement. Environmental impact between times of measurement is found to be of marked importance in children and in measures of fluid intelligence in adults, while generational differences appear to account for substantial portions of variance in studies of adult age changes on measures of crystallized intelligence.

I. INTRODUCTION

The purpose of this chapter is to pursue further a number of methodological issues raised in earlier discussions concerning the differences in status among the concepts of age change, age difference, and cultural change (Schaie, 1959, 1965, 1967). The importance of this differentiation for research design and the interpretation of developmental data seems finally to have come home to investigators interested in adulthood and old age (cf. Carp, 1968; K. F. Riegel *et al.*, 1967; C. L. Rose, 1968). Unfortunately, however, it is clear that many workers interested in childhood and adolescence are still behaving as if they were quite ignorant of the issues involved, even though they have certainly been raised as well in the child development context (Bell, 1953, 1954; Kessen, 1960; T. L. McCulloch, 1957). The present volume, of course, would seem to address itself precisely to the issue that many persons calling themselves developmental psychologists are interested in children but not in the problems of human development.

A second purpose of this chapter is to deal with some of the questions which have been raised about the utility of the general developmental model (Schaie, 1965) in generating useful strategies for an escape from the dilemma posed by the fact that none of the conventional research strategies for following behavior over time can yield clearly interpretable data. These questions have been raised in a most thoughtful manner in papers by Baltes (1967, 1968b) and by Baltes and Nesselroade (1970). An attempt will be made to explicate why it is necessary to stick to certain aspects of my earlier presentation, but it will also be shown that Baltes has taken a logical step in implementing certain strategies which ought to be taken and that our differences may well be a matter of ⋅ priorities rather than principles. Subsequently, some new strategies for properly differentiating age changes from cohort (generational) differences will be further explicated. Finally, data in the developmental literature which bear on some of the theoretical issues to be discussed in this chapter will be presented.

II. AGE CHANGES versus AGE DIFFERENCES versus CULTURAL CHANGE

It has been known for some time that data on age-related phenomena will differ markedly depending upon whether it has been collected by means of cross-sectional or longitudinal research strategies. Although the problem is quite severe in studies of development in early life, little emphasis has been given to it by child psychologists arguing perhaps that the proportion of maturational variance in any variable of interest in early life is so preponderant as to permit ignoring other sources of variation. This stance is quite wrong and dangerous of course, but thus far the matter of discrepancies between the results of longitudinal and cross-sectional studies has been discussed primarily in work on adult age changes (Birren, 1959b; Damon, 1965; Kuhlen, 1940, 1963; Owens, 1953; Schaie & Strother, 1968a, 1968b; Welford, 1961).

The reason for such discrepancies is to be sought in the nature of the developmental process. Three methods of describing developmental change have been defined in an earlier paper (Schaie, 1965) each of which confounds two parameters. Precise terms are available to denote what is being measured by each strategy as follows:

1.   The *cross-sectional* method measures *age differences* but confounds differences in maturational status with differences between generations.

2.   The *longitudinal* method measures *age changes* but confounds differences in maturational status with environmental treatment effects.

3.   The *time-lag* method measures *cultural change* but confounds environmental treatment effects with differences between generations.

What all this means is that any sample of subjects must be indexed to show its status on three dimensions: (a) the cohort C_i from which the sample has been drawn (i.e., the time interval of entry into the environment); (b) the time T_k at which the reported measurements have been taken; and (c) the age A_m of the sample at the time of measurement. Now, it is perfectly true that the last of these three parameters can always be inferred from the other two (Baltes, 1967, 1968b) but it does not follow at all that it is immaterial which two of the three parameters are independently chosen. Neither is it true that it would be possible to resolve the components of developmental change by means of a general two-factorial model. To do so, as will later be shown, one must collect data in such a way that they can be analyzed via two of the three possible two-factorial sequential strategies deducible from the three-way model. Data analysis limited to any one of the two-way models suffers from the inexorable unidirectional nature of time which must result in the spurious confounding of the third parameter which cannot be directly estimated by a single two-way design. If one begins with the three-factor model, however, one can readily derive equations which will result in independent parameter estimates by measuring over the *population* of ages, cohorts, or times of measurement.

Baltes (1967, 1968b) has actually followed this line of reasoning implicitly in describing his "cross-sectional and longitudinal sequences." The reader should note that what Baltes has done is to specify logical extensions from the general model which apply whenever more than the minimum of two levels per parameter are included in a given research design. Moreover, at the operational level, Baltes has recently conceded the necessary consequences of a three-dimensional model by publishing two research studies which employ two of the three possible strategies (Baltes & Reinert, 1969; Baltes, Reinert, & Baltes, 1970).

It is argued then that Baltes is actually following experimental strategies which I would strongly endorse, but that he is reverting to conceptual descriptions that use terms which my discussion of the general developmental model has shown to be confusing. While I have no quarrel with his terminology in describing the nature of data collection (longitudinal and cross-sectional sequences), I would propose that the design of a given study be denoted by the terms cohort-sequential (CS), time-sequential (TS), and cross-sequential (XS). These descriptions are preferable to the terms used by Baltes since they clearly imply a radically different strategy than is implied by the conventional sounding terms of cross-sectional and longitudinal sequences.

In the following it will be attempted to make more explicit the advantages of deriving operational strategies from the three-dimensional general developmental model (Schaie, 1965). For example, if the investigator is interested in differentiating the effect of generational differences from maturational age changes, he would employ the *cohort-sequential method* which in conventional terms is the most general case of the longitudinal method. In the cohort-sequential method one would study two or more cohorts (generations) at two or more ages. It is impossible, of course, to get samples of all ages for all cohorts at the identical times of measurement and thus a significant cohort by age interaction could denote either that age changes occur at different rates for different cohorts or that there is a time of measurement confound.

How do we get out of this dilemma? It is a simple matter conceptually to let the time of measurement confound become trivial with respect to cohorts by sampling two cohorts at all possible ages, or with respect to age by sampling two ages for all possible cohorts. Neither design, however, is operationally very practical, because it will encompass the lifetime of the investigator to carry out either design. The cohort-sequential approach is quite feasible for the study of short-lived organisms but it does not seem to have much promise for human investigations of any but short portions of the life-span.

An operational solution becomes much more practical, however, thus illustrating the point that it does make a difference which two of the three possible parameters we wish to study, when we consider the *time-sequential* method which is the most general case of the conventional cross-sectional approach. Here we attempt to differentiate aging effects from environmental treatment effects by studying samples with two or more different ages at two or more times of measurement. The confound here is, of course, cohort differences since we cannot study individuals of different ages at the same time of measurement unless they also belong to different generations. Again, we may let the confound become asymptotic with respect to age by sampling two ages at all possible times of measurement or by sampling *two times of measurement with respect to all possible ages of interest*. The latter approach can be used to conduct an experiment as rapidly as one reasonably expects behavioral change to occur between two measurements and is thus eminently practical. In this case one can get a reliable estimate of the environmental treatment effect for the period in question as averaged over all ages of interest. Such net environmental effect ($Td_{k \cdot ts}$) when subtracted from measures of longitudinal (Lod_m) age changes for the same period of time should result in a reasonably close estimate of net age changes (Ad_m) at time k.

If one, however, is concerned with the impact of generation differences, which issue is becoming increasingly meaningful and important, then one must begin by using the *cross-sequential* method which is the most general case of the time-lag method. Here one examines two or more samples from the same cohort at two or more times of measurement. In this instance it is, of course, necessary that members of different cohorts also differ in age at different times of measurement, age being thereby confounded in this design. Again, one can let this confound go asymptotic with respect to environmental treatment effects by sampling two times of measurement at all possible cohort levels or sampling two cohorts at all times of measurement. The former approach is clearly the practical one since it permits data collection in a minimum amount of elapsed time. In that case we obtain a reliable estimate of environmental treatment effects ($Td_{k \cdot xs}$) for the time period in question as averaged over all cohorts of interest. Such net time of measurement effect when subtracted from the appropriate time-lag measure of cultural change (Tld_k) should consequently result in a reasonably close estimate of net generational differences (Cd_i) at time k.

When only two estimates are available for each parameter, it is necessary for the third parameter to be inextricably confounded with the status of the other two rather than becoming asymptotic and thus trivial as will be the case when a large number of levels are sampled for at least one of the parameters. We will therefore now write a set of equations which may be more useful than the ones presented previously (Schaie, 1965) for the minimum two level per parameter case. The following set of six equations contains two alternate estimates each for net age differences (Ad), cohort differences (Cd) and time of measurement (or environmental treatment) differences (Td):

$$Ad_{m \cdot cs} = (1/C) \sum_{i=1}^{C} (A_n - A_m) \tag{1}$$

Operation: Sum the differences between two ages over all possible cohorts and divide by the number of cohorts over which summed (cohort-sequential method).

$$Ad_{m \cdot ts} = (1/T) \sum_{k=1}^{T} (A_n - A_m) \tag{2}$$

Operation: Sum the differences between two ages over all possible times of measurement and divide by the number of times of measurement over which summed (time-sequential method).

$$Cd_{i \cdot cs} = (1/A) \sum_{m=1}^{A} (C_j - C_i) \tag{3}$$

Operation: Sum the differences between two cohorts over all possible ages and divide by the number of ages over which summed (cohort-sequential method).

$$Cd_{i \cdot xs} = (1/T) \sum_{k=1}^{T} (C_j - C_i) \tag{4}$$

Operation: Sum the differences between two cohorts over all possible times of measurement and divide by the number of times of measurement over which summed (cross-sequential method).

$$Td_{k \cdot ts} = (1/A) \sum_{m=1}^{A} (T_l - T_k) \tag{5}$$

Operation: Sum the differences between two times of measurement over all possible ages and divide by the number of ages over which summed (time-sequential method).

$$Td_{k \cdot xs} = (1/C) \sum_{i=1}^{C} (T_l - T_k) \tag{6}$$

Operation: Sum the differences between two times of measurement over all possible cohorts and divide by the number of cohorts over which summed (cross-sequential method)

For cross-referencing purposes it should be noted that under the circumstances described above the equations given in this chapter should be substituted for those presented earlier (Schaie, 1965) as follows:

Revised Equation	1965 Equivalent Equation
(1)	(10)
(2)	(13)
(3)	(11)
(4)	(16)
(5)	(14)
(6)	(17)

All of the above equations (and consequently the three alternate sequential strategies) are feasible with short-lived organisms. In studies of human Ss, however, it is clear that only Equations 5 and 6 have any merit for translation into actual experimental designs. It will now be shown how these equations may be incorporated into what should be reasonably accurate estimates of the other components of developmental change as proposed in our earlier discussion.

To do so we shall redefine the three ways in which developmental change can be measured using a unidirectional notation; i.e., age n will stand for a later age than age m; cohort i will have entered the environment before cohort j; and time of measurement k occurred prior to time of measurement l. The following equations are required:

$$Csd_{m \cdot k} = Ad_m - Cd_i \tag{7}$$

i.e., the cross-sectional age difference between ages m and n measured at time k is composed of the net age difference Ad_m less the net cohort (generational) difference Cd_i standing for the difference between cohorts i and j.

$$Lod_{m \cdot i} = Ad_m + Td_k \tag{8}$$

i.e., the longitudinal age change from age m to age n measured for cohort i is composed of the net age difference Ad_m plus the net time of measurement difference Td_k which identifies the net environmental impact from time k to time l.

$$Tld_{k \cdot m} = Td_k + Cd_i \tag{9}$$

i.e., the time-lag cultural change from time k to time l measured at age m is composed of the net time of measurement (environmental impact) difference Td_k plus the cohort difference Cd_i which measures the net cohort difference between cohorts i and j.

It is now possible to solve for all three components of developmental change by substituting the population net time of measurement effect estimated by either Equation 5 or 6 into Equations 8 and 9 and rearranging terms as follows:

$$Ad_m = Lod_{m \cdot i} - Td_{k \cdot ts} \tag{10}$$

i.e., the estimated net maturational age difference between ages m and n equals the difference in mean scores for cohort i obtained on measurement occasions k and l minus the time of measurement effect from time k to l as averaged over all ages of interest. Equation 5 should be used here because $Td_{k \cdot ts}$ holds the effect of cohort differences asymptotic to time of measurement.

Next, we may solve for net cohort differences by the equation

$$Cd_i = Tld_{k.m} - Td_{k.xs} \tag{11}$$

i.e., the estimated net difference between cohorts i and j can be accounted for by subtracting the net time of measurement effect from time k to time l averaged over all cohorts of interest from the difference in mean scores between cohorts i and j at age m. Equation 6 is used in (11) in this instance because $Td_{k.xs}$ holds the effect of age differences asymptotic to time of measurement.

Attention should be called also to the fact that in terms of the above notation $Td_{k.xs}$ will be the proper net estimate of Td_k whenever Ad_m approximates zero, while $Td_{k.ts}$ will be the proper estimate whenever C_i approximates zero. When both Ad_m and C_i approximate zero then the two Td estimates will, of course, approximately agree with one another.

Similar equations can also be derived for the estimation of the components of developmental change beginning with Equations 1, 2, 3, and 4. As should by now be clear to the reader, the designs required for data collection in the manner suggested by these formulas is uneconomical and will therefore not be pursued further.

The above estimates of time of measurement effect are, of course, based on one time period only. As in any sound experimental plan, data should be collected over at least one further measurement interval to reassure the investigator that he has not sampled a chronological period which possesses unusual and temporally unreplicable characteristics.

It is now proposed that the developmental psychologists paradoxically should not be particularly concerned about maturational age changes in behavior once he has satisfied himself as to what component of developmental change can actually be attributed to net aging effects. In other words, our concern with age-related changes in structure and function is only a first step and part of the taxonomic concern of our discipline. Once we have cataloged the truly age-related behavior changes we can then more profitably go on to understand the impact of the environment for organisms at different life stages and, of even more interest, to concern ourselves with differences between generations. The latter issue, concerned with the question as to whether there are indeed systematic changes in the behavior of organisms from one generation to the next will now be considered in more detail.

III. THE IMPACT OF GENERATIONAL DIFFERENCES

A. The Problem

Much attention has heretofore been paid to tracing the changes in behavioral events over the life history of single organisms or of aggregates representing normative samples of organisms at various stages in the life cycle. In most instances, however, it has been assumed that the life cycle of any one member of a given species or sample of a class of members of a species can be readily compared or merged for normative purposes regardless of the historical time at which specific behavioral events have occurred.

The importance of the time at which a behavior is observed has also been considered by sociologists, anthropologists, and political scientists, examples of recent studies being those by Damon (1965), Hyman and Sheatsley (1964) and C. L. Rose (1968). These investigators and many other nonpsychologists have been directly concerned with historical time and consequent generation differences. Most developmental psychologists, on the other hand, seem to have been alerted to these problems primarily out of their concern to reconcile the apparent differences in findings yielded by cross-sectional and longitudinal studies of identical behavior dimensions. Kuhlen (1940) was perhaps the earliest investigator to call attention to the confounding effects of cultural change but the conceptual models discussed above have only recently presented us with a methodology which can point out the necessary steps which must be taken to assess the importance of the interactive effects between the development of behavioral events, the particular circumstances of the species, and the environment within which they have been historically located.

Let us now focus specifically upon generational changes in intellectual ability which are presumed to occur independently of maturational events. To do so, it will be necessary to recapitulate certain deductions from the general developmental model which do not particularly concern themselves with providing an adequate description of intelligent behavior but rather involve those dimensions which are necessary (albeit not sufficient) parameters to account for differences in intellectual development over different time periods. We must, of course, distinguish between those subdomains of the intelligence construct which have been observed or should be expected to follow different patterns of development depending on the direction of change in genetic potential and/or environmental opportunity (R. B. Cattell, 1963b; Horn, 1968; Horn & Cattell, 1966a). If we succeed in specifying those components of intellectual development which interact differentially with changes in the species of the environment we will then be in a position to make differential predictions as to the expected changes in performance on intelligence tests administered at different points in time in the same sample or at the same stage of the life cycle in different generations of organisms.

B. Generational Effects and the Structure of Intelligence

Let us first of all consider the data we have on the structure of intelligence to see how they would likely be affected by developmental change. We will here restrict our consideration to distinguish between what R. B. Cattell (1963b) has labeled crystallized and fluid intelligence, and furthermore will distinguish between measures of intelligence which are either power tests or which are largely dependent upon speed of performance. If we consider that generation differences can obtain by postulating differences in genetic structure and/or prior experience, then if we consider the development of intelligence on a life-span basis, we find cohort effects on average to be primarily a function of those factors which have operated upon the genetic matrix of the cohort (i.e., prior to the time that any of our samples entered the environment). In this case we would assume that cohort differences on measures of fluid intelligence should operate via changes in the genetic matrix of the organism which is essentially inherited; i.e., we get differences over generations in level of fluid intelligence because there has been a shift in the matrix of inherited potentialities. On the other hand, generation differences in crystallized intelligence would be assumed to be a function of differential environmental exposure of the different cohorts prior to the time they enter our scrutiny. Consequently, at birth we would expect generation differences, if measures could be obtained, to occur solely on measures of fluid intelligence, while at any later point in the organism's life-span, generation differences could and will occur in both fluid and crystallized intelligence. Moreover, we must consider here the effect of motor speed on intelligence performance. Clearly, the impact of this parameter is more readily felt in measures of fluid intelligence, as well as being itself subject to changes between generations attributable most likely to environmentally induced factors.

Considering then the parameters of fluid intelligence (FI), crystallized intelligence (CI), and motor speed (MS) as the classes of behavior most often measured via intelligence tests, we may describe age changes in these dimensions to contain the following elements in terms of the notation earlier introduced in this chapter:

$$CId = Cd + Td \tag{12}$$

$$FId = Cd - Ad \tag{13}$$

$$MSd = Td + Ad \tag{14}$$

In other words, it is suggested that measures of age changes on crystallized intelligence can be explained most parsimoniously by considering them to be the cumulation of generation-specific experiences prior to the first time of measurement plus such specific (or in Cattell's terms "epogenic") experiences as will occur for all generations over a specified period of time (R. B. Cattell, 1969b). I am thus proposing that the proper age gradient for a pure measure of crystallized intelligence would therefore be a slowly decelerating positive linear function from birth to death; the increment in function over age here being simply the cumulative acquisition of information, skills, etc. over time. The level of such gradient, however, may change over generations as the amount of input for any given time period increases or declines; i.e., the total amount of information input over the life-span of any given generation may be different from the next.

Matters are rather different when we consider fluid intelligence. Such variables are presumed to be essentially programmed into the organism via their biological determinants. Thus, with all other biological variables they must be presumed to have a species-determined time clock. Such a time clock is, of course, subject to genetic mutation. Nevertheless, it must be assumed that there will be a basic age pattern with increment in childhood and decrement in old age being quite independent of environmental information input. Furthermore, most such abilities are typically measured in ways which contain motor speed contaminants. But motor speed in itself is a biologically determined variable which should show age changes within a given generation. In contrast to fluid intelligence, however, motor speed seems to be heavily influenced by environmental circumstances (such as the introduction of labor saving technology) which will modify the need or opportunity to exercise psychomotor skills.

If the above propositions are accepted, for argument's sake, it will then follow that age changes in crystallized intelligence are erroneously reported by *both* cross-sectional and longitudinal studies even though *no* such changes are occurring. The cross-sectional age differences (at least between adult samples) must therefore refer to the net amount of information accumulation gained by the particular generation as opposed to another generation which started out with a larger or smaller amount of information in its base period prior to the common measurement point. Longitudinal age changes, on the other hand, would simply indicate environmental treatment impacts occurring over the period marked by the measurement points which is common to organisms of all ages. Time-lag measures are therefore the approach to be used in the study of crystallized intelligence.

Age changes in fluid intelligence, however, will be overestimated in cross-sectional studies if there are positive generation differences in psychomotor function and underestimated if there are negative changes. Longitudinal studies, here, will of course show the proper within generation occurrences. For motor speed, on the other hand, longitudinal studies will provide overestimates of change if environmental treatment effects tend to exacerbate, and underestimates if treatment effects compensate for age-related developments. Consequently, cross-sectional data should be most appropriate for obtaining best estimates of age differences on pure speed variables.

Having drawn attention to the differential elements contained in the major dimensions of intelligence which should interest the developmental psychologist and having related them to our proposed research strategies it is now timely to turn more specifically to the estimation of generation effects.

C. The Estimation of Generation Effects

Let us begin by reminding our reader of the most parsimonious manner by which to determine reliable estimates of time of measurement effects and of generation differences. We have indicated in the previous section that time of measurement effects can be estimated either by the time-sequential or cross-sequential method by studying samples representing either all possible ages or all possible cohorts at two points in time. Most conveniently intervals between ages and cohorts should be chosen so as to be equivalent to the interval between the two times of measurement, but this is only a convenient and not a necessary restriction (see Eisner, Schaie, & Apfeldorf, 1969; Schaie & Strother, 1968b).

In the case of two time intervals the time-sequential and cross-sequential approaches can be handled by virtually identical data except that for the time-sequential approach it becomes necessary to delete the sample from the first cohort for the second measurement occasion and add a sample one cohort interval below the last cohort used at the first measurement time. The main difference, of course, is that we pair samples at time k and l for each age level in the time-sequential method, while we pair samples for each cohort level in the cross-sequential method. The former approach assumes that we know that there are no significant cohort differences, the latter that there are no significant age changes!

But how can we be in a position to specify which of these assumptions may be true? Previously certain kinds of decision rules have been suggested (Schaie, 1965). Since that time I have worked with another empirical approach which may be somewhat more satisfying. This approach, which I have applied to the analysis of empirical data of various kinds (Schaie & Strother, 1968a, 1968b), is based essentially upon the comparison of cross-sectional and composite longitudinal age gradients.

D. The Comparison of Composite Cross-Sectional and Longitudinal Age Gradients

It must generally be argued that conventional longitudinal and cross-sectional gradients cannot be compared directly because the cross-sectional data have been collected at one point in time while the longitudinal data have been collected at many points in time. There is, however, a special type of longitudinal gradient which can validly be compared with cross-sectional data. This is a composite longitudinal gradient which is composed of segments depicting longitudinal change from time k to time l. Each segment in such a gradient is drawn from two observations of the same cohort, but every successive segment is based on a different cohort. Furthermore, just as in the cross-sectional study, we compare data based on measurements taken at the same point in time, so do we in the composite longitudinal gradient compare segments of change covering the same time interval.

To obtain comparable gradients, all that is needed, therefore, is to construct a cross-sectional gradient by averaging means over both times of measurement and to obtain average age changes for the composite longitudinal gradient by taking the difference between adjacent age levels averaged over all cohorts included in the study. The effect of this approach will be that both average cross-sectional and average longitudinal measures will have been obtained at the same points of environmental impact. The composite longitudinal gradient is furthermore constructed so as to have its point of origin coincident with the first cohort represented in the study.

What are the implications to be drawn from the comparison of gradients constructed in the suggested manner? Deducing the appropriate consequences from the general model, I would like to propose that coincidence of the two gradients could occur only if the cross-sectional age differences for a given variable were a function of maturational change alone. If, on the other hand, cross-sectional differences include the effects of differential environment opportunity and/or genetic changes in the species (in other words cohort differences) then one would expect discrepancies between the two gradients. Thus, whenever cohort differences are in a positive direction (i.e., improvement of the species with respect to a given variable), then the cross-sectional gradient will have to drop below the longitudinal gradient. In this case the performance of an earlier cohort will be below that of a later cohort even if there is no maturational age change whatsoever. In this instance the steep cross-sectional decrement represents a gradient of progressive improvement in the species. Conversely, a longitudinal gradient must fall below the corresponding cross-sectional gradient for those variables where decrement in ability occurs over the generations which have been sampled.

It is proposed that the above-mentioned gradients be routinely constructed on the basis of data involving at least two times of measurement and that the gradients be inspected to see whether the largest discrepancy is significant at a specified level of confidence. The proper error estimate for such a significance test may be conveniently obtained from either time-sequential or cross-sequential analysis. If the null hypothesis cannot be rejected, it would ordinarily be safe to assume that the assumptions of the time-sequential method have been met. If this is not the case, then, since time of measurement effects have been held constant, it must be assumed that there are significant cohort differences. In that case, the cross-sequential approach would then be called upon to yield further information.

IV. EMPIRICAL EVIDENCE BEARING UPON GENERATION DIFFERENCES IN INTELLIGENCE

There are three routes to examine evidence on the issues raised above by scrutiny of the research literature. We can look first at published data from both cross-sectional and longitudinal studies using the same or similar variables. Next, we can do a chronological analysis of available cross-sectional research data on intelligence. Such analysis will show us whether or not successive studies demonstrate shifts in peak age of performance as well as absolute magnitudes of gains and decrement. Lastly, where the design of the study permits such analysis, we can use the equations presented in the second section of this paper to attempt net estimates of generational differences for a number of intellectual abilities.

A. Comparison of Cross-Sectional and Longitudinal Findings

I have recently pursued the first alternative for information available on the five mental abilities measured by the Science Research Associates Primary Abilities Test as compared with other similar variables on which longitudinal data were available (Schaie, 1969). In Table 1 the conclusions drawn on the interpretation of various age gradients derived by conventional cross-sectional longitudinal and the new short-term longitudinal sequential strategies are reproduced. If we assume that the primary mental abilities of Verbal Meaning, Space, Reasoning, and Number are indeed measures of crystallized intelligence, while Word Fluency is primarily a measure of fluid intelligence, then it is clear that the comparisons shown in this table support the model described above. Methodologically adequate studies of these variables show the measures of crystallized intelligence to exhibit virtually no age changes while the measure of fluid intelligence is found to exhibit even greater change than previously suspected.

B. Chronological Analysis of Cross-Sectional Findings

The second approach is that of looking for the point of peak performance on intellectual measures in cross-sectional studies conducted at different points in time. At least eight major cross-sectional studies covering the broad range of adult life can be considered for this purpose. They include two studies conducted in the early thirties, the Army Alpha study of H. E. Jones and Conrad (1933) and the Otis short-form study by C. C. Miles and Miles (1932); one study in the late thirties (Wechsler, 1939); three studies in the late fifties, the revision of the Wechsler-Bellevue (Wechsler, 1958), Schaie's PMA study (1958), and Bilash and Zubek's work with the King factored aptitude battery (1960); and two studies in the mid-sixties with PMA type measures (Verhage, 1964; Schaie & Strother, 1968b).

TABLE 1

*Comparison of Inferences Drawn from Cross-Sectional
Longitudinal, and Short-term Longitudinal Studies* [a]

Variable	Cross-sectional	Longitudinal	Short-term longitudinal
Verbal meaning	Sharp decrement from middle adulthood to old age	Modest gain throughout life from young adult plateau	Modest decrement from young adult plateau; increment in successive cohorts reaching asymptote
Space	Sharp decrement from young adult peak to old age	Modest decrement from adult plateau	Almost no decrement until advanced age; steep positive cohort gradient is reaching asymptote
Reasoning	Sharp decrement from young adult peak to old age	Modest gain from young adult plateau till old age	Modest decrement from middle adulthood to old age; positively accelerating cohort gradient
Number	Modest gain and loss before and subsequent to midlife plateau	Modest gain from early adulthood to plateau at advanced age	Very modest decrement from plateau in middle adulthood; positively accelerated cohort gradient
Word fluency	Moderate decrement from plateau extending over major portion of adulthood	Moderate gains from young adult levels	Sharp decrements from young adult levels; steep decrements for successive cohorts

[a] Inferences from cross-sectional data are based on data by Kamin (1957), H. E. Jones (1959), and Schaie (1958). No long-term longitudinal studies on the PMA variables were found, but inferences are based on an examination of analogous data available from studies by Bayley (1968b), Bayley and Oden (1955), and Owens (1953). The short-term longitudinal inferences are those of Schaie and Strother (1968a, 1968b).

Examination of the above studies shows clearly that there has been a marked shift in peak age of performance on intellectual functions over the thirty-five year period under scrutiny. In the first three studies all the evidence points at the attainment of peak performance at age 20 and some decrement thereafter on all variables sampled. In the revised Wechsler standardization studies, however, peak performance ages were typically at about age 25 and decrement curves were much less marked. Schaie's initial study conducted several years after Wechsler's revision showed a further shift with average measures of intelligence now peaking in the early thirties. The Bilash and Zubek study showed some peaks at 20 but others as late as 40. It is possible, however, that this generational shift may be reaching asymptotic levels. Thus Schaie and Strother (1968b) found age gradients to be elevated over those reported in 1958, but the peak age did not show any further forward shift. Verhage's (1964) data in general agree with the latter findings.

C. Reanalysis of Sequential Data

We will next look at some empirical data, and by means of the procedures presented in this chapter, attempt to estimate the effect of generation differences in intellectual behavior. For this purpose, I shall review a set of data coming out of my own work (Schaie & Strother, 1968b). In this study we compared the data of a sample of 500 *S*s stratified in ten 5-year age groups from 21 to 70 years collected in 1956, with a similar sample (augmented by an additional age group from 71-75) drawn from the same sampling universe but tested in 1963. For this data set, as previously indicated, it is possible to obtain age, cohort, and time of measurement estimates by use of the cross-sequential and time-sequential methods. Although this study contains data on all five PMA variables and the Test of Behavioral Rigidity (TBR) (Schaie, 1960), the analysis

TABLE 2

Mean Scores for Cross-Sectional Data, Net Age Difference Estimates, and Age Change Estimates for Some Measures of Crystallized and Fluid Intelligence [a]

Mean age	Cross-sectional data (1963)				Net age change estimates				Gross longitudinal estimates			
	V	S	W	PS	V	S	W	PS	V	S	W	PS
23	53.0	58.0	50.2	53.2	53.0	58.0	50.2	50.2	53.0	58.0	50.2	53.2
28	51.6	53.5	49.4	50.2	53.2	57.3	52.2	52.7	53.9	58.8	49.6	51.2
33	54.7	55.1	51.9	52.2	52.4	55.8	53.4	51.2	53.7	58.8	48.3	48.2
38	53.6	52.6	48.8	50.3	50.8	53.7	52.3	52.0	52.8	58.2	44.6	47.6
43	53.3	52.3	50.2	51.2	50.1	51.9	53.0	50.9	52.7	57.9	42.8	45.0
48	49.4	48.8	45.2	47.7	49.1	50.0	49.8	49.1	52.3	57.5	37.1	41.6
53	50.4	49.0	48.0	48.8	48.7	49.0	47.9	46.7	52.6	58.0	32.6	35.7
58	47.7	49.6	46.7	45.5	46.9	48.3	45.6	43.3	51.5	58.8	27.8	32.8
63	45.1	44.5	44.7	43.6	44.8	46.6	43.3	38.9	50.0	58.6	22.9	27.0
68	41.2	42.3	42.0	42.0	43.4	43.2	43.2	39.1	49.3	56.7	20.2	25.7
73	40.5	39.9	43.3	43.3	43.1	41.3	44.8	40.5	49.6	56.3	19.3	25.6

Average Time-Lag per 5 years
+.65   +1.50   −2.55   −1.49

[a] Measures of Crystallized Intelligence: Verbal Meaning (V) and Space (S). Measures of Fluid Intelligence: Word Fluency (W) and Psychomotor Speed (PS). Reanalyzed data from Schaie and Strother (1968b). Cross-sectional data, $N = 50$ per age group; all scores are *T* scores with $X = 50$ and S.D. = 10.

will be restricted to two variables representative of crystallized intelligence (Verbal Meaning [V] and Space [S] from the PMA) and two measures which may be considered as having high saturations of fluid intelligence (Word Fluency [W] from the PMA and Psychomotor Speed [PS] from the TBR).

In previous reports on this study, cross-sectional data have been compared with longitudinal estimates based on the assumption that the effects of environmental impact on the longitudinal estimates had been equated since they all cover the same span of time. Equating for time of measurement effects, however, does not necessarily remove the confound, even though this can be accomplished approximately via several of the equations provided at the beginning of this chapter. As a result we reported substantial generation effects

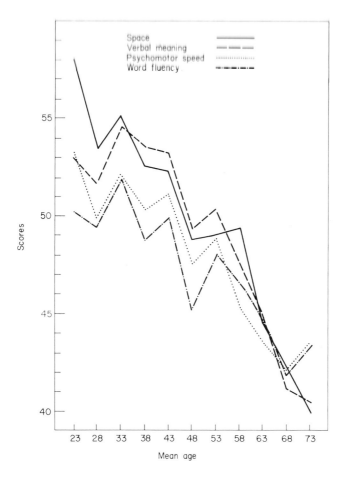

Figure 1. Cross-sectional age difference gradient. Time of measurement, 1963.

leading to overestimates of maturational change for power tests and under-estimates of maturational change for speeded tests. We failed, however, to attend to the equally important confound of the time of measurement effects although these were alluded to in passing. It is here that attending to the crystallized versus fluid types of measures dichotomy becomes helpful in understanding that the erroneous estimates of maturational change may well be time of measure-ment effects even though significant variance remains to be attributed to generational differences.

The reanalysis of our data is shown in Table 2 and Figure 1. In Table 2, the mean scores for the cross-sectional data collected in 1963 will be found listed. These data are also presented in graphical form in Figure 1. Highly significant age differences are found, which are more severe for V and S than for W and PS. Next, by use of the time-sequential method, I compared these data with similar data available for 1956, and by means of Equation 5 estimated the average time of measurement difference as estimated over all ages of interest. These Tds are listed at the bottom of Table 2. Note the positive time-lag for Space and Verbal Meaning, the measures of crystallized intelligence, and negative time-lags for Word Fluency and Psychomotor Speed. It is not clear whether this is due to negative environmental impact on the saturation of these measures on fluid intelligence or whether the results must be attributed to the speed factor with which they are undoubtedly also saturated.

Next, the data were reorganized in a cross-sequential matrix to be able to obtain longitudinal difference scores for each cohort. Equation 10 was used to estimate net age differences between all age levels included in the study. Using the youngest cohort as the base point it was then possible to compute the estimated longitudinal mean scores given in the middle block in Table 2, and graphed in Figure 2.

It must be realized, however, that these estimates assume that there will be no environmental time of measurement effect in the projected future. Such a hypothesis is directly contradictory to our findings for the most recent time period. Consequently, the data were further adjusted by adding back in the average estimate of time of measurement differences for each five-year interval. The estimates in the third block of Table 2 are therefore, given present knowledge, the most realistic estimates of scores which should be expected for the cohort born in 1940 when it reaches the specified ages.

It will be seen that the projected net age changes are actually largest for Space, next largest for Verbal Meaning and Psychomotor Speed and smallest for Word Fluency. However, as noted, these estimates completely ignore the compensatory or exacerbatory impact of environmental events which are independent of maturational trends. Thus when we correct for the expected environmental treatment effects we find, as expected, that the measures of crystallized intelligence show very little projected decrement over the adult

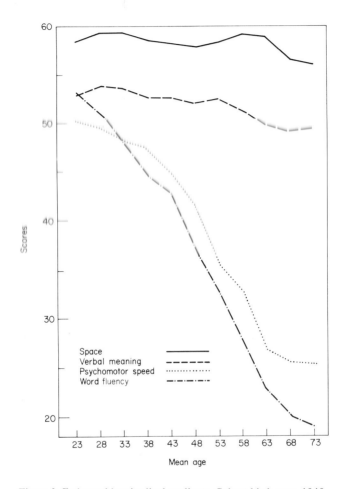

Figure 2. Estimated longitudinal gradients. Cohort birth year, 1940.

life-span while the estimates involving biologically mediated variables and those variables where speed is involved show profound projected decrement.

Finally, by means of Equation 11 it was possible to estimate net cohort differences. Using our youngest cohort as base points we have computed the estimated mean score for each of eleven cohorts at age 23, as shown in Table 3. It is of interest to note that the revised method of estimating cohort differences leads to the conclusion of average improvement on both crystallized and fluid abilities. This is in contrast to inferences drawn from our earlier analyses when no attention was paid to maintain unidirectionality of component estimates. The average cohort differences are greatest for the measures of crystallized

TABLE 3

Mean Scores at Age 23 Estimated for Eleven Cohorts [a]

Mean year of birth	Verbal meaning	Space	Word fluency	Psychomotor speed
1890	42.6	41.2	44.9	45.4
1895	43.8	42.7	46.1	46.3
1900	46.5	43.2	48.1	47.0
1905	48.4	47.5	48.5	46.5
1910	50.2	49.5	48.3	47.9
1915	49.1	49.8	45.2	47.2
1920	50.6	52.1	45.4	49.1
1925	52.2	53.2	46.3	49.5
1930	52.7	54.6	47.0	52.1
1935	50.9	54.3	48.0	51.1
1940	53.0	58.0	50.2	53.2

[a] From Schaie & Strother (1968b).

intelligence and smallest for the fluid measures, which is quite consistent with our predictions from theory. Inspection of Figure 3 moreover will show that the cohort gradients for Space and Verbal Meaning are quite steep and do not as yet tend toward an asymptote. Word Fluency on the other hand seems to be cycling towards an asymptotic phase; i.e., our youngest cohort born in 1940 is estimated to perform at the same level as the cohort born in 1900 even though there has been a dip in performance in between. Psychomotor Speed is in between in that it shows a moderate improvement gradient which appears to be leveling off.

The magnitudes of these cohort differences are indeed impressive. Moreover, in conjunction with the data presented in Table 2 and in Figures 1 and 2, these findings permit us to conclude that for some time to come we must expect cross-sectional studies to portray marked age differences on measures of crystallized intelligence due to an apparent systematic increment in performance for successive cohorts. On the other hand, longitudinal studies of the same variables will show little or no decrement because net maturational decrement in adulthood will be successfully compensated by the same increment in environmental input which produces the cohort differences in the first place.

Studies of fluid intelligence, however, will show relatively little differences among cohorts because input here is not specifically due to environmental impact and can proceed only slowly as genetic selection may become effective. If our findings of negative environmental impact on these variables are indeed replicable rather than an artifact of the particular time period studied, we would then expect marked decrement within generations, some of which is currently hidden by the apparent cycling of cohort effects such as is shown on the cohort gradient for Word Fluency.

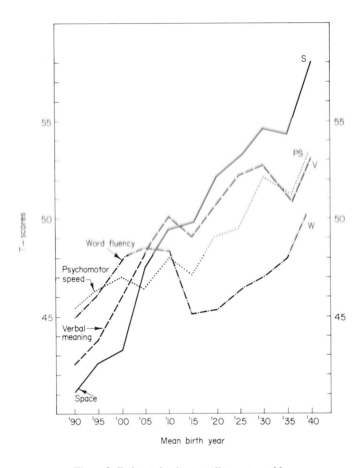

Figure 3. Estimated cohort gradients at age 23.

An attempt has been made also to reanalyze some suitable data on generational changes in children. One such set comes from the Harvard Growth Study (Shuttleworth, 1939). Six independent samples from the data pool recorded in the Shuttleworth monograph were drawn such that three four-month cohorts, three times of testing and three ages were represented. Application of sequential strategies did not lead to the detection of generation differences because the accumulation of information and the impact of environmental intervention which is not age-specific tend to be rather overwhelming during the period of early development. However, generation differences may have failed to appear also because the Binet test data examined obviously confound measures of crystallized and fluid intelligence which would be expected to show different and possibly contradictory cohort gradients (see Schaie, 1970).

Another relevant study with children where it is possible to specify at least one measure each of reasonably pure estimates of crystallized and fluid intelligence and which has been analyzed by sequential methods is the Saarbruecken cohort effects study reported by Baltes and Reinert (1969). This study is essentially a cohort-sequential design comparable data for which have also been analyzed in a time-sequential manner (Baltes *et al.*, 1970). Interestingly enough they originally identified an interaction between age and cohort level which upon reanalysis with a different set of data turns out to be a clearcut time of measurement effect. Of particular interest, moreover, is the fact that the time of measurement effects found for the variable of fluid intelligence seem to conform to bioclimatological events (season of year) while differences on the crystallized measure appear to be a function of the time of the school year; i.e., the relative amount of information acquisition as determined by the time of year.

V. CONCLUSIONS

It was the purpose of this chapter to show how the original concern with differences in findings from cross-sectional and longitudinal studies has now led to a much more sophisticated analysis of developmental phenomena by distinguishing between age differences, age changes, and cultural changes. As part of these considerations, it is necessary to deal with the structure of intelligence as consisting of variables some of which are predominantly subject to environmental input and others which are largely biologically mediated. In some ways the former overlap much with tests which in terms of the operations involved are usually called power tests while the latter not infrequently turn out to be measures with high saturation on a perceptual or motor speed factor.

The general development model was reexamined to take into account some of the most legitimate criticisms raised by Baltes and his associates. While no complete resolution of the questions raised has as yet occurred, it was possible to identify some inconsistencies in earlier formulations (Schaie, 1965) and an attempt was made to rectify these problems.

The literature on intellectual change over the life-span was examined to clarify the nature of the data available for the impact of generational differences. It was shown here, that much of the variance which has previously been accounted for differences in maturational level, must indeed be attributed to environmental treatment effects which interact in either positive or negative fashion with the maturational events.

On the other hand, a chronological ordering of cross-sectional studies of intellectual functioning covering large portions of the life-span, conducted over the past thirty years showed clear evidence of shifts in age of peak performance. Reanalysis of our own data, however, hints that these shifts may well be a combination of generational shift in talent with respective increment or decrement in the amount of environmental impact. No matter which of these inferences is correct, it remains obvious that much is yet to be learned about patterns of intellectual change over the life-span or any of its portion and that further complication of our models and strategies must be expected.

References

Adams, J. A. *Human memory.* New York: McGraw-Hill, 1967.

Adams, J. A., & Montague, W. E. Retroactive inhibition and natural language mediation. *Journal of Verbal Learning and Verbal Behavior*, 1967, 6, 528-535.

Adkins, D. The simple structure of the A.P.A. *American Psychologist*, 1954, 9, 175-180.

Ahammer, I. M. Alternative strategies for the investigation of age differences. Paper presented at the Regional Meeting of the Society for Research in Child Development. Athens, Georgia, April 1970.

Alcott, B., & Peabody, E. P. *Record of a school.* Boston: James Munroe & Co., 1835.

Alcott, B., & Peabody, E. P. *Conversations with children on the gospels.* Boston: James Munroe, 1836-1837. 2 vols.

Alexander, P. *Sensationalism and scientific explanation.* London: Routledge & Kegan, 1963.

Allport, G. *Becoming.* New Haven: Yale University Press, 1955.

Alpern, M. Metacontrast. *Journal of the Optical Society of America*, 1953, **43**, 648-657.

Altus, W. D., & Clark, J. V. The effect of adjustment patterns upon the intercorrelation of intelligence subtest variables. *Journal of Social Psychology*, 1949, **30**, 39-48.

Amelang, M., & Langer, I. Zur Kritik der Divergenzhypothese der Intelligenz. *Archiv für die Gesamte Psychologie*, 1968, **120**, 203-217.

American Psychological Association directory. Washington, D.C.: APA, 1966. Pp. 1053-1055, 1092-1093.

Anastasi, A. The influence of specific experience upon mental organization. *Genetic Psychology Monographs*, 1936, 18, 245-355.

Anastasi, A. Heredity, environment and the question "How?" *Psychological Review*, 1958, **65**, 197-208.

Anastasi, A. *Differential psychology.* (2nd ed.) New York: Macmillan, 1961.

Anastasi, A. *Psychological testing.* (3rd ed.) New York: Macmillan, 1968.

Anderson, H. E., & Slivinske, A. J. A study of intelligence and achievement at the fourth-, fifth-, and sixth-grade levels. *Journal of Experimental Education*, 1963, **31**, 425-432.

Anderson, J. E. The limitations of infant and preschool tests in the measurement of intelligence. *Journal of Psychology*, 1939, 8, 351-379.

Anderson, J. E. The prediction of terminal intelligence from infant and preschool tests. *Yearbook of the National Society for the Study of Education*, 1940, **39**, 385-403.

Anderson, J. E. *Psychology of development and personal adjustment.* New York: Holt, 1949.

Anderson, J. E. Methods of child psychology. In L. Carmichael (Ed.), *Manual of child psychology.* (2nd ed.) New York: Wiley, 1954.

Anderson, J. E. (Ed.) *Psychological aspects of aging.* Washington, D.C.: American Psychological Association, 1956.

Anderson, J. E. Dynamics of development: Systems in process. In D. B. Harris (Ed.), *The concept of development.* Minneapolis: University of Minnesota Press, 1957. Pp. 25-46.

509

Anderson, J. E. The relation between adult adjustment and early experience over a 28-year interval. *American Psychologist*, 1960, **15**, 385-386. (Abstract)

Anisfeld, M., Barlow, J., & Frail, C. M. Distinctive features in the pluralization rules of English speakers. *Language and Speech*, 1968, **11**, 31-37.

Anisfeld, M., & Gordon, M. On the phonological structure of English inflectional rules. *Journal of Verbal Learning and Verbal Behavior*, 1968, **7**, 973-979.

Anker, J., & Dahl, S. *Werdegang der Biologie*. Leipzig: Hiersemann, 1938.

Apgar, V. A proposal for a new method of evaluation of the newborn infant. *Current Researches in Anesthesia & Analgesia*, 1953, **32**, 260.

Arenberg, D. Anticipation interval and age differences in verbal learning. *Journal of Abnormal Psychology*, 1965, **70**, 419-425.

Arenberg, D. Age differences in retroaction. *Journal of Gerontology*, 1967, **22**, 88-91.

Arenberg, D. Concept problem solving in young and old adults. *Journal of Gerontology*, 1968, **23**, 279-282.

Arnhoff, F. N. Adult age differences in performances on a visual-spatial task of stimulus generalization. *Journal of Educational Psychology*, 1959, **50**, 259-265.

Asch, S. E. A study of change in mental organization. *Archives of Psychology*, 1936, **28**, (Whole No. 195).

Atchley, R. C. Respondents vs. refusers in an interview study of retired women: An analysis of selected characteristics. *Proceedings of the 20th Annual Meeting of the Gerontological Society*, 1967, p. 41.

Ayllon, T., & Azrin, N. H. The measurement and reinforcement of behavior of psychotics. *Journal of the Experimental Analysis of Behavior*, 1965, **8**, 357-383.

Babcock, H. An experiment in the measurement of mental deterioration. *Archives of Psychology*, 1930, **117**, 1-105.

Baer, D. M. An age-irrelevant concept of development. Paper presented at the meeting of the American Psychological Association, New York, September 1966.

Bakwin, H. The secular change in growth and development. *Acta Paediatrica*, 1964, **53**, 78-89.

Baldwin, A. L. *Theories of child development*. New York: Wiley, 1967.

Baldwin, A. L., Kalhorn, J., & Breese, F. H. Patterns of parent behavior. *Psychological Monographs*, 1945, No. 58.

Baldwin, B. T. William James' contributions to education. *Journal of Educational Psychology*, 1911, **2**, 369-382.

Baldwin, J. M. *Mental development in the child and the race*. New York: Macmillan, 1895.

Baldwin, J. M. *Mental development in the child and the race: Methods and processes*. (2nd ed.) New York: Macmillan, 1906.

Baldwin, J. M. History of psychology. A sketch and an interpretation. New York: Putnam, 1913. 2 vols.

Balinsky, B. An analysis of the mental factors of various age groups from nine to sixty. *Genetic Psychology Monographs*, 1941, **23**, 191-234.

Ballauf, T. *Die Wissenschaft vom Leben*. Vol. 1. *Eine Geschichte der Biologie*. Freiburg: Alber, 1954.

Baller, W. R. A study of the present social status of a group of adults who, when they were in elementary school, were classified as mentally deficient. *Genetic Psychology Monographs*, 1936, **18**, 165-244.

Baller, W. R., Charles, D. C., & Miller, E. L. Mid-life attainment of the mentally retarded: A longitudinal study. *Genetic Psychology Monographs*, 1967, **75**, 235-329.

Baltes, P. B. Längsschnitt- und Querschnittsequenzen zur Erfassung von Alters- und Generationseffekten. Unpublished doctoral dissertation, University of Saarland, Saarbruecken, Germany, 1967.

Baltes, P. B. The logical status of age as an experimental variable: Comments on some methodological issues. In K. W. Schaie (Ed.), *Theory and methods of research on aging.* Morgantown, W. Va.: West Virginia University Library, 1968. Pp. 172-173. (a)

Baltes, P. B. Longitudinal and cross-sectional sequences in the study of age and generation effects. *Human Development*, 1968, **11**, 145-171. (b)

Baltes, P. B., & Nesselroade, J. R. Toward a research methodology for the analysis of long-term developmental change: Multivariate longitudinal and cross-sectional sequences. Unpublished manuscript, Department of Psychology, West Virginia University, 1969.

Baltes, P. B., & Reinert, G. Cohort effects in cognitive development of children as revealed by cross-sectional sequences. *Developmental Psychology*, 1969, **1**, 169-177.

Baltes, P. B., & Nesselroade, J. R. Multivariate longitudinal and cross-sectional sequences for analyzing ontogenetic and generational change: A methodological note. *Developmental Psychology*, 1970, **2**, 163-168.

Baltes, P. B., Reinert, G., & Baltes, M. M. The effect of time of measurement in cognitive age-development of children: An application of cross-sectional sequences. *Human Development*, 1970, in press.

Balzert, C. Untersuchungen über Zusammenhänge von Extraversion/Introversion und der Faktorenstruktur der Intelligenz. Unpublished doctoral dissertation, University of Giessen, Germany, 1966.

Barber, T. X. Hypnotic age regression: A critical review. *Psychosomatic Medicine*, 1962, **24**, 286-299.

Barker, R. G. Explorations in ecological psychology. *American Psychologist*, 1965, **20**, 1-14.

Barnes, J. M., & Underwood, B. J. "Fate" of first-list associations in transfer theory. *Journal of Experimental Psychology*, 1959, **58**, 97-105.

Bartholomäi, F. The contents of children's minds on entering school at the age of six years. *Städtisches Jahrbuch, Berlin und Seine Entwicklung*, 1870, **4**. (Translation published in *Reports of the United States Commission of Education*, 1900-1901, **1**, 709-727. Washington, D.C.: U.S. Government Printing Office, 1902.)

Bartley, S. H. *Principles of Perception.* New York: Harper, 1958.

Bartoshuk, A. K. Human neonatal cardiac acceleration to sound: Habituation and dishabituation. *Perceptual and Motor Skills*, 1962, **15**, 15-27. (a)

Bartoshuk, A. K. Response decrement with repeated elicitation of human neonatal cardiac acceleration to sound. *Journal of Comparative and Physiological Psychology*, 1962, **55**, 9-13. (b)

Basowitz, H., & Korchin, S. J. Age differences in the perception of closure. *Journal of Abnormal and Social Psychology*, 1957, **54**, 93-117.

Bateman, B. Learning disabilities—yesterday, today and tomorrow. *Exceptional Children*, 1964, **31**, 167-177.

Bateman, W. G. A child's progress in speech. *Journal of Educational Psychology*, 1914, **5**, 307-320.

Bath, J. A. Mental ability of residents in a state school for dependent and neglected youth. *Psychological Reports*, 1967, **20**, 469-470.

Battig, K., & Grandjean, E. Beziehung zwischen Alter und Erlernen einer bedingten Fluchtreaktion bei der weissen Ratte. *Gerontologia*, 1959, **3**, 266-276.

Battig W. F. A shift from "negative" to "positive" transfer under the A-C paradigm with increased number of C-D control pairs in a mixed list. *Psychonomic Science*, 1966, **4**, 421-422.

Baumeister, A. A., & Bartlett, C. J. A comparison of the factor structure of normals and retardates on the WISC. *American Journal of Mental Deficiency*, 1962, **66**, 641-645.

Baumrind, D., & Black, A. E. Socialization practices associated with dimensions of competence in preschool boys and girls. *Child Development*, 1967, **38**, 291-327.

Bayley, N. Mental growth during the first three years: A development study of sixty-one children by repeated tests. *Genetic Psychology Monographs*, 1933, **14**, 1-92.

Bayley, N. Mental growth during the first three years. In R. G. Barker, J. S. Kounin, & H. F. Wright (Eds.), *Child behavior and development*. New York: McGraw-Hill, 1943.

Bayley, N. Consistency and variability in the growth of intelligence from birth to eighteen years. *Journal of Genetic Psychology*, 1949, **75**, 165-196.

Bayley, N. Individual patterns of development. *Child Development*, 1956, **27**, 45-74.

Bayley, N. The life-span as a frame of reference in psychological research. *Vita Humana*, 1963, **6**, 125-139.

Bayley, Comparisons of mental and motor test scores for ages 1-15 months by sex, birth order, race, geographical location and education of parents. *Child Development*, 1965, **36**, 379-411.

Bayley, N. Learning in adulthood: The role of intelligence. In H. J. Klausmeier & C. W. Harris (Eds.), *Analysis of concept learning*. New York: Academic Press, 1966. Pp. 117-138.

Bayley, N. Behavioral correlates of mental growth: Birth to thirty-six years. *American Psychologist*, 1968, **23**, 1-17. (a)

Bayley, N. Cognition and aging. In K. W. Schaie (Ed.), *Theory and methods of research on aging*. Morgantown, W. Va.: West Virginia University Library, 1968. Pp. 97-119. (b)

Bayley, N., & Oden, M. H. The maintenance of intellectual ability in gifted adults. *Journal of Gerontology*, 1955, **10**, 91-107.

Bechtoldt, H. P. Factorial investigation of the perceptual speed factor. *American Psychologist*, 1947, **2**, 304-305.

Beeson, M. F. Intelligence at senescence. *Journal of Applied Psychology*, 1920, **4**, 219-234.

Beilin, H. Developmental stages and development processes. Paper presented at the Conference on Ordinal Scales of Cognitive Development, Monterey, California, February 1969.

Beilin, H., & Kagan, J. Pluralization rules and the conceptualization of number. *Developmental Psychology*, 1969, **1**, 697-706.

Bell, R. Q. Convergence: An accelerated longitudinal approach. *Child Development*, 1953, **24**, 145-152.

Bell, R. Q. An experimental test of the accelerated longitudinal approach. *Child Development*, 1954, **25**, 281-286.

Bellugi, U. The emergence of inflection and negation systems in the speech of two children. Paper presented at the New England Psychological Association Convention, November 1964.

Bellugi, U. The development of interrogative structures in children's speech. Report No. 8, 1965, Center for Human Growth and Development, University of Michigan.

Belmont, I. B., Birch, H. G., & Belmont, L. The organization of intelligence test performance in educable mentally subnormal children. *American Journal of Mental Deficiency*, 1967, **71**, 969-976.

Belmont, L., & Birch, H. G. The relation of time of life to behavioral consequence in brain damage: I. The performance of brain injured adults on the marble board test. *Journal of Nervous and Mental Diseases*, 1960, **131**, 91-97.

Bentler, P. M. Evidence regarding stages in the development of conservation. Unpublished manuscript, University of California, 1969. (a)

Bentler, P. M. Monotonicity analysis: An alternative to factor test analysis. Paper presented at the Conference on Ordinal Scales of Development, Monterey, California, February 1969. (b)

Bereiter, C. Some persisting dilemmas in the measurement of change. In C. W. Harris (Ed.),

Problems in measuring change. Madison, Wis.: University of Wisconsin Press, 1963. Pp. 3-20.

Berger, L., Bernstein, A., Klein, E., Cohen, J., & Lucas, G. Effects of aging and pathology on the factorial structure of intelligence. *Journal of Consulting Psychology,* 1964, **28**, 199-207.

Bergmann, G. Sense and nonsense in operationism. *Scientific Monthly,* 1954, **79**, 210-214. [Reprinted in P. G. Frank (Ed.), *The validation of scientific theories.* New York: Collier, 1961. Pp. 46-56.]

Bergmann, G. *Philosophy of science.* Madison, Wis.: University of Wisconsin Press, 1957.

Berlyne, D. E. Discussion: The delimitation of cognitive development. *Monographs of the Society for Research in Child Development,* 1966, **31** (5, Whole No. 107).

Bernreuter, R. G. Implications of recent studies on intelligence. *Transactions of the New York Academy of Sciences,* 1953, **15**, 301-305.

Berrien, F. K. Cross-cultural equivalence of personality measures. *Journal of Social Psychology,* 1968, **75**, 3-9.

Bever, T., Fodor, J. A., & Weksel, W. On the acquisition of syntax: A critique of "contextual generalization." *Psychological Review,* 1965, **72**, 467-482.

Beveridge, W. I. B. *The art of scientific investigation.* London: Heinemann, 1950.

Bijou, S. W. Ages, stages, and the naturalization of human development. *American Psychologist,* 1968, **23**, 419-427.

Bijou, S. W., & Baer, D. M. *Child development.* Vol. 1. *A systematic and empirical theory.* New York: Appleton-Century-Crofts, 1961.

Bijou, S. W., & Baer, D. M. Some methodological contributions from a functional analysis of child development. In L. P. Lipsitt & C. C. Spiker (Eds.), *Advances in child development and behavior.* Vol. 1. New York: Academic Press, 1963. Pp. 197-231.

Bilash, I., & Zubek, J. P. Effects of age on factorially "pure" mental abilities. *Journal of Gerontology,* 1960, **15**, 175-182.

Binet, A. La mesure des illusions visuelles chez les enfants. *Revue Philosophique de Louvain,* 1895, p. 40.

Binet, A., & Henri, V. La psychologie individuelle. *Année Psychologique,* 1896, **2**, 411-465.

Binet, A., & Simon, T. Sur la nécessité d'établir une diagnostic scientifique des états inférieurs de l'intelligence. *Année Psychologique,* 1905, **11**, 163-190. (a)

Binet, A., & Simon, T. Méthodes nouvelles pour le diagnostic du niveau intellectuel des anormaux. *Année Psychologique,* 1905, **11**, 191-244. (b)

Binet, A., & Simon, T. Le développement de l'intelligence chez les enfants. *Année Psychologique,* 1908, **14**, 1-94.

Birch, D. Verbal control of nonverbal behavior. *Journal of Experimental Child Psychology,* 1966, **4**, 266-275.

Birch, H. G., & Lefford, A. Intersensory development in children. *Monographs of the Society for Research in Child Development,* 1963, **28** (5, Whole No. 89).

Birch, H. G., Thomas, A., Chess, S., & Hertzog, M. E. Individuality in the development of children. *Developmental Medicine and Child Neurology,* 1962, **4**, 370-379.

Birnbaum, I. Long-term retention of first-list associations in the A-B, A-C paradigm. *Journal of Verbal Learning and Verbal Behavior,* 1965, **4**, 515-520.

Birren, J. E. The significance of age changes in speed of perception and psychomotor skills. In J. E. Anderson (Ed.), *Psychological aspects of aging.* Washington, D.C.: American Psychological Association, 1955. Pp. 97-104.

Birren, J. E. (Ed.) *Handbook of aging and the individual: Psychological and biological aspects.* Chicago: University of Chicago Press, 1959. (a)

Birren, J. E. Principles of research on aging. In J. E. Birren (Ed.), *Handbook of aging and the individual. Psychological and biological aspects.* Chicago: University of Chicago Press, 1959. Pp. 3-42. (b)

Birren, J. E. Behavioral theories of aging. In N. W. Shock (Ed.), *Aging: Some social and biological aspects.* Washington, D.C.: American Association for the Advancement of Science, 1960. Pp. 305-332.

Birren, J. E. A brief history of the psychology of aging. Part I. *Gerontologist,* 1961, **1,** 69-77. (a)

Birren, J. E. A brief history of the psychology of aging. Part II. *Gerontologist,* 1961, **1,** 127-134. (b)

Birren, J. E. The psychology of aging in relation to development. In J. E. Birren (Ed.), *Relations of development and aging.* Springfield, Ill.: Thomas, 1964. Pp. 99-120.

Birren, J. E. Toward an experimental psychology of aging. Paper presented at the meeting of the American Psychological Association, Washington, September 1969.

Birren, J. E., Allen, W. R., & Landau, H. G. The relation of problem length in simple addition to time required, probability of success and age. *Journal of Gerontology,* 1954, **9,** 150-161.

Birren, J. E., & Botwinick, J. Age changes in verbal fluency. *Journal of Gerontology,* 1951, **6** (Monogr. Suppl. 62).

Birren, J. E., & Morrison, D. F. Analysis of the W.A.I.S. subtests in relation to age and education. *Journal of Gerontology,* 1961, **16,** 363-369.

Bitterman, M. E. Phylectic differences in learning. *American Psychologist,* 1965,‚20, 396-410.

Black, M. *Models and metaphors.* Ithaca, N.Y.: Cornell University Press, 1962.

Blackwell, H. R., & Smith, S. W. The effect of target size and shape on visual detection. II: Continuous foveal targets at zero background luminance. Michigan Project Report No. 2144-334-T, 1959, University of Michigan.

Bloom, B. S. *Stability and change in human characteristics.* New York: Wiley, 1964.

Bloom, M. Life-span analysis: A theoretical framework for behavioral science research. *Human Relations,* 1964, **12,** 538-554.

Bloomfield, L. *Introduction to the study of language.* New York: Holt, 1914.

Bloomfield, L. *Language.* New York: Holt, 1933.

Boesch, E. E., & Eckensberger, L. Methodische Probleme des interkulturellen Vergleichs. In C. F. Graumann (Ed.), *Handbuch der Sozialpsychologie.* Göttingen: Hogrefe, 1969.

Boigon, H. W. Problems in learning: Why do they tell me I can when I can't? *American Journal of Psychoanalysis,* 1968, **28,** 25-34.

Bolton, T. L. The growth of memory in school children. *American Journal of Psychology,* 1891, **4,** 362-380.

Bondareff, W. Morphology of the aging nervous system. In J. E. Birren (Ed.), *Handbook of aging and the individual.* Chicago: University of Chicago Press, 1959. Pp. 136-172.

Boring, E. G. A history of introspection. *Psychological Bulletin,* 1953, **50,** 169-189.

Botwinick, J. *Cognitive processes in maturity and old age.* New York: Springer, 1967.

Botwinick, J., Brinley, J. F., & Robbin, J. S. Learning a position discrimination and position reversals by Sprague-Dawley rats of different ages. *Journal of Gerontology,* 1962, **17,** 315-319.

Botwinick, J., & Kornetsky, C. Age differences in the acquisition and extinction of GSR. *Journal of Gerontology,* 1960, **15,** 83-84.

Bousfield, W. A., Whitmarsh, G. A., & Danick, J. J. Partial response identities in verbal generalization. *Psychological Reports,* 1958, **4,** 703-713.

Bowditch, H. P. The growth of children. In *Eighth annual report of the Massachusetts State Board of Health.* Vol. 1. Boston, 1877. Pp. 275-325.

Bowditch, H. P. The growth of children. In *Tenth annual report of the Massachusetts State Board of Health* Vol. 2. (Suppl.) Boston, 1879-1880. Pp. 91-109.

Brackbill, Y. Research and clinical work with children. In R. Bauer (Ed.), *Some views on soviet psychology*. Washington, D.C.: American Psychological Association, 1962. Pp. 99-164.

Bradway, K. P., & Thompson, C. W. Intelligence of adulthood. *Journal of Educational Psychology*, 1962, 53, 1-14.

Bradway, K. P., Thompson, C. W., & Cravens, R. B. Preschool IQ's after twenty-five years. *Journal of Educational Psychology*, 1958, 49, 278-281.

Braine, M. D. S. On learning the grammatical order of words. *Psychological Review*. 1963, 70, 323-348. (a)

Braine, M. D. S. The ontogeny of English phrase structure: The first phase. *Language*, 1963, 39, 1-13. (b)

Braine, M. D. S. Learning the positions of words relative to a marker element. *Journal of Experimental Psychology*, 1966, 72, 532-540.

Braine, M. D. S., Heimer, C., Wortis, H., & Freedman, A. M. Factors associated with impairment of the early development of prematures. *Monographs of the Society for Research in Child Development*, 1966, 31, 1-92.

Braithwaite, R. B. *Scientific explanation*. New York: Harper, 1953.

Braun, H. W. Perceptual processes. In J. E. Birren (Ed.), *Handbook of aging and the individual*. Chicago: University of Chicago Press, 1959.

Braun, H. W., & Geiselhart, R. Age differences in the acquisition and extinction of the conditioned eyelid response. *Journal of Experimental Psychology*, 1959, 57, 386-388.

Brenner, M. W. The developmental study of apparent movement. *Quarterly Journal of Experimental Psychology*, 1957, 9, 169-174.

Bridger, W. H. Sensory habituation and discrimination in the human neonate. *American Journal of Psychiatry*, 1961, 117, 991-996.

Bridger, W. H. Sensory discrimination and autonomic function in the newborn. *American Academy of Child Psychiatry, Journal*, 1962, 1, 67-82.

Bridgman, P. W. The present state of operationalism. *Scientific Monthly*, 1954, 79, 224-226. [Reprinted in P. G. Frank (Ed.), *The validation of scientific theories*. New York: Collier, 1961. Pp. 75-80.]

Bromley, D. B. Primitive forms of response to the Matrices Test. *Journal of Mental Science*, 1953, 99, 374-393.

Bromley, D. B. Some experimental tests of the effect of age on creative intellectual output. *Journal of Gerontology*, 1956, 11, 74-82.

Bromley, D. B. Some effects of age on the quality of intellectual output. *Journal of Gerontology*, 1957, 12, 318-323.

Bromley, D. B. Some effects of age on short-term learning and remembering. *Journal of Gerontology*, 1958, 13, 398-406.

Bromley, D. B. Age differences in conceptual abilities. In R. H. Williams, C. Tibbitts, & W. Donahue (Eds.), *Processes of aging: Social and psychological perspectives*. Vol. 1. New York: Atherton Press, 1963. Pp. 96-112.

Bromley, D. B. *The psychology of human aging*. Baltimore: Penguin, 1966.

Bromley, D. B. Age and sex differences in the serial production of creative conceptual responses. *Journal of Gerontology*, 1967, 22, 32-42.

Bromley, D. B. Conceptual analysis in the study of personality and adjustment. *Bulletin of the British Psychological Society*, 1968, 21, 155-160.

Bromley, D. B. Studies of intellectual function in relation to age and their significance for professional and managerial functions. In A. T. Welford & J. E. Birren (Eds.), *Interdisciplinary topics in gerontology*. Vol. 4. Basel: Karger, 1969. Pp. 103-126.

Bronfenbrenner, U. Developmental theory in transition. In H. W. Stevenson (Ed.), *Child psychology*. Chicago: University of Chicago Press, 1963. Pp. 517-542.

Brossard, L. M., & Décarie, T. G. Comparative reinforcing effect of eight stimulations on the smiling response of infants. *Journal of Child Psychology and Psychiatry*, 1968, **9**, 51-59.

Brown, J. Some tests of the decay theory of immediate memory. *Quarterly Journal of Experimental Psychology*, 1958, **10**, 12-21.

Brown, R. W. *Words and things*. Glencoe, Ill.: Free Press, 1959.

Brown, R. W., & Bellugi, U. Three Processes in the child's acquisition of syntax. *Harvard Educational Review*, 1964, **34**, 133-151.

Brown, R. W., & Berko, J. Word association and the acquisition of grammar. *Child Development*, 1960, **31**, 1-14.

Brown, R. W., Cazden, C. B., & Bellugi, U. The child's grammar from I to III. In J. P. Hill (Ed.), *Minnesota symposium on child psychology*. Vol. 2. Minneapolis: University of Minnesota Press, 1969.

Brown, R. W., & Fraser, C. The acquisition of syntax. In C. N. Cofer & B. S. Musgrave (Eds.), *Verbal behavior and learning*. New York: McGraw-Hill, 1963. Pp. 158-197.

Brown, R. W., & Fraser, C. The acquisition of syntax. *Monographs of the Society for Research in Child Development*, 1964, **29**, 43-79.

Brown, R. W., Fraser, C., & Bellugi, U. Explorations in grammar evaluation. *Monographs of the Society for Research in Child Development*, 1964, **29**, 79-92.

Bruner, J. S. The course of cognitive growth. *American Psychologist*, 1964, **19**, 1-15.

Bruner, J. S., Goodnow, J. J., & Austin, G. A. *A study of thinking*. New York: Wiley, 1956.

Bryk, J. A., & Kausler, D. H. Stimulus meaningfulness and unlearning in the A-B, A-C transfer paradigm. *Journal of Experimental Psychology*, 1966, **71**, 917-920.

Bugelski, B. R. Images as mediators in one-trial paired-associate learning. II: Self-timing in successive lists. *Journal of Experimental Psychology*, 1968, **77**, 328-334.

Bühler, C. *Die Psychologie des Jugendlichen*. Jena: Fischer, 1922.

Bühler, C. *Kindheit und Jugend*. Leipzig: Hirzel, 1928.

Bühler, C. *Der menschliche Lebenslauf als psychologisches Problem*. Leipzig: Hirzel, 1933.

Bühler, C. The curve of life as studied in biographies. *Journal of Applied Psychology*, 1935, **19**, 405-409.

Bühler, C. *Der menschliche Lebenslauf als psychologisches Problem*. (2nd ed.) Göttingen: Hogrefe, 1959.

Bühler, C., & Hetzer, H. Beitrag zur Geschichte der Kinderpsychologie. In E. Brunswik *et al.* (Eds.), *Beitrag zur Problemgeschichte der Psychologie, Festschrift zu Karl Bühlers 50. Geburtstag*. Jena: Fischer, 1929. Pp. 204-224.

Bühler, C., & Massarik, F. (Eds.) *The course of human life*. New York: Springer, 1968.

Bühler, K. *Die geistige Entwicklung des Kindes*. (5th ed.) Jena: Fischer, 1929.

Bürger, M. *Altern und Krankheit*. (3rd ed.) Leipzig: Thieme, 1957.

Burns, R. B. Age and mental ability: Re-testing with thirty-three years interval. *British Journal Educational Psychology*, 1966, **36**, 116.

Burt, C. The bearing of the factor theory on the organization of schools and classes. *Report of the L.C.C. Psychologist*, London, 1919.

Burt, C. The differentiation of intellectual abilities. *British Journal of Educational Psychology*, 1954, **24**, 76-90.

Burt, C. The evidence for the concept of intelligence. *British Journal of Educational Psychology*, 1955, **25**, 158-177.

Burt, C. The inheritance of mental ability. *American Psychologist*, 1958, **13**, 1-15.

Burt, C., & John, E. A. A factorial analysis of Terman Binet tests. *British Journal of Educational Psychology*, 1942, **12**, 117-127, 156-161.

Butcher, H. J. *Human intelligence*. London: Methuen, 1968.

Caldwell, B. M. The effects of infant care. In M. L. Hoffman & L. W. Hoffman (Eds.),

Review of child development research. Vol. 1. New York: Russell Sage Foundation, 1964. Pp. 9-87.

Cameron, J., Livson, N., & Bayley, N. Infant vocalizations and their relationship to mature intelligence. *Science,* 1967, **157**, 331-333.

Campbell, D. T. A cross-sectional and longitudinal study of scholastic abilities over twenty-five years. *Journal of Counseling Psychology,* 1965, **12**, 55-61.

Campbell, D. T., & Fiske, D. W. Convergent and discriminant validation by the multitrait-multimethod matrix. *Psychological Bulletin,* 1959, **56**, 81-105.

Campbell, D. T., & Stanley, J. C. Experimental and quasi-experimental designs for research in teaching. In N. L. Gage (Ed.), *Handbook of research on teaching.* Chicago: Rand McNally, 1963. Pp. 171-246.

Canestrari, R. E., Jr. Paced and self-paced learning in young and elderly adults. *Journal of Gerontology,* 1963, **18**, 165-168.

Canestrari, R. E., Jr. Age changes in acquisition. In G. A. Talland (Ed.), *Human aging and behavior.* New York: Academic Press, 1968. Pp. 169-188. (a)

Canestrari, R. E., Jr. Age differences in verbal learning and verbal behavior. In S. M. Chown & K. F. Riegel (Eds.), *Interdisciplinary topics in gerontology.* Vol. 1. *Psychological functioning in the normal aging and senile aged.* Basel: Karger, 1968. Pp. 2-14. (b)

Cannon, W. B. Henry Pickering Bowditch. *Memoirs of the National Academy of Sciences, U.S.,* 1924, **17**, 182-196.

Carmichael, L. (Ed.) *Manual of child psychology.* (2nd ed.) New York: Wiley, 1954.

Carp, F. M. *The retirement process.* Washington, D.C.: U.S. Government Printing Office, 1968. Pp. 151-160.

Carroll, J. B. The nature of the data, or how to choose a correlation coefficient. *Psychometrika,* 1961, **26**, 347-372.

Cassirer, E. *The philosophy of the enlightenment.* Boston: Beacon Press, 1951.

Cassirer, E. *The philosophy of symbolic forms.* New Haven: Yale University Press, 1953. 3 vols.

Castaneda, A. The paired-associates method in the study of conflict. In L. P. Lipsitt & C. C. Spiker (Eds.), *Advances in child development and behavior.* Vol. 2. New York: Academic Press, 1965. Pp. 1-18.

Castaneda, A., & Lipsitt, L. P. Relation of stress and differential position habits to performance in motor learning. *Journal of Experimental Psychology,* 1959, **57**, 25-30.

Castaneda, A., Palermo, D. S., & McCandless, B. R. Complex learning and performance as a function of anxiety in children. *Child Development,* 1956, **27**, 327-332.

Cattell, J. McK. Mental tests and measurements. *Mind,* 1890, **15**, 373-381.

Cattell, J. McK., & Farrand, L. Physical and mental measurements of the students of Columbia University. *Psychological Review,* 1896, **3**, 618-648.

Cattell, R. B. *The description and measurement of personality.* Yonkers, N.Y.: World Book, 1946.

Cattell, R. B. *Personality.* New York: McGraw-Hill, 1950.

Cattell, R. B. The three basic factor-analytic research designs—their interrelations and derivations. *Psychological Bulletin,* 1952, **49**, 499-520.

Cattell, R. B. *Personality and motivation structure and measurement.* New York: World Book, 1957.

Cattell, R. B. The multiple abstract variance analysis equations and solutions: For nature-nurture research on continuous variables. *Psychological Review,* 1960, **67**, 353-372.

Cattell, R. B. *Handbook for the individual or group culture fair (or free) intelligence test.* Scale 1. Champaign, Ill.: Institute for Personality and Ability Testing, 1962.

Cattell, R. B. The structuring of change by P-technique and incremental R-technique. In C. W. Harris (Ed.), *Problems in measuring change*. Madison, Wis.: University of Wisconsin Press, 1963. Pp. 167-198. (a)

Cattell, R. B. Theory of fluid and crystallized intelligence: A critical experiment. *Journal of Educational Psychology*, 1963, **54**, 1-22. (b)

Cattell, R. B. The data box: Its ordering of total resources in terms of possible relational systems. In R. B. Cattell (Ed.), *Handbook of multivariate experimental psychology*. Chicago: Rand McNally, 1966. Pp. 67-128. (a)

Cattell, R. B. Guest editorial: Multivariate behavioral research and the integrative challenge. *Multivariate Behavioral Research*, 1966, **1**, 4-23. (b)

Cattell, R. B. The meaning and strategic use of factor analysis. In R. B. Cattell (Ed.), *Handbook of multivariate experimental psychology*. Chicago: Rand McNally, 1966. Pp. 174-243. (c)

Cattell, R. B. Patterns of change: Measurement in relation to state-dimension, trait change, lability, and process concepts. In R. B. Cattell (Ed.), *Handbook of multivariate experimental psychology*. Chicago: Rand McNally, 1966. Pp. 355-402. (d)

Cattell, R. B. The theory of fluid and crystallized intelligence checked at the 5-6 year-old level. *British Journal of Educational Psychology*, 1967, **37**, 209-224.

Cattell, R. B. Continuity of personality and ability concepts in researches over the life-span. Paper presented at the American Psychological Association Convention, San Francisco, August 1968. (a)

Cattell, R. B. Fluid and crystallized intelligence. *Psychology Today*, 1968, **3**, 56-62. (b)

Cattell, R. B. *Human abilities and intelligent intelligence testing.* Unpublished manuscript, University of Illinois, 1969. (a)

Cattell, R. B. Separating endogenous, exogenous, ecogenic component curves in developmental data. Unpublished manuscript, University of Illinois, 1969. (b)

Cattell, R. B., & Cattell, A. K. S. *Handbook for the individual or group culture fair intelligence test.* Scale 3. Champaign, Ill.: Institute for Personality and Ability Testing, 1959.

Cattell, R. B., Feingold, S. N., & Sarason, S. B. A culture free intelligence test. II. Evaluation of cultural influences on test performance. *Journal of Educational Psychology*, 1941, **32**, 81-100.

Cavan, R., Burgess, E. W., Havighurst, R. J., & Goldhammer, H. *Personal adjustment in old age.* Chicago: Science Research Associates, 1949.

Cazden, C. B. Environmental assistance to the child's acquisition of grammar. Unpublished doctoral dissertation, Harvard University, 1965.

Cazden, C. B. Subcultural differences in child language: An interdisciplinary review. *Merrill-Palmer Quarterly*, 1966, **12**, 185-220.

Chapanis, A. Men, machines, and models. *American Psychologist*, 1961, **16**, 113-131.

Charles, D. C. Ability and accomplishment of persons earlier judged mentally deficient. *Genetic Psychology Monographs,* 1953, **47**, 3-71.

Charlesworth, W. R., & Zahn, C. Reaction time as a measure of comprehension of the effects produced by rotation on objects. *Child Development*, 1966, **37**, 253-268.

Chen, H. P., & Irwin, O. C. Infant speech vowel and consonant types. *Journal of Speech Disorders,* 1946, **11**, 27-29.

Chen, T. Y. L., & Chow, H. H. A factor study of a test battery at different educational levels. *Journal of Genetic Psychology*, 1948, **73**, 187-199.

Chomsky, N. *Syntactic structures.* The Hague: Mouton, 1957.

Chomsky, N. Review of B. F. Skinner, *Verbal behavior. Language*, 1959, **35**, 26-58.

Chomsky, N. *Aspects of the theory of syntax.* Cambridge, Mass.: Massachusetts Institute of Technology Press, 1965.

Chomsky, N. The formal nature of language. In E. H. Lenneberg (Ed.), *Biological foundations of language.* New York: Wiley, 1967. Pp. 397-442.

Chomsky, N. *Language and mind.* New York: Harcourt, Brace & World, 1968.

Chomsky, N., & Miller, G. A. Introduction to the formal analysis of natural languages. In R. D. Luce, R. R. Bush, & E. Galanter (Eds.), *Handbook of mathematical psychology.* Vol. II. New York: Wiley, 1963. Pp. 269-321.

Chown, S. M. Age and the rigidities. *Journal of Gerontology,* 1961, **16**, 353-362.

Christian, A. M., & Paterson, D. G. Growth of vocabulary in later maturity. *Journal of Psychology,* 1936, **1**, 167-169.

Chrysostome, F. L'organisation des traits mentaux avec l'age. *Annales de l'Association Canadienne-Française pour l'Avancement des Sciences,* 1938, **4**, 124. (Abstract)

Church, R. M. The role of fear in punishment. Paper presented at the meeting of the American Psychological Association, New York, September 1966.

Claparède E. *Le développement mental.* Neuchatel: Delachaux & Niestle, 1951.

Clark, H. H. On the use of meaning of prepositions. Unpublished doctoral dissertation, Johns Hopkins University, 1966.

Clark, M. P. Changes in primary mental ability with age. *Archives of Psychology,* 1944, pp. 291-329.

Clark, W. W. The differentiation of mental abilities at various age levels. *American Psychologist,* 1949, **4**, 291. (Abstract)

Clay, H. M. Changes in performance with age in similar tasks of varying complexity. *British Journal of Psychology,* 1954, **45**, 7-13.

Clay, H. M. An age difficulty in separating spatially contiguous data. *Journal of Gerontology,* 1956, **11**, 318-322.

Clay, H. M. The relationship between time and accuracy on similar tasks of varying complexity. *Gerontologia,* 1957, **1**, 41-49.

Clifton, R. K., & Meyers, W. J. The heart-rate response of four-month-old infants to auditory stimuli. *Journal of Experimental Child Psychology,* 1969, **7**, 122-135.

Coan, R. W. Child personality and developmental psychology. In R. B. Cattell (Ed.), *Handbook of multivariate experimental psychology.* Chicago: Rand McNally, 1966. Pp. 732-752.

Coerper, K., Hagen, W., & Thomae, H. *Deutsche Nachkriegskinder. Methoden und erste Ergebnisse der deutschen Längsschnittuntersuchungen über die körperliche und seelische Entwicklung im Schulalter.* Stuttgart: Thieme, 1955.

Cohen, J. A comparative factor analysis of WAIS performance for four age groups between eighteen and eighty. *American Psychologist,* 1956, **11**, 449.

Cohen, J. The factorial structure of the WAIS between early adulthood and old age. *Journal of Consulting Psychology,* 1957, **21**, 283-290.

Cohen, J. The factorial structure of the WISC at ages 7-6, 10-6, and 13-6. *Journal of Consulting Psychology,* 1959, **23**, 285-299.

Cohen, J. Multiple regression as a general data-analytic system. *Psychological Bulletin,* 1968, **70**, 426-443.

Cohen, R., & Wittemann, K. Eine Untersuchung zur Abhängigkeit der Intelligenzstruktur vom Neurotizimus. *Zeitschrift für Experimentelle und Angewandte Psychologie,* 1967, **14**, 71-88.

Cole M., Sharp, D. W., Glick, J., & Kessen, W. Conceptual and mnemonic factors in paired-associate learning. *Journal of Experimental Child Psychology,* 1968, **6**, 120-130.

Comalli, P. E., Jr. Differential effects of context on perception in young and aged groups. Paper presented at the meeting of the Gerontological Society, Miami Beach, October 1962.

Comalli, P. E., Jr. Perceptual closure in middle and old age. Paper presented at the meeting of the Gerontological Society, Boston, October 1963.

Comalli, P. E., Jr. Cognitive functioning in a group of 80-90 year old men. *Journal of Gerontology*, 1965, **20**, 14-17. (a)

Comalli, P. E. Jr. Life-span developmental studies in perception: Theoretical and methodological issues. Symposium paper presented at the Eastern Psychological Association meetings, Atlantic City, April 1965. (b)

Comalli, P. E., Jr. Perception and age. *Gerontologist*, 1967, **7**, 73-77.

Comalli, P. E., Jr. Perceptual changes to visual illusions in childhood, adulthood, and old age. Paper presented at the meeting of the Society for Research in Child Development, Santa Monica, California, March 1969.

Comalli, P. E., Jr., Wapner, S., & Werner, H. Perception of verticality in middle and old age. *Journal of Psychology*, 1959, **47**, 259-266.

Comalli, P. E., Jr., Wapner, S., & Werner, H. Interference effects of Stroop color-word test in childhood, adulthood, and aging. *Journal of Genetic Psychology*, 1962, **100**, 47-53.

Conant, J. B. *On understanding science*. New Haven: Yale University Press, 1947.

Conrad, R. Interference or decay over short retention intervals? *Journal of Verbal Learning and Verbal Behavior*, 1967, **6**, 49-54.

Coombs, C. A theory of data. *Psychological Review*, 1960, **67**, 143-159.

Corballis, M. C., & Traub, R. E. Longitudinal factor analysis. *Psychometrika*, 1970, **35**, 79-98.

Corman, C. D., & Wickens, D. D. Retroactive inhibition in short-term memory. *Journal of Verbal Learning and Verbal Behavior*, 1968, **7**, 16-19.

Corsini, R. J., & Fassett, K. K. Intelligence and aging. *Journal of Genetic Psychology*, 1953, **83**, 249-264.

Cowdry, E. V. (Ed.) *Problems of aging*. Baltimore: Williams & Wilkins, 1939.

Craik, F. I. M. Short-term memory and the aging process. In G. A. Talland (Ed.), *Human aging and behavior*. New York: Academic Press, 1968. Pp. 131-168.

Critchley, H. Aging and the nervous system. In E. V. Cowdry (Ed.), *Problems of aging*. (2nd ed.) Baltimore: Williams & Witkins, 1942.

Crites, J. O., & Semler, I. J. Adjustment, educational achievement, and vocational maturity as dimensions of development in adolescence. *Journal of Counseling Psychology*, 1967, **14**, 489-498.

Cronbach, L. J. Processes affecting scores on "understanding of others" and "assumed similarity." *Psychological Bulletin*, 1955, **52**, 177-193.

Cronbach, L. J. The two disciplines of scientific psychology. *American Psychologist*, 1957, **12**, 671-684.

Cronbach, L. J. *Essentials of psychological testing*. New York: Harper & Row, 1960.

Cronbach, L. J. Year-to-year correlations of mental tests: A review of the Hofstaetter analysis. *Child Development*, 1967, **38**, 283-289.

Cronbach, L. J., & Meehl, P. E. Construct validity in psychological tests. *Psychological Bulletin*, 1955, **52**, 281-302.

Cropley, A. J. Differentiation of abilities, socioeconomic status and the WISC. *Journal of Consulting Psychology*, 1964, **28**, 512-517.

Crossman, E., & Szafran, J. Changes with age in speed of information intake and discrimination. In F. Verzar (Ed.), *Experimental research on aging*. Basel: Birkhäuser, 1956.

Crovitz, E. Reversing a learning deficit in the aged. *Journal of Gerontology*, 1966, **21**, 236-238.

Cruze, W. W. Maturation and learning in chicks. *Journal of Comparative Psychology*, 1935, **19**, 371-409.

Cumming, M. E. New thoughts on the theory of disengagement. In R. Kastenbaum (Ed.), *New thoughts on old age*. New York: Springer, 1964. Pp. 3-18.

Cumming, M. E., & Henry, W. E. (Eds.) *Growing old: The process of disengagement.* New York: Basic Books, 1961.

Curtis, H. A. A study of the relative effects of age and of test difficulty upon factor patterns. *Genetic Psychology Monographs,* 1949, **40,** 99-148.

Damianopoulos, E. A formal statement of disengagement theory. In M. E. Cumming & W. Henry (Eds.), *Growing old: The process of disengagement.* New York: Basic Books, 1961. Pp. 210-218.

Damon, A. Discrepancies between findings of longitudinal and cross-sectional studies in adult life: Physique and physiology. *Human Development,* 1965, **8,** 16-22.

Davies, A. D. M. Measures of mental deterioration in aging and brain damage. In S. M. Chown & K. F. Riegel (Eds.), *Interdisciplinary topics in gerontology.* Vol. 1. *Psychological functioning in the normal aging and senile aged.* Basel: Karger, 1968. Pp. 78-90.

Davies, A. D. M., & Laytham, G. W. H. Perception of verticality in adult life. *British Journal of Psychology,* 1964, **55,** 315-320.

Davis, A., & Dollard, J. *Children of bondage: The personality development of Negro youth in the urban South.* Washington, D.C.: American Council on Education, 1940.

Davis, E. A. The development of linguistic skills in twins, singletons with siblings, and only children from age five to ten years. *Institute of Child Welfare Monographs,* 1937, **14.**

Davis, E. A. Developmental changes with distribution of parts of speech. *Child Development,* 1938, **8,** 139-143.

Dearborn, W. F., & Rothney, J. W. M. *Predicting the child's development.* Cambridge, Mass.: Sci-Art, 1941.

Dearborn, W. F., Rothney, J. W. M., & Shuttleworth, F. K. Data on the growth of public school children. *Monographs of the Society for Research in Child Development,* 1938, **3**(1, Whole No. 14).

Deese, J. On the structure of associative meaning. *Psychological Review,* 1962, **69,** 161-175.

Deese, J. *The structure of associations in language and thought.* Baltimore: Johns Hopkins Press, 1965.

DeLaguna, G. *Speech: Its function and development.* Bloomington, Ind.: Indiana University Press, 1927.

Demming, J. A. & Pressey, S. L. Tests indigenous to the adult and older years. *Journal of Counseling Psychology,* 1957, **4,** 144-148.

Denenberg, V. H., & Kline, N. J. The relationship between age and avoidance learning in the hooded rat. *Journal of Comparative and Physiological Psychology,* 1958, **51,** 488-491.

Dennis, W. Historical beginnings of child psychology. *Psychological Bulletin,* 1949, **46,** 224-235.

Dennis, W. Causes of retardation among institutional children: Iran. *Journal of Genetic Psychology,* 1960, **96,** 47-59.

Dennis, W., & Mallinger, B. Animism and related tendencies in senescence. *Journal of Gerontology,* 1949, **4,** 218-221.

Dennis, W., & Najarian, P. Infant development under environmental handicap. *Psychological Monographs,* 1957, **71** (Whole No. 7).

Dewey, J. *The child and the curriculum.* (Contributions to Education, No. 5.) Chicago: University of Chicago Press, 1902.

Doll, E. A. The average mental age of adults. *Journal of Applied Psychology,* 1919, **3,** 317-328.

Doll, E. A. Psychological significance of cerebral birth lesions. *American Journal of Psychology,* 1933, **45,** 444-452.

Doll, E. A., Phelps, W. M., & Melcher, R. T. *Mental deficiency due to birth injuries.* New York: Macmillan, 1932.

Dollard, J., & Miller, N. E. *Personality and psychotherapy.* New York: McGraw-Hill, 1950.

Dollard, J., Miller, N. E., Doob, L. W., Mowrer, O. H., & Sears, R. R. *Frustration and aggression.* New Haven: Yale University Press, 1939.

Doppelt, J. E. The organization of mental abilities in the age range thirteen to seventeen. (Doctoral dissertation, Columbia University.) *American Psychologist*, 1949, **4**, 242. (Abstract)

Doppelt, J. E. The organization of mental abilities in the age range thirteen to seventeen. *Teachers College Contributions to Education*, 1950, No. 962.

Doppelt, J. E., & Wallace, W. L. Standardization of the Wechsler adult intelligence scale for older persons. *Journal of Abnormal and Social Psychology*, 1955, **51**, 312-330.

Dron, D. M., & Boe, E. E. R-S paired associate learning as a function of percentage occurrence of response members. *Journal of Verbal Learning and Verbal Behavior*, 1964, **3**, 130-131.

Duncanson, J. P. *Intelligence and the ability to learn.* Princeton, N.J.: Educational Testing Service, 1964.

Dye, N. W., & Very, P. S. Growth changes in factorial structure by age and sex. *Genetic Psychology Monographs*, 1968, **78**, 55-88.

Eisdorfer, C. Verbal learning response time in the aged. *Journal of Genetic Psychology*, 1965, **107**, 15-22.

Eisdorfer, C., Axelrod, S., & Wilkie, F. L. Stimulus exposure time as a factor in serial learning in an aged sample. *Journal of Abnormal and Social Psychology*, 1963, **67**, 594-600.

Eisner, D. Age changes in the perceptual functioning of the aged. Unpublished master's thesis, West Virginia University, Department of Psychology, 1968.

Eisner, D., Schaie, K. W., & Apfeldorf, M. Changes in response to visual illusions in old age. Unpublished manuscript, West Virginia University, Department of Psychology, 1969.

Ekstrand, B. R. Backward associations. *Psychological Bulletin*, 1966, **65**, 50-64.

Ekstrand, B. R., Wallace, W. P., & Underwood, B. J. A frequency theory of verbal-discrimination learning. *Psychological Review*, 1966, **73**, 566-578.

Elkind, D., & Flavell, J. H. (Eds.) *Studies in cognitive development: Essays in honor of Jean Piaget.* New York: Oxford University Press, 1969.

Elkind, D., & Weiss, I. Studies in perceptual development: III. Perceptual exploration. *Child Development*, 1967, **38**, 553-561.

El Koussy, A. A. H. The visual perception of space. *British Journal of Psychology*, 1936, **7**, (Monograph Supplement).

Ellington, N. R., & Kausler, D. H. "Fate" of list 1 R-S associations in transfer theory. *Journal of Experimental Psychology*, 1965, **69**, 207-208.

Emmerich, W. Continuity and stability in early social development. *Child Development*, 1964, **35**, 311-332.

Emmerich, W. Stability and change in early personality development. In W. W. Hartup & N. L. Smothergil (Eds.), *The young child: Reviews of research.* Washington, D.C.: National Association for the Education of Young Children, 1967. Pp. 248-261.

Emmerich, W. Personality development and concepts of structure. *Child Development*, 1968, **39**, 671-690.

Engen, T., & Lipsitt, L. P. Decrement and recovery of responses to olfactory stimuli in the human neonate. *Journal of Comparative and Physiological Psychology*, 1965, **59**, 213-316.

Engen, T., Lipsitt, L. P., & Kaye, H. Olfactory responses and adaptation in the human neonate. *Journal of Comparative and Physiological Psychology*, 1963, **56**, 73-77.

Entwisle, D. R. *Word associations of young children.* Baltimore: Johns Hopkins Press, 1965.

Entwisle, D. R., Forsyth, D. F., & Muus, R. The syntactic-paradigmatic shift in children's word associations. *Journal of Verbal Learning and Verbal Behavior*, 1964, **3**, 19-30.

Erikson, E. H. *Childhood and society*. New York: Norton, 1950.

Erikson, E. H. *Kindheit und Gesellschaft*. Zürich: Pan, 1957.

Erikson, E. H. Identity and the life cycle: Selected papers. *Psychological Issues*, 1959, **1**, 50-100.

Erlenmeyer-Kimling, L., & Jarvik, L. F. Genetics and intelligence: A review. *Science*, 1963, **142**, 1447-1478.

Ertl, J. Evoked potentials, neural efficiency and I.Q. Report of the Center of Cybernetic Studies, 1968, University of Ottawa, Canada.

Ervin, S. M. Changes with age in the verbal determinants of word-association. *American Journal of Psychology*, 1961, **74**, 361-372.

Ervin, S. M. Imitation and structural change in children's language. In E. H. Lenneberg (Ed.), *New directions in the study of language*. Cambridge, Mass.: Massachusetts Institute of Technology Press, 1964.

Ervin, S. M., & Osgood, C. E. Second language learning and bilingualism. In C. E. Osgood & T. A. Sebeok (Eds.), *Psycholinguistics*. Bloomington, Ind.: Indiana University Press, 1965. Pp. 139-146.

Escalona, S., & Heider, G. M. *Prediction and outcome*. New York: Basic Books, 1959.

Eschenbrenner, A. J., Jr. Retroactive and proactive inhibition in verbal discrimination learning. *Journal of Experimental Psychology*, 1969, **81**, 576-583.

Eschenbrenner, A. J., Jr., & Kausler, D. H. Unlearning of list 1 wrong items in verbal discrimination transfer. *Journal of Experimental Psychology*, 1968, **78**, 696-698.

Estes, W. K. The problem of inference from curves based on group data. *Psychological Bulletin*, 1956, **53**, 134-140.

Eyferth, K. Gültigkeit und faktorielle Struktur des Hamburg-Wechsler-Intelligenztest für Kinder (HAWIK) bei seiner Anwendung auf schwachsinnige Erwachsene. *Diagnostica*, 1963, **9**, 11-26.

Eysenck, H. J. *Fact and fiction in psychology*. Harmondsworth, England: Penguin Books, 1966.

Eysenck, H. J., & White, P. O. Personality and the measurement of intelligence. *British Journal of Educational Psychology*, 1964, **34**, 197-202.

Fantz, R. L. Pattern vision in young infants. *Psychological Record*, 1958, **8**, 43-47.

Fantz, R. L. Visual perception from birth as shown by pattern selectivity. *Annals of the New York Academy of Sciences*, 1965, **118**, 793-814.

Fantz, R. L. Visual perception and experience in early infancy: A look at the hidden side of behavior development. In H. W. Stevenson, E. H. Hess, & H. L. Rheingold (Eds.), *Early behavior: Comparative and developmental approaches*. New York: Wiley, 1967. Pp. 181-224.

Fantz, R. L., & Nevis, S. The predictive value of changes in visual preferences in early infancy. In J. Hellmuth (Ed.), *The special child*. Vol. 1. Seattle: Special Child Publications, 1967.

Feffer, M. H., & Gourevitch, V. Cognitive aspects of role-taking in children. *Journal of Personality*, 1960, **28**, 383-396.

Feifel, H. Qualitative differences in the vocabulary responses of normals and abnormals. *Genetic Psychology Monographs*, 1949, **39**, 151-204.

Feifel, H., & Lorge, I. Qualitative differences in the vocabulary responses of children. *Journal of Educational Psychology*, 1950, **41**, 1-8.

Ferguson, G. A. On learning and human ability. *Canadian Journal of Psychology*, 1954, **8**, 95-112.

Ferguson, G. A. On transfer and the abilities of man. *Canadian Journal of Psychology*, 1956, **10**, 121-131.

Fernberger, S. W. History of the psychological clinic. In R. A. Brotemarkle (Ed.), *Clinical psychology: Studies in honor of Lightner Witmer*. Philadelphia: University of Pennsylvania Press, 1931.

Ferré, F. Mapping the logic of models in science and theology. *Christian Scholar*, 1963, **46**, 9-39.

Fischer, G., & Roppert, J. Bemerkungen zu einem Verfahren der Transformationsanalyse. *Archiv für die Gesamte Psychologie*, 1964, **116**, 98-100.

Fischer, G., & Roppert, J. Ein Verfahren der Transformationsanalyse faktorenanalytischer Ergebnisse. In J. Roppert & G. Fischer (Eds.), *Lineare Strukturen in Mathematik und Statistik unter besonderer Berücksichtigung der Faktoren-und Transformationsanalyse*. Vienna: Physica (Arbeiten aus dem Institut für Höhere Studien und Wissenschaftliche Forschung, Wien Nr. 1), 1965. Pp. 1-15.

Fiske D. W., & Rice, L. Intra-individual response variability. *Psychological Bulletin*, 1955, **52**, 217-250.

Flavell, J. H. *The developmental psychology of Jean Piaget*. Princeton, N.J.: Van Nostrand, 1963.

Flavell, J. H. Developmental studies of mediated memory. In L. P. Lipsitt & H. W. Reese (Eds.), *Advances in child development and behavior*. Vol. 5. New York: Academic Press, 1969.

Flavell, J. H., Beach, D. H., & Chinsky, J. M. Spontaneous verbal rehearsal in a memory task as a function of age. *Child Development*, 1966, **37**, 283-299.

Flavell, J. H., & Wohlwill, J. F. Formal and functional aspects of cognitive development. In D. Elkind & J. H. Flavell (Eds.), *Studies in cognitive development*. New York: Oxford University Press, 1969. Pp. 67-120.

Fleishman, E. A., & Hempel, W. E. Changes in factor structure of a complex psychomotor test as a function of practice. *Psychometrika*, 1954, **19**, 239-252.

Fleishman, E. A., & Hempel, W. E. The relation between abilities and improvement with practice in a visual discrimination reaction task. *Journal of Experimental Psychology*, 1955, **79**, 301-310.

Fodor, J. A. Could meaning be an r_m? *Journal of Verbal Learning and Verbal Behavior*, 1965, **4**, 73-81.

Fodor, J. A., & Garrett, M. Some syntactic determinants of sentence complexity. *Perception & Psychophysics*, 1967, **2**, 289-296.

Foster, J. C., & Taylor, G. A. The applicability of mental tests to persons over fifty years of age. *Journal of Applied Psychology*, 1920, **4**, 39-58.

Foster, J. C. Significant responses in certain memory tests. *Journal of Applied Psychology*, 1920, **4**, 142-154.

Foulds G. A. Mill Hill vocabulary and matrices. *American Journal of Psychology*, 1949, **62**, 238-246.

Foulds, G. A., & Raven, J. C. Neural changes in mental abilities of adults as age advances. *Journal of Mental Science*, 1948, **94**, 133-142.

Fox, C. Vocabulary abilities in later maturity. *Journal of Educational Psychology*, 1947, **38**, 484-492.

Fox, C., & Birren, J. E. Some factors affecting vocabulary size in late maturity: Age, education and length of institutionalization. *Journal of Gerontology*, 1949, **4**, 19-26.

Fox, C., & Birren, J. E. Intellectual deterioration in the aged: Agreement between the Wechsler-Bellevue and the Babcock-Levy. *Journal of Consulting Psychology*, 1950, **14**, 305-310.

Frank, L. K. The beginnings of child development and family life education in the twentieth century. *Merrill-Palmer Quarterly*, 1962, **8**, 207-227.

Frank, P. G. The variety of reasons for the acceptance of scientific theories. *Scientific Monthly*, 1954, **79**, 139-145. [Reprinted in P. G. Frank (Ed.), *The validation of scientific theories*. New York: Collier, 1961. Pp. 13-26]

Frank, P. G. (Ed.) *The validation of scientific theories*. New York: Collier, 1961.

Freeman, F. N., & Flory, C. D. Growth in intellectual ability as measured by repeated tests. *Monographs of the Society for Research in Child Development*, 1937, **2**(2, Whole No. 9).

French, J. W. *The description of aptitude and achievement tests in terms of rotated factors*. Chicago: University of Chicago Press, 1951.

French, J. W., Ekstrom, R. B., & Price, L. A. *Manual for kit of reference tests for cognitive factors*. Princeton, N.J.: Educational Testing Service, 1963.

Frenkel, E. Lebenslauf, Leistung und Erfolg. Bericht über den 12. Kongress für experimentelle Psychologie. *Archiv für die Gesamte Psychologie*, 1931, **76**, 331-335.

Frenkel, E. Studies in biographical psychology. *Character & Personality*, 1936, **5**, 1-34.

Freud, A. *Psychoanalytic treatment of children*. London: Imago, 1946.

Freud, S. Jenseits des Lustprinzips. (1920) In J. Strachey (Ed.), *Gesammelte Werke*. Vol. 13. London: Imago, 1948-1961.

Fries, C. C. *American English grammar*. New York: Appleton-Century-Crofts, 1940.

Fruchter, B. Manipulative and hypothesis testing factor-analytic experimental designs. In R. B. Cattell (Ed.), *Handbook of multivariate experimental psychology*. Chicago: Rand McNally, 1966. Pp. 330-354.

Furneaux, W. D. Some speed, error and difficulty relationships within a problem-solving situation. *Nature*, 1952, **170**, 37-38.

Furneaux, W. D. Intellectual abilities and problem-solving behavior. In H. J. Eysenck (Ed.), *Handbook of abnormal psychology*. New York: Basic Books, 1961.

Furth, H. *Piaget and knowledge*. Englewood Cliffs, N.J.: Prentice Hall, 1969.

Gaeth, J. H., & Allen, D. V. Effect of similarity upon learning in children. *Journal of Experimental Child Psychology*, 1966, **4**, 381-390.

Gajo, F. D. *Adult age differences in the perception of visual illusion*. (Doctoral dissertation, Washington University) Ann Arbor, Mich. University Microfilms, 1966. No. 67-7036.

Gallagher, J. W. Paired associate learning in children as a function of type of syntactic relationship and associative relationship. *Journal of Verbal Learning and Verbal Behavior*, 1968, **7**, 491-495.

Galton, F. Twins as a criterion of the relative power of nature and nurture. *Journal of the Royal Anthropological Institute*, 1875, **5**, 324-329.

Galton, F. Psychometric experiments. *Brain*, 1879, **2**, 149-157.

Galton, F. Visualized numerals. *Journal of the Royal Anthropological Institute*, 1880, **10**, 85-102. (a)

Galton, F. Statistics of mental imagery. *Mind*, 1880, **5**, 301-318. (b)

Galton, F. *Inquiries into human faculty and its development*. London: Macmillan, 1883.

Galton, F. On the anthropometric laboratory at the late International Health Exhibition. *Journal of the Anthropological Institute*, 1885, **14**, 205-221, 275-287.

Garrett, H. E. A developmental theory of intelligence. *American Psychologist*, 1946, **1**, 372-378.

Garrett, H. E., Bryan, A. I., & Perl, R. E. The age factor in mental organization. *Archives of Psychology*, 1935, **26**, (Whole No. 176).

Gault, U. Factorial patterns on Wechsler intelligence scales. *Australian Journal of Psychology*, 1954, **6**, 85-90.

Gebhardt, F. Über die Ähnlichkeit von Faktorenmatrizen. *Psychologische Beiträge*, 1968, **10**, 591-599.

Gerhard, M. *Der deutsche Entwicklungsroman bis zu Goethe's Wilhelm Meister.* Halle/Saale: Niemeyer, 1926.

Gesell, A. The individual in infancy. In C. Murchison (Ed.), *Handbook of child psychology.* Worcester, Mass.: Clark University Press, 1931. Pp. 628-660.

Gesell, A. *The first five years of life.* New York: Harper, 1940.

Ghiselli, E. E. The relationship between intelligence and age among superior adults. *Journal of Genetic Psychology*, 1957, **90**, 131-142.

Giese, F. *Erlebnisformen des Alters.* Halle/Saale: Niemeyer, 1928.

Gilbert, J. A. Researches on mental and physical development of school children. *Studies of the Yale Psychological Laboratory*, 1894, **2**, 40-100.

Gilbert, J. G. Mental efficiency in senescence. *Archives of Psychology*, 1935, **188**, 1-60.

Gilbert, J. G. Memory loss in senescence. *Journal of Abnormal and Social Psychology*, 1941, **36**, 73-86.

Ginsburg, H. Children's estimates of simultaneously presented proportions. *Merrill-Palmer Quarterly*, 1967, **13**, 151-157.

Gladis, M. Grade differences in transfer as a function of the time interval between learning tasks. *Journal of Educational Psychology*, 1960, **51**, 191-195.

Gladis, M., & Braun, H. W. Age differences in transfer and retroaction as a function of intertask response similarity. *Journal of Experimental Psychology*, 1958, **55**, 25-30.

Glanzer, M. Psycholinguistics and verbal learning. In K. Salzinger & S. Salzinger (Eds.), *Research in verbal behavior and some neurophysiological implications.* New York: Academic Press, 1967.

Goddard, H. H. A measuring scale for intelligence. *Training School Bulletin,* 1910, **6**, 146-154.

Goldfarb, N. *An introduction to longitudinal statistical analysis.* Glencoe, Ill.: Free Press, 1960.

Goldfarb, W. *An investigation of reaction time in older adults.* New York: Columbia University Press, 1941.

Goldschmid, M. L. Different types of conservation and nonconservation and their relation to age, sex, IQ, MA and vocabulary. *Child Development,* 1967, **38**, 1229-1246.

Goldschmid, M. L., & Bentler, P. M. The dimensions and measurement of conservation. *Child Development*, 1968, **39**, 787-802.

Goldstein, K., & Scherer, M. Abstract and concrete behavior. *Psychological Monographs*, 1941, **53**, No. 2.

Goldstein, K., & Scherer, M. Tests of abstract and concrete thinking. In A. Weider (Ed.), *Contributions toward medical psychology.* Vol. 8. New York: Ronald Press, 1955, Pp. 702-730.

Goodenough, F. L. The use of pronouns in young children: A note on the development of self-awareness. *Journal of Genetic Psychology*, 1930, **52**, 33-346.

Goodnow, J. I., & Bethon, G. Piaget's task: The effects of schooling and intelligence. *Child Development*, 1966, **37**, 574-582.

Gordon, L. V. Comments on "cross-cultural equivalence of personality measures." *Journal of Social Psychology*, 1968, **75**, 11-19.

Gordon, T., & Foss, B. M. The role of stimulation in the delay of onset of crying in the newborn infant. *Quarterly Journal of Experimental Psychology*, 1966, **18**, 79-81.

Gorham, D. R. A proverbs test for chemical and experimental use. *Psychological Reports*, 1956, 2(Monogr. Suppl. 2), 1-12.

Gottschaldt, K. Erbpsychologie der Elementarfunktionen der Begabung. In G. Just (Ed.), *Handbuch der Erbbiologie.* Vol 5/1. Berlin: Springer, 1939.

Gottschaldt, K. *Die Methodik der Persönlichkeitsforschung in der Erbpsychologie.* Leipzig: Barth, 1942.

Gottschaldt, K. Das Problem der Phänogenetik der Persönlichkeit. In P. Lersch & H. Thomae (Eds.), *Handbuch der Psychologie in 12 Bänden.* Vol. 4. *Persönlichkeitsforschung und Persönlichkeitstheorie.* Göttingen: Hogrefe, 1960. Pp. 222-280.

Gottschaldt, K. Zwillingsuntersuchungen vom zweiten bis zum sechsten Lebensjahrzehnt. In R. Schubert (Ed.), *Herz und Atmungsorgane im Alter. Kongress der Deutschen Gesellschaft für Gerontologie 1967.* Darmstadt: Steinkopff, 1968. Pp. 176-185.

Gough, P. B. Grammatical transformations and speed of understanding. *Journal of Verbal Learning and Verbal Behavior,* 1965, **4**, 107-111.

Goulet, L. R. Verbal learning and memory research with retardates: An attempt to assess developmental trends. In N. R. Ellis (Ed.), *International review of research in mental retardation.* Vol. 3. New York: Academic Press, 1968. Pp. 97-134. (a)

Goulet, L. R. Verbal learning in children: Implications for developmental research. *Psychological Bulletin,* 1968, **69**, 359-376. (b)

Goulet, L. R., & Bone, R. N. Interlist form-class similarity and interference effects. *Journal of Verbal Learning and Verbal Behavior,* 1968, **7**, 92-97.

Graham, F. K., & Clifton, R. K. Heart-rate changes as a component of the orienting response. *Psychological Bulletin,* 1966, **65**, 305-320.

Graham, F. K., & Jackson, J. C. Arousal systems and infant heart rate responses. In H. W. Reese & L. P. Lipsitt (Eds.), *Advances in child development and behavior.* Vol. 5. New York: Academic Press, 1970.

Graham, F. K., & Kendall, B. S. Memory-for-designs test: Revised general manual. *Perceptual and Motor Skills,* 1960, 7(Monogr. Suppl. 2).

Graham, F. K., Matarazzo, R. G., & Caldwell, B. M. Behavioral differences between normal and traumatized newborns: II. Standardization, reliability and validity. *Psychological Monographs,* 1956, **70**, No. 21.

Grant, D. A. Classical and operant conditioning. In A. W. Melton (Ed.), *Categories of human learning.* New York: Academic Press, 1964. Pp. 3-31.

Green, B. F. A method of scalogram analysis using summary statistics. *Psychometrika,* 1956, **21**, 79-88.

Green, D. T., & Swets, J. *Signal detection theory and psychophysics.* New York: Wiley, 1966.

Green, R. F., & Berkowitz, B. Changes in intellect with age: II. Factorial analysis of Wechsler-Bellevue scores. *Journal of Genetic Psychology,* 1964, **104**, 3-18.

Greene, E. B. An analysis of random and systematic changes with practice. *Psychometrika,* 1943, **8**, 37-52.

Greenfield, P. M., & Bruner, J. S. Culture and cognitive growth. *International Journal of Psychology,* 1966, **1**, 89-107.

Gregoire A. *L'apprentissage du langage: Les deux premières années.* Paris: Droz, 1937.

Gregory, R. L. *Eye and brain.* London: Weidenfeld & Nicolson, 1966.

Grinder, R. *A history of genetic psychology.* New York: Wiley, 1967.

Grisby, O. J. An experimental study of the development of concepts of relationships in preschool children as evidenced by their expressive ability. *Journal of Experimental Education,* 1932, **1**, 144-162.

Groffmann, K. J. Die Entwicklung der Intelligenzmessung. In R. Heiss (Ed.), *Handbuch der Psychologie in 12 Bänden.* Vol. 6. *Psychologische Diagnostik.* Göttingen: Hogrefe, 1964. Pp. 147-199.

Groos, K. *Die Spiele der Tiere.* Jena: Barth, 1896.

Groos, K. *Die Spiele der Menschen.* Jena: Barth, 1899.

Gruhle, H. W. Das seelische Altern. *Zeitschrift für Altersforschung,* 1938, **1**, 89-95.

Grunbaum, A. Operationism and relativity. *Scientific Monthly*, 1954, **79**, 228-231. [Reprinted in P. G. Frank (Ed.), *The validation of scientific theories*. New York: Collier, 1961. Pp. 83-92.]

Guilford, J. P. Zero intercorrelations among tests of intellectual abilities. *Psychological Bulletin*, 1964, **61**, 401-404.

Guilford, J. P. *The nature of human intelligence*. New York: McGraw-Hill, 1967.

Guttman, L. A generalized simplex for factor analysis. *Psychometrika*, 1955, **20**, 173-192.

Hagen, P. *A factor analysis of the Wechsler intelligence scale for children*. (Doctoral dissertation, Columbia University) Ann Arbor, Mich: University Microfilms, 1952. No. 4189.

Hagen, W. *Wachstum und Entwicklung von Schulkindern im Bild*. Munich: Barth, 1964.

Hagen, W., Thomae, H., & Ronge, A. *10 Jahre Nachkriegskinder*. Munich: Barth, 1962.

Haith, M. M. The response of the human newborn to visual movement. *Journal of Experimental Child Psychology*, 1966, **3**, 235-243.

Hall, C. S., & Lindzey, G. *Theories of personality*. New York: Wiley, 1957.

Hall, G. S. The contents of children's minds. *Princeton Review*, 1883, **11**, 249-272.

Hall, G. S. The ideal school as based on child study. *Forum*, 1901-1902, **32**, 24-25.

Hall, G. S. *Adolescence*. New York: Appleton, 1904. 2 vols.

Hall, G. S. *Educational problems*. New York: Appleton, 1911.

Hall, G. S. *Senescence, the last half of life*. New York: Appleton, 1922.

Hall, J. W., & Ware, W. B. Implicit associative responses and false recognition by young children. *Journal of Experimental Child Psychology*, 1968, **6**, 52-60.

Halstead, W. C. *Brain and intelligence*. Chicago: University of Chicago Press, 1947.

Handmann, E. Über das Hirngewicht des Menschen. *Archives Anatomy*, 1906, **8**, 14-17.

Hanfmann, E., & Kasanin, J. Conceptual thinking in schizophrenia. *Nervous and Mental Diseases Monographs*, 1942, **67**, 115.

Hanley, C., & Zerbolio, D. J. Developmental changes in five illusions measured by the up-and-down method. *Child Development*, 1965, **36**, 437-452.

Harcum, E. R. Visual detection and recognition of targets with various dependency contrasts in microstructure. *Journal of Experimental Psychology*, 1967, 73, 155-159.

Harlow, H. F. The formation of learning sets. *Psychological Review*, 1949, **56**, 51-65.

Harman, H. H. *Modern factor analysis*. Chicago: University of Chicago Press, 1960.

Harrell, W. A factor analysis of mechanical ability tests. *Psychometrika*, 1940, **5**, 17-33.

Harris, C. W. Canonical factor models for the description of change. In C. W. Harris (Ed.), *Problems in measuring change*. Madison, Wis.: University of Wisconsin Press, 1963. Pp. 138-155.

Harris, D. B. (Ed.) *The concept of development*. Minneapolis: University of Minnesota Press, 1957. (a)

Harris, D. B. Problems in formulating a scientific concept of development. In D. B. Harris (Ed.), *The concept of development*. Minneapolis: University of Minnesota Press, 1957. Pp. 3-14. (b)

Harter, S. Discrimination learning set in children as a function of IQ and MA. *Journal of Experimental Child Psychology*, 1965, **2**, 31-43.

Havighurst, R. J. Social competence of middle aged people. *Genetic Psychology Monographs*, 1957, **56**, 297-375.

Havighurst, R. J., & Albrecht, R. *Older people*. New York: Longmans, Green, 1953.

Havighurst, R. J., Neugarten, B. L. & Tobin, S. Disengagement and patterns of aging. Paper presented at the International Social Science Seminar on Social Gerontology, Sweden, 1963. Cited by G. L. Maddox, Disengagement theory: A critical evaluation. *Gerontologist*, 1964, **4**, 80-82, 103.

Hayes, K. J. Genes, drives and intellect. *Psychological Reports*, 1962, 10, 299-342.

Hayhurst, H. Some errors of young children in producing passive sentences. *Journal of Verbal Learning and Verbal Behavior,* 1967, 6, 634-640.

Haynes, J. R., & Sells, S. B. Measurement of organic brain damage by psychological tests. *Psychological Bulletin,* 1963, 60, 316-325.

Hays, W. L. *Statistics for psychologists.* New York: Holt, Rinehart & Winston, 1963.

Healy, W., & Bronner, A. F. The child guidance clinic: Birth and growth of an idea. In L. G. Lowrey & V. Sloane, (Eds.), *Orthopsychiatry, 1923-1948; retrospect and prospect.* New York: American Orthopsychiatric Association Press, 1948.

Healy, W., & Fernald, G. M. Tests for practical mental classification. *Psychological Monographs,* 1910, 13(Whole No. 54).

Hearnshaw, L. S. *A short history of British psychology.* London: Methuen, 1964.

Hebb, D. O. The effects of early and late brain injury upon test scores, and the nature of normal adult intelligence. *Proceedings of the American Philosophical Society,* 1942, 85, 275-292. (Abstract)

Hebb, D. O. *Organization of behavior.* New York: Wiley, 1949.

Heider, F. K., & Heider, G. M. A comparison of sentence structure of deaf and hearing children. *Psychological Monographs,* 1940, 52, 42-103.

Heinonen, V. A factor analytical study of transfer of training. *Scandinavian Journal of Psychology,* 1962, 3, 177-188.

Heinonen, V. *Differentiation of primary mental abilities.* Jyvaskyla, Finland: Kustantama, 1963.

Hempel, C. G. *Aspects of scientific explanation and other essays in the philosophy of science.* New York: Free Press, 1965.

Hempel, C. G. *Philosophy of natural science.* Englewood Cliffs, N.J.: Prentice-Hall, 1966.

Hempel, C. G., & Oppenheim, P. Studies in the logic of explanation. *Philosophy of Science,* 1948, 15, 135-175.

Henry, W. E. Engagement and disengagement: Toward a theory of adult development. In R. Kastenbaum (Ed.), *Contributions to the psychology of aging.* New York: Springer, 1966. Pp. 19-35.

Henrysson, S. *Factor analysis in the behavioral sciences: A methodological study.* Stockholm: Almqvist & Wiksell, 1960.

Heroard, J. *Journal, 1601-1628.* Lemy: Sovlie & de Barthe, 1868.

Heron, A. Immediate memory in dealing performance with and without simple rehearsal. *Quarterly Journal of Experimental Psychology,* 1962, 14, 94-103.

Hershenson, M. Visual discrimination in the human newborn. *Journal of Comparative and Physiological Psychology,* 1964, 58, 270-276.

Hershenson, M. Development of the perception of form. *Psychological Bulletin,* 1967, 64, 326-336.

Hesse, M. B. *Models and analogies in science.* London: Sheed & Ward, 1963.

Heston, J. C., & Cannell, C. F. A note on the relation between age and performance of adult subjects on four familiar psychometric tests. *Journal of Applied Psychology,* 1941, 25, 415-419.

Heydt, C. Der Einfluss des Alters bei Eignungsuntersuchungen mit besonderer Berücksichtigung des Verkehrs- und Betriebswesens der Deutschen Reichsbahn. *Industrielle Psychotechnik,* 1925, 2, 213.

Hill, J. P. Similarity and accordance between parents and sons in attitudes toward mathematics. *Child Development,* 1967, 38, 777-791.

Hindley, C. B. Stability and change in abilities up to five years: Group trends. *Journal of Child Psychology and Psychiatry,* 1965, 6, 85-99.

Hindley, C. B., & Munro, J. A. Longitudinal results of the changing pattern of abilities in the first 18 months of life. *Bulletin of the British Psychological Society*, 1968, **21**, 110. (Abstract)

Hoffman, M. L., & Hoffman, L. W. (Eds.) *Review of child development research*. New York: Russell Sage Foundation, 1964-1966. 2 vols.

Hofstätter, P. R. Tatsachen und Probleme einer Psychologie des Lebenslaufes. *Zeitschrift für Angewandte Psychologie*, 1938, **53**, 273-333.

Hofstätter, P. R. The changing composition of intelligence: A study in T-technique. *Journal of Genetic Psychology*, 1954, **85**, 159-164.

Höhn, E. Zur Geschichte der Entwicklungspsychologie und ihrer wesentlichsten Ansätze. In H. Thomae (Ed.), *Handbuch der Psychologie in 12 Bänden*. Vol. 3. *Entwicklungspsychologie*. Göttingen: Hogrefe, 1959. Pp. 21-45.

Holden, E. S. On the vocabularies of children under two years of age. *Transactions of the American Philological Association*, 1877, **8**, 56-58.

Holt, E. B. *Animal drive*. London: Williams and Norgate, 1931.

Holt, L. M. *Care and feeding of children*. New York: Appleton, 1894.

Holtzman, W. H. Methodological issues in P-technique. *Psychological Bulletin*, 1962, **59**, 248-256.

Holtzman, W. H. Statistical models for the study of change in the single case. In C. W. Harris (Ed.), *Problems in measuring change*. Madison, Wis.: University of Wisconsin Press, 1963. Pp. 199-211.

Holtzman, W. H. Cross-cultural research on personality development. *Human Development*, 1965, **8**, 65-86.

Honzik, M. Environmental correlates of mental growth: Prediction from the family setting at 21 months. *Child Development*, 1967, **38**, 337-364.

Horn, J. L. Fluid and crystallized intelligence: A factor analytic and developmental study of the structure among primary mental abilities. Unpublished doctoral dissertation, University of Illinois, 1965.

Horn, J. L. Short period fluctuations in intelligence. Final Report, 1966, University of Denver, Colorado, NASA Project Number DR 1-614. (a)

Horn, J. L. Integration of structural and developmental concepts in the theory of fluid and crystallized intelligence. In R. B. Cattell (Ed.), *Handbook of multivariate experimental psychology*. Chicago: Rand McNally, 1966. Pp. 553-562. (b)

Horn, J. L. Intelligence—why it grows, why it declines. *Transaction, 1967*, **4**, 23-31.

Horn, J. L. Organization of abilities and the development of intelligence. *Psychological Review*, 1968, **75**, 242-259.

Horn, J. L. Personality and ability theory. In R. B. Cattell (Ed.), *Handbook of modern personality theory*. New York: Aldine, 1970, in press.

Horn, J. L., & Bramble, W. J. Second order ability structure revealed in rights and wrongs scores. *Journal of Educational Psychology*, 1967, **58**, 115-122.

Horn, J. L., & Cattell, R. B. Vehicles, ipsatization and the multiple method measurement of motivation. *Canadian Journal of Psychology*, 1965, **19**, 265-279.

Horn, J. L., & Cattell, R. B. Age differences in primary mental ability factors. *Journal of Gerontology*, 1966, **21**, 210-220. (a)

Horn, J. L., & Cattell, R. B. Refinement and test of the theory of fluid and crystallized intelligence. *Journal of Educational Psychology*, 1966, **57**, 253-270. (b)

Horn, J. L., & Cattell, R. B. Age differences in fluid and crystallized intelligence. *Acta Psychologica*, 1967, **26**, 107-129.

Horn, J. L., & Little, K. B. Isolating change and invariance in patterns of behavior. *Multivariate Behavioral Research*, 1966, **1**, 219-228.

Horowitz, F. D. Learning, developmental research, and individual differences. In L. P. Lipsitt & H. W. Reese (Eds.), *Advances in child development and behavior*. Vol. 4. New York: Academic Press, 1969. Pp. 84-127.

Horst, P. *Factor analysis of data matrices.* New York: Holt, Rinehart & Winston, 1965.

Horton, D. L., & Kjeldergaard, P. M. An experimental analysis of associative factors in mediated generalizations. *Psychological Monographs*, 1961, 75(11, Whole No. 515).

Hotelling, H. The generalization of S's ratio. *Annals of Mathematical Statistics*, 1931, 2, 360-378.

Houston, J. P. First-list retention and time and method of recall. *Journal of Experimental Psychology*, 1966, 71, 839-843.

Houston, J. P. Proactive inhibition and competition at recall. *Journal of Experimental Psychology*, 1967, 75, 118-121.

Houston, J. P. Competition in the two-factor theory of forgetting. *Journal of Verbal Learning and Verbal Behavior*, 1968, 7, 496-500.

Hover, G. L. An investigation of differences in intellectual factors between normal and neurotic adults. Unpublished doctoral dissertation, University of Michigan, 1951.

Howard, I. P., & Templeton, W. B. *Human spatial orientation.* London: Wiley, 1966.

Hsü, E. H. Factor analysis, differential bio-process, and mental organization. *Journal of General Psychology*, 1948, 38, 147-157.

Hubel, D. H., & Wiesel, T. N. Receptive fields, binocular interaction, and functional architecture in the cat's visual cortex. *Journal of Physiology*, 1962, 160, 106-154.

Hulicka, I. M. Age differences for intentional and incidental learning and recall scores. *Journal of the American Geriatrics Society*, 1965, 13, 639-649.

Hulicka, I. M. Age differences in retention as a function of interference. *Journal of Gerontology*, 1967, 22, 180-184.

Hulicka, I. M., & Grossman, J. L. Age-group comparisons for the use of mediators in paired-associate learning. *Journal of Gerontology*, 1967, 22, 46-51.

Hull, C. L. The problem of stimulus equivalence in behavior theory. *Psychological Review*, 1939, 46, 9-30.

Hull, C. L. *Principles of behavior.* New York: Appleton, 1943.

Humphreys, L. G. Investigations of the simplex. *Psychometrika*, 1960, 25, 213-323.

Humphreys, L. G. The organization of human abilities. *American Psychologist*, 1962, 17, 475-483.

Humphries, N. W. A contribution to infantile linguistics. *Transactions of the American Philological Association*, 1880, 11, 5-17.

Hundal, P. S. Organization of mental abilities at successive grade levels. *Indian Journal of Psychology*, 1966, 41, 65-72.

Hunt, J. McV. *Intelligence and experience.* New York: Ronald Press, 1961.

Hunt, J. McV. Intrinsic motivation and its role in psychological development. In D. Levine (Ed.), *Nebraska symposium on motivation*. Lincoln, Neb.: University of Nebraska Press, 1965. Pp. 189-282.

Hurley, J. R. Parental malevolence and children's intelligence. *Journal of Consulting Psychology*, 1967, 31, 199-204.

Hurlock, E. B. *Developmental psychology.* New York: McGraw-Hill, 1968.

Hurst, J. G. Factor analysis of the Merrill-Palmer at two age levels: Structure and comparison. *Journal of Genetic Psychology*, 1963, 102, 231-244.

Husen, T. The influence of schooling upon IQ. *Theoria*, 1951, 17, 61-88.

Hutt, S. J., Lenard, H. G., & Prechtl, H. F. R. Psychophysiological studies in newborn infants. In L. P. Lipsitt & H. W. Reese (Eds.), *Advances in child development and behavior*. Vol. 4. New York: Academic Press, 1969. Pp. 128-173.

Huttenlocher, J., Eisenberg, K., & Strauss, S. Comprehension: Relation between perceived actor and logical subjects. *Journal of Verbal Learning and Verbal Behavior*, 1968, **7**, 527-530.

Huttenlocher, J., & Strauss, S. Comprehension and a statement's relation to the situation it describes. *Journal of Verbal Learning and Verbal Behavior*, 1968, 7, 300-304.

Hyatt, A. Genesis of the Arietidae. *Smithsonian Contributions to Knowledge*, 1890, *i-xi*, p. LX.

Hyman, H. H., & Sheatsley, P. B. Attitudes towards segregation. *Scientific American*, 1964, **211**, 16-23.

Inglis, J., Ankus, M. N., & Sykes, D. H. Age-related difference in learning and short-term memory from childhood to the senium. *Human Development*, 1968, **11**, 42-52. (a)

Inglis, J., Sykes, D. H., & Ankus, M. N. Age differences in short-term memory. In S. M. Chown & K. F. Riegel (Eds.), *Interdisciplinary topics in gerontology*. Vol. 1. *Psychological functioning in the normal aging and senile aged*. Basel: Karger, 1968. Pp. 18-43. (b)

Inhelder, B., & Piaget, J. *The growth of logical thinking from childhood to adolescence*. New York: Basic Books, 1958.

Inhelder, B., & Piaget, J. *The early growth of logic in the child*. London: Routledge & Kegan, 1964.

Institute of Human Development. *Annual report, 1967-68*. Berkeley: University of California, 1968.

Irvine, E. E. Children in Kibbutzim: Thirteen years after. *Journal of Child Psychology and Psychiatry*, 1966, 7, 167-178.

Irwin, O. C. Amount and nature of activities of newborn infants under constant external stimulating conditions during the first ten days of life. *Genetic Psychology Monographs*, 1930, 8, 1-92.

Irwin, O. C., & Chen, H. P. A reliability study of speech sounds observed in the crying of newborn infants. *Child Development*, 1941, **12**, 351-368.

Irzhanskaia, K. N., & Felberbaum, R. A. Effects of stimulus sensitization on ease of conditioning. In Y. Brackbill & G. G. Thompson (Eds.), *Behavior in infancy and early childhood: A book of readings*. New York: Free Press, 1967. Pp. 246-249.

Ives, W. C., & Shilling, C. W. Object identification with the Hecht-Schlaer adaptometer. Report, December 26, 1941, New London, Connecticut, S24-1 (102) WCI/fgl/aam.

Jackson, C. L. Factor structure of the Wechsler Intelligence scale for children and selected reference tests at pre-school level and after first grade: A longitudinal study. *Dissertation Abstracts*, 1965, *29*, 1125.

Jackson, D. N. Multimethod factor analysis in the evaluation of convergent and discriminant validity. *Psychological Bulletin*, 1969, *72*, 30-49.

Jacobs, J. Experiments on "Prehension." *Mind*, 1887, **12**, 75-79.

James, W. *Principles of psychology*. New York: Holt, 1890. 2 vols.

James, W. Letter to Rosina Emmet, August 2, 1896. Cited by G. W. Allen, *William James*. New York: Viking Press, 1967. P. 384.

James, W. *Talks to teachers on psychology and to students on some of life's ideals*. New York: Holt, 1899.

Janke, W. Veränderungen einfacher psychomotorischer Leistungen durch Übung. *Psychologische Beiträge*, 1965, 8, 314-342.

Janke, W., & Ritzmann, H. Untersuchungen uber den Einfluss von pharmakologischen Belastungsbedingungen auf einfache psychomotorische Leistungen. *Archiv für die Gesamte Psychologie*, 1964, **116**, 33-57.

Jastrow J. Some anthropological and psychological tests on college students—a preliminary survey. *American Journal of Psychology*, 1891-1892, **4**, 902-910.

Jeffrey, W. E. The effects of verbal and nonverbal responses in mediating an instrumental act. *Journal of Experimental Psychology*, 1953, **45**, 327-333.

Jeffrey, W. E. Variables affecting reversal-shifts in young children. *American Journal of Psychology*, 1965, **78**, 589-595.

Jeffrey, W. E., & Skager, R. W. Effect of incentive conditions on stimulus generalization in children. *Child Development*, 1962, **33**, 865-870.

Jenkins, J. J., & Palermo, D. S. Mediation processes and the acquisition of linguistic structure. *Monographs of the Society for Research in Child Development*, 1964, **29**(1, Whole No. 92).

Jensen, A. R. Estimation of the limits of heritability of traits by comparison of monozygotic and dizygotic twins. *Proceedings of the National Academy of Science, U.S.*, 1967. Pp. 149-157.

Jensen, A. R. Social class, race, and genetics: Implications for education. *American Educational Research Journal*, 1968, **5**, 1-42.

Jensen, A. R. How much can we boost I.Q. and scholastic achievement? *Harvard Educational Review*, 1969, **39**, 1-123.

Jensen, A. R., & Rohwer, W. D., Jr. Syntactical mediation of serial and paired-associate learning as a function of age. *Child Development*, 1965, **36**, 601-608.

Jerome E. A. Age and learning—experimental studies. In J. E. Birren (Ed.), *Handbook of aging and the individual*. Chicago: University of Chicago Press, 1959. Pp. 655-699.

Jesperson, O. *Analytic syntax*. London: Allen and Unwin, 1937.

Johnson, G. J., & Penney, R. K. Transfer effects of mixed and unmixed list designs in paired-associate learning of children. *Psychonomic Science*, 1965, **2**, 171-172.

Johnson, W. A. S-R, R-S independence and the interference potency of latent R-S associations. *Journal of Experimental Psychology*, 1967, **74**, 511-516.

Johnston, W. A. Bidirectional interference in an A-B, C-B paradigm. *Journal of Verbal Learning and Verbal Behavior*, 1968, **7**, 305-311.

Jones, H. E. Consistency and change in early maturity. *Vita Humana*, 1958, **1**, 43-51. (a)

Jones, H. E. Problems of method in longitudinal research. *Vita Humana*, 1958, **1**, 93-99. (b)

Jones, H. E. Trends in mental abilities. *Institute of Child Welfare, University of California*, 1958. (c)

Jones, H. E. Intelligence and problem solving. In J. E. Birren (Ed.), *Handbook of aging and the individual*. Chicago: University of Chicago Press, 1959. Pp. 700-738.

Jones, H. E., & Conrad, H. S. The growth and decline of intelligence: A study of a homogenous group between the ages of ten and sixty. *Genetic Psychology Monographs*, 1933, **13**, 223-298.

Jones, H. E., Conrad, H. S., & Horn, A. Psychological studies of motion pictures. II. Observation and recall as a function of age. *University of California Publications in Psychology*, 1928, **3**, 225-243.

Jones, L. V. A factor analysis of the Stanford-Binet at four age levels. *Psychometrika*, 1949, **14**, 299-331.

Jones, L. V. Analysis of variance in its multivariate developments. In R. B. Cattell (Ed.), *Handbook of multivariate experimental psychology*. Chicago: Rand McNally, 1966. Pp. 244-266.

Jones, M. C. A report on the three growth studies at the University of California. *Gerontologist*, 1967, **7**, 49-54.

Kagan, J. American longitudinal research on psychological development. *Child Development*, 1964, **35**, 1-32.

Kagan, J. Personality and intellectual development in the school-aged child. In I. L. Janis, G. F. Mahl, J. Kagan, & R. R. Holt. *Personality*. New York: Harcourt, Brace and World, 1969. Pp. 519-540.

Kagan, J., & Freeman, M. Relation of childhood intelligence, maternal behaviors and social class to behavior during adolescence. *Child Development*, 1963, **34**, 899-911.

Kagan, J., Henker, B., Hen-Tov, A., Levine, J., & Lewis, M. Infants' differential reactions to familiar and distorted faces. *Child Development*, 1966, **37**, 519-632.

Kagan, J., & Moss, H. A. *Birth to maturity: A study in psychological development*. New York: Wiley, 1962.

Kahneman, D. Method, findings and theory in studies of visual masking. *Psychological Bulletin*, 1968, **70**, 404-425.

Kallina, H. Das Unbehagen in der Faktorenanalyse. *Psychologische Beiträge*, 1967, **10**, 81-86.

Kallmann, F. J., & Jarvik, L. F. Individual differences in constitution and genetic background. In J. E. Birren (Ed.), *Handbook of aging and the individual*. Chicago: University of Chicago Press, 1959. Pp. 216-263.

Kamin, L. J. Differential changes in mental abilities in old age. *Journal of Gerontology*, 1957, **12**, 66-70.

Kanak, N. J., & Dean, M. F. Transfer mechanisms in verbal discrimination. *Journal of Experimental Psychology*, 1969, **79**, 300-307.

Kanner, L. Emotionally disturbed children: A historical review. *Child Development*, 1962, **33**, 97-102.

Kantor, J. R. *An objective psychology of grammar*. Bloomington, Ind.: Principia Press, 1935.

Kaplan, A. *The conduct of inquiry*. San Francisco: Chandler, 1964.

Kaplan, B. The study of language in psychiatry. The comparative developmental approach and its application to symbolization and language in psychopathology. In S. Arieti (Ed.), *American handbook of psychiatry*. Vol. 3. New York: Basic Books, 1966. Pp. 659-688.

Karelitz, S., & Fisichelli, V. R. The cry thresholds of normal infants and those with brain damage. *Journal of Pediatrics*, 1962, **61**, 679-685.

Karelitz, S., Karelitz, R., & Rosenfeld, L. S. Infants' vocalizations and their significance. In P. W. Bowman & H. V. Mautner (Eds.), *Mental retardation: Proceedings of the first international medical conference*. New York: Grune & Stratton, 1960. Pp. 439-446.

Katz, E. W., & Brent, S. B. Understanding connectives. *Journal of Verbal Learning and Verbal Behavior*, 1968, **7**, 501-509.

Kausler, D. H. *Readings in verbal learning: Contemporary theory and research*. New York: Wiley, 1966.

Kausler D. H., Fulkerson, F. E., & Eschenbrenner, A. J., Jr. Unlearning of list 1 right items in verbal-discrimination transfer. *Journal of Experimental Psychology*, 1967, **75**, 379-385.

Kausler, D. H., & Gotway, M. A. R-S learning in children. *Journal of Experimental Child Psychology*, 1969, **8**, 190-194.

Kausler, D. H., & Lair, C. V. R-S ("backward") paired-associate learning in elderly subjects. *Journal of Gerontology*, 1965, **20**, 29-31.

Kausler, D. H., & Lair, C. V. Associative strength and paired-associate learning in elderly subjects. *Journal of Gerontology*, 1966, **21**, 278-280.

Kausler, D. H., & Lair, C. V. Informative feedback conditions and verbal-discrimination learning in elderly subjects. *Psychonomic Science*, 1968, **10**, 193-194.

Kausler, D. H., & Sardello, R. J. Item recall in verbal-discrimination learning as related to pronunciation and degree of practice. *Psychonomic Science*, 1967, 7, 285-286.

Kausler, D. H., & Trapp, E. P. Methodological considerations in the construct validation of drive-oriented scales. *Psychological Bulletin*, 1959, 56, 152-157.

Kausler, D. H., & Trapp, E. P. Motivation and cue utilization in intentional and incidental learning. *Psychological Review*, 1960, 67, 373-379.

Kawi, A., & Pasamanick, B. Association of factors of pregnancy with reading disorders in childhood. *Journal of the American Medical Association*, 1958, 166, 1420-1423.

Kaye, H. Theories of learning and aging. In J. E. Birren (Ed.), *Handbook of aging and the individual*. Chicago: University of Chicago Press, 1959. Pp. 614-654.

Kebbon, L. *The structure of abilities at lower levels of intelligence*. Stockholm: Skandinaviska Test Forlaget, 1965.

Keen, R. E., Chase, H. H., & Graham, F. K. Twenty-four hour retention by neonates of an habituated heart rate response. *Psychonomic Science*, 1965, 2, 265-266.

Keeney, T. J., Cannizzo, S. R., & Flavell J. H. Spontaneous and induced verbal rehearsal in a recall task. *Child Development*, 1967, 38, 953-966.

Kelley, H. P. Memory abilities: A factor analysis. *Psychometric Monographs*, 1964, No. 11.

Kelley, T. L. *Crossroads in the mind of man: A study of differentiable mental abilities*. Stanford, Calif.: Stanford University Press, 1928.

Kellogg, W. N., & Kellogg, L. A. *The ape and the child*. New York: McGraw-Hill, 1933.

Kelly, E. L. Consistency of the adult personality. *American Psychologist*, 1955, 10, 659-681.

Kelly, G. *A theory of personality*. New York: Norton, 1963.

Kendler, H. H., & Kendler, T. S. Vertical and horizontal processes in human concept learning. *Psychological Review*, 1962, 69, 1-16.

Kennedy, W. A., Van de Riet, V., & White, J. A normative sample of intelligence and achievement of Negro elementary school children in the Southeastern United States. *Monographs of the Society for Research in Child Development*, 1963, 28 (Whole No. 6).

Kenny, P. B. A note on the formal requirements for factorial studies of differentiation of abilities with age. *Australian Journal of Education*, 1958, 2, 121-122.

Kenny, P. B. & Coltheart, F. M. M. The effect of sampling restriction on factor patterns. *Australian Journal of Psychology*, 1960, 12, 58-69.

Keppel, G. Verbal learning in children. *Psychological Bulletin*, 1964, 61, 63-80.

Keppel, G. Retroactive and proactive inhibition. In T. R. Dixon & D. L. Horton (Eds.), *Verbal behavior and general behavior theory*. Englewood Cliff, N.J.: Prentice-Hall, 1968. Pp. 172-213.

Keppel, G., & Underwood, B. J. Proactive inhibition in short-term retention of single items. *Journal of Verbal Learning and Verbal Behavior*, 1962, 1, 152-161. (a)

Keppel, G., & Underwood, B. J. Retroactive inhibition of R-S associations. *Journal of Experimental Psychology*, 1962, 64, 400-404. (b)

Keppel, G., & Zavortink, B. Unlearning and competition in serial learning. *Journal of Verbal Learning and Verbal Behavior*, 1968, 7, 142-147.

Kerlinger, F. N. The statistics of the individual child: The use of analysis of variance with child development data. *Child Development*, 1954, 25, 265-275.

Kessen, W. Research design in the study of developmental problems. In P. H. Mussen (Ed.), *Handbook of research methods in child development*. New York: Wiley, 1960. Pp. 36-70.

Kessen, W. Stages and structure in the study of children. *Monographs of the Society for Research in Child Development*, 1962, 27(2, Whole No. 104), 65-86.

Kessen, W. Questions for a theory of cognitive development. *Monographs of the Society for Research in Child Development*, 1966, **31**(5, Whole No. 107), 55-70.

Kidd, A. H., & Kidd, R. M. The development of auditory perception in children. In A. H. Kidd & J. L. Rivoire (Eds.), *Perceptual development in children*. New York: International Universities Press, 1966. Pp. 113-142.

Kimble, G. A., & Pennypacker, H. S. Eyelid conditioning in young and aged subjects. *Journal of Genetic Psychology*, 1963, **103**, 283-289.

King, W. L. Learning and utilization of conjunctive and diagnostic classification rules: A developmental study. *Journal of Experimental Child Psychology*, 1966, **63**, 217-231.

Kingsley, P. R., & Hagen, J. W. Induced versus spontaneous rehearsal in short-term memory in nursery school children. *Developmental Psychology*, 1969, **1**, 40-46.

Kirchner, W. R. Age differences in short-term retention of rapidly changing information. *Journal of Experimental Psychology*, 1958, **55**, 352-358.

Kirkpatrick, E. A. Individual tests of school children. *Psychological Review*, 1900, **7**, 274-280.

Klein, M. *The psychoanalysis of children.* New York: Norton, 1932.

Kleitman, N., & Blier, A. A. Color and form discrimination in the periphery of the retina. *American Journal of Psychology*, 1928, **85**, 178-190.

Klima, E. S., & Bellugi, U. Syntactic regularities in the speech of children. In J. Lyons & R. J. Wales (Eds.), *Psycholinguistics papers*. Edinburgh: Edinburgh University Press, 1966.

Klinger, N. K., & Palermo, D. S. Aural paired-associate learning in children as a function of free-associative strength. *Child Development*, 1967, **38**, 1143-1152.

Kodlin, D., & Thompson, D. J. An appraisal of the longitudinal approach to studies of growth and development. *Monographs of the Society for Research in Child Development*, 1958, **23**(1, Whole No. 67).

Kofsky, E. Developmental scalogram analysis of classificatory behavior. Unpublished doctoral dissertation, University of Rochester, 1963.

Koga, Y. & Morant, G. M. On the degree of association between reaction times in the case of different senses. *Biometrika*, 1923, **15**, 346-372.

Kohen-Raz, R. Scalogram analysis of some developmental sequences of infant behavior as measured by the Bayley Infant Scale of Mental Development. *Genetic Psychology Monographs*, 1967. **76**, 3-21.

Kohlberg, L. Development of moral character and moral ideology. In M. L. Hoffman & L. W. Hoffman (Eds.), *Review of child development research*. Vol. I. New York: Russell Sage Foundation, 1964. Pp. 383-432.

Kohlberg, L. Early education: A cognitive-developmental view. *Child Development*, 1968, **39**, 1014-1062.

Kohlberg, L. Continuities and discontinuities in childhood and adult moral development. *Human Development*, 1969, **12**, 93-120.

Koltsova, M. M. The physiological mechanisms underlying the development of generalization in the child. In Y. Brackbill & G. G. Thompson (Eds.), *Behavior in infancy and early childhood: A book of readings*. New York: Free Press, 1967. Pp. 250-258.

Koppenaal, R. J., Krull, A., & Katz, H. Age, interference, and forgetting. *Journal of Experimental Child Psychology*, 1964, **1**, 360-375.

Korchin, S. J., & Basowitz, H. Age differences in verbal learning. *Journal of Abnormal and Social Psychology*, 1958, **54**, 64-69.

Korenchevsky, V. *Physiological and pathological aging*. New York: Hafner, 1961.

Korner, A. F., Chuck, B., & Dontchos, S. Organismic determinants of spontaneous oral behavior in neonates. *Child Development*, 1968, **39**, 1145-1157.

Kotaskova, J. Faktorova analyza individualnich trendu vyvoje intelek tovrch schopnosti. *Psychologica, A Patopsychologica Diatata*, 1967, **3**, 5-15.

Krauskopf, J., Duryea, R. A., & Bitterman, M. E. Threshold for visual form: Further experiments *American Journal of Psychology*, 1954, **67**, 427-440.

Krechevsky, I. "Hypotheses" in rats. *Psychological Review*, 1932, **39**, 516-532.

Kristof, W. Orthogonal inter-battery factor analysis. *Psychometrika*, 1967, **32**, 199-27.

Kubo, Y. Mental and physical changes in old age. *Journal of Genetic Psychology*, 1938, **53**, 101-108.

Kuenne, M. R. Experimental investigation of the relation of language to transposition behavior in young children. *Journal of Experimental Psychology*, 1946, **36**, 471-490.

Kuhlen, R. G. Social change: A neglected factor in psychological studies of the life-span. *School and Society*, 1940, **52**, 14-16.

Kuhlen, R. G. Age and intelligence: The significance of cultural change in longitudinal vs. cross-sectional findings. *Vita Humana*, 1963, **6**, 113-124.

Kuhn, T. S. *The structure of scientific revolutions*. Chicago: University of Chicago Press, 1962.

Lacher, M. R., & Riegel, K. F. Visual recognition threshold for nouns as a function of instruction, type of word relation, and associative strength. *Journal of General Psychology*, 1970, in press.

Lachman, R. The model in theory construction. *Psychological Review*, 1960, **67**, 113-129.

Lachman, R. Machines, brains, and models. In S. Hook (Ed.), *Dimensions of mind. A symposium*. New York: Collier, 1961. Pp. 172-173.

Lair, C. V., Moon, W. H., & Kausler, D. H. Associative interference in the paired associate learning of middle aged and old subjects. *Developmental Psychology*, 1969, **1**, 548-552.

Lamb, S. M. *Outline of stratificational grammar*. Washington, D.C.: Georgetown University Press, 1966.

Lang P. J., & Buss, A. H. Psychological deficit in schizophrenia: II. Interference and activation. *Journal of Abnormal Psychology*, 1965, **70**, 77-106.

Langer, J. *Theories of development*. New York: Holt, Rinehart & Winston, 1969.

Lansing, A. I. General biology of senescence. In J. E. Birren (Ed.), *Handbook of aging and the individual*. Chicago: University of Chicago Press, 1959. Pp. 119-134.

Lashley, K. S. Persistent problems in the evaluation of the mind. *Quarterly Review of Biology*, 1949, **24**, 28-42.

Lashley, K. S. The problem of serial order in behavior. In S. Saporta (Ed.), *Psycholinguistics: A book of readings*. New York: Holt, Rinehart & Winston, 1961.

Laurence, M. W. Memory loss with age: A test of two strategies for its retardation. *Psychonomic Science*, 1967, **9**, 209-210.

Lawrence, D., & Coles, G. R. Accuracy of recognition with alternatives before and after the stimulus. *Journal of Experimental Psychology*, 1954, **47**, 208-214.

Lehman, H. C. *Age and achievement*. Princeton: Princeton University Press, 1953.

Lehr, U. Untersuchungen über Zukunftserwartungen und Zukunftsbefürchtungen älterer Menschen. In Österreichische Gesellschaft für Geriatrie (Ed.), *Proceedings of the VII international congress of gerontology*. Vienna, 1966. Pp. 249-252.

Lehr, U. Sozialpsychologische Aspekte der Heimübersiedlung älterer Mitbürger. In H. Thomae & U. Lehr (Eds.), *Altern: Probleme und Tatsachen*. Frankfurt a. M.: Akademische Verlagsgesellschaft, 1968. Pp. 439-460.

Lehr, U., & Dreher, G. Psychologische Probleme der Pensionierung. In H. Thomae & U. Lehr, (Eds.), *Altern: Probleme und Tatsachen*. Frankfurt a.M.: Akademische Verlagsgesellschaft, 1968. Pp. 345-369.

Lehr, U., & Thomae, H. Eine Längsschnittuntersuchung bei 30- bis 50-jährigen Angestellten. *Vita Humana*, 1958, **1**, 100-110.

Lehr, U., & Thomae, H. *Konflikt, seelische Belastung und Lebensalter. Forschungsberichte des Landes Nordrhein-Westfalen.* Köln (Opladen): Westdeutscher Verlag, 1965.

Lehr, U., & Thomae, H. Die Stellung des älteren Menschen in der Familie. In H. Thomae & U. Lehr (Eds.), *Altern: Probleme und Tatsachen.* Frankfurt a.M.: Akademische Verlagsgesellschaft, 1968. Pp. 381-409.

Lehtovaara, A. Beitrag zum Problem der Differenzierung der Begabungsstruktur. Einige Resultate einer finnischen Längsschnittuntersuchung bei 7- bis 15-jährigen. *Zeitschrift für Psychologie*, 1962, **166**, 42-56.

Leibowitz, H. W., & Gwozdecki, J. The magnitude of the Poggendorff illusion as a function of age. *Child Development*, 1967, **38**, 573-580.

Leibowitz, H. W., & Judisch, J. The relationship between age and the magnitude of the Ponzo illusion. *American Journal of Psychology*, 1967, **80**, 105-109.

Leicht, K. L., & Kausler, D. H. Functional stimulus learning as related to degree of practice and meaningfulness. *Journal of Experimental Psychology*, 1965, **69**, 100-101.

Leik, R. K., & Mathews, M. A scale for developmental processes. *American Sociological Review*, 1968, **33**, 62-75.

Lenneberg, E. H. *Biological foundations of language.* New York: Wiley, 1967.

Leopold, W. F. *Speech development of a bilingual child: A linguist's record.* Evanston, Ill.: Northwestern University, 1939-1949. 4 vols.

Lesser, H. S., Fifer, G., & Clark, D. H. Mental abilities of children from different social-class and cultural groups. *Monographs of the Society for Research in Child Development*, 1965, **30**, (Whole No 4.)

Levenstein, P., & Sunley, R. Stimulation of verbal interaction between disadvantaged mothers and children. *Journal of Orthopsychiatry*, 1968, **38**, 116-121.

Levine, M. A model of hypothesis behavior in discrimination learning set. *Psychological Review*, 1959, **66**, 353-366.

Levinson, B. M. Subcultural values and IQ stability. *Journal of Genetic Psychology*, 1961, **98**, 69-82.

Levinson, B. M. The W.A.I.S. quotient of subcultural deviation. *Journal of Genetic Psychology*, 1963, **100**, 103-131.

Levinson, B., & Reese, H. W. Patterns of discrimination learning set in preschool children, fifth-graders, college freshmen, and the aged. *Monographs of Society for Research in Child Development*, 1967, **32**(Whole No. 7).

Lewin, K. Eine dynamische Theorie des Schwachsinnigen. In Anonymous (Ed.), *Hommage au Dr. W. Decroly*, 1933. Pp. 313-350. [Republished in F. Weinert (Ed.), *Pädagogische Psychologie.* Cologne: Kiepenheuer & Witsch, 1968. Pp. 390-411.]

Lewin, K. *Dynamic theory of personality.* New York: McGraw-Hill, 1935.

Lewis, D. *Quantitative methods in psychology.* New York: McGraw-Hill, 1960.

Lewis, H. P. Spatial representation in drawing as a correlate of development and a basis for picture preference. *Journal of Genetic Psychology*, 1963, **102**, 95-107.

Lewis, M. M. *Infant speech: A study of the beginnings of language.* New York: Humanities Press, 1951.

Liebert, R. S., & Rudel, R. G. Auditory localization and adaptation to body tilt: A developmental study. *Child Development*, 1959, **30**, 81-90.

Lienert, G. A. Die Faktorenstruktur der Intelligenz als Funktion des Intelligenzniveaus. In H. Thomae (Ed.), *Bericht über den XXII. Kongress der Deutschen Gesellschaft für Psychologie in Heidelberg, 1959.* Göttingen: Hogrefe, 1960. Pp. 138-140.

Lienert, G. A. Factor structure of intelligence in 10, 18 and 50 years. In A. Wellek (Ed.), *Bericht über den XVI. Internationalen Kongress für Psychologie in Bonn, 1960.* Amsterdam: North-Holland Publ., 1961. P. 308. (a)

Lienert, G. A. Überprüfung und genetische Interpretation der Divergenzhypothese von Wewetzer. *Vita Humana*, 1961, **4**, 112-124. (b)

Lienert, G. A. Die Faktorenstruktur der Intelligenz als Funktion des Neurotizismus. *Zeitschrift für Experimentelle und Angewandte Psychologie*, 1963, **10**, 140-159.

Lienert, G. A. *Belastung und Regression.* Meisenheim a.G.: Hain, 1964.

Lienert, G. A. Mental age regression induced by lysergic acid diethylamide. *Journal of Psychology*, 1966, **63**, 3-11.

Lienert, G. A., & Crott, H. W. Studies on the factor structure of intelligence in children, adolescents and adults. *Vita Humana*, 1964, **7**, 147-163.

Lienert, G. A., & Faber, C. Über die Faktorenstruktur des HAWIK auf verschiedenen Alter- und Intelligenzniveaus. *Diagnostica*, 1963, **9**, 3-11.

Lindsay, R. B. Operationalism in physics. *Scientific Monthly*, 1954, **79**, 221-223. (Reprinted in P. G. Frank (Ed.), *The validation of scientific theories.* New York: Collier, 1961. Pp. 69-75.)

Lindsley, O. R. A behavioral measure of television viewing. *Journal of Advertising Research*, 1962, **2**, 2-12.

Lindsley, O. R., Hobika, J. H., & Etsten, B. E. Operant behavior during anesthesia recovery: A continuous and objective method. *Anesthesiology*, 1961, **22**, 937-946.

Lintz L., Fitzgerald, H. E., & Brackbill, Y. Conditioning the eyeblink response to sound in infants. *Psychonomic Science*, 1967, **7**, 405-406.

Lipsitt, L. P. Learning in the first year of life. In L. P. Lipsitt & C. C. Spiker (Eds.), *Advances in child development and behavior.* Vol. 1. New York: Academic Press, 1963. Pp. 147-195.

Lipsitt, L. P. Learning processes of human newborns. *Merrill-Palmer Quarterly*, 1966, **12**, 45-71.

Lipsitt, L. P. & Jacklin, C. N. Cardiac deceleration response to olfactory stimulation in human neonates. Paper presented at the meeting of the Psychonomic Society, St. Louis, November, 1969.

Lipsitt, L. P., & Kaye, H. Conditioned sucking in the human newborn. *Psychonomic Science*, 1964, **1**, 29-30.

Lipsitt, L. P., Kaye, H., & Bosack, T. N. Enhancement of neonatal sucking through reinforcement. *Journal of Experimental Child Psychology*, 1966, **4**, 163-168.

Lipsitt, L. P., & Levy, N. Electrotactual threshold in the neonate. *Child Development*, 1959, **30**, 547-554.

Lipsitt, L. P., Pederson, L. J., & DeLucia, C. A. Conjugate reinforcement of operant responding in infants. *Psychonomic Science*, 1966, **4**, 67-68.

Lipsitt, L. P., & Spears, W. C. Effects of anxiety and stress on children's paired-associate learning. *Psychonomic Science*, 1965, **3**, 553-554.

Lipton, E. L., Steinschneider, A., & Richmond, J. B. Autonomic function in the neonate: VII. Maturational changes in cardiac control. *Child Development*, 1966, **37**, 1-16.

Livesley, W. J., & Bromley, D. B. Studies in the developmental psychology of person perception. *Bulletin of the British Psychological Society*, 1967, **67**, 21A. (Abstract)

Loevinger, J. A. A systematic approach to the construction and evaluation of tests of ability. *Psychological Monographs*, 1947, **61**(4, Whole No. 285).

Loevinger, J. A. Models and measures of developmental variation. *Annals of the New York Academy of Sciences*, 1966, **134**, 585-590.

Longeot, F. Aspects différentiels de la psychologie génétique. *Bulletin de l'Institut Nationale de l'Étude du Travail et d'Orientation Professionnelle*, 1967, 23(Numero Special).

Longstreth, L. E. *Psychological development of the child.* New York: Ronald Press, 1968.

Loomis, D. J., & Hall, V. C. The effects of age and overlearning in an A-B, A-C design using high- and low-H value. *Journal of Verbal Learning and Verbal Behavior*, 1968, 7, 182-188.

Loranger, A. W., & Misiak, H. Critical flicker frequency and some intellectual functions in old age. *Journal of Gerontology*, 1959, 14, 323-327.

Lorge, I. The influence of the test upon the nature of mental decline as a function of old age. *Journal of Educational Psychology*, 1936, 27, 100-110.

Luria, A. R. *The role of speech in the regulation of normal and abnormal behavior.* New York: Liveright, 1961.

Maccoby, E. E., & Hagen, J. W. Effect of distraction upon central versus incidental recall: Developmental trends. *Journal of Experimental Child Psychology*, 1965, 2, 280-289.

Mackie, J. B., Maxwell, A., & Rafferty, F. T. Psychological development of culturally disadvantaged Negro kindergarten children: A study of the selective influences of family and school variables. *American Journal of Orthopsychiatry*, 1967, 37, 367-368.

Maddox, G. L. Disengagement theory: A critical evaluation. *Gerontologist*, 1964, 4, 80-82, 103.

Magladery, J. W. Neurophysiology of aging. In J. E. Birren (Ed.), *Handbook of aging and the individual.* Chicago: University of Chicago Press, 1959. Pp. 173-183.

Maher, B. A. Position errors and primitive thinking in the Progressive Matrices Test. *American Journal of Mental Deficiency*, 1960, 64, 1016-1020.

Maier, H. W. *Three theories of child development: The contributions of Erik H. Erikson, Jean Piaget, and Robert R. Sears, and their applications.* New York: Harper & Row, 1965.

Maleci, O., & Montonari, M. Il Test Wechsler-Bellevue in soggetti anziani normali. *Archivio di Psichologia, Neurologia e Psichiatria*, 1953, 14, 591-602.

Maleci, O., & Pessina, G. Alcune elaborazioni del punteggio Wechsler-Bellevue in soggetti normali della provincia di podora. *Rivista di Patologia Nervosa e Mentale*, 1954, 75, 1-23.

Mandler, G. From association to structure. *Psychological Review*, 1962, 69, 415-427.

Mandler, G., & Kessen, W. *The language of psychology.* New York: Wiley, 1959.

Mann, I. *The development of the human eye.* (3rd ed.) New York: Grune & Stratton, 1964.

Marbe, K. *Praktische Psychologie der Unfälle und Betriebsschäden.* Munich: Oldenbourg, 1926.

Margenau, H. Interpretations and misinterpretations of operationalism. *Scientific Monthly*, 1954, 79, 209-210. [Reprinted in P. G. Frank (Ed.), *The validation of scientific theories.* New York: Collier, 1961. Pp. 45-46.]

Margis, P. Das Problem und die Methoden der Psychographie. *Zeitschrift für Angewandte Psychologie und Psychologische Sammelforschung*, 1911, 5, 409-451.

Marinesco, G., & Kreindler, A. Des réflexes conditionnels. III. Applications des réflexes conditionnels à certains problèmes cliniques. *Journal de Psychologie Normale et Pathologique*, 1934, 31, 222-291.

Marquis, D. P. Learning in the neonate: The modification of behavior under three feeding schedules. *Journal of Experimental Psychology*, 1941, 29, 263-282.

Marshall, A. J., & Day, R. H. The resolution of grating test objects during the course of dark adaptation. *Australian Journal of Psychology*, 1951, 3, 1-21.

Martin, E. Transfer of verbal paired associates. *Psychological Review*, 1965, 72, 327-343.

Martin, E. Stimulus meaningfulness and paired-associate transfer: An encoding variability hypothesis. *Psychological Review*, 1968, **75**, 421-441.

Martin, W. E. Singularity and stability of profiles of social behavior. In C. B. Stendler (Ed.), *Readings in child behavior and development*. New York: Harcourt, Brace & World, 1964. Pp. 448-466.

Martini, F. *Deutsche Literaturgeschichte*. (15th ed.) Stuttgart: Kramer, 1968.

Matson, F. *The broken image*. New York: Braziller, 1964.

Maudsley, H. *The pathology of the mind*. New York: Appleton, 1880.

Maxwell, A. E. A factor analysis of the Wechsler intelligence scale for children. *British Journal of Educational Psychology*, 1959, **29**, 237-241.

Maxwell, A. E. Discrepancies between the pattern of abilities for normal and neurotic children. *Journal of Mental Sciences*, 1961, **107**, 300-307. (a)

Maxwell, A. E. Trends in cognitive ability in the older age ranges. *Journal of Abnormal and Social Psychology*, 1961, **61**, 449-452. (b)

McCahan, G. P. Mental organization in the age range 9 to 17 years. *Dissertation Abstracts*, 1953, **13**, 123.

McCall, R. B., & Kagan, J. Stimulus-schema discrepancy and attention in the infant. *Journal of Experimental Child Psychology*, 1967, **5**, 381-390.

McCandless, B. R., & Spiker, C. C. Experimental research in child psychology. *Child Development*, 1956, **27**, 75-80.

McCarthy, D. Language development in children. In L. Carmichael (Ed.), *Manual of child psychology*. (2nd ed.) New York: Wiley, 1954. Pp. 492-630.

McCullers, J. C. Associative strength and degree of interference in children's verbal paired-associate learning. *Journal of Experimental Child Psychology*, 1967, **5**, 58-68.

McCulloch, T. L. The retarded child grows up: Psychological aspects of aging. *American Journal of Mental Deficiency*, 1957, **62**, 201-208.

McCulloch, W. S. Mysterium iniquitatis—of sinful man aspiring into the place of God. *Scientific Monthly*, 1955, **80**, 35-39. [Reprinted in P. G. Frank (Ed.), *The validation of scientific theories*. New York: Collier, 1961. Pp. 148-156.]

McDonald, R. P., & Burr, E. S. A comparison of four methods of constructing factor scores. *Psychometrika*, 1967, **32**, 381-401.

McFarland, R. A. The sensory and perceptual processes in aging. In K. W. Schaie (Ed.), *Theory and methods of research on aging*. Morgantown, W. Va.: West Virginia University Library, 1968, Pp. 5-52.

McGeoch, J. A. *The psychology of human learning*. New York: Longmans, 1942.

McGovern, J. B. Extinction of associations in four transfer paradigms. *Psychological Monographs*, 1964, **78**(16, Whole No. 593).

McGraw, M. *The neuromuscular maturation of the human infant*. New York: Columbia University Press, 1943.

McHugh, R. B., & Owens, W. A. Age changes in mental organization—a longitudinal study. *Journal of Gerontology*, 1954, **9**, 296-302.

McNeill, D. Developmental Psycholinguistics. In F. Smith & G. A. Miller (Eds.), *The genesis of language*. Cambridge, Mass.: Massachusetts Institute of Technology Press, 1966, Pp. 15-84.

McNeill, D. On theories of language acquisition. In T. R. Dixon & D. L. Horton (Eds.), *Verbal behavior and general behavior theory*. New York: Prentice-Hall, 1968. Pp. 406-420.

McNeill, D. The development of language. In P. H. Mussen (Ed.), *Carmichael's manual of child psychology*. New York: Wiley, 1970, in press. (a)

McNeill, D. The capacity for grammatical development in children. In D. Slobin (Ed.), *The ontogenesis of grammar: Some facts and several theories*. New York: Academic Press, 1970, in press. (b)

McNeill, D., & McNeill, N. B. What does a child mean by "no?" In E. M. Zale (Ed.), *Proceedings of the conference on language and language behavior.* New York: Appleton-Century-Crofts, 1968.

McNemar, Q. The equivalence of the general factors found for successive levels on the new Stanford revision. *Psychological Bulletin*, 1938, **35**, 657. (Abstract)

McNemar, Q. *The revision of the Stanford-Binet Scale: An analysis of the standardization data.* Boston: Houghton Mifflin, 1942.

Mead, M. *Coming of age in Samoa.* New York: Morrow, 1928.

Mead, M. *Growing up in New Guinea.* New York: Morrow, 1930.

Mednick, S. A., & Lehtinen, L. C. Stimulus generalization as a function of age in children. *Journal of Experimental Psychology*, 1957, **53**, 180-183.

Meely, B. E., Olson, F. A., Halwes, T. G., & Flavell, J. H. Production deficiency in young children's clustered recall. *Developmental Psychology*, 1969, **1**, 26-34.

Meili, G., & Meili, R. Forms of behavior related to disturbance in infancy. Part I and II. Unpublished manuscript, University of Bern, 1969.

Meili, R. Beobachtungen über charakterologisch relevante Verhaltensweisen im 3. und 4. Lebensmonat. *Schweizerische Zeitschrift für Psychologie und ihre Anwendung*, 1953, **12**, 257-275.

Meili, R. Angstentstehung bei kleinen Kindern. *Schweizerische Zeitschrift für Psychologie und ihre Anwendung*, 1955, **14**, 159-212.

Meili, R. *Anfänge der Charakterentwicklung.* Bern: Huber, 1957.

Meili, R., Lohr, W., & Pulver, U. Über den Ursprung von Persönlichkeitseigenschaften. *Schweizerische Zeitschrift für Psychologie und ihre Anwendung*, 1964, **23**, 1-15.

Melametsa, L. The influence of training on the level of test performance and the factor structure of intelligence tests. *Scandinavian Journal of Psychology*, 1965, **6**, 19-25.

Melton, A. W. Comments on Professor Postman's paper. In C. N. Cofer (Ed.), *Verbal learning and verbal behavior.* New York: McGraw-Hill, 1961.

Melton, A. W., & Irwin, J. M. The influence of degree of interpolated learning on retroactive inhibition and the overt transfer of specific responses. *American Journal of Psychology*, 1940, **53**, 173-203.

Menyuk, P. Syntactic rules used by children from preschool through first grade. *Child Development*, 1964, **35**, 533-546.

Mering O. V., & Weniger, F. L. Social-cultural background of the aging individual. In J. E. Birren (Ed.), *Handbook of aging and the individual.* Chicago: University of Chicago Press, 1959. Pp. 279-335.

Merleau-Ponty, M. *The structure of behavior.* Boston: Beacon Press, 1963.

Mermelstein, E., & Shulman, L. S. Lack of formal schooling and acquisition of conservation. *Child Development*, 1967, **38**, 39-52.

Merrill, M. The relationship of individual growth to average growth. *Human Biology*, 1931, **3**, 37-70.

Merz, F., & Kalveram, K. R. Kritik der Differenzierungshypothese der Intelligenz. *Archiv für die Gesamte Psychologie*, 1965, **117**, 287-295.

Meyer, W. J., & Bendig, A. W. A longitudinal study of the primary mental abilities test. *Journal of Educational Psychology*, 1961, **52**, 50-60.

Meyers, C. E., & Dingman, H. F. The structure of abilities at the preschool ages: Hypothesized domains. *Psychological Bulletin*, 1960, **57**, 514-532.

Meyers, W. J., & Cantor, G. N. Observing and cardiac responses of human infants to visual stimuli. *Journal of Experimental Child Psychology*, 1967, **5**, 16-25.

Miles, C. C. Influence of speed and age on intelligence scores of adults. *Journal of General Psychology*, 1934, **10**, 208-210.

Miles, C. C., & Miles, W. R. The correlation of intelligence scores and chronological age from early to late maturity. *American Journal of Psychology*, 1932, **44**, 44-78.

Miles, W. R. Measures of certain human abilities through the life-span. *Proceedings of the National Academy of Sciences, U.S.*, 1931, **17**, 627-632.

Miles, W. R. Age and human ability. *Psychological Review*, 1933, **40**, 99-123.

Miles, W. R. Psychological aspects of aging. In E. V. Cowdry (Ed.), *Problems of aging*. (2nd ed.) Baltimore: Williams & Wilkins, 1942.

Milgram, N. A. Verbal context versus visual compound in paired-associate learning by children. *Journal of Experimental Child Psychology*, 1967, **5**, 597-603.

Milholland, J. E. Four kinds of reproducibility in scale analysis. *Educational and Psychological Measurement*, 1955, **15**, 478-482.

Miller, F. M., & Raven, J. C. The influence of positional factors on the choice of answers to perceptual intelligence tests. *British Journal of Medical Psychology*, 1939, **18**, 35-39.

Miller, G. A. *Language and communication*. New York: McGraw-Hill, 1951.

Miller, G. A. The magical number seven, plus or minus two: Some limits to our capacity for processing information. *Psychological Review*, 1956, **63**, 81-97.

Miller, G. A., & McNeill, D. Psycholinguistics. In G. Lindzey & E. Aronson (Eds.), *The handbook of social psychology*. Vol. 3. (2nd ed.) Reading, Mass.: Addison-Wesley, 1969.

Miller, J. G. Toward a general theory for the behavioral sciences. *American Psychologist*, 1955, **10**, 513-531.

Miller, N. E., & Dollard, J. *Social learning and imitation*. New Haven: Yale University Press, 1941.

Miller. W. R. Patterns of grammatical development in child language. In *Proceedings of the 9th international congress on linguistics*. The Hague: Mouton, 1964. (a)

Miller, W. R. The acquisition of grammatical rules by children. Paper presented at the annual meeting of the Linguistics Society of America, New York, December 1964. (b)

Miller, W. R., & Ervin, S. M. The development of grammar in child language. *Monograph of the Society for Research in Child Development*, 1964, **29**, 9-34.

Miner, J. B. *Intelligence in the United States*. New York: Springer, 1956.

Mishima, J., & Inoue, K. A study on development of visual memory. *Experimental Psychology and Research*, 1966, **8**, 62-71.

Mitchell, J. V., Jr. A comparison of the factorial structure of cognitive functions for a high and low status group. *Journal of Educational Psychology*, 1956, **47**, 397-414.

Moede, W. Kraftfahreignungsprüfungen beim deutschen Heer 1915-1918. *Industrielle Psychotechnik*, 1926, **3**, 23.

Moers, M. *Die Entwicklungsphasen des Menschlichen Lebens*. Ratingen: Henn, 1953.

Mooney, C. M. Age in the development of closure ability in children. *Canadian Journal of Psychology*, 1957, **11**, 219-226.

Moore, K. C. The mental development of a child. *Psychological Review*, 1896, **1**(Whole No. 3).

Moore, T. Language and intelligence: A longitudinal study of the first eight years. *Human Development*, 1967, **10**, 88-106.

Mowrer, O. H. *Learning theory and behavior*. New York: Wiley, 1960.

Mukherjee, B. N. The factorial structure of aptitude tests at successive grade levels. *British Journal of Statistical Psychology*, 1962, **15**, 59-69.

Munn, N. L. *The evolution and growth of human behavior*. Boston: Houghton Mifflin, 1965.

Munnichs, J. M. A. A short history of psychogerontology. *Human Development*, 1966, **9**, 230-245.

Munsinger, H., & Gummerman, K. Simultaneous visual detection and recognition. *Perception & Psychophysics*, 1968, **3**, 383-386.

Munsinger, H., & Weir, M. Infants' and young children's preference for complexity. *Journal of Experimental Child Psychology*, 1967, **5**, 69-73.

Münsterberg, H. Zur Individual Psychologie. *Zentralblatt für Nervenheilkunde und Psychiatrie*, 1891, **14**, 196-198.

Murchison, C. *The foundations of experimental psychology*. Worcester, Mass.: Clark University Press, 1929. (a)

Murchison, C. *The psychological register*. Worcester, Mass.: Clark University Press, 1929. (b)

Murchison, C. (Ed.) *Handbook of child psychology*. Worcester, Mass.: Clark University Press, 1931.

Murdock, B. B., Jr. Proactive inhibition in short-term memory. *Journal of Experimental Psychology*, 1964, **68**, 184-189.

Mussen, P. H. (Ed.) *Handbook of research methods in child development*. New York: Wiley, 1960.

Mussen, P. H., Conger, H. J., & Kagan, J. *Child development and personality*. (2nd ed.) New York: Harper & Row, 1963.

Myklebust, H. R., & Johnson, D. Dyslexia in children. *Exceptional Children*, 1962, **29**, 14-25.

Nagel, E. Determinism and development. In D. B. Harris (Ed.), *The concept of development*. Minneapolis: University of Minnesota Press, 1957. Pp. 15-24.

Neimark, E. D., & Lewis, N. The development of topical problem-solving strategies. *Child Development*, 1967, **38**, 107-110.

Nesselroade, J. R. A model for psychological states, moods, and role sets. Paper presented at the conference on Modern Personality Theory, University of Illinois, November 1967.

Nesselroade. J. R. Theory of psychological states and mood action. In R. B. Cattell (Ed.), *Handbook of modern personality study*. Chicago: Aldine Press, 1970, in press.

Nesselroade, J. R., & Baltes, P. B. On a dilemma of comparative factor analysis: A study of factor matching based on random data. *Educational and Psychological Measurement*, 1970, in press.

Neugarten, B. L. Adult personality: Toward a psychology of the life-cycle. Paper presented at the meeting of the American Psychological Association, New York, September 1966. (a)

Neugarten, B. L. Adult personality: A developmental view. *Human Development*, 1966, **9**, 61-73. (b)

Neugarten, B. L. Adaptation and the life cycle. Paper presented at the meeting of the Foundations Fund for Research in Psychiatry, Puerto Rico, June 1968.

Neugarten, B. L. Continuities and discontinuities of psychological issues into adult life. *Human Development*, 1969, **12**, 121-130.

Nikkel, N., & Palermo, D. S. Effects of mediated associations in paired-associate learning of children. *Journal of Experimental Child Psychology*, 1965, **2**, 92-102.

Nissen, H. W. Phylogenetic comparison. In S. S. Stevens (Ed.), *Handbook of experimental psychology*. New York: Wiley, 1951. Pp. 347-386.

Noble, G. E. An analysis of meaning. *Psychological Review*, 1952, **59**, 421-430.

Noble, G. E., Baker, B. L., & Jones, T. A. Age and sex parameters in psychomotor learning. *Perceptual and Motor Skills*, 1964, **19**, 935-945.

Norcross, K. J. Effects on discrimination performance of similarity of previously acquired stimulus names. *Journal of Experimental Psychology*, 1958, **56**, 305-309.

Norcross, K. J., & Spiker, C. C. The effects of type of stimulus pretraining on discrimination performance in preschool children. *Child Development*, 1957, **28**, 79-84.

Norcross, K. J., & Spiker, C. C. The effects of mediated associations on transfer in paired-associate learning. *Journal of Experimental Psychology*, 1958, **55**, 129-134.

Norman, R. D., & Daley, M. F. Senescent changes in intellectual ability among superior women. *Journal of Gerontology*, 1959, **14**, 457-464.

Nunnally, J. C. *Psychometric theory*. New York: McGraw-Hill, 1967.

Nyssen, R., & Delys, L. Contributions a l'étude du problème du déclin intellectuel en fonction de l'âge. *Archives de Psychologie*, 1952, **33**, 295-310.

Odom, R. D., & Coon, R. C. The development of hypothesis testing. *Journal of Experimental Psychology*, 1966, **4**, 285-291.

Oerter, R. *Moderne Entwicklungspsychologie*. Donauwörth, Germany: Auer, 1967.

Oleron, P. Les composantes de l'intelligence d'après les recherches factorielles. Paris: Presses Universitaires de France, 1957.

Olton, R. M. The effect of a mnemonic upon the retention of paired-associate verbal material. *Journal of Verbal Learning and Verbal Behavior*, 1969, **8**, 43-48.

O'Neil, W. M. The stability of the main pattern of abilities with changing age. *Australian Journal of Psychology*, 1962, **14**, 1-8.

Osborne, R. T. Factor structure of the WISC at pre-school level and after first grade: A longitudinal analysis. *Psychological Reports*, 1965, **16**, 637-644.

Osborne, R. T., Anderson, H. E., & Hemberger, L. The stability of basic abilities at early age levels. *American Psychologist*, 1966, **21**, 662. (Abstract)

Osborne, R. T., & Lindsey, J. M. A longitudinal investigation of change in the factorial composition of intelligence with age in young school children. *Journal of Genetic Psychology*, 1967, **110**, 49-58.

Osborne R. T., & Sanders, W. B. Differential decline in Graduate Record Examination scores with age. *Journal of Genetic Psychology*, 1955, **87**, 309-316.

Osgood, C. E. Toward a wedding of insufficiencies. In T. R. Dixon & D. L. Horton (Eds.), *Verbal behavior and general behavior theory*. Englewood Cliffs, N.J.: Prentice-Hall, 1968. Pp. 495-519.

Osgood, C. E., & Sebeok, T. A. (Eds.) *Psycholinguistics: A survey of theory and research problems*. Baltimore: Waverly Press, 1954.

Over, R. Explanations of geometrical illusion. *Psychological Bulletin*, 1968, **70**, 545-562.

Overton, W. F., & Brodzinsky, D. Perceptual and verbal factors in the development of multiplicative classification. Paper presented at the meeting of the Eastern Psychological Association, Philadelphia, April 1969.

Owens, W. A. Age and mental abilities: A longitudinal study. *Genetic Psychology Monographs*, 1953, **48**, 3-54.

Owens, W. A. Age and mental ability: A second adult follow-up. *Journal of Educational Psychology*, 1966, **57**, 311-325.

Pacaud, S. Experimental research on the aging of psychological functions. In *Old age in the modern world*. Edinburgh: Livingstone, 1955. Pp. 279-290.

Palermo, D. S. Backward associations in the paired associate learning of fourth and sixth grade children. *Psychological Reports*, 1961, **9**, 227-233.

Palermo, D. S. Mediated association in a paired-associate transfer task. *Journal of Experimental Psychology*, 1962, **64**, 234-238.

Palermo, D. S. Mediated association in the paired-associate learning in children using heterogeneous and homogeneous lists. *Journal of Experimental Psychology*, 1966, **71**, 711-717.

Palermo, D. S. Imagery in children's learning: Discussion. Paper presented at the meeting of the Society for Research in Child Development, Santa Monica, California, March 1969.

Palermo, D. S. Language acquisition. In H. W. Reese & L. P. Lipsitt (Eds.), *Experimental child psychology*. New York: Academic Press, 1970, in press. (a)

Palermo, D. S. On learning to talk: Are principles derived from the learning laboratory applicable? In D. I. Slobin (Ed.), *The ontogenesis of grammar: Some facts and several theories*. New York: Academic Press, 1970, in press. (b)

Palermo, D. S., & Eberhart, V. L. On the learning of morphological rules: An experimental analogy. *Journal of Verbal Learning and Verbal Behaviour*, 1968, 7, 337-344.

Pap, A. *Elements of analytic philosophy*. New York: Macmillan, 1949.

Papousek, H. Conditioned head rotation reflexes in infants in the first months of life. *Acta Paediatrica*, 1961, 50, 565-576.

Papousek, H. Experimental studies of appetitional behavior in human newborns and infants. In H. W. Stevenson, E. H. Hess, & H. L. Rheingold (Eds.), *Early behavior: Comparative and developmental approaches*. New York: Wiley, 1967. Pp. 249-277.

Parrish, M., Lundy, R. M., & Leibowitz, H. W. Hypnotic age-regression and magnitudes of the Ponzo and Poggendorff Illusions. *Science*, 1968, 159, 1375-1376.

Pasamanick, B., & Knobloch, C. H. Brain and behavior: Brain damage and reproductive casuality. *American Journal of Orthopsychiatry*, 1960, 30, 298-305.

Pascal, R. *Die Autobiografie*. Stuttgart: Kohlhammer, 1965.

Pawlik, K. *Dimensionen des Verhaltens*. Huber: Bern, 1968.

Pederson, F. A., & Wender, P. H. Early social correlates of cognitive functioning in six-year-old boys. *Child Development*, 1968, 39, 185-193.

Peel, E. A. Evidence of a practical factor at the age of eleven. *British Journal of Psychology*, 1949, 19, 1-15.

Peel, E. A., & Graham, D. Differentiation of ability in primary school children. *Research Review*, 1951; 1, 40-48. (University of Durham, Institute of Education.)

Peel, E. A., & Graham, D. Differentiation of ability in primary school children. *Research Review*, 1952, 1, 31-34. (University of Durham, Institute of Education.)

Pepper, S. C. *World hypotheses*. Berkeley: University of California Press, 1942.

Pfaffmann, C. The pleasures of sensation. *Psychological Review*, 1960, 67, 253-268.

Phillippe, J. Jastrow—Exposition d'anthropologie de Chicago—tests Psychologique. *Annee Psychologique*, 1894, 1, 522-526.

Phillips, A. Diagnostic education. In R. A. Brotemarkle (Ed.), *Clinical psychology: Studies in honor of Lightner Witmer*. Philadelphia: University of Pennsylvania Press, 1931. Pp. 167-176.

Piaget, J. *The origin of intelligence in children*. New York: International Universities Press, 1936.

Piaget, J. *The psychology of intelligence*. London: Routledge & Kegan 1946.

Piaget, J. *Psychologie der Intelligenz*. Zürich: Rascher Verlag, 1947. (a)

Piaget, J. *La psychologie de l'intelligence*. Paris: Colin, 1947. (b)

Piaget, J. *The psychology of intelligence*. New York: Harcourt & Brace, 1950.

Piaget, J. *The language and thought of the child*. (3rd ed.) London: Routledge & Kegan, 1959.

Piaget, J. *Psychology of intelligence*. New Jersey: Littlefield & Adams, 1960.

Piaget J. *Les mécanismes perceptifs*. Paris: Presses Universitaires de France, 1961.

Piaget, J. Nécessité et signification des recherches comparatives en psychologie génétique. *International Journal of Psychology*, 1966, 1, 3-13.

Piaget, J. *Biologie et connaissance*. Paris: Gallimard, 1967.

Piaget, J. Quantification, conservation and nativism. *Science*, 1968, 162, 976-979.

Piaget, J., Maire, F., & Privat, F. Recherches sur le développement des perceptions: XVIII.

La resistance des bonnes formes a l'illusion de Muller-Lyer. *Archives de Psychologie*, 1954, **34**, 155-202.

Pikler, E. Some contributions to the study of the gross motor development of children. *Journal of Genetic Psychology*, 1968, **113**, 27-39.

Pinneau, S. R. *Changes in intelligence quotient from infancy to maturity*. Boston: Houghton Mifflin, 1961.

Pintner, R., & Anderson, M. M. The Muller-Lyer illusion with children and adults *Journal of Experimental Psychology*, 1916, **1**, 200-210.

Platt, L. & Parkes, A. S. Social and genetic influences on life and death. New York: Plenum Press, 1967.

Pollack, R. H. Simultaneous and successive presentation of elements of the Muller-Lyer figure and chronological age. *Perceptual and Motor Skills*, 1964, **19**, 303-310.

Pollack, R. H. Ontogenetic changes in perception. In D. E. Elkind & J. H. Flavell (Eds.), *Studies in cognitive development*. New York: Oxford University Press, 1969. Pp. 365-407.

Popper, K. R. *The logic of scientific discovery*. New York: Basic Books, 1959.

Popper, K. R. *Conjectures and refutations*. New York: Basic Books, 1962.

Poresky, R., & Doris, J. Brightness and visual acuity in infancy. Paper read at the meeting of the Eastern Psychological Association, Boston, April 1967.

Postman, L. The present status of interference theory. In C. N. Cofer (Ed.), *Verbal learning and verbal behavior*. New York: McGraw-Hill, 1961.

Postman, L. Short-term memory and incidental learning. In A. W. Melton (Ed.), *Categories of human learning*. New York: Academic Press, 1964. Pp. 146-201. (a)

Postman, L. Studies of learning to learn. II.: Changes in transfer as a function of method of practice and class of verbal materials. *Journal of Verbal Learning and Verbal Behavior*, 1964, **3**, 437-449. (b)

Postman, L. Differences between unmixed and mixed transfer designs as a function of paradigm. *Journal of Verbal Learning and Verbal Behavior*, 1966, **5**, 240-248.

Postman, L., & Greenbloom, R. Conditions of cue selection in the acquisition of paired-associate lists. *Journal of Experimental Psychology*, 1967, **73**, 91-100.

Postman, L., & Keppel, G. Retroactive inhibition in free recall. *Journal of Experimental Psychology*, 1967, **74**, 203-211.

Postman, L., Keppel, G., & Stark, K. Unlearning as a function of the relationship between successive response classes. *Journal of Experimental Psychology*, 1965, **69**, 111-118.

Postman, L., & Stark, K. Proactive inhibition as a function of the conditions of transfer. *Journal of Verbal Learning and Verbal Behavior*, 1964, **3**, 249-259.

Postman, L., Stark, K., & Fraser, J. Temporal changes in interference. *Journal of Verbal Learning and Verbal Behavior*, 1968, **7**, 672-694.

Prechtl, H. F. R. Brain and behavioural mechanisms in the human newborn infant. In R. J. Robinson (Ed.), *Brain and early behaviour*. London and New York: Academic Press, 1969. Pp. 115-131.

Pressey, S. L. The new division on maturity and old age. Its function and potential services. *American Psychologist*, 1948, **3**, 107-109.

Pressey, S. L. Sidney Leavitt Pressey. In E. G. Boring & G. Lindzey (Eds.), *A history of psychology in autobiography*. Vol. 5. New York: Appleton-Century-Crofts, 1967.

Pressey, S. L., Janney, J. E., & Kuhlen, J. E. *Life: A psychological survey*. New York: Harper, 1939.

Pressey, S. L., & Kuhlen, R. G. *Psychological development through the life span*. New York: Harper & Row, 1957.

Preyer, W. *Die Seele des Kindes*. Leipzig: Fernau, 1882.

Price, L. E. Learning and performance in a verbal paired-associate task with preschool children. *Psychological Reports*, 1963, **12**, 847-850.

Price L. E., Cobb, N. J., & Morin, N. J. Associative interference as a function of amount of first-task practice and stimulus similarity. *Journal of Experimental Child Psychology*, 1968, **6**, 202-211.

Pulver U., & Lang, A. Von der 'Störbarkeit' zur 'Schüchternheit' in der Entwicklung des Kindes. I. Verhaltensweisen der Erstklässler. *Schweizerische Zeitschrift für Psychologie und ihre Anwendung*, 1961, **20**, 329-344.

Punfrey, P. The growth of the schema of proportionality. *British Journal of Educational Psychology*, 1968, **38**, 202-204.

Quarterman, C. J., & Riegel, K. F. Age differences in the identification of concepts of the natural language. *Journal of Experimental Child Psychology*, 1968, **6**, 501-509.

Quereshi, M. Y. Patterns of psycholinguistic development during early and middle childhood. *Educational and Psychological Measurement*, 1967, **27**, 353-365. (a)

Quereshi, M. Y. The invariance of certain ability factors. *Educational and Psychological Measurement*, 1967, **27**, 803-810. (b)

Quetelet, A. *Sur L'homme et le développement de ses facultés.* Paris: Bachelier, 1835. 2 vols.

Quetelet, A. *Über den Menschen und die Entwicklung seiner Fähigkeiten.* Stuttgart: Schweizerbart's Verlagshandlung, 1838.

Rabbitt, P. Age and the use of structure in transmitted information. In G. A. Talland (Ed.), *Human aging and behavior.* New York: Academic Press, 1968. Pp. 75-92.

Radcliffe, J. A. WAIS factorial structure and factor scores for ages 18 to 54. *Australian Journal of Psychology*, 1966, **18**, 228-238.

Rajalakshmi, R., & Jeeves, M. Changes in tachistoscopic form perception as a function of age and intellectual status. *Journal of Gerontology*, 1963, **19**, 275-278.

Ransom, D. An index of future growth for divisions of A.P.A. *American Psychologist*, 1956, **11**, 14-20.

Rashevsky, N. Is the concept of an organism as a machine a useful one? *Scientific Monthly*, 1955, **80**, 31-35. [Reprinted in P. G. Frank (Ed.), *The validation of scientific theories.* New York: Collier, 1961. Pp. 142-148.]

Raven, J. C. *Progressive matrices (1938). Sets A, B, C, D and E.* London: Lewis, 1938.

Raven, J. C. The comparative assessment of intellectual ability. *British Journal of Psychology*, 1948, **39**, 12-19.

Raven, J. C. *Guide to the standard progressive matrices. Sets A, B, C, D and E.* London: Lewis, 1951.

Raven, J. C. *Guide to using the Mill Hill Vocabulary Scale with progressive matrices (1938).* London: Lewis, 1954.

Rawlings, T. D. *Mental organization as function of brightness.* (Doctoral dissertation, University of Kentucky) Ann arbor, Mich.: University Microfilms, 1956. No. 61-305.

Rawlings, T. D. Mental organization as function of brightness. *Dissertation Abstracts*, 1961, **21**, 2778.

Reese, H. W. Verbal mediation as a function of age level. *Psychological Bulletin*, 1962, **59**, 502-509.

Reese, H. W. Discrimination learning set and perceptual set in young children. *Child Development*, 1965, **36**, 153-161. (a)

Reese, H. W. Imagery in paired-associate learning in children. *Journal of Experimental Child Psychology*, 1965, **2**, 290-296. (b)

Reese, H. W. The scope of experimental child psychology. In H. W. Reese & L. P. Lipsitt (Eds.), *Experimental child psychology.* New York: Academic Press, 1970, in press.

Reichard, S. Mental organization and age level. *Archives of Psychology,* 1944, **41,** (Whole No. 295).

Reinert, G. Zur Problematik der faktoriellen Differenzierungshypothese der Intelligenz. In H. Heckhausen (Ed.), *Bericht über den 14. Kongress der Deutschen Gesellschaft für Psychologie in Wien, 1964.* Göttingen: Hogrefe, 1965. Pp. 167-173.

Reinert, G., Baltes, P. B., & Schmidt, L. R. Faktorenanalytische Untersuchungen zur Differenzierungshypothese der Intelligenz: Die Leistungsdifferenzierungshypothese. *Psychologische Forschung,* 1965, **28,** 246-300.

Reinert, G., Baltes, P. B., & Schmidt, L. R. Kritik einer Kritik der Differenzierungshypothese der Intelligenz. *Zeitschrift für Experimentelle und Angewandte Psychologie,* 1966, **13,** 602-610.

Reinert, G., & Tauscher, H. Zur Differenzierung optischer Wahrnehmungsfaktoren in Abhängigkeit vom Lebensalter. Eine Untersuchung an Schulkindern. Unpublished manuscript, Universität des Saarlandes, Saarbrücken, Germany, 1969.

Reisen, A. H. The development of visual perception in man and chimpanzee. *Science,* 1947, **106,** 107-108.

Reitan, R. M. The distribution according to age of a psychologic measure dependent upon organic brain functions. *Journal of Gerontology,* 1955, **10,** 338-340.

Reitan, R. M. A research program on the psychological effects of brain lesions in human beings. In N. R. Ellis (Ed.), *International review of research in mental retardation.* Vol. 1. New York: Academic Press, 1966. Pp. 153-218.

Reuchlin, M. L'intelligence: Conception génétique opératoire et conception factorielle. *Schweizerische Zeitschrift für Psychologie und ihre Anwendung,* 1964, **23,** 113-134.

Richards, T. W. Genetic emergence of factor specificity. *Psychometrika,* 1941, **6,** 37-42.

Richards, T. W., & Nelson, V. L. Abilities of infants during the first eighteen months. *Journal of Genetic Psychology,* 1939, **55,** 299-318.

Rickert, H. *Die Grenzen der naturwissenschaftlichen Begriffsbildung.* (5th ed.) Tübingen: Mohr, 1929.

Rieber, M., & Womack, M. The intelligence of preschool children as related to ethnic and demographic variables. *Exceptional Children,* 1968, **34,** 609-614.

Riegel, K. F. Untersuchung über intellektuelle Fähigkeiten älterer Menschen. Unpublished doctoral dissertation, University of Hamburg, 1957.

Riegel, K. F. Ergebnisse und Probleme der psychologischen Alternsforschung. Teil I & II. *Vita Humana,* 1958, **1,** 52-64, 204-243.

Riegel, K. F. Ergebnisse und Probleme der psychologischen Alternsforschung. Teil III. *Vita Humana,* 1959, **2,** 213-237. (a)

Riegel, K. F. A study on verbal achievements of older persons. *Journal of Gerontology,* 1959, **14,** 453-456. (b)

Riegel, K. F. Free associative responses to the 200 stimuli of the Michigan restricted association norms. Report No. 8, 1965, University of Michigan, USPHS Grant MH 07619, Center for Human Growth and Development. (a)

Riegel, K. F. The Michigan restricted association norms. Report No. 3, 1965, University of Michigan, USPHS Grant MH 07619, Center for Human Growth and Development. (b)

Riegel, K. F. *Der sprachliche Leistungstest SASKA.* Göttingen: Hogrefe, 1967.

Riegel, K. F. Changes in psycholinguistic performances with age. In G. A. Talland (Ed.), *Human aging and behavior.* New York: Academic Press, 1968, Pp. 239-279. (a)

Riegel, K. F. Some theoretical considerations of bilingual development. *Psychological Bulletin,* 1968, **70,** 647-670. (b)

Riegel, K. F. Untersuchungen sprachlicher Leistungen und ihrer Veränderungen. *Zeitschrift für Experimentelle und Angewandte Psychologie,* 1968, **15,** 649-692. (c)

Riegel, K. F., & Birren, J. E. Age differences in verbal associations. *Journal of Genetic Psychology*, 1966, **108**, 153-170.

Riegel, K. F., & Birren, J. E. Age differences in choice reaction times to verbal stimuli. *Gerontologia*, 1967, **13**, 1-13.

Riegel, K. F., & Riegel, R. M. An investigation into denotative aspects of word meaning. *Language and Speech*, 1963, **6**, 6-21.

Riegel, K. F., & Riegel, R. M. Changes in associative behavior during later years of life: A cross-sectional analysis. *Vita Humana*, 1964, **7**, 1-32.

Riegel, K. F., Riegel, R. M., & Meyer, G. Socio-psychological factors of aging: A cohort-sequential analysis. *Human Development*, 1967, **10**, 27-56.

Riegel, K. F., Riegel, R. M., Quarterman, C. J., & Smith, H. D. Developmental differences in word meaning and semantic structure. *Human Development*, 1968, **11**, 92-106.

Riegel, K. F., Riegel, R. M., & Skiba, G. Probleme der Anpassung in Alltag. *Vita Humana*, 1962, **5**, 234-245.

Riegel, K. F., & Zivian, A. Converging and diverging relations of the Michigan restricted and free association norms. Report No. 44, 1968, University of Michigan, USPHS Grant HD 01368, Center for Human Growth and Development.

Riegel, R. M. Faktorenanalyse des Hamburg-Wechsler-Intelligenz-Tests für Erwachsene (HAWIE) für die Altersstufen 20-34, 35-49, 50-64, und 65 Jahre und älter, *Diagnostica,* 1960, **6**, 41-66.

Riegel, R. M., & Riegel, K. F. Standardisierung des Hamburg-Wechsler-Intelligenztests für Erwachsene (HAWIE) für die Altersstufen über 50 Jahre. *Diagnostica*, 1959, **5**, 97-128.

Riegel, R. M., & Riegel, K. F. A comparison and reinterpretation of factor structures of the W-B, the WAIS, and the HAWIE on aged persons. *Journal of Consulting Psychology*, 1962, **26**, 31-37.

Rivoire, J. L., & Kidd, A. H. The development of perception of color, space, and movement in children. In A. H. Kidd & J. L. Rivoire (Eds.), *Perceptual development in children.* New York: International Universities Press, 1966. Pp. 81-112.

Robbins, L. C. The accuracy of parental recall of aspects of child development and of child rearing practices. *Journal of Abnormal and Social Psychology*, 1961, **66**, 271-275.

Roff, M. A statistical study of the development of intelligence test performance. *Journal of Psychology*, 1941, **11**, 371-386.

Rohwer, W. D., Jr., Lynch, S., Suzuki, N., & Levin, J. R. Verbal and pictorial facilitation of paired-associate learning. *Journal of Experimental Child Psychology*, 1967, **5**, 294-302.

Rose, A. M. A current theoretical issue in social gerontology. *Gerontologist*, 1964, **4**, 46-50.

Rose, C. L. Secularity in longevity research. Paper presented at the meeting of the Gerontological Society, Denver, October, 1968.

Rosenthal, I. Reliability of retrospective reports of adolescence. *Journal of Consulting Psychology*, 1963, **27**, 189-198.

Ross, J. The relation between test and person factors. *Psychological Review*, 1963, **70**, 432-443.

Ross, J. R. Constraints on variables in syntax. Unpublished doctoral dissertation, Massachusetts Institute of Technology, 1967.

Rovee, C. K., & Rovee, D. T. Conjugate reinforcement of infant exploratory behavior. *Journal of Experimental Child Psychology*, 1969, **8**, 33-39.

Ruch, F. L. The differentiative effects of age upon human learning. *Journal of General Psychology*, 1934, **11**, 261-286.

Rudel, R. G., Teuber, H., Liebert, R. S., & Halpern, S. Localization of auditory midline and reactions to body tilt in brain-damaged children. *Journal of Nervous and Mental Diseases*, 1960, **131**, 302-309.

Rudner, R. Value judgments in the acceptance of theories. *Scientific Monthly,* 1954, **79,** 151-153. [Reprinted in P. G. Frank (Ed.), *The validation of scientific theories.* New York: Collier, 1961. Pp. 31-35.]

Russell, W. A. Assessment versus experimental acquisition of verbal habits. In C. N. Cofer (Ed.), *Verbal learning and verbal behavior.* New York: McGraw-Hill, 1961.

Russell, W. A., & Storms, L. H. Implicit verbal chaining in paired-associate learning. *Journal of Experimental Psychology,* 1955, **49,** 287-293.

Salapatek, P., & Kessen, W. Visual scanning of triangles by the human newborn. *Journal of Experimental Child Psychology,* 1966, **3,** 155-167.

Sameroff, A. J. The components of sucking in the human newborn. *Journal of Experimental Child Psychology,* 1968, **6,** 607-623.

Sandak, J. M., & Garskof, B. E. Associative unlearning as a function of degree of interpolated learning. *Psychonomic Science,* 1967, **7,** 215-216.

Sanders, B. S. *Environment and growth.* Baltimore: Warwick & York, 1934.

Sanders, S., Laurendeau, M., & Bergeron, J. Aging and the concept of space: The conservation of surfaces. *Journal of Gerontology,* 1966, **21,** 281-286.

Sarbin, T. R. Role theory. In G. Lindzey (Ed.), *Handbook of social psychology.* Reading, Mass.: Addison-Wesley, 1954. Pp. 223-258.

Schaie, K. W. Rigidity-flexibility and intelligence: A cross-sectional study of the adult life-span from 20 to 70. *Psychological Monographs,* 1958, **72**(462, Whole No. 9).

Schaie, K. W. Cross-sectional methods in the study of psychological aspects of aging. *Journal of Gerontology,* 1959, **14,** 208-215.

Schaie, K. W. *Manual for the test of behavioral rigidity.* Palo Alto, Calif.: Consulting Psychologists Press, 1960.

Schaie, K. W. A field-theory approach to age changes in cognitive behavior. *Vita Humana,* 1962, **5,** 129-141.

Schaie, K. W. A general model for the study of developmental problems. *Psychological Bulletin,* 1965, **64,** 92-107.

Schaie, K. W. Age changes and age differences. *Gerontologist,* 1967, **7,** 128-132.

Schaie, K. W. The short-term longitudinal study of age changes in cognitive behavior. In C. Eisdorfer (Ed.), *Proceedings of Duke conference on longitudinal methods in studies of adult life and aging.* Washington, D.C.: Government Printing Office, 1969.

Schaie, K. W. An application of the general developmental model to the reanalysis of data from the Harvard Growth Study. Unpublished manuscript, West Virginia University, 1970.

Schaie, K. W., Baltes, P. B., & Strother, C. R. A study of auditory sensitivity in advanced age. *Journal of Gerontology,* 1964, **19,** 453-457.

Schaie, K. W., & Marquette, B. Personality in maturity and old age. In R. M. Dreger (Ed.), *Multivariate personality research: Contributions to the understanding of personality in honor of R. B. Cattell.* Champaign, Ill.: University of Illinois Press, 1970, in press.

Schaie K. W., Rosenthal, F., & Perlman, R. M. Differential mental deterioration of factorially "pure" functions in later maturity. *Journal of Gerontology,* 1953, **8,** 191-196.

Schaie, K. W., & Strother, C. R. A cross-sectional study of age changes in cognitive behavior. *Psychological Bulletin,* 1968, **70,** 671-680. (a)

Schaie, K. W., & Strother, C. R. The effects of time and cohort differences on the interpretation of age changes in cognitive behavior. *Multivariate Behavioral Research,* 1968, **3,** 259-294. (b)

Scharmann, D. Beiträge zur psychologischen Lebenslaufforschung. *Psychologische Forschung,* 1955, **25,** 79-117.

Schmidt, W. H. Spontaneous and nonspontaneous formation of scientific concepts by children. *Human Development*, 1965, **8**, 222-237.

Schneirla, T. C. The concept of development in comparative psychology. In D. B. Harris (Ed.), *The concept of development*. Minneapolis: University of Minnesota Press, 1957. Pp. 78-108.

Schon, D. *The displacement of concepts*. London: Tavistock, 1963.

Schorn, M. Lebensalter und Leistung. *Archiv für die Gesamte Psychologie*, 1930, **75**, 168-184.

Schubert, R. (Ed.) *Herz und Atmungsorgane im Alter. Kongress der Deutschen Gesellschaft für Gerontologie, 1967.* Darmstadt: Steinkopff, 1968.

Schwartz, D. W., & Karp, S. A. Field dependence in a geriatric population. *Perceptual and Motor Skills*, 1967, **24**, 495-504.

Sears, R. R., Rau, L., & Alpert, R. *Identification and child rearing.* Stanford, Calif.: Stanford University Press, 1965.

Seeger, R. J. Beyond operationalism. *Scientific Monthly*, 1954, **79**, 226-227. [Reprinted in P. G. Frank (Ed.), *The validation of scientific theories*. New York: Collier, 1961. Pp. 80-83.]

Segall, M. H., Campbell, D. T., & Herskovitz, M. J. *The influence of culture on visual perception.* Indianapolis: Bobbs-Merrill, 1966.

Segel, D. *Intellectual abilities in the adolescent period.* Bulletin No. 6. Washington, D.C.: U.S. Office of Education, 1948.

Senn, M. J. E. Pediatrics in orthopsychiatry. In L. G. Lowrey (Ed.), *Orthopsychiatry 1923-48: Retrospect and prospect.* New York: American Orthopsychiatric Association, 1948. Pp. 300-309.

Shakow, D., Dolkart, M. B., & Goldman, R. The memory function in psychosis of the aged. *Diseases of the Nervous System,* 1941, **2**, 43-48.

Shakow D., & Goldman, R. The effect of age on the Stanford-Binet vocabulary score of adults. *Journal of Educational Psychology*, 1938, **31**, 241-256.

Shapiro, S. I. Aural paired associates learning in grade-school children. *Child Development*, 1966, **37**, 417-424.

Shapiro, S. I., & Palermo, D. S. Mediation in children's aural paired-associate learning. *Child Development*, 1968, **39**, 569-577.

Shepard, R. N., & Teghtsoonian, M. Retention of information under conditions approaching a steady state. *Journal of Experimental Psychology*, 1961, **62**, 302-309.

Shepard, W. O. The effect of verbal training on initial generalization tendencies. *Child Development*, 1956, **27**, 173-178.

Shinn, M. W. Notes on the development of a child. *University of California, Publications in Education,* 1893-1899, **1**, 1-424.

Shinn, M. W. *The biography of a baby.* Boston: Houghton Mifflin, 1900.

Shinn, M. W. Notes on the development of a child. *University of California, Publications in Education,* 1907, **4**, 1-258.

Shipley, E. Detection and recognition with uncertainty. Unpublished doctoral dissertation, University of Pennsylvania, 1961.

Shipley, W. C. An apparent transfer of conditioning. *Journal of General Psychology*, 1933, **8**, 382-391.

Shipley, W. C. Indirect conditioning. *Journal of General Psychology*, 1935, **12**, 337-357.

Shirley, M. M. *The first two years: Personality manifestations.* Vol. 1. Minneapolis: University of Minnesota Press, 1933. (a)

Shirley, M. M. *The first two years: A study of twenty-five babies.* Vol. 2. Minneapolis: University of Minnesota Press, 1933. (b)

Shock, N. W. Growth curves. In S. S. Stevens (Ed.), *Handbook of experimental psychology.* New York: Wiley, 1951. Pp. 330-346.

Shucard, D. W., & Horn, J. L. Some relationships between evoked potential recordings and behavioral measurements of intelligence. Unpublished manuscript, Department of Psychology, University of Denver, 1970.

Shuttleworth, F. K. The physical and mental growth of girls and boys six to nineteen in relation to age at maximum growth. *Monographs of the Society for Research in Child Development*, 1939, No. 4.

Sidman, M. A note on functional relations obtained from group data. *Psychological Bulletin*, 1952, 49, 263-269.

Siegel, A. E. Editorial. *Child Development*, 1967, 38, 901-908.

Siegel, A. W., & Stevenson, H. W. Incidental learning: A developmental study. *Child Development*, 1966, 37, 811-818.

Sigel, I. How intelligence tests restrict our concept of intelligence. *Merrill Palmer Quarterly*, 1963, 9, 39-56.

Simkin, J. S. An investigation of differences in intellectual factors between normal and schizophrenic adults. (Doctoral dissertation, University of Michigan) Ann Arbor, Mich.: University Microfilms, 1950. No. 2464.

Siqueland, E. R. Reinforcement patterns and extinction in human newborns. *Journal of Experimental Child Psychology*, 1968, 6, 431-442.

Siqueland, E. R. The development of instrumental exploratory behavior during the first year of human life. Paper presented at the meeting of the Society for Research in Child Development, Santa Monica, California, March 1969.

Siqueland, E. R., & Lipsitt, L. P. Conditioned head-turning in human newborns. *Journal of Experimental Child Psychology*, 1966, 3, 356-376.

Sixtl, F., & Fittkau, B. Critical issues in comparing factorial structures. *Scandinavian Journal of Psychology*, 1969, 10, in press.

Skeels, H. M. Adult status of children with contrasting early life experience. *Monographs of the Society for Research in Child Development*, 1966, 31, 1-65.

Skeels, H. M., & Dye, H. B. A study of the effects of differential stimulation on mentally retarded children. *Proceedings of the American Association for Mental Deficiency*, 1939, 44, 114-136.

Skutsch, R. Lebensalter, Berufsleistung und Eignungsprüfung. *Industrielle Psychotechnik*, 1925, 2, 90.

Slobin, D. I. The role of imitation in early language learning. Paper presented at the meeting of the Society for Research in Child Development, Minneapolis, March 1965.

Slobin, D. I. Comments on developmental psycholinguistics. In F. Smith & G. A. Miller (Eds.), *The genesis of language: A psycholinguistic approach.* Cambridge, Mass.: Massachusetts Institute of Technology Press, 1966. Pp. 85-91. (a)

Slobin, D. I. The acquisition of Russian as a native language. In F. Smith & G. A. Miller (Eds.), *The genesis of language: A psycholinguistic approach.* Cambridge, Mass.: Massachusetts Institute of Technology Press, 1966. (b)

Slobin, D. I. Grammatical transformations and sentence comprehension in childhood and adulthood. *Journal of Verbal Learning and Verbal Behavior*, 1966, 5, 219-227. (c)

Smith, K. U., & Greene, P. A critical period in maturation of performance with space-displaced vision. *Perceptual and Motor Skills*, 1963, 17, 627-639.

Smith, L., & Lipsitt, L. P. A study of conjugate visual reinforcement in 2- to 5-month-old infants using mobiles. Unpublished manuscript, Department of Psychology, Brown University, 1968.

Smith, T. L. The development of psychological clinics in the United States. *Pedagogical Seminary*, 1914, **21**, 143-153.

Solyom, L., & Barik, H. C. Conditioning in senescence and senility. *Journal of Gerontology*, 1965, **20**, 483-488.

Sontag, L. W. Somatopsychics of personality and body function. *Vita Humana*, 1963, **6**, 1-10.

Sontag, L. W., Baker, C. T., & Nelson, V. L. Mental growth and personality development: A longitudinal study. *Monographs of the Society for Research in Child Development*, 1958, **23**, (Whole No. 2).

Sorenson, H. Adult ages as a factor in learning. *Journal of Educational Psychology*, 1930, **21**, 451-457.

Sorenson, H. *Adult abilities*. Minneapolis: University of Minnesota Press, 1938.

Sosa, J. M. Aging of neurofibrils. *Journal of Gerontology*, 1952, **7**, 191-195.

Speakman, M. A. The effect of age on the incidental relearning of stamp values: The use of deduction in a subsidiary test. *Journal of Gerontology*, 1954, **9**, 162-167.

Spear, N. E., Ekstrand, B. R., & Underwood, B. J. Association by contiguity. *Journal of Experimental Psychology*, 1964, **67**, 151-161.

Spearman, C. General intelligence objectively determined and measured. *American Journal of Psychology*, 1904, **15**, 201-293.

Spearman, C. *The abilities of man*. New York: Macmillan, 1927.

Sperling G. Temporal and spatial visual masking: I. Masking by impulse flashes. *Journal of the Optical Society of America*, 1965, **55**, 541-559.

Spiker, C. C. Associative transfer in verbal paired-associate learning. *Child Development*, 1960, **31**, 73-87.

Spiker, C. C. The concept of development: Relevant and irrelevant issues. *Monographs of the Society for Research in Child Development*, 1966, **31**, 40-54.

Spitz, R. A. Hospitalism: A follow-up report. *Psychoanalytic Studies of the Child*, 1946, **2**, 113-117.

Spranger, E. *Psychologie des Jugendalters*. Leipzig: Quelle & Meyer, 1925.

Staats, A. W. *Learning, language, and cognition*. New York: Holt, Rinehart & Winston, 1968.

Stadius, G. Faktorbehandlung of Harnqvists Differenzierungsstudie. *Nordisk Psykologi*, 1964, **16**, 241-258.

Stahl, E. L. *Die religiöse und die humanitätsphilosophische Bildungsidee und die Entstehung des deutschen Bildungsromans im 18. Jahrhundert*. Bern: Haupt, 1934.

Stanka, R. *Geschichte der politischen Philosophie*. Vol. 1. *Die politische Philosophie des Altertums*. Wien: Sexl, 1951.

Steinhagen, K. Faktorenanalytische Untersuchungen zur Veränderung von Intelligenz-strukturen im Erwachsenenalter. Unpublished doctoral dissertation, University of Kiel, Germany, 1967.

Stern, C., & Stern, W. *Die Kindersprache*. Leipzig: Barth, 1920.

Stern, E. *Jugendpsychologie*. (2nd ed.) Breslau: Hirt, 1928.

Stern, E. *Anfänge des Alterns*. Leipzig: Thieme, 1931.

Stern, E. Der menschliche Lebenslauf als psychologisches Problem. *Allgemeine Zeitschrift für Psychiatrie und Psychisch-Gerichtliche Medizin*, 1933, **99**, 101.

Stern, E. *Der Mensch in der zweiten Lebenshälfte*. Zürich: Rascher, 1955.

Stern, W. Tatsachen und Ursachen der seelischen Entwicklung. *Zeitschrift für Angewandte Psychologie und Psychologische Sammelforschung*, 1908, **1**, 1-43.

Stern, W. Über Aufgabe und Anlage der Psychographie. *Zeitschrift für Angewandte Psychologie und Psychologische Sammelforschung*, 1910, **3**, 166-190.

Stern, W. Die psychologischen Methoden der Intelligenzprüfung. In F. Schumann (Ed.), *Bericht über den 5. Kongress für experimentelle Psychologie in Berlin, 1912.* Leipzig: Barth, 1912. Pp. 1-109.

Stern, W. *The psychological methods of testing intelligence.* Baltimore: Warwick & York, 1914. (Translated by G. M. Whipple from the 1912 German edition.)

Stern, W. *Die Intelligenz der Kinder und Jugendlichen und die Methoden ihrer Untersuchung.* (3rd ed.) Leipzig: Barth, 1920.

Stern, W. *Die differentielle Psychologie in ihren methodischen Grundlagen.* (3rd ed.) Leipzig: Barth, 1921.

Stevens, S. S. *Handbook of experimental psychology.* New York: Wiley, 1951.

Stevenson, H. W. Latent learning in children. *Journal of Experimental Psychology,* 1954, *47,* 17-21.

Stevenson, H. W. Learning in children. In P. H. Mussen (Ed.), *Carmichael's manual of child psychology.* New York: Wiley, 1970, in press.

Stolz, L. M. *Influences on parent behavior.* Stanford, Calif.: Stanford University Press, 1967.

Stone, C. P. The age factor in animal learning: I. Rats in the problem box and the maze. *Genetic Psychology Monographs,* 1929, *5,* 1-130. (a)

Stone, C. P. The age factor in animal learning: II. Rats on a multiple light discrimination box and a difficult maze. *Genetic Psychology Monographs,* 1929, *6,* 125-202. (b)

Stott, L. W. *Child development: An individual longitudinal approach.* New York: Holt, Rinehart & Winston, 1967.

Street, R. F. *A Gestalt completion test.* New York: Teachers College, Columbia University, 1931.

Strong, E. K. *Change of interests with age.* Stanford, Calif.: Stanford University Press, 1931.

Strong, R. T., Jr. The identification of primary school age children with learning handicaps associated with minimal brain disorders. Unpublished doctoral dissertation, University of Utah, 1964.

Strother, C. R., Schaie, K. W., & Horst, P. The relationship between advanced age and mental abilities. *Journal of Abnormal and Social Psychology,* 1957, *55,* 166-170.

Stroud, J. B. Experiments on learning in school situations. *Psychological Bulletin,* 1940, *37,* 777-807.

Sullivan, A. M. The relation between intelligence and transfer. Unpublished doctoral dissertation, McGill University, 1964.

Sullivan, J. P., & Moran, L. J. Association structures of bright children at age six. *Child Development,* 1967, *38,* 793-800.

Sumita, K., & Ichitani, T. A factor analytic study on the differentiation of intellectual abilities. *Tohoku Psychologica Folia,* 1956-1957, *15,* 51-85.

Sward, K. Age and mental ability in superior men. *American Journal of Psychology,* 1945, *58,* 443-479.

Swartz, J. D., & Moran, L. J. Association structures of bright children at ages nine and twelve. *Multivariate Behavioral Research,* 1968, *3,* 189-198.

Swineford, F. Growth in the general and verbal bi-factors from grade VII to grade IX. *Journal of Educational Psychology,* 1947, *38,* 257-272.

Swineford, F. General, verbal, and spatial bi-factors after three years. *Journal of Educational Psychology,* 1949, *40,* 353-360.

Sylvester, R. H. Clinical psychology adversely criticized. *Psychological Clinic,* 1913-1914, *7,* 182-188.

Taine, H. Note sur l'acquisition du langage chez les enfants et dans l'espace humaine. *Revue Philosophique,* 1876, *1,* 3-23. (Translated in *Mind,* 1877, *2,* 252-257.)

Talbot, E. *Papers on Infant Development*, 1882, **52**. (American Social Science Association, Educational Department.)

Tallard, G. A. The effect of age on speed of simple manual skill. *Journal of Genetic Psychology*, 1962, **100**, 69-76.

Tanner, J. M. Some notes on the reporting of growth data. *Human Biology*, 1951, **23**, 93-159.

Tanner, J. M. *Educational and physical growth*. London: University of London Press, 1961.

Tanner, J. M. The regulation of human growth. *Child Development*, 1963, **34**, 817-848.

Taylor, C. *The explanation of behavior*. New York: Humanities Press, 1964.

Templin, M. C. Certain language skills in children: Their development and inter-relationships. *Institute of Child Welfare Monographs*, 1957, No. 26.

Terman, L. M. *The measurement of intelligence*. Boston: Houghton, 1916.

Terman, L. M., & Merrill, M. A. *Stanford-Binet Intelligence Scale. Manual for the third revision form L-M*. Boston: Houghton Mifflin, 1960.

Tetens, J. N. *Philosophische Versuche über die menschliche Natur und ihre Entwicklung*. Leipzig: Weidmanns Erben & Reich, 1777. 2 vols.

Thomae, H. Objective socialization variables and personality development. *Human Development*, 1965, **8**, 87-116.

Thomae, H. *Das Individuum und seine Welt*. Göttingen: Hogrefe, 1968. (a)

Thomae, H. Interdisziplinäre Gemeinschaftsarbeit der Gerontologie. *Zeitschrift für Gerontologie*, 1968, **1**, 273-274. (b)

Thomae, H. Persönlichkeit und Altern. In R. Schubert (Ed.), *Herz und Atmungsorgane im Alter. Kongress der Deutschen Gesellschaft für Gerontologie, 1967*. Darmstadt: Steinkopff, 1968. Pp. 191-203. (c)

Thomae, H. Zur Entwicklungs- und Sozialpsychologie des alternden Menschen (1959). In H. Thomae & U. Lehr (Eds.), *Altern: Probleme und Tatsachen*. Frankfurt a.M.: Akademische Verlagsgesellschaft, 1968. Pp. 1-20. (d)

Thomae, H. Psychische und soziale Aspekte des Alterns. *Zeitschrift für Gerontologie*, 1968, **1**, 43-55. (e)

Thomae, H., & Lehr, U. (Eds.) *Altern: Probleme und Tatsachen*. Frankfurt a.M.: Akademische Verlagsgesellschaft, 1968.

Thomas, A., Birch, H. G., Chess, S., Hertzog, M. E., & Korn, S. *Behavioral individuality in early childhood*. New York: New York University Press, 1963.

Thomas, J. P. The effect of contour sharpness on perceived brightness. *Vision Research*, 1965, **5**, 559-564.

Thomas, J. P., & Charles, D. C. Effects of age and stimulus size on perception. *Journal of Gerontology*, 1964, **19**, 447-450.

Thompson, C. *Die Psychoanalyse*. Zürich: Pan, 1952.

Thompson, C. W., & Margaret, A. Differential test responses of normal and mental defectives. *Journal of Abnormal and Social Psychology*, 1947, **42**, 285-293.

Thompson, W. R. Development and biophysical basis of personality. In E. F. Borgatta & W. W. Lambert (Eds.), *Handbook of personality theory and research*. Chicago: McNally, 1968. Pp. 149-214.

Thorndike, E. L. *Animal intelligence*. New York: Macmillan, 1898.

Thorndike, E. L. *Notes on child study*. New York: Macmillan, 1901.

Thorndike, E. L. *Educational psychology*. New York: Teachers College, Columbia University, 1903.

Thorndike, E. L. *Educational psychology*. Vol. I. New York: Columbia University, 1913; Vol. II, III. New York: Teachers College, 1913.

Thorndike, E. L. On the improvement in intelligence scores from 14 to 18. *Journal of Educational Psychology*, 1923, **14**, 513-516.

Thorndike, E. L. *Adult learning.* New York: Macmillan, 1928.

Thorndike, E. L. *Adult interests.* New York: Macmillan, 1935.

Thorndike, E. L. Autobiography. In C. E. Murchison (Ed.), *A history of psychology in autobiography.* Vol. 3. Worcester, Mass.: Clark University Press, 1936. Pp. 263-270.

Thurstone, L. L. A method of scaling psychological and educational tests. *Journal of Educational Psychology,* 1925, **16,** 433-451.

Thurstone, L. L. Primary mental abilities. *Psychometric Monographs,* 1938, No. 1.

Thurstone, L. L. Current issues in factor analysis. *Psychological Bulletin,* 1940, **37,** 189-236.

Thurstone, L. L. *A factorial study of perception.* Chicago: University of Chicago Press, 1944.

Tiedemann, D. Beobachtungen über die Seelenfähigkeiten bei Kindern. *Hessische Beiträge zur Gelehrsamkeit und Kunst,* 1787, **2,** 313; **3,** 486.

Torgerson, W. J. *Theory and methods of scaling.* New York: Wiley, 1958. (2nd ed., 1967).

Toulmin, S. *The philosophy of science.* London: Hutchinson, 1953.

Toulmin, S. *The uses of argument.* London: Cambridge University Press, 1958.

Toulmin, S. *The philosophy of science.* (2nd ed.) London: Hutchinson, 1962.

Tucker, L. R. Determination of parameters of a functional relation for factor analysis. *Psychometrika,* 1958, **23,** 19-23.

Tucker, L. R. Implications of factor analysis of three-way matrices for measurement of change. In C. W. Harris (Ed.), *Problems in measuring change.* Madison, Wis.: University of Wisconsin Press, 1963. Pp. 122-137.

Tucker, L. R. Learning theory and multivariate experiment: Illustrations by determination of generalized learning curves. In R. B. Cattell (Ed.), *Handbook of multivariate experimental psychology.* Chicago: Rand McNally, 1966. Pp. 476-501.

Turner, E. A., & Rommetveit, R. Focus of attention in recall of active and passive sentences. *Journal of Verbal Learning and Verbal Behavior,* 1968, **7,** 543-548.

Turner, M. B. *Philosophy and the science of behavior.* New York: Appleton-Century-Crofts, 1967.

Tyler, F. T. Organismic growth: *P*-technique in the analysis of longitudinal growth data. *Child Development,* 1954, **25,** 83-90.

Tyler, L. E. *The psychology of human differences.* New York: Appleton-Century-Crofts, 1950. (2nd ed., 1965.)

Überla, K. *Faktorenanalyse.* New York: Springer, 1968.

Underwood, B. J. Speed of learning and amount retained: A consideration of methodology. *Psychological Bulletin,* 1954, **51,** 276-282.

Underwood, B. J. *Psychological research.* New York: Appleton-Century-Crofts, 1957. (a)

Underwood, B. J. Interference and forgetting. *Psychological Review,* 1957, **64,** 49-60. (b)

Underwood, B. J. Stimulus selection in verbal learning. In C. N. Cofer & B. S. Musgrave (Eds.), *Verbal behavior and learning.* New York: McGraw-Hill, 1963.

Underwood, B. J. The representativeness of rote verbal learning. In A. W. Melton (Ed.), *Categories of human learning.* New York: Academic Press, 1964. Pp. 48-78. (a)

Underwood, B. J. Degree of learning and the measurement of forgetting. *Journal of Verbal Learning and Verbal Behavior,* 1964, **3,** 112-129. (b)

Underwood, B. J. False recognition produced by implicit verbal responses. *Journal of Experimental Psychology,* 1965, **70,** 122-129.

Underwood, B. J. Some relationships between concept learning and verbal learning. In H. J. Klausmeier & C. W. Harris (Eds.), *Analyses of concept learning.* New York: Academic Press, 1966.

Underwood, B. J., & Ekstrand, B. R. An analysis of some shortcomings in the interference theory of forgetting. *Psychological Review,* 1966, **73,** 540-549.

Underwood, B. J., Ham, M., & Ekstrand, B. R. Cue selection in paired-associate learning. *Journal of Experimental Psychology,* 1962, **64,** 405-409.

Underwood, B. J., & Keppel, G. One-trial learning. *Journal of Verbal Learning and Verbal Behavior*, 1962, **1**, 1-13.

Underwood, B. J., & Postman, L. Extraexperimental sources of interference in forgetting. *Psychological Review*, 1966, **73**, 540-549.

Underwood, B. J., Runquist, W. N., & Schulz, R. W. Response learning in paired-associate lists as a function of intralist similarity. *Journal of Experimental Psychology*, 1959, **58**, 70-78.

Underwood, B. J., & Schulz, R. W. *Meaningfulness and verbal learning*. Philadelphia: Lippincott, 1960.

USES, factor analyses of aptitude tests 1944-1945. (In J. W. French, The description of aptitude and achievement tests in terms of rotated factors. *Psychometric Monograph*, 1951, No. 5.)

Uzgiris, I. C. Situational generality of conservation. *Child Development*, 1964, **35**, 831-841.

Uzgiris, I. C., & Hunt, J. McV. A longitudinal study of recognition learning. Paper presented at the meeting of the Society for Research in Child Development, Minneapolis, March 1965.

Uznadze, D. N. *The psychology of set*. New York: Plenum Press (Consultants Bureau), 1966.

Vandenberg, S. G. Contribution of twin research to psychology. *Psychological Bulletin*, 1966, **66**, 327-352. (a)

Vandenberg S. G. The nature and nurture of intelligence. Research Report No. 20, 1966, from the Louisville Twin Study, University of Louisville School of Medicine. (b)

Vandenberg S. G., & Falkner, F. Heredity factors in human growth. *Human Biology*, 1965, **37**, 357-365.

Van den Daele, L. D. Qualitative models in developmental analysis. *Developmental Psychology*, 1969, **1**, 303-310.

Van der Vaart, H. R. Adult age: An investigation based on certain aspects of growth curves. *Acta Biotheoretica*, 1953, **10**, 139-211.

Velten, H. V. The growth of phonemic and lexical pattern in infant language. *Language*, 1943, **19**, 281-292.

Verhage, F. *Intelligentie en leeftijd bij volwassenen en bejaarden.* (Intelligence and age in adults and the aged.) Groningen, Netherlands: Wolters, 1964.

Vernon, P. E. Changes in abilities from 14 to 20 years. *Advancement of Science,* 1948, **5**, 138.

Vernon, P. E. *The structure of human abilities*. London: Methuen, 1950. (2nd ed., 1961).

Vernon, P. E., & Parry, J. B. *Personnel selection in the British forces.* London: University of London Press, 1949.

Verville, E., & Cameron, N. Age and sex differences in the perception of incomplete pictures by adults. *Journal of Genetic Psychology*, 1946, **68**, 149-157.

Very, P. S. Differential factor structures in mathematical ability. *Genetic Psychology Monographs*, 1967, **75**, 169-207.

Verzar-McDougall, E. J. Studies in learning and memory in aging rats. *Gerontologia*, 1957, **1**, 65-85.

Vinh-Bang. Évolution des conduites et apprentissage. In A. Morf, J. Smedslund, Vinh-Bang, & J. F. Wohlwill, *L'Apprentissage des structures logiques*. Paris: Presses Universitaires de France, 1959. Pp. 3-13.

von Bertalanffy, L. Principles and theory of growth. In V. W. Nowinski (Ed.), *Fundamental aspects of normal and malignant growth*. Amsterdam: Elsevier, 1960. Pp. 137-144, 169-180, 196-259.

von Bertalanffy, L. *Modern theories of development*. New York: Harper & Row, 1962.

von Bertalanffy, L. *Robots, men and minds*. New York: Braziller, 1967.

von Bertalanffy, L. *General systems theory*. New York: Braziller, 1968.

von Bracken, H. Die Altersveränderungen der geistigen Leistungsfähigkeit und der seelischen Innenwelt, Übersichtsreferat. *Zeitschrift für Alternsforschung*, 1939, **1**, 256-266.

von Glaserfeld, E. An approach to the semantics of preposition. In, *Symposium on computer related semantic analysis*. Detroit: Wayne State University, 1965.

von Kerekjarto, M., & Schmidt, G. Faktoren-Analyse des Hamburg-Wechsler-Intelligenztests für Kinder (HAWIK). *Diagnostica*, 1962, **8**, 110.

Vukovich, A. Untersuchungen zur Invarianz der Faktorenstruktur von Begabungstests bei systematischer Variation der Probandengruppen. In H. Heckhausen (Ed.), *Bericht über den 24. Kongress der Deutschen Gesellschaft für Psychologie in Wien, 1964*. Göttingen: Hogrefe, 1965. Pp. 173-177.

Vukovich, A. Faktorielle Typenbestimmung. *Psychologische Beiträge*, 1967, **10**, 112-121.

Vygotsky, L. S. *Thought and language*. Cambridge, Mass.: Massachusetts Institute of Technology Press, 1962.

Wallace, J. G. Some studies of perception in relation to age. *British Journal of Psychology*, 1956, **47**, 283-297.

Wallin, J. E. W. The new clinical psychology and the psychoclinicist. *Journal of Educational Psychology*, 1911, **2**, 121-132.

Wallin, J. E. W. *The mental health of the school child*. New Haven: Yale University Press, 1914.

Wallin, J. E. W., & Krohn, W. O. Early psychological practitioner. *American Psychologist*, 1961, **16**, 259.

Walters, Sister A. A genetic study of geometrical-optical illusions. *Genetic Psychology Monographs*, 1942, **25**, 101-155.

Wapner, S., & Werner, H. *Perceptual development*. Worcester, Mass.: Clark University Press, 1957.

Wapner, S., Werner, H., & Comalli, P. E., Jr. Perception of part-whole relationships in middle and old age. *Journal of Gerontology*, 1960, **15**, 412-415.

Watson, J. B. Psychology as the behaviorist views it. *Psychological Review*, 1913, **20**, 158-177.

Watson, J. B. *Psychology from the standpoint of a behaviorist*. Philadelphia: Lippincott, 1919.

Watson, J. B. Is thinking merely the action of language mechanisms? *British Journal of Psychology*, 1920, **11**, 87-104.

Watson, J. B. Autobiography. In C. E. Murchison (Ed.), *History of psychology in autobiography*. Vol. 3. Worcester, Mass.: Clark University Press, 1936. Pp. 271-282.

Watson, J. B., & Raynor, R. Conditional emotional reactions. *Journal of Experimental Psychology*, 1920, **3**, 1-14.

Watson, J. S. Evidence of discrimination operant learning within 30 seconds by infants 7 to 26 weeks of age. Paper presented at the meeting of the Society for Research in Child Development, Minneapolis, March 1965.

Watson, J. S. Memory and "contingency analysis" in infant learning. *Merrill-Palmer Quarterly*, 1967, **13**, 55-76.

Watson, R. I. The personality of the aged. A review. *Journal of Gerontology*, 1954, **9**, 309-315.

Wechsler, D. *The measurement of adult intelligence*. Baltimore: Williams & Wilkins, 1939.

Wechsler, D. *The measurement and appraisal of adult intelligence. Manual for the Wechsler Adult Intelligence Scale*. New York: Psychological Corporation, 1955.

Wechsler, D. *The measurement of adult intelligence*. (3rd ed.) Baltimore: Williams & Wilkins, 1958.

Weiner, G., Rader, R. B., Oppel, W. C., & Harper, P. A. Correlates of low birth weight: Psychological status at eight to ten years of age. *Pediatric Research*, 1968, **2**, 110-118.

Weiner, M. Organization of mental abilities from ages 14 to 54. *Educational and Psychological Measurement*, 1964, **24**, 573-587.

Weir, R. H. *Language in the crib.* The Hague: Mouton, 1962.

Weiss, A. D. Sensory functions. In J. E. Birren (Ed.), *Handbook of aging and the individual.* Chicago: University of Chicago Press, 1959. Pp. 503-542.

Weiss, E. Leistung und Lebensalter. *Industrielle Psychotechnik*, 1927, **4**, 227.

Weisstein, N., & Haber, R. N. A U-shaped backward masking function in vision. *Psychonomic Science*, 1965, **2**, 75-76.

Welford, A. T. *Skill and age.* London: Oxford University Press, 1951.

Welford, A. T. *Aging and human skill.* London: Oxford University Press, 1958.

Welford, A. T. Méthode longitudinale et transversale dans les recherches sur le vieillissement. In Colloques Internationaux du Centre de la Recherche Scientifique (Ed.), *Le vieillissement des fonctions psychologiques et psycho-physiologiques.* Paris: R.S., 1961. Pp. 31-44.

Werner, E. E., & Bayley, N. The reliability of Bayley's revised scale of mental and motor development during the first year of life. *Child Development*, 1966, **37**, 39-50.

Werner, H. *Comparative psychology of mental development.* New York: International Universities Press, 1948.

Werner, H. The concept of development from a comparative and organismic point of view. In D. B. Harris (Ed.), *The concept of development.* Minneapolis: University of Minnesota Press, 1957. Pp. 125-148.

Werner, H., & Kaplan, B. *Symbol formation.* New York: Wiley, 1963.

Werner, H., & Strauss, A. Types of visuo-motor activity in their relation to low and high performance ages. *Proceedings of the American Association for Mental Deficiency*, 1939, **44**, 163-168.

Wertheimer, M. Principles of perceptual organization. *Psychologische Forschung*, 1923, **4**, 301-350. [Translated and abridged: In D. C. Beardslee & M. Wertheimer (Eds.), *Readings in perception.* New York: Van Nostrand, 1958.]

Werts, C. E. Paternal influence on career choice. *National Merit Scholarship Corporation Research Reports*, 1967, **3**, 19.

Wetherick, N. E. An experimental study of the relationship between problem solving ability and age in the normal human adult. Unpublished doctoral dissertation, University of Liverpool, 1964.

Wetherick, N. E. Changing an established concept: A comparison of the ability of young, middle-aged and old subjects. *Gerontologia*, 1965, **11**, 82-95.

Wetzel, N. C. Physical fitness in terms of physique development and basal metabolism. *Journal of the American Medical Association*, 1941, **116**, 1187-1195.

Wewetzer, K. H. Zur Differenz der Leistungsstrukturen bei verschiedenen Intelligenzgraden. In A. Wellek (Ed.), *Bericht über den 21. Kongress der Deutschen Gesellschaft für Psychologie in Bonn, 1957.* Göttingen: Hogrefe. 1958. Pp. 245-246.

Wewetzer, K. H. Die Faktorenstruktur der Intelligenz in ihrer Abhängigkeit von der Begabungsart. Ein Beitrag zur Typenanalyse. In K. J. Groffmann & K. H. Wewetzer (Eds.), *Person als Prozess.* Bern: Huber, 1968. Pp. 213-230.

White, S. H. Evidence for a hierarchical arrangement of learning processes. In L. P. Lipsitt & C. C. Spiker (Eds.), *Advances in child development and behavior.* Vol. 2. New York: Academic Press, 1965. Pp. 187-220.

White, S. H., Spiker, C. C., & Holton, R. B. Associative transfer as shown by response speeds in motor paired associate learning. *Child Development*, 1960, **31**, 609-616.

Whiteman, M., & Jastak, J. Absolute scaling for different age groupings of a state-wide sample. *Educational and Psychological Measurement*, 1957, **17**, 338-346.

Whiting. J. W., & Child, I. L. *Child training and personality*. New Haven: Yale University Press, 1953.

Wickens, D. D., Born, D. G., & Allen, C. K. Proactive inhibition and item similarity in short-term memory. *Journal of Verbal Learning and Verbal Behavior*, 1963, **2**, 440-445.

Wickens, D. D., & Cermak, L. S. Transfer effects of synonyms and antonyms in mixed and unmixed lists. *Journal of Verbal Learning and Verbal Behavior*, 1967, **6**, 832-839.

Wickens, D. D., & Wickens, C. A study of conditioning in the neonate. *Journal of Experimental Psychology*, 1940, **26**, 94-102.

Wicklund, D. A., Palermo, D. S., & Jenkins, J. J. The effects of associative strength and response hierarchy on paired-associate learning. *Journal of Verbal Learning and Verbal Behavior*, 1964, **3**, 413-420.

Wilcox, B. M., Appel, L., & Robbins, P. L. Operant conditioning of leg kicking responses in infants using mobiles. Unpublished manuscript, Brown University, Department of Psychology, 1965.

Willard, E. Observations on an infant during its first year by a mother. In A. A. de Sausurre & A. L. G. Necker (Eds.), *Progressive education*. Boston: Ticknor, 1835. Pp. 323-348.

Williams, H. S. Some aspects of the measurement and maturation of mechanical aptitude in boys aged 12 to 14. Unpublished doctoral dissertation, University of London, 1948.

Williams, M. The effect of past experience on mental performance in the elderly. *British Journal of Medical Psychology*, 1960, **33**, 215-221.

Williams, R. H., & Wirth, C. G. *Lives through the years*. New York: Atherton Press, 1965.

Willoughby, R. R. Family similarities in mental-test abilities. *Genetic Psychology Monographs*, 1927, **2**, 235-277.

Willoughby, R. R. Incidental learning. *Journal of Educational Psychology*, 1929, **20**, 671-682.

Willoughby, R. R. Incidental learning. *Journal of Educational Psychology*, 1930, **21**, 12-23.

Wimer, R. E. Age differences in incidental and intentional learning. *Journal of Gerontology*, 1960, **15**, 79-82.

Windelband, W., & Heimsoeth, H. (Eds.) *Lehrbuch der Geschichte der Philosophie*. (15th ed.) Tübingen: Mohr, 1957.

Witkin, H. A., Lewis, H. B., Hertman, M., Machover, K., Meisser, P. B., & Wapner, S. *Personality through perception*. New York: Harper, 1954.

Witmer, L. Clinical psychology. *Psychological Clinic*, 1907, **1**, 1-9.

Wohlwill, J. F. Developmental studies of perception. *Psychological Bulletin*, 1960, **57**, 250-288. (a)

Wohlwill, J. F. A study of the development of the number concept by scalogram analysis. *Journal of Genetic Psychology*, 1960, **97**, 345-377. (b)

Wohlwill, J. F. Piaget's system as a source of empirical research. *Merrill-Palmer Quarterly*, 1963, **9**, 253-262. (a)

Wohlwill, J. F. The measurement of scalability for non-cumulative items. *Educational and Psychological Measurement*, 1963, **23**, 543-555. (b)

Wohlwill, J. F. The age variable in psychological research. *Psychological Review*, 1970, **77**, 49-64.

Wohlwill, J. F., Fusaro, L., & Devoe, S. Measurement, seriation and conservation: A longitudinal examination of their interrelationship. Paper presented at the meeting of the Society for Research in Child Development, Santa Monica, California, March 1969.

Wolf E., & Zigler, M. J. Dark adaptation level and size of test field. *Journal of the Optical Society of America*, 1950, **40**, 211-218.

Wolfe, R. The role of conceptual systems in cognitive functioning at varying levels of age and intelligence. *Journal of Personality*, 1963, **31**, 108-123.

Wolff, G. A study on the trend of weight in white school children from 1933 to 1936. *Child Development*, 1940, **11**, 159-180.

Wolff, P. H. The serial organization of sucking in the young infant. *Pediatrics*, 1968, **42**, 943-956.

Wolfle, D. Annual report of the Executive Secretary. *American Psychologist*, 1949, **4**, 502-505.

Woodrow, H. The relation between abilities and improvement with practice. *Journal of Educational Psychology*, 1938, **29**, 215-230.

Woodrow, H. Factors in improvement with practice. *Journal of Psychology*, 1939, **7**, 55-70.

Woodrow, H., & Lowell, F. Children's association frequency tables. *Psychological Monograph*, 1917, **22**, (Whole No. 97).

Wright, R. E. A factor analysis of the original Stanford-Binet scale. *Psychometrika*, 1939, **4**, 209-220.

Wyss, D. *Die tiefenpsychologischen Schulen von den Anfängen bis zur Gegenwart.* (2nd ed.) Göttingen: Van den Hoeck & Ruprecht, 1966.

Yakorcynsky, G. K. An evaluation of the postulates underlying the Babcock deterioration test. *Psychological Review*, 1941, **48**, 261-267.

Yerkes, R. M. Comparative psychology: A question of definitions. *Journal of Philosophy and Scientific Methods*, 1913, **10**, 580-582.

Yerkes, R. M. (Ed.) *Psychological examining in the United States Army. Memoirs of the National Academy of Sciences*, 1921, **15**, 1-890.

Young, F. M. Development as indicated by a study of pronouns. *Journal of Genetic Psychology*, 1942, **61**, 125-134.

Young, R. K. Serial learning. In T. R. Dixon & D. L. Horton (Eds.), *Verbal behavior and general behavior theory*. Englewood Cliffs, N. J.: Prentice-Hall, 1968. Pp. 122-148.

Yuille, J. C., & Paivio, A. Imagery and verbal mediation instructions in paired-associate learning. *Journal of Experimental Psychology*, 1968, **78**, 436-441.

Zeidner, J., Goldstein, L. G., & Johnson, C. D. Factor analysis of visual acuity tests during dark adaptation. PRB Technical Research Note 40, November, 1954, Washington, D.C., Department of the Army.

Zigler, E. Metatheoretical issues in developmental psychology. In M. Marx (Ed.), *Theories in contemporary psychology*. New York: Macmillan, 1963. Pp. 341-369.

Zivian, M. T., & Riegel, K. F. Word identification as a function of semantic clues and associative frequency. *Journal of Experimental Psychology*, 1969, **79**, 336-341.

Zivian, M. T., Riegel, K. F., & Zeiher, H. Restricted and free associations of 12, 15, and 18 year old Germans. Report No. 29, 1967, University of Michigan, USPHS Grant HD 01368, Center for Human Growth and Development.

Zubek, J. P., & Solberg, P. A. *Human development*. New York: McGraw-Hill, 1954.

Zyve, C. I. Conversation among children. *Teachers College Record*, 1927, **29**, 46-61.

Author Index

Numbers in italics refer to pages on which the references are listed.

A

Adams, J. A., 306, 307, 309, 313, 320, *509*
Adkins, D., 24, *509*
Ahammer, I. M., 17, *509*
Albrecht, R., 45, *528*
Alcott, B., 26, *509*
Alexander, P., 119, *509*
Allen, C. K., 350, *561*
Allen, D. V., 328, *525*
Allen, W. R., 460, *514*
Allport, G., 133, *509*
Alpern, M., 235, *509*
Alpert, R., 124, *552*
Altus, W. D., 475, *509*
Amelang, M., 473, *509*
Anastasi, A., 286, 427, 433, 441, 450, 469, 475, 481, 483, *509*
Anderson, H. E., 470, *509, 545*
Anderson, J. E., 5, 10, 25, 45, 50, 150, 167, 187, 426, 427, *509, 510*
Anderson, M. M., 213, *547*
Anisfeld, M., 419, *510*
Anker, J., 58, *510*
Ankus, M. N., 81, 429, *532*
Apfeldorf M., 496, *522*
Apgar, V., 295, *510*
Appel, L., 299, *561*
Arenberg, D., 81, 274, 277, 278, 319, 325, 342, *610*

Arnhoff, F. N., 268, *510*
Asch, S. E., 469, 470, *510*
Atchley, R. C., 452, *510*
Austin, G. A., 435, 436, *516*
Axelrod, S., 277, 278, *522*
Ayllon, T., 266, *510*
Azrin, N. H., 266, *510*

B

Babcock, H., 44, 374, *510*
Baer, D. M., 124, 127, 128, 138, 140, *510, 513*
Baker, B. L., 15, *544*
Baker, C. T., 426, *554*
Bakwin, H., 7, *510*
Baldwin, A. L., 46, 72, *510*
Baldwin, B. T., 35, *510*
Baldwin, J. M., 29, 432, *510*
Balinsky, B., 426, 470, 471, 472, 477, *510*
Ballauf, T., 57, 58, *510*
Baller, W. R., 51, *510*
Baltes, M. M., 488, 506, *511*
Baltes, P. B., 9, 18, 63, 167, 169, 171, 199, 200, 201, 206, 207, 447, 465, 473, 474, 475, 476, 477, 479, 483, 486, 487, 488, 506, *510, 511, 544, 549, 551*
Balzert, C., 475, *511*
Barber, T. X., 17, 18, *511*

Barik, H. C., 260, 261, *554*
Barker, R. G., 76, 78, *511*
Barlow, J., 419, *510*
Barnes, J. M., 333, *511*
Bartholomäi, F., 27, *511*
Bartlett, C. J., 473, *511*
Bartley, S. H., 240, *511*
Bartoshuk, A. K., 294, *511*
Basowitz, H., 224, 326, *511, 536*
Bateman, B., 430, *511*
Bateman, W. G., 402, *511*
Bath, J. A., 441, *511*
Battig, K., 267, *511*
Battig, W. F., 325, *511*
Baumeister, A. A., 473, *511*
Baumrind, D., 433, 440, *511*
Bayley, N., 187, 212, 426, 432, 433, 440, 452, 453, 455, 499, *512, 517, 560*
Beach, D. H., 320, *524*
Bechtoldt, H. P., 457, 461, *512*
Beeson, M. F., 44, 450, 455, *512*
Beilin, H., 15, 205, 398, 432, *512*
Bell, R. Q., 173, 174, 486, *512*
Bellugi, U., 412, 414, 415, *512, 516, 536*
Belmont, I. B., 473, *512*
Belmont, L., 421, 473, *512*
Bendig, A. W., 469, 470, *542*
Bentler, P. M., 155, 163, 165, 166, *512, 526*
Bereiter, C., 182, 196, 202, *512, 513*
Berger, L., 472, 478, *513*
Bergeron, J., 74, *551*
Bergmann, G., 116, 117, 118, *513*
Berko, J., 405, *516*
Berkowitz, B., 470, 472, 482, *527*
Berlyne, D. E., 138, 140, 144, *513*
Bernreuter, R. G., 483, *513*
Bernstein, A., 472, 478, *513*
Berrien, F. K., 10, 154, *513*
Bethon, G., 441, *526*
Bever, T., 419, *513*
Beveridge, W. I. B., 72, *513*
Bijou, S. W., 124, 127, 128, 138, 140, 144, *513*
Bilash, I., 454, 457, 458, 461, 498, *513*
Binet, A., 32, 33, 213, *513*
Birch, D., 361, *513*
Birch, H., 431, *512, 513*
Birch, H. G., 177, 186, 188, 295, 473, *513, 556*
Birnbaum, I., 336, *513*

Birren, J. E., 5, 10, 11, 12, 13, 16, 43, 44, 45, 111, 112, 113, 150, 369, 371, 374, 430, 453, 454, 456, 457, 459, 460, 461, 487, *513, 514, 524, 550*
Bitterman, M. E., 7, 235, *514, 537*
Black, A. E., 433, 440, *511*
Black, M., 117, 118, 119, 120, 130, *514*
Blackwell, H. R., 234, *514*
Blier, A. A., 234, *536*
Bloom, B. S., 426, 427, *514*
Bloom, M., 4, *514*
Bloomfield, L., 406, 407, *514*
Boe, E. E., 329, *522*
Boesch, E. E., 107, *514*
Boigon, H. W., 428, *514*
Bolton, T. L., 32, *514*
Bondareff, W., 448, 450, *514*
Bone, R. N., 338, *527*
Boring, E. G., 228, *514*
Born, D. J., 350, *561*
Bosack, T. N., 294, *539*
Botwinick, J., 13, 249, 250, 258, 263, 265, 275, 314, 317, 454, 459, *514*
Bousfield, W. A., 351, *514*
Bowditch, H. P., 27, *514*
Brackbill, Y., 258, 261, 262, *515*
Bradway, K. P., 426, 452, 456, *515*
Braine, M. D. S., 412, 414, 419, 431, 433, *515*
Braithwaite, R. B., 118, 119, *515*
Bramble, W. J., 443, 453, 454, *530*
Braun, H. W., 259, 260, 265, 273, 274, 325, 342, 459, *515, 526*
Breese, F. H., 46, *510*
Brenner, M. W., 224, *515*
Brent, S. B., 419, *534*
Bridger, W. H., 294, 295, *515*
Bridgman, P. W., 116, *515*
Brinley, J. F., 275, *514*
Brodzinsky, D., 138, *545*
Bromley, D. B., 13, 16, 73, 79, 80, 89, 93, 95, 280, 456, 459, 461, *515, 539*
Bronfenbrenner, U., 12, 47, *515*
Bronner, A. F., 30, *529*
Brossard, L. M., 301, *516*
Brown, J., 350, *516*
Brown, R. W., 390, 405, 412, 414, 415, 435, *516*
Bruner, J. S., 321, 398, 435, 436, 439, *516, 526*

Bryan, A. I., 469, 470, 477, *525*
Bryk, J. A., 327, *516*
Bugelski, B. R., 320, *516*
Bühler, C., 4, 17, 54, 63, 64, 65, 67, *516*
Bühler, K., 63, *516*
Burger, M., 447, *516*
Burgess, E. W., 45, *518*
Burns, R. B., 389, 452, *516*
Burr, E. S., 199, *541*
Burt, C., 426, 430, 469, 470, 472, 475, 477, 482, *516*
Buss, A. H., 323, *537*
Butcher, H. J., 425, *516*

C

Caldwell, B. M., 292, 295, *516, 517, 527*
Cameron, J., 433, *517*
Cameron, N., 224, 433, *558*
Campbell, D. T., 13, 16, 18, 213, 425, 454, 455, *517, 552*
Canestrari, R. E., Jr., 81, 277, 317, 319, 323, *517*
Cannell, C. F., 453, 461, *529*
Cannizzo, S. R., 320, 344, *535*
Cannon, W. B., 27, *517*
Cantor, G. N. , 296, *542*
Carmichael, L., *517*
Carp, F. M., 486, *517*
Carroll, J. B., 166, *517*
Cassirer, E., 131, 132, 133, 135, *517*
Castaneda, A., 279, 326, *517*
Cattel, A. K. S., 441, *518*
Cattell, J. McK., 32, *517*
Cattell, J. McK., 32, *517*
Cattell, R. B., 6, 11, 63, 182, 194, 195, 196, 197, 199, 201, 202, 203, 204, 205, 207, 425, 428, 434, 436, 440, 441, 442, 443, 444, 453, 454, 455, 456, 457, 461, 478, 493, 494, *517, 518*
Cavan, R., 45, *518*
Cazden, C. B., 412, 413, 414, 516, *518*
Cermak, L. S., 325, *561*
Chapanis, A., 118, 119, 120, 125, *518*
Charles, D. C., 51, 225, *510, 518, 556*
Charlesworth, W. R., 166, *518*
Chase, H. H., 294, *535*
Chen, H. P., 403, *518, 532*
Chen, T. Y. L., 470, 471, 477, *518*
Chess, S., 186, 188, 295, *513, 556*
Child, I. L., 46, *560*

Chinsky, J. M., 320, *524*
Chomsky, N., 248, 360, 390, 406, 410, 418, *518, 519*
Chow, H. H., 470, 471, 477, *518*
Chown, S. M., 454, *519*
Christian, A. M., 453, *519*
Chrysostome, F., 470, *519*
Chuck, B., 295, *536*
Church, R. M., 288, *519*
Claparède, E., 123, *519*
Clark, D. H., 440, *538*
Clark, H. H., 388, *519*
Clark, J. V., 475, *509*
Clark, M. P., 426, 469, *519*
Clark, W. W., 470, *519*
Clay, H. M., 429, 458, 459, 460, *519*
Clifton, R. K., 295, 296, *519*
Coan, R. W., 194, 199, 201, 482, *519*
Cobb, N. J., 325, *548*
Coerper, K., 66, *519*
Cohen, J., 195, 450, 461, 470, 472, 478, *513, 519*
Cohen, R., 475, *519*
Cole, M., 319, *519*
Coles, G. R., 238, *537*
Coltheart, F. M. M., 477, *535*
Comalli, P. E., Jr., 212, 213, 214, 215, 216, 217, 218, 219, 220, 221, 222, 223, 224, *519, 520, 559*
Conant, J. B., 72, *520*
Conger, H. J., 430, *544*
Conrad, H. S., 34, 63, 450, 453, 456, 498, *533*
Conrad, R., 350, 459, *520*
Coombs, C., 155, *520*
Coon, R. C., 437, *545*
Corballis, M. C., 194, 195, 201, 204, *520*
Corman, C. D., 350, *520*
Corsini, R. J., 453, 455, 461, *520*
Cowdry, E. V., 44, *520*
Craik, F. I. M., 81, *520*
Cravens, R. B., 426, *515*
Critchley, H., 450, *520*
Crites, J. O., 440, *520*
Cronbach, L. J., 79, 195, 315, 432, 450, *520*
Cropley, A. J., 470, 477, *520*
Crossman, E., 459, 460, *520*
Crott, H. W., 470, 472, 483, *539*
Crovitz, E. 270, *520*

Cruze, W. W., 434, *520*
Cumming, M. E., 14, 45, 96, *520, 521*
Curtis, H. A., 470, *521*

D

Dahl, S., 58, *510*
Daley, M. F., 453, 455, 457, 459, *545*
Damianopoulos, E., 97, *521*
Damon, A., 169, 170, 487, 490, *521*
Danick, J. J., 351, *514*
Davies, A. D. M., 80, 217, *521*
Davis, A., 46, *521*
Davis, E. A., 389, 394, 397, *521*
Day, R. H., 234, *540*
Dean, M. F., 352, *534*
Dearborn, W. F., 167, 175, 178, *521*
Décarie, T. G., 301, *516*
Deese, J., *521*
DeLaguna, G., 361, *521*
DeLucia, C. A., 299, *539*
Delys, L., 461, *545*
Demming, J. A., 453, *521*
Denenberg, V. H., 267, *521*
Dennis, W., 26, 54, 62, 74, 434, *521*
Devoe, S., 164, *561*
Dewey, J., 37, *521*
Dingman, H. F., 468, *542*
Dolkart, M. B., 458, *552*
Doll, E. A., 34, 431, *521*
Dollard, J., 46, 142, 403, *521, 522, 543*
Dontchos, S., 295, *536*
Doob, L. W., 46, *522*
Doppelt, J. E. 426, 450, 453, 455, 457, 458, 459, 461. 470, *522*
Doris, J., 236, *547*
Dreher, G., 66, *537*
Dron, D. M., 329, *522*
Duncanson, J. P., 427, *522*
Duryea, R. A., 235, *537*
Dye, H. B., 434, *553*
Dye, N. W., 469, 470, *522*

E

Eberhart, V. L., 419, *546*
Eckensberger, L., 10, *514*
Eisdorfer, C., 277, 278, 279, *522*
Eisenberg, K., 419, *532*
Eisner, D., 213, 214, 496, *522*
Ekstrand, B. R., 310, 312, 349, 352, *522, 554, 557*

Ekstrom, R. B., 425, 439, 451, 461, 462, *525*
Elkind, D., 431, 432, 437, *522*
El Koussy, A. A. H., 457, *522*
Ellington, N. R., 347, 348, *522*
Emmerich, W., 10, 186, 188, 205, 206, 432, *522*
Engen, T., 294, *522*
Entwisle, D. R., 362, 383, *522, 523*
Erikson, E. H., 62, 124, 135, 252, *523*
Erlenmeyer-Kimling, L., 430, *523*
Ertl, J., 458, *523*
Ervin, S. M., 365, 385, 405, 412, 413, 415, *523, 543*
Escalona, S., 186, *523*
Eschenbrenner, A. J., Jr., 310, 352, *523, 534*
Estes, W. K., 168, 169, *523*
Etsten, B. E., 299, *539*
Eyferth, K., 473, *523*
Eysenck, H. J., 86, 475, *523*

F

Faber, C., 470, 473, *539*
Falkner, F., 178, *558*
Fantz, R. L., 180, 236, 298, *523*
Farrand, L., 32, *517*
Fassett, K. K., 453, 455, 461, *520*
Feffer, M. H., 181, *523*
Feifel, H., 373, 456, *523*
Feingold, S. N., 442, *518*
Felberbaum, R. A., 261, *532*
Felzen, E., 236
Ferguson, G. A., 427, 436, 481, *523, 524*
Fernald, G. M., 33, *529*
Fernberger, S. W., 29, *524*
Ferré, F., 118, 119, *524*
Fifer, G., 440, *538*
Fischer, G., 479, 480, *524*
Fisichelli, V. R., 295, *534*
Fiske, D. W., 13, 18, 425, *517, 524*
Fittkau, B., 478, 480, *553*
Fitzgerald, H. E., 258, 261, 262, *539*
Flavell, J. H., 74, 166, 184, 230, 320, 321, 341, 344, 431, 432, 435, *524, 535, 542*
Fleishman, E. A., 427, 484, *524*
Flory, C. D., 178, *525*
Fodor, J. A., 130, 138, 406, 418, 419, *513, 524*
Forsyth, D. F., 383, *523*

Foss, B. M., 301, *526*
Foster, J. C., 44, 453, *524*
Foulds, G. A., 453, 461, *524*
Fox, C., 374, 453, 457, 461, *524*
Frail, C. M., 419, *510*
Frank, L. K., 41, *525*
Frank, P. G., 116, 124, 125, *525*
Fraser, C., 390, *516*
Fraser, J., 333, 412, *547*
Freedman, A. M., 431, 443, *515*
Freeman, F. N., 178, *525*
Freeman, M., 440, *534*
French, J. W., 425, 439, 451, 461, 462, *525*
Frenkel, E., 64, *525*
Freud, A., 42, *525*
Freud, S., 62, *525*
Fries, C. C., 408, *525*
Fruchter, B., 195, *525*
Fulkerson, F. E., 352, *534*
Furneaux, W. D., 458, 461, *525*
Furth, H., 130, *525*
Fusaro, L., 164, *561*

G

Gaeth, J. H., 328, *525*
Gajo, F. D., 213, 214, *525*
Gallagher, J. W., 319, *525*
Galton, F., 43, 63, *525*
Garrett, H. E., 426, 469, 470, 472, 477,
    483, *525*
Garrett, M., 418, *524*
Garskof, B. E., 346, *551*
Gault, U., 469, 470, *525*
Gebhardt, F., 479, *526*
Geiselhart, R., 259, 260, 265, *515*
Gerhard, M., 56, *526*
Gesell, A., 40, 433, *526*
Ghiselli, E. E., 451, *526*
Giese, F., 63, *526*
Gilbert, J. A., 32, *526*
Gilbert, J. G., 44, 374, 455, 456, 458, 459,
    461, *526*
Ginsburg, H., 437, *526*
Gladis, M., 273, 274, 325, 331, 342, *526*
Glanzer, M., 402, *526*
Glick, J., 319, *519*
Goddard, H. H., 33, *526*
Goldfarb, N., 167, *526*
Goldfarb, W., 460, *526*
Goldhammer, H., 45, *518*

Goldman, R., 453, 458, *552*
Goldschmid, M. L., 166, 437, *526*
Goldstein, K., 74, 429, 460, *526*
Goldstein, L. G., 235, *562*
Goodenough, F. L., 397, *526*
Goodnow, J. I., 435, 436, 441, *516, 526*
Gordon, L. V., 154, *526*
Gordon, M., 419, *510*
Gordon, T., 301, *526*
Gorham, D. R., 456, *526*
Gottschaldt, K., 65, *526, 527*
Gotway, M. A., 319, 330, *534*
Gough, P. B., 418, *527*
Goulet, L. R., 16, 314, 317 319, 327, 331,
    338, 352, *527*
Gourevitch, V., 181, *523*
Graham, D., 470, *546*
Graham, F. K., 294, 295, 430, *527, 535*
Grandjean, E., 267, *511*
Grant, D. A., 308, *527*
Green, B. F., 158, 159, *527*
Green, D. T., 228, 240, 243, *527*
Green, R. F., 470, 472, 482, *527*
Greenbloom, R., 309, 312, 328, *547*
Greene, E. B., 427, 484, *527*
Greene, P., 178, *553*
Greenfield, P. M., 439, *527*
Gregoire, A., 402, *527*
Gregory, R. L., 215, *527*
Grinder, R., 28, 29, *527*
Grisby, O. J., 389, *527*
Groffmann, K. J., 62, *527*
Groos, K., 397, *527*
Grossman, J. L., 322, *531*
Gruhle, H. W., 63, *527*
Grünbaum, A., 117, *528*
Guilford, J. P., 425, 426, 436, 439, 469,
    480, *528*
Gummerman, K., 237, *544*
Guttman, L., 427, *528*
Gwozdecki, J., 214, 215, *538*

H

Haber, R. N., 235, *560*
Hagen, J. W., 282, 321, *536, 540*
Hagen, P., 470, *528*
Hagen, W., 66, *519, 528*
Haith, M. M., 294, *528*
Hall, C. S., 61, *528*
Hall, G. S., 27, 28, 35, 43, 62, 67, *528*

Hall, J. W., 351, *528*
Hall, V. C., 319, 325, 336, 337, 340, 341, *540*
Halpern, S., 218, *550*
Halstead, W. C., 430, *528*
Halwes, T. G., 321, *542*
Ham, M., 312, *557*
Handmann, E., 447, *528*
Hanfmann, E., *74, 528*
Hanley, C., 213, *528*
Harcum, E. R., 235, *528*
Harlow, H. F., 436, *528*
Harman, H. H., 199, *528*
Harper, P. A., 431, 443, *560*
Harrell, W., 457, *528*
Harris, C. W., 194, 198, 204, *528*
Harris, D. B., 10, 72, *528*
Harter, S., 272, *528*
Havighurst, R. J., 45, 96, *518, 528*
Hayes, K. J., 244, 428, 434, 437, *529*
Hayhurst, H., 419, *529*
Haynes, J. R., 430, *529*
Hays, W. L., *529*
Healy, W., 30, 33, *529*
Hearnshaw, L. S., *529*
Hebb, D. O., 229, 230, 431, 438, 443, 462, *529*
Heider, F. K., 389, 394, *529*
Heider, G. M., 186, 389, 394, *523, 529*
Heimer, C., 431, 443, *515*
Heimsoeth, H., 57, *561*
Heinonen, V., 469, 470, 479, 484, *529*
Hemberger, L., 470, *545*
Hempel, C. G., 72, 82, 83, 84, 85, 86, 124, 125, *529*
Hempel, W. E., 427, 484, *524, 529*
Henker, B., 298, *534*
Henri, V., 32, *513*
Henry, W., 14, 45, 96, *521, 529*
Henrysson, S., 481, *529*
Hen-Tov, A., 298, *534*
Heroard, J., 63, *529*
Heron, A., 429, 459, *529*
Hershenson, M., 229, 236, *529*
Herskovitz, M. J., 213, *552*
Hertman, M., 221, 222, 223, *561*
Hertzog, M. E., 186, 188, 295, *513, 556*
Hesse, M. B., 108, *529*
Heston, J. C., 453, 461, *529*
Hetzer, H., 54, *516*

Heydt, C., 63, *529*
Hill, J. P., 440, 441, *529*
Hindley, C. B., 426, 470, 471, *529, 530*
Hobika, J. H., 299, *539*
Hoffman, L. W., 39, 47, *530*
Hoffman, M. L., 39, 47, *530*
Hofstätter, P. R., 54, 55, 60, 64, 65, 204, 431, 432, 433, *530*
Höhn, E., 54, 64, 65, *530*
Holden, E. S., 26, *530*
Holt, E. B., *530*
Holt, L. M., 40, 432, *530*
Holton, R. B., 273, 274, *560*
Holtzman, W. H., 7, 183, 202, *530*
Honzik, M., 433, 440, *530*
Horn, A., 459, *533*
Horn, J. L., 194, 202, 204, 425, 428, 430, 435, 439, 441, 443, 444, 453, 454, 456, 457, 458, 459, 461, 462, 478, 493, *530, 553*
Horowitz, F. D., 295, *531*
Horst, P., 199, 203, 453, 455, 479, *531, 555*
Horton, D. L., 405, *531*
Hotelling, H., 195, *531*
Houston, J. P., 333, 334, 335, 336, *531*
Hover, G. L., 475, *531*
Howard, I. P., 215, *531*
Hsü, E. H., 483, *531*
Hubel, D. H., 232, *531*
Hulicka, I. M., 281, 322, 325, 342, *531*
Hull, C. L., 15, 46, 403, *531*
Humphreys, L. G., 425, 427, *531*
Humphries, N. W., 26, *531*
Hundal, P. S., 469, 470, *531*
Hunt, J. McV., 298, 432, 433, 435, 436, *531, 558*
Hurley, J. R., 434, 440, *531*
Hurlock, E. B., 4, 25, *531*
Hurst, J. G., 470, 471, 477, *531*
Husen, T., 426, *531*
Hutt, S. J., 294, *532*
Huttenlocher, J., 419, *532*
Hyatt, A., 28, *532*
Hyman, H. H., 493, *532*

I

Ichitani, T., 470, *555*
Inglis, J., 81, 429, *532*
Inhelder, B., 138, 366, *532*
Inoue, K., 429, *543*

Irvine, E. E., 441, *532*
Irwin, J. M., 332, *542*
Irwin, O. C., 301, 403, *518, 532*
Irzhanskaia, K. N., 261, *532*
Ives, W. C., 234, *532*

J

Jacklin, C. N., 295, 296, *539*
Jackson, C. L., 470, *532*
Jackson, D. N., 19, *532*
Jackson, J. C., 295, *527*
Jacobs, J., 32, *532*
James, W., 35, *532*
Janke, W., 484, *532, 533*
Janney, J. E., 25, *547*
Jarvik, L. F., 171, 430, *523, 534*
Jastrow, J., 32, *533*
Jeeves, M., 226, *548*
Jeffrey, W. E., 269, 276, 404, *533*
Jenkins, J. J., 122, 326, 362, 363, 405, 416, *533, 561*
Jensen, A. R., 319, 321, 430, 434, 440, 441, 442, *533*
Jerome, E. A., 323, 324, *533*
Jesperson, O., 360, *533*
John, E. A., 477, *516*
Johnson, C. D., 235, *562*
Johnson, D., 430, *544*
Johnson, G. J., 325, *533*
Johnston, W. A., 348, *533*
Jones, H. E., 34, 50, 63, 167, 249, 450, 451, 452, 453, 454, 456, 459, 498, 499, *533*
Jones, L. V., 195, 450, 469, 470, *533*
Jones, M. C., 453, *533*
Jones, T. A., *544*
Jostak, J., 453, 459, *561*
Judisch, J., 214, 215, *538*

K

Kagan, J., 13, 49, 50, 63, 186, 292, 298, 301, 398, 430, 440, *512, 534, 541, 544*
Kahneman, D., 235, *534*
Kalhorn, J., 46, *510*
Kallina, H., 468, *534*
Kallmann, F. J., 171, *534*
Kalveram, K. R., 477, *542*
Kamin, L. J., 453, 457, 461, 499, *534*
Kanak, N. J., 352, *534*

Kanner, L., 30, *534*
Kantor, J. R., 406, *534*
Kaplan, A., 117, 121, *534*
Kaplan, B., 126, 136, 140, 143, *534, 560*
Karelitz, R., 295, *534*
Karelitz, S., 295, *534*
Karp, S. A., 221, 222, 223, *552*
Kasanin, J., 74, *528*
Katz, E. W., 419, *534*
Katz, H., 339, 340, 343, 345, 349, *536*
Kausler, D. H., 280, 309, 310, 312, 313, 315, 319, 320, 323, 326, 327, 329, 330, 331, 347, 348, 352, 353, *516, 522, 534, 535, 537, 538*
Kawi, A., 431, *535*
Kaye, H., 294, 458, *522, 535, 539*
Kebbon, L., 473, 477, *535*
Keen, R. E., 294, *535*
Keeney, T. J., 320, 344, *535*
Kelley, H. P., 459, *535*
Kelley, T. L., 470, 477, *535*
Kellogg, L. A., 402, *535*
Kellogg, W. N., 402, *535*
Kelly, E. L., 51, *535*
Kelly, G., 139, *535*
Kendall, B. S., 430, *527*
Kendler, H. H., 320, 404, *535*
Kendler, T. S., 320, 404, *535*
Kennedy, W. A., 442, *535*
Kenny, P. B., 477, 478, *535*
Keppel, G., 307, 313, 317, 333, 334, 335, 337, 338, 339, 346, 347, 350, *535, 547, 558*
Kerlinger, F. N., 182, *535*
Kessen, W., 9, 10, 15, 72, 117, 139, 143, 152, 167, 205, 236, 319, 486, *519, 535, 536, 540, 551*
Kidd, A. H., 212, 215, *536, 550*
Kidd, R. M., 212, *536*
Kimble, G. A., 260, 263, *536*
King, W. L., 437, *536*
Kingsley, P. R., 321, *536*
Kirchner, W. R., 458, *536*
Kirkpatrick, E. A., 33, *536*
Kjeldegaard, P. M., 405, *531*
Klein, E., 472, 478, *513*
Klein, M., 42, *536*
Kleitman, N., 234, *536*
Klima, E. S., 412, *536*
Kline, N. J., 267, *521*

Klinger, N. K., 326, *536*
Knobloch, C. H., 431, *546*
Kodlin, D., 167, 171, 172, *536*
Kofsky, E., 158, *536*
Koga, Y., 44, *536*
Kohen-Raz, R., 432, *536*
Kohlberg, L., 123, 138, 158, 249, *536*
Koltsova, M. M., 261, 263, 264, *536*
Koppenaal, R. J., 339, 340, 343, 345, 349, *536*
Korchin, S., 224, 327, *536*
Korchin, S. J., 224, *511, 536*
Korenchevsky, V., 447, 449, *536*
Korn, S., 186, 188, *556*
Korner, A. F., 295, *536*
Kornetsky, C., 258, 263, 265, *514*
Kotaskova, J., 432, *537*
Krauskopf, J., 235, *537*
Krechevsky, I., 119, *537*
Kreindler, A., 265, *540*
Kristof, W., 18, *537*
Krohn, W. O., 30, *559*
Krull, A., 339, 340, 343, 345, 348, *536*
Kubo, Y., 459, *537*
Kuenne, M. R., 404, *537*
Kuhlen, R. G., 4, 13, 20, 25, 169, 445, 487, 493, *537, 547*
Kuhn, T. S., 117, 121, 122, 125, 417, *537*

L
Lacher, M. R., 370, *537*
Lachman, R., 118, 120, *537*
Lair, C. V., 280, 320, 326, 327, 353, *534, 537*
Lamb, S. M., *537*
Landau, H. G., 460, *514*
Lang, A., 65, *548*
Lang, P. J., 323, *537*
Langer, I., 473, *509*
Langer, J., 72, 141, *537*
Lansing, A. I., 457, *537*
Lashley, K. S., 417, 443, *537*
Laurence, M. W., 459, *537*
Laurendeau, M., 74, *551*
Lawrence, D., 238, *537*
Laytham, G. W. H., 217, *521*
Lefford, A., 177, *513*
Lehman, H. C., 93, *537*
Lehr, U., 66, 67, *537, 538, 556*

Lehtinen, L. C., 269, *542*
Lehtovaara, A., 469, 470, 471, *538*
Leibowitz, H. W., 16, 214, 215, *538, 546*
Leicht, K. L., 309, *538*
Leik, R. K., 160, 161, *538*
Leinert, G. A., 472, 473, 474, 475, *538, 539*
Lenard, H. G., 294, *532*
Lenneberg, E. H., 248, 396, *538*
Leopold, W. F., 402, *538*
Lesser, H. S., 440, *538*
Levenstein, P., 433, *538*
Levin, J. R., 321, *550*
Levine, J., 298, *534*
Levine, M., 119, *530*
Levinson, B., 272, *538*
Levinson, B. M., 439, 440, 441, *538*
Levy, N., 295, *539*
Lewin, K., 482, *538*
Lewis, D., 177, *538*
Lewis, H. B., 221, 222, 223, *561*
Lewis, H. P., 155, 157, *538*
Lewis, M. M., 298, 361, *534, 538*
Lewis, N., 437, *544*
Liebert, R. S., 217, 218, *538, 550*
Lienert, G. A., 470, 472, 473, 474, 475, 483, *538, 539*
Lindsay, R. B., *539*
Lindsey, J. M., 470, 482, *545*
Lindsley, O. R., 299, *539*
Lindzey, G., 61, *528*
Lintz, L., 258, 261, 262, *539*
Lipsitt, L. P., 279, 290, 291, 293, 294, 295, 296, 299, 300, 402, *517, 522, 539, 553*
Lipton, E. L., 295, *539*
Little, K. B., 194, 202, 204,
Livesley, W. J., 89, *539*
Livson, N., 433, *517*
Loevinger, J. A., 161, 190, *539*
Lohr, W., 65, *542*
Longeot, F., 180, *540*
Longstreth, L. E., 11, *540*
Loomis, D. J., 319, 325, 340, 341, *540*
Loranger, A. W., 459, *540*
Lorge, I., 373, 451, *523, 540*
Lowell, F., 385, *562*
Lucas, G., 472, 478, *513*
Lundy, R. M., 16, *546*
Luria, A. R., 361, *540*
Lynch, S., 321, *550*

M

Maccoby, E. E., 282, *540*
Machover, K., 221, 222, 223, *561*
Mackie, J. B., 439, *540*
Maddox, G. L., 96, *540*
Magladery, J. W., 449, 457, *540*
Maher, B. A., 79, *540*
Maier, H. W., 72, *540*
Maire, F., 213, *546*
Maleci, O., 451, *540*
Mallinger, B., 74, *521*
Mandler, G., 72, 324, *540*
Mann, I., 235, *540*
Marbe, K., 63, *540*
Margaret, A., 473, *556*
Margenau, H., 117, 118, *540*
Margis, P., 63, *540*
Marinesco, G., 265, *540*
Marquette, B., 10, *551*
Marquis, D. P., 301, *540*
Marshall, A. J., 234, *540*
Martin, E., 313, 327, *540, 541*
Martin, W. E., 188, *541*
Martini, F., 56, *541*
Massarik, F., 4, *516*
Matarazzo, R. G., 295, *527*
Mathews, M., 160, 161, *538*
Matson, F., 131, *541*
Maudsley, H., 30, *541*
Maxwell, A. E., 439, 459, 472, 475, *540, 541* ✶
McCahan, G. P., 470, *541*
McCall, R. B., 298, *541*
McCandless, B. R., 12, 15, 279, *517, 541*
McCarthy, D., 372, 403, *541*
McCullers, J. C., 326, *541*
McCulloch, T. L., 486, *541*
McCulloch, W. S., 119, *541*
McDonald, R. P., 199, *541*
McFarland, R. A., 212, *541*
McGeoch, J. A., 332, *541*
McGovern, J. B., 312, 346, *541*
McGraw, M., 161, *541*
McHugh, R. B., 470, 472, *541*
McNeill, D., 129, 138, 393, 396, 414, 419, *541, 542, 543*
McNeill, N. B., 10, *542*
McNemar, Q., 426, 469, 471, *542*
Mead, M., 42, *542*
Mednick, S. A., 269, *542*

Meehl, P. E., 315, *520*
Meely, B. E., *542*
Meili, G., 65, *542*
Meili, R., 65, 542
Meisser, P. B., 221, 222, 223, *561*
Melametsa, L., 481, *542*
Melcher, R. T., 431, *521*
Melton, A. W., 332, 333, *542*
Menyuk, P., 412, *542*
Mering, O. V., 55, *542*
Merleau-Ponty, M., 133, *542*
Mermelstein, E., 441, *542*
Merrill, M., 33, 168, 169, 442, 556, *542*
Merz, F., 477, *542*
Meyer, G., 452, 486, *550*
Meyer, W. J., 469, 470, *542*
Meyers, C. E., 468, *542*
Meyers, W. J., 296, *519, 542*
Miles, C. C., 450, 498, *542, 543*
Miles, W. R., 34, 44, 63, 211, 225, 450, 498, *543*
Milgram, N. A., 322, *543*
Milholland, J. E., 159, *543*
Miller, E. L., 51, *510*
Miller, F. M., 77, 78, 79, *543*
Miller, G. A., 390, 414, 429, 435, *519, 543*
Miller, J. G., 5, *543*
Miller, N. E., 46, 142, 403, *522, 543*
Miller, W. R., 412, *543*
Miner, J. B., 453, *543*
Mishima, J., 429, *543*
Misiak, H., 459, *540*
Mitchell, J. V., Jr., 481, *543*
Moede, W., 63, *543*
Moers, M., 66, *543*
Montague, W. E., 320, *509*
Montonari, M., 451, *540*
Moon, W. H., 320, 327, *537*
Mooney, C. M., 224, *543*
Moore, K. C., 27, *543*
Moore, T., 433, *543*
Moran, L. J., 484, *555*
Morant, G. M., 44, *536*
Morin, N. J., 325, *548*
Morrison, D. F., 459, *514*
Moss, H. A., 13, 50, 186, 292, *534*
Mowrer, O. H., 46, 124, *522, 543*
Mukherjee, B. N., 469, 470, 478, *543*
Munn, N. L., 212, *543*
Munnichs, J. M. A., 55, 68, *543*

Munro, J. A., 470, 471, *530*
Munsinger, H., 236, 237, *544*
Münsterberg, H., 32, *544*
Murchison, C., 36, 39, 45, *544*
Murdock, B. B., Jr., 350, *544*
Mussen, P. H., 47, 150, 430, *544*
Muus, R., 383, *523*
Myklebust, H. R., 430, *544*

N

Nagel, E., 5, 126, *544*
Najarian, P., 434, *521*
Neimark, E. D., 437, *544*
Nelson, V. L., 471, *549, 554*
Nesselroade, J. R., 9, 18, 197, 198, 199,
    200, 201, 205, 206, 207, 479, 483, 486,
    511, 544
Neugarten, B. L., 20, 96, 252, *528, 544*
Nevis, S., 180, *523*
Nikkel, N., 405, *544*
Nissen, H. W., 15, *544*
Noble, G. E., 15, 359, *544*
Norcross, K. J., 270, 271, 403, 404, 405,
    544, 545
Norman, R. D., 453, 455, 457, 459, *545*
Nunnally, J. C., 196, *545*
Nyssen, R., 461, *545*

O

Oden, M. H., 452, 453, 455, 499, *512*
Odom, R. D., 437, *545*
Oerter, R., 468, *545*
Oléron, P., 481, *545*
Olson, F. A., 321, *542*
Olton, R. M., 320, *545*
O'Neil, W. M., 470, 472, 475, *545*
Oppel, W. C., 431, 443, *560*
Oppenheim, P., 124, 125, *529*
Osborne, R. T., 455, 470, 482, *545*
Osgood, C. E., 122, 365, 406, *523, 545*
Over, R., 215, *545*
Overton, W. F., 5, 138, *545*
Owens, W. A., 451, 455, 456, 461, 470,
    472, 487, 499, *541, 545*

P

Pacaud, S., 458, 459, *545*
Paivio, A., 310, *562*
Palermo, D. S., 122, 279, 319, 326, 329,
    330, 405, 416, 417, 419, *517, 533, 536,
    544, 545, 546, 552, 561*

Pap, A., 117, 120, 121, *546*
Papousek, H., 289, 290, 293, 546
Parkes, A. S., 20, *547*
Parrish, M., 16, *546*
Parry, J. B., 426, *558*
Pasamanick, B., 431, *535, 546*
Pascal, R., 56, *546*
Paterson, D. G., 453, *519*
Pawlik, K., 480, *546*
Peabody, E. P., 26, *509*
Pederson, F. A., 433, 440, *546*
Pederson, L. J., 299, *539*
Peel, E. A., 470, *546*
Penney, R. K., 325, *533*
Pennypacker, H. S., 260, 263, *536*
Pepper, S. C., 117, 120, 121, 122, 125, 131,
    546
Perl, R. E., 469, 470, 477, *525*
Perlman, R. M., 454, 457, 461, *551*
Pessina, G., 451, *540*
Pfaffmann, C., 301, *546*
Phelps, W. M., 431, *521*
Phillippe, J., 33, *546*
Phillips, A., 29, *546*
Piaget, J., 7, 9, 124, 138, 164, 213, 215,
    248, 366, 397, 432, 435, 436, 482, *532,
    546, 547*
Pikler, E., 433, 434, *547*
Pinneau, S. R., 426, *547*
Pintner, R., 213, *547*
Platt, L., 20, *547*
Pollack, R. H., 213, 215, *547*
Popper, K. R., 72, 75, *547*
Poresky, R., 236, *547*
Postman, L., 306, 309, 312, 313, 317, 325,
    328, 333, 337, 338, 346, 347, 349, *547,
    558*
Prechtl, H. F. R., 294, *532, 547*
Pressey, S. L., 4, 13, 20, 25, 45, 445, 453,
    521, 547
Preyer, W., 26, 62, 67, *547*
Price, L. A., 425, 439, 451, 461, 462, *525*
Price, L. E., 278, 325, *548*
Privat, F., 213, *546, 547*
Pulver, U., 65, *542, 548*
Punfrey, P., 437, *548*

Q

Quarterman, C. J., 367, 376, *548,550*
Quereshi, M. Y., 484, *548*
Quetelet, A., 43, 54, 60, 61, 67, *548*

R

Rabbitt, P., 109, *548*
Radcliffe, J. A., 472, *548*
Rader, R. B., 431, 443, *560*
Rafferty, F. T., 439, *540*
Rajalakshmi, R., 226, *548*
Ransom, D., 24, *548*
Rashevsky, N., 118, *548*
Rau, L., 124, *552*
Raven, J. C., 74, 77, 78, 79, 453, 461, *524, 543, 548*
Rawlings, T. D., 470, 473, *548*
Raynor, R., 37, 288, *559*
Reese, H. W., 5, 126, 128, 130, 271, 272, 317, 319, 320, 322, 402, 404, *538, 548*
Reichard, S., 470, 471, 472, *549*
Reinert, G., 169, 171, 470, 473, 474, 475, 477, 484, 488, 506, *511, 549*
Reisen, A. H., 434, *549*
Reitan, R. M., 80, 430, *549*
Reuchlin, M., 481, *549*
Rice, L., 13, *524*
Richards, T. W., 469, 470, 471, *549*
Richmond, J. B., 295, *539*
Rickert, H., 57, *549*
Rieber, M., 440, *549*
Riegel, K. F., 67, 81, 363, 365, 367, 368, 369, 370, 371, 374, 375, 376, 380, 383, 384, 385, 386, 396, 450, 452, 456, 461, 472, 486, *537, 548, 549, 550, 562*
Riegel, R. M., 67, 375, 376, 383, 384, 452, 470, 472, 486, *550*
Ritzmann, H., 484, *532, 533*
Rivoire, J. L., 212, 215, *550*
Robbin, J. S., 275, *514*
Robbins, L. C., 17, *550*
Robbins, P. L., 299, *561*
Roff, M. A., 187, 427, *550*
Rohwer, W. D., Jr., 319, 321, *533, 550*
Rommetveit, R., 419, *557*
Ronge, A., 66, *528*
Roppert, J., 479, *524*
Rose, A. M., 96, *550*
Rose, C. L., 486, 493, *550*
Rosenfeld, L. S., 295, *534*
Rosenthal, F., 454, 457, 461, *551*
Rosenthal, I., 17, *550*
Ross, J., 201, 202, 203, *550*
Ross, J. R., 410, *550*
Rothney, J. W. M., 167, 175, 178, *521*
Rovee, C. K., 299, *550*

Rovee, D. T., 299, *550*
Ruch, F. L., 44, 327, 459, *550*
Rudel, R. G., 217, 218, *538, 550*
Rudner, R., 125, *551*
Runquist, W. N., 311, 328, *558*
Russell, W. A., 405, *551*

S

Salapatek, P., 236, *551*
Sameroff, A. J., 293, *551*
Sandak, J. M., 346, *551*
Sanders, B. S., 171, *551*
Sanders, S., 74, *551*
Sanders, W. B., 455, *545*
Sarason, S. B., 442, *518*
Sarbin, T. R., 397, *551*
Sardello, R. J., *535*
Schaie, K. W., 10, 16, 169, 171, 173, 213, 445, 447, 451, 452, 453, 454, 455, 457, 459, 461, 476, 482, 486, 487, 488, 489, 490, 496, 498, 499, 500, 504, 506, *522, 551, 555*
Scharmann, D., 66, *551*
Scherer, M., 74, 429, 460, *526*
Schmidt, G., 470, *559*
Schmidt, L. R., 470, 473, 474, 475, 477, *549*
Schmidt, W. H., 434, *552*
Schneirla, T. C., 1, *552*
Schon, D., 118, 131, *552*
Schorn, M., 63, *552*
Schubert, R., 67, *552*
Schulz, R. W., 310, 311, 328, *558*
Schwartz, D. W., 221, 222, 223, *552*
Sears, R. R., 46, 124, *522*
Sebeok, T. A., 406, *545*
Seeger, R. J., 117, 118, *552*
Segall, M. H., 213, *552*
Segel, D., 473, 474, *552*
Sells, S. B., 430, *529*
Semler, I. J., 440, *520*
Senn, M. J. E., 42, *552*
Shakow, D., 453, 458, *552*
Shapiro, S. I., 405, *552*
Sharp, D. W., 319, *519*
Sheatsley, P. B., 493, *532*
Shepard, R. N., 351, *552*
Shepard, W. O., 404, *552*
Shilling, C. W., 234, *532*
Shinn, M. W., 26, 27, *552*
Shipley, E., *552*

Shipley, W. C., 310, *552*
Shirley, M. M., 40, 156, 157, *552*
Shock, N. W., 169, 177, *553*
Shucard, D. W., 458, 461, *553*
Shulman, L. S., 441, *542*
Shuttleworth, F. K., 169, 170, 175, 505, *521, 553*
Sidman, M., 168, 169, *553*
Siegel, A. E., 19, *553*
Siegel, A. W., 283, 429, *553*
Sigel, I., 436, *553*
Simkin, J. S., 475, *553*
Simon, T., 33, *513*
Siqueland, E. R., 290, 291, 293, 300, *553*
Sixtl, F., 478, 480, *553*
Skager, R. W., 269, *533*
Skeels, H. M., 51, 434, *553*
Skiba, G., 67, *550*
Skutsch, R., 63, *553*
Slivinske, A. J., 470, *509*
Slobin, D. I., 10, 129, 413, 414, 415, 417, 419, *553*
Smith, H. D., 376, *550*
Smith, K. U., 178, *553*
Smith, L., 300, *553*
Smith, S. W., 234, *514*
Smith, T. L., 30, *554*
Solberg, P. A., 25, *562*
Solyom, L., 260, 261, *554*
Sontag, L. W., 41, 50, 426, *554*
Sorenson, H., 44, 455, *554*
Sosa, J. M., 450, *554*
Speakman, M. A., 458, *554*
Spear, N. E., 310, *554*
Spearman, C., 32, 429, 434, 469, 474, 477, *554*
Spears, W. C., 279, *539*
Sperling, G., 235, *554*
Spiker, C. C., 10, 12, 15, 126, 128, 129, 139, 270, 273, 274, 325, 405, *541, 544, 545, 554, 560*
Spitz, R. A., 434, *554*
Spranger, E., 64, *554*
Staats, A. W., 122, *554*
Stadius, G., 469, 470, 479, *554*
Stahl, E. L., 56, *554*
Stanka, R., 55, *554*
Stanley, J. C., 13, 16, *517*
Stark, K., 333, 337, 338, 346, 347, *547*
Steinhagen, K., 470, 472, 479, *554*

Steinschneider, A., 295, *539*
Stern, C., 372, 390, *554*
Stern, E., 63, 64, 66, *554*
Stern, W., 33, 63, 67, 372, 390, 482, *554, 555*
Stevens, S. S., 398, *555*
Stevenson, H. W., 259, 262, 263, 267, 271, 275, 276, 281, 282, 283, 429, *553, 555*
Stolz, L. M., 250, 251, 252, *555*
Stone, C. P., 266, 267, *550*
Storms, L. H., 405, *551*
Stott, L. W., 187, *555*
Strauss, A., 431, *560*
Strauss, S., 419, *532*
Street, R. F., *555*
Strong, E. K., 44, 63, *555*
Strong, R. T., Jr., 430, *555*
Strother, C. R., 171, 445, 447, 451, 452, 453, 454, 455, 459, 496, 498, 499, 500, 504, *551, 555*
Stroud, J. B., 427, *555*
Sullivan, A. M., 427, *555*
Sullivan, J. P., 484, *555*
Sumita, K., 470, *555*
Sunley, R., 433, *538*
Suzuki, N., 321, *550*
Sward, K., 454, *555*
Swartz, J. D., 484, *555*
Swets, J., 228, 240, 243, *527*
Swineford, F., 426, 469, 470, *555*
Sykes, D. H., 81, 429, *532*
Sylvester, R. H., 31, *555*
Szafran, J., 459, 460, *520*

T

Taine, H., 402, *555*
Talbot, E., 26, *556*
Tallard, G. A., 459, *556*
Tanner, J. M., 169, 171, 178, 190, *556*
Tauscher, H., 484, *549*
Taylor, C., 138, *556*
Taylor, G. A., 453, *524*
Teghtsoonian, M., 351, *552*
Templeton, W. B., 215, *531*
Templin, M. C., 412, *556*
Terman, L. M., 33, 442, *556*
Tefens, J. N., 59, 67, *556*
Teuber, H., 218, *550*
Thomae, H., 66, 67, *519, 538, 556*
Thomas, A., 186, 188, 295, *513, 556*

Thomas, J. P., 225, 234, *556*
Thompson, C., 61, *556*
Thompson, C. W., 452, 453, 456, 472, *515,*
    526, 556
Thompson, D. J., 167, 171, 172, *536*
Thompson, W. R., *556*
Thorndike, E. L., 34, 36, 44, 63, *556, 557*
Thurstone, L. L., 178, 224, 469, 481, *557*
Tiedemann, D., 63, 67, *557*
Tobin, S., 96, *528.*
Torgerson, W. J., 5, 158, 160, *557*
Toulmin, S., 72, 82, 87, 89, 117, 118, 120,
    124, *557*
Trapp, E. P., 315, *535*
Traub, R. E., 194, 195, 201, 205, *520*
Tucker, L. R., 195, 199, 203, 204, *557*
Turner, E. A., 419, *557*
Turner, M. B., 72, *557*
Tyler, F. T., 182, *557*
Tyler, L. E., 441, 450, *557*

U

Überla, K., 477, *557*
Underwood, B. J., 307, 309, 310, 311, 312,
    315, 317, 318, 328, 329, 333, 339, 342,
    347, 348, 349, 350, 351, 352, *511, 522,*
    535, 554, 557, 558
Uzgiris, I. C., 166, 298, *558*
Uznadze, D. N., 123, *558*

V

Vandenberg, S. G., 11, 178, 430, *558*
Van den Daele, L. D., 205, 432, *558*
Van de Riet, V., 442, *535*
Van der Vaart, H. R., 169, 179, *558*
Velton, H. V., 402, *558*
Verhage, F., 498, 500, *558*
Vernon, P. E., 426, 461, 470, *558*
Verville, E., 224, *558*
Very, P. S., 469, 470, 481, *522, 558*
Verzar-McDougall, E. J., 267, *558*
Vinh-Bang, 164, *558*
von Bertalanffy, L., 5, 135, 169, 177, *558,*
    559
von Bracken, H., 63, *559*
von Glaserfeld, E., 389, *559*
von Kerekjarto, M., 470, *559*
Vukovich, A., 477, 480, *559*
Vygotsky, L. S., 397, *559*

W

Wallace, J. G., 225, *559*
Wallace, W. L., 450, 453, 455, 457, 458,
    459, 461, *522*
Wallace, W. P., 352, *522*
Wallin, J. E. W., 30, *559*
Walters, Sister A., 213, *559*
Wapner, S., 212, 213, 214, 215, 216, 217,
    219, 220, 221, 222, 223, *520, 559, 561*
Ware, W. B., 351, *528*
Watson, J. B., 37, 287, 288, 407, 417, *559*
Watson, J. S., 298, *559*
Watson, R. I., 268, *559*
Wechsler, D., 374, 450, 458, 461, 498, *559*
Weiner, G., 431, 443, *560*
Weiner, M., 470, 472, *560*
Weir, M., 236, *544*
Weir, R. H., 397, *560*
Weiss, A. D., 212, *560*
Weiss, E., 63, *560*
Weiss, I., 437, *522*
Weisstein, N., 235, *560*
Weksel, W., 419, *513*
Welford, A. T., 44, 78, 429, 447, 458, 459,
    460, 487, *560*
Wender, P. H., 433, 440, *546*
Weniger, F. L., 55, *542*
Werner, E. E., 433, *560*
Werner, H., 7, 74, 136, 140, 141, 142, 212,
    213, 214, 215, 216, 217, 219, 220, 223,
    431, 468, *520, 559, 560*
Wertheimer, M., 228, *560*
Werts, C. E., 441, *560*
Wetherick, N. E., 79, 81, *560*
Wetzel, N. C., 187, *560*
Wewetzer, K. H., 473, 481, *560*
White, P. O., 475, *523*
White, J., 442, *535*
White, S. H., 123, 273, 274, 324, 404, *560*
Whiteman, M., 453, 459, *561*
Whiting, J. W., 46, *561*
Whitmarsh, G. A., 351, *514*
Wickens, G., 259, 260, 262, 264, *561*
Wickens, D. D., 259, 260, 262, 264, 325,
    350, *520, 561*
Wicklund, D. A., 326, *561*
Wiesel, T. N., 232, *531*
Wilcox, B. M., 299, *561*
Wilkie, F. L., 277, 278, *522*
Willard, E., 26, *561*

Williams, H. S., 426, 470, 471, *561*
Williams, M., 455, *561*
Williams, R. H., 45, *561*
Willoughby, R. R., 280, 450, 455, 456, 458, 459, 461, *561*
Wimer, R. E., 281, *561*
Windelband, W., 57, *561*
Wirth, C. G., 45, *561*
Witkin, H. A., 221, 222, 223, *561*
Witmer, L., 29, 31, *561*
Wittemann, K., 475, *519*
Wohlwill, J. F., 5, 15, 140, 151, 158, 160, 161, 164, 166, 178, 184, 191, 213, 215, 224, *561*
Wolf, E., 234, *561*
Wolf, P. H., 295, *562*
Wolfe, R., 181, *562*
Wolff, G., 171, 295, *562*
Wolfle, D., 24, *562*
Womack, M., 440, *549*
Woodrow, H., 385, 427, 481, *562*
Wortis, H., 431, 443, *515*

Wright, R. E., 477, *562*
Wyss, D., 61, *562*

XYZ

Yakorcynsky, G. к., 374, 456, *562*
Yerkes, R. M., 7, 34, 450, *562*
Young, F. M., 397, *562*
Young, R. K., 313, *562*
Yuille, J. C., 310, *562*
Zahn, C., 166, *518*
Zavortink, B., 313, *535*
Zeidner, J., 235, *562*
Zeiher, H., 385, *562*
Zerbolio, D. J., 213, *528*
Zigler, E., 5, 13, 127, 140, *562*
Zigler, M. J., 234, *561*
Zivian, A., 386, *550*
Zivian, M. T., 363, 370, 385, *562*
Zubek, J. P., 25, 454, 457, 458, 461, 498, *513, 562*
Zyve, C. I., 389, 394, *564*

Subject Index

Ability-differentiation hypothesis, 473
Abnormality, 74-76
Adaptive flexibility, 96
Adolescence
  conditioning, 259-261, 263, 265-266
  intelligence and cognition, 247-251,
    450-462, 470-473, 475, 498, 500
  language, 370, 374-376, 380-381, 387,
    417, 272-274, 276, 283
  part-whole differentiation, 221-223
  perceptual closure, 224-225
  retention-forgetting, 322, 325, 327-330,
    332-334, 337-339, 342, 348
  spatial orientation, 215-221
  speed of recognition, 225-226
  verbal learning, 322, 325, 327-330,
    332-334, 337-339, 342, 348
Adulthood
  conditioning, 259-266, 268
  creative thinking, 93-96
  illusions, 213-215
  intellectual changes, 73-81
  intelligence and cognition, 247-251,
    450-462, 470-473, 475, 498,
    500
  language, 374-376, 405
  learning, 270-283
  part-whole differentiation, 221-223
  perceptual closure, 224-225
  spatial relations, 217-221
  speed of recognition, 225-226

verbal learning, 319, 324, 326, 342
retention-forgetting, 319, 324, 326, 342
Age
  and cohort variable, 169-173
  and dependent variables, 60
  chronological, 15, 33, 317, 337
  concepts, 15-16, 129
  generalizability over, 202-203, 206
  manipulation, 16
  response changes, 150-152
  simulations, 16
Age variable, 11, 127, 141, 150-151,
    169-173, 485-486
  status of, 11, 14-15, 150-151
Age change vs. age differences, 16-18, 20,
    317
Age-differentiation hypotheses, 468-473
  age parameter, 468-473
  differentiation-integration- differentia-
    tion, 471
  general factor, 471
  group factors, 471
  integration-disintegration hypothesis,
    471
  supportive vs. negative evidence,
    469-475
Age-sensitive learning processes, 314
Age-sensitive processes, 317-331
  amount of transfer, 331
  interference proneness, 323-328, 334
  mediating capacity, 340-341

mediation-retention relationship, 342
mediational deficiency hypothesis, 317,
    320-321, 328, 343
proactive inhibition, 331-337, 343-346
production-deficiency hypothesis,
    320-321, 344-345, 353
recognition, 351
R-S learning, 329-331
retroactive inhibition, 331-343
short-term memory, 349-350
stimulus selection, 327-329
Age-specific theories vs. life-span theory,
    14-15
Aging,
    and performance speed, 223
    and visual changes, 211-226
    counterpart theory, 111-113
    differential longevity, 112
    long-term consequences, 112
    psychology of, 72-74
    sex differences, 217
    vs. development, 112
Aging patterns over life-span, 213-
    auditory, 217
    conception of, 72
    conditionability, 262-263
    creative thinking, 93-96, 108
    crystallized intelligence, 494, 499,
        501-505
    fluid intelligence, 495, 499, 501-505
    form discrimination, 226
    illusions, 213-215
    in factor structure of intelligence,
        467-484
    intellectual performance, 34, 44, 48-51,
        60, 73-76, 109, 247-253, 446-464
    language, 367-371
    learning, 268-282, 292, 319-336
    learning in rats, 266-267
    perceptual span, 225
    perceptual speed, 225
    position preference, 78
    rote vs. mediated learning, 320-323
    spatial orientation, 215-221
    stimulus generalization, 268-269
Aids and concepts, 435-438
Analogy or model, 108-111
    and explicandum, 109
    conception of, 108
    function of, 108

Animals,
    learning, 266-267, 275
Anlage, 428-431
    concept, 438
    aphasias, 429
    apprehension span, 429
    attention, 429
    development of intelligence, 429
    hereditary potential, 430
    immediate expression of, 429
    nature of, 430
    perceptual-motor integration, 429
    perseveration, 429
    short-term memory, 429
Anthropology, 42
Anxiety, 278-279
Associationism, 307
Associative learning, 310
Associative strength, 307
Associativity, 437
Attention span, 295
Attentional behavior, 297, 302
Audition, 237-238
Auditory stimuli, 290-292, 296

B

Baby biographies, 26, 63, 402
Base level, 299
Basic data relational system, 9, 201
Behavioral change, 139-140, 150, 194
Behaviorism, 37, 46, 121-122
Bentler monotonicity analysis, 163
Bilingualism, 398
Bioclimatological events, 506
Biological determinants, 495
Biotic variables, 15
Bivariate methodology, 195
Bloomfeldian linguistics, 406-409
    behavioristic approach, 407, 417
    frames-technique, 408
Body tilt, 215-216
Brain-damage
    cognition, 218
    learning, 260-261

C

Cardiac deceleration, 295
Categorical determinism, 115, 117, 145
Ceiling effects, 477

Central nervous system, 110-111, 113
Change,
    age, 150-155
    basic paradigm, 5, 9, 11
    behavioral, 127, 139-140, 150, 194
    cumulative, 111-113
    developmental change, 4-6, 21, 43, 123,
        132, 139-140
    differential, 201
    direction of, 111-113, 140-141
    environmental treatment effect,
        488-492, 502
    experimental settings for, 250
    generation/cohort effect, 169-173,
        488-492
    interrelation among, 180-182
    long-term, 11, 15, 20, 193, 204, 206
    maturational effect, 488-492, 497
    measurement artifact, 153
    nature of, 10
    nature of cause, 133, 135, 138, 140
    ontogenetic, 4, 126
    operant conditioning, 266
    organic, 111-113
    phylogenetic, 126
    qualitative, 123, 132-135, 139, 142, 151,
        154, 163-166, 179-180, 183, 190,
        193, 197, 198-199, 203, 205-206,
        248, 249, 251
    quantitative, 60, 132-134, 152, 163-166,
        177-179, 182-183, 190, 193, 197,
        198-199, 205-206, 248, 249
    sequence of, 15
    short-term, 10-11
    stages, 64, 128, 134, 143-144, 184, 203,
        205, 230-231, 249, 431-445
    structural, 123, 134-135, 139
    unidirectional, 111-113
Change-score analysis, 182
Child development, 26-42, 45-48, 53
Child study institutes, 39
    berkeley, 41
    Fels Research, 40-41
    function of, 39-41
    Iowa Child Welfare, 40
    Merrill-Palmer, 40
    Yale Psycho-Clinic, 40
Child study movement, 27, 29
Child personality development, 46
Child psychiatry, 30-31

Childhood
    conditioning, 259-264
    illusions, 212-215
    intelligence and cognition, 432-434,
        440-441, 463
    language, 367-369, 372-373, 374-379
    learning, 268-282
    part-whole differentiation, 222-223
    spatial orientations, 215-221
    retention-forgetting, 317, 319, 321-330,
        336
    speed of recognition, 225-226
    verbal learning, 317, 319, 321-330, 336
Children's clinic, 29-31
Chomsky's linguistics, 409-411
    and learning theories, 416
    competence model, 410-411, 416, 418
    performance model, 410-411, 416, 418
Chronological aging, 13, 33, 317, 337,485
Chronotypic changes, 64
Cognition, 247-253
    adult cognitive changes, 247-251
    age changes, 485-486, 488
    age differences, 485-486
    conventional research strategies, 171-174,
        486-487
    cultural change, 485-486
    developmental change, 485, 488-489
    environmental input, 248-250
    general developmental model, 486-492
    generational differences, 485, 488-492,
        493-506
    language, and 359
    time of measurement, 488-492, 496,
        504-506
Cognitive shift, 75
Color preferences, 300
Comparative developmental psychologies,
    8-9
Comparative factor analytic research,
    467-484
    ability-differentiation hypothesis, 473
    age-differentiation hypothesis, 468-473
    age parameter, 468-473
    comparability issue, 480
    construct validity of measurement, 477
    criteria for evaluation of change,
        478-480, 483-484
    developmental ability differentiation,
        474

developmental personality differentiation, 474-475
divergence hypothesis, 473
factor change, 480-484
factor structure change in tests, 481
fluid vs. crystallized intelligence, 478
heredity vs. environment issue, 478
in intelligence, 467-484
in motor behavior, 484
in perceptual abilities, 484
in psycholinguistic abilities, 484
in word association, 484
methodological issues, 475-479
secondary age parameters, 473-475
stability vs. instability in factor pattern,
469-475
Component processes, 332-346
age-degree of learning bias, 336-344
competition-at-recall, 332-346, 349
competition-differentiation composite,
333, 338, 343
list differentiation, 332-346
modified modified recall, mmfr, 336,
339-340, 342-343, 346
paced recall, 342-343
paced task, 339, 346
spontaneous recovery, 332-347, 349
unlearning, 332-350
Composite longitudinal gradient, 496-497
Concept, 118
definition, 118
descriptive, 118
development, 123
theoretical, 118-119
validation, 118
Concept formation, 434-438
concept awareness, 434
generalised solution instruments, 436
indirect measurement, 435
nullifiability, 437
Conditioning, 36, 37, 258, 307-308,
classical, 258, 288, 290, 292-294
classical vs. operant, 292
comparability of results, 258-259
in neonates, 289-294
operant and instrumental, 265-267, 288,
290, 292-294, 298-301
Conditioning capacity, 296
Conditioning stimulus, 292
Conjugate reinforcement, 297-301
Connectionism, 36

Conservation aquisition, 164-166
Content preferences, 77
Contingent vs. noncontingent reinforcement, 297-299
Counterpart theory, 111
Conventional research strategies, 171-174,
469-470, 486-487, 495
cross-sectional approach, 16, 25, 60,
171-174, 199-200, 213, 469-470,
472, 476, 487, 501
longitudinal approach, 16-17, 25, 151,
167, 199-201, 213, 469-470, 472,
476, 487-501
time-lag approach, 487
Corollary model issues, 135-144
Covariation chart, 63, 193
Covariation techniques, 201-206
differential R-technique, 205
function of, 205-206
incremental P-technique, 182
O-technique, 203
P-technique. 182, 202-203
Q-technique, 201-202
R-technique, 201-202
relationship to stages, 205-206
S-technique. 203-204, 206
T-technique, 203-204, 206
Cross-sectional sequences, 488
Cross-sequential matrix, 502-505
net age difference estimate, 489-492,
502
net cohort difference estimate, 503-504
Crystallized intelligence, 494, 499, 501-505
Curiosity reinforcers, 298

D

Dark adaptation, 235
Darwin's evolution theory, 28, 54, 58-59
Defensive responder, 296
Descriptive vs. explanatory research, 47
Detection theory, 240-243, 245
Development, 126
behavioral definition, 126-130
biological, 248-249
cognitive, 248-253
concept, 56-59, 63, 126-129
definition of, 126-130, 249, 252
descriptive term, 128-129
laws in, 20, 128
organismic definition, 126-130
structural, 207

uniformity within species, 247-253
Developmental ability differentiation
    hypothesis, 474
Developmental disciplines, 4-7, 27
    research parameters, 5-7
    study of change, 4-21
Developmental curves, 64
Developmental disciplines, 4-7, 27
Developmental function, 151-152, 176-180,
    182-191
    and age continuum, 178-179
    and level of response, 179-180
    form and shape, 151-152, 176, 179-180,
        190
    generalizability vs. specificity, 152
    rate of, 178-180, 190
    specification of, 153, 177-178, 183
    unidimensional vs. multidimensional
        variables, 152-153
Developmental personality-differentiation
    hypothesis, 474-475
Developmental psychology, 24-67
    conception of, 24-25
    historical roots, 25-42, 62-65
Developmental research methodology
    age-equivalence of tests, 18, 153
    age-related change, 10-21, 44
    age simulations, 16
    change-pattern analysis, 184-186
    convergence model, 174-175
    correlational techniques, 17
    cross-sectional approach, 16, 25, 60,
        199-200, 213, 469-476, 486-487
    culture invariant measurement, 155
    cumulative model of scaling, 158-160,
        190
    description of age functions, 12
    developmental channel approach, 187
    disjunctive model of scaling, 160-161,
        190
    explanation of age functions, 12
    idealized function approach, 187
    ipsative approach, 206
    issue of age variable, 14-15, 20, 150-153,
        169-175, 180-182, 292
    issue of homology, 14-15
    life-span approach vs. age-specific
        approach, 14-15, 17, 20
    longitudinal approach, 16-17, 25, 151,
        167, 199-201, 203, 213, 469-476,
        487-501

nomothetic vs. idiographic, 13
normative approach, 187
objectives of developmental study, 15-16
probability model approach, 166
problems and issues, 5-7, 15, 18, 149
prospective method, 17
retrospective method, 16
scales of measurement, 153-154
scalogram-analytic approach, 156, 158
time-series-analysis, 183
trifactorial model, 171-174, 487-492
two-factor model, 487-488
Differential discriminative stimuli, 298
Differential learning, 16
Discontinuity vs. continuity, 20, 141-144,
    188, 207
Discrimination learning, 269-276, 291
Discriminative vs. conditioned stimulus, 292
Doctrine of preformation, 58

E
Early experience, 292
Educational psychology, 35, 62
Effects of deprivation, 46
Eliciting stimulus, 291
Epigenesis, 58
Erikson's model of life-span changes, 257
Experimental vs. correlational techniques,
    194-195
Experimental child psychology, 36-38
Exploratory behavior, 299
External validity, 13
Extinction, 264-267, 299-300
Extrinsic stimulation, 302
Eyeblink response, 259

F
Factor analysis, 196-207
    additive model, 197
    estimation of factor scores, 199
    function of, 196-199
    longitudinal factor analysis, 201, 204
    N mode, 204-205
    three mode, 204-205
Factor model of change
    and test construction, 483
    criteria for change, 478-480, 483-484
    differential psychology, 482
    differentiation hypotheses, 467-484
    emergence of factors, 200

factor metamorphosis, 200, 482
field-theory, 482
manipulation of change, 481, 484
Factor structure of intelligence, 469-484
    simple structure, 478
    and developmental change, 476
    concept of, 478
    concept of factor metamorphosis, 482
    dedifferentiation in old age, 482
    differentiation over childhood, 482
    experimental effects on, 481
    factor change, 480-484
    implications of change in, 483-484
    invariance over adulthood, 482
    postulate of invariance, 480-481
    quantitative vs. qualitative similarity,
        478-479
    similarity rotation, 479
    stability vs. instability of, 469-479
    transformation analysis, 479
    validity of intelligence structure models,
        483
Factors
    qualitative equivalence, 199
    factor scores-factor loading pattern,
        197-199, 203
    stability coefficients, 201
First-order habits, 307-308
Fixation, 298
Floor effects, 477
Fluid intelligence, 495, 499, 501-505
Follow-up studies, 50-51
Food intake schedule, 301
Forgetting, 305-355
    component processes, 332-346
    interference theory, 306-359
    long-term forgetting, 349
    mediational devices, 306
    proactive inhibition, 331-337, 343-346,
        349-350
    retroactive inhibition, 331-343, 347-350
    retrieval, 307
    storage, 307
    trace theory, 306
Free association, 375, 381-383, 385
    paradigmatic responses, 382-384
    syntagmatic responses, 382-384
Frustration-aggression hypothesis, 46
Functional psychology, 35
Functionalism, 307

G
General developmental psychology, 6-12
General developmental model, 171-174,
    486-492
    three-factor model, 171-174, 487
    two-factor model, 171-174, 487-488
Generalized habits, 309, 321, 328
    selector mechanism, 309, 311, 334-335,
        337-339, 347
    stimulus selection, 309, 311
Generalization effects, 307
Generational effects, 169-173, 492-499
    age gradients, 494, 499, 503, 505
    chronological analysis, 498-500
    cross-sectional vs. longitudinal gradient,
        497
    cross-sequential approach, 496
    cross-sequential matrix, 500
    crystallized intelligence, 494-495,
        498-499
    differences in genetic structure, 494
    differences in prior experience, 494
    estimation of, 496, 500, 502-504
    fluid intelligence, 494-495, 502-505
    intelligence development, 492-499
    motor speed, 494, 504
Genetic psychography, 63
Genetic psychology, 26-29, 31, 35, 62
German entwicklungsnovel, 56
Gompertz function, 183
Guttman scales, 158-159 163

H
Habit-family hierarchy concept, 307, 309
Habit repertoire, 309
Habit strength, 318, 336, 341-342
Habituation, 260, 263-264, 294, 296
Heart rate acceleration vs. deceleration,
    295-297
Heredity vs. environment, 11, 286-287
Holism vs. elementarism, 136-137
Hullian S-R model, 314
Hullian theory, 119, 307-308
Humanistic psychology, 61
Hypnotic age regression, 16-17

I
Illusions
    Muller-Lyer, 212-214
    Poggendorff, 215

Ponzo, 213-215
Titchener circles, 213-215
Image, 228, 310
Imagery, 108
Individual differences, 32, 43, 295, 430-431
Infant laboratories, 299
Infants
    conditioning, 259-264, 288-300
    intelligence, 432-434
    learning, 268-283, 293-300
    retention-forgetting, 319
    verbal learning, 319
Information processing, 109-110
    chaining paradigm, 362-367, 391
    human vs. computer, 109-110
    response equivalence paradigm, 362-367, 380, 391
    reverberation, 362-366
    stimulus equivalence paradigm, 362-367, 391
Informative feedback, 307
Intelligence, 74, 93-96, 423-505
    abilities, 423
    age-related changes, 467-473
    age parameters, 80, 468-473
    anlage function, 428-431
    bioclimatological events, 506
    comparative factor analytic research, 467-484
    deterioration, 74, 76, 374, 446-450,
    differentiation hypotheses, 426
    general factor model, 483
    gestalt-process model, 483
    multiple factor model, 483
    overt behavioral measurements, 430
    stages of development, 74, 431-445
Intellectual abilities, 425
    Anderson theory, 427-428, 439
    anlage function, 428-431
    breadth validity, 425
    crystallized, 498-499
    differentiation of, 425
    emergence of linear patterns, 428
    factor composition, 428
    Ferguson theory, 427, 443
    fluid, 498-499
    individual differences in, 430-431
    issue of unity and differentiation, 426-428
    overlap theory, 428-431

primary factors, 425
simplex model, 427
structural damage, 431
structural differences in, 430-431
test-retest correlation, 426
Intelligence in adults
    alternative mechanisms, gf, gc, 455-456, 462-463
    crystallized intelligence, gc, 453-455, 462-463, 465
    intensive accultration, 445
    fluid intelligence, gf, 454-455, 457, 462-463, 465-466
    occupational adjustment, 445, 454-455
    perceptual-motor speediness, 454
    peripheral functions, gu, 456
Intelligence in children,
    intensive acculturation stage, 438-445
    sensori-motor alertness stage, 432-434
    stage of concept and aid acquisition, 435-438
Intelligence decline, 446-450, 504
    and age-differences in CNS, 447-449, 465
    and age-differences in sensorium, 446-447, 456-457
    and aging, 446-450
    and brain function, 448-449
    and memory, 458-459
    and reasoning, 458-461
    and speediness, 458-461
    behavioral evidence, 450-452
    cohort differences, 445, 452
    compensatory modes of functioning, 78
    cross-sectional studies, 450-451
    cross-sequential analyses, 452-453
    educational factor, 451
    intrusive modes, 78
    longitudinal studies, 451-452
    neurological-physiological functioning, 450, 457
    performance IQ vs. verbal IQ, 461
Intelligence development, 423
    ability differentiation hypothesis, 473-474
    adulthood and old age, 445-464
    age-differentiation hypotheses, 468-473
    alternative mechanisms, 445, 455-456, 462
    and factor analytical models, 483
    changes over age, 432-464, 502-505

childhood period, 432-445
chronological analysis, 498-499
comparison of cross-sectional studies, 498
concept formation, 434-435
crystallized and fluid intelligence, 443
crystallized intelligence measures,
  444-445, 453-454, 462
fluid intelligence measures, 444-445,
  454-455, 462
intellectual training effect, 481
long-term experimental effects, 481
performance differentiation hypothesis,
  474
personality differentiation hypothesis,
  474-475
short-term experimental effects, 481
stages vs. quasi-stages, 432
Intensive acculturation, 438-445
collective intelligence, 439
issue of culture-fair tests, 442
shaping of abilities, 441
vs. incidental learning, 442
Interference theory, 312-359
contextual cues, 312
extralaboratory interference, 338, 340
  342, 348-349
linguistic habits, 334, 349
list sequences, 312-313
proactive inhibition, 312, 323-328,
  330-331
retention interval, 333-335, 337
retroactive inhibition, 330-331, 312-313,
  323-328
Interindividual differences, 13, 16, 112, 152,
  189-191, 289
Internalization, 436
Intraindividual stability, 202, 204, 207
Intraindividual variability, 13-14, 16-17,
  202-203, 206-207
Intrinsic stimulation, 302
Introspection, 239
Involuntary behavior, 265
Ipsilateral head-turn, 289-290, 292-294,
  297-301
IQ-concept, 33

L

Lamarckian theory, 28-29
Language
analysis of arguments, 96-107

and emotional development, 397-398
and intellectual development, 397-398
and mediation, 403-404
and verbal learning, 405-406
associative behavior, 375-376
competence vs. performance model,
  410-411, 416
deep structure, 410-417
development, 358-397, 401-419
differential decline, 396
dualistic conception of, 407
egocentric vs. socialized speech, 397
identification of classes, 379-389
implicit, explicit relations, 387-389
input-output ratio, 378-379
internal logic, 96-111
meaning concept, 371-372
nature of phonological units, 411
nature of semantic units, 411
nature of syntactic units, 411
paradigmatic and syntagmatic classes,
  384
phrase or constituent structure analysis
  of, 408-409, 416
preference for word classes, 383
repertoire of relations, 371-372
semantic structure, 376-377
surface structure, 410, 417
theory of, 410-411
variables effecting identification,
  369-371
vocabulary, 372-374
word classes-relational nets, 385-387
word identification, 361-367, 367-371
Language acquisition, 358-397, 401-419
acquired distinctiveness of cues,
  403-404, 406
acquired equivalence of cues, 403-404
acquisition of word classes, 363-367
basic structure of utterances, 412
bilingualism, 402
clue words, 367-371
developmental patterns in, 402-403
function of sex in, 402-403
function of social variables, 403
function of age in, 402-403
history of research, 401
identification of elements, 367
imitation, 412-414
influence of expansion, 413-414

influence of modeling, 413-414
learning theories, 416
linguistic performance and behavior, 419
mediational deficiency, 404, 406
multiword utterances, 415
other languages, 402
overgeneralization errors, 415
performance in learning tasks, 603
phonological development, 402
secondary generalization, 403
semantic development, 402
syntactic development, 402
target words, 367-371
two-word utterances, 414
verbal learning, 404-406
Law of effect, 36
Learning, 36, 46, 257-294
  learning set acquisition, 271-272
  competition-interference prerequisite, 317
  curves, 204
  habit strength, 279
  incidental, 279-280
  infants and neonates, 288-302
  intentional, 282
  methodological paradigms, 312-350
  pacing schedule, 277-278
  paired associate, 277, 321
  rate of learning, 317-320, 336-337
  serial, 277
  stimulus exposure interval, 278
  transfer, 272
  unconditioned and conditioned behavior, 287-292
  verbal vs. visual mnemonics, 320-323
Learning sets, 271-272, 436
Libido, 61
Likelihood ratio, 240-242
Life plans, 302
Life-span developmental psychology, 3-4, 53-67, 71-72, 211-212
  classification of attributes, 9-10, 289
  classification of entities, 7-9, 20, 112, 289
  conception of, 72;111
  definition of, 12
  development and aging, 72
  explanatory mechanisms, 11-12
  explication of time continuum, 10
  generalizability of data, 13

generalizability over people, 13
history, 23-52, 53-67
interindividual variability, 13, 16, 112, 152, 189-191, 289
intraindividual variability, 13-14, 16-17, 202-203, 206-207
multidisciplinary studies, 87
natural events, 87
prescientific origins, 55-59
process-mechanisms, 11-12
psychoanalysis, 61
scientific origins, 59-67
theory construction within, 14-15;72-114
Linguistic associations, 334, 349
Linguistics, 401
  American school of, 407
  antimentalistic position, 407
  bloomfeldian linguistics, 406-407
  Chomsky, 409-411
  cross-linguistic analyses, 419
  linguistic universals, 419
  mentalistic concepts, 401, 410
  rationalistic concepts, 401, 410
Linneaus, classification scheme, 7
Loevinger method of homogeneous tests, 161, 163
Longevity and intelligence, 112-113
Longevity and sex differences, 113, 217
Longitudinal sequences, 488
Longitudinal studies, 26, 41, 48-49 54, 63, 65, 295, 469-487
  Berkeley Growth Study, 49
  Fels Study, 50
  Harvard Growth Study, 505
  Kansas City Study, 45
  longitudinal research projects, 65-66
  McFarland Guidance Study, 49-50
  Oakland Growth Study, 49
  Stanford Studies of Gifted Children, 49
Longitudinal vs. cross-sectional method, 167-175, 469-476, 486-487
LSD, 475

M
Mediation, 80, 309-310, 317, 320-323
Mediation concept, 275
  generalized habits/mediation, 308-310
  verbal mediation, 340
  verbal mediator, 321

Mediation theory, 403-405
  acquisition of syntax, 405
  and age differences, 405
  chaining paradigm, 405
  response equivalence paradigm, 405
  stimulus equivalence paradigm, 405
Mediation-retention relationship, 341
Mediational devices, 306
Memory
  decay theory, 350
  limited capacity theory, 350
  long-term, 458
  short-term, 349-350, 458-459
Memory trace mechanism, 309
Mental age concept, 33
Mental measurement, 31
Metaphysical models, 121-122, 128, 130
Methodological paradigms in learning
  free recall, 313
  paced recall, 340
  paired-associate learning, 312-313, 321
  recognition vs. recall, 313
  recognition tasks, 313
  serial learning, 313, 344
Method variance vs. attribute variance,
    18-19
Mnemonic diagram, 89
Model, 115-145
  empirical test, 135
  epistomological, 117, 125
  general, 117, 119
  levels of, 117
  mechanistic, 116-117, 123, 125,
    129-130, 130-133, 135-137,
    138-142, 144
  metaphysical levels, 115, 117, 131
  metaphysical models, 115, 120, 125,
    130
  organismic, 116, 117, 123, 124, 126,
    129, 130, 132-137, 138-143
  origin, 130
  pragmatic models, 117-118
  S-R model, 130, 132, 138, 275
  scientific theories, 115
  theoretical models, 118
  validity of, 120
Mortality rate, 60-61
Multiple abstract variance analysis, 11
Multiple regression technique, 44
Multitrait-multimethod matrix, 18

Multivariate methodology, 193-207
  comparative factor analysis, 193-196
  conception of, 195-196
  grid designs, 204
  multiple discriminant function model,
    204
Muscular tension, 295

N

Nature vs. nurture, 11, 40, 46, 478
Neutral stimulus, 293
Novelty stimulation, 298

O

Observational techniques, 72
Old age
  conditioning, 259-261, 263, 265-266,
    268
  creative thinking, 93-96
  illusions, 213-215
  intellectual changes, 73-81
  intelligence-cognition, 449-462,
    470-471, 498, 500
  language, 374-376
  learning, 270, 272-274, 277-278,
    280-281
  part-whole differentiation, 221-223
  perceptual closure, 224-225
  retention-forgetting, 319, 322, 326-327
  spatial relations, 217-221
  speed of recognition, 225-226
  verbal learning, 319, 322, 326-327, 332
Olfactory stimuli, 29
Operant activity level, 299
Operant methodology, 298
Operant responding, 298
Operationalism, 116
Optical apparatus, 231-232
Orienting behavior, 296

P

Pangenesis, 27-29
Paradigms in learning, 117, 121-122, 124
Paradox of conceptualization, 117
Parallel development, 184-185
Pediatrics, 41-42
Perception,
  simple vs. complex figures, 225
  age changes, 212-226

anatomy of, 231-232
and judgment, 239, 242, 246
and sensation, 228-229
apparent horizon, 219-221
conception of, 227
development of, 227-246
discrimination of form, 234
feedback, 229
information processing, 228-229,
    232-234
measurement methods, 238-240,
    244-245
perceptual closure, 224
perceptual field dependency, 221-223
psychophysical methods, 213
spatial orientation, 215-221
verticality, 215-216
visual acuity, 236
visual illusions, 212-215
visual mechanisms, 229-230, 234-235
Perceptual response, 65
Perceptual trace mechanism, 309
Performance differentiation hypothesis, 474
Personality development, 61, 65, 397-398
Philosophy of science, 77
Physiological maturity, 296
Piagetian theory, 74, 121
Position preferences, 76-77, 79-80, 83
Positivists, 116
Power test, 494, 502
Principle of falsification, 75
Problem solving, 80-81, 109-110
Psychoanalysis, 31, 42, 61-62, 140
    Adler, 62
    Freud, 31, 61-62
    Jung, 62
Psycholinguistics, 406-419
    associationistic, 359-360
    atomistic, 358-361
    classification of words, 380-381, 388
    current research, 401
    definition of meaning, 371-372
    history, 358-361, 406
    internal logic, 93-96
    intersecting term, 371-372, 379-380
    learning psychology, 358-359
    multidisciplinary research, 406
    operations, 390-398
    phrase structure grammar, 395
    processes,

relations, 361-397
research, 412-416
underlying principles for language
    performance, 418-419
vocabulary growth, 372-373
Psycholinguistic relations,
    bilingual conditions, 365
    class relations, 395-396
    extralingual relations, 361
    independence of, 375-376
    interlingual relations, 365-371
    intersection of relations, 361-365,
        379-380, 391
    intralingual relations, 365-397
    monolingual conditions, 365
    paradigms, 362-367
    preference, 377-379
    prepositional relations, 387-389
    strength of classes, 364-367
    transitivity of, 392, 395
Psycholinguistic paradigms, 362-367, 391
Psycholinguistic operations,
    analogical inferences, 394-395
    class relations, 395-396
    combinations, 390-396
    compounding of relations, 392-393
    linguistic transformations, 390-391
        396-398
    realistic inferences, 395
    relations of relations, 393-394
    reversibility, 398
    syllogistic reasoning, 391-392
    transformations, 390-391

R

Reaction time, 44, 292
Reactive inhibition, 96
Recall, 282
Recognition, 225-226, 229-245, 281,
        313-314, 350-352, 373
    false recognition, 351
    frequency differential, 351
    frequency theory, 352
    implicit associative response (IRR), 351
    learning-retention variant, 350
    pattern of, 227-229, 233
    representation response (RR), 351
    speed of, 225
    theory of, 351
    vs. detection, 227-230, 234-237, 243

Reinforcement, 290-292, 297-301
Reinforcement contingencies, 290-291
Research parameters, 5-7
    concept of entity, 5-7
    concept of attribute, 5-7
    concept of time, 5-7
Response, 77, 140
    attributes, 301-302
    bias, 276
    changes, 140
    classes, 306
    classification of responses, 77-78
    consistency, 295-296
    heartrate, 295-297
    latent, 309
    mediating, 130, 132
    potentiation of, 293
    preferences, 298
    propensities, 291
    rate, 299
    repertoire, 288
    system, 294
Restricted association, 376-379, 381
Retardates, 29-30
    intelligence, 29-30, 473-
Retention, 305-355
    delayed recall, 341
    free recall, 313, 331
    gestalt, 320
    immediate recall, 341, 344
    information processing, 109-110
    interference theory, 312-313, 331-350
    interlist similarity, 315
    long-term, 306, 313, 333, 344
    long-term retroactive inhibition, 339, 344
    nomological network, 314-331
    proactive inhibition, 331-337, 343-346, 349-350
    recall, 314-350, 458-459
    recognition, 350-352
    R-S recall method, 331-337, 343-346
    retrieval, 346
    retroactive inhibition, 312, 328, 330-331, 331-343, 347-350
    short-term, 80, 110, 313, 321, 344
    storage, 346
    verbal discrimination, 352-353
Retention-development relationships, 314
    age-sensitive processes, 314-331

    comparability of age groups, 317-320
    degree of learning, 317-320, 336-337
    degree of overlearning, 336
    degree-unlearning relationship, 336-337
    developmental learning processes, 314
    incidental learning, 330
    incremental theory, 318
    mediated learning and age, 320-323
    mnemonic-mediational activity, 341
    paired associate learning and age, 319-320
    qualitative dimension, 320-
    quantitative dimension, 318-319
    rote vs. mediated learning, 320-323
    R-S learning, 329-331
    stimulus selection, 327-329
    threshold, 318
Retention-forgetting model, 315-317
Retroactive inhibition, 331, 343, 347, 358
Retrospection, 87
Reversal shift vs. nonreversal shift, 275-276
Reversibility, 436-437
Rote-conditioning model, 305, 307-308

S

Saarbruecken cohort effect study, 506
Scaling procedures, 153-161
    applicability over life-cycle, 153-154
    construct validity, 153-155
    equal interval, 155, 161
    nominal, 155, 158
    ordinal, 155, 161
    response-scaling method, 155-156, 158
Scalogram analysis, 158-161
Secondary age parameters, 473-475
Selective sampling, 17
Selective drop-out, 17
Selective survival, 16, 20
Semantic structure, 380-381
Semantic-syntactic space, 375-376
Semantics, 360
Sensation, 228
Sensitivity, 239-240
Sensori-motor alertness stage, 432-434
    classical conditioning, 432
    measurement of, 433
    preconceptual phase, 435
    relation to intelligence, 433-434
    sensory deprivation vs. enrichment, 434
    transfer learning, 432, 436

Sensory systems vs. perceptual systems, 229-230, 233
Sequential patterning, 184-185, 190
Sequential strategies, 487-500
Simulation of age differences, 16
Social learning, 46
Social pressures, 113
Socialization process, 47-48
Sociological studies, 46
Specific developmental psychologies, 8-9
Speed factor in performance, 274, 277, 494, 502
Speed test, 494, 502
Stability, 186-189, 197-199, 201
Startle reflex, 296
State, 301-302
Stimulus differentiation training, 297
Stimulus events, 298
Stimulus exposure, 297
Stimulus generalization, 268-269
Stimulus properties, 296
Stimulus-response contingencies, 301
Stimulus-response units, 307
Stimulus selection, 327-329
Structural change, 9, 139-140, 142-143
Structure-function relationship, 139-140, 142-143
Styles of behavior, 292
Sucking behavior, 289, 293-295, 300
Syntactic structure, 393
System of semantics, 384

T
Tactile stimuli, 290-292
Tests
    Army Alpha, 34, 450-451, 453, 455-456, 498
    Associative Matching Task, 346
    Binet-Simon, 33
    Body Adjustment, 221-223
    California First Year Mental Scale, 432
    California Preschool Scale, 432
    CAVD, 451
    CFR, 456
    Common-Word Analogy Test, 456
    Concept Mastery Test, 452-453, 456
    Digit Symbol 1, 280
    Digit-Span, 32
    Dotted Outline, 224
    Embedded Figures, 221, 223
    Gestalt Completion, 224
    Goldstein-Scheerer, 430
    Healy Pictorial, 33
    Hidden Digit, 224
    King Factored Aptitude Test, 498
    KOHS Blocks, 431
    Letter Group, 80
    Macroscopic examination, 448
    Matrices and Analogies, 430
    Microscopic histological examination, 448-449
    MMFR, 333-334, 336, 339-343, 346
    Mutilated Word, 224-225
    Omnibus tests, 450
    Otis, 450, 498
    Paced Recall Task, 339-340, 342-343
    PMA, 477, 498, 500
    Progressive Matrices Test, 74-75
    Psychomotor speed, 451
    Psychophysical Methods, 153
    Rigidity, 451
    Rod-and-Frame, 221-223
    SASKA, 374
    Scale of moral reasoning, 158
    Simplex group intelligence, 452
    Social responsibility, 451
    Stanford-Binet, 373-374, 438, 442, 450, 452, 455-456
    Stroop Color Word, 153
    Stroop Color Word Test, 223
    TBR, 500
    Terman McNemar Group, 438, 442
    Thorndike, 451
    Thurstone Attitude Scale, 160
    Vocabulary, 372-375, 442, 456
    Wechsler, 280, 374, 431, 450, 453, 455-461, 498
    Wisconsin Card Sort, 270, 291
    Word Association method, 376
Theoretical models, 118-119, 125, 128
    analogue, 118-119
    conceptual, 118
    deployment of, 120
    descriptive representation, 119
    evaluation of, 120
    functions of, 119
    metaphorical representation, 119-120
    nature of, 118
    scale, 118-119
Theory construction, 14-15, 72-114, 116, 129, 138-139, 144

acceptance of, 125
antecedent-consequent relation, 83, 95
arrays of interrelated statements, 83-87, 97
bridge principles, 86-87
conceptual analysis, 89-92
creative induction, 81-82
deductive inference rules, 81-82
deductive-nomological explanations, 85, 95
descriptive observation, 78
eclectic, 123
explicandum, 108
field dependent logic, 81
functions of, 124
inference warrant, 83
internal logic, 81
internal principles, 86, 88
operational definitions, 77, 86-87
proto-theory, 73
role of analogies, 108-111
role of models, 108-111
taxonomy, 77
terminology, 77
translation of, 121
value judgments, 125-126
Theory of disengagement, 96-107
Theory of fluid and crystallized intelligence, 443-445, 478, 485, 493-495
Three-factor developmental model, 171-174, 487-492
Threshold, 234-235, 239-240, 295, 307, 310, 350
Thought disorder, 74
Trace theory, 306
Transfer, 310, 312-314, 316, 321, 337, 427-428, 432
amount of transfer, 317
classical research, 329
generalization of learning, 428
genotypical paradigm, 329
interference, 428
mechanism changes, 316
method, 324-328
mixed list, 330
negative, 316-317, 323, 331-332, 337-340, 427
paradigm, classical and specific, 316, 331-340
phenotypical paradigm, 329

positive, 317, 331, 427
similarity, 428
Transitivity, 437
Twin studies, 46, 63, 65
Two-factor model, 487-488
cross-sectional sequences, 487-488
longitudinal sequences, 487-488

U

Unlearning process, 332-350
analysis of associative interference, 346
associative matching task, 346
disjunctive concept learning, 347
inhibitory set, 347
interference-unlearning relationship, 346
nature of, 346
retrieval, 346-347
storage, 346-347

V

Vocabulary, 372-375
differential decline, 374-375
qualitative changes and age, 373-374
Verbal behavior, 81
Verbal learning, 305, 314, 359-360, 363, 402
active vs. passive subject, 308, 310
component processes, 332-346
conventional method, 320, 332
conventional model, 307-308
formal S-unit, 307-331
functional stimulus, 307, 313
generalized habits/mediation, 308-310
multiple process vs. single process, 307-312
nominal stimulus unit, 307, 311-331
nominal-functional disparity, 309
R-S associative learning, 312-314
R-S unlearning, 348
R-unit, 307-333
response integration, 311
response learning, 311, 314-315, 317
rote processes, 310
S-R associative learning, 311-312, 318, 329
S-R unlearning, 348
stage analysis, 311-312
stimulus-related processes, 311
Verbal discrimination learning (VD), 310, 313, 352-353

Verbal learning, 314-346
   associative learning, 352
   transfer-retention paradigm, 352
VD paradigm, 312-313, 352
Verbal mediation, 405
Vestibular stimulation, 302
Vienna circle, 64-65
Visual attention behavior, 298
Visual imagery, 321

Visual stimuli, 296
Voluntary behavior, 265

W

Word association, 405

Y

Yerkes-Dodson law, 86